For over a hundred years there has been no comprehensive history of later medieval Anglo-Latin literature (which constitutes an astonishing nine-tenths of English literary activity in the period). The century and a half since the last major work on this subject have seen the discovery and editing of many important texts. The view is commonly held that English literary culture declined after the Norman Conquest and revived only in the fourteenth century in the work of writers such as Chaucer; this view ignores the flourishing tradition of Latin literature written between England's enforced entry into the European mainstream and the rise of the vernacular and humanism. A.G. Rigg's new history reveals a very rich corpus of writings, comprising epic, lyric, comedy, satire, prose anecdote, romance, saints' lives and devotional texts. Authors such as Geoffrey of Monmouth, John of Salisbury, Gerald of Wales and John Gower are now presented in the context of the host of other Anglo-Latin writings, both major and minor. This chronological history gives quotations in the original Latin with English translations in verse or prose; Anglo-Latin metres are explained and exemplified in the Appendix.

A history of Anglo-Latin literature 1066–1422

A history of
Anglo-Latin literature 1066–1422

A. G. RIGG

Centre for Medieval Studies,
University of Toronto

CAMBRIDGE
UNIVERSITY PRESS

Published by the Press Syndicate of the University of Cambridge
The Pitt Building, Trumpington Street, Cambridge CB2 IRP
40 West 20th Street, New York, NY 10011–4211, USA
10 Stamford Road, Oakleigh, Victoria 3166, Australia

First published 1992

Printed and bound in Great Britain by
Woolnough Bookbinding Ltd, Irthlingborough, Northamptonshire

*A catalogue record for this book is
available from the British Library*

Library of Congress cataloguing in publication data
Rigg, A. G.
A history of Anglo–Latin literature, 1066–1422 / A.G. Rigg.
p.   cm.
Includes bibliographical references.
ISBN 0 521 41594 2
1. Latin literature, Medieval and modern – England – History and
criticism.   2. Christian literature, Latin (Medieval and modern) –
England – History and criticism.   3. England – Intellectual life–
Medieval period, 1066–1485.   4. England – Church history – Medieval
period, 1066–1485.   I. Title.
PA8045.E5R54   1992
870.9'003 – dc20   91–40270 CIP

ISBN 0521 41594 2 hardback

SE

In memory of
COLIN CHASE
1935–1984
colleague and friend

Contents

Acknowledgments

Like any broad survey of material, this work rests on the labours of others, especially editors of texts, many of whom are long gone. Prominent among the latter is Thomas Wright (1810–77), in whose erratic footsteps I seem to have walked for all my scholarly career. Among the living I would like to mention those colleagues and students, past and present, who have given me advice (not always taken), information and encouragement, and who have let me see their texts and studies in pre-publication state: Dr Deirdre Baker, Dr Peter Binkley, Mr Bruce Burnam, Dr Charles Burnett, Professor John Burrow, Professor James Carley, Dr Laurel Cropp, Professor Siân Echard, Ms Claire Fanger, Dr Elizabeth Stevens Girsch, Dr James Girsch, Professor Joe Goering, Professor Roger Hillas, Professor Andrew Hughes, Dr Anna Kirkwood, Professor Antonio Saiani, Professor Paul Gerhard Schmidt, Dr Richard Sharpe (whose bibliographical range in this material must be unrivalled), Dr Pauline Thompson, Professor David Townsend, Professor Nicholas Watson, Mr Bill Woodward, and Professor Norman Zacour (who not only patiently read a very ill-written first draft of the book but also persuaded me not to believe everything that John of Garland said). If I have forgotten someone, please forgive me.

The person to whom I owe most – after my wife, Jennifer, who has for so long tolerated this obsession along with all the others – saw only the first few months of this project. Colin Chase was my colleague in Medieval Latin studies in Toronto for sixteen years. His friendship and guidance while we sought to promote Medieval Latin was my constant support, and I am pleased to have the opportunity to dedicate this book to him.

Abbreviations

AB	*Analecta Bollandiana*
AH	Analecta Hymnica
ALMA	*Archivum Latinitatis Medii Aevi* (= *Bulletin du Cange*)
ALSP	*The Anglo-Latin Satirical Poets and Epigrammatists of the Twelfth Century*, ed. T. Wright, 2 vols. RS (London, 1872)
ASS	Acta Sanctorum
Bale *Catalogus*	John Bale, *Scriptorum illustrium Brytanniae . . . Catalogus*, 2 vols. (Basel, 1557–59; rpt. Farnborough, 1971)
Bale *Index*	*Index Britanniae Scriptorum. John Bale's Index of British and other Writers*, ed. R.L. Poole and M. Bateson (Oxford, 1902), reissued with introduction by C. Brett and J.P. Carley (Woodbridge, Suffolk, 1990)
Becket Materials	*Materials for the History of Thomas Becket*, ed. J.C. Robertson and J.B. Sheppard, 7 vols., RS (London, 1875–85)
Bekynton	Oxford, Bodleian Library, MS Add. A.44: see ch. 2, n. 288
Bezzola	See ch. 2, n. 12
BHL	Bibliotheca Hagiographica Latina
BIHR	*Bulletin of the Institute of Historical Research*
BJRL	*Bulletin of the John Rylands Library*
BL	British Library
BN	Bibliothèque Nationale
Carmina Burana	Ed. A. Hilka, O. Schumann, B. Bischoff, I.1–3, II.1 (Heidelberg, 1930–70)
Chevalier	U. Chevalier, *Repertorium Hymnologicum*, 6 vols. (Louvain, 1892–1912; Brussels, 1920–1)
CLP	F.J.E. Raby, *A History of Christian Latin Poetry*, 2nd edn (Oxford, 1953)
CM	*Classica et Medievalia*

COCR	*Collectanea Ordinis Cisterciensis Reformatorum* (now = *Collectanea Cisterciensia*)
Commedie Latine	See ch. 2, n. 307
CS	Camden Society
DNB	Dictionary of National Biography
EETS	Early English Text Society
EHR	*English Historical Review*
Emden BRUO	A.B. Emden, *A Biographical Register of the University of Oxford to 1500*, 3 vols. (Oxford, 1957–9)
Glastonbury Miscellany	*A Glastonbury Miscellany of the Fifteenth Century*, ed. A.G. Rigg (Oxford, 1968); see Rigg, thesis
Gransden	See Introduction, n. 12
Hauréau NE	B. Hauréau, *Notices et Extraits de quelques manuscrits latins de la Bibliothèque Nationale*, 6 vols. (Paris, 1890–3; rpt. in 3 vols., Farnborough, 1967). To be distinguished from the journal *Notices et Extraits*
Hervieux	L. Hervieux, *Les fabulistes latins depuis le siècle d'Auguste jusqu'à la fin du moyen âge*, 5 vols. (Paris, 1884–99)
*Hunt	See p. 8
JEH	*Journal of Ecclesiastical History*
JWCI	*Journal of the Warburg and Courtauld Institute*
Kingsford	See Bekynton and ch. 2, n. 288
Lapidge–Sharpe	M. Lapidge and R. Sharpe, *A Bibliography of Celtic-Latin Literature 400–1200* (Dublin, 1985)
Lehmann *Parodie*	P. Lehmann, *Die Parodie im Mittelalter*, 2nd edn (Stuttgart, 1963)
Leland	John Leland, *Commentarii de scriptoribus Britannicis*, ed. A. Hall (Oxford, 1709), completed 1545
LMP	(Reginald of Canterbury) see ch. 1, n. 63
MAe	*Medium Aevum*
Manitius	M. Manitius, *Geschichte der lateinischen Literatur des Mittelalters*, 3 vols. (Munich, 1911–31)
Mapes	See Wright
MARS	*Medieval and Renaissance Studies*
MGH	*Monumenta Germaniae Historica*
MJ	*Mittellateinisches Jahrbuch*
MPhil	*Modern Philology*
MSt	*Mediaeval Studies*
NA	*Neues Archiv*
OHS	Oxford Historical Society
PL	*Patrologia Latina*
PMLA	*Publications of the Modern Language Association of America*
Political Poems	See Wright

Political Songs	See Wright
RAM	*Revue d'Ascétique et Mysticisme*
RB	*Revue Bénédictine*
RES	*Review of English Studies*
Rigg thesis	A.G. Rigg, *An Edition of a Fifteenth-century Commonplace Book (Trinity College, Cambridge, MS 0.9.38)*, 2 vols., D.Phil. thesis (Oxford, 1966); see *Glastonbury Miscellany* for a descriptive index of this
RS	Rolls Series
Russell	J.C. Russell, *Dictionary of Writers of Thirteenth-century England*, BIHR s.s. 3 (London, 1936), rpt. with supplements (London, 1967). For Russell and Heironimus, see ch. 3, n. 74
SLP	F.J.E. Raby, *A History of Secular Latin Poetry in the Middle Ages*, 2nd ed., 2 vols. (Oxford, 1957)
SM	*Studi medievali*
Smalley *Friars*	See ch. 3, n. 66
Tanner	T. Tanner, *Bibliotheca Britannico-Hibernica* (London, 1748)
TRHS	*Transactions of the Royal Historical Society*
UL	University Library
Ward-Herbert	H.D.L. Ward and J.A. Herbert, *Catalogue of Romances in the Department of Manuscripts in the British Museum* 3 vols. (London, 1883–1910, rpt. London, 1961–2)
WIC	H. Walther, *Initia Carminum ac Versuum Medii Aevi posterioris latinorum*, 2nd ed. (Göttingen, 1969)
Wilmart *Auteurs*	A. Wilmart, *Auteurs spirituels et textes dévots du moyen âge latin* (Paris, 1932; rpt. with corrections, Paris, 1971)
WMP	(Reginald of Canterbury) see ch. 1, n. 63
Wright *Biographia*	T. Wright, *Biographia Britannica Literaria*, 2 vols. (London, 1842–46)
Wright *Mapes*	T. Wright, *The Latin Poems commonly attributed to Walter Mapes*, CS (London, 1841)
Wright, *Pol.Poems*	T. Wright, *Political Poems and Songs relating to English history from the accession of Edward III to that of Richard II*, 2 vols. RS (London, 1859–61)
Wright *Pol.Songs*	T. Wright, *The Political Songs of England from the Reign of John to that of Edward II*, CS (London, 1839)
York Historians	*The Historians of the Church of York and its Archbishops*, ed. J. Raine, 3 vols. RS (London, 1879–94)
ZfdA	*Zeitschrift für deutsches Altertum*

Introduction

Nil ego temere cano Catonibus
sed tantum paruulis balbucientibus,
qui turbi lusitant in uertiginibus
et adhuc lusitant in arundinibus
      (Walter of Wimborne, *De Palpone* 180)

Et certe longus (et forte superfluus) esset
exemplis instare labor – nam quodlibet horum
conantem quamcumque breui perstringere uersu
huius oporteret geminare uolumina libri
      (Henry of Avranches, *Vita Oswaldi* 724–7)

In 1612, after several voyages to what is now Canada, Samuel Champlain drew a map. In light of what we know now, it was not a very good map (in fact, he revised it later); its outlines were vague and its depictions of the hinterland negligible. He could probably have made a better map; if he had consulted all the natives and explored all the inlets and creeks, he would have made a very good map indeed, but he would probably never have lived long enough to complete it. This book is a bit like Champlain's map. It suffers from too sketchy a knowledge of the primary sources and even more from too little reading in secondary works. It is full of hasty generalizations, even prejudices. It is, however, a map of sorts, and, as such, it is something that has not been available before. The absence of explorers in post-Conquest Anglo-Latin literature is largely explained by the lack of any sort of guide, however inadequate. I hope that my rough sketch map – even in four hundred pages it is scarcely more than an outline – will encourage others to enter the territory and to describe it more thoroughly.

To most students of England in the Middle Ages, especially those 'in English', the literary history of the years between 1066 and 1422 appears as a large letter U – a rapid decline after the Anglo-Saxon period, descending to a nadir in the twelfth and thirteenth centuries, struggling feebly out of the pit in the early fourteenth century, and finally emerging with Chaucer, Langland and the poet of *Sir Gawain*.

In fact, the opposite is true. The high point of literary excellence in England in the Middle Ages was the twelfth and thirteenth centuries. The Latin writers of England and Wales achieved in that period a reputation across Europe that their vernacular counterparts never rivalled, before or since.[1] Although Anglo-Latin literature was thriving before the Norman Conquest, William's victory at Hastings in 1066 and Henry II's inheritance in 1154 of a large chunk of Europe (the Anglo-Angevin Empire) brought England into a close relationship with European Latin culture. The links were broken by the loss of Normandy in 1205, but the educated clergy, reinforced by the friars, maintained a continuous stream of literature that was only stemmed by the rise of vernacular English.

One reason for the general unawareness of the true literary picture is the lack of a history of Latin literature of the period. There have, of course, been some attempts to fill the gap, and these attempts illustrate the problem. Tanner's *Bibliotheca Britannico-Hibernica* (1748) and its successor, Thomas Wright's *Biographia Britannica Literaria* (1842–6), are arranged like encyclopedias; they simply list writers, with no connecting narrative, no 'history', and no distinction between 'literary' and 'non-literary'. Like Bale and Leland before them, they simply list *scriptores*. Russell's alphabetically arranged *Dictionary of Writers of Thirteenth-century England* (1936), although indispensable, suffers from the same problem. The term 'literary' certainly has its drawbacks, as I discuss below, but its absence means that reading works like Tanner, Wright and Russell in search of Anglo-Latin literature is like looking for the history of English literature in the *Dictionary of National Biography*. General histories of medieval English literature often have a chapter on 'Latin',[2] but they usually deal with the important Latin thinkers and their significance for intellectual history rather than their literary achievements in their own right. In any case, these surveys always squeeze Latin literature into a disproportionately small space compared to vernacular writings.

English studies

One explanation for the neglect of Anglo-Latin lies in the history of English studies.[3] In the early days of English as an academic subject, philology was a dominant, often predominant, element – hence the departments of English *language* and literature. This resulted in an emphasis on vernacular Germanic languages to provide the tools of comparative philology. As the medievalists in a department were almost invariably also the philologists, the study of pre-Renaissance texts had a linguistic and vernacular bias. Although these philologists were usually excellent Latinists, their prime interests were usually in Old English, for which the classical tradition was largely irrelevant. Moreover, the academic study of English had often been opposed by classicists, who saw it as an easy option (with philology its only bulwark against mushiness). Thus, even when the literary study of medieval texts began seriously, medievalists tended to resent the notion that classics had some kind of priority: rivalry between English and Classics sometimes led to an unnecessary conflict over 'relevance'. While post-medievalists could argue for the importance of classical authors (such as Virgil and Ovid), medievalists did not see the ancient authors as the starting point of their literary tradition. Sometimes this was a defence against those who sought to abolish Old English requirements and to substitute Classical Latin. C.S. Lewis argued strongly that if any language was needed for the study of medieval English, it was not Latin but Old French (Lewis himself had taken Old Norse); by Latin, of course, Lewis meant Classical Latin. In the meantime, Anglo-Latin lay neglected.

Medieval Latin studies owe a great deal to departments of English, but sometimes the attention of English medievalists has had a distorting effect on the study of Anglo-Latin. Medieval Latin writings have usually been valued according to their relevance to Old or Middle English: a text known to Chaucer is given far more attention than one that was read only by monks and clerics. This is quite right and proper: departments of English are constituted to teach and read works in English, not works written in England. English medievalists, often defensively, are often concerned to show a linguistic (and possibly literary) continuum between *Beowulf* and Virginia Woolf; the study of texts written in languages other than English is tolerable only if it serves this central purpose. Consequently, a literature that had no influence outside itself and which quite definitely died in the Middle Ages is not their concern.

Classicists and the classical fallacy

Until recently classicists, with few exceptions, have taken almost no interest in Medieval Latin, and indeed have often been hostile to or contemptuous of it. This attitude goes back to – in fact almost a definition of – the Renaissance. Humanist culture prided itself on having rediscovered classical antiquity – not only Greek but 'pure' Latin. From the sixteenth century on, the efforts of Latinists have been directed to preserving the Latin language and literature of the late years of the Republic and the early years of the Empire. Style, spelling and metre were taught according to classical models; the reform of spelling took immediate effect and was confirmed by the invention of printing.[4] As a result over a thousand years of Latin literature was dismissed as ignorant and barbaric. I recall a New Zealand professor of Latin who read the entire *Oxford Book of Medieval Latin Verse* and found only one piece that he liked (Peter Riga's poem on the hermaphrodite). Religious attitudes (not, of course, just among classicists) have also played their part. A great deal of Medieval Latin literature concerns the Virgin, the saints, and other (from a Protestant point of view) dubious topics. Anticlericalism was not confined to Protestant countries: the epithet 'monkish' has often been enough to condemn an author to permanent obscurity. In modern times even being religious at all – let alone moral – puts a medieval writer at a serious disadvantage with his reader.

This attitude of the classicists has not only deprived Medieval Latin of those who might have been its most competent editors and historians: it has had a deep effect

3

on the way in which Medieval Latin literature is read and assessed, even amongst its admirers. This is what I call the 'classical fallacy', along with its corollary, the belief that 'learning' and 'literature' are the same thing. Once we grant the superiority of the ancient authors, we have an index by which to measure and assess Medieval Latin writers – namely, their proximity to, or distance from the classics.[5] A non-classical construction or vowel quantity moves an author down the ladder; the competent use of a rare classical metre is a mark of superiority, whereas rhythmical verse and especially rhyme earn a bad mark. The use of this stylistic slide-rule goes back at least as far as John Bale in the sixteenth century: he would patronizingly allow that an author was 'not entirely to be despised, considering the time at which he wrote'. Similarly, authors are moved up or down a scale according to their knowledge of the classics, usually by means of an index of quotations.[6] A writer whose knowledge of the classics seems to be second-hand, from another writer or through a florilegium, is placed below someone who had read the original. This is one of the reasons for John of Salisbury's high reputation, not because of what he had to say or because of some originality, but because he had read the classics in the original.

The fallacy of literary progress

The 'classical fallacy' and the 'learning equals literature' equation also involve the notion of literary progress. If the Latin culture of the Middle Ages is seen solely as a slow blundering journey towards the Renaissance in search of the lost gold of the ancients, proceeding fitfully by minor 'renaissances' in the Carolingian age and the twelfth century, then any writer who was walking in the same direction is to be praised and the rest can be ignored as irrelevant. Certainly, many medieval writers look back on the ancients with admiration, but to most of them this secular view of human history would have seemed strange and possibly even heretical. In any case, this approach has led to the neglect of the many writers whose literary ideals and ambitions had nothing to do with the past or the future or their part in an imaginary cultural development.

The idea of literary progress has drawn another red herring across the path of literary history, the search for something *new*. The quest for the *first* use of rhyme, the *first* rhythmical poem, the *first* appearance of prose fiction, etc., is valuable in itself, but often leads to the neglect of works that are written in established genres and forms. The culmination of the two volumes of Raby's *History of Secular Latin Poetry* is a two-chapter account of the lyric. From this one can easily fall into the error of supposing that rhythmical lyric metres were the final achievement of Medieval Latin poetry. It is easy to forget that throughout the Middle Ages the dominant verse forms were the hexameter and elegiac couplet.

Literary historians have often gone to Medieval Latin looking for something by which to illuminate something else: the origins of courtly literature (Bezzola), a continuum of rhetorical composition (Curtius), poetic originality (Dronke), the origins of fiction (Dronke), sources and analogues for vernacular literature (almost everyone). I have no wish to disparage the work of these scholars: they have brought Medieval Latin out of its dusty cupboard and have analysed texts with enviable sensitivity. Theoretically, one should not treat Medieval Latin in isolation from other contemporary literatures. On the other hand, some isolation might not be a bad thing: it would enable us to look at Medieval Latin literature for its own sake and not for its contribution to, or relevance for, something else. Many of the authors in this book (Reginald of Canterbury or Lawrence of Durham, for example) had no influence on anyone else and are not participants in any literary movement. Their significance rests in their works for their own sake.

National versus international

Most of what I have said so far applies to Medieval Latin literature as a whole. I want to consider now the absence of any treatment of post-Conquest Anglo-Latin as a distinct literature.[7] The major histories of Medieval Latin literature do include English writers, but not as a separate tradition and only to about 1200.[8] The geographic breadth and temporal narrowness are, in fact, related, and not just because of the enormity of the task of covering all European literature for another three hundred years. The European dimension of Medieval Latin literature – it would be a mistake to call it a 'fallacy', as it was, up to a certain date, true – is reflected in the title of Curtius' great book, *European Literature and the Latin Middle Ages*, and to some extent in Dronke's title *Medieval Latin and the rise of European Love-lyric*. The impression is given that 'Latin' and 'Middle Ages' and 'Europe' are coterminous. At certain times and in certain subjects this view is correct. The early Christian poets – Ambrose, Prudentius, Avitus, Dracontius, Arator, and so on – enjoyed a readership throughout Christendom. Texts on subjects of universal importance – theology, philosophy, science, medicine – crossed national boundaries throughout the Middle Ages. In 'literary' writings, however, this 'indivisibility of Latin culture', whatever validity it had had at earlier periods, certainly broke down in the thirteenth century. One cause was increasing nationalism. Another was the emergence of vernacular literatures and the gradual replacement of Latin as the sole language of culture. This happened at different times in different countries: earliest in Italy, then France, and somewhat later in England. The different paces of cultural change across Europe – for instance, the spread of 'humanism' – broke down whatever universality had existed. Consequently, literary historians with a European perspective have found it convenient to stop at around 1200. This is entirely understandable, but it has resulted in the neglect of Latin literature at the end of the Middle Ages, even in those countries where it thrived, such as England. It has also given the quite unwarranted impression – another part of the 'literary progess' fallacy – that anything after 1200 is part of a 'decline'.[9]

Is Anglo-Latin a valid concept?

Despite the European approach, literary historians have had no problem with the isolation of national Latin literatures at specific times: Hiberno-Latin and pre-Conquest Anglo-Latin have commonly been treated as distinct literatures, and Raby often finds it convenient to subdivide into nations. Post-Conquest Anglo-Latin, however, has its own problems. In the late eleventh century England was in many ways simply a colony of Northern France. In the reign of Henry II (1154–89) the English Channel almost disappeared politically and culturally: I have serious qualms about including Peter of Blois but excluding Walter of Châtillon. Nevertheless, the loss of Normandy in 1205 led to the increasing isolation of England and particularly of its literature. There is certainly no difficulty in separating Anglo-Latin 1216–1422 as a distinct literature.

In any case, theoretical problems have never inhibited the writing of histories of 'England in the later Middle Ages': one simply extracts those bits of European history that are directly relevant to England. When the Niagara River flows out of Lake Erie and over the Niagara Falls, it enters the vast space of water known as Lake Ontario, which is divided by an arbitrary line separating Canada from the United States. At the eastern end of Lake Ontario, the river flows on in a north-easterly direction, becoming first the St Lawrence River, then the Gulf of St Lawrence, before finally emerging into the Atlantic Ocean. In its long course it is sometimes a river, sometimes a lake, sometimes part of an ocean, part Canadian, part American, but no one denies that it has a course. It would be possible to treat Anglo-Latin literature at the end of the eleventh century as part of a Norman lake and that of the second half of the twelfth century as part of an Angevin Gulf. For my present purpose I prefer to treat it all as one river.

What is literature?

The most contentious part of my title is not the prefix 'Anglo-' but the word 'literature'. I am well aware that a genre of writing called 'literature' would have been incomprehensible to the Middle Ages,[10] and is scarcely defensible even in Modern English. Neither form nor content is sufficient to separate the 'literary' from the 'non-literary'. An evident intention to amuse or entertain or to imitate a literary model (such as an epic poem) is a helpful hint that something should be included, but its absence does not necessarily mean that a work should be regarded as non-literary. On the other hand, while anything written down *can* be subjected to a literary analysis, to include everything written down would be impossible.

For the literary historian (such as the present writer) this is not a theoretical problem but a practical one. Much Anglo-Latin writing challenges the concept of 'literature' (and finds it wanting). Those with a smaller corpus of writings (such as the Anglo-Saxonist or historian of Middle English or Anglo-Norman) can avoid the issue by including almost everything, prose chronicles, instructions for anchoresses, handbooks of astronomy, and moral advice, but this option is not available to the historian of Anglo-Latin. Russell lists three hundred and fifty named English writers in the thirteenth century alone. There are no problems – other than purely theoretical – at the extreme ends of the scale. Even if Joseph of Exeter's *Ilias* was used as a school-text and Nigel Whiteacre's *Speculum Stultorum* was intended as an exemplum against discontentment with one's lot, I have no hesitation about including them. Equally, I do not anticipate complaints about the exclusion of prose treatises on mathematics or biblical concordances. The problem is in the middle; a few examples will suffice.

In the Middle Ages the letter was an art form, and treatises (*artes dictaminis*) were written on how properly to compose a letter: one is included in John of Garland's verse *Poetria parisiana*. I have discussed the model collection of letters by Peter of Blois, but a survey of letters written in England would take a book in itself. There must be thousands to the papal curia alone and even more between ecclesiastical officials: those of John of Salisbury occupy two volumes. I have, therefore, excluded letters from literature – and not without criticism.[11]

The writing of history is even more of a literary act – the organization of material, the shaping of the narration to point to conclusions and morals, the variations in style, the embellishment with verses – and again I have excluded chronicles, though perhaps with the better excuse that excellent accounts of them already exist.[12] I have not, however, been entirely consistent in excluding prose accounts of past events. It would have been unforgivable to omit Geoffrey of Monmouth, originator of the immortal saga of King Arthur, but in his own eyes – or at least as he wished to be seen – he was writing history and, with few exceptions, was accepted as a narrator of true history for several centuries. As far as I know, there is no literary category of 'accidental fiction' and no procedure for reclassifying an inaccurate historian as a novelist. Nevertheless I have included him.

The religious poems of Walter of Wimborne and John of Howden are unquestionably literary. Consequently I have also included examples of the devotional movement that lies behind them (Anselm, Aelred, Stephen of Easton). The culmination of the meditative tradition, however, is seen in Richard Rolle, and I would be surprised if he or his contemporaries regarded his Latin prose works – commentaries on biblical texts, exhortations to the heremitic life as the way of salvation – as belletristic.

The prose saint's life was also a literary form: it had a recognizable formal structure and often – depending on the saint – provided escapist entertainment, much like a romance. I have given some space to the major writers (Goscelin, John of Tynemouth), but have been unwilling to delve further into this enormous field. On the other hand, I have included miracles of the Virgin.

My procedure, therefore, has been practical and arbitrarily – though not, I hope, capriciously – selective. This book has been written to fill the gap in the literary history of England between the Norman Conquest and Chaucer: it responds primarily to the need of the student of English literature to know what was going on in Latin that was similar to the kind of thing studied in English in other periods. I include works that one would normally expect to find in the 'Literature' section of a bookstore; I exclude works that one would normally look for under 'Science', 'Philosophy', 'Religion', 'History', 'Law', 'Travel', and 'Gardening'. I have included all major works in verse and those prose works that are associated with some major literary writer or are of interest for some other reason. I have paid more attention to works and writers that are 'literary' in this narrow sense: for example, more attention is given to Reginald of Canterbury than to Anselm, to Lawrence of Durham than to Aelred, and to Walter of Wimborne than to Grosseteste.

There will be many who will be dissatisfied with my selection of material and my procedures and emphases. At the end of my opening paragraph I have suggested the remedy.

Presentation

Except where I have re-edited a text myself, quotations are given in the form in which they appear in the edition cited. This has resulted in the use of both medieval and classical spellings, such as *ratio/racio, uenus/venus, amauit/amavit, eius/ejus, proelium/praelium/prelium*. I have occasionally repunctuated a text without comment.

Footnote citations have been kept to a minimum.

Translations, except where stated, are my own. I have rendered prose by prose and verse by verse; I have tried to use rhyme where the Latin is rhymed, though not always in the same patterns (English, as Chaucer noted, suffers from a scarcity of rhymes). The translations are not intended as cribs; especially in the verse I have tried to represent the gist or the spirit of the lines rather than the exact sense, so that non-Latinists will be able to get the flavour of the original – that, at least, is my hope.

Addendum. When this volume was in proof, a book appeared that touches on many authors discussed here: Tony Hunt, *Teaching and Learning Latin in Thirteenth-Century England*, 3 vols. (D.S. Brewer, Cambridge, 1991). I have not been able to incorporate the book adequately, but where Hunt has an edition or major extract I have signalled this by adding *Hunt in the endnote.

William I to Stephen (1066–1154)

The cultural scene in 1066

Politically, this chapter is defined by the Norman Conquest at one end and the coronation of Henry II at the other. In literature, the three most notable figures at the beginning of the period all came from outside England: Godfrey of Winchester from Cambrai, Reginald of Canterbury from Noyers, and the itinerant Goscelin from St Bertin. The years 1154–5, however, saw the deaths of Henry of Huntingdon, Geoffrey of Monmouth, and Lawrence of Durham, all indigenous authors. In four reigns, covering eighty-eight years, we see the Normanization of England and the Anglicization of the Normans; the process was not complete until the early thirteenth century, but was well under way by King Stephen's death in 1154.

Even before the Conquest there was a sizable foreign element among the English clergy.[1] During the tenth-century Benedictine Reform strong ties had been established with continental abbeys such as Fleury and St Peter's at Ghent. More recently, Edward the Confessor (1042–66), after a youth spent at the Norman court, had brought over many Normans in his service; he appointed many to ecclesiastical offices, including five or six to bishoprics, and they in turn had brought other followers.[2] Their impact, however, was negligible compared to that of the Norman Conquest itself. William systematically filled vacant bishoprics and abbacies with Normans; he secured the deposition of the archbishop of Canterbury, Stigand (who had uncanonically replaced the Norman Robert of Jumièges), and in 1070 Lanfranc of Bec was consecrated in his place; in 1089 Lanfranc died, and was succeeded in 1093 by Anselm, who had followed Lanfranc to Bec. By the end of William's reign in 1100, of thirty-five abbeys only three still had English abbots: their replacements came from nine Norman monasteries.[3] These abbots in their turn, of course, brought over followers from their home monasteries. Not surprisingly, there was trouble: for example, at Glastonbury, the abbot Thurstan had to call on his armed men to quell the recalcitrant monks. At Durham, bishop Walcher was murdered in revenge for a slaying by his foreign knights. At

Canterbury, the monks of St Augustine's were in almost open rebellion, and were replaced by monks from Christ Church.

The old and new clergy did not speak the same language, either literally or figuratively. As a literary medium, the English language was almost wiped out. The Anglo-Saxon Chronicle continued to be written in English at Peterborough until 1154, but generally literary monuments (such as the *Owl and Nightingale* and Layamon's *Brut*) were rare and isolated until the fourteenth century. The language of the court and administration was French, and for many years French must have been the language of at least the superior officers of the church, both inside and outside monasteries. The language of *Beowulf*, Aelfric and Wulfstan now ranked third, behind Latin and French.

Many of the newly arrived clergy and monks held the English – and their revered saints – in contempt. Athelelm of Abingdon considered the English boors ('dixit enim esse Anglicos rusticos'),[4] and at St Albans, Abingdon, Malmesbury and Evesham the relics of English saints were dishonoured and their feasts discontinued. Lanfranc removed many saints from the Canterbury calendar, and only Anselm managed to dissuade him from extirpating St Elphege. Even the English veneration for the Virgin Mary was not spared: for doctrinal reasons (the implicit threat to the doctrine of Original Sin) both Lanfranc and Anselm opposed the feast of the Immaculate Conception.[5] The impact of the new zealous Norman monasticism on English church life was certainly revolutionary in every sense; in the end it was probably beneficial, but in the short run it trod on many toes and bruised many spirits.

From a Norman and continental point of view (which would have no admiration for works in vernacular English), Anglo-Saxon culture must have seemed barbaric and even idolatrous. Looking back in 1140 William of Malmesbury contrasted the high standards of the monasteries of his own day, both moral and literary, with what he saw as a general decay at the time of the Conquest, when any cleric who knew grammar would be an object of wonder ('stupori erat et miraculo ceteris qui grammaticam nosset').[6] This was no doubt an exaggeration, but whether these slights on late Anglo-Saxon culture were justified or not, the effect of the Norman Conquest was to drag England willy-nilly into the mainstream of the European eleventh century – what Southern calls 'England's first entry into Europe'.[7]

Links with French monasteries, strengthened by their 'English' alumni, acted like grappling hooks to draw England closer to Northern France. Bec, for example, provided not only two archbishops of Canterbury (Lanfranc and Anselm) but also Gilbert Crispin[8] and Gundulf, bishop of Rochester. It was at Bec that Henry of Huntingdon saw one of the first copies of Geoffrey of Monmouth's *Historia Regum Britanniae*.[9] The English chronicler Orderic Vitalis lived at St Evroul. Goscelin and Arnulf (one of Reginald of Canterbury's correspondents) came from St Bertin's at St Omer. From Bayeux came not only Odo, Williams I's militant bishop, but also Thomas (I), archbishop of York. Such contacts had a more lasting effect, as they caused the spread of French-Latin authors, whose works continued to dominate English Latin poetic anthologies into the thirteenth (and in some cases even the fifteenth) century. The most notable were Marbod of Rennes, Baudri of Bourgueil, and Hildebert.[10] The impact of French-Latin poets on English culture, which lasted to the reign of King John, was especially marked during the reign of Henry II, but by then the Angevin Empire was more culturally united. In this first period, before 1154, England was simply an outpost of – or perhaps a jumping-off point for – Northern French monastic culture.

Immigrant attitudes

While England was being so ruthlessly and completely Normanized, what was the attitude of the new immigrants? For some, alienation must have been severe: as late as Henry II's reign, Peter of Blois lamented that he had spent twenty-five years in a country whose language he did not know.[11] Others, however, settled quickly. Goscelin,[12] who spent all his adult life in England, was thoroughly at home. After leaving Sherborne he moved first to East Anglia and finally to Canterbury; his writings are almost entirely concerned with English saints. He seems also to have accommodated himself easily to the newly arrived Normans, who may have seemed to him more alien than the English. Godfrey of Winchester tells us nothing of his feelings, but his historical poems are entirely concerned with England; only once, on a special occasion, does he write about an event on the continent.[13] More interesting is Reginald of Canterbury.[14] Born in Faye-la Vineuse in France, he retained a strong affection for his birthplace and writes of it with evident nostalgia:

> Fagia, dulce solum, rus nobile, villa celebris,
> Te veneror solum, te laudibus effero crebris (WMP 4.7–8)

> O sweet and noble land of Faye, your fields and town renowned,
> To you alone respect I pay, and in your praise resound.

He says wrily that his muse is nourished on English beer, not French wine:

> Vitis Francigenam docet, Anglia discit avenam (LMP 1.19)

> The vine instructs the Gallic muse, but England's barley-taught.

The debate between French wine and English beer, usually at the expense of beer, goes back at least to Alcuin and continues through literature to the present day,[15] but it must have been a real part of Reginald's culture shock: in his *Vita Malchi* (IV, 27–8) even the ants disdain barley grains:

> Frumentum cernunt, praedantur, at hordea spernunt.
> Hoc dedignantur, frumenti farre cibantur.

> They spot and plunder stores of wheat, but barley they disdain:
> They don't like this – they'd rather feed on spelt of other grain.

Further, the friends and contemporaries to whom he sent copies of his *Vita Malchi* all either lived in France or were first-generation immigrants. On the other hand, his loyalties were English: he writes of 'gens Anglica nostra' (LMP 25.15), and he revered the English saints associated with Canterbury.

Contrasts: lives of Edward the Confessor

One area in which there was continuity between pre- and post-Conquest literature was hagiography, especially (once the Normans had accepted their validity) the lives of Anglo-Saxon saints.[16] This was at times a minor literary industry, expressing sometimes simple local loyalty, sometimes a broader national spirit. In the first period, the major authors were Goscelin and Folchard; in the thirteenth century Henry of Avranches wrote several verse lives, and in the fourteenth John of Tynemouth assembled the major collection known as the *Sanctilogium*.[17] The motives for rewriting these lives varied: sometimes they were historical (where new evidence appeared), sometimes simply stylistic, adapting old material to new rhetorical moulds. One of the most dramatic adjustments, however, is seen in the various lives of Edward the Confessor, where the alterations not only transform the style and structure of the earliest *Vita* but also drastically shift its political stance. First, a sketch of pre-Conquest history is necessary.

Edward was venerated both by the English (as the last successful and untainted English monarch) and by the Normans (for his nomination of William, duke of Normandy, as his heir). He was the son of King Ethelred by Emma, who later married Cnut, Danish king of England. When Cnut and all his heirs died, Edward succeeded him. He married Edith, daughter of Godwin, earl of Wessex and former adviser of Cnut; Godwin's sons included Harold (later king of England) and Tostig. Edward, who had spent his youth in exile, brought many foreign ecclesiastics to England, including Robert of Jumièges, who became archbishop of Canterbury. Godwin quarrelled with Robert, and went into exile (and Edith went temporarily to the nunnery at Wilton). Later Godwin was reconciled to Edward, and Robert left and was replaced as archbishop by Stigand. England was invaded by the Welsh and Scots, who were repelled by Godwin's sons Harold and Tostig. The two brothers eventually quarrelled, and Tostig went into exile. On Edward's death, Harold (despite his apparent earlier promise to accept William of Normandy as king) took the throne; Tostig joined Harold Hardrather in an invasion of the North, and was killed by Harold at Stamford Bridge. Finally, William invaded England and killed Harold at the Battle of Hastings.

The first life of Edward was written probably in 1066: Hastings is not mentioned but is perhaps implicit.[18] It is a prosimetrum,[19] in which the verses are in elegiac couplets with fairly regular monosyllabic Leonine rhyme. Although there are no divisions in the manuscript, it can most conveniently be divided (as Barlow has done) into two books. The first (about three times as long as the second) recounts the history of Edward, Godwin, Harold and Tostig, with frequent forebodings in the verses; the second, with the poet in despair at the loss of all his lords, describes, in prose, Edward's miracles and holy life. The structure is remarkable: even in the early part of Book I it is clear, in the verses, that disaster is impending, but the prose sections optimistically continue to recount the exploits of the Godwin family; it is only at the beginning of Book II that the poet admits that all is lost. Edward appears in Book I, always in a good light, but the attention is on the Godwins; only in Book II is he the central figure. Possibly the author planned the whole work at once as a doomed family saga, leading to a consolation for Queen Edith in the form of a record of the saintly life of her husband.

Book I. In a verse dialogue with his muse, the author promises to sing, in honour of Edith, a 'song of Edward' and praise of Godwin, from whom come the four streams of paradise. The prose recounts the miraculous acknowledgment of the unborn Edward's future kingship, even when he was apparently remote from the succession. It tells of Cnut, Godwin, Godwin's family, and Godwin's support of Edward's accession (with a physical description of the king); a poem describes the ship given by Godwin as a coronation gift. After a gap of two folios, another poem picks up the theme of the four rivers very obscurely: if they obeyed the Creator's rules, all would be well, but one river is destructive. The prose recounts Godwin's quarrel with Robert of Jumièges, his exile, Edith's retirement to Wilton, and Godwin's restoration, with poems on injustice (Godwin's unjust fall) and David's sparing of Saul (that is, Godwin's humility to Edward). After Godwin's death, Harold and Tostig are praised as models; a poem here begins with praise of them, but laments the dire effects of discord. As though there had been no mention of strife, the prose says that England thrived, guarded by the two brothers; it recalls Edward's love of hunting, and praises the virtues of Edward and Edith. Invasions by the Welsh and Scots are repelled by the brothers. Edward builds St Peter's at Westminster, Edith builds a chapel at Wilton; a poem (using Psalm 83) glorifies the Church. The final chapter of Book I describes a revolt in the North and the quarrel of Harold and Tostig, and the grief of the king and queen; Tostig goes into exile. Book II begins with another verse dialogue between poet and muse: the poet is bereft of lords, and his hope for a happy song has been dashed. Who will sing of the defeat of the Welsh? Who will sing of the Ouse choked with bodies (i.e. Stamford Bridge)? The muse advises him to please Edith by recounting Edward's virtues. The story almost begins again, with an account of the miraculous oath of allegiance to the unborn Edward, followed by his miraculous cures. A missing two folios probably contained further miracles. Finally Edward falls sick and reports a gloom-laden vision of England's future, defeated by foreigners; he commends Edith to Harold's care, and dies. Various miracles are performed at his tomb. (There is no mention of the succession.)

In 1138 Osbert of Clare, monk of Westminster,[20] rewrote the *Vita* in an attempt, initially unsuccessful, to have Edward canonized. He has transformed the apparently uneven but brooding *Vita* into a chronologically smooth, somewhat bland piece of traditional hagiography. All the Anglo-Saxon history has gone, and Godwin is mentioned only as Edith's father. After a prologue on the philosopher-king, Osbert describes Edward's lineage: by making him a younger son, he makes the prenatal oath of allegiance even more miraculous. He stresses the chastity of Edward's marriage with Edith, and recounts a true vision that Edward had, followed by Edward's apologies for his failure to visit Rome. Various miracles and visions are recounted, along with Edward's building of St Peter's and his generosity to it. His death is described, together with his vision of England's future; then there are some posthumous miracles, including one in which Edward's spirit aids Harold at Stamford Bridge.

In 1161 the campaign for Edward's canonization succeeded, and the translation of his relics was commemorated by yet another life, this time by Aelred of Rievaulx.[21] Aelred used Osbert's life as his basis, but entirely rewrote the prose in a more refined style. He added material from other sources, and began with a prologue in defence of wealth as no barrier to sanctity. He reintroduced material on Godwin (perhaps from William of Malmesbury), but for entirely hostile purposes: Aelred was naturally appalled by the ejection of Robert of Jumièges, rightful archbishop of Canterbury, and gleefully retold the story of Godwin's death, choking on a crust in the act of perjury. Aelred offered interpretations of many of the visions, and saw in Edward's final vision a prophecy of the accession of Henry II. He retained Osbert's account of Edward's ghostly assistance to Harold at Stamford Bridge, but made it serve as a kind of trap, leading Harold to his doom at Hastings. Thus, the life of an Anglo-Saxon king has been subtly transformed into service of the Norman and Plantagenet dynasties. At the end of the century, Aelred's life of Edward was versified by Alexander of Ashby.[22]

Forms: verse, the prosimetrum[23]

In this first period, although there was some rhythmical, stanzaic verse (as in Lawrence of Durham's Easter poem), the predominant verse forms were quantitative. Most poems were in hexameters or elegiac couplets (as they continued to be throughout Anglo-Latin). Many were unrhymed (e.g. Geoffrey of Monmouth's *Vita Merlini*); some, such as the *Carmen de Hastingae proelio*, have occasional monosyllabic rhyme. Others, especially Reginald of Canterbury, employed the full range of disyllabically rhymed hexameters and pentameters; these remained popular throughout the Middle Ages. What is particularly striking in this first period, however, is the use of quantitative lyric metres derived from, or based on, Horace, Martianus Capella and Boethius. Reginald of Canterbury used Sapphics in a poem recommending the reading of Horace for a mastery of metres. Goscelin (who is praised by Reginald for his ability in verse) used a wide range of lyric metres – some of his own invention – in his *Vita S. Edithae*. Gilbert Crispin used adonics. Henry of Huntingdon experimented with a variety of quantitative and rhythmical forms, often apparently trying to imitate in Latin the structures and cadences of vernacular English poetry. He also used some traditional classical lyric metres: adonics, the Fourth Asclepiad, and an eleven-syllable line perhaps based on the Sapphic line. These quantitative lyric metres disappeared from Anglo-Latin until the metrical experiments of John Seward in the early fifteenth century.

The influence of Martianus and Boethius is also seen in the prosimetrum. This form (to be distinguished from chronicles which simply quote apposite poems) regularly alternates passages of prose and verse, in which the poems summarize or comment on the prose argument. We have already discussed the anonymous *Vita Edwardi Confessoris*. Other examples include: Goscelin's *Vita S. Edithae*, Adelard of Bath's philosophical *De eodem et diverso*, and Lawrence of Durham's *Consolatio de morte amici*. The popularity of this form (used by Alain de Lille in his *De planctu naturae*) waned in England: to my knowledge, the only Anglo-Latin author who used it after this period was Elias of Thriplow.[24]

Political poetry and epitaphs

In the first three reigns of this period, before 1135, there is little political verse in comparison with later reigns, when an (admittedly selective) history of England could be written from the satirical poetry. On the Norman Conquest itself we have the *Carmen de Hastingae proelio* (though it may be a somewhat later work). The rebellion of Waltheof does not appear in literature until after 1219, when William of Ramsey wrote in his praise;[25] one of the consequences of his execution in 1076 was the murder of Walcher, bishop of Durham, in 1080, an event lamented by Godfrey of Winchester. Hints of William's devastation of the North are seen in the verse life of St Hilda, though this too may be a later poem. During the reign of William Rufus we have a poem (parts of which were quoted by William of Malmesbury, *Gesta Regum* 4.338) on the simony of Herbert Losinga in 1091, 'Surgit in ecclesia monstrum, genitore Losinga'. Rhygyfarch ap Sulien lamented the Norman invasion of Wales in 1093. The quarrels of Anselm first with William Rufus and then with Henry I resulted in his two exiles of 1097–1100 and 1103–7: his absence from England was mourned by Reginald of Canterbury and Gilbert Crispin. The disaster of the White Ship in 1120, which deprived Henry I of his heirs, elicited a poem quoted by Henry of Huntingdon. Otherwise there was little verse comment on the events of nearly seventy years. As we will see, it was the death of Henry I in 1135 and the subsequent anarchy that stirred poets to action. We must remember that before 1135 most of the writers represented the conquering aliens, and that for most of them events in England were of less interest than those in their old homes across the Channel.

One kind of contemporary event, however, did have a literary by-product: the verse epitaph was almost a genre in itself. On the death of a famous person (usually, but not always, religious) an abbey or other body would circulate to the other major religious houses a roll listing the recently deceased as a kind of newsletter; on it the members of the various communities would inscribe their prayers, often in verse. Delisle has printed a series of these rolls:[26] in one there are many poems in honour of Matilda, daughter of William the Conqueror and abbess of Caen (d. 1113), with the names of many otherwise unknown English versifiers. Orderic Vitalis records the epitaphs of many famous people, usually Norman abbots and bishops but also including Matilda, widow of William the Conqueror; some were copied from tombstones, some his own composition. He mentions that on the death of William of Fécamp his colleagues and students composed verse epitaphs:

Hildebert's was selected for inscription on the tomb, and one by Athelelm was written in the roll; as we will see, another was composed by Godfrey of Winchester. Verse epitaphs continue to appear in chronicles, and many found their way into poetic anthologies.[27]

Carmen de Hastingae proelio

The most obvious text with which to begin a history of post-Conquest Anglo-Latin literature would seem to be that on the Battle of Hastings itself, the *Carmen de Hastingae proelio*.[28] Although the author, according to the traditional view, was Guy, bishop of Amiens, its claim to a share in the Anglo-Latin heritage is strong, as it concerns the very event that caused the Normanization of England. Further, it is apparently dedicated to Lanfranc, archbishop of Canterbury from 1070, and Guy was chaplain to Matilda, wife of the Conqueror. Unfortunately for the neatness of this opening, a recent study has argued very persuasively that it was not composed in 1067 but was a literary exercise written some time after 1125 in Northern France.[29] The matter is still under debate, and the arguments are too complex to present here, but the poem is interesting enough in itself to merit inclusion. It consists of 835 lines in (usually unrhymed) elegiac couplets; it ends with a hexameter and is presumably incomplete.

The twenty-five line hexameter proemium begins:

> Quem probitas celebrat, sapientia munit et ornat,
> Erigit et decorat, L. W. salutat (1–2)

> W. greets L., whose virtue brings him praise,
> Whom wisdom guards, adorns, uplifts and decorates.

This has traditionally been interpreted 'Lanfrancum Wido salutat' ('Guy greets Lanfranc'), but other interpretations are possible. The poem proper begins with an address to William, waiting at Vimeu for a fair wind; his prayers are answered and the Normans cross the Channel. As they begin to lay waste, a messenger goes to inform Harold, who is returning from Stamford Bridge where Tostig was killed:

> Inuidus ille Cain fratris caput amputat ense (137)

> In envy Cain, with sword, strikes off his brother's head.

Harold rallies his men and sends a defiant message; William responds similarly and asserts his right to the kingdom:

> Etguardus quod rex ut ei succederet heres
> Annuit et fecit, teque fauente sibi (293–4)

> King Edward's grant declared that William should succeed
> And be his heir – and you agreed to this.

Battle begins, and the first kill goes to a Norman mummer known in French romance as Taillefer:

> Incisor-ferri mimus cognomine dictus (399)

> A mummer, who went by the name of Taillefer.

Fortunes ebb and flow, and William twice loses his horse, but is supplied with one by Eustace of Boulogne. Harold is finally killed by four knights, and the English are routed. On the next morning William, rejecting Harold's mother's request for his body, has it interred, Beowulf-like, on the edge of the cliff as a guardian against enemies:

> Per mandata ducis rex hic Heralde quiescis,
> Vt custos maneas littoris et pelagi (591–2)

> The duke's command is this: here, Harold, you remain,
> To stand on guard above the shore and sea.

William claims the kingship and consolidates his victory by taking Dover, Canterbury, and Winchester. Initially London resists, choosing the young Edgar as king; William lays siege to the city and, after some obscure negotiations and attempts at double-crossing, London finally surrenders. The extant remainder of the poem (753–835) describes William's coronation, the regalia and the ceremony.

The *Carmen*, whether a contemporary report or a later re-creation, is the literary equivalent of the Bayeux Tapestry, paralleled only by Baudri's account of the wall-paintings in Countess Adela's bedroom.[30]

Godfrey of Winchester

Godfrey (d. 1107), a native of Cambrai, joined the community of St Swithin's at Winchester in about 1070.[31] His writing was praised by William of Malmesbury ('litteratura et religione insignis fuit' *Gesta Regum* 5.444), and he was the first resident Latin poet after the Conquest. He wrote two hundred and thirty-eight epigrams and nineteen short poems, mainly epitaphs, on historical figures. The *Epigrams* are superficially in the style of Martial,[32] and the imitation was so successful that in some later continental manuscripts they were actually ascribed to Martial.[33] They are pithy comments on behaviour, addressed to fictitious persons (Damianus, Coranus, Didimus, etc.), and are compressed, allusive, and often cryptic; e.g.

> Pecte lavaque canem, curam tibi ponis inanem,
> Pontice, si studium, dum colis Elvidium (Epig. 7)

> So, Pontic, wash and comb your dog – your labour is in vain:
> You waste your time in courting Elwi's grace.

17

That is, cultivating Elvidius is as futile as washing a dog. Here, however, the resemblance ends: where Martial's epigrams are bitter and (even in disguised form) personally abusive, Godfrey's are full of commonplace moral advice. There is nothing in Godfrey about social status or personal hygiene. In his preface he says that he intends to follow the advice of Horace:

> Undique susceptum qui miscuit utile dulci,
> Undique laudatum pagina nota refert (Prol. 1–2)[34]

> A famous dictum holds him praised and everywhere revered
> Whose words combine the useful and the sweet.

Equally bland is the statement that he laughs at himself as well as others:

> . . . carpo alios, me quoque carpo simul (Prol. 6)

> . . . I others blame, but also blame myself.

In fact, the morals, though couched in the form of criticism of individuals, are, as Raby says, those of the *Distichs of Cato*, advocating temperance, caution, and wisdom. E.g.

> Deridens alios non inderisus abibis,
> Unde alios rides, Scevola, si facias (Epig. 12)[35]

> O Scaevola, your scathing tongue will not escape unscathed,
> If you are guilty of the faults you mock.

On the other hand, although the moral lessons are those of the cloister and far from pagan, they are not (despite occasional biblical echoes) specifically Christian: God is hardly mentioned, the Church never. The *Epigrams* are organized in gradually ascending size;[36] they are all in elegiac couplets, sometimes with rhyme:

> Qua doceat sedem querit Plotinus et edem;
> Querit qua doceat, non ea que doceat (Epig. 81)

> Plotinus seeks a chair and hall to teach: he seeks a place
> But not the subjects that he ought to teach.

Other kinds of rhetorical repetition are common, such as epanalepsis:

> Crimen in omne ruis, quia non peccasse superbis,
> Te iustum esse putans, crimen in omne ruis (Epig. 113, 3–4)

> You fall headlong in every sin, for bragging that you don't;
> By claiming that you're just you fall in sin.

Of Godfrey's nineteen *Historical Poems*, all but two are epitaphs of ten or twelve lines of elegiac couplets.[37] Many, especially those of people who died at Winchester, may have been known to Godfrey personally. Some may have been intended for the kind of mortuary rolls discussed above. At least three must have been literary exercises, as they are of people who had died before Godfrey went to Winchester: Cnut, d. 1035, Emma, Cnut's widow, d. 1052; Edward the Confessor, d. 1066. The structure of each epitaph is formal: biography, praise, and a dating formula, e.g.

> Urebat binis sol egoceronta diebus,
> > Cum tu deposito pondere carnis abis (*HP* 4, 9–10)

> When for two days the sun had burned the horned Goat,
> > You put aside the weight of flesh and left.

The method of death is sometimes given, as in the case of William the Conqueror's son Richard, who was killed while hunting:

> Discebas cervos fragili terebrare sagitta;
> > Mors ausa est forti figere te jaculo (*HP* 10, 7–8)

> With slender dart you learned to pierce the fleeting deer,
> > But Death was bold to fix you with his spear.

In the epitaph of William the Conqueror there is a hint of the lawlessness that followed in William Rufus' reign

> Justitiae facies erepto judice marcet,
> > Fracta gemit virtus, pax fugitiva latet (*HP* 5, 9–10)

> The judge is snatched away: the face of Justice pales,
> > Sad Virtue groans, and Peace in exile lurks.

There is pathos in the one on Wulnoth, a son of Godwin, who was a hostage through most of his life but seems to have died soon after his release in 1087:

> Exilium, carcer, tenebrae, clausura, catenae,
> > Accipiunt puerum destituuntque senem (*HP* 12, 5–6)

> A life of exile, prison, darkness, bars and chains
> > Detained you as a boy, release you old.

Two other poems (*HP* Nos. 8–9) are in hexameters; they deplore the murder in 1080 of Walcher, bishop of Durham, and call for vengeance on his murderers. The occasion of the murder was the slaying, by one of Walcher's Norman attendants, of his English adviser Ligulf, and Godfrey may be hinting that Walcher's murder was not entirely unprovoked:

> Forsitan hanc culpam contagia prima tulerunt,
> > Ut sit culpa recens scelerum vindicta priorum (*HP* 9, 19–20)

> Perhaps those former taints gave rise to this new fault,
> So this new crime was vengeance for those older deeds.

In minor ways Godfrey can be used as a literary commentary on the events of the time.

Canterbury: Anselm, Goscelin, Osbern

The principal literary centre in England was, not surprisingly, at Canterbury, where there were two communities of monks: at Christ Church, the archiepiscopal see, and St Augustine's. We have already mentioned the zealous attempts at reform by the first Norman archbishop, Lanfranc (1070–89). His successor, Anselm (who also came from Bec), seems to have been more accommodating: he had earlier persuaded Lanfranc to accept the sanctity of St Elphege, and under his regime the old Canterbury saints, as well as other Anglo-Saxon saints, were honoured by Goscelin and Reginald.[38] Anselm is famous primarily for his philosophical and theological writings, but he is also of literary interest. Despite his opposition to the feast of the Immaculate Conception, he was active in promoting devotion. His three prose *Meditationes* are emotionally highly charged; like his *Orationes* (to God, the Virgin, and the saints), they concern sin and salvation, and induce a sense of humility and vulnerability.[39] They are not 'affective' in the later style (which stresses the pathos of the sufferings of Christ and the Virgin) and they do not meditate on biblical events, but they encourage this kind of devotion. Anselm's words summarize the attitude: 'Sentiam per affectum quod sentio per intellectum.'[40]

We also have two quite long poems concerning Anselm, both in elegiacs. One is on behalf of someone called Hugh, whose life and spiritual health are in danger; the other is a lament in praise of Anselm, shortly after his death. Neither is very distinguished; their editor has shown that the attribution to William of Chester is an unlikely inference from one of Anselm's letters, and that other attributions are no more than guesses.[41]

One of the most venerable figures at Canterbury was Goscelin, the Flemish biographer, whose career we have already mentioned.[42] He wrote many prose saints' lives; only a few have been edited in recent times, but many were sources for John of Tynemouth's *Sanctilogium*.[43] In his early Wessex period he wrote lives of St Wulfsige, bishop of Sherborne, and of St Edith, founder of Wilton.[44] The *Vita S. Edithae* is his only work that contains verse: there are fourteen poems in a variety of complex quantitative lyric metres; significantly, it is for his command of verse that Reginald of Canterbury commends him:

> Carminis omne genus scit enim, sic carmine plenus (LMP 15, 11)

> For full of song he understands all kinds of song.

His other early work (1080–2) was the prose *Liber confortatorius* to Eva, a nun who had left Wilton to become a recluse at Angers; the work is moral and conventional, but has passages of autobiographical significance. Between his Wessex and Canterbury periods we have, among others, lives of Sts Wulfhild and Ivo. In

Canterbury, from about 1090, he was known especially for his music: Reginald says that he cheered everyone with his songs ('cantibus exhilaras omnes', LMP 15, 53) and addressed to him a poem mythologizing musical terminology. William of Malmesbury, who called Goscelin the best prose writer since Bede, said that he was second only to Osbern in music. Here he wrote lives of St Mildred and St Augustine of Canterbury (with miracles, translation, and an account of other Canterbury saints, Mellitus, Justus, Honorius, Deusdedit, Theodore, and Hadrian). These and other Canterbury saints were also celebrated in verse by Reginald.[45] Even if Goscelin is denied the authorship of many other lives attributed to him, he is nevertheless the major English hagiographer after Bede, and unsurpassed for many years.

We have just mentioned William of Malmesbury's praise of Osbern of Canterbury for his music. Osbern was a native Englishman; he wrote a life of St Dunstan, utilizing those by Adelard and 'Author B', but Eadmer and William of Malmesbury both felt they had to revise it because of its historical defects. At Lanfranc's request he wrote a life of St Elphege, after Lanfranc had been convinced by Anselm of Elphege's sanctity; this life was later turned into verse, as discussed below.[46]

Folchard; Dominic of Evesham

The history of prose hagiography is too vast to be attempted in this book, but in the context of Goscelin two other writers should be mentioned. Like Goscelin, Folchard came from St Bertin, and between 1068 and 1084/5 was a kind of 'acting' abbot of Thorney; he was described by Orderic (11.4.281–2) as 'karitatiuus gramaticae artis ac musicae peritissimus'. He wrote lives of St Bertin, John of Beverley (sent to Aldred, archbishop of York), Botulph, and possibly Oswald and Omer.[47]

Dominic, prior of Evesham (d. after 1130), wrote on Sts Egwin, Odulf, and Wistan, but his most important contribution to Anglo-Latin literature was his collection of miracles of the Virgin, one of the earliest made.[48]

Verse lives of saints

St Albans lives of Catherine and Elphege

The late twelfth-century manuscript Corpus Christi College, Cambridge, MS 375 (apparently written at St Albans but sent to Christ Church, Canterbury) contains two unpublished verse saints' lives. They were originally in two separate booklets, but were almost certainly by the same author. The first is a life of St Catherine of Alexandria; after a prologue, it consists of over 3400 lines of Leonine hexameters; it follows fairly closely the vulgate version of the passion, but with many long expansions, especially of the speeches.[49] The second life is of St Elphege, martyred archbishop of Canterbury. The poet says that the life had first been written in prose by Osbern,[50] and that this was sufficient for the 'gens religiosa'; a more fussy age, however, now rejects prose in favour of poetry:

> Sed uirtute tamen minor etas deliciosa
> Carmine scripta probat cui prosa dicta perosa
>
> This present fussy age, in moral virtue worse,
> Disdains mere humble prose, prefers what's clothed in verse.

The verse life is in collateral hexameters, and consists of over 3800 lines. These two lives were probably written one or two generations after Osbern. The manuscript also contains short poems for the feasts of St Alban and of Sts Peter and Paul.

Gregory of Ely: St Etheldrida

The combination of local pride with an interest in the Anglo-Saxon past is exemplified by Gregory of Ely. His verse life of St Etheldrida (Audrey), seventh abbess of Ely, was written after 1116.[51] It consists of three books of 983 Leonine hexameters (mainly with monosyllabic rhyme) and a few elegiac couplets. The material of the early part (St Audrey's life) corresponds to Bede's account, but for later events (the sack of Ely by the Vikings, the refoundation, and later miracles) there is a correspondence with the *Liber Eliensis*. Either the text is deficient or the poem was left unfinished. The narrative sticks closely to the traditional sequence of birth-life-miracles, but is also illustrated by Virgilian and other classical echoes. Gregory is especially interested in describing the new building of the cathedral and in praising Henry I for his favour to the monastery. The style is generally very pedestrian:

> Postquam septenis subiectis prefuit annis,
> Sic uiuens moritur corpusque sacrum sepelitur (1 197–8)
>
> When she in life had ruled her flock for seven years
> She passed away; her holy corpse was laid to rest.

St Hilda of Whitby

This is the appropriate place to deal with another text based primarily on Bede, an anonymous verse life of the Northern saint, St Hilda of Whitby. It could, in fact, have been composed any time between the death of William the Conqueror in 1087 and the middle of the fifteenth century, the date of the sole extant manuscript.[52] It consists of two distinct parts, possibly the work of two separate authors at different times: 1–551 in simple Leonine hexameters on St Hilda and Caedmon, and 552–609 (in *Leonini unisoni*) on the history of Whitby Abbey after Hilda. After the invocation of the muse,

> Iam mera Clio sona, iam sis ad carmina prona, (1)

> Pure Clio, now sing forth; be present for my song.

the first part is essentially based on Bede. It recounts Hilda's birth (with the miracle of the necklace), her baptism and vocation to monastic life, her stay in East Anglia and visit to Chelles (misunderstanding Bede), her foundation of a community on the Wyre, her move to Hartlepool, and finally to Sinus Fari (Whitby):

> Inde Sinum Fari peciit quo velle morari
> Prouida duxit hera; locus hic sibi venit ab era (96–7)

> Thence Lighthouse Bay this prudent mistress sought, for there
> She planned to stay: our Lady gave this place to her
> (The sense of *ab era* is unclear: perhaps Hēra = Juno = the virgin)

Her rule there is described, and her famous alumni and miracles. Here the poet adds two stories not in Bede but found also in John of Tynemouth:
(1) Hilda's petrification of noxious snakes (an aetiological myth to explain the ammonites found on the North Yorkshire coastline):

> Serpens virus habens quondam sub cespite labens
> In pelago pleno modo labitur absque veneno (238–9)

> The poisoned snake that once lay hidden in the grass
> Now slips beneath the open sea, all venom gone.

(2) her confinement of predatory birds and her resuscitation of one that seemed to be dead. These stories are followed by accounts of Hilda's death, with attendant miracles, and Caedmon's poetic inspiration:

> Mox licet invitus Cedmon cantare petitus
> Versus psallebat quales non ante sciebat (436–7)

> Then, though unwilling, Caedmon, called upon to sing,
> Produced such verses which he'd never known before.

The second half of the poem is very compressed and allusive, and is almost incomprehensible without reference to contemporary sources. It recounts the sack of Whitby by the Vikings, the flight of the monks to Glastonbury with Hilda's relics:

> Hinc decesserunt quia mortem contremuerunt;
> Hylde, scripta ferunt, cum gazis ossa tulerunt (554–5),

> They then departed, dreading death. They took away
> The abbey's wealth and Hilda's bones, as records say.

the desolation of the North (at an unspecified date), the sudden monastic vocation of a soldier Reinfrid, his refoundation of the abbey on land donated by William

Percy, complaints made to the king, and an unspecified vengeance inflicted by Begu, Hilda's former disciple.

St Cuthbert

The North's most famous saint, of course, was Cuthbert. Bede had written an *opus geminatum* (that is, a verse and prose life) on him, and this was followed in the early twelfth century by an anonymous poem of about eight hundred Leonines (inc. 'O pater Anglorum').[53] The poem relates the main events in Cuthbert's life and his miracles; each story is turned into a prayer by the author for his own reform from sin. The poem is preserved in a separate booklet attached to the famous illustrated life of Cuthbert in University College, Oxford, MS 165.[54]

Reginald of Canterbury

We return now to Canterbury. In literary terms the most interesting writer there (as a Latin poet second only to Nigel Whiteacre at the end of the twelfth century) was Reginald. Some time in the late eleventh century he left his abbey of Noyers and native Faye-la-Vineuse (of which, as we have seen, he retained nostalgic memories) to become a monk at St Augustine's.[55] We will consider below his many short poems (including several on Anselm and Canterbury saints), but his major work was his six-book verse epic on the life of the desert saint Malchus. We are lucky to have also his first draft of the poem, which provides an insight into his literary procedures. These can best be appreciated by giving first a synopsis of his source, the brief prose life by Jerome:[56]

Jerome says that as a young man he visited the Syrian town of Maronia, where he met an old man, Malchus, living chastely with an old woman; at Jerome's request Malchus then tells his story in the first person. 'When I was a young man, my parents pressed me to marry, so I fled to the desert and entered a monastery. After many years I learned that my father had died; I decided to go home to visit my mother. Despite my abbot's pleas I left and joined a caravan of travellers; we were captured by bandits and I was sold into slavery along with a woman. I was put in charge of sheep and found happiness as a kind of desert monk, but my master wished to reward my good service by marrying me to the woman, although she had a husband. At first I refused, but yielded under threat of death. In despair I planned to commit suicide, but the woman also pledged herself to perpetual chastity and proposed that we should simply feign marriage to deceive our master. We lived continently and contentedly but one day, after seeing ants at work, I remembered the pleasure of communal life and also Solomon's words, and determined to escape. We took goatskins and inflated them to cross a river, where we lost our food. We saw our master and a servant in pursuit, and took refuge in a cave. First the servant and then the master himself tried to enter the cave, but were killed by a lioness, whose den it was. We were terrified, but the lioness eventually left. Riding on our master's camels we reached freedom and settled in this monastery.' Jerome says that the story exemplifies chastity and shows that a man dedicated to Christ can die but not be overcome.

It is a brief story, sparingly told, but full of incident and drama, which Reginald exploited to the full. In his first draft, of 1076 Leonine hexameters, he made a radical change that would make possible all his later expansions:[57] he removed the framing device (Jerome's introduction) and recast Malchus' personal story into a third-person narration. This allowed him to intrude authorial observations and apostrophes, and to record events not witnessed by Malchus himself. He also dramatized the action, introducing direct dialogue (e.g. between Malchus and his father, Malchus and the abbot).

The final version is over three times the length (3344 lines), and other patterns of rhyming hexameters have been introduced. It has been divided into six books, each intended for delivery in a single performance and ending with a formula:

Quo te Musa sequor ? Sta ! Cras iterabimus aequor (III 572)

Where next from here, O Muse ? But stay ! I'll cross the sea another day.

Hic quoque restabo: quae restant, cras reserabo (IV 673)

I'll stop here too, and what remains tomorrow I'll reveal again.

Jerome's meeting with Malchus has been restored, but at the end of Book VI; Malchus' 'wife' has been given a name, Malcha, and a much larger role in the story. Many of the expansions are simply poetic amplifications of earlier ideas, but others introduce new scenes and events. In a letter to Baldwin, prior of Rochester, Reginald gives us a rare insight into a medieval poet's justification for his fictions.[58] He has not, he says, deviated from Malchus' saintly character, but he is not writing history either; those who want the truth can go to Jerome (who must be believed), but the poet is like a stream, running between banks or across fields:

Item rogat auctor multumque precatur lectorem ne in singulis versibus aut verbis aucupetur historiae veritatem. Minimum plane aut omnino nichil referre arbitratus est utrum ea quae ostendere intendebat per vera an per veri similia ostenderet. Tamen si adhuc improbus est, ait: Mittimus eum ad librum quem Hieronimus de eodem Malcho scripserit; quem assumens ac legens conferat hunc nostrum et illius. Ubi eos concordare in historia viderit, credat ambobus. Ubi discordare, non cogitur ut credat nostro; cogitur autem ut semper credat Hieronimo. Cucurrit ille via regia nec ab alveo declinavit historiae. Nos instar rivuli currentes, modo ripas tenuimus, modo arva rigavimus, dum ea quae per historiam non erant, per artem edidimus . . . quantaslibet ergo virtutes Malcho personaliter ascripserimus, non a vero deviavimus. At in reliquis, multa nos, ut suum est versificantium, confinxisse non negamus.

Further, the author begs and earnestly beseeches the reader not to search in each verse or word for the truth of history. In the author's opinion, it matters little or nothing whether he shows what he intends to show by means of the truth or the probable.

Nevertheless, if the reader is still obdurate my reply is as follows. I direct him to the book on this same Malchus that Jerome wrote; let him take it and read it, and compare Jerome's and my version. Wherever both concur in the story, he should believe both. Where they disagree, he is not compelled to believe mine; he is, however, always obliged to believe Jerome. Jerome ran along the royal way and did not diverge from the channel of history. I run along like a stream, sometimes keeping to the banks, sometimes watering the fields; things that did not exist in history I produced by art. Whatever virtues I have ascribed to Malchus personally, I have not diverged from truth, but in other matters, I do not deny that, as is the custom of versifiers, I have invented much.

A sense of his expansions can be had from an account of the largest of them. (1) After Malchus' capture by the bandits, there is a 381-line expansion (1 333–453; 11 1–265) on Malchus' misery, the bandits' feast, their drawing lots for the booty, and (based on *Aeneid* v) their games, including boxing, horse-races, discus-throwing, and a foot-race. (2) Thirty-six lines in the first version are replaced by 238 (III 1–238) describing the poverty of Malchus' dwelling (Jerome's 'speluncam semirutam') and Malchus' lamentations. (3) Reginald adds 112 lines in the authorial voice to dissuade Malchus from suicide (III 293–406). (4) Jerome had nothing to say about the married life of Malchus and his wife, except that it was chaste; Reginald first has Malchus instruct his wife on the religious life, with five lines in which he is taught to spin; in the final version, the five lines have become twenty-four, with all the details of spinning and weaving. (5) To the example of the ants, Reginald adds a similar account, based on the *Georgics*, of bees. (6) The largest expansion within the central story concerns the night of the couple's flight:

(IV 183–585) The setting of the sun in the western ocean evokes an elaborate mythological excursus. The sun is greeted by Neptune and the sea deities; there are descriptions of the 'domus Oceani', the banquet of Philosophy, the Seven Liberal Arts, the Muses, scenes of pagan mythology (such as the Labours of Hercules), and Pluto's dwelling. Finally Ocean, his attendants, and all the rivers of the world accompany the sun on his journey to the east. Meanwhile the moon (Cynthia) is shining; there is a description of her beauty and her cloak, on which are depicted stories such as Troy, Hippolyte, and Actaeon. In short, all is quiet and bright for the couple's flight.

(7) The third-person perspective allows Reginald to observe the anger of Malchus' master (whom he casts in the role of an astrologer) on discovering that the couple have fled, and his rage at his household. In the long version, the astrological observations are learnedly expanded (v 19–58). (8) When the couple safely reach Maronia, Reginald adds an account (v 502–64) of how Malchus planted a garden, with flowers, vegetables, vineyard and orchard. He ends the book with a sowing image:

Sevimus haec hodie; dabo cras sata poma Thaliae (v 565)

Today I've sown the Muse's seed, tomorrow I'll produce their yield.

(9) Book VI (not in the first draft of the poem) is indeed the 'fruit', and is entirely Reginald's creation. It begins with a series of hymns, supposedly composed by Malchus, in tristichs and tetrastichs,[59] to the Trinity, the Cross, the Virgin and the Apostles. The last, VI 288–415, to his guardian angel, in four-line stanzas of *caudati*, was often excerpted.[60] Malchus lives happily ever after, performing the roles of both Martha and Mary. Finally Reginald gives an account of Jerome and his meeting with Malchus, who agrees to tell his tale:

> Tunc sibi narravit quaecumque stilus peraravit,
> Aut suus aut noster, suus olim sed modo noster (VI 515–6)

> And then to him he did unfold what once his pen had fully told
> 'His pen' or was it his or mine ? It once was his but now it's mine.

Reginald closes with an elegiac couplet:

> Currendi finis quadrigis sive carinis
> Nostris hoc igitur pentametro dabitur (VI 532–3)

> The race is run, by boat or cart, and from my writing here I part;
> The race is run – Pentameter will see it done.

Reginald claims Thalia, muse of comedy, as his inspiration, and his motives were primarily literary. His recasting of the original tale and his expansions (including the extended role of Malcha) are all directed to making it a more entertaining and diverting story; both in structure and in its episodes it is a romance. Nevertheless its hero is saintly and his chastity remains inviolate. Further, Reginald directs the poem to monks who were forbidden to wander (*Epistola ad monachos*, p. 43):

> O monachi cari, quos non sinit ordo vagari ,

> Dear cloistered monks, who're strictly bound by rule from wandering around

and the story serves as a warning against the dangers, both physical and moral, of leaving the cloister. Reginald would have liked Chaucer's comparison of 'a monk out of his cloystre' to 'a fissh that is waterlees'.[61]

Reginald was proud of his epic, and sent copies to at least ten of his contemporaries. We have already mentioned his letter to Baldwin, prior of Rochester: in this he asks for the return of this text, after copying, by Easter. He must also have sent one to the renowned Hildebert, for we have Hildebert's gracious reply: although he was busy with administration, he says, he has read *Malchus* with pleasure, noting the 'figmentis fabularum'; he expresses delight that Reginald had made use of some of his, Hildebert's, lines.[62] In his collection of minor poems, many were written to accompany a copy of the *Malchus* and some are from the recipients.[63] In Leonine elegiac couplets he writes to Gilbert Crispin, abbot of Westminster,[64] saying that he wrote the *Malchus* at Gilbert's request; he uses the 'poem as ship' metaphor with which both Jerome and Reginald himself opened the story of Malchus (WMP No. 1 'Tiro rudis Martem'). In a poem rhyming entirely on *-orem* (WMP No. 2), he sent *Malchus* to Hugo, sub-prior of St Pancras abbey at Lewes, as his trepidation would not permit him to send it to the great prior Lanzo. He sent another copy with a poem (LMP No. 1) to Lambert, abbot of St Bertin, whom he may have known through Anselm or Goscelin.[65] Lambert replied with fulsome praise (LMP Nos. 2–4):

> Dum Statius, dum Virgilius, dum Naso legetur,
> Perpetuus liber iste tuus non emorietur (LMP 2, 13–14)

> As long as Statius', Virgil's, Ovid's works still thrive,
> Your Malchus will not die but always stay alive.

Reginald addressed a series of three poems to Anselm during his exile of 1104–6 (LMP Nos. 5–7); in the third he recounts a dream in which Anselm assured him of his speedy return and said that the *Malchus* was to be kept for him to approve and authorize:

> Quemque manu propria Malchum, dictante sophia,
> Metro scripsisti, dictasti, composuisti,
> Auctorizandum cum venero sive probandum,
> Hunc mihi custodi, nec eum prius, obsecro, prodi
> Quam veniam . . . (LMP No. 7, 44–8)

> And Malchus, – which you wrote with your own hand,
> At wisdom's voice, and versified and framed, –
> Keep it for me to authorize and pass;
> Don't publish it before I come, I ask.

A series of six poems is addressed to Arnulf, prior of the neighbouring Christ Church (LMP Nos. 8–13). The first is a propempticon to his muse, who has only a short way to go, an hour or so:

> Non est longa via quam debes ire, Thalia;
> Parvam tolle moram ! Potes ire, redire, per horam
> Unam, quo celeris apices hos ferre iuberis (LMP 8, 1–3)

> You don't have far to go, my merry muse, and so
> There's no need to be slack: to go both there and back
> A single hour will do to get this message through.

She need not be afraid as Reginald will accompany her ('Comes ibo'). He wonders what poem he can send to Arnulf, whom he praises and to whom he commends wisdom; finally he decides to send *Malchus* and asks for Arnulf's patronage. In the next poem (LMP No. 14) the muse has to carry *Malchus* overseas, to Stephen, abbot of his old abbey of Noyers:

Expers Musa maris tenus hac, transire rogaris
Aequor et ire celer, quo per mea scripta reveler (LMP 14, 1–2)

You have to go – although to you the sea's unknown –
Across to France, where by my writings I'll be known.

The next two (LMP Nos. 15–16) are to Goscelin. The first, sent with *Malchus*, praises Goscelin's poetic skills so extravagantly as almost to amount to parody: Goscelin is as full of verses as the Alps with snow, April with flowers, and so on, in over eighty such similes. The second, in a very elaborate metre, is an obscure myth explaining the nature of the octave.[66] The next four poems in the manuscript (WMP Nos. 3–4, LMP Nos. 17–18) do not accompany *Malchus*. The first two, in collateral hexameters, are to Aimeric of Faye-la-Vineuse, Reginald's home town, and to the town of Faye itself: they are full of nostalgia. The next is addressed to Anselm the younger,[67] lamenting the absence of archbishop Anselm but praising his nephew. Most of Reginald's correspondents admired the *Malchus*, but in the next poem (LMP No. 19) Thomas (II), archbishop of York, added a warning against pride:

Hoc solum timeo, ne mens tua leta tropheo
Glorificetur eo displiceatque Deo (LMP 19, 11–12)

My only fear is that you will, rejoicing in your epic's skill,
Fall prey to boastfulness, thus causing God's distress.

The next twelve poems (LMP Nos. 20–31) all concern Canterbury itself. There are poems in honour of Augustine, Lawrence and Mellitus, Justus and Honorius, Deusdedit, Theodore, Hadrian and Theodore, Mildred, Letard, and Ethelbert and Bertha (LMP Nos. 20–8); these are followed by the 'tituli' of the Canterbury saints, archbishops and abbots (LMP No. 29); finally, two poems (LMP Nos. 30–1) are addressed to the choir, exhorting them to sing in praise. This series is remarkable for an unusual kind of rhyme, not seen again until Michael of Cornwall,[68] in which the middle of a word, or the end of one and the beginning of the next, rhyme with the final syllables of the line; in the first poem the last word of one line is repeated as the first of the next:

Laudibus Aug*usti*ne, tui decus effero b*usti*,
Busti, quod cele*bra*re lira iuvat et fide c*rebra*.
Crebra tuum cla*ma*bit opus laus crebraque *fama* (LMP 20, 1–3)

The glory of your tomb, Aug*usti*ne, sing I m*ust*.
'I m*ust* ?' – on lyre and fiddle str*ing* I'm glad to s*ing*,
To s*ing* and often cry in p*raise* and glory *raise*.

Using two words:

Septima quem sup*er* *a*stra levat sors tempore s*era* . . .
Preminuit b*is* *te*rnis maior in arte mag*ister* (24, 2–4)

29

> In order *seven*th, Theodore was raised to *heaven* . . .
> In art the *mas*ter, outshone six, by none sur*passed*.
> (*Note*: Theodore was seventh archbishop of Canterbury)

Using triple rhyme:

> State ch*ori*, sensu mem*ori* cantuque son*ori*,
> O iuv*enes* sanctique s*enes*, voces date l*enes* (30, 1–2)

> Rise, singers, sing in tune, and don't forget your words;
> O young and honoured old, let gentle sounds be heard.

In all his poems Reginald shows a mastery of rhymed dactylic verse, both hexameters and elegiacs. The *Malchus* (except for Book VI) is principally in simple Leonines, but there are set pieces in collaterals, caudati, and so on. In one poem (LMP No. 18) Reginald claims to be following Virgil's advice ('numero deus impare gaudet', *Ecl.* 8, 75) and writes the poem entirely in pentameters. In another poem (WMP No. 5) he shows a strong interest in quantitative lyric metres, urging Osbern to study Horace in order to acquire a mastery of metre. The poem itself is in Sapphics:

> Discat Osbernus studio frequenti
> Regulas certas Sapphici tenoris,
> Quas potest nemo nisi per laborem
>   Discere jugem (WMP 5, 1–4)

> Let Osbern learn by constant work
> The Sapphic metre's certain rules,
> Which no one, but by labour long,
>   Can learn.

The fullest collection of Reginald's poems is in Bodleian MS Laud misc. 40, a Rochester manuscript.[69] After the opening letter to Baldwin, the *Malchus*, and the minor poems, there is a series of eighty one-line prayers, in Leonines, to the Virgin, the Cross, and Sts Michael, Theodore, Matthew and Maurice. Many of the lines are similar to Reginald's, and the prayers may be his or an imitator's.[70] Altogether, Reginald emerges as one of the most imaginative and versatile poets of this first period, matched only by Lawrence of Durham a generation later.

Eadmer

The last and youngest member of this Canterbury circle was Eadmer, an Englishman, historian and hagiographer; he was active between about 1090 and 1120, and died about 1130.[71] Because of its historical inaccuracies he found it necessary to rewrite Osbern's life of St Dunstan. One of his most interesting works is his biography of St Anselm: as an Englishman, Eadmer had been annoyed by Lanfranc's assault on the native English saints, and he was therefore pleased at

Anselm's moderation and humanity. He also wrote lives of Sts Oda, Bregwin, and Oswald, and a *Historia Novorum*. He joined the supporters of the feast of the Immaculate Conception in a treatise later ascribed to Anselm himself.

Gilbert Crispin

One of the recipients of Reginald's *Malchus* – in fact, one of those who had encouraged him to write it – was Gilbert Crispin. He had been a monk at Bec under Lanfranc and Anselm; Lanfranc summoned him to England and in 1085 appointed him abbot of Westminster, where he remained until his death in 1117.[72] His writings, which are mainly homiletic or theological, closely follow Anselm's interests; they include a life of Herluin, abbot of Bec, and two dialogues, one between a Christian and a Jew, the other between a Christian and a 'gentile' (a pagan but monotheistic philosopher). He wrote a poem to Anselm during his exile, in seventy-eight adonics, deploring the effect his absence was having on his flock:

> Quae modulando
> clara solebat
> dicere laudes
> fistula vestra
> murmure rauco
> nunc canit, atque
> lugubris extat (1–7)

> The flute which once
> Would gladly sing
> And clearly speak
> In praise of you,
> Now hoarsely croaks
> In sorrow, now
> Is full of grief.

Peter Alfonsi; Adelard of Bath

Two other writers during the reign of Henry I were Peter Alfonsi and Adelard of Bath, both primarily scientists. England's claims on Peter Alfonsi are tenuous; he was a Spanish Jew who converted to Christianity and became personal physician to Henry I.[73] His only literary work is the *Disciplina Clericalis*, a collection of moral and entertaining stories woven together in the frame of a dialogue between a father and son. It is one of the first introductions into the Western Latin tradition of Eastern (specifically Arabic) tales. It is the precursor of the collections of moral and moralized tales, such as the *Fables* of Odo of Cheriton and the *Gesta Romanorum*.[74]

Peter's astronomical works were utilized by another Englishman, Adelard of Bath.[75] His scientific works (based on Arabic and ultimately Aristotelian sources) have no place in a literary history, but his *De eodem et diverso* (1105–10) is a prosimetrum, closely modelled on Boethius.[76] It is a confrontation between Philocosmia (love of the world) and Philosophia for the allegiance of the writer. Naturally, Philosophia wins and instructs the writer on the Liberal Arts, especially geometry. The few poems simply help the work to conform to the Boethian model.

The beginning of the Anarchy

The writers discussed so far lived mainly before the death of Henry I in 1135. The drowning of Henry's heir William in the White Ship (1120) resulted in the succession of his nephew Stephen; Henry's death precipitated England into a period of chaos and anarchy. Even in 1135 writers sensed a time of trouble to come in both England and Normandy. Verse epitaphs on Henry, composed or recorded by Orderic Vitalis, Henry of Huntingdon, and Robert of Torigni, as well as chroniclers, lamented the passing of one who had brought peace and law.[77] Richard of Worcester, a monk of Winchester, wrote a typical epitaph of thirty-one lines in variously rhymed hexameters:[78]

> Deflet Normannus cum Francigena, Cenomannis,
> Sed magis et Anglis, et erit dolor omnibus annis.

> The French and Normans grieve; Le Mans and Englishmen
> Will mourn his death this year for ever without end.

The gloomy predictions proved all too true. Stephen's claim was disputed by Henry's daughter Matilda, ex-empress of Germany and countess of Anjou; she invaded England in support of the claim of her son, the future Henry II. The civil war let loose a period of anarchy when, in the words of the Peterborough Chronicle, 'Christ and his saints slept.' The anarchy was 'predicted' in Geoffrey of Monmouth's *Vita Merlini*.[79] There was almost a typology of torture: the Peterborough Chronicle lists a set of tortures inflicted by Geoffrey de Mandeville's men almost identical to those inflicted on Durham by William Cumin's supporters and reported by Simeon and Lawrence of Durham;[80] in fact it was the civil war that led to Cumin's seizure of Durham. By the end of Stephen's reign, the future king Henry II was being welcomed as a saviour by Osbert of Clare and Henry of Huntingdon.[81]

Osbert of Clare

The career of Osbert of Clare, like most of the writers in the rest of this chapter, straddled the reigns of Henry I and Stephen. He was a monk at Westminster under Gilbert Crispin and was at various times prior there, but he had troubles with the abbey and spent much time 'in exile', at Ely, Bury, and Pershore (a dependent house of Westminster, near Worcester).[82] This geographical wandering accounts for the wide range of saints whom he honoured. We have already discussed his rewriting of the life of Edward the Confessor (whose body is in Westminster).[83] He also wrote a collection of the miracles of St Edmund, for the younger Anselm, abbot of Bury, and prose lives of Ethelbert and (for Pershore) Edburga. Like the younger Anselm and others we have mentioned, he was a strong supporter of the feast of the Immaculate Conception, and in 1129 attended its celebration in London. He was therefore an enthusiastic devotee of St Anne, mother of the Virgin, and in 1136 at the request of Simon and Warin, bishop and dean of Worcester, he composed for the abbey of Pershore a set of six prayers to St Anne.[84]. Two of these are rhythmical poems. The first consists of 128 lines of couplets:

> O preclara mater matris
> quae concepit verbum patris
> Non commixtione maris,
> sed ut virgo singularis

> O mother of the mother who conceived
> The Father's word
> Without a fleshly union with a man,
> A maid unique.

The second, written in combinations of 8p and 7pp (sometimes producing the *Stabat mater* stanza), was for the use of a nun, as it is in the feminine:

> Fac ut grata vivam deo
> castitatis cum tropheo
> stricta sponsi fascia

> Grant that I may please my Lord
> And proffer chastity's reward,
> Bound firmly to the groom.

Osbert's extant letters, forty-three in all, date from between 1123 and 1154; they have been closely analysed for his biography, but some may have been intended as epistolary models. Two are in verse; the first, twenty-nine variously rhymed hexameters, is to the abbot of St Albans asking for support of a religious house. The second, 196 lines of rhythmical couplets, welcomes the young prince Henry as England's saviour, praising him lavishly:

> Angelusque cum sis Dei
> per te splendet lux diei,
> et quae regnum nox depressit
> in adventu tuo cessit

> Since you're the angel of the Lord,
> Through you the light of day shines forth.
> The night that held the realm in fear
> Has left at your arrival here.

Osbert asks Henry to be his Maecenas or Augustus, but he himself was no Virgil.

Historiography

We turn now to three historians, more or less contemporaries, a monk and two secular clerics.[85] Two of them are still esteemed as historians, but the third has been dismissed as a fabricator of tales. They are: William of Malmesbury, a Benedictine; Henry of Huntingdon, an archdeacon; Geoffrey of Monmouth, archdeacon of Oxford, later bishop of St Asaph. They lived widely apart and there is no sign that they knew each other personally, but there is some mutual borrowing, and they overlapped in their patrons.[86] William and Henry covered the time from the Romans or Bede to their own day, Geoffrey wrote about the period before the Anglo-Saxon conquest. Despite their obvious differences, each has his own significance for literary history.

William of Malmesbury

William of Malmesbury called Goscelin the best historian since Bede, but modern scholars have paid this compliment to William himself. He was born about 1090–6 of Norman and English parentage ('utriusque generis') and died in or just after 1142; he spent all his life at Malmesbury Abbey, of which he was librarian.[87] He collected, and made extracts from ancient history, classical authors, grammar, Roman law, and theology.[88]

His *Gesta Regum*, first completed to 1125 and revised later, is primarily a sober secular history, based on earlier sources or site visits, but is enlivened by anecdotes, and there are observations of literary interest. We have already mentioned his contrast between his own days and pre-Conquest illiteracy.[89] He frequently quotes contemporary poets: Hildebert (on Berengar of Tours and Rome), Godfrey of Winchester (on Serlo), and the anonymous verses on Herbert Losinga and Peter, bishop of Poitiers. When dedicating the work to Robert of Gloucester, he praises him for his love of literature. He records the discovery of Gawain's tomb 'in provincia Walarum quae Ros vocatur' (3.287) [In the province of the Gaels named Ros], and shows interest in Arthur, wishing that he was treated in proper histories instead of the 'Britonum nugae' (1.8) [trifles of the Britons]; he mentions that because Arthur's body had not been found he was expected to return ('antiquitas naeniarum adhuc eum venturum fabulatur' [ancient wailings still report that he will return]).[90]

William later revised the *Gesta Regum* and added the *Historia Novella*, covering 1125–42. In the meantime he wrote the *Gesta Pontificum*, finished in 1125 but also revised later. This deals with the ecclesiastical history of the period covered by the *Gesta Regum*, and concludes (in Book v) with a life of Aldhelm of Malmesbury. William travelled widely for information for the *Gesta Pontificum*; he mentions the Severn bore ('higram, sic enim Anglice vocant') and the unintelligible dialect of Northern England:

Sane tota lingua Nordanimbrorum, et maxime in Eboraco, ita inconditum
stridet, ut nichil nos australes intelligere possimus (3.99)

The entire language of the Northumbrians, particularly in York, is so strident and so
unpolished that we southerners cannot understand it at all.

He repeats his praise of Godfrey of Winchester, and mentions the hymn-writing of
Thomas (I), archbishop of York. He quotes a poem on Faricius, Italian abbot of
Abingdon, by the Malmesbury monk Peter Baldwin, and adds that Peter had
written a life of Aldhelm. He also quotes his own rhythmical poem on Elgiva of
Shaftesbury.

In the *De antiquitate Glastoniensis Ecclesiae* William explored the early foundation
of Glastonbury Abbey, and laid the foundations for three centuries of Glastonbury
historiography, including much Arthurian lore. He wrote the lives of Sts Wulfstan
and Dunstan, and also compiled a collection of miracles of the Virgin.

Miracles of the Virgin

Writers as early as the sixth century (Gregory of Tours, Gregory the Great) had
recorded miracles performed by the Virgin Mary, and in the following centuries
legends accumulated. The first major collections were by Guibert of Nogent and
Herman of Laon.[91] The theme was very popular in England, and 1120–30 a major
collection was assembled by Dominic of Evesham.[92] William's *De laudibus et
miraculis Sanctae Mariae* comprises first the *laudes* (in praise of the Virgin's virtues of
justice, prudence, fortitude and temperance) and then fifty-one miracles, beginning with the story of Theophilus, whose rash pact with the devil is annulled by the
Virgin. The miracles are in a direct but elegant prose, and were intended for the
encouragement of the simple:[93]

Nam ratiocinationes quidem perfectorum fidem excitant; sed simplicium
spem et caritatem accendit miraculorum narratio, ut torpens ignis iniecto
roboratur oliuo. Ratiocinationes docent eam miseris misereri posse; exempla
uero miraculorum docent uelle quod posse. (2.2)

For reasoned arguments encourage the faith of the perfect, but the hope and love of
the simple is kindled by the telling of miracles, just as a dull fire is fuelled by pouring
on oil. By arguments we learn of the capacity of the Virgin to show mercy on the
miserable, but examples of her miracles demonstrate that she has the desire to put that
ability into practice.

William's collection was the direct source of Nigel Whiteacre's verse *Miracula*.[94]
Other collections appeared quickly across Europe; their relationship and trans-
mission is very complex. Other English writers involved in the genre were Roger
of Ford, Alberic of London (in French) and John of Garland, especially his *Stella
Maris*.[95]

Henry of Huntingdon

Apparently without knowledge of William's work, Henry of Huntingdon covered roughly the same historical period. He was born before 1089, the son of Nicholas, from whom he 'inherited' his archdeaconry and for whom he wrote a touching epitaph:

> Stella cadit cleri, splendor marcet Nicholai,
> Stella cadens cleri splendeat arce Dei (p. 237)

> Now Nicholas, the clergy's shining star, has set;
> Now may this setting star shine in God's house.

He was educated in the house of Robert Bloet, bishop of Lincoln, and wrote his epitaph too. At the request of Alexander, Robert's successor, he wrote the *Historia Anglorum* from Roman times to his own days; he revised the work several times, finally bringing it down to 1154. The early part relies on Nennius (notable for an account of the marvels of Britain) and Bede; when Bede ran out he made use of the Anglo-Saxon Chronicle, and also used personal knowledge. In 1145 he inserted two separate works, *De summitatibus* and *De miraculis*, between Books VII and VIII. The *De summitatibus* consists of three letters: a list of ancient kingdoms, now fallen; an epistle *De contemptu mundi* to a friend Walter; a letter to Warin, describing his discovery of Geoffrey of Monmouth's *Historia Regum Britanniae* on a visit to Bec. The *De miraculis* contains saints' lives, from Bede and later sources. The whole *Historia* (apart from the final sense of relief at Henry II's arrival) is suffused with a sense of transience: even the dedicatory prologue to Alexander is full of warnings that he will not last for ever.[96]

Henry's literary interest, however, consists mainly in his poetry. The *Historia* is decorated with short poems, mainly in unrhymed hexameters or elegiacs. The prologue ends with one in honour of Alexander; there are set pieces on Alfred, Elfleda, Edgar, and Henry I. There is an address in the mouth of an ailing England, calling on Prince Henry (II) for aid:

> Dux Henrice, nepos Henrici maxime magni,
> Anglia celsa ruo, nec iam ruo tota ruina (p. 284)

> Duke Henry, mighty Henry's grandson, hear my plea:
> I, England, fall, but yet my fall is not complete.

and the final poem welcomes Henry, the new king:

> Rex obiit, nec rege carens caret Anglia pace:
> Haec, Henrice, creas miracula primus in orbe (p. 291)

> The king is dead, but kingless England lacks not peace:
> You, Henry, first on earth produce this paradox.

All these poems are claimed by Henry. Many others are attributed to *quidam* (two extracts from a poem on Britain, a line on Lincoln, celebrations of Henry I's victory in 1119 and marriage in 1121, and praise of Alexander); one is ascribed to *poeta* (on the disaster of the White Ship in 1120). These are probably all Henry's; certainly the epitaph on Robert Bloet is his, as it is included among the *Epigrams*. Others are introduced by *ut dictum est* (the comet of 1066, an epitaph of Matilda 1118, and a lament on the Anarchy) and are also probably Henry's work.[97]

These poems are all competent and even imaginative, but even more interesting – indeed, unique in post-Conquest literature – are his attempts to reproduce the rhythms of Old English verse. On five occasions he writes a line or couplet that is clearly an imitation of the alliterative line, as under AD 617:[98]

> Amnis Idle / Anglorum / sanguine sorduit
>
> The river Idle, with English blood befouled.

A different pattern is seen under AD 655:

> In Winwed amne / vindicata est / caedes Anne:
> Caedes regum   Sigbert et Ecgrice
> Caedes regum   Oswald et Edwine
>
> In river Winwed was avenged King Anna's death:
> The death of kings – Sigbert and Ecgric;
> The death of kings – Oswald and Edwin.

Although these are introduced by the phrases *ut dicitur* or *unde dicitur*, there is no way of knowing if they are translations or original compositions. Under AD 937, however, he attempted his most ambitious project, a translation of the Old English poem on the Battle of Brunanburh.[99] The English writers, he says, described the battle in a kind of song, using strange words and figures; they must be translated faithfully, almost word for word, so that their deeds and valour may be reflected in the words:

> De cuius proelii magnitudine Anglici scriptores quasi carminis modo proloquentes, et extraneis tam verbis quam figuris usi, translatione fida donandi sunt, ut pene de verbo in verbum eorum interpretantes eloquium, ex gravitate verborum gravitatem actuum et animorum gentis illius condiscamus.

> The English writers on this great battle, expressing themselves in a kind of song with strange words and expressions, should be rendered faithfully, so that by interpreting their speech almost word for word we may learn from the solemnity of their words the solemnity of the deeds and spirits of that race.

Purely as translation it is perhaps, as Campbell says, 'atrocious': Henry was unfamiliar with a poetic vocabulary that had been out of style for two hundred years, and he renders *hamora* ('hammers') as 'homes' and and *hæleþa* ('men') as 'health'. As an (incomplete) experiment in poetic form, however, it is bold and striking:

> Gens vero Hibernensium   et puppium habitatores
> fatales corruerunt   colles resonuerunt . . .
> telis perforati   sub scutis lanceati
> simul et Scotti   bello fatigati . . .
> terram petierunt   Marte morituri

> But the race of the Irish and rovers in ships
> Doomed descended, dales resounded . . .
> Thrust through by spears, transfixed beneath their shields,
> And likewise the Irish, shattered in battle . . .
> They sought out our land, doomed to die in fight.

The substitution of rhyme for alliteration, or the combination of the two, was probably a feature of twelfth-century vernacular poetry: it is seen, for example, in Layamon's *Brut*. To modern ears accustomed to Old English verse, the most successful Latin unit to translate the Old English half-line is the rhythmical adonic (a metre which Henry uses elsewhere):

> Non fuit bellum   hac in tellure
> majus patratum   nec caedes tanta

> In all this kingdom was never a conflict
> Greater accomplished, nor such a slaughter.

Only two books of Henry's *Epigrams* have survived, though he tells us, in the prologue to the second, that he had written six earlier ones on frivolous subjects; these two make up the number eight, which signifies beatitude.[100] In the preface to the first extant book he says that epigrams thrive on variety ('epigrammata varietate gaudent'), and, in contrast to Godfrey of Winchester's regular elegiac couplets on moral themes, Henry's certainly show variety, both in metre and content. They range in length from a couplet to twenty-eight quatrains. Most are elegiac couplets or hexameters (some in stanzas, some in rhyme schemes such as caudati, trinini salientes, and collateral adonics), but there are also glyconics, the Fourth Asclepiadic stanza, adonics, and a curious eleven-syllable line. The poems of the first book are moral or political, those of the second religious; of the twenty-four poems in the first book, only fifteen resemble Godfrey's (on love, prosperity, greed, pride, mortality, avarice, envy, and so on).

The first poem ('De veritate libri') says that epigrams are intended to expel idleness, and he tells of an abbot who ordered nuns to sew and resew garments, much like Penelope:

> Quondam sanctificus pater inclusis monialibus
> Indixit vehementius vestes ut suerent suas

Consutasque refringerent; hoc rursum peterent opus
Et gratum colerent onus . . .[101]

A saintly father once proclaimed a rule for holy nuns:
To sew their clothes, and then unstitch the finished work again,
And then repeat the task, and thus perform a pleasing work.

No. 2 is a 'satira communis', seventy-four lines of caudati, attacking clergy, bishops, monks and lay people. No. 4, in adonics, consists of moral precepts. In No. 8 ('Carmen puerile') a boy tells Henry that his teacher, after reading his students Henry's poem on the vanity of ambition (No. 7), had attempted to ingratiate himself with a lord, despite physical abuse, and had then given a false self-serving report of his fine welcome. The boy therefore doubts the value of Henry's moral teachings; Henry agrees that not all who say well do well, but that one should subject oneself even to those who are unworthy. No. 17, in adonics, laments the state of England under the Anarchy, employing the image of a polluted spring and the story of a peasant who tries to get honey from a hive but is bitten by a snake:

Sic quoque saevis   Anglia moerens
Pressa tyrannis,   sorde repleta,
Diruta fraude,   dulcia secus
Mella venenis   anxia mutat

So also England, saddened and oppressed
By fierce tyrants and filled full of filth,
Torn by treachery, in torment changes
The sweet of honey for bitter venom.

No. 21 is a mortality poem, advising the reader to cultivate himself rather than his goods or his body. In No. 24 Henry gives himself the same advice: for all his cultivation (of his verses, his garden, and his home),

O jam culta tibi bene sunt, sed tu male cultus:
Se quicunque caret, dic mihi, dic quid habet ?

Your lands are cultivated well, but you less so –
Whoever lacks himself, what does he have ?

The eight poems of the second book are all religious. No. 1 praises God through his Old Testament achievements; No. 2 consists of three Fourth Asclepiadic stanzas:

Cantemus domino carmina glorie,
Qui cernens miseros exilio datos
Se fecit miserum maximus omnium
Ut nos efficeret suos

Let's sing to the Lord songs of glory.
He saw the wretched in exile bound;

> Though greatest of all, he was debased
> To make us his own.

Another, in hexameter tristichs, is typological. Another lists all the sweet smells of nature, of which none compare with the 'virtutum perhennis usus':

> Balsama quod spirant recenter acta,
> Quod suaue spirat crocus rubescens,
> Lilia quod spirant rosis iugata . . .[102]

> . . . the constant practice of virtue:
> The scents produced by balsam freshly crushed,
> The fragrant smell of crocus' recent bloom,
> The breath of lilies mixed with roses sweet.

Another, in twenty-eight quatrains of elegiacs, presents a dialogue between an *amicus* and *amica* (or *dilectus* and *dilecta*), expressing their yearning for each other and their contempt for detractors. It is entitled *De amore virtutis per allegoriam* and is based loosely on the Song of Songs, but in fact reads like a secular love dialogue.

As Partner has shown, Henry emerges from his writings as an intriguing personality, with a pessimistic but wry view of the world. His verses show a versatile and imaginative poet.

The ap Suliens

Before turning to the Anglo-(Norman-)Welsh literature that begins with Geoffrey of Monmouth, we should mention two Welsh Latin poets who preceded the fusion of the cultures and who reflect an older literary style. Sulien, bishop of St David's (1011–91), had four sons, of whom two wrote Latin poetry.[103] John (Ieuan) wrote short verses to accompany a text of Augustine's *De trinitate* and a longer poem about the life of his father (*Carmen de uita et familia Sulgeni*). His brother Ricemarch (Rhygyfarch) was more productive; he wrote a prose life of St David, later revised by Gerald of Wales, and three poems: one on the Psalter, a short epigram on mice eating the harvest, and a lament on the Norman Conquest of South Wales, in the metre of Boethius, Cons. Phil. 1 m.2:

> Dispicitur populus atque sacerdos
> uerbo, corde, opere Francigenarum . . .
> nunc cadit e summis pompa potentum:
> queque cohors tristis, tristis et aula,
> tristitie semper atque timores (16–17, 26–8)

> The priest and the people are now held in contempt
> By the hearts and the words and the deeds of the French . . .
> The pomp of the mighty now falls from the heights,
> The court is in sadness and so is the hall,
> And sadness and terror are felt everywhere.

Both Ieuan and Rhygyfarch show learned allusions to curriculum authors, but their style and syntax are, by Anglo-Latin standards, antique. Their conquerors, however, drew on the Welsh tradition.

Geoffrey of Monmouth

No literary writer in Anglo-Latin – or indeed in any medieval language – had such an influence on posterity as Geoffrey of Monmouth. His literary bequest was the whole corpus of Arthurian literature, extending into the twentieth century, and his beneficiaries include Malory, Shakespeare, Milton, and Tennyson. His account of pre-Saxon Britain was accepted by most historians up to the sixteenth century, and his prophecies influenced political thinking up to the Tudors. In his own day his work was known to Orderic Vitalis and Henry of Huntingdon (with whom he shared a patron). He was born in Monmouth, and also used the name Arthur, perhaps indicating Welsh descent. He spent most of his career at St George's on Osney island near Oxford; in 1151 he was made bishop of St Aspah, and he died in 1155. He wrote the *Historia Regum Britanniae* (completed about 1138), the *Prophetiae Merlini* (completed before 1135), and the *Vita Merlini* (1148–51).

Historia Regum Britanniae

In the prologue to the *Historia*[104] Geoffrey expresses his surprise that the reports of Gildas and Bede on British kings ('infra mentionem quam de eis Gildas et Beda luculento tractatu fecerant')[105] did not include pre-Christian kings or King Arthur or many of his successors. He is right: Gildas lists only a few British kings, and records the resistance to the Saxons by Aurelius Ambrosius. Bede, after an account of the arrival of the Scots, begins with the invasion of the Romans, and is concerned primarily with the spread of Christianity, first among the Britons, then among the Angles and Saxons; after the arrival of Augustine in 597, he writes from an English perspective, mentioning the British only where they impinge on English history. Geoffrey certainly supplied the gap, with a sequential history of Britain from the fall of Troy to the death of Cadwaladr in AD 689. He claimed to be translating an old British book brought 'ex Britannia' by his friend and colleague Walter, archdeacon of Oxford (not to be confused with Walter Map); Geoffrey said that William of Malmesbury and Henry of Huntingdon should not attempt to write about British history, as they lacked the 'old book'. About fifty years later William of Newburgh denounced the *Historia* as a fraud, and since the sixteenth century most scholars have agreed with him. Few now accept the 'old book',[106] and argument now centres on the nature of Geoffrey's sources. He certainly used some known literary sources,[107] as well as Roman historians and (for the later period) Bede and Henry of Huntingdon, but he must also have had other sources. Myrddin (Merlin) certainly existed outside Geoffrey, and Arthurian characters appear in art before 1138. His account of Stonehenge has some support from modern archaeology. Geoffrey, however, must take the credit (or the blame) for weaving these separate strands into a complete tapestry, a consecutive history of nearly two thousand years.

For convenience, the *Historia* can be divided into five periods:

I. The first period (about a quarter of the whole) goes from the Fall of Troy to the arrival of the Romans in Britain, about twelve hundred years. Brutus, great-grandson of Aeneas, along with Trojan exiles from Greece, is given oracular advice by Diana, and discovers the island of Albion.[108] Brutus and Corineus (eponymous founder of Cornwall) expel the giants and settle in the island, which they name Britain. Much of this section is aetiological myth, explaining the origin of British customs (e.g. the Molmutine Laws), roads, and topography. Eponymous founders are supplied for countries (Albania, Cambria = Scotland, Wales), rivers (Severn, Humber), cities (Carlisle from Leil, London – earlier *Trinovantum* 'New Troy' – from Lud), and smaller districts (Ludgate from Lud, Billingsgate from Belinus). Two episodes are particularly prominent: the story of Leir and his daughters (much as Shakespeare told it), and the conquest of Rome by Brennius – a reminiscence of the historical sack of Rome by Brennus in 390/387 BC.

II. The second period (about a fifth of the whole) covers the period of Roman invasion and domination, from Julius Caesar in 55–54 BC to the appeal for help to the consul Agetius in AD 446. It occasionally touches base with 'real' history, such as Bede, but with much expansion, duplication, and often confusion. Geoffrey gives Britain a large role in the Roman Empire, stressing (and occasionally inventing) Roman-born kings of Britain.

III. The third period (about twenty-two per cent of the whole) covers about 150 years, and sets the stage for the reign of Arthur. After Rome refuses to help Britain against Norse and Pictish pirates, appeal is made to Britanny (which had been settled from Britain), and Constantine II accepts the kingship. His heirs are Constans (a monk) and Aurelius Ambrosius and Uther, both too young to rule. The ambitious Vortigern engineers Constans' succession and then his murder by the Picts, and seizes the kingship. To counter the Picts he invites the Saxons Hengist (whose daughter he marries) and Horsa. As Saxon power grows, he tries to build a fortified tower, but its foundations sink. Advised to sprinkle them with the blood of a fatherless child, he thus meets Merlin Ambrosius, who reveals a subterranean lake and two dragons fighting.[109] Eventually Aurelius and Uther depose Vortigern and defeat the Saxons. To provide a fitting victory monument, Aurelius sends Uther and Merlin to bring back Stonehenge from Ireland (where it had been brought by giants from Africa). In time Uther (now Pendragon) succeeds as king. He falls in love with Igerna, wife of Gorlois, king of Cornwall. With Merlin's aid, disguised as Gorlois, he enters Tintagel, and Igerna conceives Arthur.

IV. The reign of Arthur (about twenty-three per cent of the whole, proportionately by far the largest part of the *Historia*). Geoffrey has turned the *dux bellorum* of the *Historia Britonum* into a world conqueror: Arthur subdues all Europe, and, with Gawain's help (but the loss of Bedwer and Kei), defeats the Roman procurator Lucius at Saussy. He is set to conquer Rome itself, when he is summoned back to Britain by the news that Modred (who has again summoned the Saxons) has usurped the throne and seduced Guinevere. Although victorious at Camlann, Arthur falls with a deadly wound and is borne away to Avalon 'ad sananda vulnera sua'.[110]

v. The final tenth of the *Historia* is a kind of coda. After the death of Constantine III, British rule falls apart. The Saxons summon an African king, Gormund, who drives out the British and hands Loegria over to the Saxons. After Augustine's mission of 597, even Christian hegemony seems to pass to the invaders. An amicable *modus vivendi* with Edwin of Northumbria (dividing the island at the Humber) is broken by the British king Cadwallo, at the instigation of his nephew Brian, who appeals to the undying British hatred for the Saxons. Cadwallo's revolt is ultimately successful, and – from this perspective – the English kings (Edwin, Oswald, Penda) seem minor characters beside the British ruler. His heir, Cadwaladr, however, is driven out to Britanny. Civil war, famine and plague empty Britain. The Saxons return, and Cadwaladr is warned by an angel not to attempt to retake Britain; he goes to Rome, where he dies in 689.[111] A 79-year naval campaign by Yvor and Yni fails; the British degenerate and change their name to Welsh ('Gualenses'); the Saxons behave more wisely and peacefully establish their settlement, and under their ruler Athelstan ('duce Adelstano qui primus inter eos diadema portauit') rule over the whole of Loegria.[112]

The *Historia* makes very entertaining reading. Annalistic sections are balanced by complete tales: the story of Leir forms an almost independent exemplum. The story of Brian, Cadwallo's nephew, contains romance elements: he gives his starving uncle part of his own thigh to eat; when he goes to Edwin's court, disguised as a beggar, in order to kill the magician Pellitus, he meets his long-lost sister. There are two giant-killings, of Goemagog by Corineus and of the giant of St Michel by Arthur. The mysterious past is constantly brought into the present by topographical allusions. There is surprisingly little magic: Merlin uses technology to move the stones of Stonehenge. In fact, divine and demonic intervention are rarer in the *Historia* than in many a 'straight' chronicle. The only poems are a prayer to Diana and her oracular reply.

Geoffrey's purpose has been much debated. On one level he is simply providing a prehistory and history for Britain; by his account of Arthur's 'colonization' of Europe he suggests a common ancestry for Normans and Celts, legitimizing the Norman Conquest. Recent critics, however, have used the word 'parody' of the *Historia*:[113] Hanning and Brooke suggest that Geoffrey, while knowingly writing fiction, was aping the pretensions of his grand historiograph contemporaries, but Flint argues that he was satirizing institutions.

His sympathies are usually assumed to be pro-Celtic and anti-English, but his attacks on the Welsh in later sections (derived from Gildas) and the implication that the true homeland of the British is Britanny[114] have led others to infer that Geoffrey was himself Breton. On the other hand, there are signs of a pro-English shift after the mission of Augustine: the Welsh clergy, out of nationalist pride, refuse to help in the conversion of the English; the peace between Edwin and Cadwallo is broken by Brian's fanatical, atavistic, pan-Celtic, anti-Saxon tirade; Cadwallo allies with the pagan Penda to kill the saintly Oswald. Finally the British degenerate into barbarism, while the Saxons settle peacefully:

> At Saxones, sapientius agentes, pacem et concordiam inter se habentes, agros colentes, ciuitates et opida aedificantes et sic abiecto dominio Britonum iam toti Loegriae imperauerunt . . .

But the Saxons behaved more wisely; they were at peace and harmony; they cultivated the fields and built towns and cities, and so, having overthrown the dominion of the Britons, they now ruled over all Loegria.

The *Historia* enjoyed instant success: a copy had reached Bec by 1139, where Robert of Torigni showed it to an astonished Henry of Huntingdon. Over two hundred manuscripts are extant, making it one of the most popular histories of the Middle Ages.

Prophetiae Merlini

In Book VII of the *Historia*, where Merlin is explaining the mysteries of Vortigern's tower, Geoffrey interrupts the story: he has been asked by Alexander, bishop of Lincoln, to translate the *Prophetiae Merlini*, since Merlin's fame has spread ('de Merlino diuulgato rumore'). In fact, he must have translated them at least by 1135, when they are quoted by Orderic Vitalis, and they must have circulated separately. There are about 270 prophecies (counting each discrete sentence as a prophecy). The first thirty-two can fairly easily be seen to foretell the remainder of the *Historia*, from Vortigern and the arrival of the Saxons to the departure of Cadwaladr; the next seventeen can be matched with events up to the reign of Henry I (the Danish and Norman invasions, the wreck of the White Ship). The rest are unaccounted for; the last eighteen are what Tatlock calls a 'Götterdämmerung',[115] and foretell the disturbance of the astronomical cosmos (e.g. 'Exibit Iupiter licitas semitas et Uenus deseret statutas lineas' [Jupiter will depart from the lawful paths and Venus will abandon the fixed lines]).[116]

There is good evidence (from John of Cornwall, the Prophecy of the Eagle, and Gerald of Wales)[117] that there was a genuine Celtic prophecy literature, though Geoffrey may have elaborated on it. If he is really translating (and not just making it up), he may have selected 1–49 to fit the specific context of Vortigern's moment in history (from a twelfth-century perspective), and left the remainder vague, menacing, and capable of multiple interpretation. Some hint at a pan-Celtic uprising (and are applied in this way in the *Vita Merlini* 967–75); others, with little danger of contradiction, prophesy a breakdown of public morality, e.g. 'mulieres incessu serpentes fient, et omnis gressus earum superbia replebitur' [Women will walk like snakes, and all their steps will be filled with pride].

Later ages naturally applied them to their own times.

In style the prophecies are remarkable. There is a phantasmagoria of animal and nature symbolism, based partly on Biblical sources (Daniel, Ezekiel, Revelations, etc.), partly on Celtic tradition. We encounter simple animals (the Boar of Cornwall, the German Worm, the Boar of Commerce, the Ass of Wickedness), monstrous animals (a golden-horned goat with a silver beard, a hedgehog laden with apples), and vast trees (one with three branches rising over the Tower of London and covering the whole island).[118] Fantastic events occur: an owl sets its nest on the walls of Gloucester, and in it an ass is born; a worm will breathe fiery breath, from which will emerge seven lions deformed with the heads of goats. Mysterious numbers occur: 'from the first to the fourth, the fourth to the third, the third to the second, the thumb will be rolled in oil'. The cities named are usually in England; most have British names, but *Vadum Baculi* is certainly English.[119]

A few words must be said about Merlin.[120] In the *Historia* he is Merlin Ambrosius, the fatherless child who solves the riddle of Vortigern's tower and makes prophecies; he tells Aurelius of the Giants' Circle in Ireland, and moves it to Salisbury Plain; finally, he helps Uther disguise himself as Gorlois, thus aiding in the conception of Arthur. In the *Vita Merlini* he is Merlin Caledonius (or Silvester), but is the same person as Merlin Ambrosius, as he recalls that he had prophesied for Vortigern. Robert of Torigni, however, before 1154, and Gerald of Wales[121] distinguished the two Merlins. Geoffrey did not invent Merlin: a seer Myrddin was part of Celtic tradition, perhaps eponymously linked with Carmarthen, centre of the Demeti tribe, of whom Merlin (in the *Vita Merlini*) was king. Geoffrey's part was to change his name to Merlin (to avoid sound association with *merde*) and to substitute Merlin Ambrosius as the fatherless child for the Aurelius Ambrosius of the *Historia Britonum*.[122]

Vita Merlini[123]

Geoffrey dedicated his next work, the *Vita Merlini*, to Robert Chesney, his former colleague at Osney, who succeeded Alexander as bishop of Lincoln in 1148; Geoffrey hints that his dedication of the *Prophetiae* to Alexander had brought him no benefit. The *Vita Merlini*, in over 1500 hexameters, is Geoffrey's only long poem and his most literary work. It is set in the reigns of Constantine III, Arthur's successor, and Aurelius Conan, the usurper. Merlin is now very old:

> Ergo diu vixi, mea me gravitate senectus
> detinuit dudum (1279–80)

> Long have I lived, and by its weight old age
> Has long detained me here.

He remembers the usurpation of Vortigern, when he was a child, and has seen an acorn grow into an oak.

As the poem opens he is prophet and king of the Demeti in South Wales, married to Guendolena and brother of Ganieda, wife of Rodarchus, king of Cumbria. Distracted by grief at deaths in a battle, he departs for the woods of Calidon. He lives as a wild man, lamenting his lack of food in winter, as even the apple trees magically desert him.

> Tres quater et juges septene poma ferentes
> hic steterant mali, nunc non stant. Ergo quis illas
> quis michi surripuit, quo devenere repente ?
> Nunc illas video, nunc non. (90–3)

> Thrice four and seven apple trees stood here
> With fruit, and now they don't. So who's the thief
> Who stole ? Where did they go so suddenly ?
> For now I see them, now I don't.

A minstrel's lament for the sorrows of Guendolena and Ganieda bring him back to himself ('Fit memor ergo sui'), but the crowds at court drive him insane again, and he is put under restraint. He earns his freedom by explaining his sudden laugh when the king pulled a leaf from his wife's hair: the leaf became entangled in Ganieda's hair, he explains, when she was lying with her lover. The queen tries to destroy Merlin's credibility by tricking him into prophesying an apparently impossible triple death for a boy; later the prophecy is fulfilled,[124] but for the moment Ganieda is saved. Merlin departs, giving Guendolena permission to remarry, but he comes to the wedding riding on a stag and bringing deer as a gift, and slays the new husband with an antler. Recaptured, he again wins his freedom by explaining two laughs, one at a beggar who is sitting on buried treasure, the other at someone whose new shoes will be useless to him, as he is about to die.

Merlin returns to the forest, where Ganieda builds him a celestial observatory; here he sings a prophecy (580–688) about the invasion of Gormund up to Henry I (corresponding to *Prophetiae* 11–49). Ganieda returns to court and finds (as Merlin had foretold) that Rodarchus has died; she sings a lament for him (639–732). Merlin is joined by the bard Taliesin, who (737–940) explains the winds, rain, spirits, seas, fish and islands; the source is principally Isidore's *Etymologiae*, whose account of the Isle of Apples leads Taliesin to recall his own role in sending Arthur to Avalon to be healed under the care of Morgen and her sisters. Taliesin wonders if Arthur should be summoned back to fight the Saxons, but Merlin says that the time has not yet come; he foretells a Celtic rising in the distant future. Merlin then (979–1135) recalls his own experiences, from Vortigern's usurpation to that of the present weak king Conan.

Suddenly a new spring gushes forth, and Merlin is cured of his madness ('sanus et incolumis rursus ratione recepta'), and praises God. Taliesin (1179–1253) again draws on Isidore to explain the medical properties of springs and lakes. Merlin refuses the kingship, because of his age, and (also using Isidore) explains the nature of birds (1298–1386). The scene is interrupted by the arrival of a madman Maeldin, who in early life had eaten a poisoned apple intended for Merlin by a rejected mistress. Maeldin is cured by the waters of the spring, and decides to stay with Merlin and Taliesin. Ganieda stays too, and sings prophetic verses apparently foretelling the Anarchy of Stephen's reign. Merlin realizes that the gift has now passed to Ganieda, and he advises her to use it well.

The *Vita Merlini* is a remarkable work. Geoffrey has created setting, characters, and plot almost *de novo*, an unusual achievement for a medieval writer.[125] He has used Celtic materials – disappearing trees, triple death, magic springs, poisoned apples, – his own works on British history (both *Historia* and *Prophetiae*), and Latin scientific knowledge. Magic is assigned its due place in a divinely ruled cosmos: through the harmonious workings of nature, both 'normal' and mysterious, Merlin is restored from madness to reason, and from agitation to repose. The morality of the *Vita* is also strange: Ganieda's adultery goes unpunished (even unrebuked), and she shows no resentment towards Merlin for exposing her. Merlin shows no remorse for killing Guendolena's husband, or for his treatment of his scorned mistress. There is no sign that his life as a Wild Man is penitential.[126] Historians such as Gildas or Henry of Huntingdon imposed moral patterns on their material, usually of guilt or retribution or at least of good and evil, but Geoffrey, in creating his own material, has brought the mysterious into harmony with nature, with no reference to Christian morality.

The heritage of Geoffrey of Monmouth

A full account of Geoffrey's literary inheritance would occupy a volume, but a few Anglo-Latin beneficiaries deserve a mention. They can be divided into: those inspired by the *Prophetiae Merlini*; those derived from the *Historia* itself; and 'romances'.

Prophecies: John of Cornwall; the Eagle[127]

Sometime between 1141 and 1155 John of Cornwall, at the request of Robert Warelwast, bishop of Exeter, undertook to expound ('exponere') the prophecy of Merlin 'iuxta nostrum Britannicum'. He produced a poem of 139 hexameters (with monosyllabic Leonine rhyme) and a prose commentary on the first 105 lines; there is an intermittent interlinear gloss.[128] Less than a third of the verse prophecies come directly from Geoffrey's *Prophetiae*; the remainder are presumably direct translations from Welsh or Cornish.[129] John begins with a prophecy of the Norman Conquest:

> Eure, tuum nostris extyrpat germen ab hortis
> Auster, et exemplum decimantis habet decimatum
>
> East wind, the South uproots your seed from out
> Our fields, and figures decimation of a tenth (?)

He continues to the reign of Stephen, interpreting Geoffrey's 'aquila' as the Empress Matilda. The prose commentary, which uses some Cornish phrases, links some of the prophecies with events in twelfth-century Cornwall.

In the *Historia* Geoffrey twice mentions a prophetic eagle. During the building of Shaftesbury an eagle spoke, but he does not believe its words:

> condidit . . . oppidum Paladur, quod nunc Sephtesberia dicitur.
> Ibi tunc aquila locuta est dum murus edificaretur. Cuius sermones si ueros arbitrarer, sicut cetera memorie dare non diffugerem. (ch. 29)
>
> He founded the town of Paladur, now called Shaftesbury. While the wall was being built there (*or* until it was built), the Eagle spoke. If I thought its words were true, I would not hesitate to pass them on, like the rest, to posterity.

Later, before advising Cadawaladr not to invade Britain, Alan of Britanny consulted the 'libris . . . de propheciis aquile quae Sestonie prophetauit' [the books of the prophecies that the Eagle made at Sestonia.] (ch. 206). In the *Brut y Brenhinedd* (the Welsh translation of the *Historia*), at the first mention of the eagle, there is a set of prophecies; these are in fact translated from a Latin *Prophetia Merlini Silvestris*,[130] which circulated separately from the *Historia*. There are over forty prophecies; they do not overlap with the *Prophetiae Merlini* of Geoffrey, but there are many echoes and the style is similar. They are closely related to those ascribed to Merlin Silvestris by Gerald of Wales in his *Expugnatio Hiberniae*.[131]

Derivatives of the Historia Regum Britanniae

Considering the importance of the *Historia Regum Britanniae* for sober chroniclers and the even greater impact of the Arthurian material on vernacular literatures, it is surprising how few Anglo-Latin treatments there are of the Galfridian legacy: Arthur is almost entirely absent. Whereas the Troy story was quite productive, and Walter of Châtillon's epic on Alexander was very popular in England,[132] Arthur had no Latin literary following. This may indicate some insecurity among Anglo-Latin poets about the authenticity of the Arthurian material and about their own function and relationship to 'imaginative' fiction (an anxiety not felt by mere vernacular entertainers); a similar feeling may account for the shortage of 'romance'.

The Anglo-Latin works derived from the *Historia*, apart from the romances, are all discussed in later chapters.[133] A few non-insular works deserve mention. In the late twelfth-century poem *Draco Normannicus* by Etienne of Rouen, monk of Bec,[134] Roland, count of Britanny, writes to Arthur, now king of the Antipodes, seeking his help against an invasion planned by Henry II. Arthur writes to Henry and informs him that his army has already landed in Cornwall; Henry, distracted by the death of his mother, Empress Matilda, postpones his plans and offers to hold Britanny under Arthur's sovereignty. An anonymous thirteenth-century poet, probably Breton, turned the *Historia* into a ten-book verse epic, the *Gesta Regum Britanniae*, addressed to Cadioc, bishop of Vannes in Britanny (1236–54); it is very anti-English and looks forward to a British resurgence.[135] Finally there is the scribe Bernardus, who wrote short verses introducing and summarizing each of the nine books of the *Historia*.[136]

Prose romance

Anglo-Latin, by comparison with Middle English, French, and Welsh, has little to show in the area of 'romance'. This literary slot is perhaps occupied by some of the more exotic saints' lives (such as Cuthbert or Godric, or Reginald's *Vita Malchi*). The Latin language itself may have raised cultural expectations above the level of pure entertainment. A stylistic barrier is perhaps suggested by the author of the *De ortu Walwanii*, who writes that, just as it is more dangerous to engage in battle than to write about it,

> sic operosius sit composito eloquencie stilo historiam
> exarare quam uulgari propalare sermone

> so it is more difficult to produce a history in an elegantly
> arranged style than to relate it in the vernacular

Some scepticism about fabulous tales is seen in a Goliardic satire on the *Navigatio Sancti Brendani*, which ridicules the idea that a holy man would desert his flock because of a crazy rumour and spend seven years celebrating Easter on the back of a fish:

> Ergo nugis his qui credit, notatur stulticie,
> Quas qui scribit, et qui legit, tempus habet perdere[137]

> If anyone believes this stuff, he's noted as a fool;
> The writer and the reader of it must have time to lose.

There is, of course, no shortage of the fabulous (in hagiographic, historical, and scientific writings), but that is a matter of credulity rather than a taste for the clearly fictitious adventure tale.

Sometimes romance appears as history: in Geoffrey's *Historia* itself there is the story of Brian, which includes many romance elements. There is also a short. narrative that purports to settle finally the fate of Arthur, the *Vera Historia de morte Arthuri*.[138] In Geoffrey, Arthur was given a deadly wound and taken to Avalon 'ad sananda vulnera'. In the *Vera Historia*, however,

while Arthur is lying fatally wounded on the battle field, a handsome young man appears, carrying a poisoned slender spear of yew; he pierces Arthur, who dies. He is taken for burial, by an archbishop and two bishops, to a tomb in Gwynedd. The tomb can be entered only by squeezing through a narrow gap, so the bier is left outside. A storm ensues, and when the bishops come out they find that the body has disappeared. Some argue therefore that Arthur is not really dead; others say that the storm has somehow sealed up the body inside the stone.

Thus, the matter remains unresolved, as was no doubt intended. The story is clearly dependent on the *Historia*, and may not have been written much later, as it makes no mention of the discovery of Arthur's tomb at Glastonbury.[139]

The *Vera Historia* is really a quaint narrative rather than a romance. There are, however, a few stories which, in structure and content, can be classified as romances; one of the best is the tale of Sadius and Galo, told by Walter Map.[140] I now describe three stories that all involve Arthur and that certainly fit the romance mould. The *Historia Meriadoci* and the *De ortu Walwanii* are by the same author, named 'R' in the prologue ('Incipit prologus R.'). The most recent editor has argued convincingly that this is Robert of Torigni, abbot of St Michel, who flourished in the first half of the twelfth century.[141] Robert, as noted, was one of the first readers of Geoffrey's *Historia*. The nature of the two romances can best be conveyed by plot summaries.

Meriadoc

Meriadoc, rightful heir to Cambria, and his sister Orwen avoid the death planned for them by their usurping uncle Griffin, with the aid of the faithful huntsman Ivor, who traps Griffin's men in a tree by rousing a pack of wolves. Ivor and his wife bring up the children in the woods; detailed instructions are given on how to cook without pots. The children are abducted by Urien of Scotland and Arthur's companion Kay, but after a gap of two years they are found by the faithful Ivor and his wife, and their true lineage is revealed.

Arthur and Meriadoc seek out Griffin in his fortress on Snowdon, and finally kill him. In

Arthur's service Meriadoc defeats the Black Knight of the Black Forest, the Red Knight of the Red Forest, and the White Knight of the White Forest; by his merciful conduct he wins them as his friends, and they enter the service of the Emperor, whose daughter has been abducted by Gunebald, king of the land 'de qua nemo revertitur'. As obstacles to their quest they encounter various enchantments, a phatasmagoric forest, an untimely dawn, a palace (where none had been before) inhabited by a beautiful maiden and surly servants, and a castle of immanent terror, also occupied by a beautiful girl, where they are attacked. Finally Meriadoc reaches Gunebald's castle, where he is advised by the queen (the Emperor's daughter) to seek out Gunebald at his palace on a marshy island in the Rhine, accessible only by causeways, and to offer him his service: Gunebald, she says, will challenge him to combat, but she lends him a superior horse. Gunebald is defeated and drowns in the marsh.

The Emperor, in hope of using his daughter to secure peace with the King of France, reneges on his promise of her to Meriadoc and traps the latter with a charge of seduction. The plot backfires, as the King of France refuses to accept 'used goods'. Meriadoc allies with him, kills the Emperor, wins the girl, and gets Gunebald's lands.

De ortu Walwanii

An illicit romance between Loth, prince of Norway, and Anna, sister of Arthur, results in the birth of Gawain. The baby, accompanied by tokens of his lineage, is sent away with merchants to be brought up abroad, but is stolen by a fisherman Viamund, who rears him as his own. Viamund moves to Rome and advances in imperial society; on his death he hands over tokens of Gawain's origin to the Emperor and Pope. At first Gawain is known as 'Puer sine nomine' but for his prowess he becomes the 'Miles cum tunica armature'.

He sets out for Jerusalem to fight in single combat on behalf of the Christians against the Persians. His ships are driven ashore on an Aegean island inhabited by pigmies (their size is later forgotten) and ruled by Milocrates, who has abducted the Emperor's niece, wife of the king of Illyria. Aided by the queen herself, who lends him Milocrates' armour (destined to bring victory to whoever wears it first instead of the king), he defeats Milocrates and restores the queen to her husband. The fleet sets sail but is intercepted by Milocrates' brother, Egesarius. After a naval battle, in which the pagans use Greek fire (for which a long recipe is provided), Gawain finally reaches Jerusalem and wins the combat.

After returning to Rome, he decides to seek service with Arthur, and, carrying his tokens but still unaware of his identity, he goes to Britain. Arthur's custom is to challenge any strange knight to single combat; undeterred by the premonitions of his wife (Gwendolen), Arthur is defeated. Loth and Anna recognize Gawain. Arthur sends him off to rescue the chatelaine of Maidens' Castle in Scotland. He kills the pagan tyrant and his birth is finally revealed to him.

Structurally the two stories are similar: early alienation, rearing by peasant, rehabilitation, quest, success of quest, return to court, denouement, and final battle. They share several traditional romance elements: concealment of identity, service with a foreign ruler, abducted daughter/niece of Emperor, single combat, use of an enemy's arms against him, and also the practical information (cooking in the wild, recipe for Greek fire); the last element is common in romances[142] and some modern adventure fiction. There is little magic in the *De ortu Walwanii*, but this is amply made up in the *Historia Meriadoci* (with two enchanted castles !). Both stories are carefully plotted, with few loose ends: they are probably original constructs from romance elements rather than simple translations of vernacular romances. It is hard to resist the feeling that they are parodies: the absurd concatenation of circumstances surpasses that in the most ridiculous vernacular tales.

The date of *Arthur and Gorlagon* is unknown; it is, however, preserved in one of the manuscripts containing the *Historia Meriadoci* and could have been copied with it. Thus, if the *Meriadoc* is early, the *Arthur and Gorlagon* may be as well. Also, it has parallels in Welsh romances of the early twelfth century. The story is as follows:[143]

Arthur is challenged by his queen to discover the mind of a woman ('artem et ingenium mentemque femineam'). He takes a vow not to eat until he has learned the answer. With Kay and Gawain he sets out on his quest, visiting first Gorgol, then Torleil, and finally the third brother King Gorlagon, who agrees to tell him a story. Gorlagon constantly interrupts his tale to ask Arthur (unsuccessfully) to eat and to remind him that even when he knows a woman's mind he will be held none the wiser ('parum inde doctior habeberis'). This is his tale: a certain king had in his garden a sapling; if struck with this, with the appropriate words, he would be turned into a wolf. His wife, who was planning an affair with a pagan king, wheedled the secret from him, but when striking him she inadvertently said 'sensum hominis (*instead of* lupi) habeas !', so he retained a human mind in a wolf's body. The wolf killed the wife's new children and devastated the neighbourhood, but eventually befriended a neighbouring king, who also had a faithless wife. The wolf foiled her murderous plot (for which she was executed) and led his new friend back to his old kingdom. His former wife was forced to reveal her enchantment; the spell is reversed, and the wolf is restored to manhood and kingship. Gorlagon now reveals that he was the wolf-man; by his side sits his former wife, who is forced constantly to kiss the severed head of her ex-lover. Arthur now agrees to eat, and returns home, marvelling at the tale.

It is a well told story, exemplifying the antifeminism often found in romances (especially those involving Guinevere). A humorous tone is evident throughout, especially in Gorlagon's attempts to make Arthur break his vow; it is packed with Celtic elements (the triad of brother-kings, the delaying devices in the narrative, the vow not to eat, the parallelism of the two kings with faithless wives), and is almost certainly parodic. The most grotesque feature is that throughout Gorlagon's tale Arthur has refrained from commenting on the severed head on the table.

Northern writers

In the period 1066–1422 the Latin writers in the North of England can be treated together in a way that works for no other geographical region of England. They shared common interests – relations with Scotland, the status of York, devotion to St Cuthbert – that cut across other affiliations (such as religious orders). Northern writers seem to have been particularly interested in British pre-history, and literary attention was devoted to the history of York well into the fifteenth century.

In the first period, before the spread of the great Cistercian houses, literary culture centred mainly on the cathedral cities of York and Durham, where there were also Benedictine abbeys. We have already mentioned the verse lives of Sts

Hilda and Cuthbert, and the writings of two archbishops of York: Thomas (I) (1070–1100) wrote hymns and was mourned by Godfrey of Winchester; Thomas (II) (1109–14), recipient of Reginald's *Vita Malchi*.[144] We consider now a few other Northern writers, culminating with the great Lawrence of Durham.

Hugh Sotovagina

One of the keenest ecclesiastic disputes of the time, usually conducted with civility, was the rivalry between Canterbury and York. York, relying on a decree of Gregory the Great, claimed equal status with Canterbury, but the latter, resorting to forged documents, claimed primacy of all England.[145] Thomas (II) had expressed obedience to Canterbury (perhaps explaining Reginald's friendly attitude to him), but his successor Thurstan (1114–40) vigorously promoted York's cause and refused to accept the pallium from the archbishop of Canterbury, eventually succeeding in being anointed directly by Pope Calixtus.

These events were recorded by the contemporary historian Hugh Sotovagina, or Hugh the Chanter, a strong Yorkist.[146] His history is essentially a collection of documents, showing that only accidents had led to Canterbury's pre-eminence. Hugh was also a poet: he wrote a poem on Thurstan's victory over King David of Scotland at the Battle of the Standard (1138), of which four lines are extant. He also wrote, or compiled, a collection of proverbial and moral lore in 360 lines of elegiac couplets. The morals, both secular and religious, are commonplace and could come out of the *Distichs of Cato*, but two short pieces embedded within the poem are interesting. One is a sixteen-line allegory on the three daughters of Simony, Simon's daughter:

> Mater, Symonia est; Symon Magus est pater illi;
> Natae: Lingua, Manus, tertia Servitium

> The mother Simony, whom Simon Magus sired;
> The daughters Tongue and Hand, and Service was the third.

The other demonstrates that trial by ordeal and single combat are contrary to canon law.

Vita Thurstani: Hugh of Pontefract; Galfridus Trocope

The life of Archbishop Thurstan (d. 1140) was celebrated in an anonymous *Vita*, which may have been part of an attempt to canonize him, as it calls him 'beatus'.[147] It seems to take a pro-Canterbury line, but fortunately includes a long pro-Yorkist poem by the otherwise unknown Hugh of Pontefract, in 176 lines of elegiacs. Hugh is keen to display his learning: there is some Greek vocabulary (*enclytica*, *polis*), and the onomastic wordplay is based on Latin rather than English: Thurstan is *thus* 'incense' or *turris stans* 'standing tower'; *Eboracum* 'York' is from *ebur* 'ivory'.

Thurstan's dilemma – whether to obey the commands of his conscience or of Henry I – is described in Abelard's terms of 'Sic vel Non':

> Sic vel non causam finit, duo verbula dura . . .
> Voce negativa constans et laedere regem,
> Affirmativam dedecus esse liquet (75–8)

> The case consists in Yes or No, two small hard words . . .
>   If he says No, he's firm but hurts the king,
>   But in his Yes it's clear dishonour lies.

After recording Thurstan's death, the *Vita* quotes two poems by another unknown author, Galfridus Trocope of Nottingham.[148] The first is a brief epitaph, describing Thurstan's appearance in a dream. The second, in variously rhymed hexameters, contains conventional praise of Thurstan.

Serlo of Fountains

The English victory at the Battle of the Standard was also celebrated by Serlo, a monk of Fountains after 1138 and a founder of Kirkstall Abbey in 1147.[149] In seventy rhythmical trochaic septenarii the poem cites biblical precedents for the victory of the small English force. King David ('manu fortis', like his namesake) is praised for his bravery, but generally the Scots are mocked. Like other chroniclers, Serlo stresses the cruelty of the Picts of Galloway who behave like beasts ('efferant immaniter') but flee abjectly, covering their bare backsides with drooping tails:

> Et quas prius extulerunt caudis nates comprimunt

> They use their once-raised tails to shield their arse.

The site of their rout, Baggamora, is the moor on which they threw away their bags of bread, cheese and raw meat. They would as soon eat raw meat as cooked and horse-flesh as much as the flesh of cows that moo:

> Quam eorum que mugitum prebent animalium

> Than of those animals that like to moo.

The widows forbid their menfolk to go fighting again and invoke the curse of Patrick on the English and the Standard:

> 'Maloht Patric' imprecantes Anglis et standardio

> St Patrick's curse be on the English flag !

Serlo makes no mention of Thurstan or of the religious significance of the standard. The combination of rhythmical, fastmoving verse with invective and abusive puns (*efferant, Baggamora*) anticipates the nationalistic polemic style that we see in the fourteenth-century political verse.[150]

Visions of heaven and hell: Orm

In about 1126 a parish priest named Sigar sent to Simeon, the Durham chronicler, an account of a vision of heaven and hell experienced by a thirteen-year-old boy Orm. Visions of heaven and hell (especially hell) were very popular in England. The apocryphal (ultimately Greek) Vision of Paul was not only widely current in Latin, but was translated into Old and Middle English. Bede (*Historia Ecclesiastica* v, ch. 12) had told the story of Drihthelm's tour of heaven and hell. The Irish vision of Tundal (Tnugdal) was also very popular in England, in Latin, French and Middle English versions. Peter the Venerable, although not himself English, was possibly the author of a similar vision by the Englishman Gunthelm. Orm's vision is similar to that of Drihthelm.[151]

Lawrence of Durham

Perhaps the most interesting writer of the whole period was Lawrence of Durham. He was born about 1100 at Waltham in Essex, and soon went as a monk to Durham, of which Waltham was a dependent house. Durham is almost an island, on a high plateau surrounded (as Lawrence says) like a horseshoe by the river Wear. The isthmus at the North is dominated by the Norman castle that was then the bishop's residence; at the southern end, about five hundred yards away, was the Benedictine monastery, near where the present cathedral stands. Lawrence was at first simply a monk, but soon joined the bishop's court as an official:

> raptum sibi curia curis
> Implicat et sibi dans me mihi tollit atrox (*Hyp.* II 5–6)

> The cruel court involves me in its cares,
> And, taking me to it, takes me from me.

In 1149, after the events described in the *Dialogi*, he became prior; he died on the way back from Rome in 1154. His literary output consists of prose, a prosimetrum, and a great deal of poetry.

His first (extant) work was a prose life of the sixth-century Irish St Bridget. He sent this to Aelred, possibly a former student of his, who was at the time (1130–4) at the court of King David of Scotland, and says that Aelred's father had given him a 'semibarbaram' life of the saint, which he had tried to turn into elegant Latin.[152]

His most popular work, written in leisure moments during his service at bishop Geoffrey's court, was the *Hypognosticon*, which he tells us means 'abbreviation'.[153] It is a verse epic, in unrhymed elegiac couplets, on the redemption of man. It contains 4684 lines, in nine books: I–III Natural Law (Creation to Moses), IV–VI Given Law (Moses to Herod), VII–IX the Age of Grace (Incarnation to the present); imposed on this is the scheme of the Six Ages of the world. The first six books are essentially narrative, based on the Bible and the *De antiquitatibus Judaicis* by Josephus,[154] with many expansions by Lawrence.

Book I (1–272) extends from Creation and the Fall (stressing the need for Hope and for a proper victim to atone for sin) to the wickedness of Cain's descendants and Noah's flood, which ends the First Age.

Book II (1–366) opens with a prologue in which Lawrence laments the court duties which prevent his writing poetry. Despite antediluvian simplicity, Noah is insufficient to redeem man: Lawrence discusses good and evil (the absence of good). The sins of some of Noah's race prompts the question why God made man and then let him fall. Nemroth builds a tower to avoid a new flood, and God disperses the people: only Heber retains the old tongue (Hebrew). The Second Age ends. The delay in God's redemptive plan is to ensure man's gratitude and awareness of his own insufficiency.

Book III (1–754) describes the history of Abram (= Faith) and Lot, the wars of Sodom and its destruction, Isaac, Rebecca (the conflict of the sons in her womb), Esau (and his hunting), Jacob's trick to win Isaac's blessing, the sale of Joseph (for thirty pieces of silver), Joseph's rise to power in Egypt, Moses, the Exodus, and the flight of the Israelites into the desert.

Book IV (1–660): the failure of free will and natural law leads to the Given Law (the ten commandments) and religious rituals and sacrifices (which will end with the New Law). The history continues with revolts against Moses, entry into the promised land, Joshua's victories, the rule of judges, degeneracy, and the story of Samson; pride leads the Israelites to demand a king (Saul). The book ends with Jesse (lineal ancestor of the Virgin Mary) and the end of the Third Age.

Book V (1–824), after a modesty prologue, describes the age of kings from the capture of Jerusalem (vividly described) to its fall to Babylon: David and Jonathan, David's infatuation with Bathsheba and his penitence, David's psalter, Solomon's wisdom and his fall through love – the power of love over reason is illustrated by the story of the incestuous Amnon (II Reg. 13) – the division into ten tribes, the sins of the people despite warnings from the prophets, the fall of Jerusalem, and the end of the Fourth Age.

Book VI (1–530) begins with Daniel (= Hope) and his interpretations of dreams, mainly of the empires that will now come and go: Babylonians, Persians (including Darius and the 'riddle'), the rebuilding of the Temple, Greeks (and Ptolemy's translation of the Bible), the Jewish heroes of the revolt (Judas, Jonathan), and finally the Romans and Herod and the end of the Fifth Age.

Book VII (1–372) begins with a review of man and nature, and shows that Natural and Given Law have failed and that the time has come for the Incarnation, the time of Grace. Prefigurations of Christ are listed, Adam and Eve are addressed, and the Virgin is praised. The book ends with John the Baptist, the final precursor of Christ.

Book VIII (1–352), after celebrating the return of the Golden Age (Virgil, *Ecl.* 4) and a time of peace, describes the life of Christ from the Nativity to the Passion, Harrowing of Hell, and Ascension.

Book IX (1–554) begins with a prologue on *otia* (which caused various disasters, including the affair between Paris and Helen); Lawrence uses his idle time to write poetry, which he prefers to dice. The book describes the effects of the Holy Spirit after Pentecost: the work of the evangelists, especially John, the new sacraments which replace the old sacrifices, the martyrs and saints (especially English, particularly Cuthbert) and doctors of the church (including Anselm and Hildebert). Lawrence looks forward to the entry into heaven, and the beginning of the Seventh Age:

> Sextaque cum mundo tunc mundi finiet etas,
> Et tunc incipiet septima fine carens (IX 539–40)

> Then, with the world itself, the world's sixth age concludes,
> And then begins the seventh, without end.

The structure of the *Hypognosticon* is remarkably coherent and clear: when Natural Law failed, man needed guidance:

> Sic igitur sine lege vagum sine fine benignus
> Respicit estque vago magna medela Deus (IV 69–70)

> God's boundless kindness sees man's lawless state.
> And for his wandering provides relief.

When Given Law in turn proved inadequate, Grace stepped in:

> Tempora nanque sui voluit specialia dici
> In quibus ipsa bonum dehinc speciale daret (VII 93–94)

> Grace wanted her own age – one named for her –
> When she would give her special gift to man.

The scheme is further reinforced by the triad of Faith (Abram), Hope (Daniel), and Charity (Christ), by Lawrence's constant reflections on the process of redemption, and by typology (Lawrence increases the price paid for Joseph to thirty silver pieces to stress the parallel with Christ). The last book, described by Browne as comprising 'miscellaneous religious content',[155] is the culmination of the redemptive scheme.

Lawrence frequently amplifies the narrative: the astronomical investigations of Seth's children, the simple life before the Flood, Esau's hunting (close in expression to a scene in the *Dialogi*), and the siege of Jerusalem by David. The career of Solomon is treated very fully (V 425–720), describing first his wisdom (his judgment between the two whores who dispute over the child), his learning (surpassing that of the Seven Sages and the ancient philosophers) and his writings, and then lamenting his fall through love:

> Ille ruit, ruit ille quidem cui singula rerum,
> Cui quodcunque libet, mente videre licet.
> Femina flammigero sibi subiugat omnia telo,
> Nam quem non subdat que sibi subdit eum ? (V 563–6)

> He falls, who with his mind can see all things
> And all he may desire, and yet he falls,
> For all succumb to woman's flaming dart:
> Who could resist, when Solomon's subdued ?

This leads to a long denunciation of the prison of love, and its foul beginning and end, illustrated by the story of the incestuous love of Amnon for Tamar (II Reg. 13).[156] Another major expansion describes the debate before Darius on the relative powers of a king, wine, woman, and truth. Lawrence is always asking questions: could the just Noah save Adam ? Why did God delay the redemption ? How did God speak to man ? How could two children be in conflict in Rebecca's womb ? He also likes to bring himself into the poem: when describing David's fall, he recalls that he too had once been allowed to repent; his list of rivers that foreshadow baptism include the small River Lea at Waltham. His sense of humour occasionally emerges: he compares his frustration at not having time to write to that of a eunuch who has caught a beautiful girl:

> Et velut apprensa pulcra spado virgine triste
>   Suspirat tristis pectora, sic et ego (II 15–16)

> And just as when a eunuch grabs a fair
>   Young girl, he grieves at heart, so now do I !

Anyone who can tell him how God speaks will have Phyllis as a prize ('Phillida demus ei', Virgil, *Ecl.* 3.107). Like Neckam, [157] Lawrence (whose muse was Thalia) ascribes a sense of humour to God: when Joseph's brothers, who formerly sold him into slavery, come to beg his aid, he writes:

> Tales sepe iocos divina potentia ludit,
>   Utitur et nostris hec bene sepe malis (III 587–8)

> Such jokes are often played by God's great might,
>   Which often makes good use of our mishaps.

The *Consolatio de morte amici* is a prosimetrum in sixteen prose sections with fifteen metra (mainly elegiacs, but some other metres).[158] It is closely modelled on Boethius' *Consolatio Philosophiae*, sharing its tone and some of its arguments. Lawrence's excessive grief at the death of his friend Paganus is rebuked by a kindly but somewhat testy Consolator. The loss of temporal advantages is subjected to a Boethian analysis of the nature of fortune: Lawrence should not complain at God's plan, for all must die and their deaths are predestined; Paganus' immortal soul survives, and it was this, not his body, that Lawrence loved. The interlocutory model (in which the Consolator initially seems to misunderstand Lawrence) may be a forerunner of the role of Peter in the *Dialogi*.

In one of the metra, Consolator quotes some verses which Lawrence recognizes as his own: these are from the 'Aura puer mulier', a twenty-three-line rebuke to a friend for exhibiting the fickleness of the breeze, a boy and a woman.[159] A fifty-six-line poem on man's fallen nature, 'Tempora nec sexum metuit', is written in the margin of one manuscript of the *Hypognosticon*: this may be by Lawrence or an imitator.[160] Lawrence also wrote a poem on the Resurrexion, in dramatic form in 109 rhythmical stanzas: a dialogue between Luke and Cleophas on the road to

Emmaus, expressing their despair after the Crucifixion, is interrupted by the risen Christ, who reminds them of the prophecies and his own promise, and finally reveals himself; the apostles discuss the news, Thomas's doubts are finally resolved, and they all rejoice. This is the first piece of verse liturgical drama in Anglo-Latin.[161]

Lawrence also wrote five prose speeches, probably as school exercises to teach forensic oratory or as literary amusements, though they seem to deal with real events:[162]

(1) *Laurentius pro Laurentio*: against unjust accusations of folly and cowardice, Lawrence defends his forbearance and good sense in dealing with tyranny. (2) *Pro naufragis*: this begins with a clear allusion to Cumin (below), and rebukes the citizens of Durham for their mistreatment of shipwrecked sailors. (3) *Pro iuvenibus*: an appeal for clemency for some young men who have been condemned for taking goods from a wrecked ship; it was not they but their servants who mistreated the shipwrecked sailors. (4) *Invectio in Malgerium*: Lawrence defends himself on a charge of plotting with one Boniface against the *princeps*. (5) *Pro Milone*: a young man is defended for pressing his suit with a noble girl.

Lawrence's most original work, almost unique in Anglo-Latin, is the *Dialogi*: not until Hoccleve in the fifteenth century did an English poet again use his personal experiences as a moral exemplum. For Hoccleve, his madness and consequent alienation teach patient acceptance of God's will; for Lawrence, the same lesson is provided by his (and Durham's) suffering under the usurper William Cumin. Both poets use a series of dialogues as their structure; in both the interlocutor is at odds with the poet; both employ an informal style, and the culmination of both series is the moral 'Disce mori'.[163] The *Dialogi* has been misunderstood and misrepresented by the few scholars who have read the work: they have concentrated on incidental features (mainly the description of Durham) at the expense of the overall design. They have searched for classical allusions and metrical technique, and have ignored the Christian moral. Just as the culmination of the *Hypognosticon* is the effect of divine Grace in human history, so the power of Grace shapes the *Dialogi*.

The historical events described in the *Dialogi* (fully supported by contemporary Durham chroniclers) must briefly be reviewed. King David of Scotland, intervening on behalf of Matilda in the civil war, hoped to have his own client in the militarily important see of Durham, and so supported the candidacy of William Cumin for the bishopric. Cumin occupied Durham but, after the protests of the monks and despite forged letters of appointment, he was excommunicated. William of St Barbe was consecrated in his place, and Cumin reacted with ferocity against the monks. He withstood a siege by the new bishop, but eventually yielded in 1144.

There are four books of *Dialogi*, averaging about 550 lines of elegiacs and each representing the conversation of one day; the first two are set in Spring 1143, somewhere outside Durham, and the last two are set inside Durham in 1144. The conversations are between three friends: Lawrence and Philip, monks of Durham (in exile in the first two books) and their Breton friend Peter.

Book I: Lawrence cannot comply with Peter's request to sing spring songs because of his grief at Cumin's occupation; the monks advise Peter against visiting Durham, and Lawrence agrees instead to describe the city and its lofty impregnable site; he recalls his happy life as cantor under the former bishop Geoffrey Rufus.[164]

Book II: the next day Lawrence describes the effects of Cumin's occupation and (using the simile of a boar hunt) the search of his men for hidden wealth. Challenged by Peter he describes Durham's wealth in hawks, silver and horses, and vividly recounts the tortures inflicted by Cumin's soldiers both to extort treasure and for sadistic pleasure.[165] Lawrence is especially horrified at the irreverence of the soldiers who occupy the monastery, cooking and polishing their armour. Peter expresses his hopes for better times, and departs.

Book III: a year has passed. Peter, despite the pleas of his family, has returned to Durham and he recounts his adventures, including a storm at sea and a shipwreck. He asks how the monks have been allowed back into the monastery, and Lawrence tells him of Cumin's change of heart, which he attributes to Grace. He reviews his own life, from boyhood at Waltham to monkhood at Durham, and his success and popularity as poet and singer. The loss of this (under Cumin) he also ascribes to Grace.

Book IV: Lawrence says that in all his study of philosophy he stumbles over one word, Mors. He now knows that he needs to learn how to die ('disce mori'), a knowledge superior to everything in the Trivium and Quadrivium. Vice consists in setting falsehood over truth; the man subject to the seven deadly sins is like a ball tossed around by players:

> Utque pilam numerosa manus sibi mutua certans
> Ludicra saepe rapit, saepe jocando jacit (IV 223–4)

> As many hands, in merry strife, toss round
> The ball in play, so man is tossed by sin.

Those who love God do not die but depart to heaven, to which Nature, Law and Grace lead; he defines good conduct as the corporal acts of mercy. He tries to describe heaven, and ends with a prayer to God.

The use of personally experienced suffering, rather than divinely ordained history, to exemplify the workings of Grace is striking enough. What is even more remarkable is the tone in which the *Dialogi* is written. The stories, descriptions, personal reminiscences and even the moralizations emerge in a series of casual conversations, which are full of jokes, irrelevancies, and banter (usually, but not always, good-humoured). Peter is represented as argumentative, sceptical and sarcastic, Philip as loyal and gentle, and Lawrence as somewhat solemn. Lawrence frequently complains of Peter's insensitivity. Lawrence plays on Cumin's name, which also means the herb cumin:

> Urbs perit illa potens exsangui pota Cumino,
> Cujus odor gravis est, gustus amara sapit (I 85–86)

> Pale Cumin's draught is poisoning the town:
> The smell is pungent, bitter is the taste.

Peter affects to misunderstand, saying that the people of Durham must find garlic and mustard even harder to bear, to which Lawrence replies:

> Gaudeat an doleat Laurentius, hoc sibi Petrus
> Ponet in exiguo. (I 129–30)

> To Peter my distress or joy will count
> For nought.

On the second day, when Lawrence rises late, Peter attributes this to staying up too late the night before:

> Sed piger ad lectum, piger est consurgere lecto (II 5)

> But 'slow to bed is always slow to rise'

but Lawrence has been unable to sleep because of his grief. Peter mocks Lawrence's praise of Durham, saying it is just 'menia, saxa, domos' and that the lands are 'culta parum'. When Lawrence mentions an invasion of wolves, Peter remarks on the slack security:

> Sic est: prava lupum pascit custodia (II 227)

> And so it is: 'Ill-keeping feeds the wolf.'

On hearing about the greedy feasting of Cumin's soldiers, he says that such gluttons should have been easy to resist:

> Vosque, Philippe, premi grege miror ab hoc Epicuri,
> Mars cui mensa, suus Martia tela ciphus (II 511–2)

> I'm much surprised that you should be oppressed
> By fops whose god and arms are food and drink.

When asked why, during a calm, he puts his hands to the oars, Peter replies that a silly question deserves a silly answer:

> Ph. Quidnam facturus ? P. Emendum
> Panem. Ph. Responde seria. P. Digna dedi,
> Digna tibi responsa dedi, nam quaestio talis
> Taliter absolvi debuit (III 95–98)

> Philip: With what in mind ?
> Peter: To purchase bread.
> Philip: Please answer properly.
> Peter: And so I did –
> I gave a worthy answer, for your words
> Deserved a silly answer in reply.

Philip and Peter trade insults about their racial origins. Peter refuses to accept Lawrence's equation of divine *ultio* with *gratia*, and says he is belching up nonsense he imbibed as a boy at Waltham. Mention of the gardens at Waltham provokes Peter to remark that he likes cabbages but not garlic or onions. Lawrence replies to Peter's request with a single line and quips 'Sumne brevis ?'

Such flippancy seems to undercut the seriousness of both the history and the morality, but thus becomes part of the 'message': God's grace operates not only in ancient history but among ordinary people who behave in ordinary ways. If so, Lawrence anticipates not only Hoccleve but also the later miracle plays, in which divine history is re-enacted (often 'anachronistically') by contemporary peasants. The apparent casualness of the conversation is also misleading: it not only serves to tell the story in an entertaining way, but is structurally useful. Peter's departure and return provides the necessary year's interlude for the solution to Durham's problems, and also supplies the sub-plot of Peter's own 'exile' and 'home-coming'. If, as has been argued, the twelfth century saw the rediscovery of the 'individual', Lawrence's use of his own persona in all his major works must be a prime example.

Aelred of Rievaulx

Aelred of Rievaulx (1110–67), to whom Lawrence sent his life of St Bridget, was the first of many important English Cistercian writers.[166] Before he became a Cistercian he was at the court of King David of Scotland and he was involved in politics: he wrote an account of the Battle of the Standard of 1138. We have already discussed his rewriting of Osbert of Clare's life of Edward the Confessor.[167] More influential was his devotional writing, in which he maintained the strongly emotional spirit of Bernard of Clairvaux. Especially significant for this history is a section in his rule for female recluses, De institutione inclusarum, in which he recommends threefold meditation, on things past, present and future:[168]

> Itaque ut ille dulcis amor Iesu in tuo crescat affectu, triplici
> meditatione opus habes, de praeteritis scilicet, praesentibus,
> et futuris

> To let the sweet love of Jesus grow in your heart, you need a
> threefold meditation, namely, on things past, things present,
> and things future.

The section de praeteritis urges meditation on biblical events from the Salutation of the Virgin to the Resurrexion of Christ; it is full of affective piety, especially on the Virgin's sorrows. Aelred exemplifies this kind of devotional attitude in his De Jesu puero duodecenni, reflections on Jesus's three-day 'disappearance' in the temple. He interprets the episode in historical, allegorical and moral senses, and stresses the mental suffering of Jesus' mother, in a passage which may have influenced Walter of Wimborne.[169] Aelred's other writings stress prayer and devotion. As meditation on the life of Christ becomes central to religious literature from the thirteenth to the fifteenth century,[170] Aelred's influence must be regarded as one of the most important on Anglo-Latin literature.

Osbern Pinnock of Gloucester

Despite the close connection between 'literature' and grammar (of which literature, hardly a medieval category at all, was a minor offshoot), I have generally
excluded purely grammatical and lexical works from this history. An exception
must be made for Osbern Pinnock, monk of Gloucester.[171] His *Panormia*, or *Liber
derivationum*, dedicated to Hamelin, abbot of Gloucester (1148–79), is an alphabetically arranged list of lexical derivatives. It was written between the important
lexical milestones of Papias' *Elementarium doctrinae rudimentum* (mid-eleventh
century) and Uguccio's *Magnae Derivationes* (1190—92), which was itself later
replaced by the monumental *Catholicon* (1286) by Giovanni Balbi of Genoa. The
Panormia marks a modest advance in lexicography and was used by many other
writers,[172] but is more interesting for the exotic vocabulary of its prologue. In this
the author's sleep is disturbed by the irruption of a noisy crowd:

> ecce phalanga turmatim subeuncium domate quo decumbebam fragosa
> crepidarum plosione perstrepebat
>
> Behold, a phalanx of folk, thronging through the dwelling where I lay, resounded
> with the shattering slap of sandals.

He tries to bury his head under a pillow,

> Quo ilicet experrectus crepitaculo semiulcos meticulose
> retegens ocellos thoralque involucro prae vultu clanculo
> corrugatum obiectans exili rimula quid rerum gereretur
> limis perspicabar
>
> Forthwith, at that disturbance I awoke and fearfully unclosed
> my half-gaping eyes, and silently drew the coverlet, all wrinkled,
> in a fold over my face, and through a tiny gap, with screwed up
> eyes, I looked out to see what was going on.

He sees Grammatica lamenting her neglect (a topos reminiscent of Boethius and
later used by Gerald of Wales).[173] To remedy the problem she will pour into the
thirsty jaws of her ally ('ad me autem oculo connivente adnutabat' [Winking, she
nodded at me]) lists of words, so that he can spread them more widely. Osbern was
closely following Martianus Capella; it has been suggested that the pattern of the
prologue (reading a book followed by a dream) is an early example of what later
became a Chaucerian topos.[174]

1066–1154: summary

What were the circumstances for literary activity during this first period of Anglo-
Norman England? The principal centres were the monasteries. We have noted
William of Malmesbury's comment on the excellence of the English abbeys in his

time, and observed literary activity in all the main monastic centres, Canterbury, Durham, York, Gloucester, Winchester, Malmesbury, and St Albans. Two major writers, Geoffrey of Monmouth and Henry of Huntingdon, were secular: in succeeding centuries we will see the balance shift towards seculars, both clerical and lay.

Monks, in theory at least, needed no financial support; their motives for circulating their works and for dedicating them to an individual may have been as varied as they are now: the wish to please and honour a superior (e.g. Osbern's dedications to abbots Gilbert Foliot and Hamelin), to seek approval and advice (e.g. Reginald's wide circulation of his *Malchus*), or perhaps to achieve fame through a prominent patron (e.g. William of Malmesbury's dedication of the *Gesta Regum* to Robert of Gloucester). For there was certainly patronage of a kind. Alexander, bishop of Lincoln (1125–48), commissioned Henry of Huntingdon's *Historia Anglorum* and encouraged Geoffrey of Monmouth to translate the prophecies of Merlin; Ralph Gubiun was for a time a member of his household. Geoffrey dedicated the *Vita Merlini* to Alexander's successor, Robert Chesney (a former Oxford colleague of Geoffrey's); this dedication may have been more successful, as shortly afterwards Geoffrey became bishop of St Asaph. William of Malmesbury tells us that Robert of Gloucester encouraged literature, and he was one of the dedicatees of Geoffrey's *Historia*. William also tells us that John of Tours, bishop of Wells (d. 1122), was a patron of writers. Literature, if not a way of life, could be a profitable hobby.

Whatever social barriers remained between English and French, by 1154 the integration of Anglo-Latin and Norman-Latin culture was complete. Lawrence of Durham and his companions joke about their racial origins, but authors who wrote in Latin obliterated (at least in their books) their national distinctions. For four reigns and eighty-eight years England had been exposed to French culture and had absorbed it into its own literary heritage; Anglo-Latin authors made their mark in almost all literary genres and on almost all subjects. The years of the Anarchy, of course, had been traumatic (though no barrier to literary activity). It was in the hope of a new peace that both Henry of Huntingdon and Osbert of Clare wrote poems of welcome to the new king Henry. Politically, Henry's reign was far from plain sailing – who could have foretold the quarrel with Becket or the rebellion of Henry's sons ? – but in literary terms Henry's succession heralded an effusion of Anglo-Angevin culture, in both French and Latin, that made England an equal partner in the renaissance of the twelfth century.

Marbod, Baudri, and Hildebert

Although these three authors are not 'Anglo' in any sense, they require a brief mention, as they represent the literary 'mainstream' into which England was drawn, and they formed the staple literary reading in Latin for many generations. First was Marbod (c. 1035–1123), who was educated at Angers (where he became chancellor in 1069) and became bishop of Rennes in 1096. All his works were popular in England: the rhetorical handbook *Colores rhetorici* ('Versificaturo quedam'), his verse saints' lives (Sts Maurilius, Agnes, Lawrence, and others), a poem on the lapidary ('Evax rex Arabum'), the moral *Decem capitula*, and his personal verse epistles.[175]

One of Marbod's contemporaries, who addressed a poem to him, was Baudri of Bourgueil (1046–1130); Baudri became abbot of Bourgueil in 1089 and archbishop of Dol in 1107, but spent much of his time at St Sampson-sur-Rille. His 225 poems are mainly short and personal, but there are some classical imitations: a pair of Paris-Helen epistles in an Ovidian manner, an Ovid-Florus epistle, and six short poems in praise of Cicero. He also wrote a now fragmentary mythological poem, in 1177 lines, based on Fulgentius. Most interesting of all is an address to Adela, countess of Blois, in 1367 lines of elegiacs. The design of the poem owes much to late classical models: it describes Adela's bedroom, which has wall-paintings depicting historical scenes (including the Norman Conquest of England), a celestial map on the ceiling, a *mappa mundi* on the floor, and statues of the Seven Liberal Arts.[176]

Hildebert of Le Mans (1056–1134) is possibly the most important Latin poet of the later Middle Ages. His poems were widely diffused in English manuscripts even into the fifteenth century; another sign of – and contributing factor in – his popularity is the false attribution to him of many other poems (including Marbod's saints' lives). The little attention that has been given to him in modern times has concentrated on his poems on Rome and on his own exile, but in the Middle Ages his *Biblical Epigrams*, his poem on the Mass, and his verse Life of St Mary of Egypt were more important. He was well known to English writers: he is quoted by Henry of Huntingdon, and is the only medieval poet praised by Lawrence of Durham. Reginald of Canterbury sent him a copy of his *Malchus* (and received a kindly reply, noting Reginald's use of many of his own lines!). His prose letters were equally popular: Peter of Blois says that in his youth (the 1140s) he learned Hildebert's letters by heart. As late as 1216 Matthew of Rievaulx included Hildebert among the great doctors of the church. Hildebert once 'visited' England to stand trial before the English bishops, after a quarrel with William Rufus, but it was probably through now well established literary channels that his fame spread.[177]

Wright's 'Anglo-Latin satirical poets'

The title of Thomas Wright's two-volume collection, *The Anglo-Latin Satirical Poets and Epigrammatists of the Twelfth Century*, RS (London, 1872), is misleading: many of the texts are not English at all. Further, the collection presents other problems: the sigla listed in Vol. I are not always applied correctly, and there is no introduction to Vol. II, with the result that the reader does not know which manuscripts were being used or what were Wright's reasons for the inclusion of some of the texts. Also, modern scholarship (particularly into contemporary anthologies) has often reassigned texts to different authors: Wright was following nine-teenth-century habits in simply dipping into anthologies for material that took his fancy. There is no space here to go into the complex problems of authorship and origins of all the texts; I offer simply an annotated contents list as a guide.

Vol. I

pp. 3–145: Nigel Whiteacre, *Speculum Stultorum*. Below, pp. 102–4.

pp. 146–230: Nigel Whiteacre, *Contra Curiales*. Below p. 107

pp. 231–9: John of Salisbury, *Entheticus in Policraticum*. Below, pp. 74–5. Incorrectly entitled 'Nigelli versus ad dominum Gulielmum Eliensem' (i.e. Nigel's address to William de Longchamps); the incorrect ascription goes back to Bale.

pp. 240–392: John of Hauville's *Architrenius*. The most recent editor has shown that the author was French: *Johannes de Hauvilla: Architrenius*, ed. P.G. Schmidt (Munich, 1974).

Vol. II

pp. 3–102: Bernard of Cluny (Morlanensis), *De contemptu mundi*. As far as I know, this text has always been regarded as French, though it was certainly popular in England. Ed. H.C. Hoskier (London, 1929).

pp. 103–55: Godfrey of Winchester's *Epigrams*. Above, pp. 17–20. (Wright confuses his sigla here).

pp. 156–62: *Epigrammata miscellanea*. Wright does not give his source, but he took this set of poems from his 'A', Vitellius A. xii (= Vt),[178] where they form a block. (i)–(viii) are by Marbod; (ix) may be by Godfrey of Winchester:

(i) *De eversione fani apud Calonnam* (p. 156), an extract about the destruction of a heathen temple, from Marbod's *Vita S. Maurilii*.

(ii)–(viii) (pp. 157–60): minor poems by Marbod.

(ix) 'Res odiosa nimis' (pp. 161–2); in Vt this follows Godfrey of Winchester's historical poems (incomplete) and is headed 'Versus Godefridi prioris', and is certainly in Godfrey's style.

pp. 163–74: Henry of Huntingdon, *Epigrams*, Book I. Above, pp. 38–9. Wright quotes no source, though it must have been the unique MS Lambeth Palace 118/188, and gives no hints of the second book.

pp. 175–200: *De vita monachorum*, 'Quid deceat monachum' (often begins at 9 'Non tonsura facit monachum'). Wright's sigla here, 'A', 'B', and 'M' (!), are used quite differently: the poem is not in Vt (his 'A'), and it is Vespasian D. xix which stops incomplete (p. 187), not Digby 65 (his usual 'B'). In ascribing this popular poem to Alexander Neckam, Wright was following Bale (*Index* p. 513, *Catalogus* p. 273); Bale also ascribed it to Aldhelm (*Index* p. 18, *Catalogus* p. 84) ! Hauréau (*NE* 1, 78–80) and Manitius (3, 851–2) follow a Bec manuscript in attributing it to Roger of Caen. A Rouen MS cited by Hauréau, and Longleat MS 27 (s. xiii[1]) ascribe it to Anselm.

pp. 201–2: *Invectio in monachos*: this consists of three parts, often separated, (a) 'Sacrilegis monachis', 4 lines, 2 caudati couplets, addressed to Hugo Diensis; (b) 'Ordo monasticus ecclesiasticus', 32 lines of dactylici tripertiti; (c) 'Presul amabilis', 10 lines of dactylici tripertiti, addressed to Hugo Diensis and Hugh of Soissons. The only date appropriate for these dedicatees is 1101–3. Opinion on authorship is divided between Galo (as Wright headed it, following Vt), supported by Hauréau, Manitius and Boutemy, and Nicholas of Caen, supported by Boehmer and Wilmart.[179]

pp. 202–7: 'Quae monachi quaerunt'. This consists of 182 Leonine hexameters denouncing Black Monks for taking over the author's property. Wright attached this poem to 'Sacrilegis monachis', citing 'B' (usually Digby 65), but in fact he was here following Titus A. xx (late fourteenth century): only the antimonastic theme links the two poems. Arguments have been made for the authorship of Serlo of Bayeux.[180]

pp. 208–12: *Versus Serlonis de filiis presbyterorum*. By Serlo of Bayeux. Fuller edition by E. Duemmler and H. Boehmer, *Libelli de lite* 3 (MGH, 1897), 579–83. Ascribed to Serlo in Digby 65, presumably Wright's (unstated) source.

pp. 213–8: *De querimonia cleri*. Ascribed by Boutemy (on Vt) to Marbod.

pp. 219–29: Hugh Sotovagina, 'Philosophus quidam'. Above, p. 52.

pp. 230–1: 'Forma fuit quondam Cluniacus religionis'. 34 lines of Leonini caudati against abbots becoming bishops. In Vt, the unique copy, it precedes 'Heu stolidi' (Boutemy, Vt, Appendix No. XIV), which is internally signed by Galo. This may also be Galo's, though (*pace* Boutemy) it is in a different metre.

Under the heading *Serlonis monachi poemata* Wright prints nine poems (pp. 232–58), of which the first is by Serlo of Wilton; the other eight are together in Vt, some by Marbod, some by Serlo of Bayeux:

pp. 232–3: 'Quisquis amicitiam'. This is Serlo of Wilton's 'Mundus abit', ed Öberg, No. 80; see below, pp. 70–1. In Wright it is preceded by an eight-line prologue found only in Julius A. xi, which must have been Wright's source, which he does not cite.

pp. 233–40: *Versus Serlonis Parisiacensis ad Muriel sanctimonialem*. The title is in Vt. The authorship of Serlo of Bayeux seems certain.[181] The poet advises Muriel to stick to her vows, and paints a vivid picture of marital woes from a woman's point of view. The works of the English poetess Muriel have not survived.[182]

pp. 240–1: *Ad virginem Deo dicatam*. The title, like this whole series, is from Vt, where it is presumably associated with the last because of its similar subject. It is usually ascribed to Marbod (Boutemy, Öberg, p. 2, n.10, Manitius 3, 870. It is No. 322 in Wilmart 'St-Gatien').

pp. 241–51: *Versus Serlonis de capta Baiocensium civitate*. By Serlo of Bayeux on Henry I's capture of Bayeux in 1105.

pp. 251–4: *Invectio eiusdem Serlonis in Gillebertum abbatem Cadomi*. By Serlo of Bayeux.

p. 254: *Ad Odonem Baiocensem episcopum*. There is little doubt that this is also by Serlo of Bayeux.

pp. 255–7: 'Rus habet in silva'. 79 unrhymed hexameters, a general moral poem, usually ascribed to Marbod (Boutemy, Wilmart 'St-Gatien' pp. 39, 250).

p. 257: *Ad amicum absentem*. 12 Leonines advising a friend to avoid the perils of the city. Usually ascribed to Marbod (Boutemy, Wilmart 'St-Gatien' p. 251).

pp. 257–8: *Invectio in mordacem cinaedum*. 23 Leonines of personal invective. Probably Marbod (Boutemy, Wilmart 'St-Gatien' p. 239 n.2).

pp. 259–67: five poems by Reginald of Canterbury. Above, pp. 27–30. Presumably taken from MS Laud misc. 40.

pp. 268–428: Alain de Lille *Anticlaudianus*; new edition by R. Bossuat (Paris, 1955). French.

pp. 429–522: Alain de Lille, *De Planctu Naturae*; new edition by N.M. Häring, 'Alan of Lille "De Planctu Naturae"', *SM* 3rd ser. 19 (1978), 797–879. French.

The Appendix (pp. 523–73) contains 'Anglo-Latin Aenigmata of the Saxon period'.

2

Henry II to John (1154–1216)

I Chronological survey

England and Europe

This chapter takes England from the height of its European power to the loss of Normandy in 1205 (confirmed by the battle of Bouvines in 1214) and the effective end of its continental dominion. Henry II combined the throne of England with the French possessions of his father, Geoffrey of Anjou, and thus established an Anglo-Angevin empire that stretched, in John of Salisbury's words, from the boundaries of Britain to those of Spain:

> a Britanniarum finibus ad Hispaniae limites uirtutis suae
> protenderit et continuauerit titulos[1]

During this period there was a kind of cultural unity in which it is sometimes hard – even inappropriate – to label a writer 'English' or 'French'. John of Salisbury was born in England, but spent most of his early career and all his later life in France. Gervase of Tilbury was also born in England, but most of his career was in France in service of the Emperor. Conversely, Peter of Blois was born in France but spent most of his life in England.

These links did not depend solely, or even primarily, on political union. Long before Henry II's accession in 1154 French schools and teachers such as Bernard of Chartres, Gerald de la Pucelle and Abelard had attracted English scholars to Paris and exercised a drawing power across Europe. Nevertheless, the Angevin Empire (and close relations with the Normans in Sicily) gave England a European outlook, intensifying the links that had existed long before the Conquest. Similarly, Anglo-Latin literature in the second half of the twelfth century and the beginning of the thirteenth had a European dimension that had disappeared by 1300. French-Latin writers – Walter of Châtillon, Alain de Lille, Bernard Silvester, Matthew of Vendôme, John of Hauville, William and Vitalis of Blois[2] – enjoyed as large a public in England as they did in France, and many English writers – Joseph of Exeter and Nigel Whiteacre – were popular on the continent.

Universities and education

In the twelfth century England still lacked universities; a century passed before Matthew Paris could claim that the university ('universitas cleri') at Oxford rivalled Paris, and the great colleges were not founded until the end of the thirteenth century. Advanced education was still sought abroad, medicine at Salerno, law at Bologna, and the arts at Paris and Orléans. Geoffrey of Vinsauf summarizes them:

> In morbis sanat medica virtute Salernum
> Aegros. In causis Bononia legibus armat
> Nudos. Parisius dispensat in artibus illos
> Panes unde cibat robustos. Aurelianis
> Educat in cunis auctorum lacte tenellos[3]

> Salerno heals the sick with medicine's art;
> Bologna arms the weak in legal strife;
> At Paris arts are taught and bread's dispensed
> To feed the strong; at Orléans the young
> Are gently weaned on ancient authors' milk.

On the other hand, 'schools' were beginning to appear in England. Simon du Freine boasted of the learning to be found at Hereford; Geoffrey of Vinsauf lectured ('legit') at Northampton; William de Montibus established Lincoln as a major centre, and the reputation of Oxford, where Gerald of Wales lectured and Alexander Neckam gave sermons, was growing. It has been suggested that Robert Grosseteste could have attained a good education in England.[4]

Some claimed to see a decline in educational standards. John of Salisbury deplored the replacement of grammar by logic, and in the *Entheticus* he satirized the 'moderni' and their contempt for the ancient authors. Like Osbern Pinnock,[5] Gerald of Wales mourned the neglect of Grammar. Poets constantly moaned about their lack of material reward in contrast to medicine and law,[6] and their favourite Ovid couplet was

> ipse licet uenias Musis comitatus, Homere,
> si nihil attuleris, ibis, Homere, foras[7]

> Though Homer, with the Muses, comes himself,
> If he brings nothing else, then out he'll go.

As John of Garland was singing the same threnody nearly a century later, we may rightly wonder if the decline of grammar was any more than a topos. Certainly the professions then (as now) were more lucrative than the arts, but if grammar had declined as much as the mourners claimed there would have been no Latin literature at all in the next two centuries.

The court

In this period we begin to see more secular (that is, non-monastic) figures engaged in literary activities. Many were attached to the 'court', as chaplains, secretaries, justices and civil servants. Many European courts were foci for literary activity,[8] and Henry II's was probably the most important. Peter of Blois says that Henry's daily school was the constant throng of learned men discussing topics:

> quotidiana ejus schola est litteratissimorum conversatio jugis
> et discussio quaestionum[9]

> The constant association of the most literate men and the
> discussion of issues is his daily school.

But what do we mean by 'the court' ? Walter Map was a member of it, and he did not know: 'in curia sum, et de curia loquor, et nescio, Deus scit, quid sit curia'.[10] Like Harlequin's company (an image also used by Peter of Blois) it is constantly on the move, and when he returns to it he finds that he is a foreigner in a strange land ('extraneam uideo factus alienus'). This is probably close to the truth. Henry's wide dominions kept him constantly on the move, and neither England nor the empire had anything that could be called a capital city; only a few officials were permanent members of the 'court'.[11]

The notion of a court circle of Latin writers is even more elusive. Dedications to Henry II do not imply residence at court or even royal favour.[12] In any case, the purely 'literary' writings associated with Henry and Eleanor were usually in French. The only literary Latin writers firmly attached to the court were Walter of Châtillon (not to be regarded as English), Walter Map and Peter of Blois. Somewhat earlier, John of Salisbury (through his friendship with Becket) had a vicarious contact with the royal court, but must have resided principally at Canterbury.

Nevertheless, the court, however elusive its nature, was a frequent object of satire.[13] It was pilloried as a centre of ambition, venality, nepotism, and flattery: the *gnatonicus* (named after the obsequious Gnato of Terence's *Eunuch*) became a favourite literary type in John of Salisbury, John of Hauville, and (later) Walter of Wimborne. The bureaucracies, with their attendant vices, were portrayed as obstacles to justice and sources of corruption; the papal curia (not all courts are royal) could only be penetrated, the satirists maintained, by bribery.

Monks versus Seculars

Satire against monks was equally popular.[14] The Benedictines were regarded as soft-living and the Cistercians (against whom Walter Map had a personal grudge) were seen as hypocritical and land-grabbing.[15] The proliferation of new monastic orders was criticized not only by Map and Gerald of Wales but by Nigel Whiteacre, himself a Benedictine. One source of friction was the appointment of bishops: Gerald believed firmly that they should always be seculars, not monks. Monks, on the other hand, disliked secular canons (venomously satirized by Nigel): the monks of Canterbury were bitterly opposed to Archbishop Baldwin's proposal to establish a college of secular canons at nearby Hackington. The bishop of Coventry, Hugh Nonant, was physically maltreated by the monks there: he retaliated by expelling them and replacing them with secular canons, an event applauded by Gerald but deplored by Nigel. Fuel was added to the fire by the suspicious reputations of the crusading orders, the Templars and Hospitallers. The validity of anti-monastic criticism has been disputed,[16] but there is no doubt that the regular orders were perceived by the seculars as corrupt, self-indulgent and exploitative: antimonasticism, whether justified or not, was a literary fact.

Cistercian literature

Monks, in fact, continued to make major contributions to Latin literature in England (Nigel Whiteacre, Robert Partes, Alexander Neckam, Adam of Barking, to name only a few). The Cistercians were especially productive.[17] Serlo of Wilton was a convert to the order. At Ford in Somerset there were Roger, author of a poem on the Virgin, and Maurinus, who wrote a poem on Becket. Another Cistercian, William, cantor of Combe, also wrote about Becket. The typological poem *Pictor in carmine* is almost certainly Cistercian. At the abbey of Furness in Lancashire, Jocelin wrote several saints' lives. Other Cistercians wrote about visions of the other world: Henry of Saltrey and Ralph of Coggeshall. In the reign of John, Matthew of Rievaulx wrote a great number of poems, many in praise of Cistercians, whose austerity he contrasts favourably with Benedictine laxness.[18] He is full of praise for St Bernard, whose sanctity Walter Map had mocked.

Modern readers of St Bernard tend to associate Cistercians with intense religious devotion and ecstatic fervour; in fact, apart from Aelred and possibly Roger of Ford, most English Cistercians wrote commonplace religious and moral verse, certainly lacking frivolity and salacity but not markedly different from other monastic literature.

Serlo of Wilton

Our survey of authors begins with two writers associated with Paris rather than England. Serlo of Wilton spent his early career in Paris, but renounced the croaking of philosophers for 'a logic that fears not the "therefore" of death':

> Linquo coax ranis, cra corvis, vanaque vanis –
> Ad logicam pergo que mortis non timet ergo[19]

I leave the idle croak of frogs, the caw of crows,
And go where Death's conclusion holds no fear.

He left the world (a renunciation described in 'Mundus abit', No. 80) and became a
Cistercian monk, eventually abbot of L'Aumône; both Walter Map and Gerald of
Wales met him in his later years (and Gerald says that he was complimented by
Serlo on his looks). His major works were grammatical.[20] His 'Unam semper amo'
(with a prologue beginning 'Dactile quid latitas') was a very popular poem which,
by means of amusing contrasts, teaches how to distinguish homographs by their
vowel quantities:

Scorto nemo placet nisi dextram munere placet (2.94)

A whore's pleased only by a handsome gift.

This technique found many imitators.[21] He also wrote a series of Latin versions of
French proverbs (Nos. 44–73), e.g. No. 48:

Ki ne feit quant il poet ne feit quant il volt
Non faciet que vult, qui quando potest ea non vult.
Cum vult quis faciat, res quando potest nisi fiat ?

Who that will not when he may, may not when he will:
Who could do it when he will, excepting when he can ?

The themes of Serlo's short poems are extensive. There are poems in praise of
religious figures, secular rulers, and even a horse Gilota. There are missives to
mistresses, often accusing them of venality, and frequent discourses on the 'to-love-
or-not-to-love' theme. In one poem he laments his proneness to love and his
dissatisfaction:

Opto placere tamen, michi dum placet ulla, sed a me
Nondum tacta placet – tacta placere sinit.
Spe tantum primi coitus amo; spe satiatus
Ultra quid sperem ? Spe nichil ulterius (20: 7–10)

I long to please, while there's a girl that pleases me.
I long for one untouched – once touched she fails to please.
My love depends on hope: when hope is satisfied,
There's nothing more to hope – for hope outreaches all.

In another he cannot decide between two women ('In bivio ponor'); in another he
describes his rape of a virgin. Apart from those that celebrate contemporary
figures, these poems are probably all set pieces, with little or no relation to his own
life or thoughts.

He is a master of rhyme; in a poem to his mistress ('Cipri timent dii te', No. 18)
he consistently rhymes one word with two:

Sicque Venus iussit – Veneris tibi non leve ius sit.
Nosti que sua vis: non hostibus illa suavis (18: 22–3)

So Venus bade – don't trifle with her laws !
You know her power: she's bitter to her foes.

He aims at the maximum compression, sometimes using *distributio*, as in the lines following those quoted above:

Infestare quidem non cessat oves lupus, hostes
  Miles, aves nisus dentibus, ense, pede (20: 11–12)

The conflict never stops: wolf plunders sheep,
  Knight foes, hawk birds, with teeth or sword or claw.

This kind of writing is akin to epigrams, and Serlo associates himself with Primas, the legendary master of epigram:

Versus Primatis:
Primas Serloni: nebulo nebulas nebuloni
Serlo e contra:
Nulla tui doni sit gratia pro 'nebuloni'
(Et michi, qui quondam, semper asellus eris)[22]

Verses of Primas:
To Serlo Primas follies sends, from fool to fool.
Serlo's riposte:
The phrase 'from fool to fool' earns no thanks for your gift:
To me, as you have always been, you'll be an ass.

In another epigram he satirizes secular canons:

Nostri canonici debent a canone dici,
Namque quod est canon bene servant, apposita non (No.74)

Our canons should be from the canon named;
They keep the canon, but with 'non' attached.

Adam of Balsham

Another Parisian scholar from England, a friend and colleague of John of Salisbury, was Adam of Balsham. He was primarily a theologian, and in Paris lived on the 'small bridge' (hence his other name 'de Parvo Ponte'). He wrote, for a friend Anselm, a short prose treatise *De utensilibus* in order to display a wide variety of vocabulary. It takes the literary form of a trip home to England to visit his old home, a fairly large country house, complete with outbuildings for specialized activities such as weaving. He wanders round the buildings and fields, listing the vocabularies of each of the trades and technologies. This work was the model for Alexander Neckam's *De nominibus utensilium* and John of Garland's *Dictionarius*.[23]

Politics of the reign of Henry II

Before we turn to some writers who were involved in current affairs, it will be useful to review the major events of Henry II's reign that affected literature. In 1155 Henry appointed his friend Thomas Becket as chancellor; John of Salisbury, at this time secretary to Theobald, archbishop of Canterbury, addressed several works to Becket. In 1161 Becket became archbishop, and soon came into conflict with Henry over church-state relations. In 1164, after the Constitutions of Clarendon he went into exile in France; Henry confiscated the property of Becket's family and supporters and tried to isolate Becket by forbidding correspondence with him. In 1170 Henry had his eldest son Henry crowned as the 'Young King' by Roger, archbishop of York. This act undercut the prerogatives of the archbishop of Canterbury (and also stirred the old Canterbury-York controversy). A specious reconciliation brought Becket back to England, but he immediately excommunicated all the bishops who had assisted at the coronation. Henry's fury at this was interpreted by his henchmen as a licence to kill, and they hacked Becket to death in the cathedral on 29 December 1170. Becket was succeeded in 1174 by Richard, the monks' choice, and in 1184 by Baldwin, bishop of Worcester. In 1171 Henry began the long campaign to conquer Ireland. In 1173 his sons rebelled and a struggle began that lasted to the end of the reign. In 1183 the 'Young King Henry' died,[24] and Richard became heir. In the meantime Jerusalem was under attack by Saladin; in 1185 Eraclius, patriarch of Christian Jerusalem,[25] went to England to implore Henry to become overlord of Jerusalem. Henry, who had enough problems at home, declined, earning the wrath of Gerald of Wales. In 1187, after the battle of Hattin, Jerusalem fell and Walter Map pronounced the year an 'annus nubileus'. In 1189 Henry died in France, still fighting his sons.

John of Salisbury

John of Salisbury is considered one of the foremost writers of the 'twelfth-century renaissance'; his knowledge of the classics, his elegant Latin style and his dedication to grammar and literary studies have earned him the title 'humanist'. Born in Salisbury he studied for twelve years (1136–47) in France, at Chartres and Paris. In the *Metalogicon* (completed in 1159) he describes his studies there, the famous philosophers, and the teaching methods of Bernard of Chartres. In 1148 he became secretary to Theobald, archbishop of Canterbury, and befriended Becket. Although based in Canterbury, he spent much of his time abroad, on official business and to avoid the wrath of the king, whom he had offended by his defence of church privileges. When Becket himself was exiled in 1164, John was with him; he returned with Becket in 1170 and witnessed his murder. In 1176 he was appointed bishop of Chartres, where he died in 1180 (and was succeeded by his friend Peter of Celle).

His early work includes the *Historia Pontificalis* (a history of the papacy 1148–52) and a life of St Anselm.[26] His first collection of letters, ending with the death of Theobald in 1161, was apparently presented to Peter of Celle; the second may have been intended as a memorial to Becket. The letters are mainly administrative; though austere in tone, they exude his classical and biblical knowledge. One (Ep. 112) is a satire against certain courtiers, disguised beneath names from Roman comedy.[27]

The *Entheticus de dogmate philosophorum*, in 1852 lines of elegiacs, written after 1155 and addressed to Becket as chancellor, is John's only major verse work. It begins by addressing the book (the classical *propempticon*) and satirizing the 'moderni' for their contempt for grammar and literature; if anyone quotes old authors,

> Undique clamabunt: 'vetus hic quo tendit asellus ?
> Cur veterum nobis dicta vel acta refert ?
> A nobis sapimus, docuit se nostra iuventus;
> Non recipit veterum dogmata nostra cohors.' (43–6)

> The cry goes up: 'The ass is off again:
> He harps on ancient sayings, old men's deeds.
> We're wise within: our youth is now self-taught –
> Our group can do without the ancients' saws.'

He mocks their 'round' speech (presumably an affected accent, as *rotunditas* is praiseworthy in classical rhetoric):

> Aulicus hic noster, tumidus sermone rotundo,
> Ridet natalis rustica verba soli (141–2)

> Our courtier, puffed up with rounded speech,
> Derides his native country's homely words.

The decline of grammar, for John, is disrespect for truth, and he links it to the low level of morality in the reign of Stephen (whom he calls Hircanus). The central part of the poem (167–1290) describes true grammar and the ancient philosophies; their merits are outlined, but Christianity and theology remain supreme. At 1291 he resumes the address to the book, and describes the courtiers it will meet, including Becket himself ('qui ius cancellat iniquum'), who is warned that the court's vices are contagious. The book is told to return to Canterbury, and the inns en route are described. The *Entheticus* is a serious work, but in a literary frame.

His most famous work, also written to Becket in 1159, is the prose *Policraticus*, subtitled *de nugis curialium et vestigiis philosophorum*. This is essentially a serious work on political morality, and not 'creative' in a modern sense. It is preceded by a more lighthearted verse prologue (*Entheticus in Policraticum*), in 316 lines of elegiacs, a valediction to the book on its way to Becket at court:

It is to behave itself and say that (like Queen Eleanor) it comes from Poitiers. It should avoid the *nugae curialium* and return to Canterbury (which is highly praised, and its statue of a guardian angel described). It should tell fables and keep good company.

The argument of the *Policraticus* itself is not easy to summarize:

> *Book I*: the importance of the written text as a witness to the past. The pastimes of courtiers, e.g. hunting, dice, chess, music, magicians, augury.

> *Book II*: omens, including the true prediction of Vespasian's capture of Jerusalem; dreams, foreknowledge, free will.

> *Book III*: the search for wisdom. Pride and flattery. A quotation from Petronius introduces the theme 'all the world's a stage'. Good and bad pagans; favours won by bribery, knowledge of secrets and flattery (illustrated by tales of Roman emperors). Flattery is appropriate to someone who may legitimately be killed, i.e. a tyrant.

> *Book IV*: the contrasting natures of tyrant and prince, with many anecdotes (including Alexander and the Brahmins).

> *Book V*: how the state should properly be governed (quoting his own fiction of an address by Plutarch to Trajan). Church; duties of attendants; effects of bribery; judges, justice and laws (with some contemporary examples).

> *Book VI*: the role of armies in the state (illustrated by classical stories, but also by Harold Godwinson and the rebellious Welsh). The emperor Brennus, and a review of English history from Cnut to Henry II. The role of husbandmen. The role of Rome in the church justified by Pope Adrian with a story of how the limbs went on strike against the stomach.[28] More on flattery. John decides to leave court . . .

> *Book VII*: . . . but is persuaded by Becket to keep on writing. Short history of philosophy, with especial attention to Boethius. Avarice, ambition, excuses made for unsuitable appointees,[29] hypocrisy; praise of the monastic orders (Carthusians, Grandmontines, Cistercians); envy.

> *Book VIII*: Terence's *Eunuch* as a metaphor for life and the seven cardinal sins. The banquet of philosophy; rules for civil conduct at table. Advice against marriage;[30] list of tyrants, concluding with Stephen. *Aeneid* VI as an allegory of man. The way to attain the Epicurean goal of happiness is a life of virtue.

The *Policraticus* is rambling and diffuse; it wanders from topic to topic with no apparent plan and no beginning or end. It has justly been remarked that the one thing John of Salisbury did not know was how to write a book.[31] Apart from IV–V (on tyranny) it is hard to discern a single theme for any part of the work, let alone the whole; themes such as flattery disappear and reappear from time to time. The only thread that John provides is a constant moral earnestness:[32]

> nugis nostris . . . in quibus fuit propositi semper a nugis ad
> bona transire seria et ad id quod decet aut prodest instituere
> uitam (8: 25 fin.)

> In this work my plan has always been to pass from frivolities
> to serious matters, and to direct life to what is proper or
> profitable.

John rarely quotes medieval literature. The *Policraticus* is a tissue of classical allusion; his exempla are almost all taken from the biblical or ancient world (from historians and anecdotists like Valerius Maximus and Aulus Gellius). His use of them, however, is not that of an inquiring humanist, but that of a moralist putting the materials to his own use – what has aptly been called 'creative appropriation'.[33] He quotes liberally – either from direct knowledge or through florilegia – from classical poets such as Lucan, and especially from the satirists Juvenal, Persius, Horace, and Terence's *Eunuch*; he was fond of quoting from Petronius' *Cena Trimalchionis*, and was one of the few medieval authors who knew this work.

For those who regard the Middle Ages as a dark road leading deviously to the Renaissance, John holds out a beacon of light; they share his dismay at the decline of the study of ancient authors, and applaud his classical preferences. On the other hand, he lacks freshness: his wit is almost entirely that of his sources. Although Henry II's court was a real one, where, presumably, hunting, dicing, flattery and ambition were rife, we see it through a veil of allusion: it could as easily be the imperial court at ancient Rome. His polished style lacks a vernacular touch. The very qualities that have earned him his reputation as scholar and writer also remove him from the less erudite but somewhat livelier world of other Anglo-Latin literature.

Robert Partes

When Becket went into exile in 1164 he spent some time at the abbey of St Remi in Rheims, whose abbot was Peter of Celle, a theologian of mystical bent.[34] The exiled party included John of Salisbury and one William Partes. In 1181 Robert Partes, a monk of Reading, made a collection of his twenty-four poems, of which the first ten were addressed to the party at St Remi, including seven to his brother William. With laborious analyses of the nature of love he expresses his affection for his brother and laments the edict that forbade contact with the exiled party (an order strictly enforced by the abbot of Reading):[35]

> Penna riget, cultellus hebet, michi dextra ligatur,
>> Effluit inchaustum, scedula nulla datur;
> Rector labra suit, tenet os linguamque coher(c)et,
>> Verbo uerba premit, uerbere scripta uetat (8:41–4)

> My pen is stiff, knife blunt, my right hand tied,
>> The ink's run dry, no sheet on which to write –
> The abbot's sewn my lips and checks my tongue;
>> His word blocks mine: his whip won't let me write.

In poem 10 he laments the death of their mother Basilia in 1167, and follows this with a series of epitaphs for her, in various rhyme schemes. Two poems praise Henry I, founder of Reading Abbey, and employ onomastic wordplay in English, French and Latin (HEN + RI + CUS) in the manner of Henry of Avranches.[36] There is a short set of typological verses, probably intended for (or taken from) wall-paintings. The longest poem (No. 23) is on the murder of Becket.[37] The final poem addresses a recalcitrant student whose grammar is deficient:

> Quippe docet te uerborum confusio stultum
> Qui sic gramatice ius ledere credis inultum (24: 7–8)

> Your muddled words betray your dullard's mind:
>   You think that Grammar's laws are safely scorned.

Apart from the picture verses, the epitaphs and the last poem, there is little rhyme; most poems are in stiff elegiac couplets, adorned with a great deal of rhetoric (particularly alliteration and wordplay) but little imagery. Several of the poems to St Remi spell out greetings in acrostics. Robert's collection testifies to the continued tradition of private monastic versification.

Literature on the death of Becket

No single event in the twelfth century (even including the Schism and the Third Crusade) produced such a torrent of literature as the murder of Thomas Becket in 1170.[38] His Anselm-like exile was already an international incident, but the murder transformed it into an event comparable to the death of Julius Caesar. It may even more aptly be compared to the Sophoclean drama of Antigone in conflict with the authority of Creon. The elements of the tragedy – Church versus State, conscience versus authority, one unarmed priest against four armed knights, and especially the sacred locus – were the stuff of drama, and continued to be exploited into the twentieth century. Also, the murder seemed to fulfil a prophecy of Merlin Silvester, 'Dolor in gaudium convertetur, cum matris in utero patrem filii trucidabunt',[39] a recurrent theme in hymns and poems.

The campaign for his canonization, granted in 1173,[40] produced many prose lives, including ones by John of Salisbury, Herbert Bosham,[41] and his friend Benedict of Peterborough, who also composed a rhymed office 'Pastor caesus in gregis medio'.[42] The translation of his relics in 1220 stimulated more writing, such as a verse life possibly by Henry of Avranches.[43] Once Becket was in the liturgical calendar and Canterbury became England's major pilgrimage centre, the flow of literature, especially hymns, was endless: only a sketch can be given here. Three ubiquitous epigrams summarize the martyrdom:[44]

> Quis moritur ? presul. Cur ? pro grege. Qualiter ? ense.
>   Quando ? natali. Quis locus ? ara Dei.

Who's dead ? The bishop. Why ? His flock. But how ? The sword.
When ? On his birthday. Where ? The altar of the Lord.

Rex miles presul, edictis ense cruore,
Impugnat uiolat protegit, ecclesiam.

King, knight, and priest – by edicts, sword, and blood –
Attacks, despoils, defends – the holy church.

Annus millenus centenus septuagenus
Primus erat, primas quo ruit ense Thomas.

Eleven hundred years, and seventy
And one – the primate Thomas fell by sword.

Continental reaction

Continental reaction deserves a mention on a topic so central to Anglo-Latin.[45]
Walter of Châtillon, a former courtier of Henry II, was outraged and called Henry
a precursor of Antichrist:

rex qui perdit presulem in proditione
re vera neronior est ipso Nerone[46]

The king that killed the bishop cruelly
Out-Neroed Nero in his treachery.

Guy de Bazoches wrote two very anti-English poems, and another is attributed
(improbably) to Adam of St Victor.[47] Another anti-English poem begins with an
allusion to the Merlin prophecy and then parodies Hildebert:

Vae tibi terra ferox Anglorum, lividus orbis,
Mors tibi fit velox revocatis cladibus orbis[48]

Shame on England, cruel, spiteful land,
Where death is swift, where man's disasters thrive.

One of the most bitter treatments is the *Visio cuiusdam*, in which the case against
Henry is presented before God by two other holy victims of murder, Abel and John
the Baptist.[49]

Apologists

Not all writers saw the event entirely in black and white: Henry had some
apologists. Gerald of Wales was very hostile,[50] but Peter of Blois (Ep. 66)

exonerated Henry from blame. A very sympathetic view is presented in the *Confessio regis Henrici* by the Cluniac monk Ralph Prunimensis:[51] Henry explains his anger that the bishops, who had only fulfilled his order to crown the Young Henry, should suffer Becket's curse:

> non mireris, cum me sic arguat,
> si rex ira motus exestuat, (26/3–4)

> Don't be surprised that I – the king – should blaze
> With anger, when he criticized my ways.

but it had never been his intention that Becket should die:

> Numquam mea fuit intentio
> nec de meo factum consilio,
> ut periret Thomas in gladio
> trucidatus in templo medio (18)

> I never thought – it wasn't my intent –
> What happened wasn't done with my consent,
> That Thomas, in the midst of holy ground,
> Should perish by the sword and bloody wound.

Walter Map calles Becket 'beatus' but never mentions the murder, and has high praise for Becket's archenemy, Gilbert Foliot, bishop of London.[52]

We turn now to discussion of a few specific works.

Herbert Bosham

Bosham's life of Becket (1186–90) is accompanied by a sequel, allegorizing the saint's life in musical terms, the *Liber melorum*:[53]

The *vita*, he says, though prose, is a *canticum* from which arise three harmonies (*consonantiae*), and from these three melodies (*meli*) are composed. The *consonantiae* are between the Emperor (Christ) and the soldier (Becket), on three topics, the visible campaign (*pugna*), the visible victory (*palma*), and the invisible spiritual victory. The points of correspondence in the lives of Christ and Becket are the notes (*notulae*) from which the *meli* are composed. The three *meli* are to be played on the *cithara*, the first on the lower, solemn strings, the second on the middle, and the third on the highest, most celestial chords.

No music accompanies the text, but Bosham had hopes for it: he says that the *Vita*, though prolix, may only be abridged when parts of it are used in services in Becket's honour.

Robert Partes[54]

Partes' poem on Becket, in 248 lines of elegiacs, does not follow the traditional *vitae*:

It begins with Becket in exile. Robert denounces the specious reconciliation, and warns Becket that the omens do not favour his return, and the planets are in evil conjunctions:

> Mars furit et radiis modicum scintillat opacis,
> Arridet Marti frigida stella senis (63–4)

> Now Mars is angry, glows with sullen rays,
> And frigid, aged Saturn's star concurs.

He recognizes the potential glory of martyrdom. He denounces the murderer but passes quickly over the murder itself, glorying in the martyrdom and praising London for its offspring. He concludes with a catechism:

> Quis perimit ? Miles. Cur.? Re sine. Quomodo ? Fraude.
> Quando ? Die sacra, proh scelus, ante sacra (231–2)

> Who ? Why ? and How ? A knight – no cause – by fraud.
> What day ? A holy one – alas, before the shrine.

'A et O carissimi'

This consists of 547 lines of Goliardics in stanzas of uneven lengths, after a four-stanza prologue in which the poet cryptically reveals his name.[55] The poem proper begins 'Ante chaos iurgium':

Even before the world began God ordained that bitter would precede sweet. The narrative begins at the Council of Northampton:

> Rus Hamonis dicitur mansio regalis,
> Plaga rus cognominat septentrionalis

> The royal place is called 'the town of Ham':
> The prefix 'North' helps specify which ham.

Becket quarrels with the king and goes into exile; Henry persecutes his family and supporters. Becket secretly becomes a monk, enduring privation and flagellation, an object lesson for modern bishops. The temporary reconciliation is a trap:

> Aegras dat inducias latro viatori,
> Sabulo vis turbinis, vis procellae flori

> The thief allows his mark some futile room –
> A lull before the storm hits sand and bloom.

Foliot and the other bishops are denounced and the murderers listed:[56]

> Tres sunt, Mortis-villicus, Thrax, et Ursi-natus,
> Ut sit tetras, tribus est Brito sociatus

> FitzUrse, de Morville, Tracy, formed the band;
> To make the fourth the Breton lent his hand.

There is a dialogue with the murderers, but Becket suffers patiently in imitation of Christ and of St Denis. On his death his sackcloth is discovered. Rome is denounced for avarice (presumably for accepting Henry's penance); the poem concludes with Becket's glory and healing.

The style is dense and allusive, and thick with biblical parallels.

William of Combe

Also in Goliardics is 'Frangit inclementiam' by William, cantor of the Cistercian abbey of Combe, Warwickshire.[57] There are twenty-four stanzas:

Nature's course is overturned and a red rose blooms in winter:

> Hiems obliviscitur cursus naturalis,
> Cuius vernat medio rosa spiritalis (1/2–3)

> The winter now forgets its normal course,
> When in December blooms a martyr's rose.

Stanzas 5–15 list Old Testament parallels for the betrayal of prophets by kings and priests:

> Ruit in Achimelec Doech Idumaeus
> Regis ex imperio (10/4–5)

> Doeg the Edomite falls on Ahimelech,
> By order of the king.

As creation was effected in six days, followed by the sabbath, so Becket's six years of exile were followed by a sabbath 'above the stars'. Finally the miracles are celebrated.

William also wrote a short poem in elegiacs ('Ara fit a Thoma'), describing, in very obscure language, Becket's cure of a monk Thomas who had castrated himself.[58]

Maurinus of Ford

Maurinus was also a Cistercian, from Ford in Somerset.[59] His poem on Becket consists of a fifty-line prologue in elegiacs, and 496 lines of hexameters, mainly rhymed in various schemes. It differs from all other treatments of the story, in that three-quarters of the poem deals with events before the quarrel with Henry:

55–221 his life as chancellor ('Ante Palatinae cancellos triverat aulae' [The chancels of the royal court were once his wonted haunt]), his generosity and friendship with Henry, their comradeship in arms; 222–353 his appointment as archbishop, the symbolism of his consecration, his dedication to the church; 354–400 the poet's reply to those who found Becket proud and vain: only good endings matter; 401–33 Becket becomes very ascetic, and quarrels with the king over laws that conflict with divine law:

> Scitaque regia legibus obvia Cunctipotentis
> Solvere nititur, hincque resolvitur unio mentis . . .

Anterioris foedus amoris dissociatur,
Posterioris causa doloris materiatur

Those royal writs that flout the law of God, those he
Attacks, and so destroys their former harmony.
The bond of former love now dissipates;
The cause of future grief now takes on shape.

434–90 he goes into exile but returns to denounce the wrongful coronation ('Non honor est suus, est honor hic tuus, ungere regem' [It's not his privilege but yours, to consecrate a king]); 491–536 his death and ascension to heaven on the fifth day of Christmas, which God had reserved specially for him ! The poem concludes with a prayer.

Maurinus is one of the few poets to try to come to terms with the whole of Becket's career; he worshipped him, but he did not hide the fact that he had had critics.[60] He also lacks the vicious polemic of many poems.

'Vox vatis velata diu'

This short poem, eighty-seven lines of mixed elegiacs and hexameters in various rhyme schemes, is based entirely on Merlin's prophecy, here somewhat expanded:[61]

Merlinus cecinit quod binos Anglia reges
Temporis accessu deberet habere, sed alter
Vita priuaret patrem genetricis in aluo (3–5)

For England in the course of time would
Have two kings – so Merlin sang – but one of these
Would kill his father in the mother's womb.

It tells briefly of Becket's virtue, quarrel with Henry, exile, attempt to rebuke the bishops ('pontifices Baal'), and death; oddly, it does not explain the 'two kings', but concludes that the prophecy has been fulfilled:

En modo panditur atque recluditur illud apertum,
Iamque resoluitur ac fore cernitur hoc per apertum (81–2)

The mystery's exposed and now disclosed:
The riddle's solved and openly resolved.

Hymns

There are literally hundreds of hymns.[62] This was not just the result of Canter-bury's tourist industry: the drama of the martyrdom earned Thomas an inter-national reputation, and many hymns are continental. Some are full offices; some briefly recount the exile and murder, sometimes adding the miracles; some are of

the miracles alone; some are simply prayers to Becket as patron saint. In one Becket
has a dialogue with his murderer:[63]

> Infert miles; 'Pare regi !'
> Praesul refert: 'Non, sed legi
>   Promulgatae caelitus' . . . (3)
> 'Regis iussum fac devotus
> Et rex tuus erit totus;
>   Cuncta cedent prospere !'
> 'Regem regum, Deum meum
> Colo; nolo propter eum
>   Vel parum offendere !' (5–6)

> The knight: 'The king's command you must obey.'
> The bishop answers: 'To no king I pay
>   Allegiance, but to God's decree.' . . .
> 'Obey the king's command with fealty;
> Your king will then be yours in loyalty,
>   And everything will be all right.'
> 'My king's the King of Heaven, King of Kings;
> I worship him, and not for any thing
>   Would I do wrong against his right.'

Common themes in the hymns include: the fifth day of Christmas (29 January),
Tuesday (the day of the murder, *dies Martis*, and of other events in Becket's life),
Thomas of India, London (Becket's birthplace), Canterbury, the monk in secular
clothing, and the image of sons killing the father in the mother's womb. A
fourteenth-century Canterbury missal has a hymn with the striking image of the
sword writing the testament in Becket's blood on the church floor:

> Vicem chartae pavimentum
> Cruor supplet attramentum
>   Scribiturque gladio[64]

> The parchment is the church's holy ground;
> The ink comes from the bishop's holy wound;
>   The pen's the butcher's sword.

Roger of Ford

The Cistercian abbey of Ford in Somerset produced several notable figures: John,
who wrote a life of Wulfric and a commentary on the Song of Songs,[65] Maurinus,
and abbot Baldwin, later bishop of Worcester and archbishop of Canterbury. The
most notable poet was Roger:[66] a (lost) collection of religious and ascetic poems
suggests a fairly productive minor poet. On a visit to Germany he made a copy of
the visions of Elizabeth of Schönau and sent it to abbot Baldwin, together with
what he calls the 'extrema pars' of a poem on the Virgin Mary. This consists of 288

lines of elegiacs, with final rhyme, and is an early example of the kind of affective piety seen later in Walter of Wimborne. He contrasts the humility and virtues of the Virgin with the selfish opulence of monks:

> Ecce doces quia sobrietas uirtus specialis,
> Dum puerum modici fonte liquoris alis.
> Cur igitur monachis Montani uenter adheres ?
> Quid monachis sacies, crapula, forma teres ? (53–6)[67]

> In giving Jesus tiny draughts, you teach
> That special virtue rests in soberness.
> So why do paunches grow on monks, who need
> No wine-distended bellies, rounded flesh ?

He goes through the life of the Virgin, giving pathetic attention to the suckling of the infant Jesus:

> Huius in amplexu summi genitoris imago
> Virgineos calices circuit ore uago (115–16)

> In her embrace the great Creator's son
> With wandering mouth seeks out her flowing cups.

He develops a striking image of Christ as vegetable (cf. Rom. 14:2); thus, the Virgin's garden produces a vine to intoxicate man and a vegetable to feed him. Especial attention is given to the Assumption of the Virgin (to which Elizabeth of Schönau had personally testified). Finally he lists eight miracles of the Virgin, and asks that they be completed by Maurinus.[68] The little evidence we have suggests a poet of some originality.

Peter of Blois

Peter of Blois, brother of the playwright William, was born about 1135.[69] He was educated in France, and in 1167 went as tutor to the young King William of Sicily; in about 1170 he entered the service of Henry II, and in 1175 became archdeacon of Bath; he was secretary to three archbishops of Canterbury, and died in 1212. He felt alien in England, a wanderer like Cain, and he did not know the language (Epist. 160):

> Viginti sex annis in Anglia peregrinans linguam quam non noveram audivi . . . Numquid semper ero 'vagus et profugus' super terram ?

> For twenty-six years I have been a pilgrim in England and have
> listened to a language that I did not know. Shall I always be
> 'a fugitive and a vagabond in the earth' (Gen. 4:14) ?

Apart from moral and theological writings, including a treatise on friendship (based on Aelred) and a commentary on Job (to comfort Henry II after the revolt of his sons in 1173), Peter is now known mainly for his letters and his poetry.

Letters

About 250 letters are extant, in several recensions probably made by Peter himself; he says (Epist. 1) that Henry II urged him to collect them into one volume, and that he had had no time to polish them. In fact, they have been carefully crafted: they owe much to the *Policraticus*, which he says he had read, and are heavily ornamented by biblical and classical quotations. Their artificiality is their strength: they were used as models for epistolary composition into the sixteenth century.

They are addressed to many different people (including John of Salisbury and Alexander Neckam) and cover a wide range of topics. He was a great admirer of Henry II, and exonerates him from complicity in Becket's death; he describes his appearance and compares his love of literature favourably with that of William of Sicily (Epist. 66). He describes his own education (Epist. 101) and says that he learned Hildebert's letters by heart; his reading list of obscure classical authors, however, is derived directly from the *Policraticus*.

The letters are deliberately provocative. Borrowing heavily from John of Salisbury he denounces life at court (Epist. 14), where neither the wine nor the beer is drinkable:

> Vidi aliquando vinum adeo faeculentum magnatibus apponi, quod non nisi clausis oculis et consertis dentibus, cum horrore et rictu, cribrari oportebat potius quam potari. Cerevisia quae in curia bibitur horrenda gustu, abominabilis est aspectu

> I have sometimes seen great lords presented with wine that was so full of dregs that it had to be sieved rather than drunk, with closed eyes, clenched teeth, and a pained grimace. As for the beer that is drunk at court, it is terrible to taste and apalling to look at.

He recalls an occasion when the courtiers, eager not to be left behind when the king set out on one of his many travels, acted on a rumour of his plans and got lost in the woods for three days. In a later letter (Epist. 150) he retracts his anticurial remarks and admits that service of king and country is a noble activity. In another pair of letters (Epist. 54–5) he first argues that one Alice should not be forced to become a nun, and then congratulates her on having become one. He advises (Epist. 74) that a certain adulterer should be allowed to sate his passions rather than punished: his gambling father was to blame. He praises the plan to remove the cathedral church from Old Sarum (Epist. 104). Again probably following the *Policraticus* (Epist. 79) he advises against matrimony. Although the letters no doubt reflect a genuine correspondence, many read as though they were intended as models for *dictamen*.

Poetry

In a poem of 1174 Walter of Châtillon described Peter of Blois as one of the foremost four rhythmical poets of the age.[70] In fact, we have very few poems that can be assigned to him with certainty. With a letter to William of Aulnay (Epist. 57), urging him to persevere in his monastic vocation, Peter enclosed five poems in elaborate metres.[71] One concerns the struggle against fleshly temptation; others are on clerical corruption; another is about the capture of Richard I in 1193. The last one, 'Quod amicus suggerit', is a debate between a courtier and a 'warner': the courtier enjoys the pleasures of the court and sees no need for repentance yet:

> Grata est in senio
>   religio,
> iuveni non congruit;
> carnis desiderio
>   consencio;
> nullus enim odio
> carnem suam habuit (Dronke, p. 208)

> Religion's not for us young folk
>   (For older men it's fine).
> Since no one makes his flesh his foe,
>   My body's wish is mine. (Cf. Ephes. 5: 20)

Peter also engaged in a lighthearted debate with Robert of Beaufeu on the merits of wine against beer.[72] Peter's first rhymes entirely on -ena:

> Felix ille locus quem vitis amoenat amoena . . .
> Sed domus infelix ubi cervisiatur avena.

> Blest is that place the kindly grape has soothed,
>   But sad the house where barley's beer is brewed.

His second poem is in elegiacs, and ends lightly:

> Dum sine felle jocor, quia te cognosco jocosum,
>   Jocunde admittas et sine felle jocum

> My merriment is free from spite, since you, I know, like mirth:
>   With equal lack of bitterness, accept my merry gift.

Robert has two twenty-five line poems in favour of beer, both rhyming on -ena:

> Eloquio dulci uernans et uoce serena
> Munera commendat Bachi tua, Petre, camena

> Your Muse, O Peter, eloquent, refined,
>   Abounds with praise of Bacchus' gift of wine.

These few poems, however, are hardly enough to merit Walter of Châtillon's high praise, and modern scholars have attempted to expand the canon. Schumann added five poems in lyric metres on the rejection of sexual love,[73] but left Peter with a fairly conventional moral outlook. If recent theories are correct, however, an entirely different Peter emerges. First, Peter refers several times to his lascivious songs:[74]

ego quidem nugis et cantibus venereis quandoque operam dedi, sed
per gratiam ejus qui me segregavit ab utero matris rejeci haec
omnia a primo limine juventutis

At one time I devoted myself to frivolities and songs of love,
but at the very threshold of youth, by the grace of the God that
took me from my mother's womb, I rejected all that kind of thing.

Second, in three letters we encounter Peter's namesake, a Pierre de Blois,[75] whom
Peter rebukes for wasting his talents on fables, philosophy and law, and for leading
others astray by his amatory songs; he is very talented, and should apply himself to
theology (Epist. 76):

Te quidem in summos eminentiae titulos scientia scholaris extulerat: quum-
que debuisses aliis esse virtutum forma et speculum honestatis, per scurriles
nugas et fabulosa commenta gentilium factus es multis láqueus in ruinam . . .
In fabulis paganorum, in philosophorum studiis, tandem in jure civili dies
tuos usque in senium expendisti . . . amatoria scribis, et adinventionibus
profanis et in te et in aliis passiones desiderii suscitans . . . Insani capitis est
amores illicitos canere, et se corruptorem virginum iactitare . . . Porro omnia
quae scribis mirabili artificio et exquisitissima sententiarum verbor-
umque venustate componis . . . Hoc unum precor, ut omissis inanibus
cantilenis scribas quae Theologicam sapiant gravitatem

Your scholarly knowledge raised you to the greatest heights of eminence, but, when
you ought to have been a model of virtues for others and a mirror of upright
behaviour, you turned yourself into a deadly trap for many people by your scurrilous
nonsense and the lying falsehoods of the pagans . . . Right up to old age you have
wasted your time in pagan stories, in philosophical pursuits, and finally in civil law . . .
You write erotic literature arousing feelings of desire both in yourself and in others,
by your profane compositions . . . It is a mark of an unhealthy mind to sing of illicit
passions and to boast of one's seduction of virgins . . . Everything you write is
composed with marvellous skill and with the most exquisite charm of words and
expressions . . . I beg this one request of you, to give up pointless songs and to write
things that are redolent of theological solemnity.

Bezzola and Dronke have suggested that this second Pierre is a fiction, an *alter ego*
whom Peter can blame for his own literary backsliding. This would reflect what
Dronke calls Peter's *sic et non* style, an inclination to present both sides of a
question.[76] This new Peter/Pierre differs entirely from the old moral Peter. On the
basis of common style, metre and phraseology, therefore, Dronke has claimed for
him a further forty-two poems, mainly amatory, found in anthologies such as the
Carmina Burana, the Arundel and the Bekynton.[77] If these erotic poems (some
sexually very explicit) are ascribed to Peter, our whole picture of him is changed, as
he is thus credited with some of the most elaborate and sophisticated love lyrics in
Medieval Latin.

Walter Map

Walter Map was also born about 1135, and was part-English, part-Welsh. He describes England as his 'mater', but refers to the Welsh as his 'compatriote' and his surname is Welsh for 'son of'. For most of his life he lived close to the Welsh border ('marchio sum Walensibus'). He was probably educated first at St Peter's Abbey in Gloucester, and then studied in Paris. He enjoyed the patronage of Henry II and travelled widely with the court, both in England and Europe. He was a king's justice in Wales and the West Midlands (what would until recently have been called a 'circuit judge'). Eventually he became chancellor of Lincoln, and finally, in 1196 or 1197, archdeacon of Oxford. He died in 1209 or 1210.[78]

Even in his own lifetime he had the reputation of a wit. Gerald of Wales introduces an anti-Cistercian anecdote with the telling remark, 'Adjecit etiam archidiaconus, vel adjicere potuit . . .' (*Speculum ecclesiae* 3.14, p. 223) [The archdeacon added, or could have added . . .], that is, this is the kind of joke that Map would have made. Other contemporary sources, such as the *Distinctiones monasticae*, credit him with witty epigrams in the Primas style. By the fifteenth century his name was being attached to satirical poems, and the sixteenth-century antiquaries extended the corpus widely, ensuring his entry into literary history.[79] He was also credited with French prose Arthurian romances. The genuine canon has now been restricted to a few short Latin poems and the *De Nugis Curialium*, but the latter alone is quite sufficient to justify his reputation.

In its present form, the *De Nugis* is divided into five distinctions, each with a prologue (some have epilogues);[80] in outline, the contents are:

> *Dist. I*: satire on the court and monastic orders; some heresies.
> *Dist. II*: tales of the supernatural, especially concerning Wales.
> *Dist. III*: four long stories (Sadius and Galo, Parius and Lausus, Raso, Rollo).
> *Dist. IV*: *Epistola Valerii* (antimatrimonial); stories of Eudo, Ollo and Scaeva, and others (some revised in Dist. II).
> *Dist. V*: synopsis of English history; court satire (revised in Dist. I).

The *De Nugis* is both satirical and anecdotal; the principal objects of the satire are the court, monks, and marriage, which can be taken in order.

As noted above,[81] the *De Nugis* begins with an adaptation of a quotation from Augustine:

> 'In tempore sum et de tempore loquor', ait Augustinus, et adiecit: 'nescio quid sit tempus'. Ego simili possum admiracione dicere quod in curia sum, et de curia loquor, et nescio, Deus scit, quid sit curia

> 'I am in time, and I speak about time', said Augustine, and he added, 'I do not know what time is.' With similar bewilderment I can say that I am in the court and speak about the court, and God knows (I don't) what the court is.

He continues to reflect on the nature of the court with a dazzling array of quotations, from Porphyry, Boethius, Virgil, and the Bible, and compares life at court to the torments of Hades.[82] Then, seemingly irrelevantly, he tells the story of the visit of King Herla, an ancient British king, to a pygmy kingdom, their Rip-van-Winkle-like return hundreds of years later, and their doom to wander for ever like the Flying Dutchman. Eventually, like the punchline of a shaggy dog story, the point of the tale emerges: on the day of Henry II's coronation, the ghostly company disappeared into the river Wye near Hereford (Map's own country), and was never seen again, 'tanquam nobis suos tradiderint errores, ad quietem sibi' [As if, to gain rest for themselves, they bequeathed their wanderings to us]. Map frequently laments the distractions of court life, which keep him from writing, and rejoices (4: 2) when he is freed from it.

Reflecting on the *annus nubileus* of 1187, when Jerusalem fell to Saladin, Map, seemingly irrelevantly, mentions that Lazarus was once raised from the dead by the prayers of two women: nowadays the prayers of many thousands of monks and nuns are achieving nothing. Thus he begins his antimonastic section. He was bothered by the proliferation of new orders ('hos religionis cultus nouitas ad-inuenit' [Newfangleness devised these religious observances, 1: 26)]), and shows how each in turn – Carthusians, Grandmontines, Templars, etc. – had good beginnings but a bad end. The Templars, for example, began with great holiness, but have degenerated into such war-lust that they actually thwarted the conversion of leading Saracens to Christianity, for fear the fighting would cease ('si pax uenerit, quo deueniet gladius ?' 1: 20 [If peace comes, what will happen to the sword ?]). His harshest words and stories are directed at the Cistercians, who, according to Gerald of Wales, had deprived Map of a benefice. He disputes the miraculous powers of Bernard of Clairvaux, and shows distinct sympathy to Abelard; he mocks their hypocritical austerity and their lack of breeches. He deplores their rapacity and describes their tricks for stealing land (creating solitudes for themselves by driving everyone else away). He seizes on their claim to be like the Hebrews spoiling the Egyptians, and in a sustained piece of sarcasm (a rare device in medieval satire) continually thereafter calls the Cistercians 'Hebrews' and the rest of the world 'Egyptians'. Pointedly, he follows his account of the monastic orders with a description of popular heresies, such as Catharism.

(His anti-Cistercian satire did not go entirely unanswered. He had apparently written a poem, now lost, beginning 'Lancea Longini'; a reply to this in eighty-six lines, mainly elegiacs ('Cum monachis albis'), was made by W. Bothewald, a canon of St Frideswide's in Oxford.[83] This begs Map, in his senility, to give up the *nugae* of his youth, and not to blame all Cistercians for the faults of a few. The Pope had exempted them from tithes; their life is austere, and they use their money to succour the needy.)

The third object of Map's satire is marriage. The *Epistola Valerii* was very popular and circulated separately: it was so popular, he complains, that people did not acknowledge his authorship, not wishing to ascribe it to a 'modernus' (and indeed it is often found with the spuria of Jerome); he will now keep it by his side, in the *De Nugis*. It is in the form of a letter to a cleric John. Map hesitates to interfere ('loqui prohibeor') but urgency compels him ('ideo tacere non possum').[84] The dissuasion consists of about twenty-five antimatrimonial exempla, taken from classical sources and Jerome, all elegantly and neatly told: they were used by vernacular writers such as Jean de Meun and Chaucer. The learned allusions provided a mine for the classicizing friars, and commentaries on the *Epistola* were written by Nicholas Trevet, John Ridevall, and others.[85] It is a highly polished literary essay, and should not be taken seriously as antifeminism.

We turn now to the stories. Distinctions 2, 3, and 4.6–16 are dominated by tales of the bizarre and supernatural, both holy and demonic – mermaids, revenants, fairy lovers, acts of daring, and strange knights who win tournaments and disappear. The macabre quality is often reminiscent of the horror stories of Poe, Stevenson, and (Map's editor) M.R. James.

1.32 and 2.2–7 deal mainly with miraculous sanctity. Most of 2.8–27 is devoted to Wales and the Welsh, their customs, legends, heroes and villains.

> 3.2 (Sadius and Galo) is a carefully structured narrative containing several romance elements: the queen's lustful advances on Galo, his feigned impotence, his 'disgrace', his combat (disguised in Sadius' armour) against a giant with a magic sword, and the final discomfiture of the queen. There is a lively dialogue between the queen and a serving girl on the verification of Galo's 'impotence'.
>
> 3.3 (Parius and Lausus) is a tale of envy and treachery, and hinges on an accusation of bad breath; it illustrates the workings of bitter malice. 3.4–5 concern lecherous wives.

The stories of Distinction 3 have just, if not happy, endings, but in many of those in Distinction 4 a black side of Map's humour emerges:

> 4.6: an impoverished Eudo is offered a pact with a demon; his instinct is to reject it, but he is assured that he will have three chances to repent. His third and genuine repentance, however, is rejected by a hard-hearted bishop, and Eudo dies in flames, unshriven.[86]
>
> 4.13: Nicholas Pipe could live for long periods under the sea, helpfully warning sailors of bad weather. William of Sicily conducted an experiment to see how long Nicholas could survive away from the sea: he died.
>
> 4.14: a convert Salius cannot believe in a paradise of milk and honey, since digestion would require privies ('pereat paradisus qui tali eget tugurio !' [A curse on the Paradise that needs such an outbuilding !]).
>
> 4.16: Sceva, annoyed by a snub from his old friend Ollo, moves in on Ollo's household in his absence. Sceva, Ollo's wife, and the bribed servants determine to keep Ollo out; in a scene reminiscent of the *Geta*, the servants refuse to recognize him. Ollo almost loses his wits, is reduced to theft, and finally abandons all claims against Sceva, who continues to thrive. The unhappy end to what at first looks like a comedy resembles the *Babio* and Evelyn Waugh.

Map tells curiously garbled versions of the history of Byzantium (2.18), Britanny (4.15), and England and France (5.3–6). He says that he is presenting modern history to show both good and bad:

> hanc tibi uitandam proponimus pro ueneficiis, illam eligendam pro beneficiis; neutri subducas oculum, nisi uise penitus et agnite (5: 1)

> I set before you two ways of life, one to be avoided for its venom, the other to be adopted for its advantages. Do not take your eye off either of them, until you have seen and recognized it completely.

but the morals are not easy to find. Greed, murder, cruelty, bravery and generosity are found on all sides. He sees the good side of those he otherwise deplores (Llewelyn, 'Apollonides'), and describes good endings from bad beginnings (Henry I). Map's prejudices are very clear: he liked Louis VII and Henry II, but not the Young Henry;[87] he thoroughly disliked Queen Eleanor ('incestis oculis'), polluter of Henry's progeny, and Geoffrey, archbishop of York, who was revered by Gerald of Wales but not allowed even a bastard's descent from Henry II by Map.

In prologues, epilogues and digressions, Map tells us a great deal about himself – famous people he had met, his triumph in debate over heretics, comic scenes he had witnessed, and his own problems (no doubt exaggerated) in controlling a large household. Most important he tells us about his work, which he jotted down in spare moments at court ('raptim annotaui scedulis' 4:2), and his attitude to it. Gerald of Wales reports Map's words:[88]

> 'Multa, magister Giralde, scripsistis, et multum adhuc scribitis; et nos multa diximus. Vos scripta dedistis, et nos verba. Et quamquam scripta vestra longe laudabiliora sint et longeviora quam dicta nostra, quia tamen hec aperta, communi quippe idiomate prolata, illa vero, quia latina, paucioribus evidencia, nos de dictis nostris fructum aliquem reportavimus, vos autem de scriptis egregiis, principibus litteratis nimirum et largis obsoletis olim et ab orbe sublatis, dignam minime retribucionem consequi potuistis.'

> 'You have written many things, master Gerald, and still do; I have spoken much. You produced writings, I produced words. Your writings are more praiseworthy and will last longer than my sayings, but because my sayings are more open, being stated in the common language, whereas your writings, being Latin, are accessible to fewer people, consequently I have won some profit from my sayings, but you have not been able to get an appropriate recompense for your fine writings – for literate and generous princes have become obsolete and have vanished from the world.'

Setting aside Gerald's vanity and the fact that the De Nugis is in Latin, the contrast between *scripta* and *verba* does reflect what Map himself says:

> siluam uobis et materiam, non dico fabularum sed faminum appono . . .
> Venator uester sum: feras uobis affero, fercula faciatis (2.32)

> I put before you the stuff, the raw material, not of stories but of sayings . . . I am your hunter: I supply the beasts, you are to make the banquets.

He describes himself as a bee, settling on both bitter and sweet:

> Apis et dulcibus et amaris herbis insidet, et ex singulis aliquid cere uel mellis elicit; amator sapiencie quemlibet in aliquo poetam approbat, et ab omni pagina quam baiulauerit recedit doctior (3.3)[89]

> The bee settles on both sweet and bitter herbs, and from each one elicits some wax or honey; the lover of wisdom approves every poet in some respect, and from every page he turns he departs the wiser. (Cf. Rom. 15:4)

One of his main themes is that he is a 'modernus': nowadays, only the ancients are valued and the moderns are despised:

> Hoc solum deliqui, quod uiuo. Verumptamen hoc morte mea corrigere consilium non habeo ... Omnibus seculis sua displicuit modernitas, et queuis etas a prima preteritam sibi pretulit (4.5)

> My only fault is this, that I am alive, but I have no intention of amending it by my death ... All ages have been displeased with their own modernity, and every age since the first has preferred the past to itself.

> Mortui uiuunt, uiui pro eis sepeliuntur ... Iacent tamen egregia modernorum nobilium, et attolluntur fimbrie uetustatis abiecte ... (5.1)[90]

> The dead live, and the living are buried in their place ... The excellent deeds of modern princes lie neglected, and the trampled fringes of antiquity are lifted up ...

This attitude is in striking contrast to John of Salisbury. Both writers agreed with St Paul that everything is written for our doctrine (Rom. 15:4), but John took his examples from the classics, whereas Map (although the *Epistola Valerii* shows that he knew the classics very well) drew on oral, especially Welsh, sources and recent history. John begins by stressing the importance of the written record, but Map, while expressing amazement at the inventions and discoveries of the ancients, notes that more knowledge was passed on by word of mouth than by writing:

> Multas nobis inuenciones reliquerunt in scriptis; plurime deuolute sunt ad nos parentatim a primis (1.1)

> In their writings they have left us many discoveries; the greatest number have come down to us from the beginnings from one generation to the next.

It would be too much to claim that the *De Nugis* is a parody of the *Policraticus*, but it is certainly a pleasant antidote.[91]

Map is primarily a raconteur and a humorist (whether his humour is simple or 'black'); one of his favourite words (once applied to God) is *facetus*.[92] His style is lively, full of internal rhymes, word-play (e.g. *a matre morphoseos*), and alliteration (as quoted above, 'feras uobis affero, fercula faciatis'), but also often allusive, terse and dense. He quotes both English and French, and his Latin often contains vernacular proverbs ('Murder will out', 'The husband is always the last to know'). His seamless texture of classical, medieval and biblical allusion can be compared to

P.G. Wodehouse's humorous fusion of Shakespeare, Marcus Aurelius, Spinoza and the Bible. As modern analogues for Map I have proposed Wodehouse, Waugh, Poe, Stevenson, and the shaggy dog story. This improbable mixture suggests something of Map's spirit.

Anonymous short stories

An early thirteenth-century manuscript from St Augustine's, Canterbury, contains a collection of nine tales; these are followed by general satire on knights, women, and merchants, and by praise of the virtues of peasants.[93] In their generally amoral character, the stories resemble those of Walter Map. Two concern the pernicious effects of wealth, and several are about the inordinate sexual appetite of women. The first story has a very ambivalent Map-like ending: when a husband kills his wife and her lover, it is the husband who is, from fear, eventually confined to his house. Some are quite long (one is over fifteen printed pages) and elaborately constructed: one has a tale within a tale, in which Robert Guiscard, ruler of Apulia, manages to get a thief to reveal himself by a long story about the marital and sexual adventures of Robert's daughter. The authorship of the collection is unkown: the settings include Italy and the Holy Land (none are Celtic), but the provenience of the manuscript and the mention of a Londoner 'whom I often saw' makes English authorship quite likely. Certainly the stories (whatever their origin) were written by a single author with a fondness for alliteration and convoluted word-order:

> Sed quoniam communis est consuetudinis male meritos metuere supplicia que meruerint, miles, in quem se uolens impulit, iam trepidans in euentu, nichil conferentibus et lacrimis effluere cepit et uerborum supplicationibus (10)

> But since it is commonly customary for those who have deserved badly to dread the dire punishments that they duly deserve, the knight, already trembling at the outcome to which he had willingly exposed himself, began to dissolve into profitless tears and piteous pleadings.

Several of the stories are accompanied by poems. The collection seems to have been planned as a unit, with the satirical conclusion as a summary of the various types that appeared in the stories. The author makes extensive use of Petronius, an author known to John of Salisbury but to few others in this period.

Gerald of Wales

Gerald of Wales' writing career extends from the reign of Henry II to that of Henry III. He was born in about 1146 at Manorbier, Pembrokeshire, which he describes with great affection. He was mainly Norman, but had a Welsh grandmother, Nest, daughter of Rhys ap Tewdyr (king of South Wales) and mistress of Henry I. He was educated at St Peter's abbey in Gloucester and Paris; he travelled widely, but his active career was centred on Wales, especially St David's. During his life he changed from a pro-Norman to a pro-Welsh point of view, arguing fiercely for the independence of the see of St David's from Canterbury. Most of his career, and much of his writing, was involved with his ambition for (and aborted election to) the archbishopric of St David's. He was a prolific writer, and now occupies eight volumes of the Rolls Series. Many of his works are autobiographical – defences of his own conduct and attacks on his enemies – and are suffused with bitterness, vanity and self-esteem. Above all, however, he was a writer – anecdotist, satirist, ethnographer, scientist, and poet – and spent much time revising and polishing earlier works.[94]

His earliest works (completed about 1188) are about Ireland, which he visited as part of Prince John's expedition of 1185. The *Topographia Hiberniae*[95] describes Ireland and the Irish, with many digressions on natural history and marvels. The *Expugnatio Hibernica* describes the conquest of Ireland (with attention to the part played by Gerald's family) and the political background; it includes a severe indictment of Henry II for refusing to go to Jerusalem. He called the first version of the *Expugnatio* the 'Historia Vaticinalis', and structured it round the prophecies of the Irish Moling, Merlin Ambrosius (of Geoffrey's *Historia*), and Merlin Silvester/ Caledonius.[96] He says that he had found Merlin Silvester's prophecies on the Lleyn peninsula in North Wales, and intended to publish them, purged of their 'Britannica barbaries', as the final book of the *Expugnatio*; if published, this book would probably have been much like the *Prophecy of the Eagle*, but longer. In the event, he decided to postpone publication rather than cause offence and risk danger:

> quam in lucem cum maiorum offensa prepropere pariter et periculose
> prorumpat

> . . . than that it should burst forth too quickly and dangerously,
> causing offence to superiors.

He is at his journalistic best in his works on Wales. The *Itinerarium Cambriae* recounts his journey round Wales with Archbishop Baldwin in 1188, preaching the crusade and picking up local gossip, amusing incidents, folklore, and natural history. The *Descriptio Cambriae* did for Wales what the *Topographia* had done for Ireland, except that Gerald knew and loved Wales better, and had now mastered the art of writing entertaining geography and ethnography.[97] His inquisitiveness about natural, supernatural and anthropological phenomena is his most endearing characteristic. The *Gemma Ecclesiastica* is formally a manual of instruction for the Welsh clergy. It describes the sacraments and difficulties in administering them. It deals with abuses (lechery, concubinage, simony and avarice), and delights in anecdotes, especially miracles and examples of divine retribution. To illustrate clerical illiteracy he tells a story about a clerk who asked who the Busillis was that he had found in the Missal; when asked to point out the word, he indicated *bus illis* at the beginning of a line, preceded on the line above by *in die-*.

Three works deal directly with his campaign for the see of St David's: *De rebus a se gestis* (a polemic autobiography), *De iure et statu Menevensis ecclesiae*, and the *Liber invectionum*. The sixth book of *Invectiones* describes prophetic visions that his contemporaries had had about Gerald and his appointment to St David's, thus neatly combining his three great interests, prophecies, Wales, and himself.

The *De principis instructione* is more than a Mirror for Princes; it recounts the rise and fall of Henry II, whose downfall is attributed to divine retribution for the murder of Becket and the refusal to go to Jerusalem; the third distinction contains mainly visions foretelling Henry's downfall. In the *Vita Galfridi archiepiscopi Eboracensis* Gerald championed Geoffrey, bastard son of Henry II, in his conflict with William de Longchamps, gleefully describing William's humiliating attempt to leave England disguised as a woman.[98]

His several saints' lives honour places with which he had some connexion. The *Vita S. Remigii* and *Vita S. Hugonis* form a single work in honour of bishops of Lincoln. The *Vita S. Ethelberti*, reworked from one by Osbert of Clare, illustrates his Hereford connexions.[99] His Welsh interests are shown in his *Vita S. Davidis*, based on the life by Rhygyfarch.[100]

His vanity is fully exemplified in the pompously entitled *Symbolum Electorum*, a collection of his letters, poems and prefaces, made (he says) at the request of his friends – a request that he clearly felt was his due. The poems, in contrast to his entertaining prose, are somewhat disappointing: some, as he says, are youthful exercises in rhetoric. There is an extended cosmology, in 266 lines of elegiacs, based on Bernard Silvester, and a poem celebrating the invasion of Prince Louis in 1216.

Satire, in the sense of both melange and criticism, runs throughout his writings, but his most satirical work was his last, the *Speculum Ecclesiae*, written in 1220 when he was in his seventies. Not surprisingly, he re-uses some early material, such as the luxurious living of the monks of Christ Church (which he had observed forty years before) and the discovery of the tomb of Arthur and Guinevere at Glastonbury. On the other hand, in the *Preface* he shows his awareness of very recent events.[101] The *Preface* criticizes mispronunciations of Latin, especially among monks, and blames the decline of grammar on the fashionable pursuit of law and philosophy.[102] The *Speculum* plots the decline of religious orders from great promise into degeneracy; his anti-Cistercian stories are often supported by witticisms quoted from Walter Map. In the final distinction, he praises Rome and defends its supposed avarice by blaming the meanness of secular rulers; he quotes, with apparent disapproval, Goliardic poems against curial greed. He himself had been disappointed by lack of support from Rome, and it has been suggested that this whole section is ironic.[103] On the other hand, sustained ambiguity is not his usual style.

Gerald has been assessed many times from various points of view. There is much to interest the literary historian: his information on Welsh and Irish customs; his interest in marvels and Arthuriana (he is sceptical towards Geoffrey's *Historia*, but made use of it); his use of prophecies; his knowledge of the classics;[104] his conservative views on the study of grammar. As a satirist he is not as funny as Nigel

Whiteacre nor as subtle as Walter Map: he is a journalist rather than an ironist. He writes elegantly and with a concern for style, but although he would no doubt have sided with John of Salisbury and the 'antiqui' against the 'moderni', his interest in British things makes him very much a writer of his own time.

Gerald's circle: Simon du Freine

Gerald's acquaintances included several writers. He had met Serlo of Wilton. He corresponded with William de Montibus (defending his literary pursuits), and probably knew Joseph of Exeter. He twice mentions Maurice of Glamorgan, a poet.[105] A close friendship with Walter Map is less certain: he sent him a staff with some verses (to which Map responded similarly) and a stuffy letter advising him to turn to theology instead of frivolous literature (much like the one he had received from William de Montibus!). He reports conversations with Map and often quotes his witticisms verbatim. On the other hand, although they both satirized monks, especially Cistercians, their attitudes to Henry II and Geoffrey of York were diametrically opposed. Map mentions several literary acquaintances, but never refers to Gerald: if there was a friendship it seems to have been one-sided.[106]

Simon du Freine, a canon of Hereford, is mainly known for his Anglo-Norman *Roman de Philosophie* and *Passion of St George*,[107] but he also wrote a Latin poem in elegiacs inviting Gerald to move to Hereford, where learning and literature thrived. (Gerald's short verse reply does not mention the invitation). In a rhythmical Latin poem he rebuked a monk who had dared to attack the master, that is Gerald.[108]

Northern writers

As in chapter 1, some writings that concern the North of England and Scotland can be isolated and described separately.[109]

William of Glasgow and other poems

An isolated incident in 1164 – an attack on Glasgow by Sumorled, 'Lord of the Isles and of Argyle', and his defeat and death at the hands of Bishop Herbert – was the occasion of a poem by a William of Glasgow.[110] In eighty rhythmical trochaic septenarii it recounts the miraculous intervention of St Kentigern (also known as Mungo), who, in a scene reminiscent of the removal of Birnam Wood to Dunsinane (*Macbeth* v.v), caused the bushes to appear as soldiers, to the discomfiture of Sumorled's army:

> Tymus usta et arbusta, rubi atque filices,
> Timebantur et rebantur hostibus ut milites.
> In hac uita non audita erant haec miracula;
> Umbrae, tymi atque fimi extant propugnacula (57–60)

Thyme and bushes, ferns and rushes, put their hearts in fear,
Consternation, expectation that the foe was near.
No such blunder, no such wonder have I heard before:
Shadows, bushes, heaps of rubbish, feared as arms of war !

Several short poems concern Scotland.[111] In 'Cur sic care taces' the dead king Malcolm (d. 1165) appears to a cleric Richard to tell him about his carefree life in heaven. A very anti-Scottish poem, 'Militat ad titulos', mocks the defeat in 1174 of the Scots under William the Lion; the Scots are naturally treacherous,

Non nequit esse nocens Aquilonis filius, immo
Contrahit Arctoa de regione malum (23–4).

The North Wind's offspring blows no good for man,
Infected by the evil of the North. (Cf. Jer. 1: 14)

but they flee when they hear of Henry II's arrival and are humiliatingly defeated. 'Vix solet esse gravis' praises the newly founded abbey of Melrose and the Benedictine way of life. This is followed by a ten-stanza rhythmical poem, 'Excitare somno musa', in honour of Hugh the Chancellor, in whom Scotland rejoices.

Reginald of Coldingham

Northern writers were naturally interested in Northern saints. Reginald of Coldingham, a monk of Durham, wrote about Cuthbert and Godric.[112] Sometime after 1172 he collected the posthumous miracles of Cuthbert and addressed them to Aelred; each marvel opens with a general statement of Cuthbert's sanctity, followed by an illustrative miracle; there are 141 chapters in all. The *De ortu* (*Libellus de Nativitate*) *S. Cuthberti* may also be by Reginald, as its author states that he had earlier collected the miracles of the saint; he tells the story, now discredited, of Cuthbert's Irish paternity which resulted from a rape by an Irish king.

Godric (d. 1170), author of some English hymns, was a hermit at Finchale; Reginald knew him personally, and although he may have used other literary sources he writes primarily as an eyewitness. The *Vita* is a vast and entertaining work, mainly about Godric's miraculous powers of perception and precognition. There are initially 315 chapters; in chapters 316–51 Reginald includes some tales he regards as less certain, including a vision of Purgatory. The posthumous miracles (chapters 352–615) are mainly cures of diseases, told very succinctly, and may have formed a dossier for possible canonization.

An anonymous poem, 'Ada mundi qui elegit', in twenty-seven Victorine stanzas, briefly recounts Godric's life, concentrating on his miracles and his wonderful control over the natural world:[113]

Dictu pisces irretivit,
Aquae tumor obedivit
Fluxu sistens limitem (15/1–3)

The net was filled with fishes at his word,
And by the swollen water he was heard,
    Which promptly stopped its flow.

Jocelin of Furness

In Northern Lancashire at the Cistercian abbey of Furness, the monk Jocelin wrote
several prose lives. One is of St Patrick, but the others are of Northern saints: St
Waltheof, grandson of the rebel, abbot of the Cistercian abbey of Melrose in
Scotland, and St Kentigern (alias Mungo), protector, as we saw above, of Glasgow
in the attack by Sumorled.[114]

'Brutus'

Hugh Puiset, bishop of Durham (whose election had been supported by Lawrence), became a powerful national figure; for a short time he was one of the
vice-regents left in charge of England, until he was removed by William de
Longchamps. He was also a literary patron. He was the dedicatee of the first major
poem based on Geoffrey of Monmouth, the *Brutus*.[115] This consists of a prologue
of thirty-four hexameters *caudati* and 620 lines of unrhymed elegiac couplets. The
prologue begins with the topos of the poor rewards for poetry, but praises Puiset as
a descendant of Charlemagne and a true Maecenas. The first part (35–100) briefly
recapitulates the fall of Troy, following Dares Phrygius. The remainder (101–654)
is based closely on Geoffrey of Monmouth (*Historia* 1.3–2.7); most of it concerns
the campaigns in Greece and France, concentrating particularly on the exploits of
Corineus, great-great-grandfather of Ebraucus, founder of York. The settlers do
not reach Britain until line 457, and again attention is given to Corineus' defeat of
the giants and to the affair between the beautiful Estrildis and Locrinus, husband of
Corineus' daughter Gwendolen. The poem was clearly intended to celebrate the
founding of York, as it ends with Ebraucus:

> Conditor urbis erat, que nunc Eboracus ab eius
>   Nomine nomen habet, qui decoravit eam (649–50)

> He founded York, which from him took its name,
>   Eboracum, and he adorned it well.

Most of the poem is straightforward narrative, but occasionally the author
intrudes an opinion. He attributes Lavinia's surprising preference for Aeneas over
Turnus –

> Phrix erat inferior virtute, remotior evo,
>   Rege minor, nevis tactus et exul erat (113–4)

> The Trojan was no match in age or might,
>   But less than king, an exile, stained with faults.

to female fickleness ('sic novit femina ferre vices'). On the love affair between Locrinus and Estrildis he remarks on the attractiveness of illicit love:

> In licitis minus ardet amor, minus acriter urit;
> Plus iuvat illicitus plusque saporis habet (589–90)

> In what's allowed, love burns less ardently:
> Illicit love holds more delights and spice.

Joseph of Exeter

When Gerald of Wales and Archbishop Baldwin were preaching the Third Crusade in Wales in 1188, Baldwin was asked who would write the history of the crusade. He replied that the archdeacon (Gerald himself) would write it in prose (which he never did), and his nephew Joseph would write it in verse. We know little of Joseph except that he was born in Exeter (hence his name Iscanus) and enjoyed the friendship of Guibert, abbot of Fleury (later of Gembloux). Only twenty-five lines of his crusade epic, the *Antiocheis*, have survived, preserved by Leland. He also wrote poems in praise of virginity and St Martin, but his reputation rests securely on his great Trojan epic, the *Ylias*, written about 1185.[116]

The Troy story was already well known in England, partly through Ovid and Virgil, but mainly through the prose histories of Dares Phrygius and Dictys Cretensis. Geoffrey of Monmouth had shown the importance of the fall of Troy for the founding of Britain, and versifications of the story were becoming popular.[117] The latter, however, were brief in relation to the size of the subject and seem almost to be exercises in *abbreviatio*; they all start with the story of Paris and the abduction of Helen. Joseph's poem is the first full-fledged medieval verse epic on Troy, and it presents the whole history, from the voyage of the Argonauts to the fates of the returning Greek warriors. It is in unrhymed hexameters and classical in tone.

Book I. In classical style the opening line summarizes the epic:

> Yliadum lacrimas concessaque Pergama fatis (1.1)

> The Trojan women's tears and fated Troy.

The prologue (1–59) praises Archbishop Baldwin, contrasting him favourably with his predecessor.[118] The story begins with the sailing of the world's first ship, the Argo, under Jason and Hercules; the inhospitable reception of the Argonauts by Laomedon, king of Troy (a motive stressed throughout the poem); Hercules' punitive expedition and the first sack of Troy, the death of Laomedon and the abduction of his daughter Hesione, who is given by Hercules to Telamon.

Book II. Priam, Laomedon's son, rebuilds Troy, but is provoked by the fury Allecto (who is angry that Troy has survived). He sends Antenor to Greece to try to recover Hesione, but Telamon will not release her, despite her reluctance for the marriage:

> sola tamen duro turbat convivia vultu
> Hesione (2.138–9)

99

> Hesione alone disturbs the feast
> With solemn gaze . . .

As the Trojans debate their options, Paris describes his judgment between the three godesses, whose speeches are given in full (237–606); he says that an expedition to abduct Helen will have the support of Venus. Priam, regarding Helen as a bargaining chip to secure Hesione's release, agrees to the expedition, despite opposition from Cassandra.

Book III. Despite prophecies by Helenus and Panthus, Troilus and Antenor support the expedition, in doomladen words:

> Fortuna sequenda est . . . (3.130)
>
> Fortune must be followed . . .
>
> Stant fixa tenore
> Fata suo . . . (3.135–6)
>
> Our destiny is fixed upon its course . . .

and Paris sets off. The rape is portrayed as the easy seduction of an eager and willing victim:[119]

> Sentit Paris, ardet et audet,
> Promissorque ingens facilis presagia prede
> Ducit Amor (3.240–2)
>
> . . . Now Paris feels and burns and dares,
> And Love, that mighty trickster, offers signs
> Of easy prey to come . . .

Paris returns home to congratulations from all except Cassandra. The Greeks assemble their forces and consult the omens.

Book IV. The main actors in the drama, Trojan and Greek, are briefly described according to Dares' sketches. Some of the descriptions utilize medieval physiological and psychological theory: the Greek Merion is almost a personification of Envy. Helen's warm and impulsive nature is the product of her heart, tongue, lungs, spleen, and lascivious liver:

> At teneri titillat mollius equo
> Pruritus iecoris meriteque insignia fame
> Mergens nativi titulos incestat amoris (4.199–201)
>
> More softly than is right, her liver's itch
> Provokes her lust, and drowns her proper fame,
> Dishonouring the name of inborn love.

When the Greeks arrive in Trojan territory, Achilles and Telephus divert to Mesia; its king Teuthras bequeaths his kingdom to Telephus. Teuthras is given an elaborate burial, and there is a detailed description of his tomb, which depicts the four ages of his life.[120]

Book V. The Greeks land and the siege of Troy and the battles begin. Years pass with alternating truces and conflicts. Andromache dreams of a huge laurel tree overhanging her chamber, hewn down and dripping blood on her marriage bed:[121]

inimica securis
Hanc a stirpe metit, rorantes sanguine rami
In stratum geniale cadunt (5.433–5)

The hostile axe
Hacks down the laurel from its stock; with blood
The branches drip upon her marriage bed.

and Hector is killed; Joseph compares him to the Young Henry.

Book VI. Agamemnon hands over leadership of the Greeks to Palamedes (later killed by Troilus). Achilles falls in love with Priam's daughter Polyxena and withdraws from the fighting. Troilus seems invincible, and even Mars learned from him:

Ipse alias discit iras maioraque Mavors
Prelia, et exemplum divus mortale secutus, (6.250–1)

Fierce Mars learns further strife and greater fights:
A mortal man is model for a god !

but he is killed by an enraged Achilles. Hecuba, on the pretext of arranging his marriage with Polyxena, lures Achilles into an ambush, where he is killed. Paris behaves like a coward; when he is killed the poet damns him to Hell:

Tibi Stix odium Phlegetonque vapores,
Cochitus lacrimas, Acheron lamenta propinet (6.530–1)

On you may Styx rain hate, Phlegethon fire,
Cochytus tears, and Acheron laments !

The Greeks are reinforced by Pyrrhus. In Troy a peace party (Antenor, Aeneas and Polydamas) propose handing Helen over; Priam tries to have them killed, but the plotters admit the Greeks into the city through a gate on which is portrayed Pegasus' head; the city is sacked:

Nox fera, nox vere nox noxia, turbida, tristis,
Insidiosa, ferox, tragicis ululanda coturnis (6.760–1)

Fierce night (so truly named), confused and grim,
Fierce, treacherous, a theme for tragic style.

Priam is killed and Hecuba laments; Aeneas vainly tries to hide Polyxena ('O scelus ingens !') and is exiled as a punishment. (At this point Joseph begins to follow Dictys Cretensis.) Aeneas fails in an attempt to overthrow Antenor, who has been given the kingship of Troy as a reward for his treachery. The Greeks return home, almost all to disaster: Agamemnon is killed by the faithless Clytemnestra; Ulysses finds his wife faithful but is accidentally killed by his own son Telegonus. Only Helen survives to glory in her reputation:

Quin ipsa superbit
Accendisse duces, lacerasse in prelia mundum,
Infamem forme titulum lucrata pudende (6.956–8)

But she takes pride that she

Set lords on fire and tore the world in war,
And won renown for beauty without shame.

In an age that was usually pro-Trojan, the *Ylias* is unusually neutral. The Greeks had definitely been wronged twice, by Laomedon's inhospitality and Helen's abduction. The most strident warmongering is done by the Trojans (especially Antenor and Paris); Troy has its heroes, notably Hector and Troilus, but is plagued by traitors. Joseph has an ambivalent attitude to pagans: he deplores their beliefs and mocks their sacrifices and auguries, their faith in warring gods, and their belief in the deification of mortals.[122] On the other hand, he introduces pagan spirits and deities (Allecto in Book II, Juno and Athene in Book V) to motivate the action, much as Chaucer does with planetary gods, but there is no sense here of an overriding destiny.

From a classical perspective the *Ylias* marks a high point in Medieval Latin verse, matched only by Walter of Châtillon's *Alexandreis*. Joseph has transformed Dares' bare telegraphic prose into a 'Silver' epic, not only by tricks such as the allusive use of patronymics (e.g. 'Martia Naupli proles' = Palamedes) but by a very dense style. Here, for instance, is Paris' coy approach when he first sees Helen:

> Indefessa vagis incessibus ocia texit
> Certantesque offert vultus, incendia nutrit
> Mutua captatumque brevi lucratur amorem (3.226–8)

> With wandering steps he idles tirelessly;
> His eager looks enkindle mutual flames,
> And quickly win the love for which he sought.

He breaks the story up into its highlights and set pieces, such as the speeches in council, the individual combats, and the funerals of Teuthras and Memnon. The major classical writers on Troy had avoided the tedium of a ten-year siege either by concentrating on one episode (*Iliad*) or by relating selected episodes in flashback (*Odyssey*, *Aeneid*). In Dares, the war drags on painfully slowly, constantly interrupted by peace negotiations and two- or three-year truces. Joseph manages to follow Dares' chronological sequence, but by suppressing or compressing allusions to the passage of time, manages to give the impression of only a few weeks action. It is a remarkable poem and quite untypical of its age.

Nigel Whiteacre

Nigel Whiteacre was born about 1140;[123] his father spoke French, his mother English. He may have been educated at Paris, but afterwards became a monk at Christ Church, Canterbury; sometime before 1160 he had met Becket. He wrote verse saints' lives, miracles of the Virgin, and poems about Canterbury, and a prose *Tractatus contra curiales*[124] but his most popular work was the brilliant satire *Speculum Stultorum*.[125] This is a vehicle for satire against religious orders (excluding his own Benedictines) and institutions and for several other stories, but its fundamental humour derives from the fact that the hero, Burnellus, is an ass.

1–80 prologue to William (presumably de Longchamps) on the text's hidden meaning, the distorted values of modern society, and Avianus' fable about the ass dressed in a lion's skin ('qui quondam, semper asellus eris').

81–204 once upon a time there was an ass who wanted a longer tail to match his ears:

> Auribus immensis quondam donatus asellus
> Institit ut caudam posset habere parem (81–2)

> An ass once lived, endowed with two long ears,
> Whose sole ambition was a tail to match.

He consults the doctors, and Galen tries to dissuade him, telling him: 205–594 the story of two cows, Brunetta and Bicornis, whose tails were frozen in the mud (Bicornis cuts hers off and lives to repent in gnat-time). 595–684 Burnellus is undeterred, and Galen prescribes a mock recipe (marble-grease, a pound of peacock song, etc.) to be purchased at Salerno, the centre of medical research. 685–826 there Burnellus is tricked by a London merchant and buys ten jars of the mixture. 827–1110 on his way home he trespasses on the land of a Cistercian abbey, is set upon by dogs, and loses his jars and half his tail. After pretending to be a papal legate, he hoofs the monk Froumond fatally into the Rhône. 1111–220 depressed by the loss of his tail, he decides to go to Paris for an arts education.

1221–502 a fellow-traveller Arnold tells the story of a vengeful cock (retold more succinctly by Chaucer). 1503–656 in Paris Burnellus joins the English nation, famed for drinking and wenching, but after seven years has learned nothing new:

> Semper 'hy ha' repetit, nihil est quod dicere possit
> Affectus quovis verbere praeter 'hy ha' (1553–4)

> 'Hee-haw' is all he says and nothing else;
> Though beaten, all he says is just 'Hee-haw'.

He is depressed by his stupidity and dreams about his mother. 1657–789 he ponders about predestination: perhaps he will become a bishop (but only with full powers); he reflects on a bishop's duties. 1789–912 he worries about the future: the present provost was once caught stealing; Burnellus had released him, but now worries that he will turn out to be ungrateful. 1913–2022 he leaves Paris, and nearly forgets its name ('Haec est Roma'); he takes a vow of silence so that he can repeat 'Parisius' to himself, but a chance stranger drives this from his head by saying the *Pater* Noster. Now he can only remember the syllable *par*. 2023–412 he decides to become a monk, but which kind ? He (satirically) reviews all the orders – Templars, Hospitallers, Cluniacs, Cistercians, Grandmontines, Carthusians, Austin Canons, Premonstratensians, secular canons (particularly savagely portrayed), nuns, and the order of Sempringham. 2413–2464 he decides to form his own order (the Asinines ?):

> Qui meus ordo meo nomen de nomine sumat,
> Nomen in aeternum vivat ut inde meum (2417–8)

> From my name will this Order take its name,
> And so my name will live for ever more.

and sets off for Rome, to have it confirmed by the Pope. 2465–874 he meets Galen again, and embarks on a long attack on Rome, kings, bribery, bishops, abbots, and priors, but will not mention lay people. 2875–3236 he tells how he escaped from his master Bernard and overheard a debate between a crow, a cock and a hawk (similar in tone to the *Owl and Nightingale*); reversing the literary convention, he fell asleep and disturbed the birds by his snoring. 3237–458 he laments the passage of time and his own sinfulness; he recalls a story his mother used to tell him, of the Three Fates and the unequal distribution of gifts (particularly in the religious life). 3459–560 a sudden nosebleed leads to reflection on omens (may bad ones befall his enemies !). Bernard now reappears, reclaims Burnellus, and cuts off his ears. Burnellus denounces all rustics, vows vengeance, is taken back to Cremona, and disappears from the poem. 3561–878 tell a story (perhaps originally separate) about Bernard, the ungrateful Dryanus, and three grateful animals.[126] 3879–900 conclusion.

Some time later Nigel wrote a prose letter to William de Longchamps (now incomplete), explaining details of the allegory.[127] In the fourteenth century the poem was expanded to include satire against the friars.

His second longest poem, 2690 lines, also in elegiacs, is his three-book *Miracles of the Virgin*.[128] There are eighteen stories, based on William of Malmesbury's collection, selected for their variety and potential for poetic embellishment. They concern the saintly (Dunstan, Ildefonsus, Fulbert) and the sinful (Theophilus, who made a pact with the devil; a cleric who sought magical aid to win his girl; two dissolute monks and a charming bibulous one; an incestuous mother; a strict abbess who has a child). Sincerity, even the mechanical habit of devotion, always saves sinners. There is an illiterate but devout priest:

> Rectus homo non retor erat nec multus in arte
> Grammatica, gratus non minus inde Deo (1759–60)

> No orator but upright man, unskilled
> In grammar, no less great in God's esteem.

A Jewish boy who admires Christianity is saved from roasting. A merchant cites the Virgin as guarantor for a loan, and she miraculously proves that he had repaid it. The Virgin twice gives her milk to a sick devotee; she gets Mercury to kill Julian the Apostate, and rescues the people of Chartres from a siege. The miracles are told simply but with rhetorical embellishment, such as alliteration, and digression and authorial comment.

His life of St Lawrence, in 2345 variously rhymed hexameters, has not been published, but extracts show that he has expanded the story considerably by speeches and general reflections.[129] His life of St Paul of Thebes consists of 747 lines in the same metre;[130] it follows Jerome's life closely, beginning with the early martyrs, and then describing Paul's flight to the desert, St Antony's search for him (including his meeting with a 'centaur' and a Christian satyr), their conversations, and Antony's burial of Paul. Nigel also wrote a brief verse life of St Catherine. He has also been credited with a life of St Eustace, in 458 lines of elegiacs mixed with blocks of Leonines. Eustace was a Roman (né Placidus) who was converted by

Christ in the shape of a stag; the story of his loss of possessions, wife and children, his restoration to favour and recovery of his family, and eventual martyrdom, is told with remarkable ineptitude and repetition; it is a silly story rendered sillier by the repetitions and flat style. If it is Nigel's, it is not his best work.[131]

Many of Nigel's short poems concern Christ Church and its relationship with the archbishopric.[132] The death in 1184 of archbishop Richard, the monks' choice, prompted Nigel to write a verse history of the archbishops ('Hic Dorobernorum'), ending with his concern for the future. Richard's successor was the Cistercian bishop of Worcester, Baldwin,[133] who proposed to establish a college of secular canons at neighbouring Hackington. Nigel's views on secular canons are clear:

> His quodcunque libet lex est licitumque, sub isto
> Canone constituit vivere tota cohors (ss 2317–8)

> So what they like is licensed and the law:
> This principle's the Rule by which they live.

Prior Honorius appealed to Rome. In retaliation Baldwin suspended the prior and offending monks; they in turn went to Rome to plead their case, but in 1188 Honorius died there. Nigel wrote several poems in his honour (the common pun is his), and regarded him as a martyr.

Politics of the reign of Richard I

Third Crusade

The fall of Jerusalem in 1187 spread dismay in the Christian world. Geoffrey of Vinsauf lamented the capture of the Cross;[134] as we have seen, Gerald of Wales preached the crusade, as did many poets, though he never wrote its history.[135] Berter of Orléans wrote:[136]

> Set ad pugnam congressuris
> est athletis opus duris
> non mollibus Epicuris,

> When we're about to fight
> We need a tough man's might,
> Not feeble sybarite.

and another poem lamented the failure of leaders to join:[137]

> cordis potentes ferrei
> sic in uindictam fidei
>   mentes et manus continent;
> quod urbem sanctam pollui,
> quod loca sancta destruj
>   pari defectu sustinent

> Their breasts are bound with iron band
> When fighting for the Holy Land:
>   They rein their hearts and hands in tight.
> The holy city's foul disgrace,
> The ruin of that sacred place,
>   They suffer with no will to fight.

Immediately after his coronation in 1189 Richard left for the Holy Land, and during his ten-year reign was in England for only a few weeks. While in Palestine he was accused of complicity in the murder of Conrad of Montferrat in 1192.[138] His later adventures are discussed below.

Career of William de Longchamps

When Richard left England he placed his chancellor, William de Longchamps, in charge of the kingdom, sharing power in the North with Hugh Puiset.[139] Richard's brother John and half-brother Geoffrey agreed to stay out of the country for three years. William was consecrated bishop of Ely (January 1190) and, at Richard's instigation, was appointed papal legate (June 1190). He seems to have encouraged literature; he surrounded himself with foreign poets, who wrote poems in his honour:

> Quidam carmina, quidam cantilenas et alia huiusmodi, quae non multum constabant, offerebant[140]
>
> Some of them used to offer him poems or jingles or other things
> of this kind, that didn't amount to much.

Gerald of Wales dedicated the first edition (1191) of his *Itinerarium Cambriae* to him, and Ralph of Diceto sent him his *opuscula*. Nigel sent him the *Speculum Stultorum* and an accompanying letter. In 1190 Nigel also sent him a poem 'Postquam tristis hiems',[141] closely modelled on John of Salisbury's *Entheticus in Policraticum*: the poem is told to go to the shrine of St Audry at Ely and to behave politely at court.

William was a parvenu, a Norman who spoke no English, and physically deformed. His attempts to replenish the treasury (emptied by crusade expenses) and his lavish visitations made him unpopular, as did his championing of the Jews of York. He earned the wrath of monks (though not of Gerald) by supporting Hugh Nonant, the bishop, when he expelled the monks of Coventry. He deposed Hugh Puiset of his Northern power and foolishly absolved John from his oath to stay out of England. His most unpopular act was the arrest of Geoffrey, archbishop of York, and he was attacked for it in Gerald's *Vita Galfridi*. William attempted to flee England, dressed as a woman, but was humiliatingly caught, deprived of office (replaced by William of Coutances), sentenced and exiled in 1191. His downfall, with all its comic elements, was retold with glee by many writers, including Gerald. The account in a letter of Hugh Nonant was the basis for a poem, 'Discat cancellarius', which mocks his haughtiness, his deformity, his injustices, and above all his female disguise:[142]

> arte fit institoria
> risoria
> nouum mundi spectaculum,
> et uilia
> mutans dum abdicat
> se masculum
> mox indicat
> semiuirum per spolia

> By sewer's skill he
> Looks quite silly,
> Gives the world another wonder;
> Doffs his man's garb,
> Puts on discards,
> Only half a man thereunder.

In 1193 Nigel sent William the prose *Tractatus in curiales*.[143] After a long attack on the unfitness of the clergy and the way they are appointed (heavily indebted to John of Salisbury),[144] Nigel develops his main theme, that bishops should not be involved in politics. William, because of his secular duties, had broken every one of the oaths (carefully itemized) that he had taken on becoming a bishop; his downfall was the result of trying to serve two masters. The treatise purports to be friendly advice, but it could hardly have been welcome to William. The same theme is common in lyrics, as in 'Heu quo progreditur', where Eraclius says that Christ is put on trial again,

> cum Petrus utitur
> Pilati gladio[145]

> When Peter wields the sword of Pilate.

Richard's capture

After successes at Cyprus, Acre and Jaffa, but failure to take Jerusalem itself, Richard set out homeward in the fall of 1192. He fell into the hands of the Duke of Austria, who handed him over to the Emperor Henry VI, who held him for ransom. This outrage provoked literary comment. Peter of Blois, 'Quis aquam tuo capiti',[146] denounced the Duke of Austria as a 'vas Deo detestabile, vas scelerum', an 'idolatra pecuniae'. Delays in securing Richard's release, and the cost, were denounced in 'Insurgant in Germaniam',[147] which calls for revenge

> ne maiestatem regiam
> tam probroso commercio
> quis deinceps offendat

> Lest by commercial travesty
> We're guilty of lese-majeste.

The name of Germany is dishonoured by the transaction:

> quod extorta pecunia
> commune parit odium;
> perhenne transitoria
> merces emit opprobrium

> Extortion's fate
> Is common hate:
> A fleeting gain
> Earns lasting shame.

Geoffrey of Vinsauf's poem 'Imperialis apex' may be an appeal to the Emperor for Richard's release.[148]

Richard's death

Richard was released in March 1194 and returned briefly to England, but he and William de Longchamps (now restored to power) left immediately for the continent. In April 1199 Richard was killed by a chance arrow at the siege of Chalus. His death was twice lamented by Geoffrey of Vinsauf.[149]

Geoffrey of Vinsauf

The twelfth century saw an increased interest in the craft of poetry, and the English contribution to this new rhetoric was considerable.[150] Geoffrey of Vinsauf was English; in his 'Si liceat michi pauca loqui', he implies that he had studied at Paris and lectured at Northampton ('Hamtone'). His major works were the prose *Documentum de arte versificandi* and *Summa de coloribus* and the verse *Poetria Nova*.[151] The *Documentum* draws its precepts from classical writers such as Horace and from Sidonius Apollinaris; many of its examples are from Geoffrey's own poems.

In order, it treats:[152] the beginning of a work (recommending one of the eight 'artificial' openings), amplification, abbreviation, 'ornata difficultas' (transferred senses of words), 'ornata facilitas' (mainly *conversio* and *determinatio*, discussed below), faults to be avoided, and methods of ending. To illustrate comic style he quotes 'De clericis et rustico' (discussed below).

The *Summa de coloribus* lists the more obvious verbal tricks of rhetoric, and occasionally overlaps with the *Documentum*. To illustrate *gradatio* it quotes from 'Si liceat michi'.

The verse *Poetria Nova*, in 2116 hexameters, is much more ambitious. It was probably completed about 1200–2, but contains works probably composed much earlier. Its examples are not classical but Geoffrey's own compositions.

The prologue addresses Pope Innocent III, whose unmetrical name caused difficulties:[153]

> Papa, stupor mundi, si dixero Papa Nocenti
> Acephalum nomen tribuam; sed si caput addam
> Hostis erit metri (1–3)

> O Pope, of whom the world's in awe, you lose
> Your head if 'Nocent' is your name, but if
> I give it back I break the rules of verse.

I. He stresses the need for a plan:

> Si quis habet fundare domum, non currit ad actum
> Impetuosa manus: intrinseca linea cordis
> Praemetitur opus (43–5)[15]

> For everi wight that hath an hous to founde
> Ne renneth naught the werk for to bygynne
> With rakel hond; but he wol bide a stounde,
> And sende his hertes line out from withinne (Chaucer, *Troilus* 1.1065–8)

II. Various ways of beginning a poem are illustrated (as in the *Documentum*, but more thoroughly) by the story of Minos and Scylla.

III.A. Amplification can be achieved in eight ways: by repetition, periphrasis, comparison (all three illustrated by the words used to describe them), apostrophe, prosopopoeia, digression, description, and 'opposition'. The six examples of apostrophe (direct address) include the two poems on the death of Richard I mentioned above;[155] 'Neustria sub clipeo' calls on Normandy to lament the loss of its protector:

> Neustria sub clypeo regis defensa Ricardi,
> Indefensa modo, planctu testare dolorem (368–9)

> O Normandy, once safe beneath King Richard's shield,
> Now, unprotected, demonstrate your grief with tears.

and itself contains six apostrophes. The three examples of *prosopopoeia* (an address by an inanimate object) are: a lament by the Cross on its capture at the fall of Jerusalem:

> Crux ego rapta queror, vi rapta manuque canina
> Et tactu polluta canum (469–70);

> Hear my lament: the Holy Cross, by force despoiled,
> Polluted by the touch of heathen dogs.

an address by the famous Château-Gaillard (also in the *Documentum*), and a lament by a worn-out tablecloth:

> Ut si jam tritum dicat mensale: Solebam
> Esse decus mensae, dum primula floruit aetas (509–10)

> As if a worn-out tablecloth should say: 'I once,
> In my first bloom of youth, lent grace to dinner-time.'

'Description' includes poems on ideal female beauty and a banquet.

III.B. Abbreviation is illustrated (as in the *Documentum*) by the story of the Snow Child: an adulterous wife claims that her new child was conceived from snow; the husband sells it and says that it has melted.[156] This is reduced first to four lines, and then to two versions of two lines each, e.g.

> Vir, quia quem peperit genitum nive femina fingit,
> Vendit et a simili liquefactum sole refingit (735–6)

> The husband sells the child his lying wife pretends
> Was born of snow: 'It melted in the sun', he says.

IV.1 'Ornatus difficilis' includes transferred and metaphorical senses of words. Geoffrey explains the tension (*lis*) between figural and real, as in

> Ante Dei faciem devota silentia clamant (878)

> Before the face of God devoted silence shouts.

IV.2 'Ornatus facilis' (rhetorical tricks such as repetition, puns, exclamation) is illustrated by two long poems, both on the theme of the Fall and Redemption of man (1098–217, 1280–527).

IV.3. 'Conversio' is the substitution of one type of grammatical structure for another. The verb *doleo* has a noun *dolor*; thus, the phrase *ex hac re doleo* can be converted to:

> Ex hoc fonte mihi manat dolor. Hinc mihi surgit
> Radix vel semen vel fons vel origo doloris (1624–5)

> From this spring flows my grief; so thus comes forth
> The 'root', 'seed', 'spring', or 'origin' of grief.

(In the *Documentum*, where he expands the words *doceo* and *lego* into whole sentences, he explains the purpose of this constant interchange of expressions for the same thing:

> sic enim gradatim descendendum est, donec inveniat animus
> in quo resideat et in quo complaceat (II.3.123)

> And so we must proceed, step by step, until the mind finds the
> appropriate and satisfactory place to stop.

IV.4 'Determinatio' covers the use of different parts of speech.

IV.5 discusses various levels of style. The simple style appropriate to comic narrative is illustrated by the story 'Tres sumus expensae' (1888–909).

V deals with memory and delivery. The poem ends with an epilogue to Innocent III (which may incorporate an originally separate poem to the Emperor calling for Richard's release) and to William de Mére-Eglise, bishop of London.[157]

Some short poems in the Hunterian anthology (below) have been attributed to Geoffrey; three are rhetorical variations of each other, apparently on Henry II.

Another, 'Si liceat michi pauca loqui', which mentions his lecturing at Northampton, is a complaint against a former friend Robert.[158]

Gervase of Melkley

Geoffrey's influence was quickly felt: before 1216 Gervase of Melkley composed a prose *Ars Poetica*.[159] We know little about him: he had studied, presumably in France, under John of Hauville, and was perhaps connected with Norwich. The *Ars Poetica* is only of technical interest; it lists rhetorical and grammatical figures, with examples, and deals with word formation. It quotes liberally from ancient authors, especially Horace, Juvenal and the rhetoricians, and also from near-contemporary sources, such as Bernard Silvester's *Cosmographia*, Hauville's *Architrenius*, and the *Poetria Nova*. He also quotes freely from his own short poems, of which five are in the Hunterian anthology (Nos. 39–43). In 'Parmenidis rupes' he prays that he may be allowed to understand Aristotelian complexities before returning to theology. In 'Magnus Alexander' he lavishly praises the new bishop of Lincoln, John Grey (later a disappointed nominee for the archbishopric of Canterbury). He also wrote a long poem on Pyramus and Thisbe, of which our only copy is incomplete. He normally writes elegiac couplets, but a poem to the Virgin, 'In honorem matris Dei', is rhythmical.

Hunterian anthology

This interest in poetics is illustrated by the early thirteenth-century Hunterian anthology.[160] It contains all the major treatises by Matthew of Vendôme, Geoffrey of Vinsauf, and Gervase of Melkley. Interspersed among these are over fifty short poems, of which a few are attributable to the rhetoricians. The poems illustrate rhetorical figures at the levels of both 'ornatus facilis' and 'ornatus difficilis'. Some seem to be exercises in abbreviation, like this account of Phaeton's fall:

> Phetonti liuor Epaphi, persuasio matris,
> Dona parentis, iter exposuere necis (56/1–2)

> Epaphus' envy, mother's words, and gift
> Of Jove laid out Phaeton's path to death.

There are different treatments of the same topic (e.g. three poems on Phaeton, two on Pyramus and Thisbe, three on Apollo and the Python, two on Deucalion and Pyrrha, two on Lycaon), and examples of descriptive and vituperative verse. All the poems are hexameters or elegiacs.

Richard Pluto

In the context of education we should mention Richard Pluto, whose only extant work is a set of 'differential' verses to distinguish homographs.[161] The *Equiuoca*, in

174 lines, is a direct descendant of Serlo of Wilton's 'Unam semper amo',[162] in one of its expanded forms. Amost all the *equiuoca* are taken from there, but Richard has substituted Leonine elegiacs for Serlo's Leonine hexameters, and has attempted (often with bizarre results) to link the lines into some kind of continuous sense. Instead of Serlo's simple alphabetical sequence, the *equiuoca* are in the order: vowels A–U (including consonantal V), LMN RS BCDF P, and one couplet for QT. More significantly, Richard has systematically removed all of Serlo's amatory and hedonistic lines, substituting (perhaps for young students) heavy moralizations. For example, for Serlo's 'Est tibi, Thay, nitor, in quem super omnia nitor' [Your pulchritude provokes my one desire], Richard has substituted:

> In uacuum nitor, dum placet iste nitor (98)
>
> When vanity's my goal I waste my time.

Sometimes Richard seems to have misunderstood the intended contrast and occasionally writes what appears to be nonsense.

Comediae

The Latin verse *comediae* are also to be seen in an educational context.[163] Their performance is a vexed question and has been much debated. William Fitzstephen appears to say that instead of theatrical plays London had religious drama:

> Londonia pro spectaculis theatralibus, pro ludis scenicis, ludos habet sanctiores, repraesentationes miraculorum quae sancti confessores operati sunt, seu repraesentationes passionum quibus claruit constantia martyrum[164]
>
> Instead of theatrical spectacles or stage plays, London has holier plays, representations of the miracles performed by holy confessors or representations of the sufferings by which the steadfast martyrs earned their glory.

The Vision of Thurkill describes an infernal theatre, which implies a knowledge of what a theatre looked like, but we do not know what kind of performances were staged in it (other than in Purgatory).[165] Geoffrey of Vinsauf writes that

> illa quae (Horatius) condidit de comoedia hodie penitus recesserunt ab aula et occiderunt in desuetudinem (*Documentum* II.3.163)
>
> The rules that Horace established for comedy have today entirely departed from court and have fallen into disuse.

Does this mean that Horace's rules have fallen into disuse, or comedy itself? Is he implying that comedy might be found outside the 'aula'? He certainly never mentions live performance of comedy: he treats the *iocosa materia* of the 'De clericis et rustico' (below) in the same way as the 'Tres sumus expensae', simply as material requiring a different level of style.

In fact, only an academic context would be appropriate for the public performance of Latin. The comedies, despite their scatology and buffoonery, reek of the schoolroom and its grammatical and philosophical jokes.[166] We do have good evidence for the public delivery of Latin verse before learned audiences,[167] and this kind of setting would also suit the comedies.

There are only three *comoediae* of probable English origin, 'De clericis et rustico', *Babio*, and *Baucis et Thraso*, and only *Babio* is a full-length play. The 'De clericis', possibly by Geoffrey of Vinsauf, is based on a story by Peter Alfonsi:[168] two students try to trick a peasant out of a cake, by agreeing amongst themselves that it will go to the one who has the most wonderful dreams. One has an astral journey, the other sees the torments of hell. In the meantime the peasant has eaten the cake; he says that he had thought that they were not going to return, and so has made an individual out of what was generic:

> Hec vidi, et libum, quia neuter erat rediturus,
> feci individuum quod fuit ante genus

> I saw that neither would return, and made
> The genus 'cake' an individual

It is a short poem of seventy-two lines and consists entirely of dialogue. Geoffrey uses it to illustrate comic style:

> Consocii ! Quid ? Iter rapiamus ! Quid placet ? Ire
> Ad sacra. Quando ? Modo. Quo? Prope. Fiat ita (1–2)

> Lads ! What ? Let's go ! What's your idea ? To go
> To church. When ? Now. Where ? Not too far. Okay !

The *Babio* falls into two parts:[169]

Babio (a priest according to the prose introduction) is in love with his stepdaughter Viola; she, however, is willingly courted by a knight Croceus. In a very comic scene Babio grudgingly serves a meal to Croceus and his servants. Viola departs with Croceus.

Meanwhile Fodius, a servant, is having an affair with Babio's wife Petula. Babio feigns a trip to Soloen (the home of solecisms, Babio's trademark) in order to catch the lovers. After a failure and a beating, he repeats the ruse and is this time castrated and retires to a monastery.

The elements of the story itself are commonplace,[170] but the telling of it is erudite. The work is full of grammatical wordplay and puns, such as

> Nunc utinam michi sint dolia plena dolis (412)

> I wish this were a barrelful of tricks !

Babio himself is characterized by his solecisms, as when he says 'goodbye' (*valeas*) instead of 'hello' to Croceus, and when he tells his guests to depart instead of sit down:

> Intremus. Sedite . . . Male dixi. Dico 'sedete' –
> erro per insolitum gramatizare volens (133–4)

Come in and scoot – oh dear, I mean 'sit down'
(I try for proper speech, but get it wrong).

When he describes his beloved Viola he endows her with the foot of the prostitute Thais instead of the nymph Thetis. His ignorance of vowel quantities allows Fodius, using Serlonian *differentiae*,[171] to deceive him by an oath:

> Per Terei planum, Celei per culmina iuro,
> iuro sacras per aras: non fodit hanc Fodius (271–2)

> By Tereus' plain, by Celeus' heights, I swear,
> By sacred sties, that I don't dig your wife.

But Tereus and Celeus are not 'earth and heaven', an *ăra* is a pigsty, not an altar, and *fŏdit* simply means that he is not 'digging' Petula at the present (though he has done so in the past).

Another comic narrative possibly of English origin is the *Baucis et Thraso*,[172] in 324 lines of elegiacs; it could have been recited but not performed:

An aged bawd Baucis promotes the prostitute Glicerium (sometimes calling her Philomena, in order to sell her twice over). The braggart knight Thraso is ensnared, and his servant Davus tries to arrange the consummation. After some horseplay (involving the hostile servant Birria) and feigned coyness by Glicerium, an arrangement is made. Baucis uses a mock recipe to prepare Glicerium ('Corvi candorem, fumum, tria flamina venti' [Three puffs of wind, a raven's whiteness, smoke]), and Thraso finally gets his desire ('Glicerio fruitur atque potitus abit' [He has his way with her, and then departs].)

The story lacks the sophisticated humour of the other *comediae* and is to some extent a pastiche of traditional comic elements.[173]

Walter the Englishman: animal fables

By the twelfth century, animal fables had become part of the fabric of Latin education, and were included (along with the *Distichs of Cato* and *Ecloga Theoduli*) in the *libri Catoniani*, the easy readers. The Greek collection traditionally associated with Aesop, edited by Babrius, had entered Latin mainly through two verse renderings: the 135 fables of Phaedrus (first century AD), and the forty-two fables of Avianus (fourth century). Phaedrus' fables were turned into prose by 'Romulus', and this was the source of fifty-eight of the sixty-two verse fables by a Walter the Englishman.[174]

Walter has been tentatively identified with Walter of Palermo, at one time chaplain of Henry II and successor of Peter of Blois as tutor to the young William of Sicily;[175] according to Bale, this Walter wrote a text 'pro latinae linguae exercitiis'. Whoever he was, the fables were very popular and were the basis for Lydgate and Henryson in the fifteenth century. Their purpose is pleasure and profit, and the reader may take which he chooses:

Vt iuuet et prosit, conatur pagina presens:
　　Dulcius arrident seria mixta iocis . . .
Si fructus plus flore placet, fructum lege; si flos
　　Plus fructu, florem. Si duo, carpe duo (Prol. 1–2;5–6)

For profit and for pleasure too I write,
　　For solemn things are sweeter mixed with mirth . . .
If fruit you like, pick fruit; if flower,
　　Then pick the flower; if you like both, pick both.

The message is hidden like the nut in the shell. The fables are mostly between four and twelve lines long, with a 'moralitas' (and in one version, an extra four-line moral), in elegiacs. Appropriately the first story is of a cock who found a precious jewel and rejected it because it was of no use to him:

Nec tibi conuenio, nec tu michi; nec tibi prosum,
　　Nec michi tu prodes: plus amo cara minus (1.7–8)

Twene thee and me ys no convenience; (Lydgate)
Thou ganis not for me, nor I for the; (Henryson)
I have more love for things less dear.

The cock is a fool, for the jewel represents wisdom. The longest tale, thirty lines, is not from 'Romulus' but from Horace (*Sat.* 2.6.79 ff.), retelling the story of the country mouse whose experiences on a visit to a town mouse teach her to prefer humble security to anxious opulence:

Rodere malo fabam, quam cura perpete rodi;
　　Degenerare cibos cura diurna facit (12.23–4)

I'd rather chew the bean than constant dread,
　　For daily worries sour one's daily bread.

Politics of the reign of John

The loss of Normandy in 1205 and the defeat at Bouvines in 1214 had immense consequences for England and for language and literature, but the effects were not perceived at the time. More immediately important was the quarrel between King John and Innocent III: the Pope, faced with two candidates for the vacant see of Canterbury (John Grey, bishop of Lincoln, the king's candidate, and Reginald, sub-prior of Christ Church, the monks' choice), consecrated instead cardinal Stephen Langton. John's resistance kept Langton in exile in France and led to the imposition of a papal interdict on England from 1208 to 1214; one result was that people could not receive religious burial. In the final settlement England was made feudally subject to the Pope, a situation not formally altered for over a hundred years. John was also in dispute with the barons, and in 1215 was forced to agree to the Magna Carta (whose effects were only realized – at least by literary writers –

fifty years later). The barons remained hostile, and invited Prince Louis of France to invade and take the English crown. The situation was resolved only by the death of King John in 1216.

William de Montibus

In the late twelfth century many English cities – Oxford, Hereford, Northampton – became centres of learning because of their cathedral schools, in which scholars gave lectures in imitation of the Paris schools that most of them had attended. One of the most important was Lincoln, whose schools were administered by William de Montibus (*c*.1140–1213), who succeeded Walter Map as chancellor.[176] William had lectured in theology at Mont St Genevieve in Paris, but about 1186 returned to Lincoln at the request of the bishop, (St) Hugh. He was very influential as a teacher and popularizer, and his death was lamented by Alexander Neckam,[177] who addressed Lincoln:

> Par tibi nulla foret, si te tuus ille magister
> Informaret adhuc moribus atque fide (*Laus* 5.837–8)

> You'd have no match, if that great master lived
> To guide you in the faith and proper ways.

William's forte was organizing knowledge in digestible and easily memorable form, in both prose and verse. Nearly 150 sermons are extant, and there are several prose treatises summarizing theological knowledge, especially penance. As examples of his organization mania we have the *Numerale* (which organizes topics by number – one church, two testaments, twelve articles of faith, etc.), *Distinctiones theologice* (alphabetical discussions of words), *Similitudinarium* (images drawn from nature), *Proverbia* (quotations under 281 headings, prose and verse: there are eight pages on *Amor*, with over forty quotations from Ovid), and *Tropi* (on technical terms of rhetoric).

He was a master of the verse mnemonic: his verses can often be found scribbled on the margins or flyleaves of manuscripts. Over 150 manuscript copies are known of his 'Peniteas cito', which summarizes the sacrament of penance in (in its fullest form) 136 lines of elegiacs:

> Peniteas cito, peccator, cum sit miserator
> Iudex, et sunt hec quinque tenenda tibi:
> Spes venie, cor contritum, confessio culpe,
> Pena satisfaciens, et fuga nequitie

> Repent in haste: the judge is merciful.
> Observe these five commands: for pardon hope;
> Have heart contrite; admit the sins you've done;
> Make full amends, and flee from wickedness.

This was equipped with glosses, no doubt the material for William's lectures; parts of the poem were incorporated in his other verse works. The *Tractatus Metricus* consists of 291 lines on various theological topics, but his most impressive verse work was the *Versarius*. This consists of about 4400 lines of verse, both hexameter and elegiac, incorporating 1375 separate poems on 900 topics (alphabetically organized). A few of the poems are by other authors, but most are William's own: some contain acrostics and similar devices that are explicable only by William's glosses. Most of the topics are theological (Angels, God, Devil, Penitence, Lust, etc.), but some are on the natural world (Fire, Earth, Water), and there is a series on animals (Spider, Ox, Deer, Lion, etc.),[178] as on 'canis':

> Inuidet, immundus, redit ad uomitum canis atque
> Mordet et oblatrat, rixatur dilaceratque

> Unclean and sly, and to its vomit drawn,
>   It barks, it bites, it fights and tears apart.

Samuel Presbiter

Testimony to William's teaching is also found in MS Bodley 860, the collections of Samuel Presbiter or Priest. His *Collecta* are on fifty-four topics, with poems and glosses (of which six overlap with the *Versarius*) probably by William, and his notes from William's commentary on the Psalms. Samuel himself was probably the author of a hexameter version of Psalm 1 (inc. 'Qui non consiliis abiit que suasit iniquus') and a 5000-line poem on the Gospels (inc. 'Leprosam tetigit Christus'), which he says he wrote after he had left the school, 'post discessum a scola'. None of Samuel's work has been published.[179]

Alexander Neckam

Alexander Neckam has been described as 'one of the most remarkable scholars of the second half of the twelfth century'.[180] He was a grammarian, encyclopedist, theologian, homilist, commentator, and poet. He was born in 1157 and was the foster-brother of the future Richard I. He lived in St Albans, which boasted one of the finest schools in England, and of which he wrote fondly:

> Dulce Verolamium linquo recessurus –
> Linquere uix dixerim, cum sim reuersurus

> I'm leaving sweet Saint Albans, I'm away –
> But 'leave' is wrong, for I'll be back some day.

He was for a time a schoolmaster at nearby Dunstable, and was a student and teacher in Paris. For a time he resided in Oxford, where he delivered sermons; during this period he may have heard Gerald of Wales recite the *Topographia Hibernica* over three days in 1188, as both share the story of the barnacle goose.

Between 1197 and 1202 he became an Austin Canon at Cirencester, and was abbot there from 1213 until his death in 1217. Like many well-known writers he was credited with more than he actually wrote,[181] but the genuine canon of works is enough to justify his reputation. Only works of literary interest are discussed here.[182]

First we must mention his pedagogic works. The *Summa de nominibus utensilium* is a list of objects of everyday life, supplied (probably by Neckam) with copious French glosses. It is organized by topic (if you are setting up a household, going out for a ride, about to besiege a city, and so on), but has less narrative structure than what was probably its model, Adam of Balsham's *De utensilibus*.[183] The *Summa* was popular, but even more so was the *Corrogationes Promethei*, a grammatical treatise combined with a commentary on difficult words in the Old and New Testaments; only extracts from it have been published.[184] The *Corrogationes* was turned into verse, presumably by Neckam himself; this verse version (which is not to be confused with the verse *Corrogationes Novi Promethei*, (discussed below) has not been published.

His two sets of verse beast fables are also to be counted among his pedagogic works. The *Novus Avianus* recasts six of Avianus' fables; their function as rhetorical models is suggested by the fact that the tale of the Eagle and the Tortoise is told three times, 'copiose' (twenty-six lines), 'compendiose' (ten), and 'succincte' (four). The moralizations come before each story, giving a more sententious effect. The *Novus Aesopus* contains forty-two fables, of which thirty-seven are taken from the prose 'Romulus'; in these the two-line moralization follows the story.[185]

Neckam's longest work available in a modern edition is the prose *De Naturis Rerum*. This is not a complete work but Books I–II of a five-book commentary on Ecclesiastes (of which Books III–V remain unpublished).[186] The relationship between the 'science' (I–II) and the theology (III–V) has been explained by Hunt: in a division of the Solomonic books that goes back to Origen, the Book of Proverbs concerns 'ethics', Ecclesiastes 'physics' (vanity of vanities'), and the Song of Songs 'logic' (*inspectiva*). Thus, the *De Naturis Rerum* deals with the material world:

Book I. 1–15 harmonization of the openings of Genesis and the Gospel of St John; angels; celestial phenomena (planets, etc.); 16 the elements; 17 fire; 18–80 air and its inhabitants (23–80 birds).

Book II. 1–21 water; 22–47 fish; 48–98 earth, its minerals, plants, precious stones; 99–151 animals; 152–6 man, vision; 157–65 domestic animals; 166–72 domestic and agricultural things, buildings; 173–4 seven liberal arts, places of learning; 175–6 soldiers; 177–92 lives of the ambitious and their vices.

The structure, therefore, is the four elements and the inhabitants of each. The information comes from both classical and medieval sources (e.g. Solinus, Isidore, Marbod, Bernard Silvester, Aristotle); some is from popular lore and perhaps direct observation. There are several stories, such as the trick of the wild parrot to release its caged domestic cousin (I.37), and the execution of a nightingale for putting ideas of love into a woman's mind (1.51). The purpose of the *De Naturis Rerum* is not scientific in our sense but, as Neckam says in his preface, tropological. Each scientific fact is accompanied by a moral: the camel's hump (II.141) represents anxiety about earthly things.

Superficially, the *Laus Sapientiae Divinae*, completed 1213–15, is simply a rendition of the *De Naturis Rerum* into elegiac couplets, with some additions and reorganization:[187]

I   1–675 God, angels, celestial phenomena.

II   1–32 summary of I; 33–60 elements: fire; 61–108 air, winds; 109–952 birds, chameleon.

III   1–74 summary of II; 75–370 water; 371–670 fish; 671–1052 rivers of the world, and prominent cities (939–1004 digression on his writing poetry, the passing of time).

IV   (scientific and theoretical) 1–251 elements, winds, weather; 252–329 God's game; 330–93 time; 394–441 small things and seeds; 442–563 moisture; 564–869 earth and elements.

V   1–34 against envious detractors; 35–174 theological reflections on the earth, its origin and nature; 175–80 divisions of the world; (181–914 Europe) 181–344 Rome; 345–438 Italy; 439–650 France (563–602 Paris); 651–90 Normandy; 691–882 England; 883–914 Ireland, Orkneys; 915–72 Spain, Holy Land, Troy, Crete.

VI   1–364 metals, precious stones.

VII   1–372 herbs

VIII   1–166 crops, vegetables, vines, trees; 167–80 why grass is green.

IX   1–262 animals; 264–314 poisons; 315–424 man, vision.

X   1–36 postlapsarian disease, nature's cure; 37–172 seven liberal arts; 173–268 theology; 269–78 summary of human life; 279–344 envoy to the book, which will be welcomed in Gloucester, St Albans, Paris, or (failing these) back home in Cirencester.

In fact, the *Laus* has a totally different emphasis from the *De Naturis*. The moral applications and stories have mostly been omitted, with the result that the poem is more 'scientific' than the prose. Paradoxically, this also makes it more theological: the whole of creation is, as the title proclaims, a celebration of God's wisdom.[188] Even the barnyard cock would be an object of wonder, if it were not so common:

> Pasceret intuitus hominum recreatio mira,
> Si tam vulgaris rara fuisset avis (II. 843–4)

> Men's eyes would feast on such a wondrous sight,
> If such a common bird were rarely seen.

Creation is God's game, even a joke:[189]

En dum naturae considero ludicra, ludos
    Ejus maturos seria jure voco . . .
Lusit ab aeterno summi sapientia patris,
    Singula disponens, ars, noys, ordo, decor . . .
De facili variisque modis gaudens operatur:
    Jocundus sermo nos recreare solet (IV. 252–63)

Now when I think of Nature's quirks, I say
    Her solemn works are simply grown-up jokes . . .
For outside time, God's wisdom played: his mind,
    His art, design and grace, disposed all things . . .
He works at ease, in varied modes, in joy,
    And cheerful talk is what refreshes us.

Perhaps in imitation, Neckam's tone is often lighthearted; sympathizing with the unicorn's capture by a virgin, he writes:

Rhinoceros capitur amplexu virginis. At quis
    Consimili renuat proditione capi ? (IX.167–8)

The unicorn succumbs in maiden's lap –
    But who'd decline a similar defeat ?

Even though the halcyon is supposed to guarantee good weather, he himself will not trust the sea:

Laeta Jovis facies arrideat, haec avis ovis
    Incubet, infidum semper habebo mare ! (II.231–2)[190]

The sky may smile, this bird may warm its eggs,
    But I'll not trust the temper of the sea !

His fondness for wine is a frequent topos;[191] after describing all the waters of the world, he bids them farewell:

Delicias Thetidi praefero, Bacche, tuas.
Nunquam, Bacche, valefaciam tibi, sed mare, fontes,
    Jam valeant, valeant flumina, stagna, lacus (III.1050–2)

But Thetis, Bacchus, does not match your charms.
I'll never say farewell to you, but sea
    And spring, stream, lake and bog I bid adieu !

He is frequently reminded of his own mortality. When reflecting on the nature of time, he remarks:

Temporis amissi jacturam defleo, de me
    Conqueror, annus abit, non rediturus abit (IV.344–5)[192]

> I mourn the loss of time that's past, I weep
> For me, the year is gone and won't return.

Above all, the *Laus Sapientiae Divinae* is a pageant of the wonders of the world. If it is treated (as it sometimes is) as an encyclopedia of fascinating knowledge (the cities of the world and their poets, the marvels of Britain), then no great harm is done.[193]

The *Corrogationes Novi Promethei*, in 1630 lines of elegiacs, has nothing to do with the prose *Corrogationes*. It was written after Neckam became abbot of Cirencester in 1213.[194]

1–204 an abbot must temper fear with love, following the image of the ark of the covenant and the manna and rod. The ark was drawn by milch-cows, who left their calves shut up at home (1 Reg. 6: 10–12): the calves are our 'motus carnales', which must be restrained. 205–1178 the poem describes the sins, beginning with Anger, and showing how each one leads to the next (Sadness to Sloth to Sleep to Luxury to Lust . . .), ending with Pride. Each sin is described elaborately: there are classical and biblical archetypes (Envy = Cain, Pride = Nebuchadnezzar, Lust = Helen), typical portraits (a drunkard, an angry man), debates between Avarice and Ambition, Prodigality and Avarice, and a lively argument between Amphitryo and the lazy Birria.[195] The section on Luxury is followed by instructions for proper hospitality.[196]
1179–630 the cure for Pride is awareness of man's nature, the filth of his procreation, and his progress through life. The ages of man are described in turn – the games of boyhood (including chess) and of youth (illustrated by a wrestling match between Castor and Pollux). Finally he reaches old age and death.

It is more entertaining than Walther's 'moral-asketische' suggests, but it is somewhat of a pastiche, including not only single lines but often whole passages from classical texts (Ovid, the pseudo-Virgilian *De rosis nascentibus*).

Neckam's fondness for wine is fully expressed in the three books of the *De Commendatione Vini*; these may originally have been separate.[197]

Book I. Five short linked poems, in variously rhymed hexameters.

Book II. This is clearly intended to follow I, as it begins

> Rursus, Bache, tuas laudes describo libenter,
> Nec vereor laudis prodigus esse tue

> Again I gladly, Bacchus, sing your praise;
> I'm not afraid to lavish praise on you.

In 170 lines of elegiacs it praises Bacchus and Noah for inventing wine, which gives him all his knowledge; he reflects on the nearness of death (using some lines also used at the end of the *Corrogationes Novi Promethei*), but even then wine has its value:

> Quid mihi cum Bacho ? Quid ? Vitam, Bache, senilem
> Solaris; corpus, Bache, senile foves . . .
> Si mihi cum Bacho nihil est commune, quid ergo
> Est mihi cum vita ? Vinea vita mihi (145–50)

What's wine to do with me ? My aged bones
It warms, and gives support to my old hulk.
If wine and I were separate, my life
And I would part: the vineyard is my life.

Book III, in 182 lines of elegiacs (occasionally rhymed), is separate from II in the manuscript and may be a reworking of it. It shares several of its ideas and conceits, but develops a new theme, the beneficial effects of wine in the Eucharist:

Que sit in altari panis, que gloria vini,
Vera fides retinet. Perfide Fauste, tace (151–2)

The glory of the altar bread and wine
True faith discerns, so Faustus hold your tongue !

The opening has been playful but has led to the sublime:

Ludicra premisi, stilus ad sublimia sponte
Transiit: ascensus utilis esse solet (171–2)

I started jokingly, but then my pen
Turned to the heights, a climb with great rewards.

Like Ecclesiastes, it has led from vanity to God.

Neckam has also been credited with a set of hymns (nine to the Virgin, four to Mary Magdalen) and many short poems and epigrams. Few of his works except the *De nominibus utensilium* and the *Corrogationes Promethei* achieved much fame outside England, but within England he was very well known, especially as a wit: several epigrams are attributed to him in the *Distinctiones Monasticae*, alongside those of Primas and Walter Map. Others have rightly stressed his immense learning. I have tried to indicate his playfulness as a poet and his literary versatility.[198]

'Scribo sed ut merear'

In the context of Neckam's pageant of nature, we can mention an anonymous poem of the thirteenth century, consisting of about 1300 lines of elegiacs. It is in the form of a dialogue between 'S' and 'R' (Scriptor and Responsor ?). S asks for an account of the cosmos:

Dic quid sit mundus, quot mundos credis, et in quo
Fabrica tam celebris sit fabricata loco

Now tell me, what's the world, and are there more ?
And where did such a structure come to be ?

With constant interruptions, R obliges, with a general account of cosmology, meteorology and angelology. He neatly expresses the value of pi:

122

Si queras quantus sit circulus, ad diametrum
    Respice: ter summam multiplicata facit.
Hoc cum attendas ut septima pars diametri
    Addatur numero quem tibi summa dabit

You want to know a circle's size ? Then take
    The width across, and multiply by three.
Then calculate the seventh part of your
    Diameter, and add it to the sum.

Nothing is known for certain about the author except that at one point (fol. 97[va]) S says 'Anglia me genuit'.[199]

Stephen Langton

Stephen Langton, former cardinal and archbishop of Canterbury (1207–28), is now known mainly for his quarrel with King John. During his exile he was praised lavishly by Matthew of Rievaulx:

Iste uir angelicus et flos est Anglicus; iste
Stephanus, ecclesie decor et decus, exulat; instar
Martyris egregii Thome uelud hospes oberrat (VIII.9–11)

That man, angelic flower of English birth,
The church's glory, Stephen, is abroad
In exile, like Saint Thomas, as a guest.

His part in the translation of the relics of Becket in 1222, together with a brief biography, is recounted in a verse life of Becket attributed to Henry of Avranches.[200] In his time he had a great reputation as a theologian, and had studied in Paris at the same time as William de Montibus. He was an energetic and fluent preacher, and we have sermons from all periods of his life: six of them (ascribed to Neckam in one manuscript) form an extended commentary on the hymn 'Ave maris stella'.

He may also have been a poet, though none of the attributions is certain. He is credited in one manuscript with 'Non te lusisse pudeat', a poem of moral advice to bishops: [201]

Sis pius, iustus, sobrius,
prudens, pudicus, humilis,
in lege Dei docilis,
et ne sis arbor sterilis,
tuo te regas aptius
    officio

Be sober, just, and merciful;
Live humbly, chaste, and prudently,

> In God's law ever dutiful,
> And don't be like the barren tree:
> Behave in office properly.

In two manuscripts he is named as author of a rhymed *psalterium* to the Virgin, 'Ave virgo virginum, parens absque pari'.[202] Originally, this paraliturgical form consisted of 150 stanzas (in this case Goliardic), each of which contained a phrase from the appropriate psalm, as in st. 2:

> Ave, cuius viscera natum ediderunt,
> Cuius ad interitum gentes fremuerunt;
> Audi voces supplicum qui te pie quaerunt,
> Mali causas removens quae nos invenerunt

> Hail, Virgin, from whose womb that child was born
> Whose death gave pagans cause to wail and mourn.
> Please hear our voices when we cry to thee;
> From evil that assails us keep us free.

which corresponds to Ps. 2:1 'Quare fremuerunt gentes, et populi meditati sunt inania ?' (In time, the form simplified to three 'quinquagena').

Finally we have the testimony of the contemporary *Distinctiones monasticae* for Langton's authorship of the famous hymn 'Veni sancte spiritus':

> Veni, sancte spiritus,
> et emitte caelitus
>   lucis tuae radium;
> Veni, pater pauperum,
> veni, dator munerum,
>   veni, lumen cordium[203]

> Come, Holy Spirit, shining bright,
> From heaven send your ray of light.
> Come, paupers' father, spreading wealth,
> Come, light of hearts, restore our health.

Ralph of Dunstable

Alexander Neckam sent his nephew to be taught verse by a 'doctor Radulphus';[204] this is perhaps the Ralph of Dunstable, monk of St Albans, who wrote a verse life of Sts Alban and Amphibal, based on the prose life by William of St Albans. There are two books, in elegiac couplets, each containing 1360 lines; the first book includes a long sermon delivered by Amphibal on creation, the fall and redemption – a miniature biblical epic, which is so long that it was recorded by Tanner as a separate poem ![205]

Third Vatican Mythographer: Alberic of London ?

In the Middle Ages Neckam was often credited with the prose treatise on mythography now assigned to a nameless 'Third Vatican Mythographer'.[206] The attribution to Neckam is understandable, as he often interprets the pagan gods in a naturalistic way, but (until very recently) modern scholars have favoured the authorship of Alberic of London, author of a French version of the Miracles of the Virgin.[207] The treatise draws on a long tradition of demythologizing the classical pagan pantheon: either (1) the ancient gods were originally mortals, deified only by popular imagination (a system first propounded by Euhemerus of Messene in the fourth or third century B.C.), or (2) they represented natural elements or stages in life (Jupiter and Juno were respectively the upper and lower air, Saturn was old age). This demythologizing rested on the premiss that some essential truth must lie beneath the old stories, and so, paradoxically, it preserved them in a kind of scientific wrapper: Christian poets could continue to retell the fables, knowing that they could call on 'science' to defend them.

Alberic's treatise (if it is his) was one of the most thorough of its type and was widely influential: it was used by Petrus Berchorius (Pierre Bersuire) in the fourteenth century and Thomas Walsingham in the fifteenth.[208]

Courtesy Books: Daniel Beccles

Many Anglo-Latin writers were, for at least parts of their career, schoolteachers; one of the elementary tools of the pedagogue formed its own literary genre, the courtesy book. In succinct form, usually in verse, the courtesy books teach a combination of copybook morality and Emily Post table manners (sit up straight, keep your elbows off the table, don't talk – or eat or drink – with your mouth full, don't stare at your betters, don't wipe your nose on your sleeve), as well as less familiar instructions about spitting, belching, defecating, and collecting used salt for re-use.

This unpromising material attracted some surprisingly big names. In the early twelfth century Hugh of St Victor and Petrus Alfonsi included chapters on table manners in their prose instructional works. John of Salisbury has a section on hospitality in the *Policraticus*, as does Neckam in the *Corrogationes Novi Promethei*. John of Garland, Robert Grosseteste, John Lydgate, and even Erasmus wrote courtesy literature. A short, twenty-three line poem, 'Quisquis es in mensa', was very influential on later manuals of behaviour. Some texts were reworked so often that even their original shape, let alone their authorship, is often hard to recover.

The first major English contribution to the genre was the *Urbanus Magnus* by Daniel of Beccles in Suffolk.[209] It consists of 2839 hexameters, some rhymed; 2524–839 may once have been separate.

1–205 moral advice, religious duties. 206–419 avarice, death, heaven and hell. 420–874 social advice: choice of protector and friends; beware flattery (digression on unnatural sex); patience in adversity; do not reveal poverty or troubles to an enemy.

875–1220 table manners. 1221–65 bad masters. 1266–483 duties of servants (especially in the bed-chamber) and messengers.

1484–641 duties of a judge (with satire on lawyers and the times).

1642–885 duties of officials, soldiers, teachers, students, citizens, merchants, bird-catchers, sailors, singers, thieves, doctors, religious, princes; defence of a city. 1886–2143 adultery, satire on women.

2144–523 general care of a household; building of house and garden; behaviour of the wife, servants, entertaining, sleeping arrangements, children, guests; how servants should bear gifts and receive them. The burdens of a householder.

2524–839 daily life and food: church, purging, table service, fish, seasonings, various diets; effects of wine, beer and various foods; exercise and general health, seasons, humours (2816–33 summary diet, rhyming throughout on -osa). Epilogue.

The *Urbanus Magnus* is difficult to summarize; it is full of digressions, and changes subject abruptly and often. A great deal is proverbial. There are a few striking passages, such as Death's horse, the bier:

> Ligneus est sonipes Christi stabulatus in ede:
> Non opus est illum prebenda pascere, feno . . . (320–1)

> The wooden horse is stabled in God's house:
> This horse requires no pasture and no hay !

There is some humour on the woes of a householder:

> Perpetuas curas domino dat nomen herile . . .
> Sponse, natorum seruum decet esse suorum
> Illum seruilem, quem cura grauis terit intus (2508–13)

> The title 'master' brings uncounted cares . . .
> He must be slave to wife and children too,
> Of servile rank, consumed by heavy care.

Although he recommends sexual activity on the fourth day after blood-letting, he adds:

> Quod lux quarta docet ignorent religiosi (2697)

> The fourth day's lesson's not for those in vows !

The most striking stylistic feature (of 1–2523) is a fondness for newly coined denominative verbs (*roso, spino, boreo, brumo, peripsimo*, and many others). The poem concludes by attributing the teachings to 'old King Henry' and asking for blessings on the author:[210]

> Rex uetus Henricus primo dedit hec documenta
> Illepidis, libro que subscribuntur in isto

Explicit liber Urbani Danielis Becclesiensis
Curuamen ueli dimittite. Gaudia celi
Qui geminauit Heli, merito tribuat Danieli (2836–9)

Old Henry first taught people lacking style
These courtly lessons set forth in this book.
Here ends the 'Book of the Urbane Man' by Daniel of Beccles.
Now strike the sail ! And may that God that blessed
Elisha, give to Daniel heavenly rest.

An extract from lines 875–1599 is found in one manuscript and ascribed to 'magister Robertus Grosteste';[211] it cannot, however, be easily separated from its context, and it shares the distinctive vocabulary of the long poem. On the other hand, the last section (2524–839), found separately in two manuscripts, is self-contained and overlaps with material in the earlier part; also it lacks the distinctive vocabulary of the remainder and the internal rhyming (though it may still be by Beccles).[212]

Visions of the other world

Henry of Saltrey

We have already discussed visions of heaven and hell. The story of St Patrick's Purgatory differs slightly from the pattern. On an island in Ireland there was a kind of penitential cursus (established by St Patrick), involving a series of pits or caves, in which penitents could earn remission of their sins; in this 'purgatory' they endured demonically inflicted torments. The story is mentioned briefly by Gerald of Wales. The first full account is by the Cistercian Henry of Saltrey in Huntingdon about 1179–81.[213] He tells the experiences of a certain Sir Owen (Owein Miles), who had been sent to Ireland in 1153 as an interpreter for Gilbert of Louth; despite warnings he voluntarily entered the purgatory and witnessed infernal torments, but was rewarded with a sight of the earthly paradise and heaven.

Peter of Cornwall

Peter of Cornwall (c. 1140–1221) was an Augustinian canon; he spent most of his life at Holy Trinity, Aldgate, in London, where he became prior in 1197. His most important work for literary purposes is his *Liber Revelationum*, written about 1200.[214] In this he collected over a thousand non-scriptural visions: most were taken from written sources, such as saints' lives, but some he seems to have gathered in person. There are several that originated in Essex and Kent. One series is of visions experienced by his own grandfather Ailsi or his close kin, including a vision of hell and heaven in which Ailsi's guide was his dead son Paganus (Peter's uncle). Peter's version of the story of St Patrick's Purgatory is the most lurid: in this the knight finds himself in a hall, where he is offered his host's daughter for his pleasure.

He accepts the offer, but the girl immediately turns into a hag; the hero is then set upon by demons, who torture him sadistically and especially sexually. Peter also retold the story of the monk of Eynsham (below).

One of Peter's most famous works in his own time was his *Disputatio contra Symonem Judaeum*, which he addressed to Stephen Langton.[215] Anti-Jewish polemic is outside the scope of this book, but must be mentioned briefly, as it was a favourite theme of many Anglo-Latin writers (and was one of the organizing principles of Adam of Barking). Its proliferation may be due to increased interaction between Christian and Jewish philosophers or to local political and racial tensions: the latter reached their height in the anti-Jewish riots in York in 1189–90, suppressed (at the cost of popularity) by William de Longchamps.

Visions: Monk of Eynsham; Thurkill

In 1196 a monk of Eynsham fell into a trance; on recovery he told how he had been escorted by St Nicholas on a tour of purgatory and the earthly paradise. This story was told by Adam of Eynsham, and an abridged version was incorporated into the chronicles of Roger of Wendover and Matthew Paris; it was also included by Peter of Cornwall in his *Liber Revelationum*, and was clearly one of the best known visions of the time.

Allusion was made to it by Ralph of Coggeshall (abbot 1207–18, died 1228) in his account of the similar vision of an Essex peasant named Thurkill.[216] In 1206 Thurkill fell into a trance and was taken on a tour of purgatory and heaven by Sts Julian and Dompninus. Interestingly, the torments that he witnessed took place in an open-air theatre.

A feature common to many such visions, including Thurkill's, is that the visionary sees identifiable people (usually recently dead) in purgatory; the purpose is to ensure that a surviving relative will pray for the lost soul and make restitution for the sin; in this way the dead person may obtain some relief from torment and the survivor may avoid making the same mistakes.

Gervase of Tilbury

Gervase of Tilbury was born in England about 1152; he knew its geography well and, in addition to other visits, probably spent his last years there. Most of his life, however, was spent on the continent: he was at various times a member of the courts of Henry II, Young King Henry, William, archbishop of Reims, and William II of Sicily. From about 1190 he was in Arles and was made marshal of the kingdom of Arles by the Emperor Otto IV, a purely honorary position. He probably died about 1222. One event in his life raises modern eyebrows: when his attempt to seduce a girl was rebuffed by her insistence on her inviolable chastity, he (correctly) inferred that she was a Cathar and had her burned for heresy.

For the Young King Henry (d. 1183) he wrote a lost *Liber Facetiarum* and began collecting materials for his major work. The *Otia Imperialia*, as its title suggests, was written for the Emperor Otto to amuse his leisure hours;[217] it was completed 1213–14. It is in prose and divided into three books (*decisiones*). Book I is structured round the opening of Genesis, from Creation to Flood; Book II is geographic and historical (extending to the reign of King John); Book I and the first part of II are abridged from Peter Comestor's *Historia Scholastica*, with some additions (such as the nature of *incubi* and fauns). It is Book III, however, which has most interested modern readers; this is a collection of marvels, some from each province, and seems to be entirely Gervase's own composition. These are not miracles in our sense but occurrences that excite wonder (*admiratio*) – things or events outside human experience but within the limits of natural possibility. They combine the kind of marvels collected by Henry of Huntingdon, Gerald of Wales, and Alexander Neckam with the tales of the supernatural told by Walter Map, and have interested students of folklore as much as literary historians. We read of the discovery of Virgil's tomb, the Neapolitan legends of Virgil the Necromancer, the sight at the bottom of a lake of the gates of hell after they had been broken down by Christ, a journey to the Antipodes by a peasant in search of a lost pig, a wailing lake, water demons who lead travellers to destruction, and so on. Several of Gervase's stories, or versions of them, are also in Walter Map; the two could possibly have met at the courts of Henry II or the Young Henry. Gervase's stories are straightforward and relatively unembellished, and lack the sense of mystery and macabre that is evident in Map, but, like all tales of the marvellous, they achieve their stated aim of entertainment.

'Pictor in carmine'

The practice of reading the Old Testament in light of the New Testament is as old as St Paul, who (Gal. 4: 21–4) interprets Ishmael and Isaac as (*per allegoriam*) the old and the new laws. The system was elaborated by Augustine and became the cornerstone of biblical exegesis in the Middle Ages. An Old Testament event, while real in itself, prefigured one in the New Testament, which thus fulfilled it. Thus, both Old and New Testaments were validated, refuting the errors of Jews and pagans alike. This fusion of distinct temporal events in an atemporal scheme acquired permanence in the *Glossa Ordinaria*. Its greatest literary flowering was in the hymns of Adam of St Victor and the Victorine school. In visual art – wall paintings, stained glass windows, and pictorial bibles – the New Testament event (the antitype) was placed in a roundel, surrounded by the Old Testament prefigurations (the types) in other roundels. These were often accompanied by short verses.

The most remarkable example of typology in Anglo-Latin literature is the poem now known as '*Pictor in carmine*'.[218] Its author is unknown, but has been conjectured to be Adam, abbot of the Cistercian abbey of Dore near Hereford.[219] In the preface he laments the profane pictures in the house of God:

Dolens in sanctuario Dei fieri picturarum ineptias et deformia quedam portenta magis quam ornamenta,

I grieved that the holy house of God contained silly pictures and grotesque – not decorations but rather aberrations.

and therefore, instead of two-headed eagles and the fabled antics of the fox and the cock, he proposes a religious programme of art (where painting is permitted), for which he has supplied verses:

digerit presens calamus adaptationes quasdam rerum gestarum ex ueteri et nouo testamento cum superscriptione binorum uersuum qui rem gestam ueteris testamenti breuiter elucidant et rem noui conuenienter adaptant

The present work sets out some correspondences of the events of the Old and New Testaments; two verses are written above, which briefly explain the Old Testament story and then appropriately apply the event of the New Testament.

The work extends from the Annunciation of the Virgin to the end of the world. There are 138 'chapters', each introduced by an antitype (e.g. Colloquium Gabrielis et Virginis, Suscitat Christus Lazarum). Each antitype is followed by two or more types, usually from the Old Testament, explained in rhyming hexameter verses, usually Leonines, of between two and eight lines. There are 508 types in all, and the total number of lines in one manuscript is given as 3582.

For example, the Adoration of the Magi is prefigured by five Old Testament types: (1) Samson takes a Philistine bride (6 lines):

> Samson allophile dignatus adire cubile,
> Christe, notat gentis te sponsum dona ferentis.
> Nata Philistei coniunx Samsonis Hebrei
> Signat adherentis Christo connubia gentis.
> Nubens Samsoni gentilis nata coloni
> Gens est quam fidei Christi dat myrra Sabei (479–84)

> That Samson deigned to wed a foreign maid
> Is Christ the groom, when gentiles gifts displayed.
> A Hebrew groom, a Philistean bride,
> Are Christ and gentile, now in marriage tied.
> The bride of Samson, gentile farmer's child,
> Denotes the race to Christ now reconciled.

(2) the servants of Hiram send gifts to Solomon (8 lines); (3) the queen of Sheba sends gifts to Solomon (8 lines); (4) servants of the king of Babylon take letters and gifts to Ezechiel (10 lines); (5) golden earrings are given to Job (6 lines).

Many of the correspondences are commonplace: the Annunciation of the Virgin, for example, is typified by Moses' burning bush, Gideon's fleece, and Ezekiel's closed gate. Most, however, have no parallel elsewhere. The selection of New

Testament events is very broad (including, for example, Mary's departure into the mountain, and John the Baptist's rebuke of Herod). The selection of Old Testament types is even more ingenious, and goes deeper and farther afield than that of any earlier exegesis:

For example, Christ's first preaching (Luc. 2:47) is prefigured by: (1) Isaac digging wells (Gen. 26:12); (2) Joseph tending the flocks (Gen. 37:2); (3) the pledges given by Judah to his daughter-in-law Tamar after he had lain with her (Gen. 38); (4) David pasturing sheep (1 Reg. 16:11); (5) the destruction of Jonah's shade plant by a worm (Jon. 4:6–7).

The verses are not all Old Testament prefigurations: sometimes there are moral, allegorical, and even naturalistic parallels. For example, the six jugs of water miraculously turned into wine at the marriage feast at Cana are interpreted as: (1) the six ages of the world (*allegorica*); (2) the six ages in the life of man (*tropologica*).

The '*Pictor*' reached quite a wide audience. In England there were at least six texts of the full poem and several abbreviated versions; on the continent, the *Tabula* of antitypes and types, either in full or abbreviated, was widely distributed.

Alexander of Ashby

Alexander, prior of the Austin canons at Ashby in Northamptonshire, is another neglected writer of the end of the twelfth century. He wrote several sermons, a treatise on preaching, and a series of meditations (redolent with affective piety), but his two major verse works remain unpublished.[220] His *Festial* is extant in three manuscripts and consists of two books.[221] Book 1 is a versification of the religious calendar, compared by Bale (presumably only for its content) to Ovid's *Fasti*. In a prose prologue Alexander says that he has versified it to make it more memorable:

Ideo autem in hoc opusculo metrica breuitate usus sum, ut memorie fragilitas fortius inde iuuaretur. Hec est enim precipua metrorum utilitas, quod in eorum compendio memoria habet magnum subsidium. Hoc in me ipso expertus didici; cum enim aliquid memorie arctius inprimere studeo, nullo faciliori modo illud retinere possum quam si idem uersu uno uel pluribus complectar

In this little work I have employed the brevity of metre, in order to assist the frailty of the memory, for the particular value of verse is that, by its concise form, it greatly aids the memory. I have learned this by my own experience, for when I want to impress something on my memory more firmly, I find that the easiest way to retain it is to enclose it in one or more lines of verse.

Seventy-four feasts are versified, in the order of the ecclesiastical calendar, from St Andrew to St Catherine; there are some movable feasts (Palm Sunday and the Resurrexion), but most are of saints. All are in unrhymed elegiacs except St Lucy and the Assumption (*elegi caudati*) and St Gregory (*hexametri caudati*). The sections vary between about ten and forty lines, but 198 lines are devoted to St Giles.

Book II is more of a ragbag, as Alexander himself implies:

> Que miranda putat, commiscens utile dulci,
> Ordine quo subeunt amodo musa canet

> Combining profit with delight, I'll sing
> Some marvels in the order they occur.

He says that he will include here some lives omitted from Book I and also (something Book II does not in fact do) treat 'diligencius et diffusius' some lives that were presented obscurely before. Book II contains lives of: (1) Eustace (over 400 lines); (2) Marina, who entered a monastery disguised as a boy (about 160 lines);[222] (3) 35 lines of *hexametri caudati*, obscurely treating several hagiographic legends; (4) Maurilius, in a version most closely resembling the life by Marbod:[223] the saint causes a boy's death by neglect, flees to England, loses the keys to the church, finds them again in a fish, and returns to Angers where he resuscitates the boy (120 lines); (5) Guthlac (13 lines);[224] (6) Edward the Confessor, based on the life by Aelred (about 500 lines).[225] Except for No. 3 and Guthlac (both in *hexametri caudati*), all these lives are in unrhymed elegiacs. The book is perhaps still a draft, and is consequently of some literary interest: Alexander seems to have indulged more in experimentation with less well established legendary material.

Hugh Primas, when challenged – on a bet, as we might say – to summarize human history, did so in two neatly rhyming lines:

> Quos anguis tristi virus mulcedine pavit,
> Hos sanguis Christi mirus dulcedine lavit

> Whom serpent's poison fed on dire deceit,
> The wondrous blood of Christ cleansed whole and sweet.

Most poets, however, were more prolix. We have already considered Lawrence of Durham's *Hypognosticon* and will be looking at Adam of Barking's sprawling epic;[226] salvation history was expounded in English in the *Ormulum* in about 20,000 lines (about a sixth of the total plan) and in the *Cursor Mundi* (in about 30,000 lines). Alexander of Ashby's *Biblia Versificata*, while not as succinct as Primas, is nevertheless a model of brevity, consisting of 1358 lines in unrhymed elegiacs. His motive for writing it was, much as the *Festial*, to aid the memory:

> Vt historie ueteris et noui testamenti postquam eas didisceris memorie tue firmius inhereant, et que a memoria tua elapsa fuerunt eidem facilius occurrant, hoc metricum tibi mitto compendium in quo tamquam in speculo historias breuiter comprehensas inspicere poteris

> In order that the stories of the Old and New Testaments, once learned, may stick in your memory more firmly, and so that the memory can more easily recall what it has forgotten, I am sending you this verse abbreviation; you will be able to see the stories succinctly contained in it, as though in a mirror.

He manages to digest the essential narrative of biblical history, and even to add a few expansions. He begins with original chaos and creation:

> Ante dies omnes mundi fuit omnis in uno
> machina momento facta, iubente Deo
>
> Before all time began, in just a trice
> The word's machine was made by God's command.

the Fall of the Angels, and the creation of world and man. He covers the Heptateuch, Ruth, Kings, Daniel, and later Jewish history, from the Persians down to Ptolemy and the translations of the Bible. After this there is an epitome, in 252 lines, of the New Testament, concluding with a series of typological motifs and an account of St Paul. Alexander was mainly following Peter Comestor's *Historia Scholastica*; the same source was used by Peter Riga, but Riga's version of Genesis alone is longer than the whole *Biblia Versificata*! This laudable brevity did not stop here: in one manuscript the *Biblia* was further reduced to 703 lines.[227]

Adam of Barking

Adam of Barking seems to have been a monk at Sherborne in Dorset.[228] His major work, a vast survey of biblical history, is incomplete; it survives, in its original draft form, in what must be an autograph copy.[229] The additions, substitutions, deletions and revised orders provide a fascinating picture of a medieval poet at work. The first version of the poem consists of about 11,500 lines of verse (mainly Leonines) and interspersed prose, from fol. 39^r to 141^r. It begins with a series of addresses (the poet to the Virgin, the Virgin to Christ, Christ to the Father, and so on), culminating in the Virgin's introduction of the poet Adam to God (fol.49^r):

> Re moueor quadam, qua me meus excitat Adam,
> Excitat, hortatur, dum me rogat unde regatur . . .
> Hoc tibi sic tradam, quod et ut michi tradidit Adam,
> Unde loquela datur. Taceam – nunc ipse loquatur
>
> By Adam's urgent pleading I am stirred:
> He seeks for guidance, with his pressing words . . .
> What Adam said I'll tell you in return;
> I'll keep my peace – now let him speak in turn.

Adam now addresses three straw opponents, a Jew, a Manichee, and a gentile; he shows that Christianity fulfils earlier prophecies, and thus justifies the New Testament to the Jew, the Old to the Manichee, and the totality of Christian belief to the gentile. Prefigurations of the Incarnation (such as Aaron's rod) occupy about 1600 lines, to fol. 67^v. At fol. 68^r he poses the fundamental question: why was Christ's passion necessary? The answer is man's subjection to sin since the First Age. From this point onwards, to the end of the poem on fol. 141^r, Adam seems to have three main themes: (1) explication of the Bible from Gen. 18 to Exodus, stressing Abraham; (2) the necessity of Christ's crucifixion; (3) the scheme of the Six Ages of the world (Adam, Noah, Abraham, Moses, David, Christ). In fact, on fol. 141^r he has still only reached the end of the Fourth Age, in Exodus, but constant reference foward has meant that in practice the Fifth and Sixth Ages have already been dealt with.

We come now to the major alterations. First, he inserted four leaves (fols. 72–5) to expand his account of the Flood (Gen. 7–8). Then he wrote about 2600 lines (fols. 17–38, quires iii–iv) for insertion immediately after the account of the Flood, dealing with the events from Gen. 8:15 to 17:27 (Noah's departure from the Ark to the circumcision of Abraham). These two additions mark a change in emphasis from typology to sequential narration, and are reinforced by the most significant change of all. Quires i–ii (fols. 1–16) containing about 1680 lines, referred to in the manuscript as the *Tractatus de Adam*, cover events from the Falls of Satan and of Adam and Eve to Noah and the Flood. They thus appear to be an entirely new beginning to the poem, perhaps to be substituted for fols. 39–67, or for insertion (after further adjustments) at fol. 68^r, converting the poem from a typological justification of Christianity to a narrative on the Six Ages of the world.

The chronological sequence, however, is frequently interrupted by typology, making it frequently difficult for the reader to know which age he is actually in. The failure of organization, however, (evident even to Adam himself), should not blind us to his consistent concern with the unity and design of revealed history, the failures of natural and positive law, and the need for redemption. In addition, we must remember that Adam was primarily a poet. The incessant jingle of the rhymes is (to modern ears) tiring, but Adam at times shows considerable powers of invention. Scenes involving the fallen Satan, being non-scriptural, offered plenty of scope. Here Satan is tormented by the idea that the newly created Adam will enjoy what he himself has lost, but he plots his revenge:

> Heu quod homo, quod humus, quod fex, aqua, quod caro, fumus,
> Quod res tam uilis fruitur uice sorte herilis !
> Spes sua fallet eum, iam sperat habere tropheum:
> Quo cecidi laqueo priuabitur ille tropheo ! . . .
> Aspicit estatem, nescit nisi prosperitatem:
> Crescit hiemps, crescet, furet Eurus et unda tumescet (fol.7^r)

> Alas, that dirt, filth, water, flesh and air,
> That man, so cheap, enjoys a master's share !
> He hopes to win: his hope will cheat him yet –
> My own downfall will catch him in its net . . .
> He now sees summer time and all is well,
> But winter's nigh, gales blow, the waves will swell . . .

As Satan himself is Fraud, he will not be lacking in trickery:

> Fraus michi num deero, que fraudis opem michi quero ?
> Fraus ego, fons sceleris, suadens contraria ueris (fol.7^r)

> Shall I, Fraud, fail, when needing fraud's support ?
> I foster sin, to truth with lies retort.

Adam was also the author of a fragmentary poem 'Quid mundus quid opes';[230] in 137 variously rhymed hexameters this denounces the vanity of earthly pursuits, hypocrites, and human praise: it is time to repent, as God sees all. There is a striking image of David's fountain of life (from Ps. 35: 10):

> Hic est fons Dauid, qui iustos spe solidauit,
> Fons qui nos sacri perfudit fonte lauacri

> Here's David's spring; the just with hope it filled;
> In this baptismal font is grace instilled.

David is a figure of Christ. The poem breaks off abruptly in the middle of an account of the parable of the workers in the vineyard.

Hugh of Montacute

Another shadowy figure from south-west England is Hugh, prior of the Cluniac house of Montacute in Somerset, later abbot of Muchelney. He is apparently the author of at least three poems.[231] One describes a sea-voyage across the channel; there is no Virgilian storm, but simply a landlubber's *mal de mer*, in which any land will do as long as it's land:

> Grandis erat de littore lis, nec erat mihi cura
>   quenam terra foret, dummodo terra foret (1.27–8)

> Dispute arose ('What land is that ?'), but I
> Cared not at all, as long it was land.

When he lands, he is, as a Frenchman, full of admiration for the English:

> si non mirarer, mirum foret, utpote Gallus,
>   Gallia cui numquam tale videre dedit (1/49–50)

> You'd be surprised if I showed no surprise,
>   Whose native France had never shown the like.

The next poem is an adaptation of Hildebert's 'Anglia terra ferax', and praises the English for their generosity and joviality:

> Anglia plena iocis, gens libera, nata iocari,
>   tota iocosa, velim dicere tota iocus (2.5–6)

For England's free and jolly, born to jest,
It's full of mirth – I'd call it all a joke.

The third poem extends the praises to London, its rich markets:

Istic invenies venalia tanta, quod omnes
expositas merces vix sibi mundus emat (3.13–14)

You'll find so much for sale in London's streets
That all the world could hardly buy it up.

and the river Thames.

Hugh has also been credited, in a fourteenth-century manuscript, with the extremely popular 'Pergama flere volo'. The latter is in single-sound Leonine elegiacs, whereas Hugh's other poems are unrhymed, but the attribution has the advantage of disinterestedness, as Hugh was relatively unknown.[232]

Matthew of Rievaulx

We turn again to the North of England for the last named writer in this chapter: Matthew, precentor of the Cistercian abbey of Rievaulx. Two of his poems were written after the death of King John, but most are from before 1216. His works – verse and prose – are preserved in a single manuscript, possibly the result of an 'edition' at St Victor in Paris.[233] His name and existence were buried until Wilmart exhumed the name Matthew from under the anonymous 'N' of the manuscript (once thought to conceal 'Nicholas').

The collection begins with 54 poems, usually fairly short, in either hexameters (often rhymed) or elegiacs. The topics are all fairly serious. Many are simply moral, criticizing vices (especially those that afflict monks, such as envy or ambition, which may lead to withdrawal from the cloister). Others are on monastic duties; his devotion to the Cistercian way of life is manifest in a series of poems on the founders and early abbots and one to the neighbouring Fountains Abbey:

O fons ortorum, o porta patens miserorum,
Morbos complanas, egros medicamine sanas (xxviii.5–6)

O fount of gardens, paupers' open gate,
You cure the sick, disease alleviate.

He praises the fathers of the church and its notable writers, such as Hildebert and Peter Riga. Contemporary scholarship is also praised: a poem on the Seven Liberal Arts is followed by one in honour of William de Montibus, whose relics were translated to Lincoln in 1214:

Dux tuus et doctor fuit, urbs Lincolnia; flere
Debes; orba sedes, tanto uiduata patrono (xiii.7–8)

Deprived of such a patron, Lincoln, weep:
Your guide and teacher's dead, and you're bereft.

Another series is on major saints; there are simple religious poems, and one on the Mass, indebted to Hildebert. Several are personal, including a request to be spared the duties of precentor.

He took particular interest in current affairs: he deplored the Interdict, and wrote in sympathy to the exiled Stephen Langton; he wondered why the people should have to pay for the sins of the king (though on John's death he prayed for his soul). On the other hand, he deplored England's subjection to the papacy:

> Hoc onus abicias, dirumpe iugum, mora desit,
> Nam Rome seruire diu non expedit, immo
> Impedit. Ingenuos libertas sola tuetur (VI.34–6)

> Without delay cast off the yoke and shed
> The load: long servitude to Rome is wrong.
> For only freedom guards the freely born.

Matthew seems to have turned against Innocent III when he refused to confirm Simon Langton as archbishop of York.

The twenty-four prose pieces show a similar variety, and often overlap with the poems in their topics. There are sermons, a florilegium from the church fathers, some personal epistles (disinclination for the precentorship, an attack on a detractor, defence of the word *pertesum*), praise of Innocent III, and laments on the captivity of Jerusalem. Expecially interesting is a denunciation of envy, illustrated by Old Testament history. This is in the prose section of the collection, but in fact can be treated as a rhythmical poem:

> Liuor Duid lanceauit
> qui Goliam fortem strauit;
> liquet satis est et certum,
> fugat illum in desertum.
> Tali causa
> nefas ausa,
> donec Ydumeus
> non uerus Iudeus
> ense necat
> (quis hoc negat ?)
> sacros Dei sacerdotes:
> hoc aperte scire potes (No. 70)

> David, slayer of Goliath, suffered envy's spear:
> Envy drove him to the desert, this is plain and clear.
> Envy dared a grievous sin and caused the Edomite
> Doeg (who was not a true Jew) with his sword to smite
> The holy priests of Israel – it cannot be denied. (I Reg. 22)

Although Matthew's writings were not known even in his own time, he testifies to the strong Cistercian literary tradition.[234]

II Anonymous literature and anthologies

Anonymous literature

A chronological history of this kind is naturally organized around major – preferably named and dated – authors. Most Latin poems, however – especially the shorter ones – are anonymous. They occur in anthologies, on flyleaves, in margins, and as fill at the end of booklets or manuscripts, and scribes are sparing in providing attributions. Even poems whose authors are now known usually appear anonymously in the manuscripts: for example, we have no name for the author of the moral poems in BL MS Burney 305,[235] and only good luck and diligent scholarship has given us a name (Matthew of Rievaulx) for the poems in Paris, BN MS lat. 15157. Few of the many hundreds of such anonymous poems have achieved any fame; even when they have been edited, they usually languish in appendices to descriptions of the manuscripts. In this section, therefore, I have tried to give a flavour of the short anonymous poems (and a few prose pieces) that occur in some anthologies compiled in the late twelfth and early thirteenth centuries, concentrating on those for which English authorship is probable.

Religious and moral

As most of the anthologies of this period are monastic, religious and moral verse predominates even in collections that also contain secular poems. Many religious poems simply celebrate the mysteries of the Trinity, the Incarnation, the Mass, and so on. In MS Bodley 603 there is a long series of rhythmical poems, probably originally about 890 lines in twelve sections (now 704 lines), which ranges through the nature of God and man and man's fallen state.[236] It begins:

> Quid sit Deus queritur:
>> Nescit res mortalis;
> Omnis sensus stringitur
>> Et uox animalis,
> Cum de illo loquitur
>> Qui est immortalis

> Questions of God's nature mortal wit defy:
> Every voice and feeling fail to satisfy
> When the topic touches God who cannot die.

In addition to more common verse saints' lives, the Rufford anthology contains short lives of saints of more local interest, Breowe (Winifred) and Werburga.[237] It also (like Matthew of Rievaulx) has epitaphs and celebratory poems on early Cistercian fathers and abbots of Rufford.

An anthology in BL MS Cotton Julius D. iii, which includes Ralph of Dunstable's Life of St Alban,[238] contains several unedited poems. One is a treatise on the nature of sin. It consists, in.its present form, of 946 lines, mainly hexameters and variously rhymed.[239] The first part, based primarily on Augustine, describes the process of suggestion, delight, and consent, and their parallel in the Fall in the Garden of Eden:

> Serpens suggessit, fallenti femina cessit,
> Adam consensit, ut ab omni parte nocens sit
>
> The serpent's urging caused the woman's fall,
> And Adam too agreed, with harm for all.

The second half describes the physical consequences of Original Sin, exemplified particularly by the six stages of human life from squalid birth to old age and then decrepitude:

> Illum spectamus tripedem baculoque leuamus;
> Hunc quasi quadrupedem querimur reptare per edem
>
> Three-footed, old folk walk with aid of cane;
> The senile on all fours crawl yet again.

Man's proneness to sin is the constant theme of versifiers. The monastic anthologies have many poems on the vices, especially those likely to tempt monks: envy, gluttony, and sexual licence. The Burney anthologist, while denouncing gluttony, has an apologia by a drunkard reminiscent of Neckam:

> Non bene cantatur nisi uino uox acuatur;
> Non bene gaudemus nisi pocula sepe leuemus (III.40–1)
>
> The voice needs wine for proper elevation;
> We're never glad when lacking lubrication.

Besides, drinking is natural to the English:

> Semper in Angligena sitit os, sitit arida uena;
> Cuilibet Angligene saliunt in pocula uene (III.53–4)
>
> The English throat is always dry and English veins are shrunk;
> But every English vein's on fire when Englishmen are drunk.

Needless to say, the poet does not agree.

A favourite device to express man's sinfulness is the debate between Body and Soul (Flesh and Mind, Heart and Eye, etc.), which is in essence a discussion of causality. In the Bekynton (No. 82 App. xix),[240] Body blames Soul for leading it astray:

Tibique cogor obsequi
et exequi,
opus rectum si iudices
uel claudices
a recti semitis (4/6–10)

I'm bound to follow you and to obey
If you judge right or falsely go astray.

A similar debate, in over 600 lines of elegiacs, is ascribed in the Bekynton to 'Tur. monachus', perhaps Turaldus, a monk of Rievaulx.[241] Flesh first argues for worldly values, and then, attacked by Spirit for causing the Fall, claims that it was misled by Spirit. The argument is resolved by Discretion, who draws an analogy with the culpability of Adam and Eve to show that both Flesh and Spirit are equally culpable. The conflict of Mind and Flesh is so prominent in the Burney anthology as almost to amount to a structural principle:

Carni seruire facit omnes pene perire;
Si caro sceptra gerit, mens male serua perit (fol.12^r, p.177)

To serve the flesh risks death for everyone:
If flesh is king, the servile mind's undone.

The two wage war in the heart:

Intra cancellum cordis caro mensque duellum
in diuersa mouent, dum sua queque fouent (fol.25^r, p.174)

The flesh and mind conflict within the heart:
While each pursues its aim, they drift apart.

but can be reconciled by the concept of measure:

Panis uinumque tua sunt, homo, sic quod utrumque
In mensura sit lausque deo sua sit (fol.25^r, p. 175)

Man, bread and wine are yours, but take them both
In moderation, and with thanks to God.

The Burney has two poems on slightly less obvious themes, the nature of *fabula* and the moral responsibilities of poetry. The various senses of *fabula* are presented, usually harmful but occasionally recreative:

Dulce facit festum, recreans cor fabula mestum;
Esse solet grata, quotiens bene fabula nata (fol.53^r, p.179)

For fables cheer the sad and grace a meal;
If nobly born, a fable has appeal.

In the other, a short dream vision,[242] the dreamer is warned not to pry too closely into Nature's secrets or to reveal them too widely:

quodque tegi natura iubet paucis et honestis
est exponendum ne vili sordeat aure (p. 23)

What nature wants concealed should be exposed
To few, lest in foul ears it be debased.

Satire

The step from moral verse to satire is a short one: it is hard (and unnecessary) to draw a sharp line between denunciations of gluttony and satire on gourmandizing abbots. Most of the interesting new satire of this period is in the Bekynton, some by the pseudonymous Eraclius.[243] Much of it concerns ecclesiastical abuses, especially avarice, simony and nepotism. On unworthy church appointments, for example, see No. 76 (XVI):

> Ve quibus ebibitur
> uirtutum fonticulus;
> Indirecte labitur
> ab hoc fonte riuulus,
> cum sic distribuitur
> dignitatum cumulus,
> indignus diligitur,
> dignus fit ridiculus (st. 4)

A curse on those who greedily the well of virtues drain:
The river from this fountain flows amiss,
When honours are distributed like this,
When worthy men are mocked and scorned, and scoundrels rank attain.

Bishops are guided by avarice (No. 21, K. VI):

> Cum deberent paracliti gratis largiri graciam,
> nil intra sancta faciunt nisi per auariciam (9–10)

For though God's grace to all should freely flow,
Self-interest is all these prelates know.

Naturally, Rome did not escape censure: it is bewitched by Simon Magus' crime (No. 10, III, ascribed by Dronke to Peter of Blois):

> Arte Symon magica
> Petri domum uendicat
> et implicat (4/1–3)

Simon's cast a spell on Rome,
And claims it for his very own.

A traveller returning from Rome describes his experiences there (No. 11, IV):

Frater, a curia Romana redeo,
passus martyria que fari nequeo.
Desunt donaria, uictum non habeo,
plenus miseria consorte careo[244] (2/1–4)

I've been to Rome, I'm going home,
   I can't relate the woes I've had.
I've lost my bribes, I can't survive,
   I have no friends, I'm very sad.

Frustration with life at court was, as we have seen, a frequent topic of satirists.[245] A group of four poems in the Bekynton[246] culminates in the exasperated cry of someone fed up with his companion's criticisms of a court which he still frequents (No. 31, x):

Cur, Tigelli nec auelli
   sustines a curia
nec ab eius, quod est peius,
   abstines iniuria ? (1/1–4)

If you don't like the life at court,
   Why don't you tear yourself away ?
At least do what you really ought:
   Don't let its pleasures make you stray.

The topos of comparing the trials of the ambitious (especially courtiers) to the torments of Hell, noted in Walter Map,[247] is used in Bekynton No. 9 (II), ascribed by Dronke to Peter of Blois; it describes the revival of the

Mistica mendacia
que Grecia
   finxit ludens fabulis (3/1–3)

Mystic marvels, fabled fables, feigned by Greece.

and applies the stories of Tantalus, Daedalus, Yxion, Ticius, Lycaon, Protheus, Midas and Venus to human behaviour. Eraclius (No. 14, VI) uses it in a general satire on sins:

En uidete Tantalum rem multiplicantem,
nummis nummos addere, bursas suffocantem (5/1–2)

There look at Tantalus, making his stack,
Adding up interest, stuffing his sack.

Eraclius complains that although men will give to Gratian (i.e. the study of the law), they give nothing to the poet:

reliquas sex uncias domno Graciano,
   michi nil qui publice res heroum cano (17/3–4)

> Six more ounces for the pocket
> Of the master of the law;
> Nothing for the humble poet
> Singing epic songs of war.

The poor rewards for poetry is a common theme. In Bekynton No. 99 (xxv) the poet plans to give up the arts for law:[248]

> Hinc leges eligo quas legunt ardui
> sacrosque canones: hic sunt precipui (5/1–2)

> I've opted for the law and the decrees,
> The topic of the grand, it's sure to please.

Another poet says that neither philosophy nor poetry bring reward; therefore the student should go into law or medicine:[249]

> Ignoro propterea unde possum tegi,
> 'carmina qui quondam studio florente peregi' . . .
> dat Galienus opes et sanctio Justiniana (8/3–4, 22/4)

> So now I can't afford a coat or vest,
> 'Who once wrote verse with eager youthful zest';
> Wealth rests with Galen and Justinian.

Comic verse and prose

The spirit of comedy[250] – clearly evident in much of the satire – comes to life with rhythmical verse, and is abundant in the Bekynton anthology. Sex, drink and food – the staples of comic writing – are in good supply. There is the very popular prose story of the Adulterous Monk:[251] a monk makes love to someone's wife; when the husband appears, the monk hides in a basket; his tonsure is showing, and he is caught and castrated. This simple fabliau achieves its comic effect by its parody of biblical language. The wife protests her innocence in the words of Pilate: 'Munda sum a semine huius, tu videbis' [I am pure of this man's seed, you will see (Matt. 27:24, cf. Act. 20: 26)]. The monk laments the loss of his 'twins' as Rachel mourned the death of her children:

> Tunc humi prostratus summo crepans gutture et evigilans geminos gemit. Et factus est Rachel plorans calculos suos, et noluit consolari, quia non sunt

> Then, flat on the ground, he groaned from the bottom of his throat and awaking mourned his twins. And he became like Rachel, lamenting his pebbles, and would not be consoled, for they were no more. (Matt. 2: 18)

Drinking is always a favourite topic.[252] An extremely popular epigram of Primas denounced the mixing of wine and water,[253] and the theme was expanded by Eraclius (No. 20, IX). The poet appears before judges to argue against an opponent who is urging the marriage of the divinities that represent water and wine:

> Dicit aduersarius Thetidem Lieo
> copulari licite, sicut deam deo (5/1–2)
>
> He argues that it's quite legitimate
> For Wine and Water, both divine, to mate.

Eraclius adduces biblical authorities in favour of wine; the marriage is improper, as Bacchus is unwilling and is 'disparaged' by the match, and the pair are linked by consanguinity. The proper bride for Bacchus is not Thetis but Venus:

> Placet ut coniugio lites sint sedate:
> Venerem non Thetidem Bacho copulate[254] (24/3–4)
>
> Let marriage now this squabble set aside,
> But Love instead of Water shall be bride.

A short prose 'collacio' (No. 22)[255] parodies biblical texts and exegesis to show how wine should be honoured:

> Primum et precipuum mandatum est: Diliges dominum Lieum ex toto ore tuo et ex toto ventre tuo et ex omnibus visceribus tuis (10–11)
>
> The first and chief commandment is this: you shall love the Lord Bacchus with all your mouth and with all your belly and with all your guts.

Celebrants are to drink toasts by number (one for One Faith of Bacchus, two for Two Testaments, five for the five books of the Pentateuch, and fifty in a Jubilee Year):

> et si multiplicaveritis potaciones usque quinquagesies, erit remissio poculorum sicut ibi debitorum (44–5)
>
> And if you multiply all the potations to the fiftieth time, there will be remission of drinks, just as of debts.

The prayer concludes with a blessing on the stomach:

> ab omnibus venter tueatur adversis. Qui vivis et regnas per omnia pocula poculorum (49–50)
>
> May your belly be protected from all adversities: you who live and reign through all potations.

The excesses of gluttony form the material for the prose story 'de quodam abbate' by Magister Golyas.[256] This describes a day in the life of an abbot: his luxurious and comfortable clothing, his meeting with his mistress in church, and his vast banquet, which is followed by many toasts (by numbers) and a great deal of belching. The abbot's diet is supported by theological arguments.

The wittiest poems in the Bekynton anthology concern food. In the 'Martyr-dom of the Game' (No. 18, VIII) all the game animals ('quadrupeds, bipeds and no-footed fish') are hunted down and brought to the abbot's kitchen. There they are examined for quality and executed by various kinds of torture:

> Qualiter hec torqueant excitatur rixa:
> pars assatur uerubus ferreis transfixa,
> pars in olla coquitur sicca, pars elixa,
> pars est in craticula torta, pars est frixa (17/1–4)

> First the burning question is, what will be their passion ?
> Some are barbecued on spits, in the current fashion;
> Some are potted, cooked all dry, some are boiled in water;
> Some are grilled upon a grid, some are fried in batter.

In the 'Mysteries of the Kitchen' (No. 94, XXIII), the poet asks to be told not the measurements of the heavens but the whys and wherefores of cooking: what herbs are suitable, what food goes with what, how it should be budgeted and cooked.

> Dic et plane precipe (MS percipe) que loquar et plene,
> congruo quis congruat sapor hora cene,
> quid delfino conpetat, quid pingui balene,
> que salsa maliciam temperet murene (9/1–4)

> Tell me plainly, make it clear, give me what I'm seeking:
> What spice suits the conger eel at the hour of eating ?
> What goes best with dolphin, whale, explicate it amply,
> Which sauce counteracts the risk of the tasty lamprey ?

In the 'Case of the Salmon' (Nos. 56–7, XV), the poet brings a legal action against a salmon which has burst directly out of an abbot's stomach, killing him in the process:

> Ventrem suo domino rumpit, rupta fide,
> quem abbas crediderat cuti malefide.
> Ergo legem consulens, bone pater, uide
> quod assignes premium huic abbaticide (6/1–4)

> Salmon broke its feudal oath, bursting through the stomach
> (Abbot trusted foolishly in his fleshly tunic).
> Now, wise father, check the law, do just what you oughta:
> Find the proper penalty for this abbot's slaughter.

The salmon responds by lamenting the indignity of being beheaded, baked with pepper, stuffed into the abbot's belly, and finally drenched with wine. He has done a good deed not only for all salmon but also for the monks, who will now have a good market in fish:

Dies numerandus est cum diebus festis
in qua die periit hec salmonum pestis.
Vos uates qui scribitis de uirorum gestis,
opus hoc tam nobile scribere potestis (32/1–4)

Let this as a holiday henceforth be regarded,
When the salmons' deadly scourge finally departed.
Poets all who celebrate deeds of human glory,
Now can give attention to this heroic story.

Love lyrics

Love poems are rare in the English anthologies.[257] The Bekynton, however, has several; most are shared with other manuscripts, but one (No. 48, XIII) is unique and may be English. It is a song of spring, the time for love:

Reuirescit abies
    et ego reuiresco;
estuat meridies,
    set non ob hoc calesco:
uirginis effigies
    fert solem quo tepesco (4/1–6)

Springtime stirs me from my sloth,
    Pine-leaves are returning;
Midday sun is blazing down:
    That's not why I'm burning,
For a virgin's shapely form
    Sets my heart a-yearning.

With this minor exception (and excepting the many love poems attributed by Dronke to Peter of Blois), it is fair to say that love played little part in the Anglo-Latin literature of this period.

The Golias tradition

Although in England the spread of the 'Goliardic' corpus was mainly in the thirteenth century, its beginnings were in the twelfth.[258] Gerald of Wales writes of the anti-Roman satire of a parasite called Golias:[259]

Item parasitus quidam Golias nomine nostris diebus gulositate pariter et lecacitate famosissimus, qui Gulias (MS Golias) melius quia gule et crapule per omnia deditus dici poterit. Litteratus tamen affatim set nec bene morigeratus nec bonis disciplinis informatus in papam et curiam Romanam carmina famosa pluries et plurima tam metrica quam ridmica non minus inpudenter quam imprudenter euomuit

Similarly, in our own time there is a parasite called Golias, notorious for his gluttony and his lechery – he could better be called Gulias, as he is entirely given over to eating and drinking. He is tolerably well-lettered, but is of bad character and has not been moulded by good discipline; he has frequently spewed out many popular songs, both metrical and rhythmical, satirizing the Pope and the Roman curia without shame or prudence.

He quotes some of the anti-Roman satire 'Utar contra vicia' and a stanza on drinking ('Meum est propositum in taberna mori') from the Archpoet's *Confession*.

A late twelfth-century manuscript from Kingswood, Gloucester (Trinity College, Oxford, MS 34), ascribes to 'bishop Gulias (or Guliash)' the drinking stanza from the *Confessio*, the poem on mixing wine and water,[260] and a serious typological poem on the Trinity (*Praedicatio Goliae*).

We have already noted that MS Digby 53 ascribes the story 'De quodam abbate' to Magister Golyas;[261] the same manuscript, however, credits the poem on mixing wine and water not to Golias but to 'dominus Primas'. There is constant interchange between Golias and Primas in attributions of this kind of material. There seems to have been a real poet, Hugh of Orléans, who went under the name of Primas. The first twenty-three poems in MS Rawlinson G. 109 have been ascribed to him: there are personal complaints, sexual adventures, drinking lore, poems on Troy, and macaronic verses. One poem often ascribed to Primas is 'Pontificum spuma', a complaint about a worn cloak given to the poet by a bishop. 'Primas' became, like Golias, a legendary figure who wrote witty, epigrammatic verse. Alexander Neckam wrote:[262]

Cum uinum poto, faciem lauo corpore loto;
Tunc fundo lacrimas, tunc uersificor quasi Primas (II. 5–6)

When I've had a drink or two
    I soak my face and body too;
Next I sadly start to cry
    But then, like Primas, versify.

Another popular satire was the *Apocalypsis Goliae*:[263] in a Spring dream the poet sees the great teachers and poets of antiquity; he is shown a book with seven seals, and when these are broken he sees laid out the faults of each ecclesiastical rank, from the pope downwards. The *Metamorphosis Goliae*[264] describes the philosophers of Paris.

To this muddied stream we must add the Archpoet of Cologne; only his *Confessio* circulated in England, but its stanza on drinking (mentioned above) has done more than anything to characterize Medieval Latin poetry for modern readers. This was ascribed to both Golias and Primas, as was the satire 'Tanto viro locuturi' of Walter of Châtillon.

This tradition may seem to have little to do with England. Hugh Primas and Walter of Châtillon were French, and the Archpoet's origins are unknown.

Nevertheless it was in England that the tradition swelled; during the thirteenth and fourteenth centuries the 'Goliardic corpus' formed one of the main nuclei of poetic anthologies. The identities of the original authors, if they were ever known, disappeared, and the literature became part of the fabric of Anglo-Latin. By the fifteenth century it came to be associated with the name of Walter Map.

Anthologies

Poetic anthologies rarely enter literary histories, let alone literary consciousness.[265] They are, however, invaluable sources for the literary historian, not only for the texts of unknown and neglected poems but as indexes to contemporary taste.

Models and compilation

Sometimes the anthologies seem to have grown round the collected poems of a single author.[266] There were also, however, classical models. Excerpts from classical authors, both prose and verse, were gathered in collections such as the *Florilegium Angelicum* (used by Gerald of Wales) and the *Florilegium Gallicum*.[267] It was through such collections that many medieval writers 'knew their classics'. Another model was the sixth-century *Anthologia Latina* which contains hundreds of short epigrams somewhat in the style of Martial; throughout the Middle Ages this was augmented continually, and some eleventh- and twelfth-century poems even found their way into modern editions of the *Anthologia*. It was one of the models for Godfrey of Winchester.

Within the limits imposed by the availability of texts, compilers seem to have aimed to produce a kind of Golden Treasury, using some of the traditional material (listed below) and adding new favourites according to taste. We can only guess at the processes by which the anthologies grew. Sometimes the contents of two collections parallel each other so closely that direct copying must have been involved, either one from the other or both from a common exemplar.[268] Sometimes the common material is found in manuscripts of different date, implying copying from an earlier exemplar.[269] At other times, however, several compilers seem to have dipped into the same pool.[270] Two things should be remembered. First, short poems were not usually written in what we think of as 'books', of a substantial size and bound in hard covers; they were in small 'booklets', of one or two quires, and could easily be passed around for copying into the larger collections. These booklets were probably regarded as ephemeral and relatively valueless (certainly not the kind of 'book' that would be catalogued as part of a monastic library). Second, many of the collections – even those that can be identified with a particular monastery – may have been compiled when its owner was at a larger urban centre, where students might easily share each other's texts. There is evidence of this in some fourteenth-century anthologies, which seem to have been compiled in Oxford, even though their owners came from, and returned to, more distant places.[271] At the beginning of the thirteenth century the same kind of interchange may have taken place at centres (such as Paris or Lincoln), where there were informal communities of highly educated clerics.

Popular anthology items

Some of the perennial contents of the anthologies are so hardy that they continue to appear even in the fifteenth-century collections. Hildebert and Marbod continued to be very prominent.[272] Hildebert's life of St Mary of Egypt, his *Biblical Epigrams*, his short 'Par tibi Roma' on Rome, his antifeminist 'Plurima cum soleant', and his personal lament 'Nuper eram locuples', are all frequently encountered; his long poem on the Mass, either alone or in combination with other liturgical expositions, is also common. Marbod's lives of St Lawrence and St Maurice, his rhetorical *De coloribus*, his poem on the lapidary, 'Evax rex Arabum', and his short personal poems are all popular. The works of Peter Riga, although he was a couple of generations younger, soon joined Hildebert and Marbod.[273] His lives of Susanna and St Agnes joined the other popular verse hagiography; his *Floridus Aspectus*, itself a collection of short poems, mingled with those of Hildebert, Marbod, and the supplemented *Anthologia Latina*.

Two epitomes of the story of Troy are common ingredients: 'Viribus arte minis' by Peter of Saintes, and 'Pergama flere volo' (which may have owed some of its popularity to its attribution to Hildebert).[274]

There are many epitaphs, sometimes of local persons (especially ecclesiastical), but often of famous historical figures, such as William the Conqueror; some of these may have been taken from mortuary rolls.[275] Compilers frequently made excerpts from longer works: verses (including epitaphs) from chronicles and from prosimetra such as Bernard Silvester's *Cosmographia*, and sections from long poems such as Lawrence of Durham's *Hypognosticon*.

Satire is a common element. Old favourites like the *De contemptu mundi* by Bernard of Cluny, *De vita monachorum*, *Invectio in monachos*, and 'Quae monachi quaerunt', continue to appear.[276] In the late twelfth century these were joined by the lively satires of Walter of Châtillon, especially 'Tanto viro locuturi' and 'Propter Syon non tacebo'. The effusion of literature on the murder of Becket soon found a place in the anthologies, and some elements of the 'Goliardic' corpus began to appear.

Types of anthology

A selection of items such as this formed the core of the anthologies, round which compilers would add material to their taste. Selection of entries allows one to divide the collections roughly into types. There is a Hildebertian model, in which the verse is nearly always hexameter or elegiac. Here we might include Vitellius A. xii, BL Add. 24199, Vespasian B. xiii, Digby 104, Corpus Christi Cambridge 34,

Gonville and Caius 238, and Laud lat. 86; these share in the large pools of Hildebert's and Marbod's short poems that have proved so difficult to penetrate.[277] Interestingly, neither these nor any other anthologies collect poems in classical lyric metres, even where there are extracts from writers who wrote them, such as Henry of Huntingdon.

Another old type, but of a different kind, is Rawlinson G. 109: this shares much with the *Anthologia Latina* model, with a strong mixture of Northern French material. Satire is very prominent in it, as it is in Digby 53, which is full of epigrams and Serlonian verse, as well as Walter of Châtillon. We have already discussed the Hunterian anthology, which is primarily a handbook of rhetoric and rhetorical examples. Bodley 656 also has a large concentration of rhetorical material.

The 'Later Cambridge Songs' manuscript, Cambridge, UL Ff.1.17, is a songbook; the metres of the poems are entirely rhythmical and lyrical. This raises the question of the role of songbooks in the formation of the anthologies. The massive Bekynton anthology contains both prose and verse; the verse is both quantitative and rhythmical; the rhythmical verse, in turn, can be divided into those with regular stanzas (Goliardic and asclepiadic) and lyrics with an apparently musical basis. Many of the latter are shared with the Florence Antiphonary, an unquestionably musical songbook. Thus, musical repertories must also be regarded as a potential source for the literary verse anthology.

Select list of anthologies c. 1200[278]

1 Oxford, Bodleian Lib., Rawlinson G. 109 (*c.* 1200, Suffolk, possibly Bury St Edmunds).[279] Begins with twenty-three poems by Hugh Primas of Orléans, followed by a great melange of classical, late classical, and Medieval Latin verse (including Serlo of Bayeux, Galo, Hildebert, and Simon Chèvre d'Or). The poems range from religious, moral and satirical (including poems against doctors) to extremely erotic. There are many topical poems, including epitaphs and pieces about Northern French abbeys and churches. The anthology illustrates the way in which Gallo-Latin poetry penetrated the English tradition. Parts of the parent manuscript of this collection were copied into BL Cotton Titus A. xx, nearly two hundred years later.[280]

2 Oxford, Bodleian Lib., Bodley 603 (*c.* 1200, provenance uncertain),[281] 145 fols. Saints' lives by Hildebert, Marbod, and Peter Riga; a block of poems on Becket; short satirical poems by Walter of Châtillon; 'Quid sit Deus';[282] moral verse, and an epic on Jerusalem. The second part of the manuscript has a composite poem on the sacraments by Petrus Pictor and Hildebert. It is closely related to the fourteenth-century collection in Bodleian Lib., Digby 166.[283]

3 BL Cotton, Vitellius A. xii (*c.* 1200), fols. 109–35; a short booklet containing many poems of the late eleventh and early twelfth century:[284] Serlo of Bayeux,

Marbod, Godfrey of Winchester, Hildebert, Galo, Hugh Sotovagina, and miscellaneous poems.

4 BL Add. 24199 (*c.* 1200, Bury St Edmunds), fols. 39–89[285] (about twice the size of the Vitellius). Begins principally with short poems by Hildebert and Marbod, followed (fols. 68^v–89^v) by a collection similar to that in the Vitellius: Hildebert, Marbod, lives of Sts Andrew and Agnes (by Peter Riga), Galo, Embricho's life of Mahomet; it has some poems not in the Vitellius, including a series to an inconstant mistress. On the other hand (in contrast to the Vitellius) it lacks the Serlo of Bayeux (though it has another poem possibly by him), Godfrey of Winchester and Hugh Sotovagina.

5 BL Cotton, Titus D. xxiv (*c.* 1200, Cistercian abbey of Rufford, Notts.), fols. 5–143.[286] Extracts from Henry of Huntingdon, some poems shared with the Vitellius and Add. 24199, Marbod, Hildebert, Galo, hymns, epitaphs (especially of Cistercian fathers and abbots), moral poems, hymns, poems attributed to St Patrick, *Anthologia Latina* material, lives of Sts Mary of Egypt, Maurice, and Lawrence, extracts from Lawrence of Durham's *Hypognosticon*, 'Pergama flere volo'.

6 BL Cotton, Vespasian B. xiii (s. xiii, early: one leaf from St Albans). The poetic section consists in 'fill' at the end of booklets of other material: (a) after fol. 26^v, *Apocalypsis Goliae* and a poem by Primas; (b) after fol. 82^r, Hildebert's *Biblical Epigrams*; (c) after fol. 110^v, *Distichs of Cato*, classical excerpts, Hildebert, Marbod, epigrams, and a florilegium from Seneca. Further poetic satirical additions were made after 1300.

7 Oxford, Bodleian Lib., Digby 104 (s. xiii, early), fols. 136–60; a booklet containing miscellaneous short poems, 'Non tonsura facit monachum' (= 'Quid deceat monachum'), Hildebert epigrams, Matthew of Vendôme's *Tobias*. The verse ends on fol. 151^r; the rest of the booklet contains prose sermons.

8 Cambridge, Corpus Christi Coll. 34 (s. xiii, early). A block (pp. 440–9) within other material, containing mainly Hildebert's poem on the Mass, some biblical epigrams, another Hildebert poem, and Peter of Saintes' 'Viribus arte minis' on Troy.

9 Cambridge, Gonville and Caius Coll. 238 (124) (s. xiii, early), fols. 148–61. This single-quire booklet is itself a composite. The inner part (fols. 150–9) contains short poems by Hildebert, especially *Biblical Epigrams*, Peter Riga's *Susanna*, satirical verses, and Walter Map's *Dissuasio Valerii*. The 'outer sleeve' (fols. 148–9, 160–1) contains more Hildebert religious epigrams. From fol. 160^r the text runs on into the next gathering, beginning with extracts from Gregory, followed by Hildebert on the Mass.

10 Oxford, Bodleian Lib., Laud lat. 86 (s. xiii, early). This contains several discrete booklets. (a) fols. 27–57: Marbod's lapidary, Peter of Saintes' 'Viribus arte minis',

and verse extracts from Bernard Silvester's *Cosmographia*. (b) fols. 94–109: miscellaneous poems, some secular, mainly from earlier periods; Hildebert on the Mass. (c) fols. 110–16: Hildebert's short, mainly secular, poems and some epigrams. (d) fols. 117–23: four poems. (e) fols. 124–33: Peter Riga's *Susanna*, a series of verse proverbs, poems in praise of London, and short pieces.

11 Oxford, Trinity College, 34 (s. xii, fin., St Mary's abbey, Kingswood, near Bristol), fillers on fols. 134^v–138^v (but included in the contents list). Well-known pieces on the genealogy of the Virgin, short religious and moral pieces, rhythmical verses of 'episcopus Guliash' (see above, p. 147), riddles, verses on Becket, Gulias 'In cratere meo'. This is the earliest explicitly Golias-ascribed set of poems in Anglo-Latin (apart from the notice in Gerald of Wales).

12 Bodleian Lib., Digby 53 (ss. xii/xiii; in Bridlington in the s. xv), 69 fols. A collection of booklets compiled by several hands in a process too complicated to be described here. (a) fols. 3–26: Serlo of Wilton's *De differentiis*, Marbod's rhetorical *De coloribus*, Serlo's proverbs and short poems, Primas epigrams, short poems, grammatical verses both in the main text and round the margins; on blanks between this section and the next are two satires by Walter of Châtillon. (b) fols. 27–34: prose satires (Golias on the abbot; the Adulterous Monk); inserted here are 'Pergama flere volo' and many epigrams. (c) fols. 35–50 *Babio*, followed by more Serlo of Wilton, and short poems. (d) fols. 51–66: treatise on rhetoric; margins filled with epigrams. (e) fols. 67–8 poem on the apostles. In all there are several hundred separate items: it forms an interesting assembly of grammar, rhetoric, satire, comedy, and prose satire, and anticipates in its overall range some of the later anthologies.

13 Bodleian Lib., Bodley 656, s.c. 27644 (s. xiii, early; Lessness or Westwood Abbey, Kent); fill on fols. 146–57. Extracts from Geoffrey of Vinsauf *Poetria Nova* (not just the isolable poems) and Walter of Châtillon's *Alexandreis*, Hildebert and similar short poems, mainly religious and moral, epigrams, grammatical verses (including Serlo of Wilton), epitaphs on Godfrey de Lucy, bishop of Winchester and abbey benefactor. There are over two hundred pieces. In the margin is scribbled what might be John of Leicester.

14 Glasgow, Hunterian v.8.14 (s. xiii, early). See above, p. 111, n. 160.

15 Cambridge, University Lib. Ff. 1.17 (s. xiii, early).[287] An eight-leaf booklet of thirty-five lyrics, laid out for music. Most are hymns for feasts; there are also three love songs, a rejection of love, and some satires. Several entries are shared with the Bekynton, the *Carmina Burana*, and other anthologies, but a few are unique. Known as the 'Later Cambridge Songs' to distinguish it from the eleventh-century Cambridge Univ. Lib. GG.5.35.

16 Oxford, Bodley Add. A.44 (c. 1200), the 'Bekynton', 228 fols. (in its original form).[288] The anthology par excellence of this – perhaps of any – period of Anglo-

Latin; it has already been mentioned many times. It was originally compiled *c.* 1200 in six sections by nine hands (I–II by B; III–IV by C; V by D, E, F, and G, with additions by H and J; VI by J. It was finally assembled by A, who added a contents list). Nevertheless, each section that contains poetry or literary material is similar in type, indicating some uniformity of plan. The prose is mainly serious (*Gospel of Nicodemus*, Isidore's *Synonyma*, and sermons), but there is antimatrimonial prose (Jerome, Map's *Dissuasio Valerii*, and Theophrastus), Eraclius' prose denunciations of William de Longchamps, Hugh Nonant's letter on the same, and two biblical parodies (Adulterous Monk, *Collacio* on wine). The long verse includes a complete epic (John of Hauville's *Architrenius*, which occupies about a third of the manuscript), Bernard Silvester's *Mathematicus*, two comediae (Matthew of Vendôme's *Miles Gloriosus*, Vitalis of Blois' *Geta*), and two verse debates ('Ganymede and Helen', Turaldus on Flesh and Spirit). The themes of the seventy-five shorter poems are equally varied: religious and moral; satire on the court, on clerical abuses, on avarice, and on ambition; topical events (Third Crusade, William de Longchamps, capture and death of Richard I); love lyrics, and a lament by Dido; comic verse on wine and food. Verse forms range from hexameters and elegiacs to rhythmical stanzas and lyric sequences. Authors of the short poems are not named in the manuscript, but (in addition to those already mentioned) we can identify Peter of Blois, Walter of Châtillon, Berter of Orléans, Hildebert, and the pseudonymous Eraclius. Material is shared with the Florence Antiphonary, the *Carmina Burana*, and the *Later Cambridge Songs*, and there are two of Hildebert's ubiquitous poems; a great deal of the contents, however, are uniquely preserved here. The most striking feature of the Bekynton is its variety: it rivals the *Carmina Burana* in scope, and although there are fewer items than in the *Carmina Burana* their types and subjects are much more varied. A reading of the whole collection, in fact, would provide a student with a very solid basis in Medieval Latin literature.

In the fifteenth century the collection was expanded by, or for, Thomas Bekynton, bishop of Bath and Wells and chancellor of Henry VI. The antimatrimonial section was supplemented (by a commentary on the *Epistola Valerii* and the *De coniuge non ducenda*) and a few other poems and items were added that were appropriate to the collection (e.g. the letter from the Old Man of the Mountain, exonerating Richard I from complicity in the death of Conrad of Mont-Ferrat); rubricated titles and a new contents list were also supplied.

Conclusions

Anthologies like Rawlinson G. 109, Vitellius A. xii and BL Add. 24199 illustrate the tenacity of the Norman traditions, not only in the popularity of the older poets but also in the clear interest still felt in the affairs of Northern France. In 1200 this should not really surprise us: it is only with hindsight that we can see the futility of English attempts to hold on to continental possessions. It must have seemed quite natural to Richard, after his release from the Emperor's prison, to spend the remainder of his reign campaigning in France. The aristocracy and educated classes, both religious and secular, still felt a psychological bond with France, for various reasons: the old Anglo-Angevin empire, real estate, the spiritual community of monastic foundations, affection for the alma mater of Paris and other centres of learning, and, for many, a common language. These sentiments changed only gradually, though the change was hastened by the humiliation of England's subjection to the papacy and the invasion of Prince Louis, which awakened a sense of English identity.

We must also remember that, long though this chapter has been, only sixty-two years elapsed between the accession of Henry II and the death of King John. They were momentous years: they saw the murder of an archbishop at the apparent instigation of a king, the fall of Jerusalem to Saladin, the capture and ransom of a king (and his subsequent death in battle), the loss of Normandy, the Interdict, and a French invasion. Nevertheless, sixty-two years is a period easily encompassed within the memory of elderly people. Peter of Blois, who died in 1212, was a friend of John of Salisbury, who was a student in Paris when Stephen was king. Walter Map lived to 1210, but had met Becket and been at Henry II's court. Gerald of Wales had met Serlo of Wilton and been involved in the conquest of Ireland in 1185; he not only outlived King John but survived to 1223. The time-frame of this chapter is simply two generations.

The circumstances for writing had changed considerably since the first two generations after the Norman Conquest. As mentioned above, by the end of the twelfth century there were centres of learning in England with the potential to become universities.[289] About half the writers surveyed in this chapter were seculars; they may have held ecclesiastical offices (often merely sources of income), but their careers were in the world, not in the cloister. Even monks, of course, were not entirely cut off: Nigel Whiteacre and Matthew of Rievaulx were well up on current events, and it was common to move back into the world: Baldwin moved from the abbacy of Ford to become bishop of Worcester and archbishop of Canterbury.

Some writers, such as Adam of Barking, seem to have worked in comparative isolation and to have had no influence on anyone else. Others, however, had more effect on other contemporary authors. John of Salisbury's *Policraticus* was used by Peter of Blois and Nigel Whiteacre, and may have been parodied by Walter Map. Serlo of Wilton's differential verses found many imitators, particularly Richard Pluto. Geoffrey of Vinsauf's *Poetria Nova* influenced Gervase of Melkley and Matthew of Rievaulx. Alexander Neckam imitated Adam of Balsham and possibly heard Gerald of Wales lecture; he himself was a source for William de Montibus. Some of Walter Map's conceits turn up in Peter of Blois, and his anti-Cistercian stories were known by Gerald of Wales; his folktales are shared with Gervase of Tilbury. We do not know if Map's influence was through the written or spoken word, or if all these writers were drawing on a common fund of material.

We do not know how much personal contact there was between the writers of this period. Both Map and Gerald had met Serlo of Wilton. Peter of Blois wrote frequently to John of Salisbury, who was a good friend of Peter of Celle, with whom Robert Partes corresponded. Peter of Blois also wrote to Alexander Neckam, who certainly knew William de Montibus, with whom Gerald had corresponded. Through Archbishop Baldwin, Gerald probably knew his nephew, Joseph of Exeter. When Baldwin was abbot of Ford, two of his monks were Roger and Maurinus of Ford, who certainly knew each other. Both Gerald and Nigel Whiteacre dedicated works to William de Longchamps. Peter of Cornwall dedicated his *Revelationes* to Stephen Langton, who seems to have know William de Montibus. In the North, Reginald of Coldingham dedicated works to Aelred (who had been known to Lawrence of Durham) and to Hugh Puiset, to whom the anonymous *Brutus* was dedicated.

Many similar connexions could be made, but there is no way of knowing whether they imply acquaintanceship, let alone friendship. Certainly there were many opportunities for the writers to have met each other, especially in Paris, where many of them had been students. There were the royal courts: Henry II and Queen Eleanor (Walter Map, Peter of Blois, Gerald of Wales); the Young King Henry (Walter Map, Gervase of Tilbury); William of Sicily (Peter of Blois, Gervase of Tilbury, and, if he is Walter of Palermo, Walter the Englishman). There were the courts of administrators: Becket, when he was chancellor, and William de Longchamps. Also there were the households of archbishops and bishops: Becket, Baldwin, and Langton at Canterbury, and Hugh Puiset at Durham.

Whether or not there were 'literary circles', it is fair to say that England as a whole could boast a thriving literary community.

Popular continental writers 1154–1216

As in the section on Marbod, Baudri, and Hildebert, a brief sketch is needed of writings from outside England. Continental (mainly French) Latin literature was so popular in England that it formed a major part of the fabric of Anglo-Latin, not only in the twelfth but in succeeding centuries.[290]

Philosophical allegory was a major product of the French Neoplatonists. Bernard Silvester's *Cosmographia*, closely modelled on Martianus Capella's *De nuptiis Mercurii et Philologiae*, provided, in a prosimetrum, a scientific myth to describe the creation of the world and man.[291] It was written about 1150. Also attributed to Bernard is the *Mathematicus* or *Parricida*, a long poem about the struggle of a Roman with the doom foretold for him.[292]

In about 1160–75 Alain de Lille composed an even more influential prosimetrum, *De planctu Naturae*.[293] In this the goddess Natura laments sexual perversions and by means of a myth instructs the poet on the proper function of love and sexuality. The account of Nature as God's vicar was profoundly influential in later literature, particularly in Jean de Meun and Chaucer. In 1182–3 Alain completed his nine-book hexameter epic, the *Anticlaudianus*.[294] This is another allegory of creation; it describes an astral journey in search of a divine soul for the newly created man. Alain's treatise on preaching was influential on John of Garland.[295]

John of Hauville, once thought to be English, was the teacher of Gervase of Melkley. His nine-book hexameter epic, *Architrenius*, is another allegory.[296] The 'Archmourner' of the title seeks out Nature to ask her why he can find, in all the world, no place for ethics. It is very satirical and has a great deal on flattery (a passage that may have influenced Walter of Wimborne).

Of continental religious literary works of this period, the most influential in England was the *Aurora* by Peter Riga, canon of Rheims. This is a versification, with allegorization, of all the major books of the Bible, with interpretations based on Peter Comestor.[297] It was composed between 1170 and 1200 and revised many times. Riga also wrote a version of the biblical story of *Susanna*, which was frequently anthologized.[298] Peter's collection of short poems, the *Floridus Aspectus*, circulated widely in England, and the poems became mingled in the anthologies with those of Marbod and Hildebert.[299] According to one early (thirteenth-century) colophon, Peter Riga was English ('natione anglicus').

Walter of Châtillon was at one time attached to the court of Henry II; we have already noted his revulsion at the death of Becket.[300] He is now much admired for his love lyrics, but in England his satirical poems were more popular.[301] In his own time, however, his most admired work was the *Alexandreis*, a classical ten-book epic on Alexander. Over two hundred manuscripts of it are extant, and extracts appear alongside those of classical writers in florilegia and schooltexts of the thirteenth century.[302] It was finished in about 1182.

The Golias-Primas tradition, in which Walter of Châtillon participates, was in origin continental: its core elements are associated with Hugh of Orléans and the Archpoet of Cologne, discussed above.[303]

Matthew of Vendôme was author of a comedy *Milo et Afra* and possibly of the *Miles Gloriosus* (of which a copy is in the Bekynton). His biblical epic, the *Tobias*, was popular in England, but his most influential work was the *Ars Versificatoria*, written about 1175, a forerunner of Geoffrey of Vinsauf's *Poetria Nova*.[304] It opens with the methods of beginning and stylistic faults to be avoided. It then gives a set of examples of *descriptio*; these descriptions – a Pope, an Emperor, Ulysses, Davus (a serf), Marcia (a matron), Helen, Beroe (an ugly woman), and the Garden of Nature – often circulated separately.[305] After these, Elegia, in a dream, instructs the poet on all the colours of rhetoric, poetic metres and styles.

The English *comediae*[306] had many forerunners in France besides Matthew of Vendôme.[307] Most of them are anonymous, but William of Blois, brother of Peter of Blois (Epist. 93), was author of the *Alda*. The most popular comedy in English manuscripts was the *Geta* by Vitalis of Blois (no relation to William or Peter). This was modelled closely on Plautus' *Amphitryo*.

3

Henry III to Edward I (1216–1307)

I Chronological survey

The end of the reign of King John marked a turning point in English affairs that also led to the separate development of Anglo-Latin literature. In contrast to the twelfth century, very few continental literary texts achieved popularity in English poetic anthologies, and almost no Anglo-Latin writers (including John of Howden and Walter of Wimborne) had an audience in continental Europe.[1] The loss of Normandy in 1205, and the subsequent defeat at Bouvines in 1214, signalled the break-up of the Angevin Empire and the effective end of English dominion in France. England and France remained at odds for centuries, and gradually an insular literature developed, first in Latin and later in English. Interest shifted from foreign to domestic affairs, such as the Barons' War and wars in Scotland.[2]

The new king, Henry III, was a boy, and until 1223 England was ruled by a council of regents. The first need of the reign was to deal with the invading army of Prince Louis, which was no longer welcome now that John was dead. The decisive victory over Louis at Lincoln in 1217 is celebrated in 'Sepserat Angligenam', in 146 hexameters:[3]

England had been afflicted by a fourfold rage, caused first by pride. John's behaviour was no longer tolerable:

> Non tulit ulterius regem regnare furentem
> Vindicis ira Dei

> The wrath of vengeful God
> Could no more bear the reign of raging king.

It is not a very distinguished poem, but is frequently alliterative:

> A face fax oritur fati flammaeque furorem
> Dum furit in regem febris vindicta fugavit

> The fire of fate takes light from fire, the fever's wrath
> Makes fugitive the flame, while fuming at the king.

The thirteenth century also displayed a new xenophobia, directed at foreigners ('alienigenae') of all kinds. John's subjection of England to the papacy produced a hostility to Rome that was no longer just anti-bureaucratic but actively nationalistic.[4] The presence of the papal legate was a constant irritant: Pandulph, although praised by Henry of Avranches,[5] caused some annoyance by persuading the pope to 'nullify' Magna Carta and to excommunicate many of the barons; Matthew Paris showed sympathy for the Oxford riot against Pandulph's successor Otto. Matthew deplored the appointment to English livings of Italians who could not even speak English; he was delighted by Grosseteste's denunciation of Innocent IV as Antichrist, and supported Frederick II in his military campaign against Rome. Xenophobia also had constitutional implications: hostility to Henry III's foreign advisers led directly to the Barons' War of 1264–5.

Events in the outside world continued, of course, to impinge on England and on its writers. The effects of the Fourth Lateran Council of 1215 were far-reaching. Its concern over threats to the church, both internal and external, led to increased vigour in the Albigensian Crusades against the Cathars of southern France; the desire to retake the Holy Land, though ultimately futile, led to the breach between pope and emperor.[6] The need to combat heresy also led to a renewed stress on preaching, and thus to the establishment of preaching orders (below). The requirement for annual confession (which incidentally caused friction between the friars and secular priests) also produced a flood of pastoral literature; it has been suggested that the constant self-scrutiny required by confession contributed to the introspective literature of the fourteenth and fifteenth centuries. The Council's reinforcement of the requirement of clerical celibacy incidentally provoked some satire.[7]

Two other overseas events had a literary impact. Louis IX's acquisition in 1239–41 of relics of the crucifixion – the crown of thorns, part of the Cross, and Longinus' spear – was widely celebrated and may have contributed indirectly to the meditation on the instruments of the Passion that figures largely in devotional poetry. There was also a general nervousness that the end of the world was at hand: the arrival of Antichrist and his precursors was inferred from the activities not only of the Cathars, the friars, Frederick II, and Pope Innocent IV, but also by the depredations of the Tartars. The great invasion under Genghis Khan had begun in 1218, and by the 1240s they were menacing Western Europe and the Holy Land; Christians saw them alternately as a scourge from hell (Tartari from Tartarus) or a potential ally against the Muslims, but more commonly they were seen as a sign of the coming apocalypse.

The friars

In 1216 Honorius III (who had succeeded Innocent III) established the order of Friars Preacher (the Dominicans); in 1223 he licensed the Friars Minor (the Franciscans), who arrived in England the following year with at least one poet among their number.[8] They formed a new kind of intellectual elite – learned and devout, but not tied to a monastery or a parish. Their evangelical fervour and commitment to academic training contributed to the rise of the English universities (below); they were able to attract and to train bright English recruits. The Franciscans in particular contributed to Anglo-Latin literature: in this period we have John of Wales, Walter of Wimborne, and John Pecham. English Franciscans were also active on the 'constitutional' side in the Wars of the Barons, and may have been authors of some of the pro-baronial poems. The friars were not welcome everywhere; although the bulk of antifraternal satire in England is fourteenth century, Matthew Paris was an early opponent and wrongly interpreted a poem by Henry of Avranches as an attack on the 'novi fratres'.[9]

Rise of the universities

We have already noted that by the end of the twelfth century England could boast several centres of learning where an advanced education could be obtained.[10] During the thirteenth century first Oxford, and then Cambridge, outstripped the rest and became formally incorporated as universities. Oxford's pre-eminence was aided by the presence of many learned scholars. At the beginning of this period there was John of London, who taught John of Garland:

> Hic de Londoniis fuerat dictusque Johannes:
> Philosophos juveni legerat ante mihi[11]

> He came from London, and his name was John:
> From him when young, I learnt philosophy.

In the next generation there were the Franciscan Adam Marsh, Robert Grosseteste, and John Blund, all of whom are of tangential literary interest. John Blund, at one time a candidate for the archbishopric of Canterbury, was addressed in poems by both John of Garland and Henry of Avranches.[12] Adam Marsh was a close friend of Grosseteste's, and both were active on the 'constitutional' side in Henry III's dispute with the barons; Adam was a friend of Simon de Montfort, but neither he nor Grosseteste lived to see the Barons' War.

Grosseteste's only properly literary work, the *Château d'Amour*, was in French, but he is important for his influence.[13] The Franciscans quickly established a friary in Oxford, and Grosseteste, although not himself a Franciscan, was their first lector, perhaps lecturing on theology, philosophy, and science; later he became bishop of Lincoln (1235–53). He quarrelled frequently with the king, and also with Innocent IV, whom, in 1250, he denounced as Antichrist; this judgment was, apparently, based on sound scholarly reasoning, but it was acclaimed by those whose antipapal sentiments were more emotional, such as Matthew Paris. Grosseteste's death in 1253 was mourned by a friar Hubert in 192 lines of elegiacs, stressing his learning and sanctity:[14] he was the strength ('robur') of the church, and kindly withal:

Mestus in ecclesia, iocundus semper in aula
In camera gaudens et velut agnus erat (177–8)

Sad-faced in church, but always glad at court.
In chambers joyful, gentle as a lamb.

A student riot in Oxford resulted in the closure of the university 1209–14; some scholars made their way to Cambridge, and in the next few decades we begin to hear more about Cambridge as an institution of learning. Elias of Thriplow was a grammar teacher in the area, and Walter of Wimborne was a Franciscan lector there in the 1260s; at the end of the century Nicholas of Breckendale taught grammar there.[15] Thus, both Oxford and Cambridge grew in strength and prestige; by the middle of the century archbishop Boniface admitted that Oxford now deserved to be considered the rival of Paris. The closure of Paris 1229–31, after another student riot, may also have contributed to the rise in status of the English universities.

Much of the excitement in universities was centred on the newly discovered and translated works of Aristotle. Although Paris in 1210 banned the teaching of Aristotle in its arts faculty (perhaps another indirect boost for Oxford), the interest was too great to be suppressed and in 1231 Gregory IX requested that Aristotle be purged of 'errors' (that is, points conflicting with Christian doctrine) so that his works could be studied in schools. His significance for literature consists primarily in the attraction of scholars to Oxford, where (among others) John Blund lectured on Aristotle: it is probable that Walter of Wimborne had attended lectures on Aristotle there,[16] as his *Quatuor Elementa* shows up-to-date knowledge on the subject. The chronicler Ralph Niger wrote verses on Aristotle, but the most important direct literary result was Henry of Avranches' versification, for public delivery in a verse competition (possibly in Oxford), of Aristotle's treatise on *Generation and Corruption*. The rediscovery of Aristotle, however, may have had less tangible but deeper and more significant results, by changing the attitude of scholars to received opinion.

Alan of Meaux

We know nothing of the first poet of this period, Alan of Meaux, except that he had been provost of a college of secular canons at Beverley (1204–12) before becoming a monk at the Cistercian abbey of Meaux in Yorkshire.[17] His poem on Susanna was probably written after 1212, as (lines 1–22) he writes of his reformed way of life. His poem consists of 418 lines of elegiacs. The well-known biblical story had already attracted two poetic versions, by Peter Riga and his editor Giles of Paris,[18] but Alan's is the most elaborate. He sticks close to the biblical story, but amplifies it with classical and other biblical allusions and some reminiscences of Riga's version. After describing his own reformed life, Alan discusses the dangers of temptation, the gifts of fortune, and the duties of judges, before narrating the story. Joachim's garden is a typical *locus amoenus*, blessed by a perpetual spring and even a phoenix. The judges tell Susanna that, like Hercules and biblical heroes they have been overcome by love; their sexual appetite, although it now has less stamina, will be revived by hers; the time is ripe for love:

> Pronior in Venere, sed tardior ad repetendum
> Flamma uirilis obit, fit rediuiua tua.
> Applaudunt uolucres, arridet tempus amori;
> Cogimur ergo frui commoditate loci (241–4)

> To love more prone but in performance slow,
> Our manly flame declines, from yours revives.
> The birds rejoice, the season smiles on love:
> We're forced to take advantage of this place.

Susanna debates her options; not only is she torn between her wish to remain pure and her fear of the judges, but reflects that even if she wanted to commit adultery this would be worse than that of Paris and Helen, because of the age of the judges and their possible impotence:

> Tussis anela senum uenerisque senilis eclipsis
> Tedia coniugibus sunt onerosa suis (263–4)

> Their old men's wheezing coughs and failing powers
> Are heavy burdens for their wives to bear.

When she cries for help, she stammers:

> 'Pres' prius et 'biteros' repetens dum cincopat, uno
> Singultu nequiit dicere 'presbiteros' (289–90)

> 'El-' first, she gulps, then '-ders' she gasps again;
> She can't say 'elders' in one single breath.

The judges falsely accuse her of just having made love to a young man, and use her stammering as evidence of sated passion:

> Nouimus, et nostis, quid creber anelitus oris,
> Cincopa quid uocis significare solet (323–4)

> We know, and you know too, what panting breath
> And stammering most probably betray.

Susanna is condemned, but Daniel intervenes and convicts the judges of perjury.

The theme was evidently attractive, as it gave an opportunity to satirize not only corrupt judges but also the *senex amans*. It was told again in Goliardics, in an incomplete version preserved in a manuscript of the early fourteenth century:[19]

> Hic Susanna sepius ingredi solebat;
> Cum feruore nimio sol incalescebat,

Fontis rore gelido corpus abluebat;
Senum hoc astuciam minime latebat (16/1–4)

Susanna often used to walk this way,
When burning sun blazed in the heat of day.
She used to bathe her body in the pool;
The old men's cunning knew her daily rule.

'Distinctiones monasticae'

Collections of *distinctiones*, very popular in the thirteenth century, would not normally find a place in a literary history: they are alphabetically organized lists of what we might call polysemous words, but on an interpretive rather than a linguistic plane – that is, words that can be interpreted in different ways or that can be applied in different ways in scriptural exegis. Thus, *aquilo*, the North Wind, signifies the devil, strong temptation, gentiles, old age, or a stern countenance.

The *Distinctiones monasticae et morales*, however, is of unusual interest. It contains five books, with 281 headwords from *Altare* to *Zona*.[20] It was compiled in England in about 1225, perhaps in a Cistercian abbey in Lincolnshire. It differs from other such collections in its personal style and its frequent quotations of poetry. There are many anecdotes, such as this about an abbot during the Interdict, when bodies could not be given sacred burial:

> Referam tibi breuiter quid accidit de quodam abbate, defuncto tempore interdicti, qui plurimum uini potacione delectari consueuerat. Hic, quia in atrio benedicto non poterat tumulari, in uinea que est proxima abbatie sepultus est. De quo quidam sui ordinis monachus sic uersificatus est:
>
> > Huic, quia dilexit uiuens super omnia uinum,
> > Vinea defuncto pandit amica sinum[21]
>
> I'll relate briefly what happened to an abbot who died during the Interdict. He had been in the habit of enjoying himself a great deal in the drinking of wine. Because he could not be buried in the sanctified enclosure, his body was placed in a vineyard close to the abbey. A monk of his order wrote this verse epitaph on him:
>
> > Because this abbot, living, loved his wines,
> > The friendly vineyard now his corpse entwines.

In addition to tags from classical poets, the author quotes much medieval verse: Peter Riga, Lawrence of Durham, Stephen Langton (providing testimony for his authorship of 'Veni sancte spiritus'), and a surprising amount of medieval satire and epigrams. We find Serlo of Wilton, Alexander Neckam, Hugh Primas, Walter of Châtillon, and (valued for their uniqueness) epigrams by Walter Map. Many of the verses may be by the compiler himself. The *Distinctiones monasticae* testifies to a fusion of literature and theology outside the realm of creative writing; it is worth remembering that many anthologies of secular verse in this period come from monasteries.

Odo of Cheriton

Another religious writer who made use of secular literature was Odo of Cheriton in Kent (*c.* 1180–1247).[22] His collection of sermons, completed in 1219, frequently quotes verse, classical and medieval, religious (e.g. by Hildebert and Reginald of Canterbury) and secular, canon law mnemonics, proverbs, and the like. He had a gift for telling stories, and his sermons make frequent use of parables.[23] In 1225 or shortly after he made a complete collection of prose *Fables*, mainly animal stories from the Aesop tradition and similar sources,[24] all equipped with a moralization. Altogether there are nearly two hundred fables; they were very popular, both in England and on the continent. They had a wide influence on sermon writers and collectors of exempla, and had many imitators, such as John of Sheppey.[25]

John of Garland

Although John of Garland spent most of his career in France, in Paris and (1229–32) Toulouse, he merits a place among Anglo-Latin writers. He was born about 1195, and studied under John of London at Oxford.[26] He writes frequently about Arthurian and English history, and was in touch with leading English figures such as Fulk Bassett, John Blund, and John Mansel.[27] He was one of the most prolific writers of the age. In addition to music (not covered here),[28] his subjects include grammar, lexicography, rhetoric, metre, mythology, religion and history. His principal interests were the Crusades, heresies, and above all the Virgin Mary; these themes occur in almost all his poems. Modern preferences for simple diction and coherent stories are inappropriate in the case of a writer whose principal aim was to introduce vocabulary and recherche expressions. Raby writes that Garland 'was above all else a teacher',[29] and his works must be read in this light. The pantechnicon of medieval education – cosmology, medicine, and above all grammar – provided not only the subject matter of his writings but also the structure and metaphors.

Grammar and lexicography

One of his earliest works, written when he was 'pene puer', was the prose *Dictionarius*; perhaps in imitation of Adam of Balsham and Neckam's *De nominibus utensilium* it is a dramatized wordlist.[30] The words are, by classical standards, exotic, many derived from English or French, and supplied (perhaps by Garland himself) with copious glosses:

The parts of the body; the trades and merchants of Paris (who are all out to cheat students), their tools and wares. The bakers, like God (Sap.11:21), work by 'number, weight and measure':

> Pistores Parisius pinsunt pastam et formant panes numero, pondere, et mensura, quos coquunt in furno mundato cum tersorio

> The patisseries of Paris pound their dough, and shape loaves by number, weight and measure; they cook them in an oven that they scrub clean with a scourer. (Note: the words *numero, pondere et mensura* are in the Cotton manuscript only)

You would expect coiners to be rich, but their coins are not their own. Siege engines at Toulouse in 1218. Tools of a student (books, pen, ink, etc.); a royal park, his own garden and orchard, a visit to the countryside, the households of the rich (including their whores). Finally, a choir of maidens and matrons singing in honour of the Virgin Mary.

The *Commentarius*, written about 1246, is a wordbook that 'focuses on features . . . of the life of the nobility, especially courtiers'; it includes a text of the poem 'Aula vernat virginalis' (below).

At the beginning of his verse *Synonyma*, Garland distinguishes *equivoca* (one word signifying many things) from *synonyma* or *univoca* (many words signifying the same thing).[32] The still unpublished poem on *Equivoca* shows first the many meanings of the word *augustus* (Caesar, the month, divination, noble) and its etymology:

> Augustus, -ti, -to, Caesar vel mensis habeto;
> Augustus, -tus, -ui, vult divinatio dici.
> Mobile cum fiat augustus nobile signat.
> Augeo dat primum, dat gustus avisque secundum.

> *Augustus* with *-ti, -to*, means Caesar or the month;
> With genitive in *-tus* the augur's craft is shown.
> When it's an adjective, *augustus* 'noble' means;
> 'Increase' provides the first, 'bird', 'taste', reveal the next.
> (i.e. *augeo* 'increase', *auis* + *gustus* 'bird' + 'taste')

Conversely, the *Synonyma* is a kind of verse *Roget's Thesaurus*, showing how a single concept can be expressed by many words:

> Adstruit affirmat asseverat: tria sunt haec,
> Asserit est quartum, quae signant quatuor unum (PL 150, 1579)

> 'Proclaim', 'affirm', 'asseverate', that's three;
> 'Assert' makes four – but all mean just the same.

His shortest work, *Cornutus*, was one of his most popular.[33] There are twenty-one hexameter couplets, gnomic or proverbial, intended to introduce rare, often Greek, vocabulary:

Hic non est hagius quem cenodoxia vexat,
Quemque premit cachesis non prodest diasynaxis (14)

The man vainglory stirs is not a 'holy' man:
The sacred office does not save a man in sin.

Most of the verse grammatical works remain unpublished.[34] The *Ars lectoria* or *Accentarius* (1246–9 or 1243) is a poem of 1426 lines, designed to teach the proper pronunciation of Latin and to refute the errors of the *Graecismus* and *Doctrinale*; it also contains a list of his earlier works. The *Clavis Compendii* is a poem of about 2250 lines, apparently another wordlist, to judge from the seventy-three lines of medical terminology printed by Scheler. Even longer is the *Ars versificatoria*, containing about 4000 lines; from it Scheler printed an extract of thirty-five lines on heresy, the wars of Toulouse, and the death of Simon de Montfort.

Rhetoric

The *Parisiana Poetria* (in its final version written about 1231–5) is a fullfledged treatise on composition;[35] it takes its name from its opening poem in praise of Paris, but is not exclusively about poetry. It combines several topics: letter-writing (*dictamen*), verse composition, and prosody, both quantitative and rhythmical. This combination of disparate topics obscures any coherent doctrine, but its interest lies in this very inclusiveness. The procedure is, as the editor puts it, 'associative', and may owe much to its origin in his lectures. It quotes from classical and medieval verse, including Garland's own *Epithalamium* (below).

The examples, usually Garland's own compositions, are especially interesting and range widely in length, metre, style and topic. They include a fifty-line allegory (*elegi Leonini*) in pastoral mode; a life of St Denis, neatly conveyed in a series of possible ways to begin a poem; a 78-line exhortation (*elegi unisoni*) to join the crusade and to be virtuous, in which the virtues and vices are depicted allegorically as the heroes of the siege of Troy; a comic story in twenty-four Leonines about a well-dwelling demon called Guinehochet –

Est ex Plutonis fouea prolata colonis
Gallica uox leta, iocunda, nouella, faceta – (ch.4, 433–4)

A Gallic voice to farmers from the pit
Is novel, jolly, full of mirth and wit.

who tells a peasant that two of his sons are the village priest's, but won't say which. There is also a mnemonic for remembering the different types of legal documents.

Book VII of the *Poetria*, the longest, contains all the major examples of the craft of writing. There is what Garland calls a 'tragedy', in 126 hexameters, in which the rivalry in love between two washerwomen-prostitutes results in the fall of a besieged castle:

Bis triginta scias inclusos menibus illis
Esse, due quorum lotrices corpora cultu
Pulcre curarunt, debentes esse parate
Ad cohitus equitum, quia marcet forma uirilis
Ad caros cultus hominum si femina desit (ch. 7, 45–9)

> Know this, that sixty men were closed within the walls.
> Two washerwomen offered first-class care to keep
> Their bodies trim: they had to be prepared to bed
> Down with the knights, for masculine physique declines
> When there's no girl at hand with loving tender care.

Rhythmical verse is illustrated by three poems: a moral poem in Goliardics, a hymn in Victorines in honour of St Catherine, and a student song about their teacher (Goliardics *cum auctoritate*). Finally, there is a long section on quantitative lyric metres; Garland was the first English writer since Henry of Huntingdon to show an interest in this topic. There are three poems on the conception of the Virgin, in the Lesser Asclepiad, Iambic dimeters, and Sapphics:

O parens uirgo, pariens parentem,
Splendor estiuus sine carnis estu,
Dumus incensus, sine rore uirga
Florida, salue (ch. 7, 1409–12)

> O virgin mother, parent of your sire,
> The summer's glory, lacking summer's heat,
> The unburnt bush, the twig that, lacking dew,
> Burst into flower – Hail !

To conclude this section, he composed nineteen poems (moral, satirical, and religious) in different quantitative metres, all derived from Horace's *Odes*.

The *Exempla honestae vitae* is one of Garland's last works (1257–8).[36] It consists of 244 lines of elegiacs, exemplifying the rhetorical devices of the *Ad Herennium* by a series of moral precepts directed mainly to ecclesiastics. It is addressed to Fulk Bassett, bishop of London, and its final section ('rerum gestarum narratio') eulogizes many leading English figures: John Mansel, King Henry III and Queen Eleanor, Henry of Wingham, Philip Lovel, the younger Simon de Montfort, and the poet ('regius vates') Henry of Avranches (*inaurans = in Avrans* !).

Other pedagogy: Morale Scolarium, Integumenta Ovidii

The relative brevity of the *Morale Scolarium* (662 lines) and Paetow's thorough edition have made this one of Garland's better known poems.[37] It was written in 1241 and dedicated to Fulk Bassett (at this time dean of York), and compliments Henry's chancellor John Blund. It is mainly in single-sound Leonine hexameters.

Its obscurity and lack of focus seem to be deliberate; Garland explicitly recommends it for acquiring new vocabulary:

> Si qua sit hic rara tibi dictio, sit tibi cara:
> Mens labat ignara doctrinaque marcet avara (7–8)
>
> Keep as a treasure any unknown word you've read:
> A mind that's blank declines, and knowledge wanes unfed.

It is understandable only (and not always then) by means of the copious glosses, which were probably provided by the poet himself. He describes it as a new kind of satire:

> Scribo novam satiram, set sic ne seminet iram,
> Iram deliram, letali vulnere diram (1–2)
>
> A satire new I write, from which no quarrels grow,
> And lacking mindless wrath that wounds with cruel blow.

and describes the function of satire as follows:

> Hec est lex satire, vitiis ridere, salire,
> Mores excire, que feda latent aperire (423–4)
>
> For this is satire's law: mock vice and jump around,
> Encourage upright ways and hidden filth expound.

Arousing morality and mocking at social ills (Frederick II, the antipapal party at Rome, ecclesiastic abuses) certainly forms part of the poem, but 'jumping about' (*salire*) is its most notable feature: the poet seems incapable of holding on to a topic for more than a few lines at a time. In several sections it includes courtesy book material, including how to ride a horse;[38] attention is given to the seven rusticities and seven courtesies of Thales of Miletus, together with a dietary which introduces rare plant names. In honour of Louis IX's acquisition of relics of the Crucifixion, the central part of the *Morale Scolarium* praises the Cross in 'cross-formed' hexameters (*hexametri cruciferi* or *cancellati*):[39]

> Crux cancellavit musam michi metra novantem
> Forma triumphantem cruce regem significavit (271–2)
>
> The Cross crisscrossed my muse to bring out metres new:
> The very shape askew portrayed the king Christ-crossed.

The poem ends with praise of the Virgin as 'stella maris'. The whole work, with its obscurities and lack of organization, is a paradigm of Garland's literary technique, spinning out verses like a spider:

> Viscera protelo, me sicut aranea velo,
> Et victus zelo metra protelata revelo (231–2)

> In secret, spiderlike, my guts I far extend,
> And, overcome with zeal, my verses I expend.

The *Integumenta Ovidii* contains 520 lines of unrhymed elegiacs.[40] The tradition of demythologizing pagan stories [41] was applied in the late twelfth century to Ovid's *Metamorphoses* by Arnulf of Orléans, and Garland follows many of his interpretations closely. Ovid's stories of transformations are totally separated from their context, and are interpreted as history, nature, or morality (never religion). For example, the adultery of Venus and Mars and their capture by Venus' husband Vulcan are interpreted naturally:

> Ver Venus est, estas Vulcanus, captus adulter
> Autumpnus nobis dans aliena bona (185–6)

> By 'Venus' Spring, by 'Vulcan' Summer's meant, and 'Mars',
> Caught in the act, is Fall, that yields another's goods.

Theseus and Perithous represent the contemplative and active lives:

> Contemplativa Theseus activaque vita
> Pyrithous, tolerant sepe pericla due (363–4)

> Thus Theseus represents the contemplative life,
> Perithous the active – perils face them both.

Circe is a whore who leads men into impurity:

> Sic Circe trahit in porcos quos vivere cogit
> Immunde magica rite nociva viris (475–6)

> So Circe turns to pigs the men that she compels
> To live an impure life, by baleful wizardry.

The original stories are not provided, and the reader's knowledge of them is assumed. The poem is, in essence, a versification of Arnulf and other interpreters, and could only be used as an accompaniment (perhaps in lectures) to a reading of the *Metamorphoses* itself.

Marian poems

According to a contemporary commentator, the *Georgica Spiritualia* was in honour of the Virgin and was based on Alain de Lille's *Ars praedicandi*.[42] All that remains of it is about a hundred one- or two-line extracts, either simple hexameters or Leonines, perhaps to illustrate metre. The lines are gnomic and proverbial, and have no perceptible link between them. It has no resemblance to Virgil's *Georgics*; in its complete form it may have resembled the series of agricultural metaphors for the Virgin found in Book IV of the *Epithalamium*, with which it shares some phrases.

With good reason Garland had a high regard for his ten-book *Epithalamium*

Beatae Virginis;[43] he often refers to it and quotes from it. He originally composed it in Paris before 1225, but recited it – perhaps lectured on it – and revised it during his years in Toulouse (1229–32). It is in elegiac couplets (occasionally, in set pieces, with internal rhymes in various schemes). It is a philosophic epic in the Chartrian tradition of Alain de Lille's *Anticlaudianus*: as Alain had supplied a myth for the creation of man, so John of Garland now provided a myth for the life of the Virgin Mary. Where Alain used the astral journey, Garland's mode was the epithalamium or marriage feast.[44]

The classical epithalamium[45] had acquired several new elements by the twelfth century. First, biblical commentaries had interpreted the Song of Songs as the marriage between Christ and the human soul, or between God and the Virgin Mary. Second, the debate between the four daughters of God (Ps. 84: 11), Justice, Truth, Mercy, and Peace, ended with a kiss, and was thus also a kind of marriage. These elements had already been combined in a short *Epithalamium*, which reduced the debate to one between Justice and Mercy.[46] To these elements Garland added another: the flight of Justice from earth and her return. He combined Isaiah's lament (59: 14),

> Et conversum est retrorsum iudicium, et iustitia longe stetit,
>
> quia corruit in platea veritas et aequitas non potuit ingredi

> And judgment is turned away backward, and justice standeth afar
> off; for truth is fallen in the street, and equity cannot enter,

with the classical myth of Astraea or Justice, who had walked the earth in the Golden Age (Virgil, *Georgic.* 2. 473–4). In Virgil's Fourth Eclogue, the return of Astraea to earth heralded the return of the Golden Age, which for Christians coincided historically with the Incarnation of Christ. Garland echoes the Virgilian phrase ('rursus aurea secla ferens') precisely at the moment of the Incarnation.[47]

The philosophic epics were also encyclopedias of knowledge, and this suited Garland's pedagogic instincts. The *Epithalamium* is full of descriptions of places and buildings, character depictions of vices and virtues, lists of herbs, trees, jewels, fish and so on. Each of the ten books is preceded by a summary in Goliardic stanzas.

Book I.[48] The bride (i.e. the soul) deviates from the true path, and Justice is driven into exile by 'terrena lues'. Those under the Old Law lament and ask for help. Death and her family; Discord reports to Death her victory over Justice: the Fall of Man. The eventual victory of the Bridegroom, however, is prefigured by the victory of Samson. The story of Jael, wife of Heber, who stuck a spike in the head of Sesara, shows that we need a woman's aid. (Wordplay is illustrated in these lines on the Hebrew victory):

> Frustra securos hostes secuere secures,
>> linquitur et canibus hiis Cananea caro (1.589–90)

> Their axes hacked their foes, so over-confident,
>> The flesh of Canaanites was left for dogs to lick.

In the meantime, the Devil rules.

Book II. Description of Satan and hell. Infamia challenges Justice: satire on clergy, tricks of Parisian tradesmen, etc. Hope consoles Nature; the route to heaven. Astraea is described; she presents her complaint to God, with a list of vices, such as the promotion of the unworthy.

Book III. Description of Mercy. Mercy addresses God, asking that a woman should be man's ladder of salvation; she laments the Fall and calls for the Incarnation (she describes man's vulnerability before the enemy in terms of a wrestling match): as the world is now ending its fifth age, the time is ripe for the fulfilment of the prophecies. God agrees with Mercy. All animals are subject to death; they unite during the Flood while Noah builds the ark; God foresees all. The martyrs prepare for their struggles (described in terms a cockfight). The land of Judea is chosen for the Incarnation.

Book IV. Description of the Holy Land and its history (including allusions to Richard I and the crusades); its trees and herbs (including the thorns from which Christ's crown will be made and the most precious spice of all, the Virgin). The marriage of Joachim and Anna (Mary's parents) and their initial childlessness. The poet has a vision of an old man (i.e. Jerome) with a book that tells the story of the Immaculate Conception of the Virgin. Joachim is sadly sent away from the temple because of his childlessness; Anna prays, and an angel visits them.

Book V. The nature of dreams (used to authenticate both Joachim's and the poet's dreams). The poet is afraid to write, but Faith puts the pen in his hand,[49] telling him that

> Ieronimus transfert prudenter apocripha, ne nos
> seducat vite mors saciata favo (5.63–4)

> The sage Jerome translates apocrypha, lest we
> Be led astray by Death, too full on life's sweet food.
> (Cf. Prov. 27: 7)

The conception of the Virgin: the four humours make up her body, but for her soul God turns to the Old Testament heroines. Her birth is under the astrological sign of Virgo. Her good behaviour as a child, her presentation in the temple, and her betrothal to Joseph. She is a *rara avis*, so a parliament of birds follows, in which Christ is the phoenix.

Book VI. A reverdie (spring song) celebrates 25 March, the date of the Annunciation. The poet omits Caesar's decree and the massacre of the Innocents, and dwells on the name of Jesus. At last Peace and Justice kiss:

> Pax et iusticia sibi dantes oscula, vero
> exorto, firmant connubiale decus (6.161–2)

> When Truth arises, Peace and Justice kiss, and then
> Confirm the glory of their marriage bond.

The Virgin's physical appearance (*dactylici tripertiti*); she rejects the gifts of Fortune. Facecia rules her five senses. Where does Facecia live ? In the Virgin; the name Maria, who is 'aula virginalis'. Fama arouses Envy.

Book VII. The mystic sphere of the Virgin. Astraea returns to earth, to the dismay of Envy. Miracles of the Virgin, followed by various figures for her: 'stella maris', the fountain of wisdom and stream of eloquence (which nourishes Augustine and the fathers of the church). John the Baptist, Evangelists, martyrs.

Book VIII. The marriage feast; Livor (envy) calls on Discord to disrupt it; Discord departs. The feast begins and the virtues serve at table. The story of the *Gesta Salvatoris* (from Satan's fall to Christ's final victory) is sung. The soldiers of the Bride and Bridegroom: the apostles (each given military rank), their spiritual armour and castle. They defeat Gula, Avaritia, and Invidia.[50]

Book IX. The battle continues, with the defeat of Superbia and Luxuria and an account of Amor (both false and true). On the defeat of the sins, Death laments and is forced to praise the Virgin. Christ rises from the dead.

Book X. The Assumption of the Virgin at the appropriate time, when the sun is in the sign of Leo (the lion of justice); the joy in heaven; the Virgin's crown and glory. The poet denounces antifeminism and exhorts widows to remain chaste. He denounces Jews, and makes a final prayer.

The *Epithalamium* is a superb example of the allegorical epic: it blends biblical and classical themes and expressions; astrology is harmonized with events in the Virgin's life, and other encyclopedic knowledge (trees, herbs, spices) is put in the service of one majestic whole. Full use is made of grammar and rhetoric; here the Virgin is praised by declining *flos*:

> Flos es, floris amans, flori gratissima, florem,
> O flos, producis, flore creata tuo (1. 11–12)

> A flower you are, a flower's love, to flower dear,
> O flower, from flower born, you bear a flower.

Here is an example of punning and alliteration:

> pollice divino polus iste politur, ut aula
> polleat, ut vestis sit polimita Ioseph (6. 285–6)

> This pole is polished by a thumb divine; the hall
> Shines bright like Joseph's multicoloured cloak.

This style produced a humus of expressions and images that nourished the 'affective' devotional poems of Walter of Wimborne and John of Howden, just as typology of the Virgin had produced the symbolism on which hymn writers drew.[51]

Garland has many shorter poems on the Virgin, often embedded in longer works. One is the 'Aula vernat virginalis';[52] it describes the Virgin's womb by an architectural metaphor:

> Christus petra fundamentum,
> tenax tecti tegumentum,
>   obumbrator spiritus.
> Parietem posse patris
> stipat ut procellis atris
>   obviet oppositus (st. 2)

The rock of Christ supports the hall,
The Holy Spirit covers all,
        An ever-present shade.
The Father's might holds up the wall,
To stand opposed to thunder squall,
        A solid palisade.

Garland's last Marian poem was the *Stella Maris*, written after 1248;[53] it consists of 192 Victorine sequence stanzas, his only full-length independent rhythmical poem. This celebration of the Virgin is based on her miracles,[54] together with scientific lore ('et phisicalia et astrologica et teologica interserta'). Most of the sixty-one miracles are common in the collections (Theophilus, the Jewish boy in the oven, the illiterate priest, the merchant's pledge, and so on), but one concerns the relief of Parma, besieged by the forces of Frederick II, in 1248. The miracles are interwoven with images drawn from the Zodiac (beginning with Aries, the sign under which the Annunciation and Crucifixion took place), the seven planets, the Galaxy, and medicine:

> Stelle proles figuratur
> in vervece qui mactatur
>   et in tauri robore.
> Geminus est Deus homo,
> cancro conversivum promo
>   hunc ad nos in tempore (184–9)

> The Ram that father Abram killed
> Proclaims the child the star revealed;
>   The mighty Bull says thus.
> Christ, God-made-man, is Gemini;
> Like sideways Crab God turns, say I,
>   In time on earth to us.

The poem is accompanied by a full set of glosses, which show a knowledge of Garland's other works and may be substantially by him. The longer (Bruges) commentary, however, does not elucidate specific miracles, and the verses themselves are not self-explanatory. For example, a long story involving a woman whose nose was deformed by disease and is cured by the Virgin is told thus:

> Hec membrorum reparatrix
> nasi fuit reformatrix
>   quem amisit femina (664–6)

> She heals the limbs that humans lose;
> She built a new replacement nose
>   To cure a woman's loss.

Either the audience was expected to know the stories already, or Garland may have lectured on his own poem (as he did on the *Epithalamium* and perhaps also on the

Integumenta Ovidii). The *Stella Maris* was written all of a piece: frequently a new legend or topic begins in the middle of a stanza.

De mysteriis ecclesiae; De triumphis ecclesiae

In about 1245, after the death of the philosopher Alexander of Hales, who is celebrated in an epilogue, Garland wrote the *De mysteriis ecclesiae*, which he sent to Fulk Bassett.[55] It consists, in its present edition, of 659 unrhymed hexameters (metrically very uneven), in his typically compressed and obscure style. It is part of a long tradition of poetic interpretations of the church and its sacraments.[56] It begins with an allegorization of the church's architectural features and then of its various sacraments and offices, beginning with the service of dedication. There are sections on ecclesiastical orders and the vestments, and finally an account of the Mass itself.

The *De triumphis ecclesiae* is an eight-book poem on the crusades.[57] He implies that he started work on it in 1245, but it continues to describe the campaign of Louis IX in 1249–52: there are many signs that it is unfinished.[58] Garland describes the work in several ways. He refers to it mostly as an 'elegia', partly because of its metre, partly because of its sad topic. At the beginning his use of the opening of the *Aeneid* implies an epic:

> Arma crucemque cano, qua dux superatur Averni
> Et qua succumbit vulgus inerme suum (Prol. 11–12)

> The arms and Cross I sing, the Cross that conquered Hell,
> The Cross to which Hell's feeble force succumbed.

In Book III, Melpomene is invited to sing the 'tragica gesta' of the Tartars (3. 689–90). At the end of Book VII he writes:

> Historiis satyras et gesta tragedica junxi,
> Haec ut venturi singula vera legant (7. 499–500)

> To histories I've satire joined and tragic deeds,
> So those to come may learn the truth in full.

Elegy, epic, history, satire, tragedy – the *De triumphis*, in part, answers to all these descriptions. The modern reader is also likely to be confused by the order of narration. Rhetorical theorists (such as Geoffrey of Vinsauf) had advised against simple chronological arrangements as inelegant, and Garland took their words to heart in this poem. He says that he has mixed past and recent events, and justifies digressions for their savour:

> Pristina cum gestis intersero gesta modernis:
> Dant lavacrum nostris antidotumque malis.
> Historias condire graves digressio morum
> Cernitur, ut condit fercula secta sapor (Prol. 187–90)

I intersperse the deeds of yore with things done now:
They yield a cleansing cure for present ills.
Digressions on behaviour, as is known, add taste
To sober history, like spice with meals.

The following synopsis illustrates his procedure:

Prologue (204 lines). General: the need to unite against the Parthi (Saracens), Tartars and heretics.

Book I (414 lines). War is evil, except in a just cause:

Est tamen ecclesiam justum defendere sanctam,
Ut pereat sanctae gens inimica crucis (1. 7–8)

And yet defence of holy church is just and right,
The downfall of the holy Cross's foes.

The crusade has been frustrated by greed and ambition, and the Golden Age disturbed by greed; man's discord upsets Nature's harmony, but the Virgin will triumph. Situation in the Holy Land; quarrels among the leaders, wars between England and France. A review of British history and the fate of Arthur shows the effects of treachery.

Book II (894 lines). *Poitevin War of 1242*[59]
Leaders of the crusade; quarrel of Pope and Frederick II; Tartars; history of Jerusalem. If only the West would unite ! Origins of human greed. Henry III sets out in 1242, facing bad weather. (Weather-lore of a sailor: the poet does not disagree but deplores superstition). Henry goes to Poitou, and war with Louis begins. The horrors of war, especially for peasants. Satire on ecclesiastical abuses. Many miracles had occurred in Poitiers but now only logicians are preferred. English–French hostility goes back to 1190. The present conflict: insults traded between French and Poitevins. Valiant Louis and Henry should be on the same side ! Praise of the Cross and its legendary history.[60]

Book III (698 lines). *Review of history from 1190*
Elegiacs suit the Cross. Crusade of 1190; Richard I's quarrel with France, capture by Duke of Austria, defeat of Bretons, King John's loss of Normandy, victories in Ireland, (John of Garland's early studies in Oxford), Interdict and submission to Pope, invasion of England by Prince Louis, death of King John. In Europe the siblings of Richard I quarrel; thus the past produces the present:

Sic in praeteritis determino bella futura,
Quae simili fient aut graviore modo (3. 389–90)

And so by wars long gone I fix the course of those
To come, for they will be the same or worse.

The war in Poitou; miracles in this area. During the campaigns the plague breaks out and heresies revive. Origin of heresy.

Book IV (544 lines). *Albigensian Crusade of 1218*[61]
Roger of Beziers killed the bishop of Albi who had seduced his wife; Raymond of Toulouse was implicated and a papal emissary killed. The pope called for a crusade against Raymond;

latent heresy comes into the open; various heresies. Siege of Toulouse led by Simon de Montfort. Writers sent to combat heresy. Early fighters for the faith, including English saints and martyrs (Edmund, Kentigern, and others), Giles, St Francis; miracles of the Virgin. Heretics are unmoved by arguments and will be devoured by Antichrist. The siege of Toulouse (a city that breeds good warriors) continues.

Book V (354 lines). *Toulouse 1218–29*
Death of Simon de Montfort.[62] Calendrical heresies of Albigensians. Lament at quarrel between Pope and Emperor; good emperors, from Charlemagne; story of Roland and the traitor Ganelon, of whom many such exist today. War in Toulouse ends in 1229. A university is founded there, and teachers (including Garland) are brought from Paris. Miracles of Virgin portrayed in church at Rocamador. At Toulouse St Julian is honoured: the various St Julians. (The book ends with a prose letter describing studies at Toulouse, where students can read Aristotle).

Book VI (364 lines). *Toulouse–Paris 1229–32*
Unrest at university of Paris (which is closed) and elsewhere. Garland teaches at Toulouse, where studies flourish; struggles against the heretical Gawain. Garland teaches how the apostles and martyrs defeated paganism, but the heretics still mock. Envy causes salaries at Toulouse to stop, and Garland leaves. He is captured by pirates, but shows them a miraculous shield in the sky and is released. (Digression on the evil effects of Venus.) The poet arrives back in Paris; heresies in northern Europe. Quarrel between Pope and Frederick II, who should be available to fight heresy. The Tartars have been sent to punish our sins.

Book VII (500 lines). *Tartars; the crusade of 1245*
Cruelty of the Tartars, compared to the Jews and contrasted with examples of Saracen mercy (e.g. at Damietta in 1249). The two St Edmunds. Greeks in conflict with the church. Shortness of human life. Tartar barbarity and its origin. Toulouse campaign. Deposition of Frederick II in 1245. Excursus on sin, with a psychomachia between vices and virtues. Only peasants get to heaven:

> Vix venit ad coelum miles, vix clericus, illud
> Simpliciter credens rustica turba rapit (7. 389–90)

> The route to heaven's hard for knights and clerics too:
> The peasant's simple faith gets there with ease.

Crusade begins in 1245. Effectiveness of prayer. Miracles of the Virgin.[63]

Book VIII (630 lines). *Crusade of 1249–52*
Unlike pagan poets, Garland sings of the Cross. Progress of the crusade: Acre, (Parma relieved in 1248), Louis IX sets out (warnings against treachery), Cyprus, siege of Damietta and its capture:

> Rex dictus rocus cadit, eschec dicitur urbi
> Mathque simul: peditum vis equitumque perit (8. 273–4)

> The king (called rook) is felled, the city's first in check
> And mated too – the knights and pawns are lost.

Damietta falls again; various battles, truces, and renewals of war. Henry III will join the crusade. Death of Frederick II in 1250. Garland will leave it to others to write the end of the story, but foretells victory with the aid of the Virgin. (Brief summary of the poem.) Account of the joys of heaven.

Garland brought all his poetic tools to writing this epic; most of it is in unrhymed elegiacs, but there are occasional blocks of rhyme, in various schemes. He also employs interesting tricks such as *versus retrogradi*.[64] The real problem is structure; although the summary above gives the impression of a fairly continuous narrative in Books III–VIII of the events from 1190 to 1252, this is an illusion. The poem skips backwards and forwards in time constantly; this may to some extent be deliberate,[65] but the real problem is that contemporary history is unfinished. The dramatic conclusion for which Garland hoped – the recapture of Jerusalem – never happened, and so the poem ends optimistically but limply.

Elias of Thriplow

We turn now to a grammarian and pedagogue of quite a different stamp. The newly discovered Elias of Thriplow was a grammar teacher in Cambridgeshire – perhaps in Cambridge itself, but before its formalization as a university – and flourished about 1222, dying before 1251.[66] He was fairly well read in classical verse and prose, in theology, and to some extent in philosophy. Most of his works – *Contra nobilitatem inanem*, *Semidiales*, and *De vita scholarium atque sua* – survive only in extracts and fragments; only one work has survived intact, the *Serium senectutis*.

This is a thirteen-book prosimetrum, modelled at least in form on Martianus Capella; each book is introduced by a poem in unrhymed hexameters or elegiacs. The content is at the same time ridiculously trivial and grandiose. It represents the querulous dialogue between Elias and his friend Philip, first on the appropriateness of the phrase 'the marriage of heart and tongue' (with a long account of the punishments meted out by God and the pagan deities for lying and blasphemy), and second on the uniqueness of man's immortal soul and the uniqueness of God. The arguments are wrapped up in an extraordinary style, characterized by exotic vocabulary, heavy alliteration, hyperbolic phrases, and a syntax in which grammatically related words are widely separated in the sentence – partly for the sake of alliteration, partly to avoid hiatus, and mainly simply to obfuscate. The obscurities are greatest when the interlocutors are insulting each other:

> Talibus itaque que scrutatori studioso cuilibet sponte primis obviam veniunt in luminibus infinita coniunctim diuisimque diligenter inspectis, subtiliterque non minus et non in superficie sola sed intrinsecus investigatis, temperare pertinaciam tue procacitatis pergas tam temerarie et non minus intempestiue quam ridicule prorsus et inconcinne garrulitatis tue, quo plus iusto fluidum ligue (= lingue) loquacitatis ue lubricum tui pergas oris opitulare uel aliquando uel aliquando cacchynum

> Having diligently inspected, together and separately, and having no less subtly investigated, not only superficially but internally, such things which countlessly offer

themselves to the first glance of any careful examiner, you ought to try to temper the pertinacity of your so rash boldness in speaking and of your garrulity, as inopportune as it is quite ridiculous and inelegant, in order that you may remedy the more than appropriate fluidity of your tongue or the slipperiness of loquacity, or sometimes guffaw.

That is, don't talk so much. Elias' verse is only slightly less distorted:

> Uir sibi sensatus male per mendacia mendax
> Se sua confundens tendit ad interitum (8. 1)

> The foolish man that lies, by his deceits
> Confounds himself and marches to his death.

The taste for alliteration and strange vocabulary is partly the result of pedagogic whimsy (Walter of Wimborne and John of Garland, both teachers, exhibit it), but it becomes a stylistic feature of many thirteenth- and fourteenth-century Anglo-Latin writers.

William of Ramsey

Before we come to Henry of Avranches, the most important Anglo-Latin verse hagiographer, we must say a few words about other verse lives of saints. Until recently, from Leland to the Dictionary of National Biography, William of Ramsey was reckoned to be one of the leading verse hagiographers of the age. Russell, however, correctly reascribed the lives of Birin, Guthlac and Edmund to Henry of Avranches.[67] He then went on to infer that William was a fiction of Leland's. We know, however, of a William of Ramsey who wrote a commentary on the Song of Songs.[68] We also have a twenty-six-line epitaph on Waltheof of East Anglia, clearly by a William, apparently written after the translation of Waltheof's relics to Croyland in 1219:[69]

> Hic, Waldeve, comes, tumularis et incineraris,
> Parte tamen pociore tui super astra bearis

> This spot, Earl Waltheof, gives your mortal ashes rest;
> Your better part above the stars is blest.

This celebrates Waltheof's sanctity and mourns his betrayal by his faithless wife.

A verse life of St Neot was also attributed to William of Ramsey by Bale, and there is no need to give it to anyone else.[70] It is in unrhymed elegiac couplets, and at present consists of 675 lines, with metre and sense incomplete. It is straightforward and unadorned but fluent; its apparent irregularities are due almost entirely to the editor. It is based on the Vita Secunda printed in the Acta Sanctorum,[71] and recounts early miracles not in the Vita Prima. St Neot began his career as a Glastonbury monk under Dunstan, where his especial friend was Aethelwold; he became a priest and left for a hermit's life in Cornwall, and after a visit to Rome he established a religious community in Cornwall. He was often consulted by King Alfred, to whom he gave dire warnings of his temporary loss of his realm:

> Post modicum tempus gentes tibi bella movebunt,
> Vis tua deficiet, vis sua grandis erit,
> Et te de regno, pro quo male tutus oberras,
> Pellent, et parvo tempore solus eris (541–4)

> Not long from now the people will rebel,
> Your might will fail and theirs will grow in strength;
> They'll drive you from your kingdom, in whose rule
> You're insecure, and soon you'll be alone.

The poem breaks off after the death of Neot and the building of a church for his body, in the middle of an account of what happened to Alfred to fulfil the saint's prophecy.

Gregory: Life of St Catherine

Another poet who has mistakenly been credited with a work by Henry of Avranches is an otherwise unknown Gregory, who dedicated a verse life of Catherine of Alexandria to a bishop of Winchester.[72] The poem consists of 422 lines of unrhymed hexameters. In contrast with the St Albans verse life,[73] Gregory's account is admirably brief, though it is well stocked with poetic expansions and digressions. It follows the outline of the 'vulgate' life, but compresses the narrative and the theological arguments. It begins by stressing Catherine's firmness:

> Sepius in sexu fragili constancia mentem
> Firmat et interdum muliebres masculat actus (1–2)

> Their constancy gives to the weaker sex
> A strength of will that makes them act like men.

It dwells on Maxencius' fury at the rise of Christianity and his almost pious desire to restore the old gods:

> Jupiter, ignosce ! Non te paciemur inultum.
> Cessabit furor iste nouus; proscripta redibit
> Relligio, marcens florebit, lapsa resurget (42–4)

> Forgive me, Jove, you won't be unavenged.
> This madness new will pass, the outlawed faith,
> Though now downcast, will rise and thrive again.

In response to Catherine's urging to believe in one God, he recites the fates of those who have offended the pagan gods. The poet denounces legal trickery and describes the dishevelled scholars after their dispute with Catherine. The story is rapidly told but includes all the main details, including the wheels and the saint's translation to Mount Sinai:

> Spiritus astra petit; corpus nouitate stupenda
> Legiferi montis secreta cacumina scandit (416 –17)

> Her spirit seeks the stars, her body climbs –
> O marvel new ! – to Moses' secret hill. (i.e. Sinai)

Henry of Avranches

By any criterion Henry of Avranches must rank as the foremost Anglo-Latin poet of the century.[74] He is called 'regius vates' by John of Garland, and (ironically) 'archipoeta', 'decus vatum' and 'primas primatum' by Michael of Cornwall, who immortalized Henry by his series of flytings against him.[75] His poems were collected and quoted by Matthew Paris. In one manuscript he is called 'magnus versificator',[76] and he is referred to as 'versificator' in court records. He was one of the first truly professional Latin poets of the Middle Ages. He was able to turn his versifying skills to the most diverse and apparently unpoetic materials (including canon law, grammar, medicine, and science). Poetry was his profession in a more precise sense, as he is one of the first poets known to have received direct payment for his poems: from 1243 to 1260 he was paid, in wine or money, from the Exchequer of Henry III, at a fairly generous rate.

He was Norman by birth, and frequently taunted by Michael of Cornwall for his origin, but spent much of his early career, in the 1220s, in England, writing verse saints' lives for episcopal and monastic patrons. In the 1230s he spent some time in Italy, mainly at the papal curia, writing verse for a variety of patrons. If we can trust the evidence of vituperative poetry, he was a teacher at Angers (his own account) and at Oxford and Paris (according to Michael of Cornwall). From 1243 he was presumably mainly in England or at least in Henry III's service; oddly, we have few poems of this period, and his share in the debate with Michael of Cornwall (1254–5) is not extant. For convenience I have divided his writings by topic rather than chronologically, into hagiography, other religious poems, education and philosophy, debates and public poetry, and court poems. Despite the attention paid (for historical reasons) to his secular poems, his saints' lives form quite the greatest part of his extant poetry.

Saints' lives

All but two of the saints' lives (Crispin-Crispinian and Francis) concern English saints; of these, two (Becket and Hugh) are modern, but the remainder are of the Anglo-Saxon period.

Oswald

In about 1227–9 Henry wrote a hexameter life of Oswald for Peterborough Abbey; there are two versions, the longer containing 1151 lines.[77] Basically it follows Bede, with some additions from Reginald of Durham.[78] The opening lines, based on Ovid's *Metamorphoses*, provide almost a paradigm for Henry's poetic procedures, and are mentioned by Michael of Cornwall:

> In nova fert animus antiquas uertere prosas
> carmina . . .
>
> My spirit urges me to turn old prose
> To poems new . . .

After addressing several monastic officials, Henry recounts Oswald's genealogy, stressing God's hand in distinguishing his character from that of his father and brothers. He describes Oswald's recovery of the Northumbrian crown, his struggles against the British, his victory, by means of the Cross, at Heavenfield, his invitation to Aidan to help spread the Christian faith, his death at the hands of Penda, and the miracles associated with the spot of ground on which he died. Great stress is laid on his right hand, which, because of his generosity, remained uncorrupted after death.

Several of Henry's distinctive topoi and stylistic features appear: detailed medical descriptions of the onset of a fever and of diabolic possession, and a fondness for onomastic wordplay: Roger, prior of Peterborough ('rosam geris'), Cedwalle ('cedem velle', 'cedes vallant'), and Aidan ('ab auxiliando').

Birin

Henry wrote the life of Birin for the powerful Peter des Roches, bishop of Winchester and adviser to Henry III during his minority.[79] It contains 658 hexameters and was probably written around 1225, when Dorchester and Winchester were competing for the relics of the saint. Henry begins by announcing his intention to write the lives of three saintly bishops of Winchester – Birin, Swithin, and Aethelwold – and of Martin of Tours (Peter was dean of St Martin's at Angers). Only that of Birin is extant.

Birin's birth at Rome, which now rejoiced in Christianity. The description of his piety illustrates Henry's style:

> Hic est cos, dos, flos et ros: cos relligionis,
> dos fidei, flos ecclesie, ros dogmatis; hic est
> libra, liber, lumen, limes, scola scalaque: libra
> consilii, liber eloquii, lumen rationis,
> limes honestatis, scola morum, scala salutis (103–7)
>
> He's whetstone, dower, flower, and dew: religion's file,
> Faith's dowry, flower of church, and dogma's dew;
> A balance, book, light, path, and school and steps:

The scale of counsel, book of eloquence, the light
Of reason, honour's path, a moral school, and step of health.

He is sent on a mission to Britain, where he will have to face beer:

> nescio quod Stigie monstrum conforme paludi –
> ceruisiam plerique uocant. Nil spissius illa
> dum bibitur, nil clarius est dum mingitur, unde
> constat quod multas feces in uentre relinquit[80] (253–6)

> A hellish brew of mud-like hue
> That they call beer is rather queer:
> For though it's thick when in the glass,
> You'll find that when you come to pass
> Water, there is nothing thinner
> Than that which comes out from your inner
> Parts. You see, it must be true,
> It left the dregs inside of you.

When crossing the Channel he absentmindedly forgets the corporal for the Mass, and confidently walks across the water to retrieve it; this miracle is explained in terms of natural physics. On arrival in Britain he delivers a long sermon on creation, fall and salvation, and makes many converts. An old blind and deaf woman shouts at Birin as though he were deaf himself. After his death he works many miracles, and we find one of Henry's favourite topoi, the mutually attested miracles:

> ceci claudos ibi cernere possunt
> currentes, surdi mutos audire loquentes (653–4)

> The blind can see the cripples run,
> The deaf can hear the dumb exchanging speech.

This life also contains examples of Henry's ability to employ proverbs ('consilium-que minus dat consultatio maior' [The more consultation, the less good advice.], 'articulus compellit anum trottare' [Need makes an old wife trot.]) in amusingly apposite circumstances.

Guthlac

Henry dedicated his life of Guthlac to Henry, abbot of Croyland; it consists of 1669 hexameters.[81]

Prenatal signs of Guthlac's sanctity; interpretation of his name:

> Dictus ibi Guthlacus, id est, interprete lingua
> Anglorum, 'Belli munus' (56–7)

> Named Guthlac, meaning, by its English roots,
> 'The gift of war' . . .

After early life as a (just) bandit, he reforms and accepts the tonsure at a monastery, where he becomes proficient in learning. He decides to become a hermit (Henry explains the different merits of monastic and heremitical lives), and takes up residence on the island of Croyland. He dispels the resident demons, and from then on the Devil wages a constant vendetta against him: the physical appearance of demons and their animal noises. Satan's attempts to trick Guthlac and to have him killed are foiled; he tries to take him to hell, but is thwarted on its brink by Bartholemew. Guthlac addresses the demons on the philosophical reasons for Satan's fall. Like many saints celebrated by Henry, he had a close rapport with animals (for example, crows bring back a lost glove), which Guthlac himself explains:

> Cui sanctus, 'Mundum fugientibus omnia cedunt
> ad solamen', ait, 'confortandisque ferarum
> commansuescit eis feritas auiumque uolatus' (986–8)

> 'To those who leave the world,' said Guthlac then,
> 'All creatures offer solace: for their aid
> The beasts grow mild and flights of birds are tame.'

He comforts King Ethelbald in his exile. His final fever is described by the simile of a marsh drying up, and his death is explained in medical terms. His flesh says farewell to his spirit.

Edmund

The life of Edmund (perhaps intended for Bury St Edmunds, though it lacks a preface) consists of 598 lines in elegiacs.[82] It follows Abbo of Fleury's life closely, with an extra miracle.

Prenatal signs of Edmund's sanctity; his name ('et mundus') signifies purity; his virtues as a king. Satan fails to subvert him and sends the Danes Ynguar and Ubba; when Edmund refuses to submit to them they use his body as target practice and then hide his head. Like deer afraid to come out of hiding even when the wolf has gone, the English are slow to emerge, but eventually are led to the king's head (which calls out 'Here, here' to them), guarded by a wolf. Many miracles occur at Edmund's burialplace, including the mutually attested ones:

> Contractum, mutum cecus surdus uidet, audit
> ire, loqui: nouitas est utrobique duplex (566–7)

> The blind and deaf behold and hear the lame
> And mute both walk and speak, a strange exchange.

The life is followed in the manuscript by two hymns to Edmund.

Fremund

The life of King Fremund, in 546 hexameters, is one of the earliest accounts of this obscure and possibly fictional saint.[83]

The birth of Fremund ('freta mundi . . . migret') to a childless couple is foretold by a three-day old infant. He becomes king and Henry debates whether *ius* or *pietas* dominate more in him. He abdicates in order to become a hermit on a fantastic island. He rejects the devil's temptation to return to his filial and royal 'duty', but responds to his parents' request for help against Edmund's murderers, Ynguar and Ubba. An angel makes his force appear a thousand times larger and he defeats the Danes, although still outnumbered two to one. He is killed by a traitor Oswi, but forgives him. Three infirm women find his tomb, which is also revealed by a sow and her litter. There are two accounts of mutually attested cures. A pilgrim in Jerusalem is told three times to return home to reveal Fremund's burialplace. News of the burial is taken to Birin at Dorchester. Various miracles occur.

Hugh of Lincoln

Hugh, bishop of Lincoln (d. 1200), was canonized in 1220; Henry's verse life, in 1306 hexameters, was written shortly after and follows the *Magna Vita* by Adam of Eynsham.[84]

It begins in high style, imitating Virgil:

> Arma virumque cano, quo judice nec caro cara
> nec mundus mundus fuit, abscissisque duabus
> alis, non potuit antiquus serpere serpens (1–3)

> The arms and man I sing, to whose purview
> The flesh was cheap, the world impure. Both wings
> Cut off, the ancient serpent lost its threat.

His birth in Burgundy, where he enters a monastery. He resists the advances of a beautiful woman (who is described in rhetorical style), and decides to avoid all women by becoming a Carthusian. He is sent to take charge of the Carthusian house at Witham in England. He has many dealings with King Henry II, and always succeeds in bringing him onto the side of the church. He is made bishop of Lincoln. From early days he had befriended animals:

> Non homines solum vel bruta domestica nutrit:
> Curam nempe gerit avium curamque ferarum,
> Et mansuetus eas sibi commansuescere sentit, (344–6)

> Not men alone but farmyard beasts he fed;
> He cared for birds, wild animals as well.
> A gentle man, he felt their gentleness.

and later had a pet hedge-sparrow and, at Lincoln, a swan. Great attention is paid in the poem to his rebuilding of Lincoln Cathedral and the symbolism of its architecture.[85] Hugh's final disease is described in medical terms, as is the miraculous cure of a knight's cancer.

Thomas Becket

The Cambridge manuscript of Henry's poems contains four poems on Becket. The Short Life, 270 lines of elegiacs, is certainly in Henry's style;[86] after general praise of the saint it recounts his history from the Council of Northampton, his exile, the reconciliation, the murder (with a dialogue with the murderers), and a brief mention of the miracles at the tomb. The *Revelationes post martirium*, 192 lines of elegiacs, is also in Henry's distinctive manner;[87] after lamentation on the murder, it recounts several visions and miracles that followed, including the restoration of a eunuch's testicles.[88]

The first two entries in the manuscript, on the life and translation of Becket, are really a single poem in 1870 hexameters.[89] Henry's authorship is far from certain;[90] it is as much a celebration of Stephen Langton as of Becket.

1–769 life and passion of Becket, beginning with his birth in London. (This section is almost a verbatim verse rendering of John of Salisbury's prose life.)
770–827 world events and disasters after Becket's death.
828–1585 the quarrel between King John and Stephen Langton, the Interdict, reconcilation with Innocent III, and England's subjection to the papacy. Parallels between Becket and Langton are drawn in almost typological fashion.[91]
1586–870 the translation of Becket's relics to the High Altar of Canterbury in 1220, under Langton's direction, followed by an elaborate account of the banquet afterwards.

Crispin and Crispinian

This short life describes the early martyrs in Gaul, their poverty (when they supported themselves as shoemakers, whose patrons they became) and their obduracy under torture.[92]

Francis of Assisi

Henry's longest life is the *Vita Francisci*; it consists of 2585 hexameters, divided into fourteen books in order to bear the acrostic dedication to GREGORIUS NONUS.[93] It is based directly on the first *Vita* by Thomas of Celano (1228), written shortly after Francis' canonization.[94] Henry has provided many poetic expansions and embellishments.

Books I-III. Francis follows his father, a dishonest merchant, but after a fever (medically described) begins to repent; his Senses and Reason debate within him, and he hesitates between virtue and evil. He plans to join a merchant going to Apulia, but a dream causes another repentance. He struggles with the seven deadly sins and their family (all neatly linked) and is given spiritual armour. He sells the merchant's goods and tries to give the proceeds to a church. He lives in poverty and his old friends think him mad. He comes out of hiding to face his father, who beats him and locks him up, but his mother frees him. He again faces his father and hands over the hidden money. He renounces all his rights and departs, dressed in pauper's clothes.

Books IV-V. Enjoying a crisp winter day he walks along singing, and is set on by robbers, who, finding him emptyhanded, throw him into a snowdrift. This illustrates the falsity of Juvenal's line 'cantabit vacuus coram latrone viator'.[95] During Spring run-off he is forced to stay in an inhospitable monastery. He cures lepers and repents of his rudeness to a beggar. He repairs his old church (now occupied by holy women) and rebuilds the church at Assisi. He decides to follow the unglossed words of the Gospels:

> In plerisque tamen valet allegoria, sed ipsam
> Littera praecellit, ubi nulla parabola mentem
> Palliat auctoris, sed rem sua verba loquuntur (5.26–8)

> Though allegory counts, the literal
> Must take first place, where no decoding masks
> The author's mind: the words mean what they say.

Dressed in a simple tunic with a cross, Francis preaches, though himself untaught. He has a vision of his future Order, and Henry offers encouragement.

Books VI-VIII. The disciples, now twelve in all, miraculously reassemble at Francis' prayer. (Henry foresees the end of the world as prophesied by Joachim of Fiore.) Francis goes to Rome to have his newly written rule confirmed by Innocent III.[96] The friars, called Minors, go out to preach against heresy; they are miraculously fed. Francis teaches them to pray; they have a vision of a chariot and of Francis on a cross. He is penitent for taking meat during sickness. He wants to seek martyrdom by going to preach to the Saracens but is needed to combat heresy at home. He stows away on a ship; during a storm and famine he miraculously feeds the sailors and the storm subsides. After several attempts he reaches Damietta, which is under siege; he crosses the Nile and is beaten by the Saracens; their king admires him and he is allowed to teach monotheism (!) and Christian doctrine. They are impressed but he has no assistance to convert them all, and so returns. He persuades animals and birds to praise God.

Books IX-XI. He silences swallows whose cries make him inaudible. He releases a hare and a fish. When he is sick God changes water into wine to cure him. Miraculous cures: he and three friars cure a possessed woman by drawing her into the shape of a cross. He preaches before the new pope Honorius:

> Non solum lingua loquitur sed corpore toto
> Nutibus et signis, extraque movetur ut intus,
> Et motus artis per motos explicat artus (10.12–14)

> He speaks not only with his tongue: with nods
> And signs, his whole physique (both in and out)
> Is moved; his moving limbs display his mind.

In Florence he prophesies that Hugelino will be Pope (= Gregory IX). He rebukes a friar for disbelieving a pauper; he rescues a sheep and nuns send him a tunic from its wool. His 'simplicitas clemens': all creatures, including the 'artis ficta', should worship God. His appearance and character. He builds a Christmas creche, and miracles occur there.

Books XII-XIV. After eighteen years ministry he is told that he will die in two years; he opens the bible and finds the description of the crucifixion. He feels Christ's wounds, and suffers, especially in the eyes. Attempted cures are unsuccessful and the rest of his body starts to fail. He feels death is near and returns to Assisi. He comforts the friars and says farewell, and dies; Christ's stigmata are seen on him. Cures (some mutually attested) occur at his tomb. Pope Gregory visits his sepulchre and preaches. Francis is canonized.

Other religious poems

In 1241 Louis IX displayed in Paris the relics of the Crucifixion that he had obtained from Jerusalem. Henry celebrated the events in a poem of 427 lines, in his 'difficult' style.[97]

After praise of Paris (a more suitable home for the relics than Jerusalem) and Louis, Henry explains the symbolism of the relics. For example, the perfect circle of thorns symbolizes the heavenly kingdom. The Cross is a complex mathematical symbol of triangle, quadruplex and perpendicular; also, Death and Life contend on the battleground of the Cross, under Justice as umpire. The wood of the spear is the Church, the iron tip Christ, and the blood and water are the sacrament. Louis is urged to a six-year programme to stamp out blasphemy: those who swear by the relics should be informed on, even by relations, and the money from fines should be used to help the poor.

Other poems include a celebration of All Saints, from angels to widows, in 102 lines,[98] and an explanation of the nature of the star of the Epiphany. A verse sermon placed in the mouth of St Andrew, as he hung from his cross, demonstrates to the Achaians (by philosophical methods and terminology, in the manner of Guthlac preaching to the demons) that the world was created by one God. Somewhat longer (about 500 hexameters) is a versification of a prophecy by Hildegard of Bingen;[99] Matthew Paris has headed the poem 'de novis fratribus', but in the poem as in the original the pale-cheeked emissaries of Satan, fanatically poor and chaste, are probably to be interpreted as Cathars. Like many of Henry's poems, the style is remarkably prosaic, following the original closely:[100]

> Heus, mons esse Syon debetis, nam benedicti
> et consignati sanctis celestibus estis;
> inde quod essetis habitacula sancta decebat
> que thus et mirram redolerent, in quibus esset
> esse beneplacitum Domino. Nec talia certe
> estis, sed reuocat lasciuia uos puerilis

> Mount Sion you should be, for you are blest
> And have a place among the heavenly saints.
> So holy habitations you should be
> Which smell of scent and myrrh, for that would be
> A pleasing gift for God, but you're not such,
> For youthful lechery has called you back.

In a Peterborough catalogue Henry is credited with 'Tropi de beata Virgine'. Several poems in the Cambridge manuscript answer this description, including two on the joys of the Virgin and also 'Anna partu solvitur'.[101] The latter is also found in Rawlinson C. 510,[102] which also contains a poem to the Virgin, 'Ave maris stella vera mellis stilla', which is ascribed in another manuscript, Digby 172, to 'M. Henricus versificator magnus'.[103]

Grammar, rhetoric, philosophy, law

Like John of Garland, Henry wrote versified grammars. In 161 lines he versified the opening of Donatus' *Ars minor* on parts of speech, using his very literal style:[104]

> Nomen cum casu communiter aut proprie rem
> aut corpus signat (2–3; ed. reads *significat*)

> A noun and case can designate a thing
> Or person, commonly or properly.

Unlike Garland, he approved of the *Graecismus* and *Doctrinale*, and his *Comoda grammatice* reflects this.[105] It is over 2200 lines long, and was written some time after 1241; it has a long section of *equivoca* or *differentiae* in the manner of Serlo of Wilton and Richard Pluto.[106]

Another poem that falls under the heading of grammar or education is the *Antavianus* ('de apologis Auiani');[107] this retells nine fables of Avianus, using elegiacs, like the original. The stories are 'medievalized' by the use of figures such as *distributio* and a joke about German beer-drinking, when the pine-tree says:

> Nautis, Hispanis, Siculis, Francis, Alemannis
> sum malus, thus, pix, hasta ciphusque simul (7.5–6)

> I'm mast for sailors, scent for Spain, for France
> A spear; for Sicily I'm pitch; I'm mug
> For Germans' beer.

One of Henry's most extraordinary feats was his versification of Aristotle's newly discovered treatise on *Generation and Corruption*.[108] From the prologue, which is in rhythmical verse, it is clear that this was delivered to a university audience (perhaps Oxford) as part of the kind of verse competition discussed below. It is a very literal rendering of the prose, as the following shows:

> Antiqui dicunt hii quod generacio simplex
> alterat; hii quod non. Qui silicet omne quid unum
> dicunt, ex uno generantes omnia, restat
> ipsis dicendum quoniam generacio simplex
> alterat[109]

> Some ancients say that generation's change:
> Some disagree. Now those that say all's one,
> Producing all from this, must now conclude
> That simple generation's change.

Images from *Generation and Corruption* are common in Henry's other poems. In the *Vita Francisci* we read that a well-fed body would be too costly if it resulted in mental deterioration:

> constaret nimii generatio carnis
> si generaretur per eam corruptio mentis[110] (3.30–1)

> The generation of the flesh would cost
> Too much, if mind's decay ensued.

Henry's facility at versification is nowhere more evident than in his two summaries of canon law, one of Gratian's *Decretum*, the other of the collection of *Decretals* (the *Liber extra*) compiled for Gregory IX in 1234.[111] The second part of Gratian's *Decretum* (1139–55) consisted of thirty-six *causae* on different topics of canon law; each *causa* contains several *questiones*, 172 in all. Henry's poem gives the answer to each *questio* in a single line of verse; the initial letters of each line spell out, in acrostic, a five-line poem, which is given at the beginning. Thus, the sixth word in the poem is *ortus*, showing that *Causa* 6 had five *questiones*, as follows:

> Omnes infames sileant et crimine noti.
> Replicet ut presul non inde notabitur actor.
> Testis vel iudex non est aliunde petendus.
> Unius ecclesie reprimet tamen altera lites.
> Si cadat accusans reus ultra non teneatur.

> The suspect, marked by crime, should hold their tongue.
> Though bishop counter, plaintiff won't be blamed.
> No judge or witness should be sought elsewhere.
> One church's claim will quash another's writ.
> If plaintiff yields, defendant's free to go.

Knowledge of the short poem would enable one to remember the order of the *causae* and the number of *questiones* in each, and, by providing the initial letter to the line, would aid one in remembering the summary answer.[112]

The collection of *Decretals* compiled under Gregory IX consists of five books, each divided into *rubricae*; each *rubrica* contains a number of decretals, totalling nearly two thousand. Henry's mnemonic poem on the *Decretals* takes the form of a satire on Roman venality (with the theme 'give, give !'). Its mnemonic character is purely visual: some words are given rubric initials, and by counting the letters between these initials one finds the number of decretals in that rubric. Thus, it indicates only the number of decretals, not their contents.

Debates, verse competitions, public poetry

Verse debate can be divided into two types: (a) both halves are written by the same person, to exploit an interesting contrast (e.g. Cluniac-Cistercian, Winter-Summer); (b) the poet is on one side only, and presents his case as a partisan. Henry practised both types.

A debate between the city of Rome and Innocent III concerns the rival claims to the Empire of the elected but deposed Otto IV (supported by the city) and the young Frederick II (supported by Pope Innocent); it consists of 401 hexameters, full of logical terms and arguments.[113] The bitter dispute is referred to a General Council, which says that it has no power to depose the pope (as the city had requested) but insists that Otto be restored. As the Lateran Council of 1215 in fact decided in favour of Frederick, the poem must have been written before this date.

In the Cambridge manuscript there are two debates between a *clericus* and a *miles* on the well-worn theme of their superiority as lovers.[114] Only the second is ascribed by Matthew Paris to Henry. The first is in hexameters (*caudati* in the first part), in which each states his case; the clerk calls on 'ladies' (*domine*) to judge, and lines 51–60 seem to be the judgment, with no winner. The second poem, in elegiacs, is written from a third-person perspective; the contestants make their case before a single 'lady' (*domina*); the knight speaks first, and the clerk turns his words against him; judgment is deferred. The manner of both poems is artificial and argumentative, but not at all in Henry's manner in other debates. On the other hand, we have Matthew's testimony for Henry's authorship of the second debate.

We turn now to competitions in which the poet is a partisan. We have William Fitzstephen's testimony to public verse contests in London schools:[115]

> Pueri diversarum scholarum versibus inter se conrixantur; aut de principiis artis grammaticae vel regulis praeteritorum vel supinorum contendunt. Sunt alii qui in epigrammatibus, rhythmis, et metris, utuntur vetere illa triviali dicacitate; licentia Fescennina socios suppressis nominibus liberius lacerant; loedorias jaculantur et scommata; salibus Socraticis sociorum vel forte majorum, vitia tangunt, vel mordacius dente rodunt Theonino audacibus dithyrambis

> Boys from different schools compete in verses; they debate about the principles of grammar or the rules for preterites or supines. Some employ the well-established loquacity of the trivium in epigrams, rhythms and metres; with Fescennine licence they excoriate their fellows freely (though under concealed names); they hurl abuse and taunts; with Socratic witticisms they touch on the faults of their peers or even of their superiors, or more bitingly, with Theonine tooth, they tear with daring dithyrambs.

Adults seem to have entertained their audiences in similar ways.[116] We lack Henry's share of the great flyting with Michael of Cornwall in 1254–5,[117] but his attack on Bordo and Siler gives a good example of the style. This was a staged contest before Michael, bishop of Angers (sometime between 1240 and 1260).[118]

Henry says that he has been presumptuously challenged by John Bordo and Peter Siler. He defends himself against charges of a hunched back, association with jesters, blindness, drunkenness and unsociability. His counterattack condemns his opponents for temerity, plagiarism and lack of skill. He relies especially on wordplay. Bordo (*bordo*) is first a burro or donkey; his brother Peter, a mule, may or may not be of the same species. Later Bordo is a bee or horsefly. Peter Siler (rock + willow) is both hard and soft; if he is not pliable enough to bind barrels, he must be used as a broom:

> Molles sunt sileres, set petre sunt rigide res . . . (287)
> O uimen natum nobis, Siler, ad famulatum,
> Fraude dolos uincis nec uini dolia uincis . . .
> aut suberis dominis aut fies scopa latrinis (309–13)

> A willow's soft enough but stones are hard and tough . . .
> O willow-withy, meant for human betterment,
> You're only good at lies but not for barrel-ties . . .
> You'll bend, or have to clean the floor of the latrine.

Peter is suffering from leprosy, caused by sexual indulgence; Bordo has a fat prebend and refuses to serve Henry, his former master. His curacy of Bazoches is a disaster; he is a doctor of medicine, but unable to cure Peter. First Bordo, then Peter, admit their defeat, as their tears show.

In *Bordo-Siler* Henry employs hexameter rhyme in various patterns; he does not come close to Michael of Cornwall's virtuosity with metre, but finding 220 rhymes on *-ere* was certainly a feat.[119]

We also have a forty-line fragment of a similar flyting by Henry (probably originally about ninety lines) against William of Laval, beginning with elegi collaterales:[120]

> Nos tua barbaries dampnat, Willelme, latinos,
> Cordis enim caries liuida prodit in os
>
> Your crude and boorish ways condemn our Latin race;
> Your rotten heart betrays its malice in your face.

It continues in Leonini unisoni, in groups of from four to eight lines. Many of the insults (with the same rhymes) are in Michael of Cornwall.[121]

Competition did not necessarily take the form of insults. We have already mentioned that the versification of *Generation and Corruption* was part of a verse competition, heard before a university audience, from whom Henry pleads for a fair hearing:

> rogo supplex obnixius
> ut tua iurisdictio,
> qua nichil iuridicius,
> vel amore vel odio
> partis flectetur neutrius
> sed consistat in medio[122] (9–14)
>
> I humbly beg this court on bended knee
> That you maintain impartiality.
> Your skill in law is peerless,
> So favour-free and fearless,
> Defer to neither part
> But always stand apart.

Henry used his talents as a poetic debater in the service of others, often at the papal curia (though this could be a fiction). As these poems are not connected with England, I mention them only briefly.[123] On behalf of (and partly in the persona of) Simon de Sully, archbishop of Bourges, he presented the claim of Bourges over Bourdeaux, a claim settled by the curia in 1232. He writes in the persona of the Dean of Maastricht, who has wrongfully been expelled from his church. In the persona of the abbot of Lorsch he claims that he has been deprived of his castle of Starkenburg, by the connivance of the archbishop of Mainz. In this context we might also place Henry's poem to the pope in favour of the candidacy of John Blund, archbishop-elect of Canterbury (1232),[124] and two poems on behalf of bishop Milo, defending him against charges of maladministration (there are also two poems to Milo).

Occasional and personal poems[125]

There are many short poems, of which only a few (particularly those relating to England) can be mentioned. Henry's mannerisms, especially the onomastic wordplay and analytical argumentation, are evident in most of them. He wrote about the removal of Salisbury Cathedral from Old Sarum to its present site: the old position on a hill hurt one's eyes, ear, heart and liberty (each fully explained), so its move into the valley was essential. Dean Ham of York (died 1220) is caught by the hook of death ('ab hamo mortis'). Eustace of Falconberg, whose election as bishop of London in 1221 was under dispute, is well-standing (*eu* + *statio*).

Peter des Roches (de Rupibus), bishop of Winchester (and dedicatee of the *Vita Birini*), is the foundation and capstone of his church:

> cur petra dicare, cur et de rupibus, a re
> non a fortuna provenit (No. 155, 2–3)

> You're named a 'rock' and from 'des Roches'
> For cause, and not by chance . . .

Henry wrote several poems to or about the courtier Robert Passelewe, later bishop of Chichester, who is 'dew, spring, incense' (*ros* + *ver* + *thus*), and who passes over the water (*transgressor aque, migrans laticem* = 'passa l'eau'), and at his death

> Robertus aquas transiens
> portum salutis attigit (No. 148, 7–8)

> Robert now has crossed the seas
> And reached salvation's port.

Fulk Bassett, bishop of London (and patron of John of Garland), is a support ('fulcit enim fulco', *bas* + *sita*). A begging letter to Richard Marsh, bishop of Durham, has a curious tone ('parcus, non cupidus; largus, non prodigus'), and hints that Henry has pleaded for the bishop and so earned the displeasure of the prior and convent; this is interesting in view of Hotoft's poem on him.[126]

Ralph Neville, bishop of Chichester, is praised for his *ius* and *pietas* in phrases reminiscent of the *Vita Fremundi*. William of York (Eboracum) is denoted by the properties of ivory ('proprietas eboris, eboris si propria noris'). There are two poems to Stephen Langton, archbishop of Canterbury, and one to the papal legate Pandulph ('totus dulcedine fusus'). Henry had a lot of fun with Geoffrey Bocland's name, playing on *gaude, fri* (free), *līber* (book), *līber* (free), and *land*:

Liberat a viciis liber omnes, liber es ergo,
    cum sis de Bocland, de regione libri.
A viciis igitur liber, gaudere teneris:
    ex hoc Gaufridi nomen et omen habes (No. 42, 1–4)

Books free all men from vice, so you are free,
    Since you're from Bocland, region of the book,
So, being free from vice, you must rejoice.
    From 'Geoffrey' comes your name and destiny.

An unidentified John (not necessarily the king) is praised for his name, which means 'gratia divina'.

Although we cannot mention all the continental figures to whom Henry addressed poems, we should note that there are three to the Emperor Frederick II (*fride* = *pax*, *ric* = *regnum*) from Henry (*Henris* = *in risu*).[127] In one, as noted above, he urges the codification of civil law; in another he immodestly describes himself as 'poesis ego supremus in orbe professor' (B.103).

Finally among the occasional poems, remembering the school and university context of much of Henry's writing (particularly the flytings), we should mention two student poems asking for suspension of classes for Easter and Christmas vacations ('Ferienlieder'), that are preserved among Henry's poems and could be his, and also one addressed to someone graduating in Canon Law.[128]

Summary

Henry began his writing career before 1215,[129] and still engaged in debate with Michael of Cornwall in 1255; he continued to receive payments from the royal exchequer after 1260.[130] He was active in England, France, Italy, and possibly Germany; he is charged with being a *solivagus* by Siler and Bordo, and defends himself by saying that he travels to collect poems:

Vt meritis fame per secula lauder et a me
Discatis scioli michi nota poemata soli
(Que minus attente didicistis), meque docente
Vt sapiant homines terrarum uisito fines (167–70)

Some lasting fame to earn, and so you too can learn,
Young dunces, poems known to me and me alone
(You haven't learned them quite), and so that others might
Through me in wisdom grow, to foreign lands I go.

His literary range is equally wide. His saints' lives show a facility for lucid narrative, but he also shows an interest in versifying apparently untractable material; frequently he employs both styles, by including in the saints' lives passages of medical, philosophical or logical technical language. He is adept, as he tells us, at converting 'old prose into new poems', and at adapting a classical tag or proverb into a new context. He can find a central image (such as the site of Old Sarum, or the etymology of a name), and build a poem round it.

For most his poems he uses unrhymed hexameters and elegiacs, but in his vituperative verse (Bordo-Siler, William of Laval) he uses various complexes of Leonine rhymes. This polemic style, though not entirely new to Anglo-Latin,[131] was fully developed by Henry and Michael of Cornwall, and became a marked feature of the political poetry of the thirteenth and fourteenth centuries. Henry employs rhythmical verse for hymns and for the introductions to some long poems (Generation and Corruption, Bourges–Bordeaux). In a rhythmical poem to Ralph Neville, he employs a run-over rhyme:[132]

> O qui flos es Anglicorum
> quorum sicut sedas placita
> ita tibi regis et illorum
> lorum regendum subigitur (No. 40, 1–4)

> You who of the English flower
> Now are, just as you confer ease
> On pleas, so rule of them and king's
> Things is passed to you to handle.

(The stumbling rhythm produced by this rhyme scheme is more than fully reflected in my translation).

He uses this again in the prologue to Bourges–Bordeaux. The device is a striking feature of Michael of Cornwall's hexameters. Henry's interest in metre is illustrated by the story that he obtained papal permission to turn amphimacri (*caritas, unitas, trinitas*) into anapaests, so that they would fit into dactylic verse.[133] He was, in every sense, a poet's poet.

Michael of Cornwall

Michael of Cornwall – 'Merry Michael', as Camden calls him – suffers from polyonymous anonymity: he has many names but no identity. He is usually surnamed 'Cornubiensis'; his religious poem is headed 'Magister Michael le Poter de Cornubia'; to the antiquarians he was 'Michael Blaunpayn'.[134] He must have been a poet of some stature, but only three works can definitely be assigned to him: the flyting with Henry of Avranches, a short religious poem, and an admonition to the doctors attending John Mansel's broken leg.[135]

For verbal wit and metrical virtuosity, the *Versus contra Henricum Abrincensem* surpass anything yet written in Anglo-Latin.[136] They are Michael's three parts of a public verse contest against Henry of Avranches held in 1254–5.[137]

Part I (1–368). (Delivered before the abbot of Westminster and the dean of St Paul's, London, in Spring 1254, and again later in the same summer at Somersham in Huntingdon-shire, before the bishop of Ely and the clergy of Cambridge University).

Why do you rebuke me ? You are a good poet, but by exalting yourself you put me down. We are both good and here to entertain our patrons. You are older and have more strength, but cannot match me in philosophy:

> Si maior me sis, quia sit magis ipsa poesis
> Nota tibi, non es adeo tamen ad raciones
> Promptus Aristotilis ut ego, liquet unde tibi lis (37–9)

> In verse (because you know it) you leave me far behind,
> But Aristotle's logic confounds your feeble mind:
> At this I am the quicker – and that is why you bicker.

You call me 'Cornish goat', but the term suits Normans better. Metres are worthless; I am a philosopher. You charge me with plagiarism:

> Inproperas nobis et non semel, immo modo bis
> Quod vatum versus furamur (96–97)

> You've criticized me wrongly not only once but twice
> For stealing poets' verses.

You have no reason to be proud, but it is the Norman way. You will have to teach grammar, though you don't know arts or grammar well:

> Ignorans artes pueros elementa docebis
> Declinans partes, nec nobis inde nocebis;
> Immo nec ars neque pars clero probat esse probum te.
> Dic: 'Dominus que pars ?' Raciones sunt michi prompte (191–4)

> In arts you are a numbskull, you'll end up teaching boys
> To parse their Latin grammar (that won't upset my poise).
> But neither art nor grammar will prove you're up to scratch.
> 'What part of speech is "Master" ?' In quickness I'm your match.

Arthur honoured Cornwall as invincible, unlike Normandy. You are a foreigner. Your name means 'into laughter'.[138] Like me you are shortsighted, but I have a good memory:

> Virtus visiva tibi deficit amodo, necnon
> Vis memorativa; michi debilis illa, sed hec non (255–6)

> Your eyesight now is failing, your memory is poor;
> My own eyes, too, are ailing, but my mind's quite secure.

You recited frivolities in the royal court:

> In domini regis tua frivola cur legis aula,
> Cui rudis ipsa gregis satis esset ydonea caula ? (275–6)

> Your drivel isn't fitting within the royal hall:
> You really should be sitting inside a cattle stall.

You used to be a swineherd and now hang thieves and clean sewers:

> Contra me cur es, latebras qui queris opacas,
> Suspendens fures ville purgansque cloacas,
> Qui nutrire sues et porcos sepe solebas ? (311–13)

Your rivalry defies belief: you lurk in shady lanes,
You hang the borough's petty thief and clean the sewage drains.
You used to be a farmhand and feed the hogs and swine.

You should yield and write 'Tu autem'.[139]

Part II (369–626). (On the Friday after the Purification of the Virgin, 5 February 1255, before Hugh Mortimer, official of the archbishop of Canterbury, at St Mary-le-Bow in London).
Why are you bothering me again ? (559 you have already lost once). You and your thieving companions, including Nicholas,[140] deserve to hang for breaking into my chest and stealing verses and books and other things. I appeal to the fair judge Hugh (frequently praised in this section; his name means 'huc go, i.e. come here'). Henry has charged me falsely; he and his companion should feed the crows. Henry deals in pitch, not peace. Let him try to read without a candle and hear his mistakes:

> Labiis labetur iniquis
> Et leget acsi sit sua littera tota litura.
> Sepeque transmisit sua sic in iurgia iura,
> In loculos oculos, in crimina carmina transfert,
> In scopulos populos, cui musas ipse Sathan fert (506–10)

> He'll stumble in his speech:
> He'll read as if the letter were all a silly scrawl;
> He'll often spell out 'righteous' as if it read as 'brawl';
> He'll turn 'eyes' into 'boxes' and 'songs' as 'sins' abuse;
> He'll turn 'folk' into 'pebbles', for Satan is his muse.

You asked for a truce, Henry, but broke it; you must be deleted from the book of life. You gave the queen's robe to a whore:

> Rustice stulte, sine sensu quid proposuisti,
> Robam regine meretrici quando dedisti ? (571–2)

> You boorish, senseless peasant, what were you planning for
> In giving as a present the queen's dress to a whore ?

593–626 run-over rhyme, with indiscriminate insults.

Part III (627–1276). (Delivered later in 1255, before Aymer de Valence, bishop-elect of Winchester, and the bishop of Rochester.)
You are a pseudopoet, not an archpoet, and know more about whores than metres. Devil's spawn, you will sell anything. You wander in various lands; you plant your poems among mine. You claim to make old new, saying that my themes are trite:

> Res agito tritas, ut dicis, nilque tenellum,
> Et quando recitas vetus incipit esse novellum.
> Quis tua fert opera per fines sive per horas,
> In nova tam vetera metra dum transferre laboras ?[141] (693–6)

> You say my themes are jaded and offer nothing fresh,
> But when you treat what's faded, it shines (so you profess).
> But who can bear your prating, from any point of view,
> When you strive in translating old poems into new ?

You say you taught me rhetoric. You and Colin Smhud stole my thirty-years savings. Your appearance is indescribable, but your account of mine is unjustifiable. (823–922 insults by vocalic series).[142] You have been defeated twice already. Your own country provides nothing; you get everything from England:

> Nil tua propria dat tibi patria dulce, Chymera,
> Sola sed Anglia pocula, prandia donat et era (973–4)

> Look, your homeland, though your own land, gives you nothing sweet;
> Only England gives you drink and cash and food to eat.

You tried to ingratiate yourself with King Louis, who should give Normandy back to England. 1207–76 runover rhyme, concluding by wishing Henry in hell:

> O li- mes sceleris, celer hiis ad Tartara visis
> Vi sis conductus, ductus, fur, ad fora luctus (1275–6)

> O road of crime, this rhyme is done: may you soon be led,
> Dead, to hell, O thief, to place of grief, without relief.

How serious or factual is all this? Poetic abuse is a well-established literary convention, from classical times to Dunbar. The objects of the satire are equally standard: the victim's name, race, parentage, appearance, physical defects, lack of skill and knowledge, stinginess, gluttony, sexual habits, and so on; specific events are often mentioned. Is it all, then, a fiction, sustained solely for the sake of the contest, like the bragging of modern boxers? Certainly, allegations about parenthood probably have no more force than calling someone 'bastard' or 'whoreson'. Also, this would be a curious occasion on which to bring a serious charge of theft. On the other hand, to be effective the humour should have some correspondence to fact, however slight, and many details in Michael's poem do correspond to known facts about Henry's biography. His Norman birth is implied by his name; we know that he wrote for Henry III (Michael calls him 'hystrio regis') and Louis IX; his works include philosophy and grammar; in the Bordo-Siler poem he admits to being shortsighted, and he is never reticent about his talents. It is also true that there are many echoes of Henry's verses in Michael's poem which might substantiate a charge of plagiarism. It is even possible that he held some office that involved hanging thieves and civic sanitation. We will never know if Henry and Michael were once teacher and student, now bitter rivals, or simply skilled competitors who put on a good show for their audience.

The flavour of the polemic can best be observed by reading it out loud. There is wordplay in both Latin,

> Cur non mercaris mea carmina? Non metricaris
> Sed meretricaris. Meretrices cumque sequaris
> Que dant se caris et vilibus, igne secaris
> Luxurie (835–8)

> Why don't you buy my verses? You don't know how to scan
> But scandalize by whoring. To whores (whom any can

Enjoy, both high and lowly) to go when you began,
You burnt yourself on Venus.

and the vernaculars:

In maiestate non fidus es, immo malignus,
In *mauvestate* confidis carcere dignus (717–8)

One can't trust in your majesty, your evil will is plain;
In fact, you are a travesty, and ought to be in chains.

Ad quid grata canam ? Non est tibi gracia digna,
Immo *grucia*, nam non fers nisi verba maligna (731–2)

Why should I sing so graciously ? Such grace is not your style,
But grouching's more your destiny – your words are full of bile.

Rhymes of one word with two are common (*vide*: *tibi de, metricos*: *metri quos, soles*: *sol es*); words are sometimes divided in order to provide a rhyme (*pro crimine furti*: *urti-ca punctus* 617–8). The most striking feature of the three diatribes is the variety and complexity of dactylic rhyme schemes.[143] They become more complex in Part III, which eschews simple Leonines entirely. The one form that needs especial comment is the runover rhyme; we have seen one example of this in Henry of Avranches.[144] The final syllables of one line rhyme with the first of the next line; this resembles the Irish *devi*, and Michael's Cornish ancestry may be significant; on the other hand, there is a similar device in Reginald of Canterbury.[145] Here is an example:

Eris collector, lector non historiarum
Harum quas recito. Cito cessa, false relator !
Lator rumorum, morum corruptor, omissis
Missis, inmensis mensis vis sepe vacare (1224–47)

Money-grubber, you're no lover of such histories
As these I read, so now concede, you lying teller,
Seller of rumour, the soul's doomer, and then having missed
The eucharist at vast repast you want to sate yourself.

Michael used runover rhyme in a short, twenty-one line poem on the Fall of Man:[146]

Cur, homo, delinquis linquis-que Deum ? Tibi dira
Ira Dei restat. Est ad mala cor leue. Pruris,
Uris . . .

O man, why dost thou slide and set aside thy God ? For you the dire
Ire of God remains. To stains your heart is prone. You yearn
And burn . . .

In 1243 John Mansel, Henry III's counsellor, broke his leg while on military service. This no doubt painful but relatively trivial event earned two literary notices, one of which was a short poem by Michael of Cornwall.[147] In varying rhymed hexameters it threatens the surgeons with dire punishments if they do not do the job well:

> Et ne frangatur crus ipsum, neve trahatur
> tibia cum crure violenter, sit tibi cure (11–12)

> Your constant care should be his leg, lest it suffer fraction,
> And make quite sure his tibia is not pulled out in traction.

Matthew Paris

Matthew Paris, monk of St Albans (d. 1259), is of tangential interest for literary history; he was possibly the greatest, and certainly the most entertaining, English chronicler of the Middle Ages.[148] He was, as we have seen, the owner of a volume of Henry of Avranches' poems. He wrote a prose life of the two King Offas of Mercia, as Offa II was founder of St Albans, and lives of Stephen Langton and Edmund Rich of Abingdon.[149] He had a wide range of interests: world history (including the customs of the Tartars), scientific curiosities, heraldry, hagiography, art, architecture, and everyday happenings and gossip. He translated Ralph of Dunstable's verse life of St Alban into French verse.[150] At St Albans he was at the centre of news – Henry III himself made at least nine visits to the abbey during Matthew's time – and was, for a monk, widely travelled: he visited Norway to advise on Benedictine reforms. His attitudes are thoroughly English and, if not sophisticated, those of the 'man in the street'. He rarely misses a chance to denounce the avarice of Rome, even siding with Frederick II; he detested the giving of English benefices to Italians who, if they bothered to reside at all, could not speak English; he gleefully tells of the physical discomfiture of the papal legate in an Oxford riot against him. Like most people, he deplored the Poitevins in Queen Eleanor's entourage and Henry III's foreign advisers (though he seems to have liked the ones he actually met); he sided with the barons in their constitutional struggle but did not live to see the tragic outcome. He disliked the proliferation of new orders, and is one of the first Englishmen to denounce the mendicants as pious frauds: we have already noticed his interpretation of a poem by Henry of Avranches as an attack on the friars,[151] and Vaughan gives several examples of his journalistic adjustment of a story to suit his own prejudices.

The wars of the barons 1264–65

The whole of Henry III's reign, after he attained his majority in 1227, was one long constitutional crisis, a series of tugs-of-war with the barons over the Magna Carta of 1215. The Charter was refined and reaffirmed several times during the reign, but the issue (which could be expressed in constitutional or practical terms) came down to the simple question whether the king could choose his own advisers. The issue, for all its ultimate constitutional importance for the nature of the monarchy, might have remained purely theoretical, if the flames had not been fanned by xenophobia and nationalism. In the early days the reforming party, or 'constitutionalists', followed the ideas of Grosseteste and Adam Marsh, first Franciscan lector at Oxford (1247–49); Franciscans seem to have been very active in the constitutional party. In the 1250s the leadership of the barons fell to Simon de Montfort, earl of Leicester, brother-in-law of the king, son of the hero of Toulouse, and himself, ironically, a 'foreigner'.

'Pange plorans Anglia'

The dispute did not surface as a literary theme until the dramatic events of 1264–65. After the intervention of Louis IX in 1264, resulting in the Mise of Amiens, several barons left Simon's cause. Their defection is lamented in a short poem of twelve Goliardic stanzas, 'Pange plorans Anglia':[152]

> Sic res publica perit, terra desolatur,
> Invalescit extera gens et sublimatur;
> Vilescit vir incola et subpeditatur,
> Sustinet injurias – non est qui loquatur (4/1–4)

> The common weal is dying, the land is desolate,
> Our enemies are stronger and seek to dominate.
> The natives are downtrodden, reduced to servile state,
> They suffer depredations – there's none to remonstrate.

The poet calls on the Earl of Gloucester, Simon de Montfort, and Earl Bigot to finish what they have begun:

> Si velletis prosequi quod jam inchoastis
> Consequi poteritis quod desiderastis (11/1–2)

> If you'll just follow through on what you once began,
> You'll certainly achieve your long awaited plan.

Song of Lewes

Later in 1264 Simon's forces astonishingly – miraculously, some felt – defeated the far superior royalist army led by Prince Edward at Lewes in Sussex. The victory was celebrated in the Song of Lewes, consisting of 968 lines of Goliardic couplets with internal rhyme.[153] It was written shortly after the battle; its author, conjectured by Kingsford to have been a friar, was probably a member of Simon's household. The first part (1–484) describes the causes of the conflict, the campaign, and the battle. Like many political poems, it is loaded with Old Testament allusions. It begins with Psalm 44:2:

Calamus velociter scribe sic scribentis
Lingua laudabiliter te benedicentis (1–2)

Hear my tongue in benison with hosannas lauding,
Like a busy writer's pen, readily recording.

and compares Henry and Simon to Aman and Mardochaeus and to Goliath and David. It deplores the immoral behaviour of the royal army on the night before the battle, and attacks foreign mercenaries and merchants, arguing that the royal party is anti-English. It describes the battle and the capture of two kings (Henry and Richard of Cornwall) and their heirs, and then denounces the character of Prince Edward: his heraldic leopard indicates a lion's ferocity but a pard's unreliability. The second part (485–968) deals with the central constitutional dispute:

En radicem tangimus perturbacionis
Regni, de quo scribimus, et dissencionis (485–6)

Here I've touched the very heart of this new uprising,
Why the kingdom falls apart – this is my surmising.

The king's argument is presented first (489–526), that he would not be king if he were not free to choose his own advisers and that his enemies are trying to enslave him:

Quare regem fieri seruum machinantur
Qui suam minuere uolunt potestatem (514–5)

Thus to make the king a slave – this is their ambition
Who upon the royal power seek to place restrictions.

The constitutionalist reply (535–968) is that the king is below God; he is required to rule justly, and this can only be done with the advice of those affected, that is, the native people. Interspersed through the poem are specific demands: castles are to be entrusted to Englishmen; the justiciar, chancellor and treasurer are to be made responsible to Council; foreigners are to be dismissed, and escheats and wardships given to Englishmen:

Eschetis et gardiis suos honorare
Debet rex (297–8)

Englishmen should be endowed with escheats and wardships;
This the king is bound to do.

The king is to take the advice of the barons and the commonalty (*communitas*, *universitas*). The threat to the king's position is implicit:

Si princeps errauerit, debet reuocari,
Ab hiis, quos grauauerit iniuste, negari (731–2)

> If a prince from right has erred, this must be corrected,
> And by those he's wrongly hurt he should be rejected.

It is not surprising if the people rebel:

> Si uero studuerit suos degradare,
> Ordinem peruerterit, frustra queret quare
> Sibi non obtemper(e)nt ita perturbati –
> Immo, si sic facerent, essent insensati ! (965–8)

> If he tries to oust his own from their proper birthright
> (Social order overthrown), it is clear as daylight
> Why they won't his rule obey and rebel, for who so
> Would submit to tyranny would be fools to do so.

Hymns and offices

Within a year the tables were turned. In 1265, at the battle of Evesham, Simon was defeated and killed, and his body was mutilated. His death, far from suppressing his memory, raised him in popular imagination to the rank of martyr or even saint. The Melrose Chronicle records that the Franciscans

> ex optimis gestis eius venerandam de illo ediderunt hystoriam, scilicet lectiones, responsoria, versus, hymnum, et alia[154]

> From his outstanding deeds produced a venerable narrative, namely lessons, responses, verses, a hymn, and other things.

Fragments survive of a rhymed office in his honour (also mentioned in a Peterborough catalogue).[155] There are three hymns, and at the end of an Evesham collection of miracles is part of another hymn:

> Salve, Symon Montis-fortis,
> > totius flos milicie,
> Duras penas passus mortis,
> > pro statu gentis Anglie

> Simon, count of Leicester, flower of knighthood, hail !
> Death's dire pains you suffered that England might prevail.

The music for this has not survived, but it was given a setting as a motet along with another hymn:

> Miles Christi gloriose
> Symon certans in agone
> > pro iusticia

> Simon, Jesus' splendid knight,
> Fighting always for the right.

'Ubi fuit mons'

Another lament is found in the legal collection made by one Walter of Hyde; it consists of fifty-seven three-line stanzas:[156]

> Ubi fuit mons est vallis
> Et de colle fit iam callis,
> Heus et strata publica (1/1–3)

> Once a mountain, now a vale,
> From a hill you're now a trail,
> Now a public street.

It compares Simon to classical and biblical heroes, and also to Becket, even including his wearing of a hair-shirt; the death of Simon's standard-bearer, Guy de Balliol, is lamented, and the poet fears for England's fate:

> Ne subuertant alieni
> istam terram dolo pleni,
> super hanc considera (57/1–3)

> Lest the strangers, full of lies,
> bring this land to its demise,
> Take good thought for her.

The Anonymous of Ramsey

A badly damaged manuscript in the British Library, Cotton Otho D. viii, contains a prose chronicle on the Wars of the Barons, interspersed in which is a series of poems in variously rhymed hexameters. Both prose and poems are probably by the same author; the chronicle was written in Ramsey Abbey and addressed to 'sanctissime pater H.', probably Abbot Hugh of Solgrave (died 1267).[157] The poems include an attack on Queen Eleanor, verses on the famine of 1258 and on the Provisions of Oxford, an attack on Louis IX for his support of Henry (the Mise of Amiens), and a brief account of the causes of the conflict. Finally there is a much longer poem, consisting of 228 lines, incomplete in its present form. It is built round the contrast between the savage revenge of the royalists after Evesham and Simon's mercy to those he defeated:

> Illos salvavit Mons Fortis quos superavit:
> Carceribus dati sunt multi, non cruciati (1–2)

> De Montfort spared his conquered foes, confined
> In chains, but not to cruel death consigned.

It begins by reviewing events from the Battle of Lewes, the defection of Gilbert of Clare, and the fall of Kenilworth, to the final rout at Evesham where Simon's body was mutilated:

> Sic sic truncatus, sic omnino spoliatus
> Et sic castratus summos patitur cruciatus (99–100)

> Alas, dismembered, spoiled in every way,
> Truncated and castrated where he lay.

The second half of the poem laments the consequences of Evesham: the natural disasters, the depredations made at Ramsey by its former protege Berengarius, the revenge taken against London for its hostility to Queen Eleanor, and the disinheriting of the barons executed by Robert Waleran:

> Exhaeredati proceres sunt rege jubente
> Et male tractati, Waleran R. dicta ferente (200–1)

> The barons lost their title to their lands;
> Count Waleran fulfilled the king's commands.

The poem, in addition to being damaged and incomplete, is often very obscure. The poet uses Greek numerals to indicate the date, and is fond of onomastic wordplay: Kenilworth is town of dogs:

> Jure canum villa Keynworth vocatur et illa (49)

> This Kenilworth is rightly 'Dog-town' named.

Evesham is 'domus Evae'. When lamenting the death of someone from Holwell the poet names himself Michael:

> Spiritus in coelis ejus prece sit Michaelis (56)

> 'Now may he rest with God' is Michael's prayer.

Russell conjectured that he might be Michael of Cornwall.[158]

Thomas Wykes

In contrast with the pro-baronial stance of most writers, the chronicler Thomas Wykes was an ardent royalist.[159] In about 1272, just after Edward I became king, Wykes wrote a poem in his honour:[160]

> Eaduuardi regis Anglorum me pepulere
> Florida gesta loqui; pudor est famosa tacere (1–2)

> The prowess of King Edward made me write;
> To pass great deeds in silence is not right.

This reviews the career of Edward from the revolt of the barons –

> Anglorum proceres legem fingendo novellam
> Ubere de regno terram fecere misellam – (13–14)

The English barons feigned a new decree
And brought this fertile realm to misery.

the battles of Lewes and Evesham, and his subsequent campaigns in England, to his taking the cross in 1268 and his departure on crusade:

Impiger Eaduuardus devitans otia, signum
Mox crucis assumpsit, cupiens exsolvere dignum
Obsequium Christo, qui se liberavit ab isto
Turbine bellorum; sequitur pia turba virorum (45–8)

The tireless Edward took the Cross; he yearned,
Avoiding sloth, to do some useful turn
For Christ, who saved him from the storm of war.
A pious troop to him allegiance bore.

It concludes with an account of Edward's narrow escape from assassination in the Holy Land.

John of Wales

We should here make a brief mention of John of Wales, a Franciscan (died 1285).[161] His political views, derived mainly from ancient sources, seem to have coincided with those of the *Song of Lewes*. His works have not been published since the Renaissance. He is a prototype of the 'classicizing friars'.[162] as his preaching aids draw heavily on classical sources. His major works include the *Breviloquium de virtutibus antiquorum principum et philosophorum*, *Communiloquium* and *Compendiloquium*; the first was a source for Gower, the second for Chaucer. John was not, however, as once thought, the author of a commentary on the *Epistola Valerii* of Walter Map.

Metrical Historia Regum Angliae

We turn now briefly to another kind of historical poem, the *Historia Regum Angliae*, which consists of 646 lines of Leonini caudati.[163] Its purpose is summarized in its opening lines:

Anglorum regum cum gestis nomina scire
qui cupit, hos versus legens poterit reperire (1–2)

To know the names of England's kings and all their deeds
Is clear to anyone who in these verses reads.

With the utmost brevity it extends from Brutus to Henry III. It was written in the reign of Edward I in the North of England, possibly at St Peter's Abbey, York; it is interesting that another epitome of British history, the *Brutus*, was also associated with Northern England.[164] It was based on a prose epitome of British and English history also written in the North.[165] Lines 1–404 deal with pre-Saxon Britain; like its source, the poem omits or drastically reduces all the interesting stories, keeping to the bare outline, and it minimizes marvellous events and prophecies, such as that of Diana's oracle. Lines 405–510 cover Anglo-Saxon England, and the lines on King Alfred illustrate the brevity of the style:

> Alfredus quartus frater post regna subiuit,
> Vnctum quem regem Leo papa manu redimiuit.
> Non erat huic similis aliquis longe neque late,
> Consilio, sensu, virtutibus et probitate (431–4)

> Then brother Alfred, fourth in line, reigned in this land;
> As king he was anointed by Pope Leo's hand.
> There was no one to match him, neither far nor near:
> In prowess, prudence, worth and wit he had no peer.

Lines 511–646 have slightly more detail; they stress Northern, especially Scottish, affairs, and deal with post-Conquest kings down to Henry III:

> Qui quinquaginta sex annis rex fore scitur;
> Hinc obit annosus et Londoniis sepelitur (645–6)

> For six and fifty years he reigned, so say the wise;
> He died when full of years, and now in London lies.

Another version of the poem, in B.L. Cotton Titus A. xix (probably also from St Peter's, York) is much expanded; its redactor has added, especially in the post-conquest section, other poems, both in the body of the text and in the margins. Some of these additions are from Henry of Huntingdon, but others are probably the work of the reviser himself. In two manuscripts there is a continuation, in elegiac couplets, to the reign of Richard II.[166]

Religious literature: themes and forms

The second half of the thirteenth century witnessed, especially in the poems of John of Howden and Walter of Wimborne, a dramatic shift in the direction of religious literature. This seems, therefore, the appropriate place for a review of continuities and innovations.

Traditional genres

World history (such as Lawrence of Durham's *Hypognosticon*, Alexander of Ashby's *Biblia versificata* and Adam of Barking's epic on the Six Ages of the world) lost its popularity as a theme. Even Old Testament stories (like Alan of Meaux's *Susanna*) were rare, except where they were absorbed, by typology, into narrations of the life of Christ. Explication of formal aspects of religion (such as John of Garland's *De mysteriis ecclesiae*) also ceased to be a popular theme of poets.

Saints, on the other hand, remained perennially popular; writers could always find an excuse for rewriting the life of a favourite saint – anniversaries, translation of relics, rededication of a church, or simply the pleasure of retelling a good story. In this chapter alone we have seen the major contribution to hagiography of Henry of Avranches, as well as verse lives of St Catherine, St Neot, and Waltheof. Prose and verse hagiography remained popular well into the fifteenth century, including saints both old and new, English and foreign.

Another way of honouring a saint, using both words and music, was through the liturgy; this could also be the occasion for reading parts of a prose life. There was nothing new about this: offices to saints, with hymns in their honour, had long been part of Christian ritual. In the twelfth century, however, we see the rise of a new liturgical form, the Rhymed Office. Benedict of Peterborough's 'Pastor caesus', in honour of Thomas Becket, was used as a model for other offices.[167] The genre is part literary, part musical, and needs far more attention than can be given here. On one level a rhymed office can be read simply as a text, a concatenation of poems in various metres (both rhythmical and quantitative), on related or consecutive topics concerning the saint – a kind of operetta. In performance, however, an office could not be perceived as a single text: even individual stanzas of hymns would be interrupted by the singing of psalms, and the whole office would be constantly 'interrupted' by essential components such as the Magnificat or readings from the Gospels or the prose life of the saint. In any case, the whole office would be spread through the day's cycle of worship, thus making an appreciation of the whole 'text' impossible. To a literary critic it is as though an artist painted a picture and then cut it up into small pieces, distributing them among other pictures. Nevertheless, we know that both words and music were often written by the same person, showing that at one moment the whole text was a unified conception in someone's mind.

We have just mentioned the rhymed office on Simon de Montfort; another 'political' figure was similarly honoured in the fourteenth century, Thomas of Lancaster; both, interestingly, were victims of kings, as Becket had been. In 1246 another saint entered the English calendar, Edmund Rich of Abingdon, archbishop of Canterbury (1233–40); prose lives were written by Matthew Paris and Eustace of Faversham,[168] and there are several rhymed offices in his honour.[169]

Edmund Rich was credited with a Psalterium in honour of the Virgin Mary, 'Ave virgo lignum mite'.[170] It obeys the original rule, that each stanza should contain a word or phrase from its corresponding psalm. In fact it is probably not Edmund's: neither of his biographers credits him with any literary work. Another 150-stanza poem to the Virgin, in three quinquagena (but without echoes from the psalms), is the Digby version of Walter of Wimborne's 'Ave virgo'.[171]

Despite their obvious importance for literary history, I have had to neglect the massive topic of hymns, except where they can be ascribed to a known author,[172] but a brief word on hymn metres is necessary. Early Christian hymn writers, such as Ambrose and Prudentius, wrote in classical quantitative lyric metres (iambic trimeter, trochaic septenarius, etc.), and their hymns remained central to the daily office. From the twelfth century, however, hymn writers began to employ new rhythmical stanzas, based on accent, especially the regular Victorine sequence (popularized by Adam of St Victor and his followers) and the complex rhyme schemes of the isometric sequence. During the thirteenth century new stanzaic forms came into use,[173] and in the fourteenth century Richard Ledrede used vernacular dance tunes as the basis for his hymns.[174]

New developments

By the middle of the thirteenth century a new kind of religious literature began to predominate over other types. This does not preach the faith (which is assumed) or even morality, but aims at a purely emotional response. It is sometimes labelled 'sentimental' or 'pathetic', and concentrates on the moments in Christian history of maximum pathos, especially the Nativity (with scenes of breastfeeding the child) and the Crucifixion (with the horrors of the physical suffering of Christ and the mental sorrows of the Virgin). Its roots, of course, are as old as the Gospels themselves and the central Christian paradox that the creator died for his creatures, the guiltless for the guilty. Expression of man's guilty sympathy can appear at any time in Christian literature: compassion and gratitude for Christ's sacrifice is not unique to the late Middle Ages. Nevertheless, it is much more prominent from the twelfth century on. It gained strength from the increasing habit of private devotion and meditation. We have already mentioned Anselm's *Meditations* and the instructions given by Aelred to meditate 'on things past'.[175] Although the Cistercians were not the only, or even the earliest, writers to concentrate on this kind of devotion, the influence of St Bernard was powerful. We have already seen the stress laid on the Nativity and the suckling child by Roger of Ford.[176] Alexander Neckam also shows it:[177]

> Constituamus ergo pre oculis mentis matrem dulcedinis et filium dulcedi- nem sese dulciter amplexantes. Videor quidem michi uidere nunc matrem leticie maternis brachiis leniter filium suum sustentantem, nunc osculum prebere sidereis pueri ocellis, nunc fronti niuee, nunc genis purpureis, nunc collo lacteo, nunc labiis roseis

> So let us set before our mind's eye the mother of sweetness and her son, sweetness itself, sweetly embracing in each other's arms. It seems to me that I can now see the mother of joy gently holding her son in her motherly arms; now she presses a kiss on the child's starry eyes, now on his snowy forehead, his damask cheeks, his milky neck, and his red lips.

In another passage Neckam actually 'quotes' the words of the Virgin in Egypt when she learns of the slaughter of the Innocents.

Another proponent of this kind of devotion was Stephen of Easton, abbot of the Cistercian abbey of Fountains in Yorkshire from 1247 till his death in 1252.[178] He has fifteen prose devotions on the Joys of the Virgin and the life and passion of

Christ; he also wrote treatises on meditation, a 'triple exercise' and a 'Speculum Novitii'.

The style of the devotional poems will be exemplified below, in the accounts of John of Howden and Walter of Wimborne; despite its essentially simple and sentimental message, it is not artless and it is far from 'sermo humilis'. It abounds in rhetorical devices – particularly all forms of repetition, especially anaphora, and alliteration and wordplay. The Old Testament (in itself of no concern to the poets) is omnipresent in the form of typological figures for Christ and the Virgin. The prophets and their prophecies are constantly invoked. In Howden's *Cythara*,[179] Christ is not so much prefigured by Old Testament persons and emblems, but actually *is* them; he is, for example, in stanza 4 the flower on Jesse's root, the curative fishpond, the fruit of life, the mystic lamb, Joseph, the rock that gave forth water in the desert, fragrant clothing, David, David's stone, and light that always shines. Similarly, the Virgin in Howden's *Viola* is, or is figured by, David's sling, Gideon's fleece, Moses' burning bush, Noah's ark and basket, the law given on Sinai, and so on. Astronomical imagery (the constellations, planets and zodiac) is common in Howden, just as it is in John of Garland. Walter of Wimborne made great use of the huge compilation of epithets for the Virgin collected by Richard of St Laurent, the *De laudibus Beatae Virginis Mariae*, written 1239–45.[180]

John of Howden

The only thing we can be sure of about the poet John of Howden is that he was a clerk of Queen Eleanor (wife of Henry III and mother of Edward I) and that he witnessed documents in 1268–9.[181] He was thus a contemporary of Walter of Wimborne, with whom he shares many themes and expressions; unfortunately, we cannot be sure of the direction of the borrowings. The principal theme of his poems, expressed at great length in several different metres, is the Passion of Christ.[182]

The *Philomena* consists of 1131 quatrains of ten-syllable lines (4p + 6pp). It is, in Blume's phrase, lyric in epic form, dwelling passionately on Christ's life and suffering, but within a basic narrative structure:

sts. 1–3. Prologue to the Word and the Virgin
4–237. Nativity, ministry, betrayal, and crucifixion. In all his actions, Christ was driven by Love:

> Tuum, Amor, dulce dominium
> Sic, sic domat Regem regnantium (22/1–2)
>
> O Love, your sweet dominion
> Thus tames the king of kings

Love writes its signature on Christ's forehead with the thorn:

> Spina scribit Amoris unici
> Chirographum in fronte simplici (155/3–4)

The signature of unique love
Is etched on Jesus' brow.

238–400. Love is asked why it caused the crucifixion.
401–819. The passion: the poet asks Love to write Christ's suffering on his own heart:

> Scribas ibi qua patientia
> Liber subit servi supplicia (496/1–2)

> Write there the strength he showed, though free,
> beneath the servile pains.

820–965. The departure ('Ecce migrat') of the King.
966–1057. Miracles at the crucifixion; the Resurrection and Ascension; the Assumption of the Virgin
1058–131. Praise of the Virgin; epilogue, echoing the opening.

Other themes are interspersed within the outline structure. The poet prays for strength to face his own death; he laments his inability to follow Christ in death, and asks for the compassion to grieve with him:

> Mors et dolor, simul irruite
> Et cor mihi, rogo, confodite !
> Mentis petram rigentem scindite,
> Condolentem dolenti facite ! (174)

> Come, death and grief, come both at once,
>   And pierce my heart in twain;
> My mind's tough hardness dissipate,
>   And make me share your pain.

His own heart is hard:

> Non est motum cum flos confringitur
> Et mors vitae venam aggreditur (949/1–2)

> My heart's not moved when flower is crushed
>   And death attacks life's vein.

He can only grieve with Christ:

> Duc me tecum ut finem videam,
> Ut migranti saltem condoleam (177/1–2)

> Take me with you to see your end,
>   To grieve when you go hence.

He prays for a mystic union between Christ and his mind, in which Christ is the incense and his mind the thurible. He asks for a marriage with Christ, in which he will learn

> In Amoris flammam defluere
> Et in eius mucronem ruere (619/3–4)

> To flow toward the flame of Love
> And fall upon its sword.

He dwells on the mental anguish of the crucifixion, as in the judgment before Pilate when the Lamb sees the butchers:

> Scribas, Amor, et crebro replices . . .
> Pupillarum labentes latices
> Quando cernit agnus carnifices (533)

> Love, write it now and many times . . .
> How, when the Lamb his butchers sees,
> The tears pour from his eyes.

The physical torments are described by very striking metaphors. The crown of thorns is a garland of laurel to erase the thorns of our sins:

> Cum te laurus, Rex summe, deceat,
> Spineale te sertum laureat,
> Et te spina pungens illaqueat,
> Spinas nostras ut spina deleat (143)

> O King, whom laurel wreath befits,
> Your head is crowned with thorns;
> The piercing thorn entwines you fast,
> Our thorns to crush with yours.

Christ is the anvil beneath the hammer:

> Caro candens livet sub malleo,
> Fit et incus ex osse niveo (185/1–2)

> Bright flesh grows blue from hammer blows;
> The anvil's Christ's white bone.

He is 'furrowed by the ploughshare of love':

> Ecce migrat, habens sub latere
> Cor Amoris aratum vomere (859/1–2)

> He goes: within his side he bears
> A heart by Love's blade ploughed.

Like Noah's ark, Christ has a window in his side:

> Scribas, Amor, aratis literis
> Velut arcae fenestram lateris;
> Arca nova fenestram veteris
> Repraesentat scissura vulneris (565)

> Love, write the window of his side,
> Like Noah's ark's, inscribed.

The new ark with the wound recalls
The window of the old.

Howden often uses the language of astronomy and mathematics:[183] the line is made into a circle; the sphere of the deity is given the shape of the square of humanity. The old typological emblems are common, but Christ is the gloss on the Old Law:

Legis glosam quare digladiant
Hi quos legis decreta cruciant ? (792/1–2)

Why do those whom the Law torments
Transfix its gentle gloss ?

The *Philomena* is highly rhetorical. In the process of devotion, like 'telling beads', repetition is very common, and anaphora is one of the commonest devices in the poem. For example, of stanzas 491–819, one hundred and twenty-three begin 'Scribe' or 'Scribas'; of stanzas 820–946, sixty-four begin 'Ecce migrat'. Alliteration and wordplay are common:

Vitae lator latrones mediat,
Florem furum fermentum sauciat;
Vitae vitem virus excruciat,
Fel molitur, ut mel inficiat.
Clamor cribrat carmen canentium (742–3/1)

The source of life between two thieves –
Their yeast infects the flower.
The venom burns the vine of life,
Bile strives for honey's blight,
Shrieks shred the singers' song.

There are frequent apostrophes to personifications or inanimate objects, such as the iron of the nails, parts of Christ's body, the Cross, Nature, the instruments of the crucifixion, and death. Praise and wonderment are often expressed, as in Walter of Wimborne, by the topoi of Inexpressibility and Outdoing:

Tuum, Virgo, vincit praeconium
Ciceronem et Titum Livium;
Mare laudis mergit Virgilium,
Augustini premit ingenium (49)

For Tully's style and Livy's pen
The Virgin can't depict;
Her floods of praise drown Virgil too,
And pass Augustine's wit.

Both Howden and Wimborne express devotion to the names of Jesus and Mary, an increasingly popular theme.[184]

I have quoted extensively from the *Philomena* in order to illustrate the style and intensity of this new kind of devotion. It is important to stress that the verses are written and are for reading, thus implying that they are for private meditation rather than public singing.[185]

The *Canticum Amoris* may have been an earlier version of the *Philomena*. It is in the same metre, but much shorter; it breaks off, at the foot of a verso page, in the 240th stanza. It follows the life of Christ fairly closely, from Annunciation to the Assumption of the Virgin, and all the motifs of the *Philomena* are to be found in it. It shows that all of Christ's life, from Incarnation to Passion, was under the compulsion of Love; one hundred and seventy-seven stanzas begin with the word *Amor* in the nominative or vocative:

> Amor iubet, et *ave* mittitur
> flori cuius candor non leditur,
> et cor a ve nostrum eripitur,
> *ave* quando puelle promitur (2)

> Love gives the word, and 'Hail' goes forth
> To flower, whose sheen is saved,
> And keeps our heart from Eve's lament
> When 'Hail' goes to the maid.

The (relative) brevity and conciseness of the poem make it somewhat more accessible to the reader than the *Philomena*. Although the narrative sequence is complete by stanza 240, there is no way of knowing how much of the poem has been lost.

The *Cythara* also concerns the sufferings of Christ, with many of the themes and expressions of the *Philomena* and *Canticum Amoris* (e.g. the power of Love over Christ, the 'fenestration' of his side, Christ as anvil), but the metre is quite different. There are three quinquagena; each of the 150 stanzas consists of twelve eight-syllable lines (8pp), rhyming aabaab bbabba:

> Quam iuste felix fierem,
> si spinis cor configerem
>   compassionis intime;
> si crucem sic recolerem,
> quod cruci me coniungerem
>   quam irrigassent lacrime.
> Set, Ihesu benignissime,
> quod impedit hoc adime;
>   nam me beatum crederem,
> si mentis petram pessime
> vi crucis invictissime
>   compaciendo frangerem (45)

> How happy I would rightly be,
> If with the thorns of sympathy
> My rigid heart I pierced,

> If I could so recall the rood
> To fix my body to its wood
>   And soak it with my tears.
> But, kindly Jesus, please remove
> Whatever holds me back from love,
>   For I'd be born anew
> If by the Cross's matchless might
> I broke my stubborn stony heart
>   By feeling pain with you.

The title is explained in the heading:

> Hec meditacio vocatur 'cythara' eo quod verbis amoriferis quasi quibusdam
> cordis musicis ad delectacionem spiritualem legentes invitat

> This meditation is called the 'Cithara', because it invites its readers to spiritual delight
> by words full of love, like musical strings.

The first quinquagenum concerns Christ; the second (in which each stanza begins
Ave) is addressed to the Virgin; the third, using the examples of the good
Samaritan, the prodigal son, and Peter, stresses mankind's sinfulness and need for
mercy.

The *Quinquaginta Cantica*, Howden's longest poem after the *Philomena*, is in a
quite different style from the easy rhythms and repetitious rhetoric of his other
poems. It is a series of meditations in fifty cantica of varying length, totalling 723
stanzas in all. The stanzas are quatrains of twelve-syllable lines with no fixed
rhythm, rhyming abab, abcb, or abba.[186] Each canticum is given to a persona, and
introduced in a manner reminiscent of the exegesis of mystical texts, e.g.

'The voice of one mystically magnifying the Lord Saviour and inviting the faithful to his
glorious praises' (Cant. 1)

'Here Christ addresses the soul or the church, and introduces his love, by recalling his death'
(Cant. 28)

The style is that of the Psalms, Prophets and Song of Songs, sometimes by direct
borrowing;[187] Howden is recreating the language of the Old Testament, but in
verse and with a gloss. Thus,

> 'The voice of Christ addressing the Father'
> Cordis affectus proprii me corrodit,
> calicem michi largiens acriorem;
> telo me caritas atroci confodit,
> quam ipsa morte sencio forciorem (399)

> I'm eaten up by bitter drink
>   Poured by my loving heart.
> Love's stronger far than death itself
>   And stabs me with its dart.

The rough rhythms, changing rhyme schemes and more strained word-order are, I believe, deliberate: unlike the poems that induce devotion by repetition, the *Cantica* require close and attentive reading.

Howden's other long poems are all on, or to, the Virgin. The *Quindecim Gaudia* contains seventeen stanzas in the metre of the *Cythara*.[188] The *Viola* is a tour-de-force of rhyming reminiscent of Michael of Cornwall. It consists of five blocks, each of fifty seven-syllable lines (7p), rhyming entirely on the same syllables in each block (*-aris, -ina, -oris, -atis, -ura*), heaping up epithets for the Virgin:

> Maria laus divina,
> virginea regina,
> vitis propinas vina,
> languenti medicina,
> tu salus repentina,
> salvificans piscina,
> tu summitas cedrina . . . (51–7)

> Mary, praise divine,
> Virginal regine,
> Vine, dispending wine,
> To sick medicine,
> Giving health on time,
> Fishpond anodyne, (cf. Jo. 5: 2)
> Cedar-tree sublime.
> (Cf. Dunbar's *Ane ballat of Our Lady*,
> 'Hale sterne superne')

The *Quinquaginta Salutaciones* consists of fifty stanzas, with a scheme of rhymes and rhythms that is easier to illustrate than describe:

> Ave, stella maris,
> virgo singularis,
>   vernans lilio;
> que cum salutaris,
> veri gravidaris
>   solis radio,
> pectus nunc preconio
>   reple; que cum replebaris
> dudum Dei filio,
>   tactus inexperta maris,
> nos replesti gaudio (st. 1)

> Greetings, lodestar of the sea,
> Matchless maiden, fresh to see,
>   Like the lily bloom.
> When you heard the angel say

'Hail', the true sun's shining ray
    Came into your womb.
Fill my heart with adoration:
    With God's own son you once were filled
In a wonderful gestation
    By man's embrace quite undefiled.
Giving cause for celebration.

Each stanza begins *Ave*, and concerns primarily the Virgin's suffering at the Crucifixion.

Finally we should mention two short poems, the *Lira* on God's cosmic powers, and *O mira creatura*. Their content is not remarkable, but their metre is significant: they are the first poems we have seen in Anglo-Latin that have refrains, thus establishing a link with vernacular lyrics and the later hymns of Richard Ledrede.[189]

Walter of Wimborne

Walter of Wimborne began his career as a schoolmaster at the college of secular canons at Wimborne in Dorset; he joined the Franciscans and may have studied at Oxford; about 1260–6 he was a Franciscan lector at Cambridge, and seems to have been a member of the community at Norwich.[190] In his religious poems he shares John of Howden's subject matter, intensity of feeling, style and expressions, but as the exact dates of both poets are uncertain there is no way of determining the direction of borrowing. His poems show a wider range of interests than Howden's and a broader literary background.

His satires, which are general and impersonal, belong to his early years as a schoolteacher. The *De Palpone* consists of two hundred quatrains of rhythmical asclepiads:[191]

The ambitious are wasting their time. There is only one art, surpassing Aristotle and alchemy, that brings quick wealth and that is flattery, which comes from the court:

Ars de qua tocies est facta mencio
ab aula prodiit, et adulacio
uocari meruit, ut appellacio
in prolem transeat de matris gremio (12)

The skill I've many times recalled
Sprang from the court, and so is called
'The art of fawning', so its name
Would pass to offspring from its dame.
(i.e. *aula* – adu*lari*)

Truth-tellers are banished from court: they are insane and as bad a fastday. The flatterer is an adulterer, breaking the proper marriage between Heart and Tongue. He turns with the wind like a pennant, and changes colour as easily as the chameleon. He defies logic and can make black white; his sweet words turn the foolish into wise, the ugly into beauties. May

Wimborne be preserved from this pestilence ! The poem is not for the wise but for young schoolboys, still beardless, wiping their noses on their sleeves and still suffering beneath their teacher's rod.

In all his poems, but especially the *De Palpone*, Walter weaves together allusions from widely differing sources – Terence's famous passage on the parasite Gnato (popularized by John of Salisbury), Solinus' geography, Persius, Juvenal, Horace, John of Hauville, and the Bible. He blends the literary allusions skilfully:

> Palpo Diogenis contempnens olera
> laudat uel leuigat tiranni scelera;
> minutam scabiem appellat ulcera,
> leprosi Naaman uerrucas tubera (90)[192]

> The fawner cynic's greens reviles;
> At royal faults he blinks and smiles.
> To him a stinking ulcer's naught,
> The leprous Naaman's sore's a 'wart'.

The next three satires, each in a different metre, deal with the theme of the power of money. This topic is one of the most popular themes of medieval satire,[193] but Walter manages to ring some changes on it. The *De Symonia* at present consists of 209 stanzas of rhythmical asclepiads.[194]

The crime of Judas has revived, but worse than before:

> Judas antiquitus qui philargirie
> ardebat facibus semel nepharie
> uendebat dominum caterue Stigie;
> nunc autem uenditur Christus cotidie (19)

> Of old did Judas burn with greed
> And once performed a heinous deed:
> He sold his Lord to get his pay,
> But Christ is now sold every day.

Money builds castles, controls kingdoms, and is more powerful than Caesar or Alexander. Money is lord everywhere. Truth should depart or learn to serve the purse; in the law courts, only money wins. Only one thing can resist money, and that is death. Death makes all equal, king and pauper, young and old, beautiful and ugly, rich and poor, wise and foolish. Mother earth swallows all her children. Death threatens on all sides, but still we play:

> mors minax miseris minatur rictibus
> et tamen miseri uacamus lusibus (153/3–4)

> Grim death displays his fearful gape,
> But we, poor fools, just play and jape.

Everything is a messenger of death – birds, fish, flowers, trees – for every alteration is a kind of dying. Despite these warnings the walls of Jericho still stand. We can only wash our hearts clean of sin and pray for heaven.

The *De Mundi Vanitate* consists of 154 Victorine stanzas. It shares with the *De Symonia* the theme 'money is invincible, except by death', but whereas about three-quarters of the latter concerns death, in the *De Mundi Vanitate* the proportions are reversed.

In the law courts the rich go free and the poor are punished:

> Quando diues fornicatur
> iura uolunt quod plectatur,
> > sed mundatur munere;
> pauper peccat et nudatus
> fustigatur ut reatus
> > emendetur uerbere (11)

> Now when a rich man fornicates
> He should be flogged, the law dictates,
> > But he is cleansed by cash.
> If poor man sins, his body's stripped
> And he is then severely whipped
> > To purge the guilt by lash.

Only money has any eloquence:

> aduocatus et patronus
> > est in consistorio (17/2–3)

> The patron and the advocate
> > Before the bishop's court.

Judges favour only the fat and pregnant purse which is about to give birth. In court you need the help of the brothers Red and White (Gold and Silver). When the poor man gets a friend, the seas will dry up, lead will float, and pigs will fly:

> tunc uolabit sus pennata,
> tunc uidebit oculata
> > talpa lince clarius (109/4–6)

> Then pigs will put out wings and fly
> And moles will have a keener eye
> > Than even does the lynx.

Truth is banished and, as in the *De Palpone*, flattery reigns, yet we refuse to take heed:

> O quam multi modo stertunt
> dormientes, nec aduertunt
> > quod mors stat ad ianuam (151/1–3)

> O how many now lie snoring
> Fast asleep and quite ignoring
> > That Death stands at the door.

The poem ends with a dedication to the boys of Wimborne.

The *De Mundi Scelere* lacks a section on death, but is otherwise a translation of the first part of the *De Mundi Vanitate* into rhyming (mainly Leonine) hexameters. It even includes the impossibilities, e.g.

> Cum depannatus, cum pauper et attenuatus
> Carus erit mundo, testudo fiet arundo
> Et lepus athleta, pastor lupus, auca poeta (49–51)[195]

> When starving beggars dressed in rags are loved at sight,
> Then lyre will be a pipe, the hare will stand and fight,
> The wolf will keep the flock, the goose will poems write.
> (*testudo* and *arundo* could mean several things).

Walter may also be the author of two other poems on secular themes.[196] One consists of fifty-three hexameters, variously rhymed, on the subject of giving gracefully, quickly and cheerfully:

> Dona Deo grata non sunt que sunt uiciata
> Per sordes dantis, sua non se sacrificantis (44–5)

> Gifts tarnished by the donor's sins displease God's eyes,
> If giver gives not self but goods in sacrifice.

The theme is found in John of Hauville's *Architrenius*, a favourite source of Walter's. The other poem, 18 hexameters, is perhaps a fragment of a poem on Old Age, emphasizing that not all the old are wise:

> Multi dumescunt mento qui mente uirescunt (8)

> There's many bearded chin with only green within.

Some time after he became a friar, Walter wrote a long prose treatise on the *Four Elements*;[197] about two-thirds is extant, and occupies four hundred densely written columns. The scientific analysis of the elements, earth, water and air, is derived from ancient authorities (such as Pliny, Solinus, Martianus, Remigius and Macrobius) and from the more recently available Aristotle and Arabic writers.[198] The scientific expositions, however, are merely preliminary to a moral and religious exegesis: some general physical property of the element is interpreted in terms of Christ or the Virgin, or given a moral application. The interpretations include many themes found in the poems: flattery, the adultery of Tongue, wife of Heart, the vanity of earthly things, and the honey and wine of the Virgin. The treatise is illustrated by quotations not only from patristic authorities but also from classical and medieval poems, including Walter's own.

Walter's religious poems are dominated by his devotion to the Virgin Mary. The *Ave Virgo* consists of 164 Victorine stanzas in praise of the Virgin. It is not narrative but exclamatory: the terms of praise are taken not only from traditional typology (Gideon's fleece, Jesse's rod, etc.) but from the amazing collection of

Marian symbolism compiled by the Dominican Richard of St Laurent in 1239–
45.[199] Using these images, and some of his own, Walter was able to create some
very vivid metaphors for the Virgin. She is the ship full of new wares, in full sail,
bringing light to the world:

> Aue, uirgo, celi clauis,
> aue, nouis noua nauis
>> onerata mercibus,
> per quam plena plenis uelis
> est allata lux de celis
>> cecis et errantibus (4)

> Ave, Virgin, heaven's key,
> O hail, new vessel on the sea
>> Weighed down with novel wares:
> On windfilled sails you bring the light
> From heaven to those who here lack sight.
>> And wander in despair.

With her needle she binds together God and mud, highest and lowest:

> que coniungis Deo limum
> et cum summo suis imum
>> acu prouidencie (9/4–6)

> Our clay to God you bind and tie,
> And sew together low and high
>> With wisdom's needle point.

Walter also uses terms from grammar. The Virgin is metonymic (since she contains
her container), zeugma (uniting Breath and Word), a denominative adjective
(*Dei + fera*); in her a rootword becomes a derivative. With the play on grammatical
cases beloved of satirists, Walter writes:

> Tu mortis es ablatiua,
> quia prolis genitiua
>> sine culpa genite;
> tu fletus es abstersiua,
> restauratrix et datiua
>> libertatis perdite (61)

> Removing death you're ablative,
> Since of a son you're genitive,
>> Conceived immaculate.
> You wash away our tears and pain;
> As dative you give back again
>> Our long-lost free estate.

Walter signs the poem:

> memor, oro, sis Gauteri,
> qui fex est et alga cleri
> Minorumque scoria (158/4–6)[200]

> Remember, please, your poet begs,
> Your Walter, who's the clergy's dregs
> And dross of Minorites.

The culmination of Walter's poetic career was the *Marie Carmina*, in 644 quatrains of rhythmical asclepiads. In it he employs the rhetorical and rhyming skills, the lexical inventiveness, and many of the themes of his earlier poems.

1–214 the conception, nativity and suckling of Jesus. The poet is overawed by his task:

> Si iam in calamos mundus decideret
> et omnis athomus attente scriberet,
> nec tantus numerus laudi sufficeret
> nec calcem uirginis digne describeret (4)

> If all the world turned into quills
> And atoms scribes, for all their skills
> This host could not her praise reveal
> Nor even match the Virgin's heel.

The Virgin places the pen in his hand.[201] The conception and quickening is described by a metaphor of honey attracting a kiss from honey:

> Cum mel in melculi centro suscipitur
> circumferencia magis extenditur (18/1–2)

> With honey's centre honey blends –
> The circle's outer ring extends.

Christ is the bread baked in the pure oven of the Virgin; he is the wine contained in her wine-cask and poured in her tavern. Its liquor made the apostles drunk, and the poet longs to drink himself to death on it:

> ut dicant angeli iocundis uultibus
> cum ad me uenerint 'Viuat multibibus !' (165/3–4)[202]

> So when the angels come they'll joke
> With merry face, 'God bless this soak !'

The name MARIA is the only sufficient word of praise.

215–310 Let us suppose that God turns back time. The poet now becomes the ass that helps the Holy Family escape to Egypt. On their return, Jesus, to the distress of his parents, disappears for three days, having stayed in the temple. The poet presents a case against Christ in the court of Christ's Clemency; as witnesses, he produces the Virgin's services to the child, her tears, and God's own words. Jesus is ordered to return to his parents; the trial has lasted three days.

311–433 Christ's willing subjection to his parents is an example against pride; the futility of pride in strength, beauty, riches, knowledge and clothing.
434–541 A council in hell meets to discuss the problem:[203]

> Sedet Tartarea furuaque concio
> de supraposito tractans negocio;
> tandem sentencie fit promulgacio
> ut solis lampadem tollant de medio (434)

> The devil's swarthy court convenes
> To see what this new business means.
> At last the sentence they proclaim,
> To quench the sun's resplendent flame.

Judas is hired for the job; the poet rushes after him, saying that he would have made a better offer than thirty pence, but is too late. The four elements once helped God's people, but have now deserted Christ. The poet sees the cross being made, and kills first the carpenter and then the smith that made the carpenter's axe.
542–644 Christ is led before Pilate, who gives a bad judgment; the ingratitude of the Jews. The theft of one rose from a garden[204] (the incarnation) does not merit crucifixion, or, if it does, the Virgin deserves to die too; she should be allowed to share her son's fate. The poet pleads to Christ to stop his mother's tears, and asks that when he dies he should become the Virgin's footstool.

The *Marie Carmina* provides a striking example of the extremes to which 'meditation on things past' can lead.

Walter, like Howden, makes full use of rhetorical tricks such as anaphora, repetition and alliteration:

> Multi mortalium per mundi maria
> solent Mercurii mercari precia (*De Palpone* 3/1–2)

> Across the seas do many range
> By trade to make a good exchange.

He is very fond of wordplay:

> Cupidinariis in mentem ueniat
> quod mors marsupio se non humiliat;
> nil confert loculus cum caro careat (*De Symonia* 128/1–3)

> Let greedy men on this reflect:
> To purses Death won't genuflect,
> Cash won't avail the rotting flesh.

Sometimes vernacular puns may lie behind his choice of words, as in *mors surda* 'deaf death'. He employs very striking images: earth the cruel mother, consuming her own children; the rich man sitting like a firedog in the flames; the swarm of bats and owls pouring from hell to put out the sun. His vocabulary is very rich; the *De Symonia*, perhaps for pedagogic reasons, is full of recherche words of both Greek and Latin origin. Many seem to be his own coinages (such as *empostatocon* 'stable', *philopragmon* 'busy about affairs'). He coins diminutives for pathetic effect:

> In uentris decubat lustro leunculus
> sed nullum territat eius denticulus;
> hic enim desinit esse mordaculus,
> iam ex leunculo factus agniculus (*Marie Carmina* 22)

> The little lion's in his lair,
> His tiny teeth give none a scare;
> His tiny bite he's now unlearned,
> From lion cub to lambkin turned.

To modern readers, Walter's principal defect is his prolixity. As Raby says of Howden, 'the poet's power of invention, remarkable as it is, is not always sufficient to remove all sense of tedium'.[205] Some medieval readers seem to have felt the same: three of Walter's poems were considerably abbreviated by medieval scribes without significant loss of sense.[206]

John Pecham

The last major literary writer of the century was John Pecham, the first Franciscan archbishop of Canterbury (1279–92), a philosopher, theologian, scientist, and poet.[207] Most of his writing seems to have been done in his early career, when he lectured in Paris, Oxford and Rome. His religious poems are more structured and 'intellectual' than those of Howden or Wimborne, but there are many signs of affective piety.

Unlike Howden's poem of the same name, Pecham's *Philomena*, in eighty-seven Goliardic stanzas, actually concerns a nightingale.[208] The poet sends the bird, messenger of Spring, to a distant friend:

At the approach of death the nightingale flies to the top of a tree and sings through each of the canonical hours; its song is so intense that at None it dies of exhaustion. So also the pious soul, knowing its end is near, sings at dawn of its gratitude to God for being created in his image. At Prime it gives thanks for Christ's incarnation, to which he was impelled by Love:

> Tibi quis consuluit sic te dare gratis
> Nisi zelus vehemens, ardor caritatis ? (27/3–4)

> Freely thus to give yourself, who advised this action ?
> Who but burning charity, who but zealous passion ?

The soul would have liked to be present to tend for the child:

> O quam dulce balneum ei praeparassem,
> O quam libens umeris aquam adportassem (33/1–2)

> I'd have gladly given him such a pleasant bathing,
> Gladly on my shoulders borne water for the basin.

At Terce it sings of Christ's ministry, and at Midday of the Passion, with the nightingale's note *oci* ('kill'):

> Tunc exclamat milies 'Oci' cum lamentis,
> 'Oci, oci miseram', quia meae mentis
> Turbat statum pallidus vultus morientis
> Et languentes oculi in cruce pendentis (50)

> Now a thousand times she cries 'Oci' with compassion,
> 'Oci, oci, wretched me', since his pale expression
> Rocks my equanimity, looking at him dying:
> As he hangs upon the Cross, see, his eyes are crying.

At None the soul, like Christ, dies but is not to be mourned, for now it is with God.

There are many echoes of Howden and Wimborne; Christ is the new wine ('fundens carnis dolium'), and all his actions are done 'ad amoris signum'. As the dates are uncertain, there is no way to be sure of the direction of the literary influence.

In 1326 or shortly after, an Italian priest, John Judoci, presented to the diocese of Morin a copy of two poems which he remembered from his youth as having been composed by Pecham when he was in Rome in 1276, one on the Virgin, the other on the sacrament of the Mass. The former, *De deliciis Virginis Gloriosae*, consists of twenty-seven regular Victorine stanzas; it celebrates the life of the Virgin, from her conception to the Assumption.[209] There is no explicit numerical list of the joys; it is more restrained than many poems on the Virgin:

> Salve, caelitus assumpta,
> Non mens sola, sed resumpta
>   Corporis substantia,
> Ubi sola te transcendit,
> Olim in te qui descendit,
>   Incarnati gloria (22)

> Greetings on your rise to heaven,
> Not just in your mind, but given
>   Body from afresh.
> There your fame is just transcended
> By his glory who descended
>   Into you as flesh.

In this context we should mention that Pecham may have been the author of the eleven-stanza prologue to the *Psalterium* on the Virgin by Stephen Langton.[210] This prologue is in rhythmical asclepiads, and thus has a flavour of Walter of Wimborne:

> Mente concipio laudes depromere
> Beatae virgini, quae nos a carcere
> Ducit per filium, genus in genere
> Mihi vivificans effectus opere

My plan is Mary's praise to sing,
For she through Jesus helped to bring
Us out of prison, kind in kind
For me reviving . . .

(I do not understand the last line and a half; *effectus opere* seems to mean 'by act of effect')

The other poem copied by Judoci, 'Ave vivens hostia', is a graphic poetic compression of the mystery of transubstantiation, in fifteen Goliardic stanzas with internal rhyme:[211]

Sumptum non consumitur corpus salvatoris,
Idem totum sumitur omnibus in horis;
Forma panis frangitur dente comestoris,
Virtus carnis sugitur morsibus amoris (9)

Christ the Saviour's body, not used up but partaken,
Every hour it stays the same, though it has been taken.
Outwardly the bread is crushed through the eater's chewing;
By love's bites the flesh is drained, constantly renewing.

Just as human lovers thirst to know each other's secret thoughts, so God wishes to enter the heart of the faithful in the form of food:

Moris est amantium invicem sitire,
Ut arcana cordium possint introire,
Sic vult rex regnantium caritatis mirae
Cibando fidelium intima subire (12)

Just as lovers share a thirst, each to each appealing,
So that they can penetrate to their inmost feelings,
So the king of kings, from love, is forever seeking
Entry into faithful hearts through the route of eating.

Pecham also wrote another poem on the nature of the Eucharist, 'Hostia viva vale', in eleven collateral elegiacs:[212]

Vivens panis, ave, cum numine iuncte suave,
Me prohibens a vae, mis memor, eia, fave (3–4)

Hail, living bread, with God so sweetly bound,
Remember me, from sorrow keep me sound.

As a philosopher, Pecham seems to have felt challenged by the problem of expressing mysteries such as transubstantiation. Similarly he used his scientific knowledge to describe the nature of the Trinity. He wrote a rhymed office, 'Sedenti super solium' for Trinity Sunday,[213] and other hymns for the same office.[214] As the author of a *Perspectiva communis* he was able to use the language of optics to describe the relationship between the persons of the Trinity:

Lux Deus est intermina,
De qua res manat gemina,
  Tam amor quam imago.

Lux non decisa radium
Diffundens per hoc medium
  Multiplicat ardorem:
Sic pater gignit filium
Cum ipso spirans tertium
  Concorditer amorem (1 Vespers, 3/3–4/6)

God is light that has no end;
From it comes a double strand:
  Love and its reflexion.
Light unbroken sends its ray
Through the air, and on its way
  Magnifies its flame.
Thus begets the Father son;
Both breathe forth in unison
  Love, the third in name.

Similarly he used the three parts of the mind (memory, understanding, will), God's plural voice ('faciamus hominem'), and Abraham's three visitors:

In his vidit indicium
Trium, quorum fastigium
  In nullo separatur (2 Nocturns, 1/7–9)

Abram saw a sign in these
Of the Three, whose majesties
  Always stand as one.

The birth of the son is the continuing result of self-reflection by the Eternal:

Aeternae mentis oculo
  Dum pater in se flectitur,
In lucis suae speculo
  Imago par exprimitur (AH 50, No. 391, 2)

When in the eye of timeless mind
  The Father's turned towards himself,
Then in the mirror of his light
  An equal image shows itself.

Four poems with melodies, on contemporary events, probably date from his Paris period.[215] The first, *Planctus almae matris ecclesiae*, consists of forty-four six-line stanzas in two abecedary series.[216] It is a complaint by the church on its present-day afflictions, particularly the Schism:

> Cum enim unicus Deus
> Sit et fides unica,
> Unicus sit sponsus meus
> Spes ecclesiastica.
> Crescit tamen pharisaeus
> Et pestis schismatica (3)

> Since God and holy faith are singlefold,
> The church's hope, my spouse, as one must hold,
> Yet Pharisee and schism's plague grow bold.

(*Pharisee* was often interpreted as 'divided')

She is torn apart by heresies and the depredations of pagans:

> Bethel sanctam rapuere,
> Peremerunt incolas,
> Jerusalem fedavere,
> Violarunt violas,
> Misquetas ibi fecere,
> Fugarunt christicolas (24)

> They've killed the folk and Bethel seized by might,
> They've fouled Jerusalem, crushed flowers bright,
> They've set up mosques, put Christians to flight.

The fault lies with the spirtual failings of the church's leaders. The second poem is a general lament by mankind for its physical and spiritual state. The third, *Exhortatio Christianorum contra gentem Mahometi*, is a call to all nations to take up the cross,

> Ut exstirpes sata vana
> Acta Mahometica, (7/9–10)

> Uproot the worthless crops by Muslims sown,

probably referring to the second crusade of Louis IX in 1270. The last poem is an individual's acknowledgment of his sinfulness.

Pecham's fame resulted in the false ascription to him of several other poems. We have already mentioned Langton's *Psalterium*.[217] Until recently he was credited with the *Defensio Fratrum Mendicantium*, a verse debate between World and Religion written before 1274;[218] it is especially concerned with the status of mendicant friars, a topic of considerable interest to Anglo-Latin poets of the next century. A fourteenth-century scribe tentatively attributed to him a penitential poem.[219]

Monastic versifiers

Chroniclers frequently decorated their narratives with verses, either their own or by someone else. In this chapter, for example, we have seen that Matthew Paris quoted Henry of Avranches, whose poems he owned; Rishanger incorporates a poem into his account of the Barons' War, and the Anonymous (Michael ?) of Ramsey writes substantial poems.[220]

John of Cella, abbot of St Albans (1195–1214), wrote three epigrams now recorded in the abbey chronicle; one was to Stephen Langton, another on the extortions of Richard Marsh, bishop of Durham and adviser to King John:

> Non erit Abimelech requies, regnante Saul, nec
> Pax stabilis donec desinat esse Doech

> Abimelech will have no rest while Saul
> Is king, nor stable peace till Doeg fall.

The third was written on his deathbed.[221]

Between 1201 and 1240 the author of the annals of the Cistercian abbey of Waverley inserted several verses, mainly couplets, on both local and national events.[222] There are many epitaphs; the first, on abbot John, is signed Simon, and it is possible that others are by him. One poem concerns the channelling of underground springs by a monk named Simon:

> Vena novi fontis ope Symonis in pede montis
> Fixa fluit jugiter, fistula format iter

> Below the hill the new spring's stream runs true,
> By Simon fixed and channelled through a flue.

Hotoft, a monk of Durham, wrote a tart six-line epitaph on Richard Marsh, rhyming entirely on -itis;[223] he warns others to beware:

> Qui populos regitis, memores super omnia sitis
> Quod mors immitis non parcit honore potitis

> You who guide a flock, above all be aware
> That cruel death does not the lofty spare.

The author of the Worcester Annals (in this section probably the sacristan Nicholas Norton) included several short poems, probably his own compositions, mainly on local events.[224]

The most prolific of these monastic versifiers was Henry de Burgo, a monk of Lanercost: between 1280 and 1292 the Lanercost Chronicle includes fourteen of his poems.[225] They are between two and sixteen lines each; most are in hexameters (usually rhymed) but one is in Goliardics. The subjects include his personal affairs (two poems on his wrongful imprisonment when he was on the archbishop's business), local events (including theft, the burning of Carlisle, and several epitaphs), and national affairs. He writes on the execution of David of Wales in 1283 and the death of Queen Eleanor in 1290. His poem on the proclamation of Edward I's overlordship of Scotland in 1291 makes a suitable transition to the next section:

Facti concordes proceres et pacificati
Sunt, qui discordes fuerant ad bella parati.
Vivas, Scotia, tu, secure sub dominatu
Edwardi regis quia vives ordine legis (p. 143)

The chiefs, once quarrelsome and keen to fight,
Are reconciled and now in peace delight.
So under Edward's rule may Scotland thrive,
Secure and, sheltered by the law, survive.

Scottish wars of Edward I[226]

Edward's campaigns in Scotland earned him the name 'Hammer of the Scots', and two poems and a prose parody celebrate English triumphs. The 'Ecce dies veniunt', in thirty Leonine hexameters and elegiacs, seems to deal with 1297, when John Baliol abdicated as king of Scotland and the rebellious Andrew of Moray died.[227] It draws a parallel with the fall of Troy, and uses a prophecy of Merlin:

Merlinus scribit quod turba superba peribit;
Latrans exibit canis, et bos profugus ibit (19–20)

For Merlin says the prideful crowd its weird will dree,
The barking dog come forth, the ox in exile flee.

'Ludere volentibus' consists of over sixty Goliardic stanzas *cum auctoritate*.[228] It denounces the alliance of the Scots, French and Welsh, and glories in their defeat by Edward at Falkirk in 1298. The *auctoritates* are taken from both classical and medieval verse, including John of Garland ('Scribo novam satiram, sed sic ne seminet iram').[229] The most distinctive formal feature of the poem is the use of concatenation, a device common in vernacular Northern poetry of the next century: a word from the last line of one stanza is repeated as the first of the next:

Johannes jam Scotiae clemens rex et castus,
Regni tenens regimen, ut rex erat pastus;
Hunc tandem deposuit gentis suae fastus:
Exulat ejectus de sede pia protoplastus.[230]

Exulat et merito, quia, sicut legi,
Spopondit homagium Anglicano regi (45–50)

King John of Scotland, merciful and chaste,
Was regnant king and fed to royal taste.
His own folk overthrew him in their pride;
Like Adam, from his home he's now exiled.

And exile he deserved, for, as I've found,
He pledged allegiance to the English crown.

In 1306 the Scots rebelled and Robert Bruce was crowned king. Edward's response was swift and ruthless: Bruce escaped but his supporters were hanged or imprisoned. These events were celebrated gleefully in a biblical parody, *Lectio actuum Scotorum*.[231] It begins with the story (Judic. 9: 8–15) of how the trees chose a king. When John Comyn, Edward's counsellor in Scotland, proclaims his loyalty to Edward, Bruce says

Quid adhuc egemus testibus ? Audivimus ex ore eius blasphemiam (Matt. 26: 65) (49–50)

What further need have we of witnesses ? We have heard blasphemy from his mouth.

It concludes with Edward's vengeance:

Respondit rex: Gladius intret per colla eorum, et arcus eorum potencie confringatur (Ps. 36: 15) (238–9)

The king replied: Let the sword enter through their necks, and let the bow of their power be broken.

Grammar in verse

Two English writers of the second half of the thirteenth century followed the tradition of versified grammar set by John of Garland and the *Doctrinale* and *Graecismus*. Nicholas of Breckendale (Brakendale) was a Cambridge scholar from 1255 (when he was charged with homicide) into the 1260s.[232] He was thus roughly a contemporary of Elias of Thriplow and Walter of Wimborne, both teachers. He wrote a poem on deponent verbs in about 630 lines.

Nearly a generation later an Oxford scholar, Adam of Nutzard, wrote two verse treatises on verbs.[233] The first consists of about 450 lines on 'neutral' (i.e. intransitive) verbs, arranged alphabetically. A short example will suffice:

Bello, belligero, bombizo, bauloque, balo,
Et barbarizo, boo, bito, buccino, burso

I fight, wage war, and buzz, and sway and bleat;
I barbarize and roar, I go, I trumpet, pack.

(*baulo* may = *ballo* 'throw' (Latham) or 'vacillate' (Catholicon)).

The second, in about 100 lines, is a similar list of deponent verbs. Neither Nicholas nor Adam can claim much attention from either grammarians or literary historians, but they testify to the continuing link between grammar and poetry.[234]

II Anonymous satire and anthologies[235]

Anonymous satire

Rivalry between the monastic orders, especially Benedictines and Cistercians, continued to be a staple of the anthologies; it was some time before the friars replaced monks as objects of satire. Some of these poems may date from earlier, but they are discussed here as they first appear in collections of the mid- or late thirteenth century.

A 'discipulus Goliae' is given as the author of a poem *De grisis monachis*.[236] The poet calls on his muse to write briefly; five Goliardic stanzas with internal rhyme in praise of the Cistercians are countered by seven stanzas satirizing them for their many defects, including lack of breeches. Finally the poet tells his muse to desist:

> Circumdate labia, precor, musa mea,
> aut propter convitia jam non eris mea;
> propter dicta talia judicaris rea;
> turpe est per turpia quaerere trophaea (53–6)

> Button up your lips, my muse, please cut out your squalling,
> Or you'll have to take your leave for this vulgar brawling.
> For abusive words like these you'll be judged as sinning:
> Shameful is by shameful words to attempt the winning.

There are two verse debates between Benedictines (Cluniacs) and Cistercians. 'Dum Saturno coniuge', in forty-two Goliardic stanzas, begins with a traditional Spring setting in a plesaunce.[237] The poet is called on to judge between two quarrelling, drunken monks:

> Quos delectat avium vox et decor prati,
> sedent hic sub tilio duo cucullati;
> regulam deregulant vino crapulati,
> nec juri nec domino deferunt abbati (41–4)

> Two whom song of birds delights and the meadow's splendour,
> Misapplying Benet's Rule on a drunken bender,
> Sit beneath a linden tree, cowled in monkish habit,
> Not deferring to the law nor the lord their abbot.

(I have reversed lines 2–3 for the sake of the rhyme)

The arguments concern their style of living, the Cluniacs in towns, the Cistercians in rural but palatial isolation, and the reputed austerity of the Cistercians. Finally the poet has to intervene before they come to blows.

De Mauro et Zoilo ('Nuper ductu serio') contains sixty-five Goliardic stanzas.[238] The poet finds a place in the south ('plagam ad australem') full of monastic communities, where two monks are quarrelling. The Cistercian (Zoilus) is dressed in poor cloth, but is sharper in wit and intellect. The debate ends on a more friendly note, with the Cistercian and the poet both saying that the two orders have their merits.

The *Metra de monachis carnalibus* was almost certainly composed in England, though a later redaction enjoyed popularity on the continent.[239] It consists of twelve hexameter lines, each followed, like a liturgical response, by a verse from the Psalms:

> Quis nescit quam sit monachorum nobile vulgus ?
> – In omnem terram exiuit sonus eorum et in fines orbis terre verba eorum
> (Ps. 18: 5)
>
> Omnia consumunt nec eos possunt saciare
> – volucres celi et pisces maris, qui perambulant semitas maris (Ps. 8: 9)

> The monkish crowd, a noble host they are –
> 'their sound is gone out through all the earth and their words to the end of the world'.
> They eat the lot, nor would be satisfied
> 'by the fowl of the air, and the fish of the sea, whatsover passeth through the paths of the seas'.

In MS Digby 65 there is a rather feeble reply to it, beginning:[240]

> Quis nescit quam sit speciosa cohors monachorum ?
> Lacrima, leccio, parca refeccio luxus eorum

> Monastic glory's known to one and all:
> Their treats are reading, tears, and dinners small.

A slightly more serious tone is found in *Versus de praelatis* ('Cum sint plures ordines').[241] It warns those placed in authority not to neglect their flocks: they have a tendency, once they are made bishops or abbots, to withdraw from the cloister:

> Cum tenetis baculum et vices abbatis,
> thalamos incolitis, et vos elongatis
> a claustri dormitorio, cum vestris privatis
> laeti multipliciter 'Wesheil' decantatis (25–8)

> When you've got the bishop's staff and the rank of abbot,
> Far from abbey dorterhouse bedrooms you inhabit,
> With your private company merrily carousing,
> Calling 'Cheers' and 'Bottoms up', happy spirits rousing.

Still in the cloister we have the burlesque 'Quondam fuit factus festus.[242] This exists in several versions, some continental, but was certainly English in origin. The abbot of Gloucester (or Leicester) holds a feast; he calls for a drink for all the brothers, but the prior intervenes to say that they have had enough. A young canon interrupts angrily, and he and the prior indulge in a slanging match. The humour consists not so much in the drunkeness and abuse as in the language itself, which is deliberately bad Latin; it shows wrong inflexions, incorrect parts of speech, and a mixture of vernacular words:

> Abbas est sedere sursum
> et prioris iuxta ipsum;
> ego miser stetit dorsum
> inter rascabilia (st. 2)

> Abbot sit him on the upside
> And the prior be on his side;
> Sorry me is standing downside
> In among the riff-raff.

The reader may, according to taste, regard this as rather puerile classroom humour or as part of the long tradition of English nonsense verse.

Satire on gluttony remained popular.[243] The *Missa Gulonis* is a parody of the Mass:[244]

> V. Introibo ad altare Bachi
> R. Ad eum qui letificat cor hominis
> Confiteor reo Bacho omnepotanti et reo vino coloris rubei et omnibus ciphis eius et vobis potatoribus me nimis gulose potasse per nimiam nauseam rei Bachi, Dei mei, potatione, sternutatione, ocitatione. Maxima mea crupa, mea maxima crupa.

> V. I shall enter into the altar of Bacchus.
> R. To him who gladdens the heart of man.
> I confess to the malefactor Bacchus, the all-drinker, and to the malefactor wine of red colour, and to all his goblets, and to you boozers, that I have overindulged in imbibing, with great throwing-up of the malefactor Bacchus, my God, by boozing, sneezing, and yawning. Great is my rump, mine is the greatest rump.

In similar vein is a verse letter from an English goliard named Richard to the disciples of Golias in France, recommending to them a Mr William de Conflatis ('of Puffery') and asking them to ensure that he is well-treated.[245]

> mero delectabili calices implete;
> tempus cum sit frigidum ad prunas sedete;
> vinum meracissimum manibus tenete;
> calices si fuerint vacui, replete;
> ut bibat et rebibat, saepe suadete (20–4)

> With the finest vintage wine keep the goblets flowing;
> Sit down by the fireside, when the cold wind's blowing;
> With the very purest wine keep your spirits glowing.
> Never let the cup run dry – always fill it, brother;
> Press him first to have a drink, then to have another.

Among its many decrees, the Fourth Lateran Council of 1216 also reaffirmed the need for clerical celibacy. An unlooked-for effect of this edict was two comic poems. The *Convocacio sacerdotum* contains, in its longest form, forty-five Goliardic stanzas and is still incomplete.[246] In response to the papal edict, a council of clerics was assembled from all England. The legate calls for silence, and an old priest begins; each priest in turn denounces the requirement of celibacy, e.g.

> Surgit quintus presbiter et respondit ita:
> 'Hec sunt noua friuola diu satis trita.
> Per reginam glorie que est polo sita,
> Non Malotam deseram, donec priuor uita' (45–8)

> Then the fifth priest took his stand and his case he stated:
> 'All these novel arguments long have been debated.
> By the Queen of Glory who up to heaven ascended,
> I'll not give my sweetheart up till my life has ended !'

Another has an unusual argument:

> Ne sint in ambiguo uota mee mentis,
> Natus sum in partibus anglicane gentis.
> Natura cuiuslibet est uiri uiuentis
> Iungi cum uxoribus et non cum iumentis
> (Bodley MS st.31; Trinity MS st.27)

> Lest there's any doubt at all as to my persuasion:
> I was born within the bounds of the English nation.
> For all virile living men this the proper course is
> To have sex with their own wives, not with cows or horses.

The second poem on the subject, 'Prisciani regula', is kept distinct from the *Convocacio* in the English manuscripts, but no context is provided and it seems almost to be a collection of supplementary stanzas.[247] It laments that once 'sacerdos' was declined according to the masculine and feminine ('per hic et haec'), but is now confined to the masculine. Priests will now have to take mistresses or other men's wives:

> Quid facis, O pontifex, unam adimendo ?
> sed tu crimen cumulas, plures largiendo.
> Minus malum crederem unam permittendo
> parcere sic aliis, nuptas muniendo (5–8)

> Pope, think what effect you have, if we lose our sole mate:
> By supplying other 'wives', you increase the crime rate.
> Surely it would do less harm, if with one we tarried
> And thus spared the other girls and the newly married.

(Note: Harley MS has *nephas minuendo* for *nuptas muniendo*)

The decree flouts the biblical commandment to be fruitful and multiply. The humour of both poems rests in the fact that despite the Gregorian reform all these priests still have wives or concubines.

General laments on the wickedness of the world were all too common. A more interesting treatment of the theme is seen in the *De quatuor raptoribus*;[248] this lays the blame on four brothers, whose names mean 'robber', 'rich and hard', 'trickster', and 'I will do it later':

> Competenter per Robert 'robur' designatur,
> Et per Richard 'ryche harde' congrue notatur;
> Gilebert non sine re 'gylur' appellatur;
> Gofrey, si rem tangimus, in 'yeo fray' mutatur (57–60)

> Robert means 'a robber man' by interpretation,
> And for Richard 'rich' and 'hard' is the designation.
> Gilbert – and appropriately – has a 'guileful' nature;
> Geoffrey, 'jeo fray' (that's in French) means 'I'll do it later'.

Satire on places occupies a small but solid place in Anglo-Latin literature. The *Descriptio Northfolchiae*, apparently by a monk of Peterborough, consists, in its earliest form, of 175 rhythmical asclepiadic stanzas of varying length.[249] Messengers are sent out by Caesar to describe the world; they report that the worst province is Norfolk, which ought to be destroyed:

> Quidam de nunciis stans dixit talia:
> 'Audi me, domine, transiui maria;
> Terrarum omnium lustraui spacia,
> Sed detestabilis non est prouincia,
> Vt verum fatear, sicut Norfolchia' (9–13)

> One of the messengers said; 'If you please,
> Caesar, please hear me. I've been overseas;
> All over Europe I've gone and I've seen:
> None of your provinces ever has been,
> As that of Norfolk is, quite so obscene.'

Its inhabitants are greedy and stupid. If they find wheat in a field, they denounce it as the devil and beat it (a detail of primitive magic); when asked directions, they say 'Go as the crow flies'; when they do not want to be disturbed, they call out 'We're not at home'; they keep bread until it is mouldy; Norfolk peasants mistake a beetle for a dove and a toad for a partridge. The poem seems to have been popular in Oxford in the fourteenth and fifteenth centuries, and new stories were added. Norfolk was a common object of satire: there are allusions in both Chaucer and Langland. This is the fate of those who, like Frisians and Newfoundlanders, dwell on the fringes of civilization.

A rather inept reply, the *Impugnatio descriptionis Northfolchiae*, was written by a

Norfolk resident, John of St Omer.[250] This simply praises Norfolk and denies the truth of each of the stories.

A poem in eighty-two Leonine hexameters mocks the people of Stoughton near Leicester for their unsuccessful attempt to persuade the king to grant them their freedom from the local abbey in 1276–7.[251] They proclaim their wisdom with a malapropism (*solamen* for *consilium*):

> Omnes prudentes, magnum solamen habentes (8)

> We all are wise, consolers great have we.

A crowd of them go to London, but spend all their money on bribes and return empty-handed. The humour is parochial, listing all the locals involved (such as Kit who speaks like a fat frog, 'Christiana . . . quasi turgida rana'). They are condemned to perpetual servitude:

> Quid faciet servus, nisi serviet ? et puer eius
> Purus servus erit, et libertate carebit:
> Judicium legis probat hoc et curia regis (80–2)

> What's serf to do but serve ? His son also
> Will be a serf, no freedom he'll enjoy:
> The law and royal court have said it's so.

Sometimes the vernacular is used:

> Rustice Willelme, causam tibi supplico: *Tel me*
> Ad quod venisti ? (24–5)

> Now, peasant Will, what is your claim ?
> Please tell me why you came.

In addition to the biblical and liturgical parodies already discussed,[252] we should finally mention one on the political events of 1286–9. Edward I had been on campaign in Gascony, leaving England to be governed by the justices. On his return he purged all the corrupt officials, and the story is presented in the *Passio iusticiariorum Anglie*, a tissue of biblical phrases and lines.[253] One of the officials was the powerful selfmade man, Adam de Stratton:

> Rex vero transiens per medium eorum ibat (Luc. 4: 30) et intravit paradisum suum, ut quereret hominem quem creaverat, et dixit: Adam, Adam, ubi es ? (Gen. 3: 9) Olim quidem debui perdere te, sed pecunia tua oravit pro te. Redde rationem villicationis tue (Luc. 16: 2). Respondit Adam: Fodere non valeo, mendicare erubesco (Luc. 16: 3) (36–40)

> The king passed through the midst of them and entered his paradise to seek the man that he had created, and he said 'Adam, Adam, where art thou ? At one time I ought to have destroyed you, but your money has prayed for you. Give an account of thy stewardship.' Adam replied: 'I cannot dig; to beg I am ashamed.'

The satire concludes with some triumphant verses, one of which puns on *scaccarium*, which is both a chessboard and the Exchequer:

> Est Adam de Strat in scaccario per escheke mat.
> Sumitur ille rocus nec minor ille locus,
> sed caveant gentes in banco nunc residentes (89–91)

> To Adam of Stratton, in chequers 'Checkmate !'
> His rook has been captured – it's no minor fate,
> And all that reside at the Bank should go straight.

Anthologies

Popular items

Most of the favourite anthology items of the end of the twelfth century, including the Goliardic tradition, remained popular in the thirteenth.[254] A few newer poems, mainly continental, joined the pool. The antimatrimonial *De coniuge non ducenda* was extremely popular.[255] It was written shortly after 1222; its text was very fluid, and scribes seem to have felt free to improvise; basically it consists of about fifty asclepiadic stanzas. The protagonist, named Gawain in the best manuscripts, was about to marry, but three angels representing the Trinity (Peter of Corbeil = *potencia*, Lawrence of Durham = *sapiencia*, John Chrysostom = *gracia*) come down to dissuade him. Each in turn argues the disadvantages of married life, not, as often, from a clerical, otherworldly point of view but for the ordinary working man.

Examples of Body-Soul debates have already been discussed.[256] In this period (though it was probably written earlier) the most popular was the *Visio Philiberti*:[257] the dreamer sees a soul as it leaves its body; it denounces its flesh for ladening it with sins and dooming it to hell. Flesh retorts that Spirit should have controlled the body better. Finally two demons carry the soul off. Almost as popular was another debate in the same vein, that between Heart and Eye by Philip the Chancellor (d. 1236/7);[258] both agree that they are equally culpable. A more light-hearted debate, frequently found in anthologies, is that between Water and Wine:[259] in a drunken sleep, the dreamer sees Bacchus and Thetis arguing, mainly from biblical precedents, about their primacy: the victory goes to wine, who gives eloquence to the dumb, liveliness to the lame, and the capacity to feel no pain; it causes men to sing 'Gloria in excelsis'. Finally among the debate poems we may mention that between a philosopher and a priest.[260]

Another satirical tradition that remained popular into the Reformation was the Devil's Letter.[261] These letters, addressed formally and couched in traditional epistolary formulae, thank the Church for its good work on Satan's behalf. The opportunities for satire were limitless, and there were many versions of the letter. The most popular in England was the 'Princeps regionis gehennalis', dated 1109 (and mentioned under this year by Matthew Paris) but probably written in Italy 1261–74.[262] It satirizes both real ecclesiastical orders (such as the Friars of the Sack) and fictitious ones: traditional churchmen, even among the mendicants, were scandalized by the number of novel sects that kept appearing, and in 1274 the Second Council of Lyons suppressed all new orders except the Franciscans, Dominicans, Augustinians and Carmelites.[263]

Select list of anthologies c. 1216–1307

Not surprisingly, these anthologies show less interest in continental affairs than the 'Norman' types mentioned above.[264] Apart from the traditional favourites (Hildebert, Marbod, Walter of Châtillon, etc.) and the few new ingredients mentioned in the last section, the contents tend to be more distinctively English in selection. Otherwise, the old models survive as the basic types. There is markedly more rhythmical verse (especially Goliardic and asclepiadic), but hexameters and elegiacs, commonly rhymed, remain very common.

1 Oxford, Bodleian Lib., Rawlinson C. 510 (Bardney, Lincs., c. 1250), fols. 230–60 in a composite manuscript.[265] This contains devotional poems in four blocks. (a) fols. 230^r–235^r Henry of Avranches' 'Ave maris stella'; lost leaf with English lyric; 15 Joys of the Virgin; three sorrowful things; 'Ave Sunamitis'; 'Dulcis Ihesu memoria'; 'Planctus ante nescia'; 'In sapientia disponens'. (b) fols. 235^v–249^r conductus and motets from Notre Dame in Paris. (c) fols. 250^r–255^r litany of English saints; three hymns, including one by Henry of Avranches. (d) fols. 258^r–260^r eleven poems, mainly on the Virgin.

2 Cambridge, Corpus Christi Coll. 481 (s. xiii); two blocks, pp. 371–457, 566–85. Mainly moral and satirical verse: prose letter of Aristotle to Alexander on health; two debates between Body–Soul and Heart–Eye; 'Viri venerabiles viri litterati; *Apocalypsis Goliae*; 'Viri venerabiles sacerdotes Dei'; 'Noctis crepusculo brumali tempore'; fables of Odo of Cheriton; various mortality poems.

3 Oxford, Bodleian Lib., Digby 65 (s. xiii); 168 fols. There are four parts. Parts I–II are similar and closely resemble the older Hildebert style of anthology. Known authors in these sections include: Hildebert, Marbod, Serlo of Bayeux, Galo, Hugh Sotovagina, Henry of Huntingdon, Bernard of Cluny, Reginald of Canterbury (extracts from *Vita Malchi*), and Serlo of Wilton (proverbs). There are epitaphs (many from the early twelfth century), epigrams (in the *Anthologia Latina* style), saints' lives, biblical epigrams, Troy poems ('Pergama flere', 'Viribus arte'), personal poems, and satire ('Quid deceat monachum', *Metra de monachis carnalibus* and rebuttal). Part III contains *Pictor in Carmine*. Part IV contains John of Garland's *Epithalamium Beatae Virginis*.

4 BL Cotton Vespasian B. xiii,[266] additions on fols. 130^v–132^v, made c. 1300. These include: Thomas Wykes on Edward I (above, pp. 203–4), a poem on Prince Louis' invasion (above, p. 157), a set of short poems mainly ascribed to Gulias, and part of the Archpoet's *Confession*, here addressed to 'presul couentrensium', as though it were English.

5 BL Sloane 1580 (s. xiii), two blocks in separate parts of the manuscript. (a) fols. 24ʳ–26ʳ Walter of Châtillon 'Eliconis rivulo', debate between Cluniac and Cistercian (above, p. 230), 'Viri venerabiles viri litterati'. (b) fols. 158ᵛ–162ʳ booklet of Walter of Châtillon's satirical poems, followed by Philip de Thaun's French *Livres des creatures*. In other parts of the manuscript there are religious poems, including Stephen Langton's 'Veni sancte spiritus'.

6 BL Harley 978 (after 1264, Reading, Berks.); consists of six parts, of which (e) contains most of the Latin poems.[267] (a) fols. 2–13 antiphonary, with text of English 'Sumer is icumen in'. (b) fols. 14–21 calendar. (c) fols. 22–39 mainly medical lore; fillers include the goliard's poem (above, p. 232) and short verses. (d) fols. 40–*75 Aesop's Fables in French; (filler) *Visio Philberti*. (e) fols. 75–117 seven poems headed 'Golyas episcopus' (including *Apocalypsis, Confessio*, poems often ascribed to Hugh Primas, and one by Walter of Châtillon), *De Mauro et Zoilo* (above, pp. 230–1), poems on avarice, two poems on the murder of Becket (see above, pp. 78–9 and nn. 49, 51), a group of Walter of Châtillon's satirical poems, debates between Phyllis and Flora, philosopher and priest, the well-known poem on the Trinity often ascribed to Golias ('Multis a confratribus), *Metamorphosis Golie, De coniuge non ducenda*, French poem, *Song of Lewes* (above, pp. 199–201), and some prose material on Becket. (f) fols. 118–62 lays of Marie de France.

7 BL Harley 2851 (s. xiii, after 1290); 187 fols. Five parts, probably all by the same compiler. (a) fols. 2–18, fol. 1, Alan of Meaux's *Susanna* (above, pp. 160–1), religious poems and extracts, four pieces attributed to a 'Guleardus' ('Raptor mei pillei', *Confessio*, 'Pontificalis equs', part of *Apocalypsis*). (b) fols. 19–130 mainly saints' lives and exempla; at the end *Visio Philberti* and other mortality poems and some older poems. (c) fols. 131–42 antifeminist verse and prose. (d) fols. 143–55 miscellanea including Marvels of Britain, medical verses, and *Passio iusticiariorum* and *Missa Gulonis* (above, pp. 232, 235–6). (e) treatise on confession, prayers. On blank leaves between (d) and (e) are extracts from Bernard of Cluny, including the antifeminist sections.

8 BL Cotton Vespasian A. xix, fols. 55–60 (s. xiii ex.), a distinct booklet. Several Goliardic favourites, including two ascribed to Golias. Poem on avarice ('In terris nummus'), part of *Confessio*, 'Cum sint plures ordines' (above, p. 231), satire on Cistercians (above, p. 230), *Apocalypsis, Metra de monachis carnalibus*, 'Utar contra vicia', 'Acusativus Rome' (against Roman avarice), verses between Pope and Emperor, 'Sacerdotes mementote' (well-known poem warning priests who handle the Eucharist to be pure).

9 Cambridge, Trinity College, 0.2.45 (Cerne Abbas, Dorset, s. xiii, after 1248), pp. 309–50, a two-quire booklet, in a collection which is mainly mathematical and computistical. *Apocalypsis*, a unique antimonastic poem 'Si tunicatorum vitam', *Confessio*, prose allegory, *Praedicatio* ('Nostris a consortibus pridie rogatus' = 'Multis a confratribus'), French satires, *Descriptio Northfolchiae* (above, pp. 234–5), part of *Convocacio sacerdotum* (above, p. 233), Adulterous Monk (above, p. 143). In the early part of the manuscript is a collection of short proverbial verses (including some Primas epigrams); these, together with the scientific material, link this manuscript closely with BL Cotton Cleopatra B. ix, from the neighbouring Abbotsbury.

Conclusions

During the thirteenth century Anglo-Latin literature changed character, both in content and style. To some extent this resulted from external causes: political events, rising xenophobia, the establishment of the orders of friars, and the rise of English universities.[268]

In hexameter and elegiac verse, rhyme became more frequent and more elaborate. There is an increase in the use of rhythmical stanzaic verse (Goliardics, asclepiads, Victorine sequence) for both religious and secular poetry, and the rhyming patterns in these forms also became more elaborate, as in John of Howden. In religious literature, affective piety was pushed to its limits, not only in sentiment but also in style;[269] the diminutive coinages of Walter of Wimborne offer an extreme example. The fondness for exotic vocabulary and new coinages (on both Latin and vernacular roots) signals a new freedom and a departure from classical norms. These developments are most evident in the invective poems of Michael of Cornwall and Henry of Avranches, where lexical inventiveness and complex punning and rhyming become part of the fabric of the verse. We see here the emergence of a polemic style that continued to develop through the fourteenth century to the point where vigorous sound patterns were sometimes achieved at the expense of the syntax.

Both prose and verse were increasingly penetrated by vernacular words, idioms, and syntactic patterns. Sources of imagery also changed: Henry of Avranches, John of Howden and John Pecham all used scientific vocabulary for religious purposes. There is a shift away from classical literature as a source of literary allusions and towards the Bible, and from classical styles and forms towards a new and less controlled language. This shift does not necessarily imply ignorance: Walter of Wimborne often quotes classical authors (and has even been included as a forerunner of the 'classicizing' friars), but he does not attempt to *seem* classical in the manner of, say, John of Salisbury or Joseph of Exeter. In prose, at opposite extremes, we see the informality of Matthew Paris and the convolutions of Elias of Thriplow: neither writer aimed at the classical veneer of, for example, Peter of Blois. Similarly, the apparent objects of invective changed: whereas twelfth-century epigrammatists sought to imitate Martial, hiding the objects of their satire under classical pseudonyms, their thirteenth-century counterparts addressed real opponents.

It is possible to see, in this shift from the classics, a decline in educational standards, as had been lamented by many twelfth-century writers and reflected in John of Garland's strictures on the errors of the *Doctrinale* and *Graecismus*. The matter is debatable, but even if the criticisms are valid, there are compensations in the liveliness of the language and the openness to new sources of expression and idiom.

These developments raise the interesting question of the daily use of Latin. If it was a normal means of communication among the educated classes, it is not surprising that its linguistic character should change through constant use. Of course, Latin had been used publicly for a long time – for example, in monastic chapter houses and in the verse competitions implied by the stories about Hugh Primas and Maurice of Glamorgan. The difference by the end of the thirteenth century is simply one of scale: the growing universities housed large communities of Latin-speaking scholars and students, who were obliged by statute to teach, preach, and be examined in oral Latin.

Finally, we should consider patronage. Most writing probably remained a private activity, in monasteries and universities, either amateur (by students) or professional (by professors like John of Garland). There are signs, however, that some writers sought for lay or ecclesiastical patrons. The obvious example is Henry of Avranches, most of whose writing was written for or on behalf of potential patrons, and who finally succeeded in acquiring regular payments for his service as a poet from Henry III. The exact relationship between other writers and their dedicatees is not ascertainable; we do not know, for example, why the colophons to John of Howden's poems stress that he was a clerk of Queen Eleanor. The political poems on behalf of Simon de Montfort and Edward I may have been entirely disinterested statements of opinion; they may also, however, suggest that some magnates found it useful to retain the services of an articulate writer or spokesman. This question arises more frequently in the fourteenth century, when political poetry becomes almost a literary genre of its own.

4

Edward II to Henry V (1307–1422)

I Chronological survey

Historical background; the status of Latin

This chapter – and the whole book – ends at the death of Henry V: after 1422 we begin to see humanistic influences in England. Although some characteristically medieval forms and themes continued to appear (described in the Epilogue), Latin in England acquires a new name, 'Neo-Latin', with its own history. In this chapter, therefore, we are witnessing the demise of Anglo-Latin as a distinct insular literature (although its practitioners were unaware of any such development); in 1422 England rejoined the continental tradition, as it had done in 1066 and 1154.

Between 1307 and 1422 England went through many political and social upheavals. Edward II's reign, characterized by the *affaire Gaveston* and the defeat by the Scots at Bannockburn, ended in his deposition and appalling murder at Berkeley Castle in 1327. His son, Edward III, after a brief minority, quickly removed his mother Isabella and her lover Roger Mortimer from power, and embarked on a reign of military glory. In 1339 he laid claim (legal from an English point of view, but ultimately impractical) to the throne of France, and so began the Hundred Years War, with its initial successes at Crecy and Poitiers. Domestically, although Bannockburn was avenged and the Scots kept in their place, things were less sanguine: the Black Death of 1348–9 reduced the population to one third, causing immense labour problems and incidentally taking the lives of several writers. Edward's son, the Black Prince, won great victories in France and Spain, but his premature death in 1376 brought the gloomy prospect of a boy king. By the end of Edward III's reign, his court was an object of satire and ridicule. In the second half of the century the squabbles between friars on the one hand and monks and secular clergy on the other provoked a great deal of satire. Richard II's reign saw the Peasants Revolt of 1381 and its horrors, and the rise of the Lollard movement. In 1399 Richard was deposed, in the first move of a dynastic struggle that became the Wars of the Roses, which was not settled until 1485. Henry V suppressed the heretic

Oldcastle, and revived the claim to the French throne, with a brilliant victory at Agincourt.

All these events had an impact on literature, but the most important cultural development of the century – and not only for literature – was the replacement of French by English as the language of the court, of parliament, and of all official business. This was partly the result of hostility towards France and, by implication, to the Norman Conquest itself; Robert Holcot reports that William the Conqueror had deliberately suppressed English and required French as the language of instruction.[1] It was also a natural, perhaps inevitable, development. English had never entirely died out as a literary medium, and was used for romances, lyrics, and especially religious instruction and biblical exegesis; the development of popular preaching (stimulated by the Fourth Lateran Council of 1215 and the arrival of the friars) ensured the use of English by educated writers at a popular level. The rise of a new merchant class also brought English into use at a higher social level: even in the thirteenth century some political satire was written in English. The displacement of French, almost complete by 1400, led to the rise of English and the decline of Latin as the natural language for literary expression: by 1422 English was the obvious medium for a budding writer who hoped for patronage, a wide popular audience, and possibly eternal fame. Such a development would have seemed inconceivable in 1307.

There are other signs of the change. In the thirteenth century John of Howden had written in both Latin and French;[2] in the fourteenth century we see more English–Latin bilingualism. The Franciscan William Herebert wrote (or at least recorded) his sermons in Latin, but he translated Latin hymns into English.[3] Richard Ledrede used vernacular songs for the tunes of his Latin hymns. Richard Rolle wrote his commentaries and major mystical works in Latin, but his many lyrics and a Psalter are in English. Richard Maidstone wrote in both English and Latin. Chaucer and Langland successfully staked their reputations on the future of the English language, but John Gower played safe by using English, French and Latin.

During the fourteenth century, however, Latin continued to be used as a successful literary medium, written apparently without serious effort or strain, though often with some departures from classical norms (Rolle consistently uses *sentiui* for *sensi*, and often has *-e* as the ablative of third declension parasyllabic nouns and adjectives) and with a strong vernacular flavour in both vocabulary and syntax. Ironically, the decline of a distinct Anglo-Latin style in the fifteenth century was due more than anything to the progress of humanism and the establishment of Classical Latin standards as the norm. On the other hand, this final period did not produce any major Latin writers – apart, perhaps, from John Gower – whose intention was primarily literary: there was no Lawrence of Durham, no Joseph of Exeter. It was a period in which more attention was paid to writing about literature than to practising it: there were literary histories, library catalogues, commentaries on literary texts, and collections of stories and saints' lives. Nevertheless, there is much in this period to interest the modern literary historian.

Political literature in the reign of Edward II

In popular imagination the troubled reign of Edward II had two especially low points: the king's affection for his Gascon favourite, Piers Gaveston, and the defeat of the English at Bannockburn. Both were the subject of literature.

Piers Gaveston

On his accession Edward recalled the banished Gaveston and made him earl of Cornwall; his pride, his extravagance, his influence over the king (ascribed to witchcraft) and his foreign origin earned him widespread hatred. In 1311 the Ordainers banished him once again, and, although the king revoked the ordinance, Gaveston was captured and summarily executed on the orders of Thomas, earl of Lancaster. The general jubilation was expressed in the *Vita Edwardi Secundi*, which occasionally breaks into verse:[4]

> De causa Petri gaudent omnes inimici,
> Atque dolent pauci nisi qui sunt eius amici

> Now all his foes rejoice at Peter's end
> And there are few to grieve except his friends.

Two popular hymns by Venantius Fortunatus had often been parodied, but never so successfully as in two songs of triumph on Gaveston's death:[5]

> Vexilla regni prodeunt, fulget cometa comitum –
> Comes dico Lancastrie, qui domuit indomitum[6] (1–2)

> The banners of the realm go forth, the Earl's bright star appears,
> I mean the Earl of Lancaster, who tamed the untamed Piers.

There are several very clever twists:

> Trux crudelis inter omnes, nunc a pompis abstinet . . .
> Flexis ramis arbor alta ruit in prouerbia,
> Nam rigor lentescit ille quem dedit superbia[7] (19–23)

> Harsh and cruel above all others, now from pomp restrained . . .
> Like the proverb, falls the high tree with its branches bowed,
> Softer grows his wonted stiffness where he once was proud.

Ten years later, in 1322, Edward had his revenge. His execution of Thomas of Lancaster led to a popular veneration which equated the earl with Becket: miracles were credited to him, and a rhymed office was composed in his honour:[8]

> Gaude, Thoma, ducum decus, lucerna Lancastriae,
> Qui per necem imitaris Thomam Cantuariae

> Joy to Thomas, barons' glory, light of Lancashire,
> By your death you follow Thomas, Canterbury's sire.

The office includes another parody of Venantius Fortunatus ('Pange lingua gloriosi comitis martyrium') and other poems in the same metre, perhaps suggesting common authorship with the Gaveston poems.

Robert Baston; Bannockburn

In 1314 Edward marched North in an attempt to relieve the siege of Stirling by Robert Bruce; despite superior numbers the English force was routed by skilful Scottish strategy and English incompetence, and the defeat was regarded as a national disaster, especially because of the death of the earl of Gloucester. In anticipation of victory Edward took with him Robert Baston, a Carmelite friar and noted poet ('famosiorem metristam in universo regno Angliae' [the most famous metrical artist in the whole realm of England.]). Baston was captured and compelled by Robert Bruce to celebrate the Scottish victory, which he did:[9]

> De planctu cudo metrum cum carmine nudo;
> Risum retrudo, dum tali themate ludo (1–2)

> In grief I forge a verse that lacks finesse;
> My mirth is quenched when I this theme address.

He describes the assembling of the English host, their boasting before the battle, Robert Bruce's exhortation to the Scots, and his preparation of ditches and caltrops to ensnare the English horses:

> Machina plena malis pedibus formatur equinis,
> Concava cum palis ne pergant absque ruinis (55–6)

> An evil block they make for horses' hooves
> To cause their fall, with spikes inset in grooves.

In a tour-de-force of hexameter rhymes reminiscent of Michael of Cornwall he describes the rout on the Monday ('atra dies lunae'):

> Hic fremit, hic tremit, hic pavet, hic cavet, iste ligatur,
> Hic legit, hic tegit, hic metit, hic petit, hic spoliatur:
> Crescit inedia, corpora, praedia diripiuntur,
> Heu mulieres, miles et heres inficiuntur (97–100)

> Some shout, some doubt, some shake and quake, and some are bound and tied;
> Some steal, conceal, some reap and seek, some from their goods are pried;
> Starvation spreads: the farms, the dead, are torn apart for plunder;
> A woman fair, a knight, an heir, are victims of this blunder.

Sometimes he breaks a word in two for a dramatic rhyme:

> Quid fruar ambage ? de tanta quid cano strage ?
> Vix poterit tragae- dia pandere schismata plagae (113–14)

No need for words of doubt to sing of this great rout,
For scarce could tragic tale the woeful wounds unveil.

His authorship is fairly certain, as he signs the poem:

> Sum Carmelita, Baston cognomine dictus,
> Qui doleo vita, in tali strage relictus (128–9)
>
> My name is Baston, I'm a Carmelite,
> My life I grieve, abandoned in this fight.

We do not know, however, how he acquired his reputation as a poet: the poems ascribed to him in the sixteenth century are not his.[10]

With less detail but equal passion the defeat was lamented in 'Me cordis angustia', in twenty-eight stanzas of Goliardics with internal rhyme.[11] The poet has contempt for Edward's venture:

> Rex coepit militiam suam adunare,
> Inconsultus abiit Scotos debellare (15–16)
>
> To form his troops the king began,
> To fight the Scots without a plan.

He is concerned mainly with the death of the earl of Gloucester and his betrayal by a certain Bartholemew; he warns against treachery in general:

> Sibi quisque caveat istis intersignis
> Jam fidem ne praebeat talibus indignis, (75–6)
>
> Let each beware by signs amiss
> Of putting trust in knaves like this.

and offers consolation to the city of Gloucester.

A different perspective on the battle is provided by an anonymous Scots poet, who wrote sixty-eight variously rhymed hexameters, glorying in the victory; he gives few details, but manages to indicate the principal causes of the English defeat:[12]

> Inter saxosum fontem castrumque nodosum
> Corruit Anglorum gens perfida, fraude suorum (60–1)
>
> Between the knotty fort and stony well
> By treachery the faithless English fell.

It is primarily a song of triumph:

> Scotorum coetus vigeat, virtute repletus,
> Et rex sit laetus, vertens in gaudia fletus (65–6)
>
> Long live the Scottish host, so fierce in fight,
> God bless the king who turns our dark to light !

Richard Ledrede

If England and Scotland were troubled, Ireland was scarcely less so, torn between native Irish, Anglo-Irish settlers and English administrators. In 1317 Edward Bruce, brother of Robert, claimed the throne of Ireland in an attempt to drive out the English, but was killed in 1318. Into this turbulent scene came Richard Ledrede, no pacifier or trimmer himself.

Born about 1275, he became a Franciscan, and was for a time at the London Greyfriars; he was appointed bishop of Ossory in 1317. An avid persecutor of heresy, he quickly quarrelled with Alexander Bicknor, archbishop of Dublin, and with the influential Power family. In 1324 he prosecuted Alice Kyteler for witchcraft. In 1329 he himself was charged with heresy; he went first to Avignon to vindicate himself, and did not return to Ireland until 1349. His whole episcopacy was full of charges and countercharges, and he was frequently deprived of his temporalities. He died in 1360.

His collection of sixty hymns, probably made not long after 1317, makes a pleasant contrast with his career.[13] Like General Booth, Ledrede did not see why the Devil should have all the best tunes. A note in the manuscript says that the bishop made the songs in order to provide an alternative to lewd secular songs:

> episcopus Ossoriensis fecit istas cantilenas pro vicariis ecclesie cathedralis sacerdotibus et clericis suis ad cantandum in magnis festis et solatiis ne guttura eorum et ora deo sanctificata polluantur cantilenis teatralibus turpibus et secularibus

> The bishop of Ossory made these songs for the vicars of the cathedral church and their clerks, to sing at major feasts and entertainments, so that their throats and mouths, consecrated to God, would not be polluted by obscene and secular theatrical songs.

Thirteen of the hymns are accompanied by tags or 'cliches' (one Latin, two French, the rest English), indicating the tune to which the hymn was to be sung. Many of the tunes were clearly from secular love songs: 'Harrow ieo su trahy / Par fol amour de mal amy', 'Haue god day my lemmon'. Most of the metres and stanza schemes are unlike anything we have seen before in Anglo-Latin;[14] most are in some form of carol, originally intended for dancing, entitled by Colledge 'rondeau simple', 'rondeau à tercet', and the like, characterized by refrains and repetitions, as in this Christmas carol (No. IV):

> Nato Marie filio
> Congaudeat ecclesia
> Verbo rerum principio
> Nato Marie filio
> Celi terreque domino
> Collaudet mundi machina
> Nato Marie filio . . . etc.

Mary's son is born,
Now let the church rejoice, –
The word, beginning of the world, –
Mary's son is born.
The lord of heaven and the earth –
Let all the world rejoice,
For Mary's son is born . . .

or this, for Easter Sunday (No. xx):

Resurexit dominus
Cantemus alleluya
Christus dei filius
Resurexit dominus
Pridie qui mortuus
Surexit die tercia
Resurexit dominus
Cantemus alleluya

Now risen is the Lord,
Let's alleluya sing,
For Christ the son of God –
Now risen is the Lord –
Who died the day before
Arose on the third day, –
Now risen is the Lord,
Let's alleluya sing.

These new metres mark the penetration of Latin by the vernacular at a musical level.

More than half the hymns were written for Christmas or Epiphany or adjacent feasts such as Innocents and the Circumcision;[15] there are several for Easter, and some for Ascension and Pentecost. The sentiments are simple and pious; there is no subtle theology or rhetoric or even elementary symbolism. They simply celebrate the occasion of the feast, or ask God or the Virgin for help. In only one group (Nos. XLVIII–LV) is there any sign of the affective piety that was so characteristic of the thirteenth century: these eight poems are derived entirely from Walter of Wimborne's *Marie Carmina*.[16] Each deals with a specific topic, including the Annunciation (with one devoted to the theme of the 'bread in the oven'), the Nativity, and the flight into Egypt. The first five simply rearrange the asclepiadic quatrains, but the remainder are in six-line stanzas, of which the third and sixth consist of half-lines, thus:

Conuertit genitor in matrem filiam,
Antiqus prosilit ad puericiam
In paruo spacio[17] (53. 19–21)

Father changed daughter to mother,
The ancient one boyhood resumed
In a very small space.

As already mentioned, the *Marie Carmina* lent itself to abridgment; two eight-stanza poems derived from it are found in a Paris manuscript, BN lat. 3757, a fourteenth-century book that formerly belonged to the London Greyfriars. There can be little doubt that the Franciscan house in London had a copy of the *Marie Carmina*, and that Ledrede saw it there.[18] The effect of Ledrede's adaptations is to reduce the 'epic-lyric' character of the long poem back to simple lyric. His poetic output is relatively slight, but his significance for the development of the religious lyric is considerable.

William of Wheatley

Before turning to a more innovative religious writer we must briefly mention William of Wheatley, a grammar teacher in Lincoln. In addition to commentaries on philosophical texts, he wrote, in 1316, two hymns in honour of St Hugh of Lincoln, with his own commentary on them.[19] They are relatively simple celebrations of the saint, and may have been intended for teaching purposes. He may, for example, have used the lines

Nunc apud qui te dominum
Fecit pastorem gentium

Now with the lord that made you
Shepherd of his flocks.

to show students how to disentangle the word-order (= 'nunc apud dominum, qui te fecit pastorem gentium').

Richard Rolle

Richard Rolle, mystic and hermit of Hampole in Yorkshire (died 1349, probably in the Black Death), is the first major writer since 1066 to write in both English and Latin.[20] His English writings are not the concern of this book: they include a translation of the Psalter with commentary, meditations on the Passion, an allegory on the bee and stork (applied to the contemplative life), and religious lyrics with a strong emphasis on love. They are less self-centred than his Latin writings; they are more amenable to the modern reader, and not just because they are in English.[21]

His Latin writings include biblical exegesis (the Psalter, Psalm 20, the Nine Readings for the Dead, Revelations 1:1–6:2, Song of Songs 1:1–3), instruction manuals (*Judica Me, Emendatio Vitae)*, and what can loosely be called guides to salvation (*Incendium Amoris, Melos Amoris, Contra amatores mundi*); there is one poem to the Virgin, *Canticum Amoris*.[22] At first sight his Latin prose works seem to fall outside the 'literary' scope of this book: Rolle is primarily a religious exegete and apologist.[23] On the other hand, he represents the culmination of the developments in religious devotion that we have observed since Anselm, and merits inclusion if only to complete the picture.

Although he shares some features with the earlier writers we have considered, he marks an entirely new departure, in several ways. First, he claims to have had three mystical experiences – *calor*, warmth (whose astonishing physical sensation he decribes in the *Incendium*), *dulcor*, and *canor*, song (which surpasses even religious music, which he finds distracting). These experiences gave him, in his opinion, the authority to write confidently about the true way of salvation, namely the heremitic way of life. He spends much of his time justifying his particular form of contemplation against his detractors and expressing his distaste for the monastic life.[24]

Second, he stresses Love as the only possible way to come to God. This may not seem unusual: it is the message of the Gospels and St Paul, and is central to St Bernard and subsequent devotional writers. The replacement of carnal love by spiritual is a common topos. In Rolle, however, it is defined only in terms of contemplation (*amor proximi* is given only slight attention), and all his works could be read as an extended commentary on I Cor. 13.[25] We have already seen the passionate account of Love in John of Howden – the Love of God that drove Christ to sacrifice himself for man.[26] Rolle shares this: in the *Incendium* he has many passages that seem to echo the *Philomena*,[27] and in the *Melos* he writes, like Howden, that it was Love that caused Truth to be wounded;[28] he describes Christ's crucifiers, the defeat of Satan, the pathos of the Nativity and Crucifixion, Christ's address from the Cross, and the ingratitude of the sinner. For the most part, however, Rolle is concerned with the love of the contemplative for God. The desire of the *amans* to be united with the *amatum* provides a sexual metaphor that lies at the heart of Rolle's message.[29] Paradoxically, the combination of this stress on Love with his preference for the heremitic life leads to an unfortunate impression of exclusiveness: Love of God is all; this Love can best be achieved by contemplation; contemplation requires solitude; *ergo*, only hermits are secure of their place in heaven, and they will mock their detractors on Judgment Day.

Rolle also differs from his predecessors in his use of the Bible. Like most religious writers of the period, his language is almost entirely biblical,[30] but the texts from which he quotes (and on which he comments) are unusually restricted: they are, predominantly, the Psalms, the Minor Prophets, the Song of Songs, St Paul's epistles, and Revelations. This arises partly from his use of the Song of Songs to express mystical love (common enough in this kind of writing), partly from his self-appointed role as a holy outcast – persecuted and reviled, but sure of his own salvation and the damnation of his enemies. More importantly, he makes no use of the narrative parts of the Bible. Typology, even as a form of expression, is almost completely absent. The Gospel parables are ignored, as are most of the details of the life of Christ except the Nativity (briefly) and the Passion. God, for Rolle, is revealed not through history – or even through Christ's own words and deeds – but by direct personal contact.[31]

It is unnecessary to provide synopses of his Latin prose writings. The *Incendium*, *Contra amatores mundi*, and *Melos* are repetitive accounts of Rolle's way to God – fervent expressions of love, his own religious way of life and experiences,[32] his division of humanity (based on I Jo. 2:15) into lovers of the world (damned) and lovers of God (saved), mingled with his customary justifications of his own conduct, and denunciations of his detractors, of monastic life, and of the dangers of women. None of this has much to do with 'literature', at least as defined here. Nevertheless, features of his style are worth comment. The lyrical nature of his writing is illustrated in this passage from the *Incendium*, in which he describes how he first tried to be like the nightingale:

> In principio enim conuersionis mee et propositi singularis, cogitaui me uelle assimilari auicule que pre amore languet amati sui, sed languendo eciam letatur adueniente sibi quod amat, et letando canit, canendo eciam languet, sed in dulcedine et ardore. Fertur enim philomena tota nocte cantui et melo indulgere, ut ei placeat cui copulatur. Quanto magis cum suauitate maxima canerem Christo meo Ihesu, qui est sponsus anime mee per totam uitam presentem . . . ut langueam et languendo deficiam pre amore[33]

> At the start of my conversion and singular plan I thought that I would make myself like the tiny bird that languishes for the love of its beloved: as it languishes it rejoices at the approach of its beloved, and in its joy it sings, and in its song it languishes, but in sweetness and desire. All night time, they say, the nightingale gives itself to song and melody, to please the one to whom it is joined. All the more would I sing with the utmost sweetness to Christ, my Jesus, who is the bridegroom of my soul throughout the present life . . . so that I might languish and in my languishing grow weak for love.

Alliteration is an incidental feature of many of Rolle's works, but it is the very basis of the *Melos Amoris*, which begins

> Amor utique audacem efficit animum, quem arripit ab imis dum eterni auctoris incendium amicam inflammat et suscipit in sublimitatem supra sophiam secularem ut non senciat nisi sanctitatem

> Love, you see, lends spirit to the soul. It lifts it up from the lowest depths, when the fire of the eternal father inflames his favourite and snatches her up to the summit above worldly wisdom, so that her senses know nothing but sanctity.

This extraordinary style is kept up for over 150 of the 191 printed pages, diminishing only slightly towards the end (where he is quoting from his other works). The marked stress patterns often allow a division into four-stressed lines, and many scholars have seen the style as a reflection of a native alliterative verse pattern: alliteration was certainly a feature of Northern English poetry of the time, as Chaucer suggests. No English verse, however, maintains the same consonant or vowel for so long. Alliteration is also a stylistic ornament in Wimborne and

Howden, but not on this scale. It is possible that Rolle is actually trying to represent the divine *canor* that he had experienced.[34] That the *Melos* was perceived in the Middle Ages as poetic is illustrated by a set of six extracts from it in a Douai manuscript, entitled *Carmen prosaicum*; these preserve none of the cohesion of the argument (such as it is), but represent simply the lyrical and ecstatic quality of the writing:

> O paruulorum pater, qui punis potentes,
> Pactum pepigi properare pacifice
> Ad panem paradisi.
> Tu pastum pretende, ne peream pergendo.
> Porta pingatur, ut pareat perpure,
> Quia puto quod paries pie perdurabit[35]

> O protector of the little ones, who punish the powerful,
> I have pledged a promise to proceed peacefully
> To the provisions of paradise.
> Provide the provender, lest I perish on my pilgrimage.
> Let the portal be painted, that its appearance may be pure,
> For I predict that the protecting wall will be permanent in piety.

Little need be said about his other prose writings, except that they reflect the same concerns – love and sin, salvation and damnation, his own authority, and the preferential status of hermits.

The *Judica me* is a guide for a friend who had become a priest. It takes its starting point from the opening of several psalms (e.g. Ps. 42: 1 Judica me, Deus, et discerne causam meam de gente non sancta), and deals with the general theme of judgment; this leads to a consideration of Judgment Day and those who will be saved. The second part is abridged directly from William of Pagula's *Oculus Sacerdotis* (completed 1327–8), a manual of instructions for parish priests, dealing particularly with hearing confessions, combined with a sermon on Judgment Day. This is followed by a few stories about those who, although they appeared holy to the world, were damned.

The commentary on Psalm 20 (on kingship) ultimately reverts to the topic of authority. His commentary on the Psalter itself runs to 650 pages of modern typed paper.

The *Tractatus super Apocalypsim* (dealing only with the opening sections up to 6:2) draws some parallels between his own circumstances and those of John, such as the need for a visionary to have solitude, but most of his interpretations are moral. He takes John's *ostium apertum* to be a mental perception ('non corpori sed spiritui') and does not seem to accept that John's account of his visions may have been autobiographical: that is, he does not allow John's experiences the same physical reality that he claimed for his own.

His commentary on the first two and a half verses of the Song of Songs is structured as a sermon. Each of the seven phrases is stated and analysed as a *thema*; this is followed by a *prothema* (from another part of the Bible); then *thema* and *prothema* are brought together. The interpretation, as an expression of mystical love, is standard, but he takes the opportunity to write about his own personal history. The 'Oleum effusum' section (Cant. 1:2), however, is a lyrical praise of the Holy Name, prefaced by praise of the Virgin, linking the phrase 'meliora sunt ubera tua vino' with the Nativity.[36]

The *Expositio super novem lectiones mortuorum* expands on the nine readings from the Book of Job that are used in the service for the dead. The commentary concentrates on sin and the need for repentance.

The *Canticum Amoris*, Rolle's only Latin poem, is addressed directly to the Virgin. It consists of thirty-nine stanzas, and, imitating a feature of Northern English verse, is cyclic: the last line of stanza 28 echoes the opening ('Zelo tui langueo'; cf. Cant. 2:5, 5:8).[37] It is an ecstatic song of love-longing to the Virgin, who is described physically in the manner of rhetorical treatises. The poet is bound and wounded by love, and pleads for mercy:

> En rigore vulneror stringentis amoris
> et in plaga penetror dulcore decoris:
> digiti sunt graciles candentis coloris:
> lucidi, laudabiles, nasus, mentum, auris (53-6)

> I'm pierced by binding love's unbending dart
> And stabbed by beauty's sweetness in my heart.
> Her slender fingers dazzle, shining white,
> Her lovely nose and chin and ear delight.

The poem is full of clashing images:

> fecunda formositas, scala scaturizans,
> non valebunt exprimi, nitor neumatizans (118-19)

> Steps spreading life with fertile loveliness,
> Her breathing brightness, cannot be expressed.

(*scala scaturizans* 'ladder that scatters water'; *(p)neumatizans* 'breathing', but perhaps with the connotation of musical neums; cf. Latham 'prolong a neum')

The density of one stanza recalls Walter of Wimborne's honey image:

> Preclara progenies iure generantis
> mellis est millesies dulcior stillantis;
> cinamomo redolet dulcedo durantis[38] (69-71)

> The dripping honey's offspring from its sire
> Is sweeter by a thousand times; the mass
> That hardens has the scent of cinnamon.

The religious implications of Rolle's approach to God fortunately lie outside the scope of this book. We should note that his works were enormously popular; the *Incendium Amoris* was translated into English by Richard Misyn. On Rolle's death there was an attempt to have him canonized, and a rhymed office was composed in his honour.[39] This often echoes his own words and experiences:

> Melos canorus
>   ardorem sequitur
> et dulcor ingens:
>   Deo laus redditur (1 Nocturns)

> A tuneful melody comes after heat,
> Then sweetness vast, then praise to God is meet.

In the last chapter[40] we discussed the way in which biblical poetry (on the history of the world, or on the reconciliation of Old and New Testaments) gave way to meditative verse and affective piety, stressing the pathos of the Nativity and Crucifixion and the sufferings of the Virgin, involving the reader and writer closely with the action, especially through meditation on 'things past'. Rolle has gone much further than this: it is almost as though he would prefer to throw away all the texts – even those of sacred history – and achieve a union with the divinity entirely by silent contemplation. He could never entirely achieve this, of course; he used texts and he produced even more himself. Nevertheless, he has narrowed the reading matter necessary for religious contemplation, and has to some extent dispensed with scholarship and the paraphernalia of glosses and interpretations. He has tried to free the contemplative from the burden of the past.

Learning and the love of books

By contrast, the fourteenth century was also a period of literary histories, library catalogues, and learned commentaries. The value of the written record – what Chaucer calls 'the key of remembrance' – had already been stressed by John of Salisbury.[41] In 1344 Richard of Bury, bishop of Durham (a friend of Edward III and former member of his household), wrote a prose essay called the *Philobiblon*, an elegant praise of books both as repositories of knowledge and also as artefacts; in a prosopopoeia, the books themselves complain satirically about their misuse by clerks, monks and friars, and their sufferings in the ravages of war.[42] In a short verse the *Philobiblon* satirizes monks who prefer Liber (Bacchus) to *liber* (book): 'Liber pater praeponitur libro patrum':

> Liber Bacchus respicitur
> et in ventrem traicitur
>   nocte dieque.
> Liber codex despicitur
> et a manu reicitur
>   longe lateque

Liber Bacchus is respected,
Into bellies soon injected
Every night and day.
Liber codex, disregarded,
From the hand is soon discarded
All along the way.

Richard denounces readers with drippy noses and dirty hands, who leave books open, mark their place by inserting straws, and even rip out blank leaves. He proposed to establish a library at Oxford, and outlined the rules for borrowing. He was also a literary patron, supporting scholars such as Robert Holcot.

The first attempt at a universal literary history was continental – the thirteenth-century *Dialogus super auctores* by Conrad of Hirsau. In England, at the beginning of the fourteenth century, an unknown Franciscan compiled an incomplete *Registrum librorum Angliae*. Somewhat later the Aristotelian philosopher Walter Burley wrote the *De vita et moribus philosophorum*, with biographies and excerpts from the ancient philosophers. At Bury St Edmunds, Henry of Kirkstede (died after 1378) wrote a *Catalogus scriptorum ecclesiae*, an alphabetical list of all known writers, both Christian and pagan, from classical times almost to his own day; each entry gives dates, lists of works, and opening and closing words.[43] This work, until recently ascribed to 'Boston of Bury', was the starting point for the literary histories that continued with Thomas of Walsingham,[44] and went on through John Bale, Thomas Tanner, and Thomas Wright, ending up in the *Dictionary of National Biography*.[45]

Besides Richard of Bury there were many private collectors of books. In 1372 the Austin friar John Ergom witnessed the catalogue of books in the priory library at York;[46] he had donated his own personal collection, which included not only standard theological works but many books of prophecies (his especial interest) and texts of classical and medieval poetry; his MS 490 is a 'Goliardic' anthology. The will of William Rede, bishop of Chichester (died 1385), shows that he owned what must have been one of the largest private libraries in England.[47] Some of his books had come from Nicholas of Sandwich and Thomas Trillek, bishop of Rochester (died 1373).

At this time there was also a reawakening of interest in classical antiquity. Beryl Smalley has identified a number of Franciscan and Dominican friars, many centred in Oxford, that she calls the 'classicizing friars'.[48] Prominent among them were Nicholas Trevet, Thomas Waleys, John Ridevall, Robert Holcot, and John Lathbury.[49] They wrote commentaries on various books of the Bible (applying historical and literary texts to them), Augustine's *De civitate dei* (Trevet, Waleys, Ridevall), Boethius, Seneca's tragedies,[50] Livy, and Walter Map's *Epistola Valerii* (Trevet, Ridevall).[51] They combined their pastoral and theological duties with an interest in the pagan past, and so laid a foundation of tolerance for later humanistic pursuits.

John Ridevall

One work by a 'classicizing friar' calls for separate comment. John Ridevall's *Fulgentius Metaforalis* (based on the fifth-century *Mythologiae* of Fulgentius) utilizes the mythography attributed to Alberic of London.[52] It begins with an account of idolatry and its origins, and then proceeds to the five major gods, Saturn and his descendants. The attributes of each god are first summarized in a verse 'picture' of seven lines. The allegorization is primarily psychological: Prudence (Saturn) is the source of Memory (Juno), Understanding (Neptune), Providence (Pluto), and Benevolence (Jupiter). The traditional iconography of each god is similarly explicated: Pluto is 'inferis prelatus', superior to the monsters and what they signify.[53]

Moral tales and exempla

We have already mentioned the moral tales collected by Peter Alfonsi and the fables of Walter the Englishman and Odo of Cheriton.[54] In the thirteenth and fourteenth centuries, partly as a result of the increased emphasis on preaching, the number of stories and of collections of stories increased considerably. Stories are found in sermon collections, preaching manuals, exempla collections (the distinctions are not always easy to draw), and the sermons themselves. Their purpose was primarily moral; certainly they were intended to amuse and entertain, but the preachers collected and used them only – or so they tell us – because of their moral applicability.[55] The modern tendency to classify the tales according to folklore elements or literary structure would have seemed strange to a medieval preacher, who would distinguish them according to their allegorical meaning (God, the Devil) or the vice or virtue exemplified.

Even within the moral framework a distinction must be made. Some stories and fables are 'free-standing', the moral evident from the story itself. Most animal fables are of this kind: the tale of the Town and Country Mice simply teaches one to be content with simple pleasures. There was a growing tendency, however, towards allegorical interpretations (thus extending the range of stories considerably), as in the following:

Science tells us that the bodies of those who have been poisoned do not generate worms unless they are struck by lightning.

Moralitas: lightning is the grace of penitence, which removes the poison of sin.[56]

A king proclaims that anyone who can outrun his beautiful daughter will win her hand in marriage; the unsuccessful contestants will lose their heads. A poor suitor named Abibas delays the girl in the race by distracting her first with a garland of roses (which she throws in a well), second with a silk girdle (which she tears in three parts), and finally with a silken box containing a ball with the inscription 'Qui mecum ludit numquam de ludo saciabitur' [He who plays with me will never get satisfaction from the game.]. The last distraction succeeds, and Abibas wins the race and the girl.

Moralitas: the king is Christ; his daughter is the soul; the proclamation means that one should protect oneself against sin. Abibas is the Devil; the garland is pride (which must be thrown into the well of humility); the girdle is lechery (which must be destroyed by the triple actions of prayer, fasting and alms). The box is the heart, which has two strings to keep it shut (fear of God and of eternal punishment); the ball is avarice, and those who play with it will be caught by the Devil.[57]

Cosdras, emperor of Athens, learns from an oracle that his Dorian enemies will not prevail if he is killed by an enemy sword. The Dorians therefore avoid hitting him. He disguises himself, is killed, and thus saves his people. Everyone grieves.

Moralitas: Cosdras is Christ, who changes clothes at the Incarnation. When a soldier pierces Christ's side, the human race is saved. The devils grieve at losing mankind; the apostles grieve for Christ.[58]

Exempla vary greatly in length: the *Gesta Romanorum* includes the full-length stories of Apollonius of Tyre and St Eustace. The immediate source is usually some other medieval collection (such as Peter Alfonsi); the ultimate sources are sometimes the Old Testament, Eastern, classical (Aulus Gellius, Valerius Maximus), patristic (Augustine, Gregory's Dialogues), and medieval (Caesarius of Heisterbach, Gervase of Tilbury); sometimes natural science provides the exemplum.

Many collections of exempla were assembled in England. The *Speculum laicorum*, possibly late thirteenth century, was once attributed to John of Howden.[59] Some of the French exempla by the English Franciscan Nicholas de Bozon (early fourteenth century) were translated into Latin.[60] The *Fasciculus Morum*, a treatise on the vices and virtues, contains many exempla.[61] The massive *Summa Praedicantium* by the Dominican John of Bromyard (compiled by 1348) is alphabetically organized under topics, especially the vices and virtues, to make it accessible to preachers looking for suitable sermon exempla.[62] The Dominican Robert Holcot (died 1349 in the Black Death) has already been mentioned as a 'classicizing friar'; he compiled two substantial collections of exempla, the *Moralitates* and the *Convertimini* (named for its opening word).[63]

The task of isolating the 'original form' of any one collection – and thus of determining its author, place of composition, or even date – is almost impossible, and calls into question the very notion of 'text'. Even Holcot's *Convertimini* exists in many different arrangements. Even when a medieval writer alludes to his source for a tale, we can never be sure if he is referring to a collection in the form in which we have it today: scribes acted as compilers and redactors, adding and subtracting items. This problem is nowhere more evident than in the shape-shifting collection known as the *Gesta Romanorum*, which has been claimed, with about equal success, for both England and Germany.[64]

By the title *Gesta Romanorum* modern scholars are usually referring to the 1872 edition by Oesterley; this has no manuscript authority, and is based on the 'Vulgärtext' contained in the printed editions of the late fifteenth century, together with two groups of stories from unspecified manuscripts. The 1890 edition by Dick is of the 220 tales assembled in an Innsbruck manuscript dated 1342; 170 of these tales overlap with those in the Oesterley edition, but in a different order. Third, there is an Anglo-Latin group (itself very unstable, appearing in several configurations); this lies behind the Middle English translation and the version printed by Wykyn de Worde in 1510–15. The vague title, which simply means 'the stories of the Romans', leads to further confusion, as it can be applied to any number of sources. The Oesterley edition begins: 'Incipiunt historie notabiles atque magis principales collecte ex gestis romanorum et quibusdam aliis notabilibus gestis cum moralisationibus eorundem' [Here begin the notable and chief stories collected from the deeds of the Romans and from certain other well known deeds, together with their moralizations.]. The Innsbruck manuscript calls the collection 'Gesta imperatorum moralizata' [The deeds of the Emperors, moralized.]

Trying to discover the 'original' form of the *Gesta Romanorum* is like asking what was the original configuration of colours in a kaleidoscope. Suffice it to say that *a* collection of this type, sharing many tales with the continental collections, was widely diffused in England during the fourteenth century, and that many of the tales are of English origin.

John of Sheppey

John of Sheppey, bishop of Rochester (1352–60), was a noted writer of sermons, which are full of exempla and which are also notable for the inclusion of several Middle English poems, possibly of his own composition. He also made a collection of seventy-three Aesopic fables in prose, following 'Romulus' and Odo of Cheriton.[65] They are very abbreviated moral fables, with a concise statement of the moral and no allegorizations:

> Contra cupidos. Canis, flumen transiens, partem carnis tenebat in ore, et, cum vidisset carnis umbram in aqua, aperuit os ut umbram caperet, et sic amisit quod tenebat
>
> Against the greedy. A dog that was crossing a river had a piece of meat in its mouth. When it saw the reflection of the meat in the water it opened its mouth to grab the reflection, and so lost what it had.

John of Tynemouth

We turn now to a different kind of collection. Literary historians have generally neglected John of Tynemouth, an ungrateful disservice to one of the most indefatigable and influential hagiographers.[66] His *Sanctilogium* contains 156 prose lives of the saints of England, Ireland, Scotland and Wales, with very few omissions.[67] The lives vary between one and thirty printed pages, the average being about six. The order is calendrical, from Edward the Confessor (5 January) to Egwin (30 December).[68] The dates of the saints range from the early conversion period (some of which probably incorporate unhistorical or mythical figures) to the late thirteenth century; the latest two are Thomas de la Hale (Thomas of Dover), a monk murdered by French invaders in 1295 (John confuses this invasion with that of Prince Louis in 1216 !), and Thomas, bishop of Hereford (died 1282, canonized 1320).

Consequently, the nature of the lives varies considerably. On the one hand there are the sober, well authenticated lives of Thomas Becket and Hugh of Lincoln. On the other, there are Carantoc, an Irish saint who tamed a serpent for King Arthur, and Kyned:

Kyned was born near King Arthur's court; he was a cripple, the offspring of incest between a father and daughter. He was rescued from exposure by birds, and brought up to manhood by the birds and wild animals. He was fed by angels by means of a breast-shaped bell, which had magical properties.[69]

The element of the miraculous does not, of course, diminish with the modernity of the saint, but with later saints the miracles are usually associated with the relics.

John's sources are wide-ranging. He used other hagiographers, such as Goscelin, Eadmer, Reginald of Coldingham, Aelred, William of Malmesbury, and especially Bede. For Welsh lives (in which the *Sanctilogium* is very rich, and of which he may have made a separate collection) he used a collection now in BL Cotton Vespasian A. xiv. Early Anglo-Saxon saints, often from Bede, are very prominent. Although he must have been aware of verse lives (such as Henry of Avranches'), he makes no use of them. The style is very even, partly because of John's techniques of abridging and expanding, but more because they are written in a common hagiographic style, without significant rhetorical embellishment. There are few direct addresses to the reader and even fewer personal remarks (except on his search for sources). Each life is followed by a short prayer or Collect, suggesting that the *Sanctilogium* was intended for liturgical use or for reading in a chapter house; the uneven length of the lives would make this difficult. He often calls the work a 'liber', implying a literary motive.

Most of the lives, until near the end, are followed by one or two supplementary stories, 177 in all, call *narrationes* or *incidentiae*. These are sometimes linked with the preceding life (by date or similar connexion), but usually seem to be randomly chosen; they are often supernatural or demonic. After the life of Gilbert of Sempringham there are visions of heaven and hell; St Patrick is naturally followed by St Patrick's Purgatory, in the version by Henry of Saltrey,[70] and the vision of Tundale. Many of the *narrationes* are taken from Vincent of Beauvais' *Speculum Maius* (1247-59). As they are not calendrically determined, they give a good insight into John's literary preferences.

Northern literature; Farne Island

In chapters I and II some Northern writers were considered as a distinct group;[71] a similar grouping could be made for the later periods. The metrical *Historia Regum*

Anglie, originally written at St Peter's, York, after 1272, was provided with a continuation to 1399, probably also made in York.[72] The vigorous invective of the poems on the Battle of the Standard and the attack on Glasgow is seen again in the poems on Bannockburn and an anonymous Scots writer, and in Thomas Varoye's poem on Otterburn.[73] One of the poems on Neville's Cross may also be of Northern origin.[74] In the fifteenth century there is Richard of Esk and the *Chronicon Metricum* of the Church of York.[75]

Probably from about this period is an anonymous 'Exhortacio ad contemplacionem' in seventy-two Goliardic stanzas.[76] It is a morality poem, but placed in an interesting context. It describes the lonely island of Farne in Northumberland, south of Lindisfarne and a frequent sanctuary of hermits. After listing all the islands in the group it gives a brief life of St Cuthbert, who lived there for nine years. It mentions 'Cuthbert's birds', eider ducks which breed on the island:

> Magne velud anseres sunt plures earum,
> Rostris, forma corporis, colore pennarum (23/1–2)

> Many of them look like geese, big and strong, together,
> With their beaks and outward shape and their coloured feathers.

The poem describes the hardships of life on Farne – the storms, isolation, and privation – which suit only those who have given up the world. The hermit who lives there must meditate, and one of his meditations may be on the fact that big fish eat little fish, but are themselves caught on the hook and roasted over the fire:

> De marinis piscibus potest contemplari
> Quod magni minoribus querunt saturari,
> Sed hos captos protinus hamo pugillari
> Frustatim in ignibus evenit versari (38)

> Of the fishes in the sea it's a cause of wonder:
> First the big ones on the small try to sate their hunger,
> But the big ones soon on hooks find themselves suspended,
> Cut in pieces, then on spits turned and grilled, upended.

The rich now prey on the poor, but will be rewarded by damnation. The rest of the poem is given to the theme of Dives and Lazarus and the need for repentance.

Hundred Years War

In 1329 the young Edward III gave homage for his French territories to the new king of France, Philip of Valois. Somewhat later, however, when he had begun to quarrel with Philip over these lands, he realized his constitutional slip. Through his mother Isabella he was grandson of Philip IV, and so had a better claim to the throne of France than Philip Valois, who was merely Philip IV's nephew. Philip, now Philip VI, invoked Salic Law (which had already been used earlier to exclude Joan of Navarre) to argue that not only could a woman not succeed to the throne, but the line could not pass through a woman either. The validity of Salic Law was disputed by Edward III, and in 1337 he set about his wars of conquest in France. In 1339 he made a symbolic gesture and quartered his arms with the fleurs-de-lys of France, as these verses tell:[77]

> Rex sum regnorum bina ratione duorum:
> Anglorum cerno me regem jure paterno;
> Jure matris quidem rex Francorum vocor idem.
> Hinc est armorum variatio bina meorum,
> M. ter centeno cum ter denoque noveno

> Of two realms I am king by double cause:
> I'm king of England by paternal laws;
> My mother's right my claim to France restores.
> The change of royal arms reflects this line,
> In A.D. thirteen-hundred thirty-nine.

The first major English victories were at sea at Sluys and on land at Crecy in 1346. The English army, accompanied by the Queen and ladies of court, settled in for the siege of Calais. Meanwhile, the Scots under David Bruce, taking advantage of Edward's absence and encouraged by the French, attacked Durham in 1347; they were soundly defeated at Neville's Cross by Henry Percy and William de la Zouche, archbishop of York, and King David was captured. Later in 1347 Calais fell to the English.

These events were celebrated in several contemporary Latin poems and in the verse prophecy of John of Bridlington.[78] Common stylistic features suggest that 'Francia feminea', 'Corda superborum', and 'Cantica leticie' (and possibly 'Si valeas paleas' and 'Annis bis sex C') are all by the same author, whom I have labelled the 'Anonymous of Calais'. They share a fondness for mixed Leonine rhymes of all kinds, including elegiac couplets and cruciferi, a racy and pugnacious style, jingoistic denunciations of the French and Scots, puns, animal symbolism, vernacular words, and a disregard for regular syntax.

Battle of Crecy

The version of the poem on Crecy in MS Bodley 851 consists of 346 lines.[79] It begins with a typical denunciation of France:

> Francia, foeminea, pharisaea, vigoris idea,
> Lynxea, viperea, vulpina, lupina, Medea (Wright, p.26)

> Foppish Frenchies, pharisee-like, won't come out to fight,
> Linxy, slinky, foxy, wolfy, sorceress of night.
> (*vigoris idea* 'a shadow of strength').

Using an old pun it criticizes the choice of Philip as king:

Phy foetet, lippus oculis nocet, ergo Phi-lippus
 Dux nocet et foetet, sordida fata metet (Wright, p. 27)

Phi's a stinker, lip's a squinter; therefore Duke Philippe
Hurts the eye and smells so high – a sordid fate he'll reap.
(*phew* + *lippus*)

Philip's cowardice is contrasted with the courage of Edward the boar (*aper singlaris*, a 'sanglier'); Edward will say 'checkmate' and will be the ferret to Philip the hare:

In proprio climat tibi dicet aper cito 'chekmat';
Nec dices liveret, lepus es, aper est tibi firet (Wright, p.29)

The boar, in your very own state, will quickly to you say 'checkmate';
You won't, for you're nought but a hare; the boar'll be your ferret out there.

Philip cannot cure the King's Evil, and his consecration was defective; Edward argues that his homage of 1329 was an error:

 Philippo feci feodum sub lege minorum;
 Major id infeci cum magna laude meorum (Wright, p.31)

I gave my pledge to Philip when I was under years;
Now older, I renounce it, and England gladly cheers.

The poem reviews the process of Philip's succession: Salic Law, instituted by the 'butcher' Hugh Capet, is invalid, as it contradicts God's law (Num. 27: 1–11) and did not Christ succeed to Judea in right of his mother Mary?[80] The poet then recounts the English victory over the French 'hogges et koghes' at Sluys, at Poissy, and finally at Crecy:

 In Cressi crevit laus Anglica, Francia flevit,
 Decrevit, saevit, fugiens ut mos inolevit (Wright, p.36)

At Crecy England's fame grew great; French courage bled,
Declined; they raged, inflamed, and true to form they fled.

Like all the chroniclers, the poet gives credit to the English archers:

 Est mundo toti notus tuus arcus et omen (Wright, p.39)

To all the world your bow is known, its hidden power.

Finally, Edward is advised to trust in God and to avoid truces.

Battle of Neville's Cross

Neville's Cross: 'Corda superborum'
 The version of this poem in MS Bodley 851 contains 181 lines, and begins:

 Corda superborum Scotorum destrue, Christe;
 Hostibus Anglorum Scotis, bone Christe, resiste[81] (Wright p.42)

O Christ, the hearts of boasting Scots confound;
To England's foes stand firm and hold your ground.

The Scots take advantage of Edward's absence abroad:

> Dum rex longinquas abiit noster regiones,
> Scoti felones guerras movere propinquas.
> Falso credentes boream virtute carere,
> Insurrexere pomposo corde tumentes (Wright, p.43)

> While Edward went to visit foreign shores
> The felon Scots waged even closer wars.
> They wrongly thought the North devoid of might
> And in their pride began a rebel fight.

The English are led by the archbishop and by Henry Percy, who is compared to the heroes of old, biblical, classical, and medieval:

> Virtus Sampsonis, Joab ars, sensus Salomonis,
> Totus divinus, urbanus, ut ille Gawynus[82] (Wright, p.45)

> A Solomon, a Joab, Samson – wise,
> Skilled, strong – like Gawain, godlike, civilized.

David Bruce is finally captured by John Copeland:

> Copland cognomen, est Johannes sibi nomen . . .
> A re nomen habens, cui cognomen 'cape terram' (Wright, p.46)

> His last name Copland, with the first name John:
> The nickname 'Cop-land' was an apt surname.

The poet recounts a scatological story that David soiled the font at his baptism:

> Dum puerum David praesul baptismate lavit,
> Ventrem laxavit, baptisterium maculavit (Wright, p.46)

> The bishop once baptized the royal child,
> But David's weakened bowels the font defiled.

After further insults at David (mentioning his infidelity to his wife Joanna, Edward III's aunt) and the Scots, the poet advises England to put its faith in God, warning that the Scots were defeated because of their sins.

Neville's Cross: 'O miranda bonitas'
The English victory over the Scots was celebrated in another poem, not by the 'Anonymous of Calais', in sixty-one Goliardic stanzas.[83] It has occasional concatenation between stanzas, a Northern feature,[84] and its frequent praise of Cuthbert suggests a poet from Durham. Although its style and content differ from 'Corda superborum', it is equally hostile to David Bruce. Taking advantage of

Edward's absence and breaking the truce, the Scots first attack Liddle; plundering and despoiling churches, they reach Durham, and Cuthbert's aid is invoked. The poet stresses disagreements between King David and William Douglas, who first tried to dissuade the king from sacrilege, and then recognized the true nature of the English force; David would not believe him:

> Wilham, illa agmina quae sic indicasti
> Ex defectu cerebri forte machinasti;
> Extra cursum solitum quia vigilasti,
> Tu ex uno homine duos aestimasti (29, p.67)

> The columns, Douglas, that you saw so plain
> May just be aberrations of your brain.
> You've stayed awake past what you're used to do,
> And from one man you thought that there were two.

Douglas stands firm despite David's taunts, but the Scots are routed. Archbishop William de la Zouche is described as performing a gruesome kind of ordination, and the image is sustained over several stanzas:

> Tunc archiepiscopus, de Zouch qui est dictus,
> Ad creandos ordines venit valde strictus.
> Quotquot ordinavit, senciebant ictus,
> Exhinc inperpetuum frater benedictus ! (44, p.69)

> Then archbishop William, de la Zouche by name,
> To ordain the many ranks strongly girded came.
> All that he ordained like this suffered for it sore.
> Bless our brother for this deed now and ever more !

David is captured by Copeland; as in 'Corda superborum', his infidelity to his wife is stressed; thanks are given to God for protecting Cuthbert's rights.

'Si valeas paleas'

A short poem of twenty-six lines, possibly by the 'Anonymous of Calais', mocks the French and Scots in turn.[85] It begins with four lines from the poem on Crecy, starting

> Si valeas paleas, Valoyes, dimitte timorem;
> In campis maneas, pareas, ostende vigorem (Wright, p.40)

> Valois, if you're worth a straw, set aside your fright;
> Hold the field and stand revealed, then come out and fight.

It celebrates the English victories over the Scots at Halidon Hill (1333) and Neville's Cross:

> Ad Duram fleres, si bellum triste videres:
> Occiderant proceres, pater occidit, occidit haeres (Wright, p.41)

Durham would bring forth your tears at so sad a war:
Fathers fell and heirs as well, and leaders were no more.

'Annis bis sex C'

The Titus manuscript has a short poem summarizing Crecy and Neville's Cross:[86]

Annis bis sex C, quater X, bis ter, simul et C,
Carmina pando lyra tunc contingentia mira (Wright, p.52)

Twelve hundred, forty-six, a century as well,
My lyre unfolds a song of wonders that befell.

There are ten lines on Crecy, and then eight lines and two rhythmical stanzas on Neville's Cross.

Siege of Calais

After a protracted siege, Calais finally surrendered in 1347; a truce was agreed between the English and French, and Edward returned to England with Queen Philippa; the storms in the channel prompted him to remark that he always had good weather when he left England, but bad weather when he returned. This occasion – probably just before he left – prompted another poem from the 'Anonymous'.[87] It begins triumphantly:

Cantica laetitiae mundi flos, Anglia promat:
Hostes justitiae fortes ubique domat (Wright, p.53)

Let England, flower of earth, sing joyful song:
She slays the foes of right although they're strong.

It turns quickly, however, into a series of severe warnings: first, against returning home before the war is finally won:

Ergo Deo mire placet ire, vetando redire
Usquequo perfecta fiat victoria recta (Wright, p.54)

God wants them to advance, forbids retreat,
Until the time that victory's complete.

then against lechery:

Subjecti Veneri multi fortes periere,
Effecti miseri confusi succubuere.
Armis invictum somnus, luxus, gula, victus
Turbant, confundunt, turbant, sua viscera fundunt (Wright, p.55)

The brave are often felled beneath love's sway,
Reduced to misery, in disarray;

> They win in war, but sloth, greed, drink and lust
> Disturb, confuse, and turn their guts to dust.

and finally against a truce, which in Cornish means 'sorrow':[88]

> Bellans, victor eris; treugas cape, decipieris;
> Lingua Cornubica designat treuga dolores (Wright, p.57)

> By arms you'll win, but truces will betray,
> For 'truce' in Cornish tongue spells out 'dismay'.

The warning against sexual sin is echoed by John of Bridlington, and may have been prompted by an affair between Edward and Joan of Kent, 'la plus belle dame de tout le roiaulme d'Engleterre et la plus amoureuse'. There is good reason to believe that 'the fair maid of Kent' was present at the siege.[89]

John of Bridlington's Prophecy

The prophecy that goes under the name of John of Bridlington, was, according to my interpretation, written in 1349–50, though some sections had been written in the 1330s.[90] It is political satire on the events of 1327–49 in the guise of prophecy.[91] It consists of twenty-nine poems divided into three distinctions; it is in variously rhymed hexameters, Leonines, single-sound, collaterals (in couplets and quatrains), and, once, hexametri tripertiti.

The poet begins by describing how he took to his bed during a fever and dreamed of the future:

> Febribus infectus, requies fuerat michi lectus:
> Vexatus mente dormiui nocte repente;
> Noscere futura facta fuerat michi cura;
> Scribere cum pennis docuit me scriba perennis (1.1.1–4)

> Inflamed by fever, troubled in my head,
> I fell asleep while resting in my bed.
> To know the future was my great desire;
> The Scribe Eternal did my pen inspire.

The second poem (1.2) 'foretells' the disastrous reign of Edward II ('Rex insensatus est bellis undique stratus' [A witless king, by wars around oppressed.]); he will give birth to a Bull, and the Bull's sire will be 'pierced in the dark regions':

> Eius et interiet genitor terebratus in atris;
> Arte sue matris regnum rapiet sui patris (1.2.14–15)

> His sire will die, impaled in dark, alone;
> By mother's craft he'll take his father's throne.

The next few poems are in praise of the Bull (Edward III), mentioning his capture of his mother's lover, Roger Mortimer:

capiet Mare Mortis
Illicitis scortis solitum cameris et in hortis (I.3.12–13)

the 'sea of death' he'll seize,
in bowers and bedrooms steeped in sultry sleaze.
(*mortis mare* = Mortimer)

They describe his attempts to make peace with the Scots, their treachery and defeat at Halidon Hill ('in sacro monte'), and the Bull's claim on the French throne through his mother, paralleled by Christ's inheritance through Mary,[92] followed by his quartering of the arms of France:

Coniunget flores leopardis deliciarum,
Per pugnatores dum regnum queret auarum (I.6.19–20)

His leopards with the 'flowers of joy' he'll mix
When with his knights a greedy realm he seeks.
(*flos deliciarum* = fleur de lys)

I.7 and II.1 deal with the early campaigns, and II.2 with Crecy and Neville's Cross ('teste noue cruce uille'). II.3–10 centre on the siege of Calais, and II.3 and II.8 specifically warn against the dangers of lechery: the Bull will spend his energies on the oversexed Diana ('simia lactata'); he should beware of the examples of Samson, Solomon, and David:

Dauid peccauit quia Barsabe clunagitauit,
Et magis errauit, Uriam cum nece strauit (II.8.15–16)

Bathsheba's swaying rear was David's curse,
And in Uriah's death his sin was worse.

III.1 seems to refer to the beginning of the Black Death, the return of Edward and Philippa to England, the storm at sea, and a fire:

Namque repentina fiet gregis ipsa morina;
Rex cum regina transibunt absque ruina;
Classes quassabit moys et pir tecta cremabit (III.1.19–21)

A sudden murrain will the flock assail;
The king and queen without a loss will sail;
Sea ships will overturn, fire houses burn.

III.3 again refers to 'Diana's' hold over the Bull, but in III.5 his moral reform is predicted. After III.8 – that is, after the events of 1349 – the prophecies become very vague. In III.10 there is an allusion, as in the 'Anonymous of Calais', to the legend that Hugh Capet was the son of a butcher. Finally, in III.12 the poet adds that he has no proof of his prophecies: only God knows the future for sure:

Solus secura nouit Deus ipse futura;
Omnia formauit veluti voluit et amauit (III.12.16–17)

God only knows how all will be fulfilled;
All things he shaped just as he loved and willed.

The poem cleverly imitates many of the features of the Merlin prophecies. Animal symbolism is common: Edward II is the Goat, Edward III is the Bull, Philip Valois the Cock, and David Bruce the Crab. The source of the imagery is part heraldic, part allegorical (the Crab's sideways walk). Another method of concealing names, still employed in heraldry, is punning: as in the Crecy poem, Phi-lippus is 'phew' (a sniff at a noisome smell) and *lippus* 'half blind'. William de la Zouche and Henry Percy are concealed in

> Suspicor et clerus penetrans cognomine verus
> Viscera Scotorum penetrabunt belligerorum (II.2.14–15)

> Suspect and piercing, clerk, by surname true,
> Will pierce the warlike Scottish bellies through.

That is, *suspicor* = French *souchier* (*Zouche*), *penetrans* = *perce*, pierce. Another kind of word-play is clipping:

> Qui capitat staurum bene formabit sibi taurum,
> Sed capitans taurum taurum conuertet in aurum (III.3.19–20)

> Behead the stores and Taurus will be yours;
> Behead the bull; with gold you will be full.

If you behead the store (*staurum*) you reform the Bull (*taurum*), that is, reconcile him to yourself, and if you behead *taurum* you will turn the bull into gold. Another favourite device of the poet, useful for giving dates, is number symbolism, or what Elmham calls 'apices numerales':[93] M = 1000, D = 500, C = 100, etc., so that *vix* can mean 'scarcely' or 14 or 16, and *dvx* can mean 'leader, duke' or 515. Thus,

> Vix cum vi culli bis septem se sociabunt (II.6.1)

> Twice seven scarce will join with force of cowl.

is VIX = 16, CVM = 1105, VI = 6, CVLLI = 206, plus 14 (*bis septem*), totalling 1347, the date of the siege of Calais. Similarly,

> Lux cuculum fallit, dum ter sex cantica psallit (II.10.23)

> Light tricks the cuckoo while thrice six sings songs.

means 65 (LXV) + 1265 (MCCLVVV) + 18 (*ter sex*) = 1348. Decoding Bridlington is much like solving a crossword puzzle, but with no assurance that the solution is correct or even that a clue is intended.

The Prophecy is essentially a literary satire on the times, veiled under the riddles and word-puzzles that delighted medieval poets, and expressed with the vigour of the polemic style. It shares the anti-French, anti-Scottish rhetoric and high moral tone of the poems of the 'Anonymous of Calais'. Nevertheless, political 'prophecy' was a dangerous hobby: in 1402 a friar was hanged for quoting verses from this Prophecy in an apparently pro-Yorkist manner.

John Ergom

In several manuscripts John of Bridlington's Prophecy is accompanied by a prose commentary. It is signed internally in a cryptogram similar to those in the Prophecy itself:

> si super consequentiae notam caput miserationis velitis
> adjungere, nomen obscurum et obsequium salutare (Wright, p.123)

> If you will join the initial of mercy to the note of consequence, (I send) an obscure name and salutary service.

That is, if you add the first letter of *miseratio* (M) to the note of consequence (Ergo), you get Ergom. We have already mentioned John Ergom, Austin friar of York, and owner of books, including prophecies.[94] His commentary was written between 1362 (as it mentions an exchange of prisoners and the death of the Duke of Lancaster) and 1364 (as it does not mention the death of King John II of France). He is our source for the methods of decoding the Prophecy, and has sometimes been credited with its authorship. His interpretations, however, though often brilliant and ingenious, are in my opinion sometimes wrong. In order to include later events, such as the battle of Poitiers, he is often forced to distort the natural interpretation of the poems.[95]

Poems relating to Oxford

Oxford had now achieved eminence as a university and could boast many fine scholars. On the other hand, its students were young and brash, and prone to drinking and fighting; there was frequent violence. In 1333–5 feuds between northern and southern students resulted in the secession of the northerners to Stamford in Lincolnshire, where a small studium already existed; eventually Edward III intervened and Stamford was suppressed. These events prompted the writing of two short poems, possibly by the same author.[96] The first, in variously rhymed hexameters, exults in the killing of one Fulk, a southerner who had been supported by the laity. The second is addressed to Richard Fitzralph, chancellor (1332–4),[97] mocking his attempts to suppress Stamford ('vada saxosa'); the poet vows never to return to 'bloody Oxford':

> Cum boue cornuto vada sanguinolenta refuto;
> Pascua permuto; loca fertiliora saluto

> The bloody Ford and horned Ox I spurn;
> I'll graze elsewhere, to richer fields I'll turn.

Twenty years later, in 1355, there was trouble of a different kind in the St Scholastica Day riots. Hostility between 'town' (led by Bereford and Bedeford) and 'gown' broke out after a tavern killing; the townspeople attacked and killed several students. Several poems on these events are preserved in MS Bodley 859.[98] The first, in seventy-one stanzas of internally rhymed rhythmical asclepiads, is in the form of a dialogue between a worried university and a sympathetic student. It is fiercely anti-town in its description of the mayhem:

> Domos assailiunt in ignominia;
> Securi feriunt necnon et ascia;
> Post haec extrinsecus ponunt incendia;
> Fortes intrinsecus defendunt hostia (89–92)

> On homes the cowards launch attacks,
> And hack with hatchet and with axe.
> Outside they set their fires alight;
> The brave their doors defend and fight.

Its style is similar to that of Richard Tryvytlam, a friar.[99] Similarly, 'O rex Anglorum', in thirty lines of collateral hexameters, begs Edward III to come to the rescue of the students. Some short verses deal with events no longer identifiable, but the leaders of the town, Bereford and Bedeford, are recognizable in

> Urgent ursina vada perturbando bovina,
>   Et vada dicta precis sunt vada dicta necis[100] (V.1–2)

> 'Bear's fords' the 'Ox's fords' oppress, distress;
> The 'fords-that-pray' are named 'the fords-that-slay'.

The final poem, in a hundred lines of collaterals, reviews the riots and attacks, and is full of vernacular phrases:

> Invadunt aulas, 'bycheson, cum forth' geminantes;
> Fregerunt caulas simul omnia vi spoliantes (VII. 43–4)

> They break into the halls – 'Come out, you s.o.b.' –
> And smash up all the stalls and plunder all they see.

Mendicant controversy

The four orders of friars – Franciscan, Dominican, Carmelite, and Augustinian – are prominent in the literary activity of the late thirteenth and fourteenth centuries.[101] In time, they also became the subject of the literature.[102] Their critics, especially the secular clergy and monks, objected to the friars' unregulated life (the consequence of their combative role in preaching and refuting heresy), their mendicancy (seen as a hypocritical distortion of Christ's poverty), and their privileges to hear confessions and to bury the dead (originally the prerogative solely of the secular clergy). In Paris in the 1250s William of St Amour attacked them as precursors of Antichrist; although his works were condemned (and the predicted millennium did not occur), his emotive antifraternal language – especially the use of key biblical phrases – remained influential to the end of the Middle Ages. His portrayal of friars is the principal source for Jean de Meun's character Faux Semblaunt. Hildegard of Bingen's prophecy was widely interpreted as the coming of the friars.[103]

The literature must be read in light of the political history of the disputes. Fortunes varied with the favour or disfavour of the current Pope. In 1250 Innocent IV's bull *Cum a nobis petitur* gave the friars wide privileges, which he restricted somewhat by *Etsi animarum* in 1254. In 1255 Alexander IV restored the privileges in *Quasi lignum vitae*. In 1274 the Second Council of Lyons forbade future recruitment to all orders except the Franciscans and Dominicans; the Carmelites and Augustinians were put on temporary hold but later allowed to proceed.[104] In 1300 Boniface VIII produced a compromise bull *Super cathedram*, requiring a bishop's approval for some of the friars' sacramentary functions. In 1349 both pro- and anti-mendicant factions appealed against *Super cathedram*.[105] In England the controversy grew heated as a result of a series of bitter antimendicant sermons by Richard Fitzralph, archbishop of Armagh, who wrote a tract *Unusquisque* (asking for the repeal of *Super cathedram* and the restoration of all rights concerning the cure of souls to the secular clergy) and a longer work, *De pauperie salvatoris* (by 1356), against mendicancy.[106]

In Oxford, there were further sources of friction. A university statute of 1251-2 required an arts degree before proceeding to theology, and lectures on Lombard's *Sentences* had to be given before one could lecture on the scriptures (contrary to practice in Paris). Both rules hindered the friars, who were skilled in biblical knowledge and exegesis. A period of strife ended in 1320, when the friars submitted to the university, but resurfaced in 1349 when (as mentioned above) the friars appealed to Rome. In 1358 a statute (repealed in 1366) forbade the recruitment to mendicant orders of boys under 18, a major source of new blood.

The tone and content of the satires is serious, but there is also an element of playful artifice. The first two, 'Sedens super flumina' and 'Quis dabit meo capiti', are exact matches and may even have been part of a public verse contest.[107] The fifth, *De supersticione*, may be a reply to the fourth (Tryvytlam).

'Sedens super flumina'

This contains twenty-six stanzas, each (as in the reply) consisting of six lines, a Goliardic quatrain plus a Goliardic couplet with the opening phrase 'With an O and an I'.[108] Sitting by the waters of Babylon (Ps. 136: 1), the poet laments his deception by the friars, who made him wear their habit; he has now rejected it, but is not an apostate because he never took vows:[109]

> With an O and an I, non apostatavi,
> Professus cum non fueram, sed regulam probavi (11–12)

With an O and I – I am not backsliding,
Since I only 'proved the rule', didn't make it binding.

Friars, who prospered after the plague, tell lies and destroy marriages; the four orders are the four apocalyptic beasts of Daniel (Dan. 7: 2–7):

> Hii bis bini ordines bis binis notantur
> Bestiis, ut notule Danielis fantur (31–2)

> These four orders can be seen in the beastly quartet
> Seen in dreams by Daniel, as he has reported.

The seven branches that support them are the Seven Deadly Sins. Their conclusion that Christ was a beggar is illogical and inconsistent with the friars' opulent feasting:

> With an O and an I, dives purpuratus
> Lazari sub gremio iacet sed velatus (47–8)

> With an O and an I – in his fancy dressing
> Dives lurks in leper's lap, signs of wealth suppressing.
> (Luc. 16: 19–26)

Throughout England women confess only to friars:

> Quere totam Angliam: vix invenietur
> Quin mariti femina fratri confessetur (61–2)

> All through England you will find, if you should inquire,
> Married women bare their souls only to a friar.

Friars lack philosophical skills and resort to abuse. By hearing confessions they have nullified the decree *Omnis utriusque* of the Fourth Lateran Council (which enjoined annual confession to one's parish priest):

> With an O and an I, scimus quod huc usque
> Cassarunt hunc canonem 'omnis utriusque' (131–2)

> With an O and an I – through them the injunction
> 'Every man and woman must . . .' now has ceased to function.

When the Son of Man has nowhere to lay his head (Matt. 8: 20), look at the fine holes these foxes have:

> With an O and an I, ecce vulpes isti
> Quales habent foveas in despectu Christi (155–6)

> With an O and I – see the comfy dwellings
> That these foxes have, when Christ must himself go begging.

'Quis dabit meo capiti'

The reply to 'Sedens' has thirty similar stanzas, but with internal rhyme in the quatrain. In stanzas 1–2, echoing Jeremiah (Jer. 9: 1; Lament. 1: 1), it laments the divisions in the church and the attacks on the mendicants:[110]

> Primi plura replicant contra mendicantes;
> Sermones intoxicant, virus ventilantes;
> Vulpes, lupos nominant pie conuersantes (25–7)

> First upon the mendicants they heap accusations,
> Spreading spite and bitterness by their condemnations,
> Crying 'Fox' and 'Wolf' at friars in their holy stations.

The antimendicants hurl their abuse at St Paul's Cross in London. There are two beasts of the Apocalypse, both called Richard; the first is Fitzralph, the other (probably Richard Kilwyngton) equally savage:

> Fyzrawffe feram pessimam verbi voco ducem,
> Et secundam bestiam equam puto trucem (43–4)

> Fitzralph is the savage beast, first in accusation;
> No less fierce is the next in my estimation.

The argument that Christ's poverty was the result of the Old Law is absurd, for Christ was above the law. Deuteronomy allows a poor man to beg, but in any case the friars do work for their living, as preaching is work:

> Wyt an O and an I, senes sic ignorant
> Quod qui plebi predicant optime laborant (113–14)

> With an O and an I – thus these dotard screechers
> Know not that the highest task is the job of preachers.

Perhaps referring to occasional hypermetric lines in 'Sedens', the author attacks the antimendicants for their poor verse:

> Hii simul et clerici rixas, rithmos edunt,
> Et sicut sunt inscii, legem metri ledunt (139–40)

> With the clerics they pour forth verse vituperation;
> Metric blunders demonstrate faulty education.

They attack the friars for their immorality, but there are more clergy in the Tun (a famous London prison) than friars; they are jealous of the friars' fine churches because they have neglected their own. The author is still secular, but he intends to become a friar:

> Adhuc moror seculo sed frater futurus[111] (176)

> Though I now live in the world, I'll become a friar.

'De astantibus crucifixo'

A more light-hearted touch is seen in a short poem of seventeen hexameters. Someone wonders why crucifixion scenes in the friars' churches have two new figures. On being told that they are Dominic and Francis, he exclaims that a mystery has been cleared up:[112]

> Nam satis audiui quod cum Domino crucifixo
> Famosi fuerunt duo latrones crucifixi (14–15)

> I've often heard it told that with Our Lord
> Two thieves were crucified at Calvary.

Now he knows their names.

Richard Tryvytlam

In about 1358–60 a Franciscan, Richard Tryvytlam (a Cornish name), wrote the *De laude universitatis Oxonie*, in 496 lines of rhythmical asclepiads.[113] As a grateful alumnus he praises the city of Oxford:

> Tu firma meniis, aruis irrigua,
> Pratis pulcherimis mire melliflua (25–6)

> Protected by strong walls, well watered in your fields,
> Your meadowland so fair a fruitful harvest yields.

The university surpasses Athens, Rome and even Paris in its learning; it is the 'City of the Sun' (Isa. 19: 18). In her dotage, however, she allows some of her children (monks) to attack others (friars), despite their faithful service. Some monks stay at home and serve God, but others indulge in hunting and good living. Some think it a virtue to persecute the friars:

> Se Deo facere putant obsequium
> Dum fratres pauperes premant ad vltimum (233–4)

> They think they're duty-bound to serve God in this way,
> By crushing humble friars, the black, the white, the grey.

Three monks in particular are the dragon, leopard and beast with lamb's horns seen by John in the *Apocalypse*; they follow the condemned teaching of Wymund (i.e William) of St Amour. The first is from Glastonbury, shrine of saints, burial-place of King Arthur, famous for its scholars, but disgraced by John Seen.[114] Defying his abbot's orders he is often drunk, and during his hangover he preaches against the friars:

> Nutant vestigia, caligant oculi,
> Lingua collabitur, pes deest gressui . . . .
> Tamen in crastino cum sol caluerit,

273

Digesto paululum vino quo maduit
Hic plebi predicat et fratres inficit (305–12)

His gait is unsteady, his eyes are a blur,
His tongue starts to tremble, his foot will not stir . . .
Yet on the next morning – the sun's in the sky,
The wine that he soaked in is almost quite dry –
His sermon the friars will hotly decry.

The leopard is Richard de Lincoln, abbot of Louth Park: the Cistercian reputation for abstinence is diminished by this lecherous glutton. The last, the two-horned beast, is Uhtred of Boldon, famous for his anti-fraternal writings. He is rightly named 'Owt-rede',

Cum sit improuidus et sine consilio . . .
Balbutit pocius quam profert sillabas,
Cum suas euomet veneni faculas (463–74)

He's lacking in foresight, of wit he's devoid . . .
He stammers his words out and can't get them right;
He vomits his poison and spits out his spite.

Oxford should restrain these three beasts.

De supersticione Phariseorum

It was probably in reply to Tryvytlam that an anonymous monk ('Ab uno de monachis amatore cleri') wrote this poem of 220 lines in Goliardic couplets.[115] Friars have fabricated an occasion out of their pride. The university has been compared to the sun; the sun is both the material sun and God; as the sun is the glory of the world, Oxford is England's glory. The material sun obeys the commands of its superior, God. Anyone who looks at the sun with a straightforward eye (Matt. 6: 22) thrives, but those who stare at it proudly are dazzled. Those who gratefully guard the privileges of the university are honoured, but some are proud:

Jacobiti scilicet, per hanc eruditi,
Lacte matris optime pessime nutriti (55–6)

Namely the Dominicans, Oxford-educated,
On the finest mother's milk wickedly inflated.

They try to enslave the university and destroy the clergy's rights:

Rem preclari nominis captant emulari;
Quia sunt Dominici vellent dominari (79–80)

Having such a splendid name, out of emulation
Since they are Dominicans they seek domination.

Some dogs are grateful but others bite you as soon as they have been fed (an allusion to the pun *Domini-canes*). They preach holiness and piety, but their deeds do not match their words:

> Mores enim mali sunt, licet sermo sanus –
> Vox quidem vox Jacob est, Esau sunt manus (147–8)

> Though their words are sound enough, of their deeds be wary:
> Jacob's voice is plain to hear; Esau's hands are hairy.
> (Gen. 27: 22)

They are wolves in sheep's clothing; they are Pharisees, which means 'divided', and wish to seem too just. They should beware of the end of Gaveston and the Templars. The humble rest with God, but the proud belong to Satan, to whom we entrust them.

'*Achab diu studuit*'

A poem of six stanzas with refrain is preserved in the anti-fraternal collection in Bodleian MS Digby 98.[116] Ahab coveted Naboth's vineyard and at Jezebel's suggestion had Naboth falsely accused and killed (3 Reg. 21). A like-minded Jacobite (i.e. Dominican) tried to do the same, but Naboth has prevailed: the Dominicans renounce the world but have been revealed as hypocrites, since they keep company with the rich:

> Dic, falsa religio, simulata vestibus,
> Omni vacans studio dolis atque fraudibus,
> Quid astas diuitibus in conclaui regio,
> Ut Christi scolaribus noceas mendacio ?
>   Acabita Jacobita, caue tibi consulo,
>   Tua vita ne unita sit totali seculo (st. 3)

> Say, religious hypocrite, clothed in outward seeming,
> Spending all your energy on deceit and scheming,
> Why do you frequent the court, with the rich consorting,
> Words of Christ's true followers twisting and distorting ?
>   Achabite and Jacobite, take heed, be affrighted,
>   Lest your life to worldly strife henceforth be united.

The ass has put on a lion's skin and innocence is expelled. Some specific incident may be behind the poem; otherwise it is more interesting for its metre.[117]

'*Belial apostatarum prepositus*'

The popular '*Princeps regionis gehennalis*', with its satire against novel religious orders, has already been mentioned.[118] Its form, the congratulatory letter from the

Devil, was employed for anti-monastic purposes in 'Belial apostatarum preposi-tus'.[119] It is dated 'anno incarceracionis nostre 1305' [In the year of our Incarcer-ation 1305.] (presumably referring to Anno Domini 1305), and addressed to monks 'qui modernis temporibus residetis in habitu monachali' [who these days reside in monastic habit.]. Unlike Christ, the monks have accepted Satan's offer; their cloisters are filled with soldiers and women, and the monks eat and drink luxuriously:

> Venaciones diurnas diligitis, in claustris residere contempnitis, et quod inter alia nobis valde complacuit, ad philosophorum mores et opera studiosissime declinatis, vestras fimbrias dilatatis, redeuntes ad vomitum velud canes (p.119)

> You love to go hunting every day, and hate to settle in the cloister; what is especially pleasing to me is that you give especial attention to the lives and works of (pagan) philosophers; you have wide fringes, and return like dogs to your vomit

Walter of Peterborough: the war in Spain

Walter of Peterborough, monk of Revesby, Lincolnshire, wrote for both Edward the Black Prince and John of Gaunt, duke of Lancaster; he may have been John of Gaunt's confessor:[120]

> Natus eram Burgi, Petri nutritus in aula,
>   Nomine Walterus, arte poeta ducis.
> Ordine sum tanti ducis inter sacra sacerdos,
>   Revesbiis monachus, vester ubique puer (Wright, p.100)

> In Borough born and raised in Peter's house,
>   My name is Walter, poet of the duke;
> By office I'm the mighty duke's own priest,
>   A monk of Revesby, everywhere your child.

The only extant full-length poem by him is on the English expedition to Spain and the battle of Najera in 1367.[121] In 1365 Pedro the Cruel had been deposed from the throne of Castile by his illegitimate brother Henry of Trastamara; the campaign to restore him was led by the Black Prince and John of Gaunt.[122] The poem consists of a prologue (102 lines, in unrhymed elegiacs), the main poem (560 lines in single-sound elegiacs), and an eight-line epilogue.

Prologue: addressed to John Marton, treasurer of John of Gaunt, who is praised for sharing the name John. After some autobiographical remarks, it praises Edward the Black Prince and John of Gaunt, stressing their lineage through six regnant Edwards.

Poem: it begins with a Lucan-like evocation of fraternal strife:

> Bella referre paro fratrum de germine claro:
>   Plus claros raro protulit ulla caro.

> Nam tres contra tres inierunt proelia fratres,
>> Per multas matres causa fuere patres (Wright, p.101)

> The wars of high-born brothers I declaim:
>> Few lines have bred a stock of greater fame.
> Fraternal trio with three brothers strives,
>> Because of fathers and their many wives.

The poem does not exploit the theme of fraternal strife;[123] it is simply a panegyric and record, with few poetic flourishes. It recounts the exiled Pedro's approach to the Black Prince, Edward III's permission for him and John of Gaunt to fight in Spain, the crossing of the Pyrenees, the surrender of Salvatierra, the penetration of Henry's guerilla bases in the mountains, and the final battle at Najera. There are many lists of the English heroes (Chandos, Knolles, etc.) and detailed accounts of battle formations and tactics, such as the dangerous (and sometimes fatal) ascent of the mountains. Walter was almost certainly present on the campaign. The poem must be regarded as a record of facts rather than an epic, but it is still depressingly flat, with frequent fillers to provide the necessary four rhymes:

> Praeco procedit, responsum principis edit,
>> Litera succedit, nuntius ergo redit (Wright, p.105)

> The prince's herald takes the answer back,
>> Then with a letter turns home on his track.

The metre and syntax are often defective, with no compensatory vigour:

> Illic plagatus est miles de Burlee vocatus,
>> Sed cito curatus est equitare ratus (Wright, p.109)

> The knight of Burley there received a wound,
>> But, quickly cured, his mount he soon resumed.

Epilogue: the poet addresses his verses and laments that they have brought no reward:

> Laudes sperabam seu praemia danda putabam;
>> Frustra sudabam, vos, metra, quando dabam (Wright, p.122)

> I hoped for praise or monetary gain:
>> In writing verse my labour was in vain.

Swine never appreciate pearls.

Walter seems to have been a prolific poet. Under the entry for 1366 the Peterborough Chronicle records that in that year 'the whole story of sacred history was for the first time discovered in the fables of Ovid's *Metamorphoses* by Walter of Peterborough, formerly monk of Revesby'. Walter himself describes the poem, written for John of Gaunt ('duce pro nostro'), in his prologue to the poem on Najera:

> Sacra Jhesu cecini sub carmine clausa poesis
>> Prodens in lucem quae latuere prius:

Chronica quicquid habet, ab Adam docet ad Julianum
De transformatis in tribus ille libris (Wright, p.98, prints *libros*)

I sang Christ's truth, in poetry enclosed;
I brought to light what lay concealed before.
The three books of the Metamorphoses
Relate man's tale right down to Julian.

The work is not extant: none of the Christian interpretations of the *Metamorphoses* answer to this description.[124]

Walter also says that he wrote a *Theotecon* (a poem on the Virgin Mary) for the Black Prince, whose poet he claimed to have been at the battle of Poitiers in 1356:

Principe pro nostro scripsi quondam Theotecon
In Pictavensi marte, poeta suus (Wright, p.97)

At Poitiers, as poet to our prince,
I wrote the Holy Mother's praise in verse.

This also has not survived: a glossator says that it consisted of 5000 lines.

He is credited, by the scribe of MS Digby 166, with three stanzas attacking a homosexual abbot:

Tolle sodomiticum, deprecor, abbatem
Qui tot tuos docuit tantam feditatem

God, please fire this sodomite, please remove this abbot,
Who has taught your many monks such a filthy habit.

These are attached to a Goliardic poem, often ascribed to Alain de Lille, on whether the love of virgins is superior to that of experienced women.[125]

Whatever Walter's failings as a poet in our eyes, he is interesting for his professional status. He clearly implies that he had some sort of status as the poet of the Black Prince and John of Gaunt; the disappointed epilogue may be no more than a joke. On the other hand, he also says that he wrote the poem on Najera at the command of his abbot:

Balsama tanta metro mandare monet meus abbas (Wright, p.100)

My abbot bids me set such balms in verse.

It may be that he simply hoped to win favours by his poems, but poetry was not his profession in the way it was, say, for Henry of Avranches.

'Gloria cunctorum'

The anonymous poem 'Gloria cunctorum', eighty lines of single-sound Leonines, covers the same events as Walter of Peterborough's poem, but makes a striking contrast.[126] Whereas Walter goes through the whole story and campaign

278

chronologically, the 'Gloria cunctorum' spends thirty-six lines on the background (Pedro's exile, the appeal to the Black Prince, Edwards III's permission), and a single couplet on the victory:

> Proelia junxerunt, ubi plures morte ruerunt;
> Multi fugerunt, capti bis mille fuerunt (Wright, p.95)

> They joined in battle; many fell down dead, –
> Two thousand captives seized, – and many fled.

The rest of the poem praises the English heroes (John of Gaunt, Offord, Chandos, Knolles, etc.) and is lavish in praise of the Black Prince, who surpasses Solomon, Samson, Simeon, and the Nine Worthy:

> Tres portant flores gentiles ut meliores;
> Tres sunt victores Judaei lucidiores;
> Tres nostrae fidei sunt ejusdem speciei –
> Compar nullus ei, dum extat dux aciei (Wright, p.96)

> Three pagans take the flower as proven knight;
> Three Jewish victors shine in glory bright;
> Three Christians are of the same degree –
> But in the fight there's none as brave as he.

It ends with praise of Edward III and Philippa for their offspring and with a prayer for their marriage bed. It lacks the detail of Walter of Peterborough, but amply compensates in liveliness.

Anticlericalism and Lollards

In the 1370s and 1380s religious controversy shifted from the conflict between friars and monks (or friars and secular clergy) to one between conservatives and reformers on the whole ecclesiastical establishment.

The first point at issue was church wealth and the 'Donation of Constantine' (which had supposedly endowed the church with its secular authority and possessions); this originally theological dispute had a more immediate relevance – the taxability of church wealth for the depleted treasury and the war effort. Added to this were the teachings of Wycliffe on the doctrine of 'dominion' (concerning the authority of unworthy priests and the validity of their absolutions and administration of the sacraments) and ultimately on the nature of the Eucharist itself. In addition there was a general undercurrent of anticlericalism (to which anti-fraternal and anti-monastic satire had doubtless contributed); several conservatives saw a connexion between Wycliffe's teachings and the social unrest of the Peasants' Revolt. There were several attempts to suppress Wycliffe's doctrines, notably at the Council of London of 1382 (also known as the Blackfriars Council or Earthquake Council). Attempts to weed out Lollards – the image of 'tares among the wheat' recurs constantly in anti-Wycliffite writing – were successful at an official level, and in the early fifteenth century Archbishop Arundel ruthlessly searched out heretics. Underground, however, with varying degrees of sophistication, the Lollard movement persisted and led to an armed revolt under Sir John Oldcastle in 1413 (he was executed in 1417). The suppression of Oldcastle is a concern of Thomas Elmham.[127]

'Vox in Rama'

This unpublished poem, probably by a Benedictine monk, consists of twenty-four six-line Goliardic stanzas with an 'O-and-I' refrain.[128] It begins with the lament of Rachel in Rama (Matt. 2: 18) and the divisions in the church; perhaps alluding to Wycliffe it says that people are deceived:

> Serpens item sibilat in sciendi ligno
> Et plebem sophisticat elencho maligno (9/1–2)

> In the tree of good and ill Satan spins temptation,
> Blinding folk with logic's tricks by sophistication.

It laments the alliance of clergy, king and people in their attack on ecclesiastical possessions and their attempts to seize it for the treasury. A few people now try to undo what has been agreed by popes and emperors:

> Quod sancti iam sanxerant et lex iubet stare
> Et pape et cesares solebant mandare
> Ut sint res ecclesie libere et clare,
> Pauci modo pueri querunt eneruare (16/1–4)

> What the saints have sanctified and the law demanded
> And by popes and emperors used to be commanded,
> That the church own property free and unrestricted,
> These few kids now want to see quashed and contradicted.

He calls on the pope to protect Christ's heritage:

> With an O and an I – zelum Dei gere,
> Christi patrimonium serua et tuere (29/5–6)

> With an O and an I – come, for God be zealous,
> Keeping Christ's inheritance, vigilant and jealous.

The reformers claim to be restoring the church to its original nature, but by that argument princes should return to sheep-tending and lawyers to ploughing; the church has now grown up and must be honoured differently:

> Tunc cepit ecclesia et nunc est adulta,
> Et decet ut aliter nunc quam tunc sit culta (37/1–2)

> Now the church has come of age (then it was beginning);
> Different customs from the old now are right and fitting.

Their arguments rest on the infernal books of Ockham.[129] The ancient right of sanctuary shows the superiority of church over state. Saints died for church property and laid anathemas on those who stole it.

'Heu quanta desolatio'

This pro-Wycliffite poem, in forty-nine stanzas of the same metre, was written shortly after the Council of London of 1382.[130] It laments the state of the realm:

> Heu quanta desolatio Angliae praestatur,
> Cujus regnum quodlibet hinc inde minatur (Wright, p.253)
>
> O what desolation now England suffers sadly;
> On all sides the realm's beset, bruised and battered badly.

God's wrath is evident in the persistence of the plague, the Peasants' Revolt,[131] and the earthquake on the opening day of the Council. This the reward for sin – for false measures by merchants,

> Si status conspicimus, nullus excusatur,
> Quod in shopis venditur male mensuratur, (Wright, p.254)
>
> If we look at each estate, all of them are targets:
> Measurements are all amiss in the shops and markets,

lecherous clerics, proud prelates, and false friars. No better are the Benedictine monks ('sunt maledicti'), with their hunting and gluttony. The poet had planned to become a monk but changed his mind and returned to 'the rule of Christ';

> Haec ego qui feceram, monachus agressus,
> Per hos rasus fueram, sed nondum professus[132] (Wright, p.258)
>
> Once I thought to be a monk (what a sad confession !),
> Took the tonsure at their hands – didn't make profession.

The first to speak at the Council is John Wells,[133] who is refuted in an exchange with Wycliffe and Nicholas Hereford:

> Nichol solvens omnia jussit Bayard stare.
> With an O and an I, Wellis replicabat,
> Sed postquam Nichol solverat, tunc Johannes stabat (Wright, p.260)
>
> Nick, refuting everything, said 'Proud Bayard, hold it !'
> With an O and an I – Wells made replication,
> But Nick's answer then led to John's humiliation.

Other anti-Wycliffites speak in turn and are denounced by the poet, who notes that Piers (presumably Piers Plowman) can testify to the degeneracy of modern friars:

With an O and an I, fuerunt pyed freres;
Quomodo mutati sunt, rogo, dicat Pers (Wright, p.262)

With an O and an I – they wore motley habit;
For the tale of how they've changed, ask Piers – he will have it.

(Pied friars: here Carmelites, whose habits were brown and white. There may be an allusion to an earlier sect of pied friars; the charge, of course, is implicitly moral. See *Pierce the Plowman's Crede*).

Their arguments are finally demolished by Philip Repingdon; they flee to the bishop of London, and bribe him to denounce Hereford and Repingdon. An appeal is to be made to the pope.

'Praesta Jhesu'

A poem of about the same date, 'Praesta Jhesu quod postulo', presents the anti-Wycliffite arguments in fifty-six twelve-line stanzas.[134] The poet asks that the gardener should remove the weeds from the garden of the church:

> Hortolanus in hortulo
> secat salutis sarculo
> veprem ne crescens noceat (1/4–6)

> Gardener with saving hoe
> Cuts the bramble in the row,
> Lest it spread and choke.

He says that John Ball, on his deathbed, admitted that Wycliffites had been the prime cause of the revolt:

> Monstrans Wycleffe familiam
> causam brigae primariam
> quae totum regnum terruit (13/7–9)

> Showing that to Wycliffe's crew
> Was the Rising mainly due
> Which had scared the realm.

He presents the Wycliffite doctrines in detail, and refutes them, stressing the duty to obey those in authority, the efficacy of sacraments even administered by bad priests, the importance of oral confession, the case for both ecclesiastical possessions and mendicancy (thus demonstrating how much alliances had shifted), and the efficacy of the Eucharist and the reality of transubstantiation. He calls on Christ to come into the garden and bind the foxes that are destroying the vineyards:

> Liga vulpes erroneas
> quae sic devastant vineas
> et gravem pestem instruunt[135] (54/4–6)

Tie the erring foxes up
When they tear the vineyards up,
    Spreading utter ruin

Consideration of the Lollards has brought us into the unhappy reign of Richard II (1377–99). At the age of ten he succeeded his grandfather Edward III (after the death of his father, the Black Prince, in 1376), and his reign sadly fulfilled the biblical warning, cited in Piers Plowman, 'Vae terrae ubi puer rex est'. His twenty-two years as King witnessed the Peasants' Revolt of 1381, the disastrous Norwich Crusade of 1383, the overthrow of his council by the Lords Appellant and the Merciless Parliament of 1386–7, his quarrel with the city of London in 1392, his capricious and vindictive measures after 1396, and finally the invasion of Henry of Lancaster in 1399, leading to his deposition and death. These events are reflected in the literature.

'Prohdolor accrevit' (Peasants' Revolt)

In 102 lines of mixed Leonines, this laments the reversal of roles:[136]

Servit nobilitas et rusticitas dominatur,
Ad res illicitas omnis plebs praecipitatur.
Garcio bacchatur et ingenuos agitatur;
Judex damnatur, reus et in sede levatur (Wright, p.227)

Nobility are serfs and peasants rule the roost;
At what was once outlawed the plebs are now unloosed.
The serving lad runs wild, the noble is distraught;
The judge is in the dock, the felon rules his court.

(Note: if Wright's ingenuos is correct, agitatur must be deponent).

The king is weak and still unfeared; he would have lost his head if Walworth had not beheaded the peasants' leader. The poet mourns the murder of the archbishop of Canterbury, Simon Sudbury,

Sic moritur Symon de bacca dictus et austri[137] (Wright, p.228)

Simon, named for 'berry' and for 'South', is dead.

Just vengeance is taken, and peace returns,

Sic mediante Deo respirat pax recidiva
Ne duce stramineo pereat plebs crismate diva[138] (Wright, p.229)

Thus by the grace of God the peace is now restored,
Lest 'Straw-duke' kill the folk anointed by the Lord.

Canterbury is blamed as the source of the rebellion; the poet prays God for mercy on a sinful land and, in a list similar to Gower's, names the leaders of the peasants:

283

Jak Chepe, Tronche, Jon Wrau, Thom Myllere, Tyler, Jak Strawe,
Erle of the Plo, Rak to, Deer, et Hob Carter, Rakstrawe (Wright, p.230)

(No translation is needed. Note *to* 'too').

Thomas Varoye (Battle of Otterburn)

In August 1388 England suffered another disaster. A Scottish raiding party, led by
the earl of Douglas, attacked Newcastle; they withdrew, pursued by Henry
Hotspur of Northumberland, but in the ensuing battle at Otterburn the English
were humiliatingly routed. Douglas and other Scottish leaders were killed, but
Hotspur was captured, and for many years Scotland dominated the North. The
battle is famous in English literature for two later ballads ('Battle of Otterburn' and
'Chevy Chase'); it was also celebrated by Thomas Varoye, canon of Glasgow and
provost of Bothwell, in a 342-line poem.[139] It begins with a prologue that laments
that the two kingdoms cannot live in peace:

> Insula jam Britonum duo continet optima regna,
> Pacis quodque bonum quibus exulat arte maligna (p.406)

> Two splendid kingdoms share this blessed isle,
> But peace is banished by the devil's guile.

It lists the Scots' leaders, and gives set speeches, first to Hotspur as he urges the
English to pursuit –

> Armetis, detis pugnam Scotis; fugitivi
> Sunt, timidi, pavidi; capientur carcere vivi – (p.408)

> To arms ! Attacks the Scots ! They run in flight:
> They'll soon surrender, cowering in fright.

and then to Douglas before the battle:

> Victores eritis, non dubitetis,
> Et vobis eveniet vespera felix
> Vosque coronabit gloria belli (p.410)

> You'll win the day, of this be sure,
> The setting sun will seal your joy
> And victor's crown will grace your brow.

There is a detailed account of the battle, of the Scottish grief when they count their
dead, and of their return home. The poem is pro-Scots but not vindictively
anti-English.

Metrically it is a remarkable tour-de-force, very reminiscent of Robert Baston's
poem on Bannockburn and sometimes approaching Michael of Cornwall's
virtuosity.[140] In addition to the usual assortment of vigorously rhymed hexa-

meters (including cruciferi and collaterals with double internal rhyme), there is one block with run-over rhyme:

> Iam fragor armorum Scotorum moenia sternit,
> Cernit et hic pugiles agiles, dum buccina clangit,
> Frangit turma fores, modo res arctissima crescit (p.408)

> Now clash of Scottish arms the walls lays low,
> And lo, the light-foot fight. The trumpet sounds,
> The army pounds the gates: the fates close in.

The section including Douglas' speech quoted above is in the metre of Boethius, *Consolatio Philosophiae* 1 m.2. Also, in two parts, one of twenty-two lines, he employs an octameter (like a hexameter, but with eight feet):

> Hic feritur, feriens ferit et perit; iste moritur sanguine fuso;
> Hic rapitur, rapiens rapit; hic capitur capiens: sic sors variatur[141](p.411)

> He's struck; the striker strikes, and falls; another sheds his blood and dies;
> He's seized, the seizer seizes; this one grabs, is grabbed; so fortunes change.

Richard Maidstone

Many writers – Walter of Peterborough, Wycliffe, Chaucer – can be associated with John of Gaunt, uncle of the king. To these may be added Gaunt's confessor, the Carmelite friar Richard Maidstone. He wrote a pro-mendicant treatise and (in English) a verse translation of the Penitential Psalms.[142] His contribution to Anglo-Latin literature is a 548-line poem on the pageant that welcomed King Richard into London in August 1392; its detailed knowledge suggests that Maidstone may have been one of the organizers.[143] The king, enraged by the city's refusal to provide him with money, had suspended London's ancient privileges, removed the mayor and sheriffs from office, and taken himself and his court to York; the reconciliation (effected by a 'gift' of £10,000) was celebrated with elaborate pageantry. Perhaps following the lead of Gower, Maidstone uses unrhymed elegiac couplets and calls London 'Troy'.[144]

Maidstone begins by quoting Cicero on friendship, invoking the name Richard that he shares with the king. In the allegorical language of the time, the bridegroom (Richard) has been separated from his bed-chamber (London) by 'perfida lingua'[145] but has now set aside his anger:

> Non poterat mordax detractans lingua tenere
> > Quin cuperet thalamum sponsus adire suum.
> Qui libertates solitas tibi dempserat omnes
> > Nunc redit, et plures reddere promptus eas (Wright, p.283)

> But biting mordant tongue could not hold back
> > The groom from entry to his bridal suite.

For he who once withheld your wonted rights
Returns and will restore them many fold.

The Warden instructs the city to prepare a welcome and, with the aldermen, goes to greet
the king, followed by representatives of all the guilds in livery,

Hic carpentarius, scissor, sartor, ibi sutor,
Hic pelliparius, fulloque, mango, faber (Wright, p.285)

The carpenter, the tailor, the mender and the shoesmith,
The skinner and the fuller, the monger and the blacksmith.

The king's majesty is like Troilus and the queen is dazzling in her jewels. The king accepts the
keys and sword of the city and its surrender. They pass through Southwark, pardoning a
criminal, and at London Bridge are presented with two destriers and a palfrey. In the city a
carriage carrying some ladies overturns, with a display of female thighs:

Femina feminea sua dum sic femina nudat,
Vix poterat risum plebs retinere suum (Wright, p.290)

When thus the ladies bared their lovely thighs,
The people scarcely could restrain their mirth.
(*femina* (2) has a short *e* in Classical Latin; I have corrected Wright's hyperclassiciza-
tions *foemina* etc.)

Pageants line the route. In Cheapside a boy and girl descend miraculously from a tower and
present wine and crowns. At St Paul's, God and angels are represented. At Temple Bar there
is a forest, full of wild animals, and in the middle is John the Baptist, the king's favourite
saint, to soothe his anger:

Hujus ad intuitum, si quid sibi manserat irae,
Extitit exstinctum protinus usque nihil (Wright, p.294)

On sight of this, if any wrath remained,
It disappeared and vanished utterly.

The king and queen are presented with gold tablets representing the Crucifixion, to arouse a
sense of mercy. At Westminster the queen fulfils an earlier promise and intercedes with the
king: not since Arthur's day have such gifts been bestowed on a king. King Richard warns
the Londoners of the dangers in pride in their wealth, but pardons them, restoring their keys
and ancient privileges. The crowd cries 'Long live the King'.

The poem illustrates the heraldic function which poets were beginning to perform
in the later Middle Ages.

John Gower

John Gower is now more famous for his English poetry than his Latin, and until
recently his reputation was second only to that of Chaucer. Although Lydgate was
soon dropped from the 'laureate triad', Gower held his place until, in this century,
he was replaced in critical esteem by Langland and the Gawain poet. The epithet

'moral', however, which was given to him by Chaucer, refers not to his English verse but to his French *Mirour de l'Omme* (*Speculum Meditantis*) and especially his Latin *Vox Clamantis*. Gower was the last major medieval English writer to use Latin and French as a literary medium: where Chaucer and Langland sensed (and to some extent fostered) an English-reading public, Gower hedged his bets on literary immortality by using all three major languages.[146] In 1390 he claimed Richard II as a literary patron, but became disillusioned and in 1399 heartily welcomed the usurpation of Henry IV.[147]

His major Latin poem, in over ten thousand lines, is the *Vox Clamantis*, the first substantial Anglo-Latin work in unrhymed elegiac couplets since Henry of Avranches.[148] The first book, entitled the *Visio* by Wickert, must be treated as a separate work; it contains 2150 lines on the Peasants' Revolt.

Book I (*Visio*).[149] In the fashion of English and French dream-visions, it begins with a *sententia*:

> Scripture veteris capiunt exempla futuri,
>> Nam dabit experta res magis esse fidem (I, Prol. 1–2)

> Of ancient books those yet to come take heed,
>> For thing experienced commands belief.

Gower gives his name in a cryptogram; may John, author of Revelations, aid his tearful poem. A pleasant day, described by means of an *aubade* (dawn song, complete with the Sun's chariot), *reverdie* (spring song) and *locus amoenus*, is followed by a sleepless night of anxiety. At dawn the poet finally falls asleep, and dreams that on a Tuesday morning (Mars' day) he goes out to pick flowers. He sees the peasant rabble turned by God's wrath into irrational beasts – asses, oxen, swine, dogs, cats, foxes, fowls, midges, and frogs. Domestic animals refuse to perform their proper functions, and tame animals become wild. Roused by the jay (Wat Tyler) and John Ball, the peasants assemble:

> Watte vocat, cui Thomme venit, neque Symme retardat,
>> Bette que Gibbe simul Hykke venire iubent (1.783–4)
> Tom comes thereat when called by Wat, and Simon as forward we find;
> Bet calls as quick to Gibb and to Hykk, that neither would tarry behind.

(Translation by Fuller, cited by H. Morley, *English Writers* IV (London, 1889), 180).

They are armed with rustic implements, which are more horrific than comic:

> Ascia, falx, fede quos roderat atra rubigo,
>> Gestantur, que suo cuspide colla secant (1.855–6)

> They carry axe and scythe befouled with rust,
>> Whose jagged edge scores deep its bearer's neck.

(Note *que* = *et*, as often in Gower)

Young and old march on New Troy, sack the Savoy, and murder the priest Helenus (i.e. Sudbury). Terrified by the breakdown in public order and feeling surrounded by foes, the poet flees, and would have crawled inside a tree if he could:

> Si potui, volui sub eodem cortice condi,
>> Nulla superficies tunc quia tuta fuit (I.1443–4)

> I longed to hide myself beneath the bark,
>> For nowhere on the surface then was safe.

He feels totally alone, and not even Sophia (Wisdom) can console him. With others he boards a ship (later in the dream interpreted as the Tower of London, and, in a marginal note, as his disturbed mind); this is assailed by storms and a sea monster, and almost sinks. His prayers to God and the Virgin are answered by Neptune: William Walworth kills Wat Tyler, and calm returns. The battered ship drifts in search of a haven: the poet disembarks on an island, which, he is told by an old man, is Brutus' island, now inhabited by lawless men. Terrified again, the dreamer faints and everything disappears. A heavenly voice tells him to write of his dream, and he awakes at cockcrow. He gives thanks to God, but is aware that the peasants are still rebellious. He decides to obey the voice and to write of his dream.

This bare synopsis cannot convey the nightmarish quality of the *Visio*, the terror at the unrestrained violence, and the panic and sense of isolation. The verbal debt to Ovid and other writers (stressed by Macaulay) does not detract from the conceptual originality. In the beast-vision section, each episode uses classical and biblical analogues to portray a society in fear and disarray.[150] Most Medieval Latin dream-visions are simply frames for fiction (such as debates between gods or abstract personifications), but Gower, by means of abrupt transitions in the narrative sequence, has managed to imitate the quality of a nightmare.

The remaining eight thousand lines of the *Vox Clamantis* can be treated more summarily. Essentially, there are three sections: estates satire (III.i–VI.vi), advice to Richard II (VI.vii–xviii), and decline of the world (VI.xix–VII.xxiv). These are framed by discussions of the nature of Fortune (II and VII.xxv). Books II–VII can stand alone, and were probably composed separately.[151]

Book II. Readers should not look for originality but for the hidden meaning; the work is called *Vox Clamantis*. Men blame Fortune and her wheel for their ills, but she does not exist. Scriptural examples show that just men have control over nature and that sinful men are overthrown: God is in charge of everything.

Book III. The poet speaks with the voice of the people:

> A me non ipso loquor hec, set que michi plebis
>> Vox dedit, et sortem plangit vbique malam (III, Prol.11–12)

> I speak these words not from myself, but as
>> The people's voice, lamenting fate, dictates.

He will write of the three estates:

> Sunt clerus, miles, cultor, tres trina gerentes,
>> Hic docet, hic pugnat, alter et arua colit[152] (III.1–2)

> The cleric, knight and ploughman have three tasks,
>> As teacher, fighter, tiller of the soil.

Satire on the secular clergy, particularly bishops and priests for their lechery and luxurious living; they encourage sin in order to reap the fines. (This section, which denounces the Donation of Constantine, is very reformist in tone. It is especially concerned with wars of Christian against Christian, encouraged by church leaders (especially the pope) out of avarice.)

Book IV. Satire on monks, nuns, and friars, using the traditional stereotypes (the hunting monk, the lecherous nun). The book concludes with Burnellus' Order of Ease.[153]

Book V. Soldiers fight for love instead of for Christ; warnings against the enticements of women (mainly from Ovid). Peasants, their laziness, wandering, and unfaithfulness:

> Nos magis hesterna facit experiencia doctos
>> Quid sibi perfidie seruus iniqus habet (v.599–600)

> Events of yesterday make us aware
>> What treachery lurks in an evil serf.

Merchants: Usury and Fraud, the two daughters of Avarice, and their activities in banking, property and trade.[154] Corruption in local government; gossip.

Book VI. Lawyers and officers of the law thrive on discord and are guilty of avarice:

> Vndique casus adest legis, quo pendulus hamus
>> Aurea de burse gurgite dona capit (vi.73–4)

> All round lies Case-at-law, whose hanging hook
>> Can catch the gifts of gold from purse's stream.

Nevertheless, law is necessary and the king is its head:

> Dux si perdat iter, errant de plebe sequentes,
>> Et via qua redient est dubitanda magis (vi.499–500)

> If leader lose his way, his flock will stray:
>> The way back home will be the more in doubt.

This leads to a long section of advice to Richard II, particularly to follow the example of his father, the Black Prince.[155] The world is in decline:

> Poma cadunt ramis, agitantur ab ilice glandes,
>> Marcescunt flores, defluit orta seges (vi.1201–2)

> The apples fall and acorns drop from oaks;
>> The flowers droop, the ripened harvest wilts.

Good rulers have passed away, and the chaste have been succeeded by the unfaithful.

Book VII. As in Nebuchadnezzar's dream (Dan. 4), gold has been succeeded by two major evils, the iron of avarice and the clay of lechery. Fiction and love stories are preferred to scripture. Death ends all, and the Seven Deadly Sins terminate in filth. The need to repent before the Last Judgment: the good will be saved, but even in his beloved England sin prevails. Fortune is not to blame. He has spoken as the spirit commanded him in his sleep and as the voice of the people told him. The world's fate is in the hands of men:

Mundus erit talis, fuerit viuens homo qualis;
Obstet vitalis quilibet ergo malis (VII.1477–8)

This world will be like every living wight:
Against what's wrong all living men should fight.

Although the overall compass of *Vox Clamantis* II–VII is impressive, the ideas and expressions are for the most part commonplace. It is hard to believe that the literary topos of Fortune was taken so seriously as to need such an elaborate refutation. The estates satire deals with plurals – monks, merchants, lawyers – rather than Chaucer's more effective individual characterizations (*the* Monk, *the* Merchant, *the* Man of Law). Where Chaucer delineates a character by means of his everyday skills and tools, Gower spells out his moral deficiencies.[156] But perhaps it is unfair to compare Gower with the genius of Chaucer just because they were contemporaries; the *Vox Clamantis* is a good place to find traditional satire assembled altogether, and there are many amusing, if not original, portraits. One of the most surprising things about it, in view of the exempla with which the *Confessio Amantis* is packed, is the absence of exemplary stories.

Four poems written before 1399 deserve mention. The *Carmen super multiplici viciorum pestilencia* (1396–7), 321 lines of unrhymed elegiacs mixed with single-sound Leonines, denounces Lollardy (the tares in the wheat of simple faith) and more general sins. The *De lucis scrutinio*, 103 Leonines, explores the shortcomings of all the estates, from the two popes to the peasants. Although presumably written before Gower's blindness, its sustained image of dark and light would be appropriate for someone whose eyesight was failing:

Hec Gower scribit, lucem dum querere quibit;
Sub spe transibit, vbi gaudia lucis adibit:
Lucis solamen det sibi Cristus. Amen (101–3)

This Gower writes, while he can seek the light.
He'll pass in hope and reach the joys of light.
May Christ grant him the comfort of His light.

'Ecce patet tensus' has lost its second half; its account of the powers of Cupid was probably followed by a prayer for grace to avoid sin. 'Est amor in glosa' has nineteen lines on the oxymora of love,[157] followed by eight lines in praise of married love, probably to be associated with Gower's own marriage in 1398:

Hinc vetus annorum Gower sub spe meritorum
Ordine sponsorum tutus adhibo thorum (7–8)

Now old in years, in hope of what I've earned,
Now wed, my bed I seek, quite unconcerned.

Gower's last major work, in any language, was the *Cronica Tripertita*. Despite its title, this is far more (and less) than a versified chronicle; events have been selected and shaped to form, for the Lancastrian cause, what is almost a drama. It describes the humiliation of Richard II in 1387, his revenge in 1397, and his downfall in 1399.

The three parts, in Leonines, mirror the structure: Part I (219 lines) the work of man, 'opus humanum'); Part II (347 lines) the work of the devil ('opus inferni'); Part III (4389 lines) the work of God, 'opus in Christo'.

Part I. Richard's reign began with an insurrexion, but his heart was hardened. With his young council he plotted against three barons in order to seize their wealth:

> Et sic qui cati pellem cupit excoriati
> Fingebat causas fallaci pectore clausas (1.25–26)

> Like one that flays the cat to get its skin,
> His crafty breast feigned causes closed within.

Forewarned, the Swan, Bear and Horse, and 'the one that bears S', supported by the Northern Moon,[158] defeated the king's forces under the Boar at Radcot Bridge in 1387. The king's councillors were executed or exiled.

Part II. Ten years later, in 1396–7, Richard treacherously attacked the three nobles, and deposed and exiled Thomas Arundel, archbishop of Canterbury.[159] The king's henchmen composed mocking songs on Gloucester, Arundel and Warwick:

> Non Olor in pennis, nec Equs stat crine perhennis . . .
> Vrsus non mordet quem stricta cathena remordet (II.314–6)

> The Swan's been plucked, the Horse has lost its mane . . .
> The Bear can't bite when tethered by a chain.

Part III. The poet sees happy times ahead:

> Tristia post leta, post tristia sepe quieta,
> Si bene pensemus, satis hec manifesta videmus (III.1–2)

> Grief follows mirth, but grief then yields to glee;
> If we reflect, this truth is plain to see.

Like a mole Richard digs traps for his enemies, and to extend his tyranny he forces people to sign blank charters. He exiles Henry of Derby (now duke of Lancaster) and tries to disinherit him, but Henry, with the archbishop, returns and lands at Grimsby. Richard 'flees' to Ireland,[160] and his accomplices Scrope, Green and Bushey are captured. Richard returns, unrepentant but unsupported; again like a mole he tries to hide, but is captured, put in the Tower, and deposed. Henry is crowned king and annuls Richard's wicked laws. A plot against him, by those he had mercifully spared, is foiled. Unconsolable, Richard dies of grief in the Tower. Gower concludes with a series of contrasts between the two kings:

> R. pestem mittit, mortem pius H. que remittit;
> R. seruitutem statuit, pius H. que salutem (III.467–8)

> R. sends the plague, H. tempers death's decree;
> While R. enslaves, with mercy H. sets free.

The *Cronica Tripertita* shares many of the features of fourteenth-century political poetry: the Leonine rhyme and the fondness for onomastic wordplay. Michael de la Pole is 'de puteo Michaelis'; Nicholas Brembre, mayor of London, is 'tribulus . . .

qui proceres pungit'. It is also the first major piece of Lancastrian propaganda, the precursor of the poems of Thomas Elmham.[161]

Gower wrote a few other short poems before his death, mainly in honour of Henry IV.[162] He combined all his Latin poems into a presentation copy (now All Souls College, Oxford, MS 98), and sent it, with a dedicatory epistle of forty-nine Leonines ('Successor Thome, Thomas'), to the restored archbishop of Canterbury, Thomas Arundel. By the time he did this he was blind:

> Cecus ego mere, nequio licet acta videre,
> Te tamen in mente memorabor corde vidente (17–18)

> Entirely blind, with eyes I cannnot view,
> But in my mind, my seeing heart sees you.

One of his last poems is a touching statement of resignation that he cannot see to write any more:

> Quicquid homo scribat, finem natura ministrat,
>   Que velut vmbra fugit nec fugiendo redit;
> Illa michi finem posuit, quo scribere quicquam
>   Vlterius nequio, sum quia cecus ego

> A man may write, but Nature writes the end;
>   She, like a shadow, flees without return.
> She wrote the end for me, and so I can
>   No longer write a thing, for I am blind.

Although the Latin verses that accompany Gower's English poem *Confessio Amantis* do not constitute a discrete Latin work, they deserve mention, as they utilize Latin in a unique way. The content of the Latin verses is determined by the English poem, which, in eight books, recounts the Lover's 'confession' to Genius, priest of the God of Love. In each chapter of each book the Lover confesses under the headings of the cardinal sins and their branches; the sins are those against love, but they are placed in a wider moral context. Each chapter is preceded by a short Latin poem (in unrhymed elegiacs, until the end) which encapsulates the sin. As the English poem explains and exemplifies the sin at length (with a story), Gower was free to use the Latin somewhat differently.[163] Unlike the easy verse of the *Vox Clamantis* and *Cronica Tripertita*, the sense is compressed into a syntactically tight, often cryptic and almost riddling epigrammatic unit, often with a resonance outside the immediate context. He makes constant use of etymological relationships to strengthen his point, as in IV.vi, against sluggardliness:

> Quem *prob*at armorum *prob*itas Venus ap*prob*at, et quem
>   Torpor habet re*prob*um re*prob*at illa virum

> Venus approves whom prowess proves in arms,
> Reproves the reprobate in Torpor's grip.
> (Translation from Echard and Fanger).

where the underlying word is *probitas* 'prowess'. His concern with 'right rule' in the kingdom leads to a series of puns on the root *reg* in VII.vi (*regimen, recte, rex, regna, regat*), which is reinforced by the English words 'right' and 'rule' (*regula*). Most importantly, the Latin poems hinge on a single central image, a relatively rare structure in Medieval Latin verse and one that comes to be a characteristic of short vernacular poems.

More Northern writings

Chronicon Metricum Ecclesiae Eboracensis

The metrical history of the church of York was written while Thomas Arundel, Gower's dedicatee, was archbishop of York (1388–96).[164] It was compiled from old records and intended for inclusion on a *tabula*, a wooden triptych containing historical monuments of York (still extant):

> Haec ex archivis de multis paucula scripsi;
> Ne lateat latebris, tabula sic publice fixi (13–14)

> From many deeds I've written just these few
> And placed them on a board in public view.

It consists of 512 lines of elegiacs and hexameters, with occasional rhyme, in no fixed pattern. It draws on Geoffrey of Monmouth, Bede, and later histories such as the *Vita Thurstani*.[165]

It describes the founding of York by Ebrauc, grandson of Brutus, and his establishment of a pagan (*phanaticum*) temple there under one of the three British *archiflamines*. This lasted for 1200 years until the conversion of the Britons to Christianity by Fagan and Damian:

> Sic archipraesul fugat archiflaminis umbram (68)

> Archbishop puts to flight archdruid's shade.

Christianity was driven out during the invasions and settlement of the Angles, Saxons and Jutes, apart from two brief restorations by Aurelius and archbishop Samson and then by Arthur and archbishop Piramus. Augustine's mission to the English led to the baptism of King Edwin by Paulinus in 627 and the renovation of York, under Oswald, Wilfrid, and Egbert. Moral degeneracy of the English led to the Norman Conquest, and the burning of York and the loss of many of its possessions; archbishops Thomas (I) and Thurstan tried to protect its rights. The poet then turns back to the time of Ebrauc to give a history of Scotland and the arrival of the Scots:

> Pervaga Scotica gens Hibernica rura relinquens
> Occiduis residet partibus Albaniae (425–6)

> The wandering Scottish race leaves Ireland's fields
> And settles in the West of Albany.

This leads into an account of the suffragan bishoprics of York in Scotland and the Orkneys, and a final prayer to St Peter and St Andrew (patron saint of Scotland) to bring the Scottish churches back into the fold of York.

The poem is a testimony to civic pride rather than literary talent, but demonstrates the monumental function of Latin verse.

Execution of Archbishop Scrope

Arundel's successor as archbishop of York, Richard Scrope, was executed by Henry IV in 1405 for his leadership of a rebellion. His death, like the deaths of Simon de Montfort and Thomas of Lancaster, produced almost a cult of veneration, of which the present poem is an example.[166] It consists of seventeen or twenty-one rhythmical stanzas.[167] The poet calls for tears to help him lament:

> Quis meo capiti dabit effundere
> Vt fontem lachrimas, vultum suffundere,
> Per dies noctesque aquas deducere,
>   Deflenti mortem presulis ? (Wright, p.114, corrected)

> O would my face had tears to weep
> Like fountains running down my cheek,
> By night and day in grief to steep
>   And mourn the bishop's death. (Jer. 9: 1)

He stresses the lack of due process, the death of the archbishop's young companion, the saintly patience, and the parallel with Thomas Becket and Simon Sudbury:

> Ast Thomam militum audax atrocitas,
> Symonem plebium furens ferocitas,
> Ricardum callide saeva crudelitas
>   Obtruncant christos Domini (Wright, p.116)

> For Becket, knights' atrocity,
> For Simon, peasants' cruelty,
> For Richard, sly barbarity
>   Caused God's elect to die.

The request to the reader not to 'pollute the father with the cup of poison' seems to refer to Henry's attempts to silence and discredit the cult. The poet mentions the persecution of Scrope's household (that is, of the rebels) and laments the state of England.

Richard Esk

Richard Esk was a minor monastic versifier. In 1412 he wrote seventy-two contorted and inelegant lines, in variously rhymed hexameters and elegiacs, to introduce the two volumes of the register of Furness Abbey.[168] He mentions the early founding of the abbey in 1124 and its change of site in 1127 under the patronage of Count (later King) Stephen. Richard was fond of cryptograms. He says that the scribe, John Stell, wrote not with a bird's feather but with a silver pen:

> Istorum capita dant *arbor gen*teque *tum*ba
> Quo scripsit calamum per paradigma suum (63–4)

> The heads of tree and race and tomb spell out
> And show the kind of pen with which he wrote.
> (*ar* + *gen* + *tum* = silver)

and his own name is concealed thus:

> Est dives durus cape denam pro decanona:
> Hec metra dictantis sic nomen habes vice prona[169] (67–8)

> He's rich and hard; for 'nineteen' insert 'ten':
> By neat exchange the poet's name you'll ken.

Further legacy of Geoffrey of Monmouth

The metrical history of York is a reminder of the continuing popularity of the *Historia Regum Britanniae*, of which three examples may be given.

John Bever

At the beginning of the fourteenth century John Bever, also known as John of London (died 1311), wrote the *Brutus abbreviatus*, a condensed version of Geoffrey's *Historia*.[170] He decorated it with several poems, mostly in unrhymed elegiacs, expanding on the content. The longest is fourteen lines of antifeminist outrage by Arthur when he hears of Guinevere's treachery:

> Mundum perdomui, dominoque suo mihi servit,
> indomitata manet femina sola mihi (Hammer, p.131)

> I tamed the world which serves me as its lord;
> The female sex alone resists my power.

Albina's sisters

The story of 'Albina's sisters' provides a missing pre-Galfridian link to explain the presence of giants on the island that Brutus colonized. It appears first in French verse (*Les Granz Geans*) and then in Latin prose,[171] and is related to the biblical mention of giants (Gen. 6: 1–4). Thirty sisters plot to murder their husbands; their plan is betrayed by the youngest sister, and the remaining twenty-nine are set adrift in a boat. They arrive at Cornwall, which they name Albion after their leader

Albina; they are visited by invisible incubi, from whose seed they give birth to horrible giants, which proliferate and live in caves.

Metrical Historia Regum Angliae continuation

The thirteenth-century verse epitome of English history was provided with a continuation from Edward I to Richard II.[172] Unlike the original (which was in Leonines), the continuation, probably also written at St Peter's in York, is in unrhymed elegiacs, as was becoming fashionable by the end of the fourteenth century. More space is given to each reign than in the original,[173] but it remains an epitome rather than a verse amplification; for example, the deposition of Richard II is condensed into four lines:

> Rex ad Hibernica regna ferocia vi properauit.
> Appulit interea dux sua iura petens.
> Rex renuit regnum; dux rex fit, sicque coronam
> Suscipit et regnum sceptra tenendo regit

> The king to fierce Ireland goes in force;
> The duke, meanwhile, invades to seek his rights.
> The king resigns; the duke's made king and crowned;
> He holds the sceptre and commands the realm.

Ghost stories

Whatever its origins, the category 'short story' is a useful one for the study of medieval literature, even if it does not correspond to any medieval literary genre. There are, for example, comic and satirical stories, the collections of anecdotes in Walter Map and Gervase of Tilbury, the narrations attached by John of Tynemouth to his saints' lives, and the many collections of sermon exempla.[174] A similar case could be made for what appears at first sight to be a purely modern genre, the ghost story. Visions of the other world were always popular, and Peter of Cornwall had collected local stories of visions and dreams.[175] Shortly after 1400 a monk of Byland Abbey in Yorkshire collected fourteen ghost stories;[176] the compiler seems to have been more fascinated by the supernatural than concerned to provide a moral application (such as the need for confession and absolution).

The tales are full of local allusions, and all but two were probably based on genuine reports. The ghosts take various forms – bullock, crow, dog, goat, horse, and even a bundle of hay. There is a churchyard ghost, a vicar who put out his mistress's eye, a spoon-stealing canon, and a woman who had given her brother false charters in order to disinherit her husband. The ghosts make odd requests and offer advice; one helps to carry a sack of beans. In one story a necromancer provides a vision of a theft; in another a man sees his stillborn and unbaptized son carried along in the boot in which he had been buried.

296

Thomas Walsingham

Thomas Walsingham, monk of St Albans (c. 1345–1422, prior of Wymondham, 1394–6), is known primarily as a historian, a worthy successor to Matthew Paris.[177] For most of his career he was in charge of the abbey library as its *scriptorarius*. Three of his works are of interest for literary history.[178]

The *Prohemia poetarum* is a collection of bio- and bibliographical accounts of the major poets, similar to the *accessus ad auctores* compiled by Conrad of Hirsau.[179] About thirty poets or anonymous works are included, in no particular order, from classical (Virgil, Horace, etc.) to medieval (such as Walter of Châtillon and John of Hauville). Walsingham seems to have taken his *accessus* from any available source and imposed no pattern on them: some follow the late classical model established by Servius (*vita, titulus, qualitas*, etc.), others simply give plot summaries. Entries vary in length from two lines to several folios: Virgil has twelve folios, but by far the longest section is that on Seneca's tragedies, unfinished after twenty-four folios; this interest in Seneca is evident in the *Dites ditatus*. The *Prohemia* is not original, but testifies to the growing interest in antiquity and literary history.

Walsingham dedicated his *Arcana deorum* to Simon Southerey, prior of St Albans from 1396/97 to after 1405, because of the latter's deep understanding of poetry ('novi vos omnes res poeticas apprehendisse profundius' [I know that you have attained a deeper understanding of everything that concerns poetry.]). He directed it, like Boccaccio's *De genealogia deorum*, to those opposed to literary studies,[180]

> qui dicunt res poeticas figmenta frivola sive vana, et nonnullos intrare volentes ad cognoscendum poemata non permittunt, cum ipsi nec intrent nec sint habiles ad intrandum
>
> They say that poetry consists of frivolous and empty fictions; if anyone wishes to enter into the subject to become acquainted with poems, they will not allow them to do so, since they themselves do not enter and are incapable of entering.

The *Arcana* is a fable-by-fable interpretation of Ovid's *Metamorphoses*, prefaced (like Petrus Berchorius' *Ovidius Moralizatus*) by an account of the pagan gods. Each book of the *Metamorphoses* is divided into fables and subordinate tales, with incipits; each fable is then narrated *ad literam*, with quotations and often with supplementary fables from other sources, and is then explicated. It is entirely derived from earlier interpretations.[181] Its interest lies in what Walsingham chose to omit: he eschews Christian allegorical interpretations (in which myths stand for God, the Devil, the Virgin Mary, prelates, etc.), preferring natural or historical explanations of the fables. The story of Pyramus and Thisbe (IV.ii), for instance, is history ('historia, et expositione non indiget' [history, needing no explanation]). The stones, or 'mother's bones', that Deucalion throws over his shoulder to repopulate the earth after the flood (I.xxxii), are interpeted simply as fugitives reappearing from their caves. Witchcraft, such as Medea's (VII.iii), is accepted as real and needed no explanation. Sometimes he adds his own comments: on the practice of changing the names of men after they have been deified, he remarks 'unde inolevit usus mutandi nominis pape' [From which arose the custom of changing the name of the pope.] (XIV.xiii). It is perhaps important that a near-contemporary of Chaucer and Gower (both of whom used Ovid extensively) did not allegorize the Ovidian fables but accepted them as concealed history. The *Arcana* is a polished and readable work, showing a thorough knowledge of Ovid and his commentators and a discriminating judgment in selecting and rejecting interpretations.

His literary and antiquarian interests are fully exemplified in his *Dites ditatus*.[182] This is based on the *Ephemeris belli Troiani*, which claimed to be an eye-witness account of the Trojan War by Dictys Cretensis, a Cretan follower of Idumeneus, a supporter of the Greeks. Walshingham's punning title is explained in the colophon:

historia Troiana a Dite greco declarata et historiis et poematibus ampliata diversis ac ditata. Unde placuit ditanti hunc tractatum vocare 'Ditem ditatum'

The Trojan history by Dictys the Greek set out and amplified and enriched with various stories and poems. Hence the enricher was pleased to call the treatise 'Dictys enriched'.

He retains the original prose (occasionally rephrasing or abbreviating) as the core, and adds his own expansions. It becomes a kind of narrative encyclopedia, in which the story is a peg on which to hang information – geographic, antiquarian, and mythographic. Mention of a person or place frequently prompts an excursus on the background; the longest is prompted by the arrival at Troy of the African Memnon, which elicits an extensive account of Africa and India, mainly from Solinus but with a section on the jewels of India, illustrated by quotations from Marbod's poem *De lapidibus*; this section also has accounts of Scythia and Thrace. Walsingham's information on pagan antiquity (including a section on pagan burial rites) comes from Servius and Lactantius especially, but for mythology he often used his own *Arcana deorum* (incidentally giving a full account of all the gods). His expansions are literary as well as encyclopedic. When Helen arrives in Troy she presents to Priam her claim to Trojan affinities: Walsingham recasts the *oratio obliqua* into direct speech, for dramatic effect. When Ulysses and Ajax both claim the arms of Achilles, Walsingham provides a prose paraphrase, in direct speech, of the *armorum iudicium* from Ovid (*Metamorphoses* 13. 1–398). The prose is frequently enlivened by quotations from the *Ilias latina*, Ovid, Seneca (especially the *Thyestes*), and other poets; mention of Oenone prompts extracts from Ovid's epistle. The *Dites ditatus* is an extremely readable work, both entertaining and instructive.[183]

The question is often asked whether Walsingham was more 'medieval' or 'humanist'. He was neither; he was simply a monk working with the available tools and reflecting the ethos of his time. He was deeply interested in classical literature and antiquity, but he did not, as later humanists did, reject the medieval inheritance.

Monk of Westminster: praise of Henry V

When the abbot of Westminster left England for the Council of Constance in 1414, the abbey was placed under the protection of Henry V. An anonymous monk took the opportunity to praise the king in 274 hexameters, variously rhymed.[184] He says that he was resting in bed and imagined himself speaking with the king:

> Sub modico tecto pausans in paupere lecto
> Regem praesentem quasi cernens meque videntem (4–5)

> In humble house, as I lay on my straw,
> The king in person eying me I saw.

He gives an account of Henry's birth and upbringing (carefully avoiding any reference to Henry IV), his coronation, appearance, manners, household –

> Tota domus redolet regis nunc tempore sani,
> Ut redolere solet quondam laus Octaviani – (147–8)

> The king's whole house smells sweetly nowadays,
> As sweet as once was sung Augustus' praise.

and his suppression of the Lollard uprising of Sir John Oldcastle:

> Sic pugil ecclesiae, patriae protector ubique,
> Miles Messiae, domitor fit gentis iniquae (173–4)

> The church's hero, shield of all this land,
> The Saviour's knight thus tamed that wicked band.

He goes on to itemize Henry's gifts to the abbey, including the body of Richard II, and his address to the monks, and ends with a prayer to be said daily for the well-being of the king.

Thomas Elmham

Thomas Elmham or Elmam (he spells his name both ways in acrostics) was a chaplain of Henry V. He began as a monk of St Augustine's, Canterbury, but in 1414 entered the Cluniac order and became prior of Lenton, near Nottingham; in 1416 he became vicar-general of the order. His writings include both prose histories and several poems.[185] He wrote mainly in unrhymed elegiacs, occasionally in simple Leonine hexameters. By any standards other than those of his age his style is crabbed and his scansion deplorable, but much of this results from word-play of various kinds.

The story of Henry V's wild youth and riotous companions, well known to us from Shakespeare, is reflected by Elmham in a very outspoken set of poems.[186] In the first (thirty-six lines) he notes that the depredations of Henry's courtiers make his arrival in England sad and his departure welcome for his subjects:

Errores solitos quos nunc tua curia nutrit
    Corrige ne feriat te grauis ira Dei (Wright, p.119)

The wonted errors, nourished by your court,
    Correct, lest God's fierce anger strike you down.
(Note: *nutrit* MS, *mittit* Wright)

The second poem is a warning to Henry V, as though from the lips of the dying Henry IV. It consists entirely of epanaleptic couplets:

Dilige mente Deum, fili, virtuteque tota,
    Hoc tu si facias, fit tibi vera salus.
Vera salus tibi fit, si corde Deum venereris . . . (Wright, p.120)

Love God, my son, with all your mind and power;
    If you do this, then true salvation's yours.
Salvation's yours, revering God at heart.
(Wright reads *sit* for *fit* twice)

The old king advises his son to choose good company and religious confessors, and uses his own dying state as a moral lesson. The poem ends with acrostics spelling REX HENRICUS and THOMAS ELMAM. Finally there is a short poem on the death of Henry IV, lamenting the transitoriness of FORTUNA:[187]

Fingit, Ovat, Recipit, Tradit, Variat, Negat, Aufert
    Quot rara promittit, fine perire solent (Wright, p.122)

Feigns joy, gets, gives, says yes and no, deprives –
    What Fortune sends will perish in the end.

Elmham's longest verse work is the *Liber metricus*, in 1350 lines of elegiac couplets.[188] This reflects the later adulation of Henry V as a pious and victorious monarch. It deals with Henry's first *lustrum*, that is, the five-year period 1412/13 to 1416/17; it follows closely the narrative sequence and often the wording of the *Gesta Henrici Quinti*.[189] The main events of Henry's early reign were the continuing war with France, the Lollard rising of Sir John Oldcastle, and the attempts to resolve the papal Schism. These are reflected in the *Liber metricus*:

Year One: Henry IV's death; Henry V's succession and coronation; Oldcastle's conviction for heresy, escape and armed rebellion. The Dauphin's insult to Henry V:

Parisiusque pilas misit, quibus ille valeret
    Ludere cum pueris, ut sua cura fuit (157–8)

From Paris he sends balls for Henry's sport,
    To play with boys, as fitting for his age.

Year Two: invitation to Emperor Sigismund; frustrated negotiations with France; beginning of the Council of Constance

Year Three: expedition to France (beginning with a thwarted plot against the king); successful siege of Harfleur; campaign in Europe and victory at Agincourt; triumphal pageant in London

Year Four: Emperor Sigismund's visit to England; relief of the French siege of Harfleur; skirmishes in the Channel; pamphlets distributed by Oldcastle

Year Five: expedition to Normandy; Scottish attack; restatement of Henry's claims to Normandy, Aquitaine and France. Election of Pope Martin V. Capture and execution of Oldcastle

The constant intrusion of minor details (such as the deaths or promotions of bishops) robs the poem of a firm structure, but it is framed by the rebellion and execution of Oldcastle in the first and last year, and the central year (the longest section in the poem) is glorious for the victories at Harfleur and Agincourt; thus, Henry's piety and military prowess are structurally prominent. Elmham was also well aware of the significance of the number five: in the fifth year of the reign of Henry the Fifth, Martin the Fifth became pope:

> Hen Quinti quinto Mar Quintus papa fit anno (1189)

> In Henry Five's fifth year was Martin Five made pope.

The poem's most striking feature is the constant use of *apices numerales* or chronograms, as in the opening line:[190]

> Hier*u*sa*lem* psa*lle* ! Babi*lon* t*u* fa*lle*re *c*essa ! (43)

> Jerusalem, rejoice ! Cease, Babylon, your lies !

that is, MCLLLLLLVVII = 1412. Similarly, on Oldcastle's heresy:

> H*ic* *I*on O*l*d*c*aste*l* *Ch*risti fuit insidiator (83)

> This year Christ's foe, John Oldcastle, intrigued.

that is, DDCCCLLVIIIIIIII = 1413. As in his other works, he is fond of acrostics: the arrival of the Emperor is spelled out SIGISMUNDUS IMPERATOR PIUS (928–31). He also uses clippings, as in his account of the service of thanksgiving for the relief of Harfleur:

> Gloria post toto sunt repetenda choro
> Can Jubi Con Lau Be Laud Exul in ordine psalle (908–9)

> The 'Glory' first, then all the choir should sing
> 'Cantemus', 'Jubilee' and all the rest.

That is, after the *Gloria*, sing '*Can*temus summe trinitati *Jubi*late, *Con*fitemini, *Lau*date, *Be*nedicite, *Laud*ate, *Exul*tavit cor meum'. The *Liber* ends with a collect to the Virgin and, in two manuscripts, an acrostic poem to the Virgin signed THOMAS ELMHAM MONACHUS.[191]

John Seward

It is fitting that the last author of this chapter is a schoolmaster. John Seward was born in 1364 and died in 1435; he taught grammar in London, and was writing during the reign of Henry V; one of his dedicatees was Simon Southerey, prior of St Albans.[192] His works have not been published,[193] they include works on prosody, treatises on allegory and mythology, and verse experiments in the form of epigrams. He was involved in literary and grammatical interchanges and disputes with others of his kind, and thus testifies to a group of proto-humanist London schoolmasters.[194] The significance of Seward is his interest in classical prosody: his metrical experiments are unrhymed and quantitative, not rhythmical, and are often derived from classical or Boethian lyric metres, such as the dactylic tetrameter catalectic:

> Trux Sathanas patriota tuus
> Qui celebrare solet missas

> Your countryman, fierce Satan,
> Who celebrates the mass.

No doubt, as Weiss says, the classical interests and efforts of writers such as Seward and Thomas Walsingham cannot be classed as 'humanist'.[195] Nevertheless, they are in marked contrast to most of the Anglo-Latin literature of the fourteenth century, and start a trend towards classicism which remained unbroken until 'humanism' and 'Neo-Latin' came into its own. Latin was becoming an object of study rather than a casually used tool; this signals the beginning of its retreat into the schoolroom.

II Anthologies and anonymous verse

Many of the anonymous poems of this period have already been discussed under separate headings – political literature of the reigns of Edward II, Edward III (Hundred Years War, mendicant and Lollard controversies, war in Spain), Richard II (Peasants' Revolt), and Henry IV – and are not given further attention here. The increased political content of the anthologies is striking.[196]

Popular anthology entries

The anthologies of this period continue to include the favourite items, particularly satires in rhythmical metres, that first became popular in the late twelfth and thirteenth centuries:[197] *Apocalypsis Goliae, De coniuge non ducenda, Visio Philiberti* (Body and Soul debate, often combined with 'Ecce mundus moritur', a general lament on the vanity of the world), Wine and Water debate, satires of Walter of Châtillon, the Troy poem 'Pergama flere volo', etc. Earlier anthologies have sometimes been utilized for large blocks of material: for example, Digby 166 has a complete series of Walter of Châtillon poems matching a set in Bodley 603, and Titus A. xx shares most of the material in one of its booklets with the much earlier Rawlinson G. 109.[198]

A few other popular anthology items, probably dating from the late twelfth or thirteenth centuries and not necessarily English, should be mentioned here, as they occur in some of the collections of the fourteenth and fifteenth centuries. In *Dives and Lazarus*, Dives argues unsuccessfully before Abraham that he, rather than Lazarus, deserves a place in heaven.[199] 'Omnis caro peccaverat' is a combination of several types of rhythmical stanza on the subject of Noah's flood.[200] 'Cur mundus militat' is extremely popular in both English and continental anthologies: it is a general statement on the vanity of earthly things.[201] Parodies on the gospels and the liturgy, the Devil's letter, and burlesque continued to be popular.[202]

Miscellaneous items of interest

I describe here a few of the more interesting or indicative entries in some of the anthologies of the period. As earlier subject headings have already absorbed easily classifiable material, this is rather a ragbag of remnants.

Religious poetry continues to be prominent. In Digby 166 there is a versified Pater Noster, followed by a penitential poem,[203] and also a long unpublished poem on the Virgin by one 'Peter', consisting of a prologue ('Laudibus eximie') and seventy-six quatrains ('Venter puellaris'). Material on saints is naturally ubiquitous. The *Glastonbury Miscellany* has an epitaph for Joseph of Arimathea (supposedly buried at the abbey) and a hymn and collect to the two Saint Josephs, senior and junior.[204] The same manuscript has a hymn to the obscure saint Uritha of Chittlehampton in Devon, and there must be many similar pieces. Poems on the sins and the need to repent are even more common; we have already mentioned the one improbably attributed to John Pecham.[205] The mortality theme – the inevitability of death – is omnipresent in medieval literature;[206] nevertheless, it seems, if anything, to be even more dominant in the fourteenth and fifteenth century anthologies. It is well exemplified in the fourteenth-century poem 'Iam nunc in proximo mors stat ad hostium'.[207] There are seventeen stanzas of rhythmical asclepiads: death addresses the poet daily, reminding him of the inevitability of judgment. The poet reflects on the 'three things':

> Pro tribus doleo dolore nimio:
> Scio quod moriar, sed tempus nescio;
> Ignoro penitus que retribucio
> Post mortem dabitur: sic sum in dubio (33–6)

> For three things I am sad: in fear I cower.
> I know that I must die, but not the hour;
> And third, what after death will be my fate
> I do not know, and thus my fear is great.

A few satirical poems are worth special note. One, from the early fourteenth-century Harley 913, attacks the venality of judges, sheriffs and their clerks; it begins by quoting the Beatitudes:[208]

> Beati qui esuriunt
> Et sitiunt et faciunt
> justitiam
> Et odiunt et fugiunt
> injuriae nequitiam

> Blest are those that hunger
> And those that thirst are blest
> For sake of righteousness
> And for it do their best.
> Blest are those that shun and flee
> Injustice and inequity.

'Totum regit seculum' consists of sixty Goliardic stanzas, with each final line a Leonine hexameter.[209] It is a general estates satire, on the pope, cardinals, king, bishops, abbots, monks, friars, knights, rectors, priests, clerks, townspeople, merchants, peasants, and the poor. It first describes the proper behaviour of each estate and then shows how they behave in practice; for example, peasants sweat six days in labour, but then indulge themselves:

> Et dies dominicus datus requiei
> ad gulam tribuitur – rubor faciei
> denotat facillime reos hujus rei;
> sic praecepta Dei deludunt ut Pharisaei (205–8)

And the Lord's day, given us as a day for quiet
Is reserved for gluttony – their indulgent diet
Shines upon their reddened face with their veins expanded.
So like Pharisees they mock what the Lord commanded.

Satire on an unusual theme is seen in the *Ingratitudo* by Stephen Deverell, monk of Glastonbury.[210] In twenty-five stanzas of rhythmical asclepiads it denounces the vice of ingratitude, the very thought of which brings a blush to the face. It has been the cause of disasters and crimes from the fall of Satan to Nero's treatment of his city, his mother, Seneca, and St Peter. These historical examples are followed by a series of impossibilities; the list is based on John of Howden's *Philomena*, where they are the events that will take place before the Virgin's praises have been adequately sung.[211] The ingrate will do good when the lamb puts the wolf to flight:

> Suos dampnatos Auernus euomet,
> Liuens Olibrius agnus deueniet,
> Et Babel sydera turris pertransiet;
> Auarum fuluor auri tunc saciet (85–8)

> Then all its prisoners Hell will set free;
> Raging Olibrius lamblike will be.
> The builders of Babel heaven will scale;
> To satisfy misers gold will not fail.

Conversely, another poet speaks ironically on behalf of wandering, pleasure-loving clerks, who know how to show gratitude for favours received, and equally how to repay the niggardly:[212]

> qui dat nobis, eum nos publice laudamus;
> qui non, coram omnibus illum diffamamus (2/3–4)

> He who gives us what we ask wins a fine oration;
> He who doesn't earns our scorn and our reprobation.

To the parodies already discussed we may add a satire on indolence in Harley 913; this takes the form of a liturgy on the Seven Sleepers of Ephesus.[213]

Another poem from Digby 166 sets out the various trials suffered by soldiers, lovers, and students.[214] It reflects some aspects of the traditional debate between clerks and soldiers for the love of a woman, but concludes that all three ways of life have their rewards:

> Tamen in officio quisque delectatur
> et dulci remedio laborem solatur.
> Dum laboris sarcina fama relevatur,
> ars, amor, milicia sic corroboratur (st. 10)

> Each, however, takes delight in his occupation
> And consoles his daily task with sweet compensation.

Since the burden of the task glory renders lighter,
Each one takes his strength from this – clerk and swain and fighter.

One of the most unusual pieces of the late fourteenth century, written between 1375 and 1401, is the *Stores of the Cities*.[215] It consists of seven tristichs of very rough Leonine hexameters; English words mingle with Latin, and the ending of the word *ciuitatis* is distorted throughout the poem for the sake of the rhyme. It lists the prominent features or commercial products of seven English cities, London, York, Lincoln, Norwich, Coventry, Bristol and Canterbury. The verses on London illustrate the style:

> Hec sunt Londonis: pira pomusque regia thronus,
> Chepp, stupha, Coklana, dolium, leo, verbaque vana,
> Lancea cum scutis – hec sunt staura ciuitutis

> These are London's: apple, pear, throne and royal dwelling,
> Cheap, Stews, Cock Lane and the Tun, lion, story-telling,
> Soldiers with their lance and shields – all this London's selling.

In the same manuscript there is an interesting dream-vision. The common features of this genre (in both Latin and the vernaculars) are the dream opening, a plesaunce, an instructor, a list of famous practitioners of the topic of the poem, and a presiding deity. These features all appear in *Gregory's Garden*, an allegory on music consisting of twenty-seven stanzas of rhythmical asclepiads.[216] The dreamer refers to himself as 'Peccator nimium polluti labii', an allusion to the first stanza of the hymn 'Ut queant laxis', on which Guido of Arezzo had based his system of musical notation (*ut re fa sol la*).

The dreamer runs through *devia* (between waking and sleeping), and comes to the garden of Gregory, codifier of liturgical chant. He is instructed by an eagle who explains the meaning of what he has seen so far. He follows the eagle and comes into the garden, where he sees the famous teachers of music: Tubal, Pythagoras, Boethius, Gregory the Great, Guido of Arezzo, and finally Franco of Cologne. The gathering is presided over by Orpheus, who is playing the organ. The components of the organ are explained by the eagle: the shutters are the frail human substance, the keys are the senses, the bellows are the vital spirit, the pipes are the praises of the faithful, and Orpheus himself is Reason which presides over all. The eagle departs and the poet calls on all to sing God's praises:

> Cessauit visio; iam pono terminum,
> Et locum volucer petit ethereum.
> Nunc regem seculi sonet vox hominum
> Et omnis spiritus collaudet dominum (105–8)

> Here the vision ended; here I make my end;
> Then I saw the eagle to the skies ascend.
> Now let human voices praise creation's king,
> And let every spirit praises to him sing.

Select anthologies

To illustrate the varying types and contents of the anthologies, I have selected three from the beginning of the fourteenth century and three from the end.

(a) Cambridge, Univ. Lib., EE.6.29 (s. xiv, first quarter; provenance unknown; in s. xv property of Thomas Suwell, priest of Wingfield, Suffolk), 141 fols. It contains over forty full-length poems and hundreds of short verses (between one and ten lines). Apart from the Wine and Water debate and a fragment of *De coniuge non ducenda*, the poems are entirely moral and penitential, with many on Death, the deadly sins, and the decline of the world. Most are known from elsewhere (there is an extract from Bernard of Cluny), but there are a few unique and unpublished items.

(b) BL Harley 913 (s. xiv, first quarter; Franciscan, Anglo-Irish, probably from Kildare), 64 fols. Trilingual (English, Latin and French); the English (which predominates) includes the satirical *Land of Cockayne*. The Latin entries include: the dog-Latin 'Quondam fuit factus festus', biblical and liturgical parodies (Seven Sleepers, *Missa de potatoribus*, Adulterous Monk), Devil's letter, *Metra de monachis carnalibus*, and the satire on the courts 'Beati qui esuriunt'. Not all the verse is satirical: Pecham's poems on the Trinity are also included.[217]

(c) Cambridge, Corpus Christi College, 450 (c. 1320, Durham). This is the collection of a Durham lawyer who had studied at Bologna, and the contents are primarily legal. The fourth quire, however, began as a Goliardic anthology, containing *Apocalypsis Goliae*, *De coniuge non ducenda*, some Primas epigrams, *Confessio Goliae*, 'Utar contra vicia', the poem in Goliardics on Susanna, the B-text of Walter of Wimborne's *De Palpone*, and some short items. Later in the manuscript, as fill, there is a Primas epigram and three Troy poems, including 'Pergama flere volo'.[218]

(d) Oxford, Bodley 851 (c. 1375, Oxford; owned by John Wells, monk of Ramsey), in its earliest form 133 fols., in three parts, fols. 7–77, 78–123, 124–39.[219] John Wells, the prominent anti-Wycliffite, was scholar of Gloucester College, Oxford, from 1376, prior studentium 1381–, and died in Peruggia in 1388.[220] Part I contains the sole copy of Walter Map's *De Nugis Curialium*; Part III contains the Z-version of Piers Plowman. Part II, the Latin poetic anthology, originally contained Walter of Wimborne's *Ave Virgo* (now acephalous), *De coniuge non ducenda*, debate between Heart and Eye, Michael of Cornwall's flyting against Henry of Avranches, Troy poems 'Pergama flere' and 'Viribus arte minis', John of Bridlington's Prophecy, *Babio*, Nigel Whiteacre's *Speculum Stultorum*, and the *Apocalypsis Goliae*.

Later additions, made in the late fourteenth and early fifteenth centuries, include: the poems on Neville's Cross and Crecy, an extract from the Devil's letter, the poem on Archbishop Scrope's execution, *Convocacio Sacerdotum*, *Geta*, and *Miles Gloriosus*.[221]

This manuscript is closely related to Trinity College, Cambridge, O.9.38 and Cotton Vespasian E. xii (below, pp. 311–2); all three were probably compiled in

Oxford. For both its unique items and its representative qualities it is one of the most important collections of the age.

(e) BL Cotton Titus A. xx (c. 1375, probably from a large abbey in the London area, perhaps St Albans), 182 fols. Compiled by several hands in different stages. There are sixty-nine separate poems, including, in their possible order of entry, the following:[222] Michael of Cornwall's flyting against Henry of Avranches; De modo cenandi; Nigel Whiteacre's Speculum Stultorum; fourteen poems (Nos. 32–45), of which all but two are shared with Rawlinson G. 109; Babio, Geta, Pamphilus; pseudo-Virgil De rosis; Apocalypsis Goliae; Peter Riga Susanna; short satires; Visio Philiberti (Body and Soul), Convocacio Sacerdotum; Proba Cento Vergilianus, poems on Neville's Cross and Crecy, Metra de monachis carnalibus, extracts from William de Montibus and Matthew of Vendôme, pseudo-Virgil Moretum, other short poems; Embrico of Mayence Vita Mahometi; Descriptio Northfolchiae and the reply to it; Praedicatio Goliae (on the Trinity); poems on the battle of Najera, the siege of Calais, B-text of Walter of Wimborne's Marie Carmina.[223]

The range is from late classical (Proba and the pseudo-Virgilian poems) to close to contemporary (Battle of Najera in 1367). Like the Bekynton anthology it would provide a student with a good range of the whole of Medieval Latin literature. Textually it is very closely related to the late fifteenth-century Rawlinson B. 214[224]

(f) Bodleian Library, Digby 166 (s. xiv, second half, probably Oxford); a collection of small booklets, each purchased for two or three shillings.[225] Parts I, II and the beginning of III, mathematics and science; Part III end, Troy material; Part IV Odoric of Pordenone's expedition to China; Part V Devil's letter, dissolution of the Order of the Sack, prose antifeminist texts. Part VI is the main verse section, containing thirty-three items, including: duties of Lover, Knight and Clerk, Apocalypsis Goliae, block of Walter of Châtillon's satires (closely related to that in Bodley 603), Praedicatio Goliae, praise of benefactors, miscellaneous Goliardic satires, versified Pater Noster, Confessio Goliae, poems on Becket, poems to the Virgin, Defensio Fratrum Mendicantium, Dives et Lazarus, Visio Philiberti (Body and Soul debate, with extra stanzas), and De coniuge non ducenda.

In the fifteenth century a like-minded owner added more science (Honorius Augustodunensis, Imago Mundi) and more poems: Alain de Lille's 'Vix nodosum' with its continuation, Walter of Peterborough's poem on the Battle of Najera, debates between Wine and Water and between Heart and Eye, and the Convocacio Sacerdotum.[226]

Conclusions

By the early fifteenth century Anglo-Latin was being pulled in several directions, and, as we will see below, continued to be for some time. On the one hand, as is evident in the 'classicizing friars', the bibliographers, and Thomas Walsingham, there was a strong interest in classical antiquity. This trend is also reflected in the renewed use, by Gower and others, of the unrhymed elegiac couplet and especially in John Seward's interest in quantitative lyric metres. It is interesting to observe the presence in Titus A. xx of ancient material like the *De rosis* and the *Moretum*. On the other hand, the 'medieval' pull was still strong; the anthologies still have a high proportion of rhythmical verse. Stylistically, verse was far from classical, even when unrhymed: Gower, for example, commonly uses *que* for *et*, as well as other common medievalisms and some syntactic liberties of his own.[227] The sources of literary expression were by now almost entirely biblical rather than classical. Poetic embellishment was not only not classical but had almost ceased to be derived from medieval rhetorical precepts; it consisted rather in word-play and tricks with cryptograms, chronograms and acrostics.

The anthologies have a different message. Many of the favourite pieces from the twelfth-century anthologies maintained their popularity, though (with the exception of the older block in Titus A. xx) the *Anthologia Latina* style of epigram disappeared. On the other hand, they all show a strong interest in contemporary politics, something not seen at all in the early collections of poetry.

Monasteries, as always, remained powerful centres of learning and literature. The universities, of course, attended by both monks and friars as well as secular clergy, were the major literary centres. To these we can now add another locus for writing, the grammar school: as Elias of Thriplow and Walter of Wimborne had been schoolteachers, so now we have the literary circle of John Seward. The normal occupations of writers had also changed; although Walter of Peterborough was a monk, he seems to have spent some time with the expeditions of the Black Prince and John of Gaunt; Richard Maidstone seems to have been involved in the arrangements for a London pageant. As far as we know, John Gower, the most important Latin poet of the age, was not in orders at all. The circumstances for writing had certainly changed considerably since 1066.

Epilogue

The new and the old

By 1422 it must have become clear to any poet with pretensions that the future (and the present, in terms of size of audience) lay with English: both Lydgate and Hoccleve, Chaucer's principal successors, wrote entirely in English.[1] Anglo-Latin continued as a literary medium, but it began to bifurcate into two streams, the new 'humanism' and the old medieval tradition; both prospered side by side for some time.

The beginnings of English humanism have been studied thoroughly by Schirmer and Weiss.[2] Its impulse was not, like Italian humanism, towards pagan antiquity (English Latin writing remained very pious and theological into the sixteenth century) but to the stylistic elegance now favoured in the papal curia. Weiss characterizes humanism in fifteenth-century England as 'utilitarian', 'a means rather than an end'. There were few poets among the early humanists and little 'creative writing'; the influence of humanism was mainly on prose, epistolary and historiographical, and the first experimental signs are the 'florida verborum venustas', a kind of Latin Euphuism, in the prose of John Whethamstede.[3] The impact of the 'new learning' in England can best be observed in the acquisition of books, especially for university libraries, and in the to-ings and fro-ings between England and Italy; in this, the Hundred Years War played its part, as Paris and the French universities were less attractive prospects for foreign study.

The leading figure in the English movement was Humphrey, duke of Gloucester, founder of the Bodleian Library in Oxford, brother of Henry V, and uncle of the new young king. He corresponded enthusiastically with Italian humanists: one of his proteges was Tito Livio Frulovisi, who wrote an elegant prose life of Henry V for the instruction of the young Henry VI.[4] Several Englishmen went to Italy to study; all were accomplished Latinists, and some of them learned Greek. Two leading English ecclesiastics were major patrons of the new learning: John Whethamstede, abbot of St Albans, and Thomas Bekynton, bishop of Bath and Wells, and chancellor of Henry VI. Both collected books and encouraged students, and Bekynton greatly influenced the epistolary style of the Chancery.

The medieval tradition did not, however, come to an abrupt halt in 1422; older works were still valued and copied, and in some cases we owe their preservation to fifteenth-century scribes. Rhythmical verse was still composed: the *Castrianus*, in 150 lines of Goliardic couplets, is a courtesy book for the scholars of Eton College.[5] Also in Goliardic couplets is a long poem on the archbishops of York, ending in 1455.[6] Many other examples could be found; it is often only assumptions about the decline of medieval verse forms that have led editors to assign rhythmical poems in fifteenth-century manuscripts to earlier periods.[7] Rhymed hexameter and elegiac verse was even more common.[8] In 1431 a Glastonbury monk named John Matthew, at the request of the abbot Nicholas Frome, wrote a Leonine epilogue to the eleventh- or twelfth-century satire 'Non tonsura facit monachum'.[9] In the same manuscript, Bodley 496, is a long poem in *hexametri caudati* by a Carthusian monk named Stoon in honour of the late Richard Fleming, bishop of Lincoln (d. 1431);[10] it is based on Richard's epitaph for himself in the same metre. As late as the 1550s we find a poem in Leonines attacking the financier Sir Richard Gresham.[11]

Older themes continued to be of interest,[12] and one links neatly with the beginning of this book: it is a verse life of Edward the Confessor, addressed to Henry VI.[13] It is an abridgment of the life by Aelred, and consists of 536 unrhymed hexameters (with a rhyming epilogue). It is an accomplished piece of work, but the couple of Greek words do not outbalance the distinctively medieval use of *distributio* or the use of *que = et*, *ve = vel*, and *posse = potentia*. Most interesting is the author's objection to vernacular literature and the apparent allusion to Piers Plowman:

> Tantaque simplicitas nostris succrevit in annis
> Quod vulgi plus sermo placet, quem dictat arator
> Vulgari lingua, quam mellica musa Maronis (27–9)

> In recent years simplicity's the rage:
> The vulgar tongue, such as the ploughman speaks,
> Wins more applause than Virgil's honeyed muse.

Fifteenth-century anthologies

The continuity of the medieval tradition can best be appreciated through the poetic anthologies.[14] Although Thomas Bekynton was, as mentioned, a patron of humanist studies, he not only owned a large volume of medieval poetry but also took the trouble to index it and to supplement it with further medieval prose and verse.[15] I have selected four anthologies for brief description.

a) Cambridge, Trinity College, 0.9.38 (after 1438, owned by a Glastonbury monk who probably compiled it in Oxford), 89 fols., compiled in booklets.[16] The first booklet contains *Apocalypsis Goliae*, *De coniuge non ducenda*, *De virtute clavium*, *De quatuor raptoribus*, *Gregory's Garden*, Debate between Wine and Water, 'Quondam fuit factus festus', *Stores of the Cities*; then a booklet of English prose and verse, followed by Walter of Wimborne's *De Symonia*; other items include Stephen

Deverell's *Ingratitudo*, Tryvytlam's *De laude Oxonie* and other pro- and anti-mendicant satire, *Descriptio Northfolchiae*, hymns to the St Josephs, 'Iam nunc in proximo', poems on Piers Gaveston, verse life of St Hilda. Latin prose includes the 'Wager Story', *Alma Redemptoris Mater* (an analogue to Chaucer's *Prioress's Tale*), Leonardo Bruni's translation of Boccaccio's story of Tancred of Salerne, the History of the True Cross, and the Lives of Pilate and Judas, and a contemporary account of events at the Council of Basel, written in 1434.[17]

b) Bodley 496, Part A (s. xv, 2nd or 3rd quarter, written mainly by Thomas Graunt, Fellow of Oriel College, Oxford, 1425–35, treasurer of St Paul's, 1454–74), 254 fols. Includes: *Praedicatio Goliae*, Quilichinus of Spoleto's verse *Historia Alexandri*, *Apocalypsis Goliae*, Nigel Whiteacre *Speculum stultorum*, the fables of Walter the Englishman, 'Non tonsura facit monachum' with epilogue by John Matthew, hymns, Stoon on Richard Fleming, debate between Wine and Water, *De coniuge non ducenda*, mortality and penitential poems, verses from Geoffrey of Vinsuaf.[18]

c) Oxford, Bodleian Lib., Rawlinson B. 214 (after 1469, Holy Cross, Waltham, written by John Wilde), 228 fols.[19] This is very closely related to Titus A. xx, and includes: Walsingham *Dites ditatus*, Elmham's verse history of Britain, Whetham-stede's verses, poems on the wars with France and Spain (particularly Crecy and Neville's Cross), 'Ludere valentibus', battle of Najera, Elmham's poems to Henry V and his *Liber metricus* and other poems, 'Cantica leticie', *Apocalypsis Goliae*, 'Noctis crepusculo', 'Meum est propositum gentis imperite', *De coniuge non ducenda*, 'Totum regit seculum', debate between Wine and Water, poems on Norfolk, *Metra de monachis*, Walter of Peterborough on battle of Najera, exposition of the *Metamorphoses* preceded by pictures of the gods and an accessus. This carefully planned collection contains both well known satires and up-to-date material.[20]

d) BL Cotton Vespasian E. xii (before 1482, property of John Russell, New College, Oxford, 1447–, chancellor of Oxford, chancellor of England, d. 1494), 122 fols.[21] It is related to the *Glastonbury Miscellany* and to Bodley 851, and to other manuscripts in this group, which probably circulated in Oxford. Its contents include; *Apocalypsis Goliae*, Diana's prophecy from Geoffrey of Monmouth, Nigel Whiteacre *Speculum Stultorum*, Petrarch's story of Griselda (the source of Chaucer's *Clerk's Tale*), *De coniuge non ducenda*, Walter of Wimborne *De Palpone*, moral sentences, Martin of Braga, verse mythography 'Iubiter et Iuno', *Praedicatio Goliae*, extracts from Seneca; there is also a quotation from John of Salisbury's *Policraticus*. Apart from the Stoic philosophy (popular in the Middle Ages), the nearest item to the 'Renaissance' is Petrarch's story.[22]

Thus, the old and the new lived side by side for a while, until eventually the rising classical standards restricted the composition of Latin verse to a few cognoscenti, who then came to despise the literature that had dominated English culture for nearly four hundred years.

APPENDIX: METRE[1]

1 Historical sketch

The metres used by post-Conquest Anglo-Latin poets are, for the most part, those used by their continental counterparts. They depend either on length of syllable (quantitative) or on accent (rhythmical). Quantitative dactylic verse (hexameters and elegiac couplets) dominated Medieval Latin poetry in both rhymed and unrhymed forms.

The unrhymed hexameter, at one time the dominant verse form, does not appear again after Henry of Avranches (mid-thirteenth century) until after the end of our period. The unrhymed elegiac couplet seems to have fallen out of favour in the mid-thirteenth century and was not common again until the end of the fourteenth century when it was used by John Gower and Richard Maidstone. Quantitative lyric metres were never very popular, but they were used by experienced poets (Goscelin, Reginald of Canterbury, Henry of Huntingdon, and Lawrence of Durham) until the middle of the twelfth century; after that, with two minor exceptions,[2] they do not reappear until the early fifteenth century. On the other hand, rhymed dactylic verse (such as the Leonine hexameter) was popular throughout the whole period; rhyme schemes grew more complex from the thirteenth century onwards.

Rhythmical verse was also very common throughout the period, especially after the middle of the twelfth century. The most popular forms were Goliardics, rhythmical asclepiads, and the Victorine sequence, followed by arrangements of six-, seven-, eight- and ten-syllable lines. Stanza schemes became more complicated from the twelfth century; refrains appear in the late thirteenth century; in the fourteenth century Richard Ledrede experimented with the metrical forms of dance tunes.

2 Quantity versus rhythm

A Quantitative verse depends on the length of the syllable; this is determined either (a) naturally, or (b) by position.

A syllable is long if the vowel in it is long by nature, e.g. *līber* 'free, child, Bacchus' (distinguished from *lĭber* 'book'). Classical Latin *æ* and *œ* (Medieval Latin *e*) are always long, and many inflexional vowels (such as the ablative singular -*ā*) are always long. Otherwise the length of vowels could only be known by learning them individually; as there were few reference tools, this learning must have taken place in school, where differential verses would have been invaluable aids:[3]

Scorto nemo plăcet nisi dextram munere plācet

A syllable is long 'by position' if a short vowel is followed by two or more consonants (e.g. *dēxtram, Pērgama, impulerīt Frigios, erubeāt dum*).[4] A short vowel remains short, however, when it precedes a consonant plus liquid or labial (*r* or *l*) when the combination begins the next syllable (e.g. *fugă fregerit*).[5]

A vowel is 'elided' before a following vowel:

Ēxŏrĕre ēt vūltūm ruga leviore resumens

Similarly, a vowel followed by *m* is elided before a following vowel:

Dūctōrem īn mĕdiīs expectat cimba procellis

Medieval poets do not always obey the 'rules' of elision; sometimes they seem to avoid juxtaposing vowels.

Even in Classical Latin it was sometimes possible to shorten a final long vowel (especially -*o*) for the sake of metre; this licence is taken a lot further by medieval poets.

A common medieval licence is to lengthen a short final vowel at the caesura of a hexameter or pentameter:

Si fueris lotā, si uita sequens bona tota[6]

Short and long vowels are combined to form a 'foot': e.g. $--$ (spondee), $-\smile\smile$ (dactyl), $\smile-$ (iamb), $-\smile$ (trochee), $-\smile\smile-$ (choriamb). These 'feet' are combined, in established patterns, to make the quantitative metres described below in 4.I.A–B.

B Rhythmical verse, on the other hand, depends not on length but on accent – that is, on the alternation of accented and unaccented syllables. The rule for accentuation is as follows: if the penultimate syllable of a word is long, the accent falls on it (*amátur*); if the penultimate syllable is short, the accent falls on the antepenultimate (*amábĭlis*). The conventional way to describe rhythmical metres is to give the number of syllables and the accentuation at the end of the line or half-line; p = paroxytonic accent, pp = proparoxytonic accent. Thus, the line

Meum est propósitum in taberna móri

is described as 7pp + 6p. As rhythmical verse is always stanzaic (divided into stanzas of a fixed length), it is also necessary to indicate the number of lines and the rhyme scheme of the stanza. The Goliardic quatrain is 4(7pp + 6p) aaaa.

Some rhythmical lines result from the prose accentual reading of a quantitative line;[7] others may be based on music.

3 Rhyme

Rhyme is always used with rhythmical verse; it is common in quantitative hexameters and elegiacs, but is not used with quantitative lyric metres. Final rhyme (at the end of the line)

314

forms couplets, quatrains, and other stanzas. Internal rhyme (in the middle of the line) may operate just within the line or may rhyme with a word in the same position in the next line (collateral).

The line quoted from Serlo (p. 314) shows that even in quantitative verse there is no need for rhyming syllables to have the same vowel length, as long as the vowel and consonant correspond (*plăcet: plācet*).

Monosyllabic rhyme (on the final syllable only) is fairly rare, but occurs sporadically throughout the period, as in John of Cornwall:[8]

> Eure tuum nostr*is* extyrpat germen ab hort*is*
> Auster, et exempl*um* decimantis habet decimat*um*

and in the thirteenth-century satire on Stoughton:[9]

> Quid faciet serv*us* nisi serviet ? et puer e*ius*
> Purus servus er*it* et libertate careb*it*

Disyllabic rhyme requires identity of the last two syllables, in both vowels and consonants. The most skilful kind of rhyming is that between one word and two, as in Serlo of Wilton:[10]

> Nosti que *sua vis*: non hostibus illa *suavis*

Michael of Cornwall is especially fond of this rhyme:[11]

> Et videam*us si* duo simus iudicis h*uius*
> Iudicio i*ussi* tam protelare di*u ius*

Another trick is to divide a word in the middle and to place the rhyme on the first half, as in Reginald of Canterbury:[12]

> Crebra tuum c*lama* -bit opus laus crebraque f*ama*

Similarly, Robert Baston rhymes[13]

> Vix poterit tr*agae* -dia pandere schismata pl*agae*

Split rhymes are found in the 'run-over' schemes of Michael of Cornwall:[14]

> queris suspendia l*atro*
> *Atro* -ci tigno digno tibi fur furibunde (598–9)

Thirteenth- and fourteenth-century poets display many elaborate tours-de-force of rhyming. A rhythmical poem to the Virgin by John of Howden consists of five blocks, each of fifty lines rhyming on the same sound (*-aris, -ina, -oris, -atis, -ura*).[15] In his attack on Bordo and Siler, Henry of Avranches has a passage of 110 lines with internal rhymes, rhyming both internally and finally on *-ere*, a total of 220 *-ere* rhymes.[16] In his *Altercacio* with Henry, Michael of Cornwall has five blocks of twenty lines, each rhyming internally and finally on the vowels in alphabetical sequence (*-aris, -eris, -iris, -oris, uris*).

It should be noted that in Anglo-Latin *c* before a front vowel (*e* or *i*) rhymes as /s/, *sc* as /ss/, final *d* as /t/, *qu* as /k/, *anct* as /ant/.

4 Illustration of metrical types

1 Quantitative verse: A. *Unrhymed*

(i) Dactylic verse

(a) *Hexameters.* The hexameter (meaning 'six feet') consists of six dactyls (−˅ ˅) or spondees (−−). The line always ends −˅ ˅− ˵ (corresponding to the rhythmical pattern of the North American pronunciation of 'stráwberry íce-cream). In every line there is a caesura, or word break, in the middle of the third foot. The 'strong caesura' occurs after the first long syllable of the third foot. The 'weak caesura' occurs after the first short syllable of the third foot, when that foot is a dactyl. The weak caesura is always accompanied by secondary caesurae in the second and fourth feet (a factor important for some kinds of rhymed hexameter). Scansion of hexameters is illustrated by some lines from Joseph of Exeter's *Ylias*:

> Ȳlĭădūm lăcrĭmās / cōncēssắquĕ Pērgắmă fắtīs
> Prēlĭā bīnă dŭcūm / bĭs ădāctām clādĭbŭs ūrbēm
> Īn cĭnĕrēs quĕrĭmūr / flēmūsquĕ quŏd Hērcŭlĭs īrā . . .
> Nōs ĕtĭām / nōscēndă ⋮ fŭgis / ? Mēcum īnclĭtă mēcūm
> Ēxŏrēre ēt vūltūm / rūgā lĕvĭŏrĕ rĕsūmēns
> Plēbēām / dīgnārĕ ⋮ tŭbām / stĕrĭlĭsquĕ vĕtūstās

(b) *Pentameters; elegiac couplets.* The pentameter ('five feet') consists of two 'hemiepes', that is, the first half of a hexameter line up to the strong caesura −˅˅−˅˅˵, repeated. The second half of the line has only dactyls−˅ ˅−˅ ˅−and so produces the rhythm 'blúeberry píe'.

The pentameter is rarely found alone,[17] but Reginald of Canterbury (LMP No. 18) has one poem consisting entirely of them:

> Īmpắrĕ cūm nŭmĕrō gāudĕăt īpsĕ dĕŭs,
> Pār cōmpōnĕ sŏphōs dīspărĕ Mūsă mŏdō . . .
> Cārmĕn ĭnēquālī pōllĭcĕ vōcĕ pĕdē
> Vērsū pēntămĕtrō scīlĭcĕt ēdĕ mĕlōs

Usually the pentameter is found in combination with a hexameter, forming the elegiac couplet, one of the most common verse forms in the Middle Ages. I give examples from Godfrey of Winchester and Lawrence of Durham:[18]

> Ūndĭquĕ sūscēptūm quī mīscŭĭt ūtĭlĕ dūlcī
> Ūndĭquĕ lāudātūm pāgĭnă nŏtā rĕfērt

> Fēmĭnă flāmmĭgĕrō sĭbī sŭbiŭgăt ōmnĭă tēlō
> Nām quēm nōn sūbdāt quē sĭbī sūbdĭt ĕūm ?

(c) *Octameter.* Thomas Varoye produced an unusual line consisting or eight dactylic or spondaic feet, i.e. a hexameter with two extra feet:[19]

> Sōl rădĭōrūm lūmĭnă cōndēns Āntĭpŏdēs pĕtĭt Hēspĕrŭs īnstăt
> Ēt mŏrĭtūr pĕrĕūntĕ dĭē lūx tūnc ăcĭēs hæ cōngrĕdĭūntŭr

(d) *Five-foot dactylic line*. Lawrence of Durham has a curious poem (*Consolatio* met. 14) consisting of five dactylic feet, as though two long syllables have been omitted after the caesura:

> Quām mĭchĭ sēmpĕr ămōr tŭŭs ēxtăt ămōrī
> tām dŏlŏr īstĕ mĭchī fĭt ămīcĕ dŏlōrī

(It rhymes finally in couplets).

(ii) Lyric metres

These metres, often in stanzas, consist of various combinations of feet (iambic, trochaic, choriambic, dactylic, spondaic); their appearance in Anglo-Latin is discussed above (p. 313 and n. 2). They were known through the *Odes* of Horace (whose study Reginald recommends for the mastery of writing verse), Boethius's *Consolatio Philosophiae*, and Martianus Capella's *De nuptiis Mercurii et Philologiae*. Medieval poets made further variations.

(a) *Sapphics*. The Sapphic stanza consists of three lines of $- \smile -- / - \smile \smile - / \smile - -$, followed by an adonic $- \smile \smile - - \underline{\smile}$ (below). Reginald recommends study of them:[20]

> Dīscăt Ōsbērnūs stŭdĭō frĕquēntī
> rēgŭlās cērtās Săpphĭcī tĕnōrīs
> quās pŏtēst nēmō nĭsĭ pēr lăbōrēm
> dīscĕrĕ jūgēm

(b) *Adonics*. An adonic is simply the last two feet of a hexameter $- \smile \smile - \underline{\smile}$. Sometimes they are laid out with two per line, but this is not metrically necessary. Henry of Huntingdon is very fond of them:[21]

> Sīc quŏquĕ sævīs
> Ānglĭă mœrēns
> prēssă tўrānnīs
> sōrdĕ rĕplētă
> dīrŭtă frāudĕ
> dūlcĭă sēcŭs

(c) *Iambic dimeters*. This metre had been popular for the hymns of the early church, and was therefore well known through the liturgy.[22] The line consists of two iambic metra, $\underline{\smile} - \smile -$, comprising two iambic feet (with the licence of an opening spondee):

> Dĕūs crĕātŏr ōmnĭūm
> pōlĭquĕ rēctōr vēstĭēns
> dĭēm dĕcōrō lūmĭnē
> nōctēm sŏpōrīs grātĭă

Surprisingly it found no imitators in Anglo-Latin except in the metrical examples in John of Garland's *Parisiana Poetria*, but it may lie behind the rhythmical line 8pp (below).

(d) *Anacreontics*. This line consists of $\smile \smile - \smile - \smile - \smile$. It is used by Lawrence of Durham,

Consolatio met. 13:

> ăgĕ sīntnĕ frūctŭōsă
> tĭbī vōtă vōxquĕ nōstră

Anacreontic lines occur among some of John of Seward's verses:[23]

> rĕvĕrēndĕ mī măgīstēr . . .
> sĭmĭlī stīlō rĕmīttĕ

(e) *Glyconics.* The Glyconic line consists of $--/-\smile \smile-/\smile\underline{\smile}$. It was known to medieval poets through Boethius and as the last line of the Fourth Asclepiadic stanza (below, itself rather rare outside Horace). The only Anglo-Latin occurrence I know is in Henry of Huntingdon, who writes them in pairs:

> Quōndām sānctĭfĭcŭs pătēr
> īnclūsīs mŏnĭālĭbŭs
> īndīxīt vĕhĕmēntĭŭs
> vēstēs ūt sŭĕrēnt sŭās

Henry has occasional rhymes, and sometimes has a 'contracted nucleus' ($---$ for $-\smile\smile-$) and sometimes an opening dactyl:

> Ōtĭă lūxŭrĭăm dŏcēnt
> ōtĭă līvōrēm mŏvēnt

(f) *Lesser Asclepiad.* This line, with two choriambs at the centre, $--/-\smile\smile-/-\smile\smile-/\smile-$, was well known from the opening of Horace's Odes. It is important for the development of the rhythmical asclepiad (see on 12pp below), but as far as I know it occurs in Anglo-Latin only in John of Garland's *Parisiana Poetria*.

(g) *Fourth Asclepiadic stanza.* This stanza consists of three Lesser Asclepiads (f) followed by a Glyconic (e), as in Lawrence of Durham, *Consolatio* met. 3:[24]

> Ōptāntēm vĕtĭtīs cūrrĕrĕ cūrrĭbŭs
> īnfērrīquĕ lŏcīs ēxĭtĭālĭbŭs
> Fētōntēm tĕmĕrīs nītĭtŭr āusĭbŭs
> ābstērrērĕ sŭŭs pătēr

(h) *Boethius, Cons. Phil. I met. 2.* This consists of a hemiepes $-\underline{\smile\smile}-\underline{\smile\smile}-$ and an adonic $-\smile\smile-\underline{\smile}$. It is used by Rhygyfarch:[25]

> nūnc cădĭt ē sūmmīs pōmpă pŏtēntūm
> quēquĕ cŏhōrs trīstīs, trīstĭs ĕt āulă
> trīstĭtĭē sēmpēr ātquĕ tīmōrēs

and also by Thomas Varoye:[26]

> Vīctōrēs ĕrĭtīs nōn dŭbĭtētĭs
> Ēt vŏbīs ēvĕnĭēt vēspĕră fēlīx

(i) *Other variations on the hemiepes.* Two other poems also use the hemiepes as the opening of the line. Henry of Huntingdon combines it with two and half iambs:[27]

> Bālsămă quŏd spīrānt rĕcēntēr āctă
> Quŏd suāuĕ spīrāt crŏcŭs rŭbēscēns

Lawrence of Durham, *Consolatio* met. 5, combines it with four or five other syllables:

> Quās Lĭbĭē pārtēs pĕrăgrāuĕrĭt
> Cēsărēās ăcĭēs vītāns Cătō
> quē mărĭs āc tērrē tŭlĕrīt mălă

(j) *Elegiac-choriambic tristich.* Reginald of Canterbury (LMP No. 16) follows an elegiac couplet with a line consisting of two choriambs and an adonic:

> Fēmĭnă iūnctă vĭrō sŏbŏlēm crĕăt ōrdĭnĕ mīrō
> Dē mărē fĭt mŭlĭēr, dē mŭlĭērĕ pŭēr
> Mīră Dĕī vēllĕ făcīt mīră pŏtēstās

(k) *Dactylic tetrameter catalectic.* This metre, consisting of four dactylic metra with the last syllable(s) 'suppressed', was quite popular in Classical Latin, but I know of only one example in Anglo-Latin, in John Seward:

> Trūx Săthănās pătrĭōtă tŭūs
> quī cĕlĕbrārĕ sŏlēt mīssās

I *Quantitative verse*: B *Rhymed*

The only rhymed quantitative verse in Anglo-Latin is dactylic, either hexameter or elegiac.[28] All patterns except *caudati*, *dactylici tripertiti* and *hexametri tripertiti* make use of the strong or weak caesura (above, I.A.i(a)). The most common forms are *Leonini*, *collaterales*, *unisoni*, and *dactylici tripertiti*, but all are quite common.

(i) Hexameters

(a) *Leonine.* The simple Leonine depends on rhyme between the strong caesura and the end of the line:

> Linquo coax ranis, cra corvis vanaque vanis;
> Ad logicam pergo que mortis non timet ergo[29]

> Illos salvavit Mons Fortis quos superavit;
> Carceribus dati sunt multi non cruciati[30]

(b) *Unisoni.* 'Single-sound' Leonines are usually in couplets, thus requiring four rhymes:

> Hinc decesserunt quia mortem contremuerunt;
> Hylde, scripta ferunt, cum gazis ossa tulerunt[31]

> Hec est lex satire, vitiis ridere, salire,
> Mores excire, que feda latent aperire[32]

Sometimes, however, they run on for more than a couplet: Michael of Cornwall, for example, has five blocks of twenty lines each, thus requiring forty rhyme-words for each section.[33]

(c) *Caudati.* 'Tailed' Leonines rhyme finally only. Sometimes they are in couplets, as in Lawrence of Durham, *Consolatio* met. 2:

> Multi multa quidem nos sepe simulque videmus;
> non tamen ut fiant hec omnes scire valemus

More often they are in quatrains, as in Reginald of Canterbury's hymn to his guardian angel:

> Angele, qui meus es custos pietate superna,
> me tibi commissum serva, tueare, guberna;
> terge meam mentem vitiis et labe veterna
> assiduusque comes mihi sis vitaeque lucerna

(d) *Collaterales.* In collaterally rhymed hexameters, caesura rhymes with caesura, final syllable with final syllable, as in Michael of Cornwall:

> Nec minus in bellis decorabit nos dyadema,
> Seu sit pax vel lis: quod qui negat, est anathema (205–6)

Thomas Varoye reinforces the parallelism by providing an extra rhyme in the penultimate syllable.[34]

> Anglus se victum scit quaerens carcere victum
> Ac videt ut Pictum Scotum fore corpore pictum (259–60)

(e) *Cruciferi.* Cruciform hexameters, also called 'cancellati' (lattice-form) by John of Garland, are those in which the caesura of one line rhymes with the end of the next, and vice versa:[35]

> Crux cancellavit musam michi metra novantem,
> Forma triumphantem cruce regem significavit

(f) *Dactylici tripertiti.* Lines of this kind (as in 'hexametri tripertiti' below) lack the traditional caesura; instead they are divided up into three sections, with the second and fourth feet rhyming together, and the ends of the lines rhyming in couplets. All three books of Bernard of Cluny's *De contemptu mundi* are written in it:[36]

> Hora novissima, tempora pessima sunt, vigilemus;
> Ecce minaciter imminet arbiter ille supremus

Collateral rhyme between the two lines is very common, as in Michael of Cornwall:

> Hystrio sordide, vernula perfide, servule nequam,
> Garcio fetide, vatibus invide, rem fugis equam (955–6)

Robert Baston divides the lines into even smaller units of dactyls, with double internal rhyme:

> Hic fremit, hic tremit, hic pavet, hic cavet, iste ligatur,
> Hic legit, hic tegit, hic metit, hic petit, hic spoliatur

(g) *Hexametri tripertiti.* These are like 'dactylici tripertiti', in lacking the traditional caesura, but the units consist of a dactyl and spondee rather than two dactyls, as in John of Bridlington (with collateral rhyme):[37]

> Arcus habentes, tela ferentes, se sociabunt,
> Arma gerentes, regna regentes qui penetrabunt (1.7.19–20)

Michael of Cornwall achieves the same rhythm, but with a split rhyme and without making use of inflexions:

Inclite rex O gallice flexo crure pudice
Me tibi vexo filaque texo rex Lodowice (983–4)

(h) *Combined dactylici and hexametri tripertiti.* Robert Baston combines types (f) and (g) in couplets:

Crescit inedia, corpora, praedia diripiuntur,
Heu mulieres, miles et heres inficiuntur (99–100)

(i) *Trinini salientes.* 'Jumping threesomes', like types (a)–(e), depend on the caesura, but in this case it is the caesurae in the second and fourth feet that carry the rhyme, as in Michael of Cornwall (with collateral rhyme):

Henriolo dare pauca volo non multa scienti
sed sciolo qui fraude dolo fert frivola genti (1009–10)

(j) *Triple rhymes.* Lines with triple rhyme are like Leonines (a), in rhyming the caesura with the end of the line, but they add another internal rhyme, as in Michael of Cornwall:

Si cupias scire reperire reperta polire
Hic potes audire prodire poemata mire (1047–8)

or, using just spondees,

Dignus culpari non laudari reprobari
Non acceptari dampnari non dominari (1098–9)

Reginald of Canterbury (LMP No. 30) employs a similar scheme, but uses the second- and fourth-foot caesura, without collateral rhyme:

State chori sensu memori cantuque sonori
O iuvenes sanctique senes voces date lenes

(k) *Run-over rhyme.* The pattern in which the final rhyme of one line is carried over to the first syllable of the next line is similar to the Irish *devi*, and Michael of Cornwall (who makes great use of it) and the Scotsman Thomas Varoye may have been following Celtic practice. Its first appearance, however, is in a poem by the French immigrant Reginald of Canterbury:

Laudibus Augusti -ne tui decus effero busti
Busti quod celebra- re lira iuvat et fide crebra
Crebra . . . (LMP No. 20, 1–3)

In a sense this is cheating, as the run-over rhyme is achieved simply by repeating the word. Michael of Cornwall is more inventive: not only does he avoid repeating a word, but he introduces a pair of internal rhymes (at the caesura and the following syllable) and uses split rhyme:[38]

Quare compescas escas ? Es namque gulosus
O sus, sordida res ares et corpore marces
Arces corque metris me tris -tem dat tua Musa
Usa . . . (1228–31)

(ii) Elegiac couplets

The four rhyme patterns in elegiac couplets correspond to the simplest types of hexameter rhyme, (a)–(d) above.

(a) *Elegi Leonini.* These employ simple rhyme between the caesura and the end of the line, as in one of the poems on the Oxford riots of 1355:[39]

> Urgent ursina vada perturbando bovina
> Et vada dicta precis sunt vada dicta necis

(b) *Elegi unisoni.* This pattern is common, and is used by Walter of Peterborough throughout his poem on the Spanish campaign of 1367:[40]

> Bella referre paro fratrum de germine claro
> Plus claros raro protulit ulla caro

(c) *Elegi collaterales.* These are also quite common; they are used by Henry of Avranches in his poem against William of Laval:[41]

> Nos tua barbaries dampnat, Willelme, latinos,
> Cordis enim caries liuida prodit in os

(d) *Elegi caudati.* When these occur, they are usually in couplets. Roger of Ford's poem on the Virgin is entirely in this metre:[42]

> Huius in amplexu summi genitoris imago
> Virgineos calices circuit ore uago

(iii) Mixed dactylic rhyme schemes

Unrhymed hexameters are almost never found in combination with unrhymed elegiacs: the two verse forms seem to have been regarded as distinct.[43] With rhyme, however, the situation changes. Although some poets stick firmly to one kind of rhyme (especially *Leonini* and *unisoni*), for others the main object seems to have been to combine as many types of rhyme pattern as possible. Michael of Cornwall, Robert Baston, and Thomas Varoye are the main proponents of this virtuosity, and Varoye, as noted, even includes other metrical types, such as 'octameters' and the metre of Boethius, *Consolatio Philosophiae,* 1 met. 2. The 'Anonymous of Calais' does not use run-over rhyme, but mixes all other kinds of hexameter and elegiac rhymes.[44]

II *Rhythmical verse*

With the exception of Henry of Huntingdon's rhythmical adonics,[45] all rhythmical verse is rhymed and arranged in stanzas – occasionally couplets, but usually quatrains or more complex arrangements. The present description is organized into: A. lines of the same length (arranged in increasing size), B. stanzas combining lines of different lengths.[46]

A *Lines of the same length*

(i) Seven syllables (see also 13- and 15-syllable lines)
  (a) 7pp, aabccb, 'Veni sancte spiritus' (p. 124):

Veni sancte spíritus
et emitte caélitus
lucis tuae rádium
Veni pater páuperum
veni dator múnerum
veni lumen córdium

(b) 7pp, abababab: quoted on p. 141.

(c) 7pp, ababbaba (or one quatrain of 14 syllable-lines with internal rhyme) with refrain: quoted on p. 275.

(d) 7p, 250 lines, in blocks of 50 on the same rhyme (p. 214):

Maria laus divína
virginea regína
vitis propinas vína . . . etc.

(ii) Eight syllables (see also 15- and 16-syllables and Victorines)

(a) 8p, couplets, aabb . . . (p. 33):

O preclara mater mátris
quae concepit verbum pátris . . .

(b) 8pp, 12-line stanza, aabaab bbabba, quoted in full on p. 212 (cf. also p. 282).

(c) 8pp, six-line stanza, aabccb, quoted in full on p. 105.

(d) 8pp, ababab . . ., with changes in order: p. 190.

(e) 8p8pp, abab, poem on Simon de Montfort (p. 201):

Salve Symon Montis-fórtis
totius flos milície
Duras penas passus mórtis
pro statu gentis Ánglie

(iii) Ten syllables

This line is always divided 4p + 6pp and always appears in quatrains. It is the metre of John of Howden's *Canticum Amoris* and *Philomena*:[47]

Ave vérbum ens in princípio
caro fáctum pudoris grémio
Fac quod frágret praesens laudátio
et placéris parvo praecónio (st. 1)

(iv) Twelve syllables (rhythmical asclepiad)[48]

This line arises from the rhythmical reading of the classical quantitative Lesser Asclepiad (above, p. 318 (f));

Māecēnās átăvīs ēdĭtĕ régĭbŭs

producing 12pp or 6pp + 6pp.

(a) Quatrains of rhythmical asclepiads, aaaa, were very common in Anglo-Latin in the thirteenth and fourteenth centuries, perhaps because of the popularity of the *Apocalypsis Goliae* and the *De coniuge non ducenda*. Walter Wimborne has three poems in this metre:[49]

> Multi mortálium in mundi stádio
> certatim cúrsitant sed casso stúdio,
> nunquam uidélicet potiti bráuio
> dum uie néscii uadunt in áuio (*De Palpone* st. 1)

(b) as in (a) but with internal rhyme throughout, in a twelfth-century satire on Rome (p. 142):

> Frater a cúria Romana rédeo
> passus martýria que fari néqueo.
> Desunt donária, uictum non hábeo,
> plenus miséria consorte cáreo

(c) as in (b), but with internal rhyme in couplets, in a poem on the Oxford riots of 1355 (p. 269):

> Domos assaíliunt in ignomínia,
> Securi fériunt necnon et áscia;
> Post haec extrínsecus ponunt incéndia,
> Fortes intrínsecus defendunt hóstia

(d) John of Howden's twelve-syllable line in *Quinquaginta Cantica* does not scan regularly as 6pp + 6pp, or even as 12pp, but it is presumably to be regarded as a rhythmical asclepiad. The stanza arrangement also differs from the usual quatrains.[50]

(e) As it is based directly on a known poem, this is the appropriate place to mention Richard Ledrede's stanzaic adaptation of Walter of Wimborne's *Marie Carmina*. Ledrede has six-line stanzas, 2(2(12pp)1(6pp)), aabccb; it is quoted on p. 247.

(v) Thirteen syllables (Goliardics)
The Goliardic line, 7pp + 6p, is probably the most famous in Medieval Latin literature; it can best be remembered by the tune of the carol 'Good King Wenceslas'.[51] It is used commonly, but not exclusively, for satire.

(a) The most frequent arrangement is in quatrains, aaaa, as in the *Psalterium* attributed to Stephen Langton:[52]

> Ave cuius víscera natum edidérunt
> Cuius ad intéritum gentes fremuérunt;
> Audi voces súpplicum qui te pie quaérunt,
> Mali causas rémovens quae nos invenérunt

(b) A variation favoured by Walter of Châtillon is the Goliardic stanza *cum auctoritate*, in which the final line of each stanza is a hexameter (usually from a well-known text) rhyming with the first three lines. It is seen in the poem on the battle of Falkirk of 1298:[53]

> Johannes jam Scótiae clemens rex et cástus,
> Regni tenens régimen, ut rex erat pástus;

Hunc tandem depósuit gentis suae fástus:
Ēxŭlăt ējēctūs dē sēdĕ pĭā prŏtŏplāstŭs

(c) Sometimes there is internal rhyme throughout the stanza, as in John Pecham's 'Ave vivens hostia':[54]

Moris est amántium invicem sitíre
Ut arcana córdium possint introíre,
Sic vult rex regnántium caritatis mírae
Cibando fidélium intima subíre

(d) Sometimes the internal rhyme is in couplets, as in Rolle's *Canticum*:[55]

En rigore vúlneror stringentis amóris
et in plaga pénetror dulcore decóris;
digiti sunt gráciles candentis colóris;
lucidi, laudábiles, nasus, mentum, aúris

(e) In a poem against the friars (p. 274) there are Goliardic couplets:

Rem preclari nóminis captant emulári;
Quia sunt Domínici, vellent dominári

(f) The *Song of Lewes* (pp. 199–201) has Goliardic couplets with internal rhyme:

Si princeps erráuerit, debet reuocári,
Ab hiis quos grauáuerit iniuste negári

(g) Quatrain and couplet are combined in a six-line stanza, aaaa bb, in which the opening of the couplet is the English phrase 'With an O and an I', in the antifraternal 'Sedens super flumina' (p. 270).

(h) The reply to 'Sedens super flumina' was 'Quis dabit meo capiti' (p. 272). This also uses the six-line stanza with 'O and I' refrain, but also has internal rhyme throughout the quatrain:

Quomodo iam cíuitas sedet desoláta,
Sola nec est cáritas nec pax illi dáta;
Suppressa fit véritas, falsitas eláta,
Ciuium lex únitas sic est extricáta:
    Wyt an O and an I, sic lege neglécta
    Seruit urbs Jerúsalem Chaldeis subiécta (st. 2)

(vi) Fifteen syllables

The fifteen-syllable lines may have been derived from an accentual reading of the classical trochaic tetrameter catalectic ('trochaic septenarius'), which consists of four trochaic metra –⏑ –⏓ with the final syllable 'suppressed':

Pāngĕ līnguă glōrĭṓsī prœlĭūm cērtā́mĭnĭs

Rhythmically, it divides into 8p + 7pp, and when the two halves of the line are separated, with rhyme, new stanza systems emerge (see below on 8p8p7pp, the Victorine).

(a) The satire on Piers Gaveston (p. 243) uses the full line, rhyming finally in triplets, and is a parody of the Venantius Fortunatus hymn:

Pange lingua necem Pétri qui turbauit Ángliam,
Quem rex amans super ómnem pretulit Cornúbiam:
Vult hinc comes et non Pétrus dici per supérbiam (1–3)

(b) Serlo of Fountains (p. 53) rhymes them finally in couplets:

David ille manu fórtis, sceptrum tenens Scóticum,
Armatorum multa mánu regnum intrat Ánglicum (1–2)

(c) Another poem from Scotland, by William of Glasgow, shows a couplet, as in (b), but divides the line 4p + 4p + 7pp, rhyming aabccb (p. 96):

Tymus ústa et arbústa, rubi atque fílices,
Timebántur et rebántur hostibus ut mílites

(d) John Pecham's *Planctus almae matris ecclesiae* (pp. 225–6) has the line divided 8p7pp with internal rhyme, in sets of three, ab ab ab. This could also be laid out (as I have it above) as a six-line stanza:

Cum enim unicus Déus sit et fides única
Unicus sit sponsus méus spes ecclesiástica;
Crescit tamen pharisáeus et pestis schismática

(vii) Sixteen syllables (on 8p8pp, see above, p. 323)
This line could have arisen from the accentual reading of two classical iambic dimeters $\underline{\smile}-\smile-$ / $\underline{\smile}-\smile-$. This is certainly the case in the satire on Piers Gaveston (p. 243) that parodies Venantius Fortunatus' hymn 'Vexilla regis', which is rhythmically 16pp, rhyming in couplets:

Vexilla regni pródeunt, fulget cometa cómitum,
Comes dico Lancástrie qui domuit indómitum

There is one other example of 16pp in couplets, in a poem attacking avarice (p. 141):

Vides quanta tiránnide nunc princeps mundi séuiat,
iustus a terra périit, non est qui bonum fáciat (K.VI.5–6)

B Lines of different length

In theory there is no limit to the variety of stanza arrangements and rhyme schemes. Some are too long or too complex to describe here, such as the isometric sequences of Peter of Blois.[56] Some poems consist of several different stanzaic patterns.[57] Sometimes lines of the same length rhyme together; sometimes long lines rhyme with short.

(a) *8p7pp* (Victorine stanza). This stanza, 2(2(8p) 1(7pp)) aabccb, is named for Adam of St Victor in Paris; it is also known as the 'Stabat mater dolorosa' stanza. It was one of the most popular hymn metres, used at length in John of Garland's *Stella Maris* and Walter of Wimborne's *Ave Virgo*. Walter also used it for satire in the *De Mundi Vanitate*:[58]

Mundi uolo uanitátem
et fortune leuitátem
breuiter descríbere,

que non habent firmaméntum
sed fugacem uincunt uéntum
fugiendo própere (st. 1)

(b) *8pp7p*. This resembles the Victorine, but with reversed rhythm: 2(2(8pp) 1(7p)), aabaab:
see p. 225.

(c) *8pp5p*. 2(2(8pp) 1(5p)) aabaab: Richard of Bury (p. 253).

(d) *12pp8pp*.[59] This is a combination of three rhythmical asclepiads and 8pp, repeated to
form an eight-line stanza: 2(3(12pp) 1(8pp)) aaabcccb. It is used in the lament for the death
of Archbishop Scrope (p. 294).

(e) *13p7pp*. This is a combination of a Goliardic stanza with 7pp, repeated, producing a
ten-line stanza, 2(4(13p) 1(7pp)) aaaabccccb. It is used by William of Combe in his poem on
Becket (p. 81). I quote half a stanza:

> Frangit incleméntiam rigor hiemális,
> Hiems oblivíscitur cursus naturális,
> Cujus vernat médio rosa spiritális,
> Thomas rubet sánguine tempore natális
> Natus ipse dénuo

I now describe a few stanza schemes that combine three or more different lengths of line.

(f) *8p4p6p*. 2(8p) 2(8p) 2(4p) 2(6p) 2(4p) 2(8p) aabbccddeeff. This stanza scheme of
Matthew of Rievaulx (quoted in full on p. 137) was not recognized as verse by its editor.

(g) *4p6pp4pp7pp8pp*. 4(4p)6pp4pp4pp6pp7pp4pp8pp4pp6pp. This is the stanza scheme of
the debate between Body and Soul (of which only a part is given on p. 140):

> Homo nátus ad labórem
> tui státus tue mórem
> sortis consídera
> propénsius; me párcius
> querelis áspera.
> Questus ergo réprime
> nec ánime
> quod misere commíseris
> quod páteris
> miser imprópera

(h) *6p5pp7p7pp8p*. 2(6p)1(5pp)2(6p)1(5pp)1(7pp)1(7p)1(7pp)1(8p)1(7pp) aabaabbabab.
This is the stanza of John of Howden's *Quinquaginta Salutaciones*, which consists of fifty
stanzas: see p. 214 where one stanza is quoted in full.

(i) *7pp7p8pp4pp*. 3(7pp7p) 3(8pp) 1(4pp) abababcccd; this is the complete stanza scheme of
a love lyric in the Bekynton anthology, from which a few lines have been quoted (p. 146).
The same rhymes are maintained in all four stanzas. There is a three-line refrain, 3(12pp)
ddd.

> Bruma, grando, glácies,
> nix, rigor hiemális,
> cedunt; redit spécies
> et decor estiuális;
> mitigatur rábies
> plage meridiális.

327

Ventus in auram vértitur,
maris procella stérnitur,
nauis a nauta régitur
    secúrior.
    Serenus est aer, aura salúbrior,
      marina resident, fit unda púrior;
      qui modo non amet est ferro dúrior

5 *Other poetic devices*

Abecedary. The initial letters of each stanza or line are in alphabetical order: see pp. 225–6.

Acrostic. The initial letters of a series of words, or of each line of a stanza or poem, spell out a word or name, e.g. pp. 76–77, 188, 300–1.

Alliteration. Repetition of the same initial consonant or vowel. This is usually decorative, as in John of Howden and Walter of Wimborne, but sometimes structural (see pp. 37–8, 250–1).

Anaphora. Repetition of the opening word or phrase of a line or stanza, a favourite device of John of Howden and Walter of Wimborne.

Apices numerales or *Chronogram.* Indication of a date by use of the roman numerals M, D, C, L, X, V, I, concealed in words: see pp. 267, 301.

Concatenation. Repetition of part of the last line of one stanza in the opening of the next (pp. 228, 262), a device of Northern poems.

Cyclic structure. The opening line of a poem repeated at the end of the poem, as in John of Howden's *Philomena* (pp. 208–12) and Richard Rolle's *Canticum Amoris* (p. 252 and n. 37), another Northern device.

Epanalepsis. Repetition of half of one line in the following line (see pp. 18, 300).

Onomastic wordplay. The interpretation of a name (of a person or place) according to its supposed etymology. English, French and Latin are used to extract meaning from a name, as in Richard = rich + hard, Passelewe = passa l'eau, Percy = pierce, Eboracum (York) = ivory. Examples can be found throughout Anglo-Latin, and it is a common device in Old English literature.

Psalterium. A poem of 150 stanzas, each of which contains a word from the appropriately numbered psalm. In time, the practice of echoing a psalm ceased and the term simply meant a poem of 150 stanzas. See pp. 124, 206.

Quinquagenum. A set of fifty stanzas, usually addressed to the Virgin Mary, a poetic form frequently used by John of Howden.

Refrain. A line or group of lines repeated after each stanza: see pp. 215, 246–7, 328. The O-and-I phrase that introduces the last two lines of the Goliardic verses on pp. 270–2 is another kind of refrain.

Retrograde verses. Verses in which a line, or series of lines, can be reversed, with the metre intact but the sense usually changed. See p. 176 n. 64.

6 Peculiarities of Anglo-Latin verse

I have not made a close analysis of contemporary European Latin verse, but I would be inclined to regard the following features as characteristically Anglo-Latin:

(a) alliteration as a structural device, as in Henry of Huntingdon and Richard Rolle;

(b) concatenation and cyclic structure, both of which are characteristic of Northern English poems of the thirteenth and fourteenth centuries;

(c) run-over rhyme, which (although used by Reginald of Canterbury) may owe something to Celtic practice (Welsh, Irish or Cornish);

(d) the O-and-I device, which appears in several fourteenth-century English poems.

Notes

Introduction

1 At the risk of causing offence, I use the term 'Anglo-Latin' to include Latin writings in Wales and by Welshmen. The term 'British Latin' (used by R.A. Browne to mean Latin written in the British Isles) is now usually confined to British writers before the Norman Conquest. The triple coinage 'Anglo-Cumbro-Latin' is something we can well do without. I have also, unsystematically, included some works by Scotsmen. It is worth noting here that in the period under discussion the rival to Latin was not English but French. Anglo-Norman (using the term to cover all French written and spoken in England to the end of the Middle Ages) was the language of the court and of most aristocratic households. It overlapped with Latin in chronicles, law, administration, theology, hagiography, science, and epic and lyric poetry. Although it did not match Latin in sheer volume, it had the field to itself in romance and was certainly the language of polite literature. Some of the Anglo-Latin writers (Simon du Freine, John of Howden, John Gower) also wrote in French.

2 See, for example, the two excellent chapters by W. Lewis Jones and J.E. Sandys in the *Cambridge History of English Literature*, Vol. 1 (Cambridge, 1907, rpt. 1932), pp. 156–216. To my knowledge, the only scholar to attempt to give a balanced account of all writers of the English Middle Ages, English, French and Latin, is Henry Morley, *English Writers. An Attempt towards a History of English Literature*, 5 vols. (London/New York, 1887–90); volumes 2–3 include many of the authors discussed here.

3 In most English-speaking universities the Medieval Latinists have most often been employed by departments of English, for no self-evident reason. Certainly only departments of English would be likely to be interested in the literary history of England (including Latin), but of course most Medieval Latin is not English. For the early history of the Oxford School of English, see D.J. Palmer, *The Rise of English Studies* (London, 1965).

4 The reform of pronunciation (recommended by Erasmus) was considerably slower. In James Hilton's *Goodbye Mr Chips*, the conservative teacher of classics is rebuked by his headmaster for continuing to say Cicero (with a sibilant) rather than Kikero.

5 This is related to the 'progress fallacy' discussed in this volume on pp. 4–5.

6 The point can be illustrated by the edition of Lawrence of Durham's *Hypognosticon* by Sr Mistretta (for a Classics Department). Her notes are full of allusions to classical authors

330

such as Virgil and Lucan, but, although the Bible could not possibly have supplied all Lawrence's knowledge of Jewish history, she never once inquires into possible medieval sources (it turns out that Lawrence was using Josephus). Nor, although she was in religious orders, does she ever look for an overall moral and religious purpose for the epic.

7 Pre-Conquest Latin has been served much better: see the collection of papers, *Insular Latin Studies*, ed. M.W. Herren (Toronto, 1981), especially M. Lapidge's 'The present state of Anglo-Latin studies', pp. 45–82.

8 Manitius, DeGhellinck, and Raby (*Secular Latin Poetry*) all end in 1200, and after this point Bezzola confines himself to vernacular writers. Raby's *Christian Latin Poetry* extends to 1300.

9 The word 'decline' or 'déclin' is used by both Raby and DeGhellinck of Latin literature after 1200.

10 For some very perceptive comments on the topic, see J.A. Burrow, *Medieval Writers and their Work* (Oxford, 1982), ch. 1.

11 For a guide to the subject, see Giles Constable, *Letters and Letter-Collections*, Typologie des sources du moyen âge occidental 17 (Turnhout, 1976).

12 See Antonia Gransden, *Historical Writing in England c. 550–1307* (London, 1974) and *Historical Writing in England* II. *c. 1307 to the early Sixteenth Century* (London, 1982); Nancy F. Partner, *Serious Entertainments: the Writing of History in Twelfth-century England* (Chicago/London, 1977).

1 William I to Stephen (1066–1154)

1 In general, see David Knowles, *The Monastic Orders in England . . . 940–1216*, 2nd ed. (Cambridge, 1963); Margaret Gibson, *Lanfranc of Bec* (Oxford, 1978), useful especially for Canterbury; Richard W. Southern, *St Anselm and his Biographer* (Cambridge, 1963).

2 For example, Herman, a Lotharingian, who had probably come to England with Edward, became bishop of Winchester in 1045 and of Sherborne in 1058; at Sherborne he was joined by another monk from St Bertin's, Goscelin (above, pp. 11, 20–1), who stayed at Sherborne until 1078 and eventually settled at St Augustine's, Canterbury.

3 'In all, between 1066 and 1135 notices remain of over sixty overseas abbots appointed to some twenty English houses', Knowles, *Monastic Orders*, p. 112.

4 Knowles, p. 119; on pp. 78–82 Knowles discusses the criticisms of the state of English monasticism immediately after the Conquest.

5 The feast was celebrated in London in 1129, and had the enthusiastic support of Anselm's nephew, Anselm of Bury, and of Osbert of Clare (see this volume, pp. 32–33).

6 *Gesta Regum* III.245 (Vol. II, 304).

7 Richard W. Southern, 'England's first entry into Europe', in *Medieval Humanism and other Studies* (Oxford, 1970), ch. 8; the implied later 'entry' was Britain's membership in the European Common Market.

8 On Crispin, see this volume, p. 31.

9 See this volume, pp. 41–4.

10 A brief account of these writers is given on pp. 63–4.

11 See this volume, ch. 2, pp. 84–7.

12 The most succinct account of Goscelin is by Barlow, *Edward the Confessor* (below, n. 18); see also above, n. 2, and pp. 20–21.

13 That is, his epitaph on William, abbot of Fécamp. Orderic Vitalis (11.4.270–1) tells us (this volume, pp. 15–16) that there was a kind of competition to supply the best epitaph for William. William died in 1107; the date 1108 given by some scholars seems to arise from the assumption that Orderic began the year in March rather than at Christmas.

14 See this volume, pp. 24–30.

15 *Two Alcuin Letter-Books*, ed. Colin Chase (Toronto, 1975), I, 5, pp. 27–8. The debate was continued by Peter of Blois and Robert of Beaufeu (see this volume, p. 86); see also pp. 143–4 and nn. 252–3.

16 In this context we should mention a Winchester manuscript, compiled in the early twelfth century, Oxford, Bodleian Library, Digby 112. This contains not only the poems of Godfrey of Winchester (see this volume pp. 17–20) but several lives of Anglo-Saxon saints and other material of that period. See Lapidge (cited above; Introduction, n. 7), p. 63.

17 See this volume, pp. 257–8.

18 *The Life of King Edward who rests at Westminster*, ed. Frank Barlow (London, 1962). It refers to the battle of Stamford Bridge in September 1066; it was certainly written before the death of Queen Edith (before 1075) and before the deposition of Stigand (1070). It may allude to the Norman Conquest in Edward's vision, in which he is told: 'tradidit deus post obitus tui diem anno uno et die una omne hoc regnum a se maledictum in manu inimici' (Barlow, p. 75). Bloch's theory that it was written in the early twelfth century has no support. The authorship is unknown. Barlow infers that the author was not English (because of some objective remarks about the *Angli*) and probably Lotharingian (because of his admiration for Count Baldwin of Flanders), but authorial distancing is not uncommon, and any member of Godwin's household would feel kindly towards Baldwin, who sheltered both Godwin and Tostig in their exiles. Barlow proposes either Goscelin or Folchard, but the style is utterly unlike anything else of theirs.

19 See this volume, pp. 14–15.

20 See this volume, pp. 32–3.

21 Text in PL 195, 737–90. On Aelred, see this volume, p. 61.

22 See this volume, pp. 131–3.

23 For a full account of Anglo-Latin metres, see Appendix, pp. 313–29.

24 See this volume, pp. 176–7.

25 See this volume, pp. 177–8.

26 Leopold Delisle, *Rouleaux des morts du IXe au XVe siècle* (Paris, 1866), especially Nos. XXXVI, XXXVIII; No. XXXI is printed in ASS, October, III, 736–65. See further Christopher Cheney, 'Two mortuary rolls from Canterbury: devotional links of Canterbury with Normandy and the Welsh March', in *Tradition and Change: essays in honour of Marjorie Chibnall*, ed. Diana Greenway, Christopher Holdsworth and Jane Sayers (Cambridge, 1985), pp. 103–14.

27 In BL Add. 24199 there is a mournful poem on the tomb and the universality of death, which has conquered 'Regem Guillelmum'. This is presumably William Rufus, as the poem says

> Intempestiue cecidit sensitque sagittam
> Cui nunquam dederat missa sagitta fugam

(unless this can mean 'the arrow of death'). If so, it is unusual: most writers condemned

William Rufus, but this is lavish in praise of his prowess and justice. See p. 151 and n. 285; the poem (WIC 5626a) is No. XI, pp. 40–2, in Boutemy's Appendix.

28 *The Carmen de Hastingae Proelio of Guy, Bishop of Amiens*, ed. Catherine Morton and Hope Muntz (Oxford, 1972).

29 Ralph H.C. Davis, 'The *Carmen de Hastingae Proelio*', *EHR* 93 (1978), 241–61; the core of the argument is that lines 329–34 must be addressed not to William I but to one of his sons. For further discussion, see *Proceedings of the Battle Conference on Anglo-Norman Studies*, ed. R.A. Brown, 2 (1979), 1–20.

30 See this volume, p. 64.

31 The fullest account of Godfrey, with an edition of the *Epigrams*, is in *Der 'Liber Proverbiorum' des Godefrid von Winchester*, ed. H. Gerhard (Würzburg, 1974), replacing Wright, *ALSP* (see n. 37). I am not inclined to accept Godfrey's authorship of a poem to the Virgin Mary (*AH* 32, 20–1) or of a poem *De Nummo* (John A. Yunck, 'The *Carmen de Nummo* of Godfrey of Cambrai', *Annuale Medievale* 2 (1961), 72–103); both are in a manuscript that contains his poems, but it is a poetic anthology containing many texts. Godfrey went to Winchester when Walchelin was appointed bishop in place of the deposed Stigand, who held Winchester as a plurality. Walchelin appointed his brother Simeon as prior, but in 1082 Simeon left to become abbot of Ely and Godfrey succeeded him. Godfrey wrote epitaphs of both Walchelin and Simeon.

32 Imitations of Martial were quite common at the time; they are evident in the *Anthologia Latina* and its later descendants, such as the collections in Paris BN MS lat. 3761 and Zurich, Zentralbibliothek MS C58/275. On epigrams, see W. Maaz, 'Epigrammatisches Sprechen im lateinischen Mittelalter', in *Mittelalterliche Komponenten des europäischen Bewusstseins*, ed. F. Wagner and J. Szövérffy (Berlin, 1983), pp. 101–29.

33 In one manuscript they are ascribed to Horace, because of the opening of the prologue (this volume p. 18).

34 Horace, *Ars poetica* 343.

35 *Disticha Catonis* III, 7: 'Alterius dictum aut factum ne carpseris umquam, / Exemplo simili ne te derideat alter.' Cf. Raby, *SLP* 2, 89.

36 Nos. 1–101 (couplets), 102–198 (quatrains), 199–218 (6-line), 219–31 (8-line), 232–4 and 234 and 237 (10-line), 238 (14-line), 235 (16-line), 236 (18); in Wright's text, the last six lines of 234 belong to 238.

37 Ed. Wright, *ALSP* 2, 148–55. They concern: (1) Cnut d. 1035; (2) Emma, Cnut's wife d. 1052; (3) Edward the Confessor d. 1066; (4) Edith, Edward's wife, d. 1075 at neighbouring Wilton; (5) William the Conqueror d. 1087; (6) Matilda, William's wife, d. 1083; (7) Lanfranc d. 1089; (8)–(9) Walcher d. 1080; (10) Richard, William's son; (11) a blind monk Aethelric; (12) Wulnoth d. after 1087; (13) Simeon of Ely d. 1093; (14) Wulfstan, bishop of Worcester d. 1095; (15) Robert Losinga, bishop of Hereford, d. 1095; (16) Walchelin d. 1098; (17) Thomas, archbishop of York, d. 1100; (18) Serlo, abbot of Gloucester, d. 1104; (19) William of Fécamp, d. 1107 (see n. 13 above).

38 See Southern, *St Anselm*, pp. 217, 249.

39 *S. Anselmi Cantuariensis Archiepiscopi Opera Omnia*, ed. Franciscus Salesius Schmitt, Vol. III (Edinburgh, 1946), 5–91.

40 *Meditatio* 3, p. 91.

41 Richard Sharpe, 'Two contemporary poems on Saint Anselm attributed to William of Chester', *RB* 95 (1985), 266–79. For a life of Anselm based on John of Salisbury's *Vita*, see Daniel J. Sheerin, 'An anonymous verse epitome of the Life of Saint Anselm

("Tange Syon citharam")', *AB* 92 (1974), 109–24. In PL 158, 119–24, there is a poem on Anselm's miracles (inc. 'Cum patris Anselmi'), with other miracles and the collections of Alexander the monk; cols. 141–2 contain some epitaphs.

42 See above, nn. 2 and 12, and p. 11. The fullest account of Goscelin is by T.J. Hamilton, *Goscelin of Canterbury: a critical study of his life, works, and accomplishments*, Ph.D. thesis, 2 vols. (Univ. of Virginia, 1973). Many of his lives are in PL 155, 11–120.

43 See this volume, pp. 257–8.

44 C.H. Talbot, 'The Life of Saint Wulsin of Sherborne by Goscelin', *RB* 69 (1959), 68–85 (cf. Grosjean in *AB* 78 (1960), 201–6). A. Wilmart, 'La légende de Ste. Édith en prose et vers par le moine Goscelin', *AB* 56 (1938), 5–101, 265–307 (St Edith is not to be confused with Queen Edith, benefactress of Wilton). C.H. Talbot, 'The *Liber confortatorius* of Goscelin of St Bertin', *Analecta Monastica* 3rd ser. (Rome, 1955 = *Studia Anselmiana* 37), 1–117; on this see also A. Wilmart, 'Eve et Goscelin', *RB* 46 (1934), 414–38; 50 (1938), 42–83. For other works by Goscelin, see Marvin L. Colker, 'Texts of Jocelyn of Canterbury which relate to the history of Barking Abbey', *Studia Monastica* 7 (1965), 383–460; D.W. Rollason, 'Goscelin of Canterbury's account of the translation and miracles of St Mildrith (BHL 5961/4): an edition with notes', *MSt* 48 (1986), 139–210; M.L. Colker, 'A hagiographic polemic', *MSt* 39 (1977), 60–108; Richard Sharpe, 'Goscelin's St Augustine and St Mildreth: hagiography and liturgy in context', *Journal of Theological Studies* n.s. 41 (1990), 502–16.

45 See this volume, pp. 29–30.

46 For the life of St Dunstan, see *Memorials of St Dunstan*, ed. W. Stubbs, RS (London, 1874), pp. 69–161; for St Elphege, see H. Wharton in *Anglia Sacra* (London, 1691; rpt. Farnborough, 1969), 2, 122–47; see this volume, pp. 20–1. A life of St Odo is generally attributed to Eadmer, this volume, pp. 30–1.

47 PL 147, 1083–200, contains texts of the lives of Sts Bertin, John of Beverley, Omer and Oswald; for a better text of John of Beverley, see *York Historians* 1, 239–60. The life of St Botulph is in *ASS*, June IV (17 June), pp. 324–30.

48 For a survey, see J.C. Jennings, 'The writings of Prior Dominic of Evesham', *EHR* 77 (1962), 298–304. The *Chronicon Abbatiae de Evesham*, ed. William Dunn Macray, RS (London, 1863), contains texts of the lives of Egwin, Odulf, and Wistan, with miracles; for a new text of Book 1 of the life of Egwin, see Michael Lapidge, 'Dominic of Evesham's "Vita S. Ecgwini episcopi et confessoris"', *AB* 96 (1978), 65–104. The miracles of the Virgin have been edited by J.C. Jennings, *Prior Dominic of Evesham and the survival of English tradition after the Conquest*, B. Litt. thesis (Oxford, 1958); the prologue is printed by R.W. Southern, 'The English origin of the Miracles of the Virgin', *MARS* 4 (1958), 176–216. On the tradition of the miracles, see this volume, p. 35.

49 A text of the prose vulgate version may be found in *The Life of St Katherine*, ed. E. Einenkel, EETS o.s. 80 (London, 1884; rpt. New York, 1973).

50 See this volume, p. 21.

51 Elizabeth Stevens and Pauline Thompson, 'Gregory of Ely's verse life and miracles of St Aethelthryth', *AB* 106 (1988), 333–90.

52 The manuscript, Trinity College, Cambridge, 0.9.38, was compiled by a Glastonbury monk, who would have been interested by the translation of Hilda's relics to Glastonbury. For a text of the poem, see A.G. Rigg, *An Edition of a Fifteenth-century Commonplace Book*, 2 vols., D. Phil. thesis (Oxford, 1966), 1, 167–85, II, 393–422. On the

manuscript, see my *Glastonbury Miscellany* and this volume pp. 311–12.

53 Text in *Miscellanea Biographica*, ed. J. Raine, Surtees Soc. 8 (London/Edinburgh, 1838), pp. 89–117; the poem is not 's. xiv' as WIC has it.

54 For a later life of Cuthbert, see on Reginald of Durham, this volume, p. 97.

55 See this volume, p. 11.

56 PL 23, 55–62, occupying only six full columns.

57 *Vita Sancti Malchi*, ed. Levi Robert Lind, Illinois Studies in Language and Literature 3–4 (Urbana, Ill., 1942). The short Merton text is on pp. 153–76.

58 Lind, pp. 37–41. This important passage has not, to my knowledge, been noticed by historians of literary theory.

59 The hymns are mainly in Leonine hexameters; the three- or four-line stanzas are determined by syntax. One is in monorhymed caudati ending in -*isti*.

60 'Angele qui meus es custos pietate superna', WIC 973.

61 *Canterbury Tales*, Gen. Prol. 180–1. The dangers of leaving the cloister were stressed also by Anselm in letters (in *Opera Omnia*, ed. F.S. Schmitt, Vols. 3–5 (Edinburgh, 1946–51)) to Lanzo (Epist. 37) and Warner (Epist. 335), and in his firm refusal to those monks who wished to visit him in his exile (Epist. 355); he warns them specifically of the danger of capture by bandits. Interestingly, Gundulf and his companions, en route to the Holy Land, 'horrendas formidabant Sarracenorum insidias', *The Life of Gundulf, Bishop of Rochester*, ed. Rodney Thomson (Toronto, 1977), p. 27.

62 PL 171. 292 (Epist. xv, 7).

63 The minor poems are to be found in Wright, ALSP 2, 259–67 (abbreviated WMP), and F. Liebermann, 'Raginald von Canterbury', *Neues Archiv* 13 (1888), 519–56 (abbreviated LMP). I have corrected some of Wright's errors.

64 See this volume, p. 31.

65 This poem contains the remarks about beer cited above (p. 11).

66 The three-line stanza consists of an elegiac couplet with Leonine rhyme followed by a line of two choriambs and an adonic.

67 Anselm, abbot of Bury, was nephew of the archbishop Anselm; he was an active supporter, with Osbert of Clare, of the feast of the Immaculate Conception.

68 See this volume, pp. 193–8.

69 Not only was Baldwin prior of Rochester, but he was succeeded by Arnulf, prior of Christ Church and addressee of LMP Nos. 8–13.

70 N.K. Rasmüssen, 'Benedictions de Matines attribuées à Réginald de Cantorbéry', *CM* 25 (1964), 215–23.

71 There are too many works to list here. For a full study, see Southern, cited above n. 1; also *The Life of St Anselm, Archbishop of Canterbury*, ed. R.W. Southern (London, 1962; rpt. Oxford, 1972).

72 The works have recently been re-edited: *The Works of Gilbert Crispin, Abbot of Westminster*, ed. Anna S. Abulafia and G.R. Evans, Auctores Britannici Medii Aevi 8 (Oxford, 1986). The fullest study is by J. Armitage Robinson, *Gilbert Crispin, Abbot of Westminster* (Cambridge, 1911).

73 The most recent study by Jacqueline H.L. Reuter (née Beaumont), *Petrus Alfonsi: an Examination of his Works, their Scientific Content and their Background*, D.Phil. thesis (Oxford, 1975), notes that although Peter was in England for a long time and worked with Adelard, the idea that he was Henry I's physician (not mentioned in court records) is first found in a manuscript of the late twelfth or early thirteenth century. There are

several editions and translations of the *Disciplina Clericalis*. I use the edition by Alfons Hilka and W. Söderhjelm (Heidelberg, 1911); *The Scholar's Guide*, transl. J.R. Jones and J.E. Keller (Toronto, 1969).

74 See this volume, pp. 163, 255–7.

75 *De eodem et diverso*, ed. H. Willner, *Beiträge zur Geschichte der Philosophie des Mittelalters* 4, 1 (1903). For a survey of Adelard's works, see article by Marshall Clagett in *Dictionary of Scientific Biography* (New York, 1970), pp. 61–64.

76 On the prosimetrum, see this volume, pp. 14–15.

77 See Dietrich Lohrmann, 'Der Tod König Heinrichs I von England in der mittellateinischen Literatur Englands und der Normandie', *MJ* 8 (1973), 90–107. We have lost a poem addressed to Henry I by Richard Belmeis, bishop of London (d. 1128); it is mentioned in a Peterborough catalogue and by Tanner.

78 WIC 2935; ed. Wright, *Biographia* 2, 180–1.

79 See this volume, pp. 45–6.

80 See this volume, p. 59.

81 See this volume, pp. 33, 36–9.

82 See *Letters of Osbert of Clare, Prior of Westminster*, ed. E.W. Williamson, with a life of Osbert by J. Armitage Robinson (Oxford, 1929); M. Bloch, 'La vie de S. Édouard le Confesseur par Osbert de Clare', *AB* 41 (1923), 5–131, with a contentious argument about the date (above, n. 18). On the death of Gilbert Crispin in 1117, Osbert may have been the logical choice as abbot, but Henry I appointed Herbert, a Norman from Bec, in 1121. Osbert seems to have been 'banished'; he went first to Ely, then Bury; in 1134 he returned to Westminster as prior, but after 1139 he went into exile again; he returned to Westminster after the deposition of abbot Gervase in 1146.

83 See this volume, pp. 13–14.

84 A. Wilmart, 'Les compositions d'Osbert de Clare en l'honneur de Sainte Anne', *Annales de Bretagne* 37 (1926), 1–33, rpt. in Wilmart, *Auteurs spirituels*, ch. 15, pp. 261–86.

85 Generally I have excluded historians from this history, despite their intrinsic literary value. For an excellent survey, see Antonia Gransden, *Historical writing in England c. 550–1307* (London, 1974) and *Historical Writing in England, 1307 to the early Sixteenth Century* (London, 1982). I have excluded Orderic Vitalis for different reasons: although born in the Severn valley, he spent most of his life as a monk at St Evroul. His thirteen-book *Historia Ecclesiastica*, ed. Marjorie Chibnall, 6 vols. (Oxford, 1969–80), mainly concerns Normandy and England from about 1066–1141, though he also deals with the crusade. He includes many verse epitaphs and other poems; some of his own verses form prologues to each book. He provides our first literary reference to the 'familia Herlechini' (see this volume, pp. 69, 89).

86 William dedicated the *Gesta Regum* and *Historia Novella* to Robert, earl of Gloucester, illegitimate son of Henry I. Geoffrey dedicated the *Historia Regum Britanniae* to Robert (among others), but his *Prophecies of Merlin* was commissioned by Alexander, bishop of Lincoln, for whom Henry wrote his *Historia Anglorum*.

87 There is an extensive bibliography on William; the most comprehensive account is by Rodney Thomson, *William of Malmesbury* (Woodbridge, Suffolk, 1987), which subsumes all Thomson's earlier studies of William. Editions of texts include: *Gesta Regum*, ed. W. Stubbs, 2 vols. RS (London, 1887–9); *Historia Novella*, ed. K.R. Potter (London, 1955); *Gesta Pontificum*, ed. N.E.S.A. Hamilton, RS (London, 1870); *The*

early History of Glastonbury, ed. and tr. J. Scott (Woodbridge, 1981); *Vita Wulfstani*, ed. R.R. Darlington CS 3rd ser. 40 (London, 1928); *Vita Dunstani*, in *Memorials of St Dunstan*, ed. W. Stubbs, RS (London, 1874).

88 *William of Malmesbury: Polyhistor. A Critical Edition*, ed. H.T. Ouelette (Binghamton, 1982).

89 See this volume, p. 10.

90 Much has been made of the word *naeniae* in connexion with Welsh prophecies. It should be noted that Reginald of Canterbury calls his own verses 'nenias' (ed. Lind, p. 38).

91 PL 156, 563–78 and 967–1018.

92 See n. 48 above. Important studies include: A. Mussafia, 'Studien zu den mittelalterlichen Marienlegenden', *Sitzungsberichte der kaiserliche Akademie der Wissenschaften in Wien*. Philosophisch-historische Classe 113 (1886), 917–94; 115 (1888), 5–92; 119 No. 9 (1889), 1–66; 123 No. 8 (1891), 1–85; 139 No. 8 (1898), 1–74. A. Poncelet, 'Miraculorum B.V. Mariae quae saec. VI–XV latine conscripta sunt Index postea perficiendus', *AB* 21 (1902), 241–360. R.W. Southern, 'The English origins of the Miracles of the Virgin', *MARS* 4 (1958), 176–216.

93 *El libro 'De laudibus et miraculis sanctae Mariae' de Guillermo de Malmesbury*, ed. José M. Canal, 2nd ed. (Rome, 1968); P.N. Carter, *An Edition of William of Malmesbury's Treatise on the Miracles of the Virgin Mary*, D.Phil. thesis, 2 vols. (Oxford, 1959).

94 See this volume, p. 104.

95 See this volume, pp. 83–84, 125, 172–3.

96 *Historia Anglorum*, ed. T. Arnold, RS (London, 1879). The best study of Henry is by Nancy F. Partner, *Serious Entertainments* (Chicago/London, 1977), pp. 11–48.

97 The only poem in the *Historia* that is certainly not his is one which he attributes to Walo on the death of William of Flanders. Several poems in the *Historia* were anthologized in Bodleian MS Laud lat. 86, and in the Rufford anthology: see this volume pp. 151, 152.

98 Similar verses are found under AD 635, 641 and 823. The rhythm would work better for those in AD 617, 635 and 641 if the specifying genitive (e.g. *Anglorum*) were omitted as a gloss, but lines with three units appear in the Brunanburh poem.

99 The poem is discussed by D. Abegg, *Zur Entwicklung der historischen Dichtung bei den Angelsachsen*, Quellen und Forschungen zur Sprach- und Culturgeschichte der germanischen Völker 73 (Strassburg, 1894), pp. 103–11. See also Alistair Campbell, *The Battle of Brunanburh* (London, 1938), p. 148, and Edith Rickert, 'The Old English Offa saga I', *MPhil* 2 (1904), 29–76 (on pp. 65–66). For a full discussion, see A.G. Rigg, 'Henry of Huntingdon's metrical experiments', *Journal of Medieval Latin* 1 (1991) 60–72.

100 In the manuscript, the two books of epigrams are numbered as XI–XII of the *Historia* but they are clearly unconnected with it. Only the first book has been published, by Wright ALSP 2, 163–74; for an account of the second, see M.R. James and C. Jenkins, *A Descriptive Catalogue of the Manuscripts in the Library of Lambeth Palace* (Cambridge, 1930–2), pp. 193–6, on MS 118, where the prologue and incipits are printed. I have benefited from a transcription made by Bruce Burnam. Leland also records eight books *de amore* and eight books *de herbis, aromatibus, gemmis*.

101 The line consists of two glyconics, sometimes with the nucleus (the choriamb) contracted to three long syllables. There is frequent rhyme. Wright prints *refrigerent*.

102 I have not found this metre elsewhere; the line seems to consist of a dactylic hemiepes (i.e. the first half of a hexameter line) plus two and a half iambs.

103 The poems are edited by Michael Lapidge, 'The Welsh-Latin poetry of Sulien's family', *Studia Celtica* 8–9 (1973–4), 68–106.

104 I quote from *The Historia Regum Britannie I: Bern, Bürgerbibliothek MS 568*, ed. Neil Wright (Cambridge, 1985). Other standard editions include those by Acton Griscom (London, 1929), the basis for the Penguin translation by Lewis Thorpe (Harmondsworth, 1966), and by Edmond Faral, *La légende Arthurienne: études et documents*, 3 vols. (Paris, 1929); the last contains texts of Geoffrey and pseudo-Nennius.

105 I take *infra = intra*; I see no support for 'apart from' (Thorpe).

106 Recently some scholars have argued that the 'first variant version' of the *Historia* antedates it and represents the 'old book' in some way. The arguments have been closely analysed and refuted in the most recent edition: *The Historia Regum Britannie of Geoffrey of Monmouth: II The First Variant Version: A Critical Edition*, ed. Neil Wright (Cambridge, 1988), Introduction.

107 The pseudo-Nennius *Historia Britonum* has the descent from Brutus, Vortigern's encounter with the 'fatherless child' (here Ambrosius Aurelius, not Merlin), who explains the sinking foundations of the tower and reveals two dragons, and the twelve battles of Arthur (here called a *dux*). The *Annales Cambriae* mention Arthur's victory at Mount Badon and (with no details) the deaths of Arthur and Medraut at Camlann. Some saints' lives mention Arthur in the company of Bedwer and Kei.

108 The claim of Trojan descent (like Rome, and also being made at this time by Normans and French) is in the *Historia Britonum*.

109 See on the *Prophetiae Merlini*, this volume, pp. 44–5.

110 The legend that Arthur would one day return (made more explicit in the *Vita Merlini*) was known to William of Malmesbury. For a different account of Arthur's death, see on the *Vera Historia*, this volume, p. 49. The legend became proverbial for a foolish hope.

111 In Bede Cadwaladr (Cædwalla) was the West-Saxon king of the Gewissae, but for Geoffrey (as in the *Vita Merlini*) the Gewissae were the British inhabitants of Gwent. Thus Geoffrey has turned a Saxon into the last British heir.

112 Geoffrey apparently jumps straight from the eighth to the tenth century, as Athelstan (925–39) was the first Saxon king of all England. In the first variant version (above n. 106) the order has been changed so that Athelstan appears to be more or less contemporary with Cadwaladr: see R.W. Leckie, *The Passage of Dominion* (Toronto, 1981). In the metrical *Historia Regum Angliae* and its source (this volume, pp. 204–5), Athelstan is placed at the beginning of the West-Saxon line.

113 Christopher Brooke, 'Geoffrey of Monmouth as a historian', in *Church and Government in the Middle Ages*, ed. C. Brooke, D. Luscombe, G. Martin and D. Owen (Cambridge, 1976), pp. 77–91; Valerie I.J. Flint, 'The *Historia Regum Britanniae* of Geoffrey of Monmouth: parody and its purpose. A suggestion', *Speculum* 54 (1979), 447–68; R.W. Hanning, *The Vision of History in Early Britain* (New York, 1966).

114 Britanny sent Constantine II to Britain's aid, and offered refuge to Cadwallo and Cadwaladr.

115 J.S.P. Tatlock, *The Legendary History of Britain* (Berkeley/Los Angeles, 1950).

116 Cf. Lucan, *Pharsalia* I, 637–90.

117 See this volume, pp. 47, 94.

118 A similar tree appears in Nebuchadnezzar's vision and in a vision before the birth of St Aethelwold.

119 Old English *stæp-ford* had only recently been assimilated to Stafford.
120 The literature is immense. See Paul Zumthor, *Merlin le Prophète: un thème de la littérature polémique de l'historiographie et des romans* (Lausanne, 1943).
121 See this volume, pp. 94.
122 The *Historia Britonum* took the name Aurelius Ambrosius from Gildas, but there he is a general.
123 Ed. John Jay Parry, Univ. of Illinois Studies in Language and Literature 10, 3 (Urbana, 1925); and Basil Clarke (Cardiff, 1973). Both editions have facing translations.
124 It is a Celtic story, told of Lailoken; it was treated in Latin verse by Hildebert.
125 It seems to have been little known; the complete text is extant in only one manuscript. Extracts were included in Higden's *Polychronicon*, which gave the poem more popularity from the fourteenth century on.
126 *Pace* Penelope B.R. Doob, *Nebuchadnezzar's Children: Conventions of Madness in Middle English Literature* (New Haven/London, 1974), pp. 153–8.
127 Prose commentaries were made by Suger and 'Alanus' and there are at least three anonymous ones: see Curley (next note), p. 220.
128 Michael J. Curley, 'A new edition of John of Cornwall's *Prophetia Merlini*', *Speculum* 57 (1982), 217–49. At least once the interlinear gloss disagrees with the prose commentary in its interpretation.
129 The phrase *per plana Reontis* (80) is explicable only by reference to Welsh prophetic writings.
130 *Brut y Brenhinedd*, ed. J.J. Parry (Cambridge, Mass., 1937), pp. 225–6.
131 See this volume, p. 94. For later use of the verse prophecy tradition, see on John of Bridlington, this volume, pp. 265–8 and n. 91.
132 There is, for example, what is now known as the St Albans Compilation, a life of Alexander the Great based mainly on Orosius; it was the basis for an Old French version and for two fifteenth-century compilations. It was attributed by Bale to two separate authors: Ralph Gubiun, abbot of St Albans (d. 1151), and Galfridus of Hemlington, who is said to have dedicated it to abbot Ralph. This Ralph is not to be confused with the Ralph of St Albans who wrote a verse life of St Alban (this volume, p. 124).
133 On the first variant version, used by Wace and written before 1154, see this volume, p. 41, n. 106. Other works include: the verse *Brutus*, this volume, pp. 98–9; the verse *Historia Regum Anglie* and its continuation, pp. 204–5, 296; the verses of John Bever, p. 295; the prose account of Albina's sisters, pp. 295–6.
134 *Chronicles of the Reigns of Stephen, Henry II and Richard I*, ed. Richard Howlett, RS (London, 1885), 2, 585–781.
135 *Gesta Regum Britanniae*, ed. Francisque Michel, Cambrian Archaeological Association (Bordeaux, 1862).
136 J. Hammer, 'Some Leonine summaries of Geoffrey of Monmouth's *Historia Regum Britanniae* and other poems', *Speculum* 6 (1931), 114–23. The *Historia* (in a Douai manuscript) is preceded by a text of 'Pergama flere' (this volume, p. 136 and n. 232), and the whole text is introduced and concluded by sets of dactylici tripertiti, summarizing the settlement of Britain, with some more verses denouncing the 'British hope'.
137 C. Plummer, *Vitae Sanctorum Hiberniae* 2 (Oxford, 1910), 293–4.
138 Michael Lapidge, 'An edition of the *Vera Historia de morte Arthuri*', *Arthurian Literature* I (1981), 79–93.
139 The manuscripts are early thirteenth century. Lapidge suggests that the story was

certainly written before the settlement of the dispute over the archbishopric of St David's in 1203.

140 See this volume, p. 90.

141 *The Rise of Gawain, Nephew of Arthur (De ortu Waluuanii nepotis Arturi)*, ed. and tr. Mildred Leake Day (New York, 1984), and the same author's *The Story of Meriadoc (Historia Meriadoci)* (New York, 1988). These replace the editions by J. Douglas Bruce (Göttingen/Baltimore, 1913). If Robert is the author, he should not properly be in this book, but the matter is not entirely settled and the manuscript tradition is entirely English. If he is not the author, the stories could be much later, as late as the thirteenth century.

142 Compare the breaking of the deer in *Sir Gawain and the Green Knight*, or the scene in *Sir Degare* where the hero is taught how to remove the shaft from a broken spear (which he later applies to a dead knight).

143 G.L. Kittredge, 'Arthur and Gorlagon', *Harvard Studies and Notes in Philology and Literature* 8 (1903), 149–275.

144 See this volume, pp. 22–4, 29, 35.

145 The conflict was one of the minor causes of the murder of Becket (who objected to the coronation of the young Henry 'III' by Roger, archbishop of York: this volume, pp. 73, 79 and n. 52), and was still a topic of Latin literature in the fourteenth and fifteenth centuries.

146 *History of the Church of York 1066–1127*, ed. C. Johnson, rev. M. Brett, C.N.L. Brooke and M. Winterbottom (Oxford, 1990); poem in ALSP 2, 219–29; the poem on the Standard is almost all lost. The surname Sotovagina may be French or may conceal the English placename element *-skeith*.

147 The *Vita* is in *York Historians*, Vol. 2; it was probably written shortly after Thurstan's death in 1140, at the Cluniac monastery of Pontefract, where he spent his last days. Hugh's poem is in 2, 261–5, Galfridus' in 2, 267–9.

148 He is described by John of Hexham (who calls him Turcople) as 'vir celebris peritiae in scholari eruditione' (*York Historians* 2, 268).

149 See *Serlo de Wilton: poèmes latins*, ed. Jan Öberg (Stockholm, 1965), pp. 7–9; Serlo seems to have thought that King Stephen was present at the battle, unless 'Stephani standardium' simply means 'the English standard'.

150 See this volume, pp. 260–4.

151 Hugh Farmer, 'The vision of Orm', *AB* 75 (1957), 72–82; for a short survey, see C.J. Holdsworth, 'Visions and visionaries in the Middle Ages', *History* n.s. 48 (1963), 141–53. For the visions described by Peter of Cornwall, Henry of Saltrey, the monk of Eynsham, and Thurkill, see this volume, pp. 127–8.

152 The life is in *Vitae Sanctorum Hiberniae*, ed. W.W. Heist, Subsidia Hagiographica 28 (Brussells, 1965), pp. 1–37, and in ASS 1 Feb (Feb. 1, 172–85). The letter to Aelred is printed by A. Hoste, 'A survey of the unedited work of Laurence of Durham, with an edition of his letter to Aelred of Rievaulx', *Sacris Erudiri* 11 (1960), 249–65.

153 *The Hypognosticon of Lawrence of Durham: a Preliminary Text with an Introduction*, ed. M.L. Mistretta, Ph.D. thesis (Fordham, New York, 1941). Lawrence tells us that before he had finished it, his copy was lost and he had to restore it from memory, which he did in a month. It was very popular: it is extant in at least seventeen manuscripts, some (e.g. Titus D. xxiv) containing extracts; it is quoted in the *Distinctiones monasticae* and by Matthew of Rievaulx; see this volume, pp. 136–7, 162–3.

154 Copies of the Latin translation of Josephus were available at Durham in the twelfth century. For an edition of Books I–V, see *The Latin Josephus*, ed. Franz Blatt (Copenhagen, 1958).

155 R.A. Browne, *British Latin Selections AD 500–1400* (Oxford, 1954), p. 56.

156 It was this passage that gave Lawrence the reputation for antifeminism that led to his being cast as one of the 'angels' in the *De coniuge non ducenda*.

157 See this volume, pp. 119–20.

158 *Consolatio de morte amici*, ed. U. Kindermann (Breslau, 1969). The metres besides elegiacs are: m.2 hexametri caudati; m.3 Fourth asclepiadic stanza; m.5 hemiepes + 4 or 5 syllables; m.12 hexameters; m.13 anacreontics; m.14 dactylic pentameters.

159 Ed. Kindermann, *Consolatio*, Appendix I, p. 190.

160 Cornelia Braun-Irgang, '*Tempora nec sexum metuit* – ein poetischer Text zum Thema "De corruptione hominis"', *MJ* 20 (1985), 128–46. The poem occurs at the beginning of Book IV, but as it concerns man's general corruption, rather than the degeneracy that preceded the Law, it is hard to fit into the Hypognosticon as it stands.

161 U. Kindermann, 'Das Emmausgedicht des Laurentius von Durham', *MJ* 5 (1968), 79–100.

162 U. Kindermann, 'Die fünf Reden des Laurentius von Durham', *MJ* 8 (1973), 108–41.

163 *Dialogi Laurentii Dunelmensis monachi et prioris*, ed. J. Raine, Surtees Soc. 70 (Durham, 1880).

164 This recalls the Prologue to *Hypognosticon* II.

165 See this volume, p. 32.

166 Most of the works mentioned here are in *Aelredi Rievallensis Opera Omnia*, ed. A. Hoste and C.H. Talbot, Vol. I *Opera ascetica*, CCCM I (Turnholt, 1971); see also PL 195; *Quand Jésus eut douze ans*, ed. A. Hoste (Paris, 1958); *Relatio de Standardio*, in *Chronicles of the reigns of Stephen, Henry II and Richard I*, ed. R. Howlett, 3, RS (London, 1886), 179–99. Other English Cistercian writers include Alan of Meaux, Roger of Ford, Stephen of Easton, and the anonymous *Pictor in carmine*, this volume, pp. 160–2, 83–4, 207–8, 129–31.

167 See this volume, p. 14.

168 Chs. 29–31, Hoste and Talbot, pp. 662–73.

169 See this volume, p. 220.

170 See this volume, pp. 207–8.

171 *Thesaurus Novus Latinitatis*, ed. A. Mai, *Classici auctores e vaticanis codicibus editi* 8 (Rome, 1836); the prologue is printed by G. Goetz, *Corpus glossariorum latinorum* I (Leipzig, 1923), 197–201. For the preface, see R.W. Hunt, 'The "lost" preface to the *Liber derivationum* of Osbern of Gloucester', *MARS* 4 (1958), 267–82. Osbern also wrote a commentary on the Book of Judges, dedicated to Gilbert Foliot, bishop of Hereford (1148–63), former abbot of Gloucester, later bishop of London.

172 See on the *Babio*, this volume, pp. 113–14.

173 See this volume, p. 95.

174 Linda E. Marshall, 'Osbern mentions a book'. *Philological Quarterly* 56 (1977), 407–13.

175 His works are in PL 171; for a full list, see M. Lapidge and R. Sharpe, *A Bibliography of Celtic-Latin Literature 400–1200* (Dublin, 1985), pp. 230–4. See also *Liber decem capitulorum*, ed. R. Leotta (Rome, 1984), *De lapidibus*, ed. J.M. Riddle, tr. C.W. King (Wiesbaden, 1977).

176 *Baldricus Burgulianus: Carmina*, ed. Karlheinz Hilbert (Heidelberg, 1979).

177 His works are in PL 171. See also *Carmina Minora*, ed. A.B. Scott (Leipzig, 1969); A.B. Scott, D. Baker, A.G. Rigg, 'The *Biblical Epigrams* of Hildebert of Le Mans: a critical edition', *MSt* 47 (1985), 272–316.

178 Described by A. Boutemy, 'Notice sur le recueil poétique du manuscrit Cotton, Vitellius A. xii du British Museum', *Latomus* 1 (1937), 278–313, and on a closely related collection, 'Le recueil poétique du ms. Additional 24199 du British Museum', *Latomus* 2 (1938), 30–52. Basic work on the canon of Marbod is by A. Wilmart, 'Le florilège de Saint-Gatien. Contribution à l'étude des poèmes d'Hildebert et de Marbode', *RB* 48 (1936), 3–40, 147–81, 235–58.

179 B. Hauréau, *Notices et Extraits* 5 (1892), 229–33; Manitius 3, 943; Boutemy 'Deux poèmes' (n. 181 below), p. 261 n.1; H. Boehmer 'Carmina in Simoniam et romanorum avaritiam', in MGH *Libelli de lite* 3, 699–701; Wilmart, 'St-Gatien', p. 36. In my article in *MSt* 39 (1977), 302, I unthinkingly followed Boehmer. The poet Galo is well attested: he was a friend of Baudri of Bourgueil and is associated, as a poet, with Thierry of Chartres in a poem in Rawlinson G. 109 (*MSt* 43 (1981), 487) and in Neckam's *Suppletio defectuum* (see this volume, pp. 119–21; Hunt, pp. 5–6 n.26; Wedge, p. 80). Poem No. 66 in Vt is signed 'Galo' in line 37, and Boutemy ascribes the preceding poem No. 65 (see below on Wright pp. 230–1) to Galo. See also Wilmart, 'St-Gatien', p. 15 n. 3. Henry of Huntingdon mentions a poet Walo who wrote an epitaph on William of Flanders (d. 1128), but he is too late.

180 B. Hauréau, *Notices et Extraits* 5, 228, refers to Meyer (*Archives des missions* 1868, p. 148) for 'proof' that the poem is by Serlo. Boutemy, 'Deux poèmes' (next note), supplies variant readings for 'Quae monachi quaerunt' from four other manuscripts.

181 On Serlo of Bayeux, see Manitius 3, 869–72. The most succinct account is by Öberg, *Serlo de Wilton* (on whom see this volume, pp. 70–2), pp. 1–2. The account by Boehmer in *NA* 22 (1897), 703–38, is described by Wilmart, 'St-Gatien' p. 246 n.1, as so confused that he would not recommend anyone to read it. Two poems are added to the canon by A. Boutemy, 'Deux poèmes inconnus de Serlon de Bayeux et une copie nouvelle de son poème contre les moines de Caen', *Le Moyen Age*, 3rd ser. 9 (1938), 241–69.

182 J.S.P. Tatlock, 'Muriel: the earliest English poetess', *PMLA* 48 (1933), 317–21; A. Boutemy, 'Muriel: Note sur deux poèmes de Baudri de Bourgueil et de Serlon de Bayeux', *Le Moyen Age*, 3rd ser. 6 (1935), 241–51; A. Wilmart, 'L'Élégie d'Hildebert pour Muriel', *RB* 49 (1937), 376–80.

2 Henry II to John (1154–1216)

1 *Policraticus* (below, n. 27), 6: 18, p. 49.

2 On continental authors, see this volume, pp. 155–6.

3 *Poetria Nova* (below, n. 151), 1008–12.

4 Richard W. Southern, *Robert Grosseteste: the Growth of an English Mind in Medieval Europe* (Oxford, 1986), ch. 3, pp. 49–62.

5 See this volume, p. 62.

6 See this volume, pp. 142–3.

7 *Ars amatoria* 2, 279–80.

8 Another such court was that of Henry I of Champagne ('Henry the Liberal'). Simon Chèvre d'Or wrote his *Ylias* at Henry's request, and there is a poem on his death in 1182 in Bekynton (this volume, pp. 152–3) No. 90, ed. *AH* 21, 180. See J.F. Benton, 'The

court of Champagne as a literary centre', *Speculum* 36 (1961), 551–91.

9 Epist. 66.

10 *De nugis curialium* (below, n. 78), I 1, p. 2.

11 E. Türk, *Nugae Curialium: le règne d'Henri II Plantagenêt (1154–1189) et l'éthique politique* (Geneva, etc., 1977), notes that most officials appear only once in the records.

12 C.H. Haskins, 'Henry II as a patron of literature', in *Essays in Medieval History presented to T.F. Tout* (Manchester, 1925), pp. 71–7; W. Stubbs, *Seventeen Lectures on the study of Mediaeval and Modern History* 3rd ed. (Oxford, 1900), chs. 6–7; R.R. Bezzola, *Les Origines et la formation de la littérature courtoise en occident 500–1200*, Part III *La Société courtoise: littérature de cour et littérature courtoise*, Vol. I *La Cour d'Angleterre comme centre littéraire sous les rois angevins 1154–1199* (Paris, 1963), pp. 3–207; P. Dronke, 'Peter of Blois and poetry at the court of Henry II', *MSt* 38 (1976), 185–235; Rita Lejeune, 'Rôle littéraire d'Aliénor d'Aquitaine et de sa famille', *Cultura neolatina* 14 (1954), 5–57.

13 See this volume on John of Salisbury (pp. 73–6), Walter Map (pp. 88–93), and Peter of Blois (pp. 84–7); on other satire, see pp. 141–3. A long passage on nepotism and unsuitable clerical appointments in John of Salisbury, *Policraticus* 7: 19 was repeated almost verbatim by Nigel Whiteacre, *Contra curiales* (this volume, p. 107).

14 Nor was it new: see this volume pp. 65–6, for Serlo of Bayeux and several anonymous antimonastic poems.

15 In addition to anti-Cistercian satire by English writers, see R.M. Thomson, 'The satirical works of Berengar of Poitiers', *MSt* 42 (1980), 89–138. A copy of Berengar's satire is in the Bekynton anthology, this volume, pp. 152–3.

16 D. Knowles, *Monastic Order*, pp. 662–78.

17 See this volume, p. 61, on Aelred of Rievaulx. For an anthology from the Cistercian abbey of Rufford (with many poems on Cistercians), see this volume, p. 151. For a survey, see Holdsworth (n. 65 below).

18 See this volume, pp. 136–7. This is No. 41 (ed. Wilmart No. XIX).

19 *Serlo de Wilton: poèmes latins*, ed. Jan Öberg (Stockholm, 1965), No. 78. See also A.C. Friend, 'The proverbs of Serlo of Wilton', *MSt* 16 (1954), 179–218; 'Serlo of Wilton: the early years', *ALMA* 24 (1954), 85–110.

20 Nos. 1 and 3 seem to be verse prologues to lost prose grammatical treatises on grammatical structure and on first syllables. A poem on noun declensions, 'Declinent tuti pueri' (Öberg, Appendix Ia: 4) may also be Serlo's.

21 There is an expanded version of 'Unam semper' in Öberg, App. IIa, and two sets of 'versus interpositi' in the principal manuscript, Oxford, Digby 53 (this volume, p. 152), in Öberg, App. II B 1–2. On Richard Pluto's bowdlerized version of 'Unam semper', see this volume, pp. 111–12. Two word-plays in the *Babio* (this volume, pp. 113–14) may derive from Serlo.

22 This is No. 75; the last line is from Avianus *Fables* 5.18.

23 *De utensilibus* ed. B. Hauréau, *Notices et Extraits* 34 (1891), 45–54; ed. *Hunt, I, 165–76. On the similar works by Neckam and Garland, see this volume, pp. 118, 163–5.

24 There is an account of the 'Young Henry' and his death in Walter Map, *De Nugis* 4: 1, and a lament in Bekynton (this volume, pp. 152–3) No. 43 (Kingsford, No. 1).

25 'Eraclius' was also the pseudonym of a satirist in the Bekynton anthology; see A.G. Rigg, 'Eraclius Archipoeta: Bekynton Anthology Nos. 14, 15, 20, 77', *MAe* 53 (1984), 1–9.

26 For an anonymous versification of John's life of St Anselm, see ch. I, n. 39.

27 *Policratici sive de nugis curialium et vestigiis philosophorum libri VIII*, ed. C.C.J. Webb, 2 vols. (Oxford, 1909); *Metalogicon*, ed. C.C.J. Webb (Oxford, 1929); *The Letters of John of Salisbury*, Vol. I ed. W.J. Millor and H.E. Butler, rev. C.N.L. Brooke (London, 1955), Vol. II ed. W.J. Millor and C.N.L. Brooke (Oxford, 1979); *John of Salisbury's Entheticus Maior and Minor*, ed. J. Van Laarhoven, 3 vols. (Leiden, 1987); *Historia Pontificalis*, ed. Marjorie Chibnall (London, 1956, rpt. Oxford, 1986). The *Vita Anselmi* is in the old edition by J.A. Giles, V, 305–57 (Oxford, 1848), rpt. PL 199. There is an invaluable collection of essays in *The World of John of Salisbury*, ed. Michael Wilks, Studies in Church History, Subsidia 3 (Oxford, 1984), with current bibliography.

28 For an amusing verse version of this story, *Carmen de membris conspirantibus*, see Giles, V, 299–304 (PL 199, 1005–8; Manitius 3, 261). Pope Adrian IV, the Englishman Nicholas Breakspear, was a friend of John's; he died in 1159.

29 The whole of this passage ('He is a boy' – so was Daniel; 'He is illiterate' – Peter and Andrew were not philosophers, etc.) was taken over directly by Nigel Whiteacre, this volume, p. 107.

30 The antimatrimonial section was taken over by Peter of Blois, and may have been known to Walter Map (this volume, pp. 89–90).

31 C.N.L. Brooke, *Letters* (n. 27 above), I, xlv. Its rambling nature is illustrated by the translations. The earliest translator (Dickinson 1927) was interested in the political theory, so he translated Books IV–VI and parts of VII and VIII; his successor (Pike 1938) picked up most of the missing parts. The two translations now have to be fitted together like a jigsaw puzzle with a few missing pieces.

32 For the possibility that Walter Map was parodying the *Policraticus*, see this volume, p. 92 and below, n. 91.

33 Peter von Moos, 'The use of *exempla* in the *Policraticus* of John of Salisbury', in Wilks (n. 27 above), pp. 207–61.

34 See this volume, pp. 73–4.

35 William H. Cornog, 'The poems of Robert Partes', *Speculum* 12 (1937), 215–50.

36 On Henry of Avranches, see this volume, pp. 179–93.

37 See this volume, pp. 79–80.

38 According to legend, Becket himself made a slight contribution to literature. The Virgin appeared to him in a vision and asked him why, in view of his constant celebration of her seven earthly joys (a frequent topic in hymns) he paid no attention to her heavenly joys. Consequently Becket composed a seven-stanza hymn in regular Victorines, 'Gaude flore virginali / Quae honore speciali' (AH 31, 198–9, No. 189).

39 It is quoted by Gerald of Wales, *Expugnatio* (this volume, p. 94), p. 74, and is found in the Prophecy of the Eagle (this volume, p. 47, n. 130).

40 A copy of Alexander's letter of confirmation is found in the anthology Bodley 603 (this volume, p. 150).

41 On Bosham's *Liber melorum*, this volume, p. 79.

42 AH 13, 238–42, No. 92. Nos. 93–4 are also full rhymed offices: No. 94 ('Adest Thomae martyris') is on the translation of the relics.

43 This volume, pp. 183–4, nn. 90–1; this was based on John of Salisbury's life.

44 WIC 16084 (10705), 16742, 1267 (1165, 1172); the first is a catechism, the second employs *distributio*. They appear in scores of anthologies, separately or in combination. The first and third are in Trinity College, Oxford, 34; all are in Bekynton (this volume, pp. 152–3). In one manuscript of Alexander of Ashby's *Festial* (this volume, pp. 131–2),

the first epigram has been substituted for Alexander's own verse on Becket. The verses enjoy a popularity similar to 'In fourteen hundred and ninety-two / Columbus sailed the ocean blue'.

45 Provenance is not always easily decided; distancing by hostile references to England may indicate continental origin. Dating (especially of the hymns) is also difficult. Many poems on Becket are found in J.A. Giles, *Anecdota Bedae, Lanfranci et aliorum. Inedited tracts*, Caxton Soc. 12 (London, 1851; rpt. 1967); there are also some in Édélestand Du Meril, *Poésies populaires latines antérieures au douzième siècle* (Paris, 1843) and *Poésies populaires latines du moyen âge* (Paris, 1847), both rpt. Bologna, 1969. I have omitted from discussion several short poems printed by Giles, including *Carmen compendiosum* (Giles, pp. 196–200), which is in a manuscript that contains otherwise non-English saints' lives. I have also omitted Simon Chèvre d'Or's life of Becket, ed. Francis R. Swietek, *MJ* 11 (1976), 177–95, and the *Thomais* in *Thomas Becket: Actes du colloque international de Sédières 19–24 Août 1973*, ed. Raymonde Foreville (Paris, 1975).

46 *Moralisch-Satirische Gedichte* (this volume, p. 156 n. 301), No. 16, 17/3–4. The murder is also the theme of 'Orba suo pontifice' (St Omer, No. 16) and mentioned in the *Alexandreis*. Walter could conceivably be the author of 'A et O carissimi' (this volume, pp. 80–1).

47 The Guy de Bazoches poems are in AH 50, 524–6; the poem ascribed to Adam of St Victor (AH 55, 361–2, No. 328) was written from Sens, where Becket had stayed ('Exsultavit tanto viro / Senonensis Gallia').

48 Giles, No. 45, pp. 205–6; the poem is in Bodleian MS Douce 287, a collection of Becket materials from Lessness Abbey in Kent. The Hildebert poem is Scott, No. 37, inc. 'Anglia terra ferax'.

49 P.G. Schmidt, 'Die Ermordung Thomas Beckets im Spiegel zeitgenössischer Dichtungen', *MJ* 9 (1973), 159–72.

50 Especially in the *De principis instructione* (this volume, p. 95).

51 Ed. Schmidt, 'Die Ermordung'.

52 Foliot had opposed Becket's election as archbishop and participated in the coronation of Young Henry; this is mentioned in 'A et O' 'Complex eis additur ex te, Trinovantum, / Novans in cognomine secularem cantum' (i.e. a *foliot*). Map praises him in *De Nugis* 4: 5. I owe to Bill Woodward of Toronto the observation that Reginald of Durham (this volume, pp. 97–8) was hostile to Becket, comparing him unfavourably with his own saint, Godric, and Foliot was praised by Northern writers. Hugh Puiset, bishop of Durham, as well as Roger of York, had also taken part in the coronation.

53 In PL 190, 1293–1404 (based on Giles' edition of 1845); the Rolls Series edition of Bosham omits the *Liber Melorum*.

54 On Partes, see this volume, pp. 76–7. The poem is No. 23, pp. 245–9.

55 Giles, pp. 114–33; also (lacking prologue) in DuMeril 1847, pp. 70–93. Even the manuscripts with the prologue vary in *A et O, A et A, Anima*. The key to the authorship is in the lines:

> Nominant me G. et s. medium dent horum
> Edidit me phare rus circa castri forum;
> Totum cibus solum est ubi sto locorum

Presumably this means a name G——s (Gualterus, Guilelmus, Gervasius, etc.). In the second line one manuscript has altered *phare* to *falte*, giving *falterus* (Walter?), but does *me* mean the poet or the poem? *circa castri forum* might suggest Châtillon, but there are many other possibilities, as there are for a land that means 'food'.

56 See n. 52 above. The murderers were Hugh de Morville, William de Tracy, Reginald FitzUrse, and Richard le Breton.

57 Giles, pp. 191–5. Each Goliardic quatrain concludes with a seven-syllable (7pp) line, linking pairs of stanzas.

58 Giles, p. 195. Henry of Avranches also seems to allude to this: see this volume, p. 183.

59 Giles, pp. 170–87. Maurinus was known to Roger of Ford (this volume, pp. 83–4). He is almost certainly the Maurice of Ford listed by Leland, Bale, and the bibliographers.

60 Two hymns, AH 9, 258–9, mention that in his early career he was 'adolescens fere Saulus' and 'praedo et vastator pacis'.

61 Pauline A. Thompson, 'An anonymous verse life of Thomas Becket', *MJ* 20 (1985), 147–54. The two kings are Henry II and the Young Henry.

62 The indexes to WIC and Chevalier are good starting points, but the latter did not cover AH Vols. 53–5 and both have some omissions; a great number of Becket hymns and offices remain in manuscripts.

63 AH 55, 364–5. No. 330, from MS Bodley 509, a major collection of Becket material.

64 AH 8, 218, No. 287.

65 C.J. Holdsworth, 'John of Ford and English Cistercian writing 1167–1214', *TRHS* 5th ser., 11 (1961), 117–36; '*Another Stage . . . a Different World': Ideas and People around Exeter in the Twelfth Century*, Inaugural Lecture, 27 October 1978 (Exeter, 1979).

66 On the (now destroyed) collection of poems, see Paul Faider and Pierre Van Sint Jan, *Catalogue des manuscrits conservés à Tournai* (Gembloux, 1950), pp. 149–53. On the extant poem, written between 1170 and 1178, see A.G. Rigg, 'Roger of Ford's poem on the Virgin: a critical edition', *Cîteaux* 40 (1989), 200–13.

67 On the stomach of Montanus, see Juvenal, *Sat.* 4.107.

68 On miracles of the Virgin, see this volume, p. 35.

69 *Petri Blesensis Bathoniensis archidiaconi opera omnia*, ed. J.A. Giles, 4 vols. (Oxford, 1847), rpt. in PL 207, with some notes from the edition by Pierre de Goussanville (Paris, 1667). *L'Hystore Job: an Old French Verse Adaptation of 'Compendium in Job' by Peter of Blois*, ed. Joseph Gildea (Liège/Villanova, Penn., 1974). *Un traité de l'amour du XIIᵉ siècle: Pierre de Blois*, ed. M.-M. Davy (Paris, 1932). On the canon of the letters, see E.S. Cohn, 'The manuscript evidence for the letters of Peter of Blois', *EHR* 41 (1926), 43–60; R.W. Southern, 'Some new letters of Peter of Blois', *EHR* 53 (1938), 412–24. For a full study, see R.W. Southern, 'Peter of Blois: a twelfth-century humanist?' in *Medieval Humanism* pp. 105–32. On the poems (discussed below, pp. 85–7), see Peter Dronke, 'Peter of Blois and poetry at the court of Henry II', *MSt* 38 (1976), 185–235. On William of Blois, see this volume, p. 156.

70 Walter of Châtillon, *Moralisch-satirische Gedichte*, No. 3, 1, 7–8, ed. Strecker, p. 41:

> inter quos sunt quatuor rithmice dictantium . . .
> Stephanus flos scilicet Aurelianensium
> et Petrus qui dicitur de castro Blesensium.
> Istis non inmerito Berterus adicitur,
> set nec inter alios quartus pretermittitur
> ille quem Castellio latere non patitur,
> in cuius opusculis Alexander legitur (i.e. himself)

71 Giles 4, 337–48; Giles' second poem conflates several poems into one; Dronke divides them into five, but his 19 and 37 may be a single poem.

72 E. Braunholtz, 'Die Streitgedichte Peters von Blois und Roberts von Beaufeu über den Wert des Weines und des Bieres', *Zeitschrift für romanische Philologie* 47 (1927), 30–8; A. Wilmart, 'Une suite au poème de Robert de Beaufeu pour l'éloge de la cervoise', *RB* 50 (1938), 136–40.

73 For the growth of the canon, see Dronke, pp. 191–2, note 27. Schumann's suggestion was made on *Carmina Burana* No. 31.

74 Epist. 76; he also refers to 'versus et ludicra quae feci Turonis' (Epist. 12) and declines to send to William of Aulnay (Epist. 57) his 'lasciviores cantilenae'.

75 Epist. 76–7 and 114; in the last Peter writes to John of Salisbury at Chartres (1176–80), thanking him for showing favour on one 'qui me totum gerit animo, vultu, nomine, cognomine et statura'. The neat idea of calling this second Peter 'Pierre' was proposed by Wedge (n. 186 below), p. 73, note 55.

76 Examples of the *sic et non* tendency include the poem and letters on the court ('Quod amicus suggerit', Epist. 14, 150), the wine–beer debate, and the letters about the nun Alice. It should be noted that if Pierre is really a fiction, he has been given a family and history (Epist. 76).

77 On the Bekynton anthology, see this volume, pp. 152–3.

78 Biographical details are summarized in the most recent edition of the *De Nugis Curialium*, ed. M.R. James, rev. by C.N.L. Brooke and R.A.B. Mynors (Oxford, 1983).

79 For a survey of the process of ascriptions of anonymous satire, see A.G. Rigg, 'Golias and other pseudonyms', *Studi medievali*, 3rd ser. 18 (1977), 65–109.

80 The present arrangement reflects neither the original order of composition (for there are conflicting dates) nor Map's final intentions (for there are inconsistencies and some sections appear twice). He seems to have written it over several years, mainly in the 1180s (but with one passage of about 1192), and then reshuffled the material according to a plan never completed. The *Epistola Valerii* was written earlier and later incorporated into the *De Nugis*.

81 See this volume, p. 69.

82 The topos is used by Eraclius and others, this volume, pp. 141–2, and by Peter of Blois, Epist. 14, who also refers to the courtiers as 'milites Herlewini' (= Herla, Harlequin).

83 Ed. Wright, *Mapes*, pp. xxxv–xxxvii.

84 The same formula is used by Peter of Blois (Epist. 95, 'Loqui vereor et tacere non expedit') and in the story of the Adulterous Monk (see this volume, p. 143).

85 See this volume, p. 254.

86 The problem of late repentance occurs also in 1.14 (reworked from 4.7), but here the issue is the obstinacy of the bishop.

87 There is a curious analogue to the coronation of the Young Henry in a story told in 2.7: a Hungarian usurper manages to get himself crowned by an unauthorized archbishop ('Ille regem se fieri ab alio eiusdem regni archiepiscopo, ad quem nichil de coronacione regis pertinebat, obtinuit').

88 *Expugnatio Hibernica* (this volume, p. 94), pp. 264–5.

89 Similarly 3.2.

90 Similar lamentations for modernity are in 1.12 and 3.3.

91 There are, however, curious parallels. First, the title, which is one of the subtitles of the *Policraticus*. Lewis Thorpe (*MAe* 47 (1978), 6–21) has suggested that the title *De Nugis*

Curialium is purely scribal, as Map does not call it this in the body of the text; Thorpe suggests *De faceciis*. On the other hand, the fact that *de nugis* is not derivable from the text is an argument in favour of its genuineness, and Bothewald (this volume, p. 89) refers to the *nugae* of Map's youth. Second, both have reviews of English history from Cnut to Henry II, and both omit William I; in the *Policraticus* the list is preceded by Brennus, in Map by the unknown Apollonides. Both writers mention the unruliness of the Welsh. Both authors have antimatrimonial passages. Map's antimonastic section parallels one in John, who mainly praises the orders, in a similar sequence (though John does point to examples of hypocrisy in each order). John denounces hunting at length; Map describes himself as 'uenator uester'.

92 Note that *facecia* is a virtue in John of Garland's *Epithalamium*. Compare also the topos of God's *ludus* in Lawrence of Durham, above p. 57, and in Alexander Neckam, below pp. 119–20.

93 *Analecta Dublinensia. Three medieval Latin texts in the library of Trinity College, Dublin*, ed. Marvin L. Colker (Cambridge, Mass., 1975), Part 3 'A collection of stories and sketches: Petronius Redivivus', pp. 181–257.

94 Almost all the works are in *Giraldi Cambrensis Opera*, ed. J.S. Brewer, J.F. Dimock, and G.F. Warner, 8 vols. RS (London, 1861–91); many of these editions have been replaced. For a full up-to-date bibliography, see Lapidge-Sharpe, pp. 22–8.

95 Gerald tells us that he recited this work over three days in Oxford (*De rebus a se gestis*, in *Opera* I, 72–3).

96 On the two Merlins, carefully distinguished by Gerald, see above, pp. 45, 47. In the *Expugnatio* Gerald quotes Merlin Ambrosius three times and Merlin Silvester eleven times (some quotations are repeated); most of the latter are in the *Prophecy of the Eagle*. In later editions, he reduced the number of prophecies: see *Expugnatio Hibernica: the Conquest of Ireland by Giraldus Cambrensis*, ed. A.B. Scott and F.X. Martin (Dublin, 1978).

97 The *Cambriae Epitome*, ed. Wright *Mapes*, pp. 131–46, versifies the *Descriptio*, using also the *Itinerarium*, in 406 lines of octosyllabic couplets.

98 On this event, see this volume, pp. 106–7; on Nigel Whiteacre's attitude to William, see p. 107. On Walter Map's view of Geoffrey, see p. 91.

99 On Osbert, see this volume, pp. 32–3; on Gerald's connexion with Hereford, see p. 96.

100 R. Bartlett, 'Rewriting saints' lives: the case of Gerald of Wales', *Speculum* 58 (1983), 598–613, illustrates the twelfth-century polish that Gerald gives to his rough sources. On Rhygyfarch, see this volume, pp. 40–1.

101 For a discussion and restoration of the badly damaged text, see R.W. Hunt, 'The preface to the *Speculum Ecclesiae* of Giraldus Cambrensis', *Viator* 8 (1977), 189–213.

102 See this volume, pp. 68–9.

103 Jill Mann, 'Giraldus Cambrensis and the Goliards', *Journal of Celtic Studies* 3 (1981), 31–9. In defending Rome, Gerald uses Christ's words.

104 Like many writers, Gerald made use of florilegia: see A.A. Goddu and R.H. Rouse, 'Gerald of Wales and the *Florilegium Angelicum*', *Speculum* 52 (1977), 488–521.

105 Gerald, *Opp.* 1.170–2, 8.310–1. Maurice had visions; in one a former friend, now dead, challenged him to complete the verse line 'Destruat hoc regnum rex regum . . .'; when Maurice failed, the dead friend continued '. . duplice plaga', predicting the Interdict. On verse competitions, see this volume, pp. 188–91.

106 For the view that they did not know each other, see A.K. Bate, 'Walter Map and

Giraldus Cambrensis', *Latomus* 31 (1972), 860–75. If this opinion is correct, it follows that parts of the *De Nugis*, as well as the *Epistola Valerii*, circulated in the twelfth century.

107 See M. Dominica Legge, *Anglo-Norman Literature and its background* (Oxford, 1963), pp. 183–7. The Latin poems are in the *Symbolum Electorum*. For important additional lines in the Hereford invitation, see R.W. Hunt, 'English learning in the late twelfth century', *TRHS* 4th ser. 19 (1936), 19–42 (text on pp. 36–7).

108 Bale's identification of the monk as Adam of Dore (*Catalogus* p. 240; *Index* p. 4) seems to be purely conjectural. On Adam, see this volume p. 129 and n. 219.

109 On Matthew of Rievaulx and Alan of Meaux, see this volume, pp. 136–7, 160–2.

110 In *Symeonis monachi Opera Omnia*, ed. Thomas Arnold, 2 vols. RS (London, 1882–85), 2. 386–8, and in Raine (next note), pp. 78–80.

111 In Raine (ch. 1, n. 163), Appendix, Nos. VIII, IXa–b, x.

112 *Libellus de vita et miraculis S. Godrici*, ed. J. Stevenson, Surtees Soc. 20 (London/ Edinburgh, 1847); *Libellus de admirandis Beati Cuthberti virtutibus*, ed. J. Raine, Surtees Soc. (London/Edinburgh, 1835); *Vita S. Oswaldi regis et martyris* ed. Arnold (see n. 110), 1.326–85. On Reginald's preference for Godric over Becket, see above, n. 52.

113 Ed. Stevenson (see n. 112), pp. xxxvii–xl.

114 The lives of Sts Waltheof and Patrick are in ASS 3 August (August 1, 242–78) and 17 March (March 2, 536–77). That of St Kentigern is in *Lives of St Ninian and St Kentigern*, ed. Alexander P. Forbes, Historians of Scotland 5 (Edinburgh, 1874), pp. 159–242, translation pp. 27–119.

115 Ed. P.G. Schmidt, '*Brutus*: eine metrische Paraphrase der "Historia regum Britannie" für den Durhamer Bischof Hugo de Puiset', *MJ* 11 (1976), 201–23. Schmidt dates the poem December 1189 – 25 March 1990, and suggests that it was written in support of Puiset's stance on the disputed election to the archbishopric of York. Puiset was also the dedicatee of a work by Reginald of Coldingham.

116 *Joseph Iscanus. Werke und Briefe*, ed. Ludwig Gompf (Leiden, 1970), contains all the works. Five manuscripts of the *Ylias* are extant, and about eleven are known to have existed; this shows a modest popularity (though not on the scale of the *Alexandreis*, of which there are over 200), but it was widely read: extracts appear in florilegia, and it was known to Chaucer.

117 Very popular was 'Pergama flere volo', sometimes attributed to Hildebert; on the attribution to Hugh of Montacute, see this volume, p. 136. This was often linked with, even intertwined with, 'Viribus arte minis' by Peter of Saintes. Somewhat longer, also popular in England, was the *Ylias* of Simon Chèvre d'Or.

118 I.e. Richard, the monks' candidate.

119 This was the usual interpretation, as seen in the Epistles of Ovid and Baudri of Bourgueil.

120 This long digression is important structurally: when the weary Greeks are about to abandon the siege in Book VI, Telephus sends reinforcements.

121 In Dares, Andromache's forebodings are expressed in a single line: 'Andromacha uxor Hectoris in somnis vidit Hectorem non debere in pugnam procedere.'

122 See III.4–13, 454–73, IV.215–45, VI.573–88.

123 His name was corrupted to Wireker in the sixteenth century; for arguments against surnaming him 'de Longchamps', see *MAe* 56 (1987), 304–7. The fullest account of Nigel is by Boutemy, *Contra curiales* (n. 132).

124 See this volume, p. 107.

125 *Speculum Stultorum*, ed. J.H. Mozley and R.R. Raymo (Berkeley/Los Angeles, 1960). Some lines (201-2, 915-16, 2051-4) suggest a date of composition 1179-80, but others (2211-22) indicate 1187-8; the prologue to William (if it is de Longchamps) also suggests a date closer to his rise in 1190, though the prologue may have been added later.

126 According to Matthew Paris (2.413-6), the story was a favourite of Richard I, who used it when raising money for the Crusade. It was retold by Gower, *Confessio Amantis* v 4937-5162.

127 J.H. Mozley, 'The *Epistola ad Willelmum* of Nigel Longchamps', *MAe* 39 (1970), 13-20. Nigel's interpretations are rather dull.

128 *Miracles of the Virgin Mary in Verse*, ed. J. Ziolkowski (Toronto, 1986). On the tradition of the Miracles, see above, p. 38.

129 Extracts in J.H. Mozley, 'The unprinted poems of Nigel Wireker', *Speculum* 7 (1932), 398-423.

130 Leo M. Kaiser, 'A critical edition of Nigel Wireker's *Vita Sancti Pauli Primi Eremitae*', *Classical Folia* 14 (1969), 63-81.

131 H. Varnhagen, 'Zwei lateinische metrische Versionen der Legende von Placidus-Eustachius', *ZfdA* 24 (1880), 241-54. For the attribution, see Boutemy (n. 132 below), pp. 69-70.

132 The Canterbury poems are printed in *Nigellus de Longchamp dit Wireker*, Vol. I: *Introduction*; *Tractatus contra Curiales et officiales clericos*, ed. A. Boutemy, Université Libre de Bruxelles, Travaux de la Faculté de Philosophie et Lettres 16 (1959).

133 On Baldwin, see also this volume, pp. 83, 99.

134 See this volume, p. 109.

135 According to Leland (*Commentarii*, p. 228), a (lost) epic on the Third Crusade was written by a William de Canno (Reed ?), 'Anglus natione', in 'heroico carmine', dedicated to archbishop Herbert Walter and Stephen Turnham, the military commander. William accompanied Richard of Holy Trinity, author of the prose *Itineratio Peregrinorum*. The latter occasionally quotes hexameter verses and some rhythmical stanzas; these are not attributed but could perhaps be from William's poem. The epic is not to be identified with the Old French poem on the Crusade, as this was by an Ambroise and is not dedicated to Hubert or Stephen. In any case Leland clearly implies that the poem (entitled *Odocporicon Ricardi* by Bale, *Catalogus* p. 242) was in Latin.

136 Bekynton, No. 98, Wilmart No. xxiv. On Walter of Châtillon's praise of Berter, see above, n. 70.

137 Bekynton No. 92, Kingsford, No. iii. Only Henri IIᵉ of Champagne is praised.

138 The charge was denied by Walter Map (*De Nugis* 5.6) and the Old Man of Mountain, whose letter exonerating Richard was added to the Bekynton anthology (No. 1) in the fifteenth century.

139 There is a succinct account of William in Boutemy (above, n. 132).

140 *Tractatus*, p. 199. One such poem is printed by Boutemy, *Tractatus*, pp. 246-7, 'Divina providentia'.

141 Boutemy, *Tractatus*, pp. 115-18, 144-9, replacing the text in Wright, *ALSP* 1.146-53. It has sometimes been taken as the prologue to the *Tractatus*, but it was surely written before William's disgrace.

142 Bekynton No. 103, Kingsford No. II. A copy of Hugh Nonant's letter is also in Bekynton, No. 104. I read *mutans* for Kingsford's *nutans*.

143 It must have been written while Richard was in captivity in 1193, but still calls William 'legate', although he had lost the position in 1191 on the death of Pope Clement III. Nigel's use of the term may be ironic or polite (suggesting that William would one day be restored).

144 About a quarter of the *Tractatus* comes from the *Policraticus*, which is acknowledged only once. See this volume, p. 75 and n. 29.

145 Bekynton No. 77, Kingsford No. VII. The fifteenth-century owner of this anthology must have found this material ironically apt: Thomas Bekynton, bishop of Bath and Wells, was also Henry VI's chancellor.

146 Giles, 4.343–5; also in Bekynton, No. 42.

147 Bekynton No. 85, Kingsford No. IV.

148 This poem is Bekynton No. 108 (with some additional lines), where it is applied to Richard's capture. It also forms lines 2081–98 of the *Poetria Nova* (below), where it is usually interpreted as an appeal to Pope Innocent III on behalf of King John. It may have been originally separate and adapted to a new context.

149 *Poetria Nova* lines 326–66, 'Anglia, regnorum regina', is a 'prophecy' of Richard's death; oddly, it also foretells that England will become a slave ('eris de principe serva'), a phrase which Matthew of Rievaulx (this volume, pp. 136–7) applies to England's subjection to the papacy in 1213! The second poem on Richard, 'Neustria sub clipeo' (see this volume p. 109), often appeared separately.

150 For Marbod's *Colores rhetorici*, see this volume, p. 64. For Matthew of Vendôme's *Ars versificatoria*, see this volume, p. 156. English interest in verse composition is also seen in John of Garland, this volume, pp. 165–6.

151 These are all edited by Edmond Faral, *Les arts poétiques du XIIᵉ et du XIIIᵉ siècle* (Paris, 1924; rpt. Paris, 1962). We do not know what 'de Vino Salvo' means, but he is often referred to as 'Galfridus Anglicus'. For the minor poems, see on the Hunterian Anthology, this volume, p. 111.

152 As the topics overlap, fuller discussion is given on the *Poetria Nova*, this volume, pp. 108–10.

153 Henry of Avranches also employs the topos of Innocent's unmetrical name.

154 Used by Chaucer, (*Troilus* I.1065–69), to describe Pandarus' scheming.

155 See this volume, p. 108, n. 149.

156 The story is also told in the 'Modus Liebinc' in the eleventh-century *Cambridge Songs*, ed. K. Strecker, *Die Cambridger Lieder* (Berlin, 1955) No. 14.

157 See n. 148.

158 It is in the Hunterian anthology, below, p. 111; for the 'De clericis et rustico', see this volume, p. 113.

159 *Gervais von Melkley: Ars Poetica*, ed. Hans-Jürgen Gräbener (Münster, 1965); for short poems, see below, n. 160.

160 The manuscript is Glasgow University, Hunterian v.8.14; see Bruce Harbert, *A Thirteenth-Century Anthology of Rhetorical Poems* (Toronto, 1975); E. Faral, 'Le manuscrit 511 du Hunterian Museum', *SM* n.s. 9 (1936), 18–121. Those by Geoffrey are Nos. 11–13, probably 14, and 33; by Gervase, Nos. 39–43, and by Matthew of Vendôme, No. 2 and perhaps others.

161 The poem was added, with Marbod's *De coloribus*, in the thirteenth century to Bodleian Library, MS Laud misc. 363, a St Albans manuscript later owned by Richard of Bury. The surname Pluto may suggest 'Rich' or the town of Diss in Norfolk. Leland

(*Commentarii* p. 234) had seen a poem *Unde malum* in the Cistercian convent at Warden in Bedfordshire. Bale (*Catalogus* pp. 220–1; *Index* pp. 356–7) added some prose works, the date 1180, and the conflicting information that he wrote a prose history for Richard, duke of Normandy (tenth or eleventh century!). Leland conjectured that he was a Canterbury monk. *Equiuoca*, ed. A.G. Rigg, *Latomus* 50 (1991), 563–80.

162 See this volume, p. 71.

163 For comedies by Matthew of Vendôme and William and Vitalis of Blois, see this volume, p. 156.

164 In *Becket Materials*, Vol. 3, p. 9.

165 See this volume, p. 128.

166 For example, in the *Geta*, Geta has brought back 'miranda sophismata' from Athens and worries about his own non-existence. Birria remarks that 'Insanire facit stultum dialectica quemuis.'

167 See this volume on Henry of Avranches and Michael of Cornwall, pp. 188–91, 193–7.

168 Ed. E. Cadoni, in *Commedie Latine* II, 351–80; it is No. 14 in the Hunterian anthology (above, n. 160). The case for Geoffrey's authorship is simply that he quotes from it in the *Documentum*.

169 Ed. A.D. Fulgheri, in *Commedie Latine* II, 129–301, and also in *Three Latin Comedies*, ed. Keith Bate (Toronto, 1976), pp. 35–60. English authorship is assumed simply because the manuscript tradition is entirely English. Interestingly, in view of the wordplay, one copy of the *Babio* is in Bodleian MS Digby 53, which contains Serlo's differential verses (this volume, p. 152).

170 The castration motif seems to me insufficient to connect the play with either Abelard or the story of the Adulterous Monk (this volume, p. 143).

171 See this volume, p. 71. The play on *ara* and *fodit* is in 'Unam semper' line 12 and *Appendix* IIa. F 2. Fulgheri also notes a debt to Osbern Pinnock's *Panormia* (see this volume, p. 62).

172 Ed. G. Orlandi, in *Commedie Latine* III, 243–303; the evidence for English authorship is its presence in the English section of Bern MS 568.

173 The possible influence of comedy should not be neglected. In Walter Map, Ollo's rejection by his servants is reminiscent of the *Geta*, and the stichomythic dialogue between queen and servant in the story of Sadius and Galo is very 'dramatic' (this volume, p. 90).

174 The best text of Walter's fables is in *Ysopet-Avionnet: the Latin and French Texts*, ed. Kenneth McKenzie and William A. Oldfather, Univ. of Illinois Studies in Language and Literature 5, No. 4 (Urbana, 1919). For 'Romulus', see *Der lateinische Äsop des Romulus und die Prosa-Fassungen des Phädrus*, e.g. Georg Thiele (Heidelberg, 1910). On Neckam's versions of Phaedrus and Avianus, see this volume, p. 118; on Henry of Avranches' version of Avianus, see this volume, p. 187.

175 Peter of Blois, Ep. 66. John of Garland mentions an English Walter in Paris in the early thirteenth century. There are too many English Walters to be sure, and Ward-Herbert 2.309–17 are doubtful even about ascribing the fables to any Walter, preferring to refer to the collection as the 'Anonymus Neveleti'.

176 For a full study with texts, see Joseph Goering, *William de Montibus (c. 1140–1213): the Schools and Literature of Pastoral Care* (Toronto, 1992). Lincoln was also fortunate in its bishops at this time: (St) Hugh of Burgundy, John of Oxford, and John Grey.

177 On Alexander, see this volume, pp. 117–22; these lines echo Hildebert's poem on

Rome, ed. Scott, No. 36. William was also praised by Gerald of Wales and Matthew of Rievaulx (p. 136).

178 Some of the characteristics of the animals correspond to those in Neckam's *De Naturis Rerum* (this volume, pp. 118–19) but not the *Laus Sapientiae Divinae*. A block of the animal verses appears in the fourteenth-century anthology BL Titus A. xx (this volume, p. 308), and have been edited by Peter Binkley, in *Scintilla: a Student Journal for Medievalists* 2–3 (Toronto, 1985–86), 66–100.

179 See Goering (this volume, n. 176), p. 45.

180 Raby, *SLP* 2.118. The fullest account is by R.W. Hunt, *The Schools and the Cloister: the Life and Writings of Alexander Nequam (1157–1217)*, ed. and rev. Margaret Gibson (Oxford, 1984), based on Hunt's thesis of 1936. I prefer the form Neckam, as argued by Wedge (n. 186 below).

181 A list of spuria is given by Hunt, pp. 147–9; they include Alberic of London's *Mythography* and Stephen Langton's commentary on the *Ave maris stella* (this volume, pp. 125, 123–4); see also, p. 65.

182 The *Sacerdos ad altare* (a priest's instruction manual) has an interesting list of books suitable for study in school; ed. *Hunt, 1, 250–73.

183 A. Scheler, 'Trois traités de lexicographie latine du xiie et du xiiie siècle', *Jahrbuch für romanische und englische Literatur* 7 (1866), 58–74, 155–73; also ed. *Hunt, 1, 177–89. On Adam of Balsham, see this volume, pp. 72–3.

184 Paul Meyer, 'Notice sur les *Corrogationes Promethei* d'Alexandre Neckam', *Notices et Extraits* 35, 2 (1897), 641–82. The title has been interpreted as 'the collections of (a) a teacher, (b) a man condemned to idleness, (c) a scholar who has only his leisure hours to devote to his studies' (as Prometheus, chained to the rock, used the time free from torment to study the heavens).

185 The *Novus Avianus* and *Novus Aesopus* are in L. Hervieux, *Les fabulistes latins depuis le siècle d'Auguste jusqu'à la fin du moyen âge*, 5 vols. (Paris, 1884–99), 3.462–7; 2.787–812.

186 *Alexandri Neckam: De Naturis Rerum*, ed. T. Wright, RS (London, 1863), pp. 1–354. There is a full study by G.F. Wedge, *Alexander Neckam's De Naturis Rerum: A Study together with Representative Passages in Translation*, Ph.D. thesis (Univ. of Minnesota, 1967). (Not Univ. of Southern California, as reported in Dissertation Abstracts).

187 Ed. Wright (see last note), pp. 357–503. For convenience I follow the ten-book division used by Wright; the seven-book division of other manuscripts possibly has greater authority, but both versions may be authorial. The *Laus* was finished after the death of William de Montibus in 1213 (v. 837–48: see above, p. 116).

188 He frequently rebukes the manichean opinions of Faustus: 1.556–73 (for saying that Sun and Moon copulate), 1.109–16, 638–9; iii.7–8; v.897–8. In the *De Commendatione Vini* (below), iii.147–68, where he explains the miracle of transubstantiation, he tells Faustus to be silent.

189 As Wisdom played, so can his Muse: ii.697–8 'Ludit in effectu vario sapientia summa, Fas erit ut ludat nostra Thalia semel'. God's joke is also a theme in Lawrence of Durham (see this volume, p. 57); it is mentioned by Bernard Silvester, *Mathematicus* 176, 'Saecula nostra jocus ludibriumque diis' (quoted by John of Salisbury *Policraticus*, 1, p. 194), but this is not quite the same thing.

190 Similarly, iii.331–70.

191 See also iv.554–7, viii.27–34; it is, of course, the theme of the *De Commendatione Vini* (below).

192 The vulture (II.437–62) reminds him of death also, but defends itself.

193 The *Laus* is probably unfinished; the uneven length of books is cured in the seven-book division, by making VI–VIII and IX–X into two books only, but there are also two major supplements (still unpublished) of 1456 and 1796 lines, called the *Suppletio Defectuum*; these sometimes overlap with material covered in the *Laus*.

194 Extracts are given by M. Esposito, 'On some unpublished poems attributed to Alexander Neckam', *EHR* 30 (1915), 450–71; H. Walther, 'Eine moral-asketische Dichtung des XIII. Jahrhunderts: *Prorogationes Novi Promethei* des Alexander Neckam', *MAe* 31 (1962), 33–42. A new edition has been prepared by Laurel Cropp, Ph.D. thesis (Toronto, 1991). There is some evidence for a lost prosimetrum entitled *Corrogationes Novi Promethei* (see Hunt, p. 60), but the text as we have it is much more unified than Hunt suggests.

195 This was almost a topos in contemporary poetry: in addition to the plays *Geta* and *Pamphilus, Gliscerium et Birria*, the attempt to rouse the sleeping Birria is used by Geoffrey of Vinsauf, *Poetria Nova* 1365–80, to illustrate man's unwillingness to repent.

196 On 'courtesy' literature, see this volume, pp. 125–7.

197 Book I is in Esposito (n. 194); Books II–III are in H. Walther, 'Zu den kleineren Gedichten des Alexander Neckam', *MJ* 2 (1965), 111–29.

198 Most of Neckam's verse works are in the huge anthology Paris, BN lat. 11867 from Cirencester; most of the minor poems from here have been printed by Esposito and Walther 'Kleinere Gedichte' (above). Another Cirencester manuscript, Cambridge, UL Gg. 6.42, is a florilegium of Neckam's works, both prose and verse.

199 In the prologue 'S' objects to being called a 'philomena'. This has led to confusion with the two poems called *Philomena* by John of Howden and John Pecham (this volume, pp. 208–12, 222–3) and to bibliographical references to the works of Bonaventure. My knowledge of the poem is based on a cursory reading of the unique copy in Bodleian MS Digby 41, fols. 93–100, a thirteenth-century booklet. When this present book was about to go to press my attention was kindly drawn by Professor P.G. Schmidt to an edition of the poem about to be published by Axel Bergmann, *Carmen de mundo et partibus: ein theologisch-physikalisch Lehrgedicht aus der Oxforder Handschrift Bodleian Digby 41* (Frankfurt am Main, 1991). I have not see the edition, but am informed that Bergmann dates the poem to after 1242, perhaps about 1250 (in which case it should be in my third chapter); he attributes it to Robert Grosseteste (this volume, ch. 3, n. 13).

200 Matthew of Rievaulx (this volume, pp. 136–7), No. 24 (VIII). On Henry of Avranches, see this volume, pp. 183–4.

201 *Carmina Burana* No. 33; for stylistic reasons, Bischoff associates several other poems with it (see *Carmina Burana* II.1, pp. 58–9). The poem is also in the Bekynton anthology (this volume, pp. 152–3). The attribution to Stephen is made in the near-contemporary MS Bodley 57.

202 AH 35, 153–71, No. 11. The poem was attributed by the antiquaries to John Pecham (this volume, pp. 222–6), but they may be referring only to the eleven-stanza prologue ('Mente concipio laudes conscribere'), which is in a different metre (rhythmical asclepiads).

203 AH 54, 234–5, No. 153. For the authorship, see (among others) Raby, *CLP* p. 343.

204 Hunt (n. 180 above), pp. 12–13. For extracts from Ralph of Dunstable, see W. McLeod, 'Alban and Amphibal: some extant lives and a lost life', *MSt* 42 (1980), 407–30; he prints lines 1–48 and 359–422.

205 Equally, there is no evidence for the attribution to Ralph of the unedited poems that follow in the manuscript BL Cotton Julius D. iii (*De motu peccandi* (this volume, p. 139), *De duodecim mensibus anni, De virtutibus imitandis*, etc.).

206 *Scriptores rerum mythicarum latini tres*, ed. George H. Bode (Zelle, 1834, rpt. Hildesheim, 1968), pp. 152–256. The title 'Mythographus Vaticanus' derives simply from the manuscript in which the text is found.

207 E. Rathbone, 'Master Alberic of London: "mythographus Tertius Vaticanus"', *MARS* 1 (1941–3), 35–8. The attribution has been disputed by C.S.F. Burnett, 'A note on the origins of the Third Vatican Mythographer', *JWCI* 44 (1981), 160–6.

208 On Thomas Walsingham's *Arcana Deorum*, see this volume, pp. 297–8.

209 *Urbanus Magnus Danielis Becclesiensis*, ed. J. Gilbart Smyly (Dublin, 1939). The word 'Magnus' has been added to distinguish the poem from others called *Urbanus*. Bale (*Catalogus* p. 221; *Index* pp. 59–60) misread the manuscript as *Ecclesiensis*; even if this had been correct, it should have been translated 'of Eccles', not 'Church' (which led to the ghost 'Daniel Church' in some bibliographies.) The fullest study of courtesy literature is by Servus Gieben, 'Robert Grosseteste and medieval courtesy-books', *Vivarium* 5 (1967), 47–74.

210 'Old King Henry' is probably Henry I, but this does no more than place the poem after 1135; even if it is thought to imply the existence of a more recent Henry, this only advances the date to 1154. The earliest manuscript is *c.* 1200; there are extracts in MS Rawlinson C. 552, which must be after 1198, as it has the opening of the *Poetria Nova* referring to Innocent III. Bale's date for Daniel of 1180 is unreliable, in view of his misunderstanding about Daniel's surname.

211 The extract, in Trinity College, Oxford, MS 18, is called *Liber Curialis*; as it calls Grosseteste 'magister' rather than 'episcopus', it may have been made before 1235, but this is uncertain. Another extract from the full text is in MS Bodley 310 (s. xiv).

212 It is printed in *The Babees Book*, ed. F.J. Furnivall, EETS 32 (1868), pp. 34–57; there is an extract from this section in BL Arundel MS 52.

213 *Das Buch vom Espurgatoire S. Patrice der Marie de France und seine Quelle*, ed. Karl Warnke (Halle, 1938); other texts are available, as in PL 180, 975–1104. I call him Henry for convenience, following Matthew Paris and the bibliographers, but he is simply 'H' in the manuscript. On earlier vision literature, see this volume p. 54.

214 The work is, not surprisingly, unpublished. There are extracts in: M.R. James, *A Descriptive Catalogue of the manuscripts in the Library of Lambeth Palace* (Cambridge, 1932), pp. 84–5; C.J. Holdsworth, 'Eleven visions connected with the Cistercian monastery of Stratford Langthorne', *Cîteaux* 13 (1962), 185–204; Robert Easting, 'Peter of Cornwall's account of St Patrick's Purgatory', *AB* 97 (1979), 397–416; Peter Hull and Richard Sharpe, 'Peter of Cornwall and Launceston', *Cornish Studies* 13 (1986), 5–53; Robert Easting and Richard Sharpe, 'Peter of Cornwall; the visions of Ailsi and his sons', *Mediaevistik* 1 (1988), 207–62.

215 R.W. Hunt, 'The disputation of Peter of Cornwall against Symon the Jew', in *Studies in Medieval History presented to F.M. Powicke*, ed. R.W. Hunt, W.A. Pantin, R.W. Southern (Oxford, 1948), pp. 143–56, with edition of the preface and a full account of Christian debates with Jews. Among Anglo-Latin writers on the subject we should mention: Petrus Alfonsi, *Dialogi cum Judaeo*; Gilbert Crispin, *Disputatio Judaei cum Christiano* (dedicated to Anselm); anon. *Dialogus inter Christianum et Judaeum de fide catholica* (dedicated to Alexander, bishop of Lincoln); Bartholemew, bishop of Exeter,

Dialogus contra Judeos ad corrigendum et perficiendum destinatus (dedicated to Baldwin, bishop of Worcester); Peter of Blois, *Invectiva contra perfidiam Judaeorum.*

216 *Visio Thurkilli, relatore, ut videtur, Radulpho de Coggeshall,* ed. P.G. Schmidt (Leipzig, 1978); P.G. Schmidt, 'The Vision of Thurkill', *JWCI* 41 (1978), 50–64.

217 *Otia Imperialia,* ed. G.W. Leibnitz, *Scriptores rerum Brunsvicensium illustrationi inservientium* I (Hannover, 1707), 881–1004; additions and corrections in II (1710), 751–84. Selections in F. Liebrecht, *Des Gervasius von Tilbury 'Otia Imperialia'* (Hannover, 1856), and in *MGH Scriptores* 27 (Hannover, 1885), ed. F. Liebermann and R. Pauli. There are several biographies, e.g. H.G. Richardson, 'Gervase of Tilbury', *History* n.s. 46 (1961), 102–14.

218 Ed. Deirdre F. Baker, Ph.D. thesis (Toronto, 1990). There is a full account by M.R. James, 'Pictor in Carmine', *Archaeologia* 94 (1951), 141–66. There is a convenient list of other published window-verses in *Dictionary of Medieval Latin from British Sources,* ed. R.E. Latham, D.R. Howlett, and others, III (London, 1986), lvii. See also on Robert Partes, this volume, p. 77.

219 A flyleaf inscription in one of the earliest manuscripts of the poem (Bodleian MS Rawlinson C. 67) reads 'Versus ade dorensis'; the flyleaf is not adjacent to the poem, which (at least now) is not the first entry in the manuscript. Gerald of Wales mentions two Adams who were abbots of the Cistercian abbey of Dore near Hereford, but does not mention that either wrote poetry. The sentiments of the prologue of 'Pictor' resemble those of Bernard of Clairvaux, as shown by James, but this does not prove Cistercian authorship.

220 For manuscripts of these poems, see Russell. One work has been edited: T.H. Bestul, 'The *Meditationes* of Alexander of Ashby: an edition', *MSt* 52 (1990), 24–81. For a discussion of the treatise on preaching, with extracts, see Fritz Kemmler, *Exempla in Context: a historical and critical study of Robert Mannyng of Brunne's 'Handlyng Synne'* (Tübingen, 1984), pp. 69–76. Alexander is no longer credited with the *Eulogium Historiarum sive temporis,* ed. F.S. Haydon, RS (London, 1858).

221 One manuscript contains Book I only.

222 The story is in PL 73. 691–4.

223 Marbod's verse life of Maurilius (PL 171. 1635–48) was popular in anthologies.

224 The section on Guthlac is evidently incomplete, as it stops at the point where he is rescued from the gates of hell by Bartholemew. Nevertheless, its thirteen lines manage to cover thirty-three of Felix's fifty-three chapters, and it must be regarded as an exercise in *abbreviatio.* The lines are squeezed in at the end of a quire in MS Bodley 40, but they may be all that Alexander wrote, as the same lines are in Bodley 527.

225 See this volume, p. 14

226 See this volume, pp. 54–7, below, pp. 133–5. On Peter Riga, see p. 156.

227 Exeter College, Oxford, MS 23.

228 Our only knowledge of Adam comes from Leland (*Commentarii,* p.232). Leland's authority (doubted by Russell) is strengthened by the fact that the author names himself Adam: as Leland does not seem to have read the poem itself, he must have had external testimony for his account.

229 Corpus Christi College, Cambridge, MS 277. See M.R. James, *A Descriptive Catalogue of the Manuscripts in the Library of Corpus Christi College, Cambridge,* 2 vols. (Cambridge, 1912), 1.40–1, the only published account of the poem.

230 Longleat MS 27, fols. 128va–129rb; see also next note.

231 A.B. Scott, 'Some poems attributed to Richard of Cluny' in *Medieval Learning and Literature: Essays presented to Richard William Hunt*, ed. J.J.G. Alexander and M.T. Gibson (Oxford, 1976), pp. 181–99. These three poems, with some others, are ascribed to Richard by Bale, but Scott shows that Bale's attribution is improbable; they are together in Longleat MS 27, where the first two are ascribed to Hugh of Montacute (and the third is clearly linked to the second).

232 'Pergama flere volo' is *Carmina Burana* No. 101; for the ascription to Hugh, see 1.2. p. 148. It is also variously ascribed to Hildebert, Benignus of Fleury, Primas, and (in a fifteenth-century note) to Hugo Diuensis, perhaps the Hugh of Die addressed by Serlo of Bayeux. Citations from 'Pergama flere' by Neckam, *Corrogationes Novi Promethei*, and Matthew of Rievaulx (Poem No. 44) do not affect the ascription to Hugh of Montacute, as we do not know his exact dates.

233 A. Wilmart, 'Les mélanges de Mathieu préchantre de Rievaulx au début du XIIIᵉ siècle', *RB* 52 (1940), 15–84. I am grateful to James Girsch for his unpublished edition of some of the poems. For another poetic collection with a strong Cistercian flavour, see this volume on the Rufford anthology, p. 151.

234 An additional five-leaf gathering in the manuscript contains a further sixteen pieces on similar subjects. I would be inclined to ascribe these also to Matthew, but Wilmart is doubtful.

235 A. Wilmart, 'Quelques poèmes moraux d'un manuscrit Burney', *SM* n.s. 12 (1939), 172–82; see further this volume, pp. 139–41.

236 David Carlson, '"Quid sit Deus": a rhythmical series from the poetic anthology Bodley 603', *MJ* 18 (1983), 197–225; on the manuscript, see this volume, p. 150. The manuscript could also be French.

237 J.H. Mozley, 'The collection of Mediaeval Latin verse in MS Cotton Titus D. xxiv', *MAe* 11 (1942), 1–45. See also this volume, p. 151.

238 See this volume, p. 124.

239 The anthology (in an early thirteenth-century hand) is on fols. 125–96. For an account of the poem, with extracts, see A.G. Rigg, 'De motu et pena peccandi', in *Poetry and Preaching in the late Middle Ages*, ed. J. Alford and R. Newhauser (forthcoming).

240 For a full account of the Bekynton anthology, see this volume, pp. 152–3.

241 A. Wilmart, 'Un grand débat de l'âme et du corps en vers élégiaques', *SM* n.s. 12 (1939), 192–209. The poem, 'Cogis me litem describere spiritualem', is in the Bekynton anthology and Bodley 527 (from Waverley).

242 'Nature talamos', ed. Raby *SLP* 2. 22–23.

243 The antimonastic satire of the early twelfth century (*De vita monachorum*, *Invectio in monachos*, and 'Quae monachi quaerunt', this volume, pp. 65–6) remained popular in this period. For satire on clerical abuses in the Bekynton anthology, see Nos. 10–11 (on Rome), 15–17 (prose, by Eraclius, aimed at William de Longchamps), 21, 76, 77, 80, 84, 86 (of which 84 and 86 are found elsewhere); the manuscript also has satires by Walter of Châtillon. See also this volume, pp. 105, 107–8 (on political satire in the Bekynton), and pp. 231–6. On Eraclius, see pp. 142–4.

244 Similarly, No. 78 (xvɪɪ).

245 See this volume, pp. 69, 74–6, (John of Salisbury), 85–6, (Peter of Blois), 88–9 (Walter Map).

246 Nos. 28–31: of these 'O curas hominum' and 'Aristippe quamvis sero' are in *Carmina Burana* (Nos. 187, 189), and 'Adulari nesciens' is in the Florence Antiphonary (printed in

AH 21, 124, No. 180). No. 31 is unique to the Bekynton.

247 See this volume, p. 89.

248 See this volume, pp. 68–9.

249 Ed. K. Strecker, 'Quid dant artes nisi luctum', *SM* n.s. 1 (1928), 380–91. The poem was once attributed to Robert Baston (this volume, pp. 244–5). It is in Goliardics 'cum auctoritate'; in the lines quoted here, the *auctoritas* is the opening of Boethius' *Consolatio Philosophiae*.

250 In MS Rawlinson G. 109 (this volume, p. 150) there is satire on doctors, a story of three stammerers who misunderstand each other, and poems on blunders and cheating in sex. In MS BL Add. 24199 (this volume, p. 151) there is a short poem about a drunken man who unknowingly has his drunken wife debauched. As these manuscripts draw most of their material from continental sources, I have not included them here.

251 Ed. Lehmann, *Parodie*, No. 14, pp. 224–30; to Lehmann's manuscripts may be added: Bodley 57 fols. 143ʳ–144ʳ; Digby 53 fol.33ᵛ; Harley 3724 fol.44ᵛ; Herdringen (now lost), fol.101ʳ. There is a very abbreviated version in BL Harley 913 (this volume, p. 307). For the formula 'loqui prohibeor . . . tacere non possum', see above, note 84. The Bekynton also contains Map's *Epistola Valerii* and Theophrastus *De nuptiis*, which are inherently comic.

252 See this volume, p. 86 (Peter of Blois and Robert of Beaufeu on wine and beer), pp. 121–2 (Neckam on wine).

253 Frequently printed, as in *Carmina Burana*, No. 194:

> In cratere meo Thetis est sociata Lyeo;
> Est dea iuncta deo, sed dea maior eo.
> Nil valet hic vel ea, nisi cum fuerint pharisea
> Hec duo; propterea sit deus absque dea

The editors list forty-seven MSS, but there are many more.

254 Similarly No. 49 (XIV), which is also *Carmina Burana* No. 202.

255 Ed. Lehmann, *Parodie*, No. 15, pp. 231–2.

256 Ed. Wright, *Mapes*, pp. xl–xliv; it is preserved in MS Digby 53.

257 Rawlinson G. 109 has several love poems and explicit sexual adventures (one of which has been erased), and BL Add. 24199 has a few poems to an inconstant mistress. As above (n. 250) I have discounted these manuscripts.

258 For an account of the growth of the Goliardic corpus and legend, see A.G. Rigg, 'Golias and other pseudonyms', *SM* 3rd ser. 18 (1977), 65–109. On the spread in the thirteenth century, see this volume, pp. 236–8. The choice of Eraclius as a pseudonym may have arisen in a similar way: see my article cited in n. 25 above.

259 The passage is in the *Speculum Ecclesiae* (see this volume, p. 95 and n. 103). The text is taken from *Carmina Burana* I. 1. p. 79.

260 See above, n. 253.

261 See this volume, p. 144 and n. 256.

262 See this volume, pp. 121–2; Esposito, p. 453.

263 K. Strecker, *Die Apokalypse des Golias* (Rome, 1928); there are over fifty manuscripts.

264 R.B.C. Huygens, 'Mitteilungen aus Handschriften: III. Die Metamorphose des Golias', *SM* 3rd ser. 3 (1962), 764–72.

265 Exceptions are the eleventh-century *Cambridge Songs*, the *Arundel Lyrics*, and of course the *Carmina Burana*. Although florilegium is simply a Latin calque on Greek *anthologia*

(both meaning 'gathering of flowers'), I follow custom in applying the former to collections of excerpts, the latter to collections of complete poems.

266 Such single-author collections include BN lat. 11867 and Cambridge UL Gg.6.42 (Neckam), Vespasian D. xix (Nigel Whiteacre), Digby 4 and Digby 168 (Walter of Châtillon), Bodleian Lat. misc. d.15 (Matthew of Vendôme), BN lat. 15157 (Matthew of Rievaulx). Sometimes these collected works, often shorn of attributions, would mingle with each other and in turn be anthologized. This seems to have happened to the poems of Hildebert, Marbod and Peter Riga, whose short poems are now inextricably tangled up with each other.

267 See n. 104 above. For a full account of the *Florilegium Gallicum* (with bibliography of other extracts) see Rosemary Burton, *Classical Poets in the 'Florilegium Gallicum'* (Frankfurt, 1983).

268 This is very evident in the case of Vitellius A. xii and BL Add. 24199 (this volume, pp. 150–1): either both were copied in the same scriptorium, or one was loaned for copying. The same applies, in the later thirteenth century, to Trinity College, Cambridge, O.2.45 and BL Cleopatra B. ix.

269 See this volume, pp. 150, 303, 308, on the relation between Rawlinson G. 109 and Titus A. xx, and between Bodley 603 and Digby 166.

270 This is particularly true of Rawlinson G. 109 (see description cited in n. 279 below) and the 'Hildebertian' manuscripts (this volume, p. 149). In the fourteenth century there seems to have been a 'pool' of poetry in Oxford (see this volume, pp. 307–8, 311–12).

271 See this volume, pp. 307–8, 311–12.

272 See this volume, pp. 63–4.

273 See this volume, p. 156.

274 See this volume, p. 136 and n. 232.

275 See this volume, pp. 15–16.

276 See this volume, pp. 65–6.

277 See Wilmart, 'Saint-Gatien', cited above, ch. I, n. 178.

278 The list includes not only manuscripts and booklets but also blocks of material that form discrete units (and thus may go back to earlier booklets).

279 A.G. Rigg, 'Medieval Latin Poetic Anthologies (IV)', *MSt* 43 (1981), 472–97.

280 See this volume, p. 308.

281 A.G. Rigg, 'Medieval Latin Poetic Anthologies (III)', *MSt* 41 (1979), 468–505.

282 See this volume, p. 138.

283 See this volume, p. 308, and the study cited in n. 281.

284 A. Boutemy, 'Notice sur le recueil poétique du manuscrit Cotton Vitellius A. xii du British Museum', *Latomus* 1 (1937), 278–313. This manuscript was one of the main sources for Wright's editions in ALSP (see this volume, pp. 64–6).

285 A. Boutemy, 'Le recueil poétique du ms. Additional 24199 du British Museum', *Latomus* 2 (1938), 30–52.

286 J.H. Mozley, 'The collection of Mediaeval Latin verse in MS Cotton Titus D. xxiv', *MAe* 11 (1942), 1–45; supplementary notes by R.W. Hunt, *MAe* 16 (1947), 6–8.

287 Otto Schumann, 'Die jüngere Cambridger Leidersammlung', *SM* n.s. 16 (1943–50), 48–85.

288 A. Wilmart, 'Le florilège mixte de Thomas Bekynton', *MARS* 1 (1941), 41–84; 4 (1958), 35–90; C.L. Kingsford, 'Some political poems of the twelfth century', *EHR* 5 (1890), 311–26. I refer to items by the numbers in Wilmart's description; roman

numerals refer to the entries edited in the second part of his article. K followed by a roman numeral refers to an edition by Kingsford.

289 See this volume, p. 68.

290 I have excluded from consideration the works of Hilary of Orléans, once known as Hilarius Anglicus. There is no evidence that he was English, and his works did not circulate in England. For an edition of his literary works, see N. Häring, 'Die Gedichte und Mysterienspiele des Hilarius von Orléans', *SM* 3rd ser. 17 (1976), 915–68.

291 *Bernardus Silvestris: Cosmographia*, ed. P. Dronke (Leiden, 1978).

292 Text in PL 171.1365–80; there is a copy in the Bekynton. For a summary of the arguments about authorship, see A.B. Scott, 'The poems of Hildebert of Le Mans: a new examination of the canon', *MARS* 6 (1968), 81.

293 N.M. Häring, 'Alan of Lille: "De Planctu Naturae"', *SM* 3rd ser. 19 (1978), 797–879.

294 *Alain de Lille: Anticlaudianus*, ed. R. Bossuat (Paris, 1955).

295 See this volume, p. 168.

296 *Johannes de Hauvilla: Architrenius*, ed. P.G. Schmidt (Munich, 1974). There is a copy in the Bekynton.

297 *Aurora: Petri Rigae Biblia Versificata*, ed. P.E. Beichner, 2 vols. (Notre Dame, 1965).

298 See this volume on Alan of Meaux, pp. 160–2.

299 PL 171, 1381–1442. See A. Boutemy, 'Recherches sur le "Floridus Aspectus" de Pierre la Rigge', *Le Moyen Age* 54 (1948), 89–112, and *Latomus* 8 (1949), 159–68, 283–301.

300 See this volume, p. 78.

301 *Moralisch-Satirische Gedichte Walters von Chatillon*, ed. K. Strecker (Heidelberg, 1929); *Die Lieder Walters von Chatillon in der Handschrift 351 von St. Omer*, ed. K. Strecker (Berlin/Zurich, 1925; rpt. 1964). A large block of Walter's satirical poems is in Bodley 603 (above, p. 150), and was copied into Digby 166. They are also in Digby MSS 4 and 168.

302 *Galteri de Castellione Alexandreis*, ed. M.L. Colker (Padua, 1978).

303 See this volume, pp. 146–8.

304 *Mathei Vindocinensis Opera*, ed. F. Munari; Vol. 1 (Rome, 1977) is a study of the manuscripts; Vol. 2 (1982) contains *Piramus et Tisbe, Milo, Epistule*, and *Tobias*. Vol. 3 (1988) has the *Ars Versificatoria*, which can also be read in Faral, pp. 106–93.

305 For example, they are in BL Titus A. xx, this volume, p. 308.

306 See this volume, pp. 112–14.

307 The standard edition of the *comediae* is *Commedie Latine del XII e XIII secolo*, 5 vols., Publicazioni dell' Istituto di Filologia Classica e Medievale 48, 61, 68, 79, 95 (Genoa, 1976–86), in progress. Each text is separately edited. The earlier edition is *La 'comédie' latine en France au XII* siècle, ed. G. Cohen, 2 vols. (Paris, 1931); here also each comedy is separately edited.

3 Henry III to Edward I (1216–1307)

1 For a summary of new interests and styles in literature in this period, see this volume, pp. 239–40.

2 See this volume, pp. 198–204, 228–9.

3 Ed. Wright, *Pol. Songs*, pp. 19–27.

4 For an early reaction, see on Matthew of Rievaulx, this volume, p. 137.

5 See this volume, p. 191.

6 These events figure prominently in the writings of John of Garland, this volume, pp. 173–6.

7 See this volume, pp. 233–4.

8 For the arrival of the Franciscans, see Thomas of Eccleston's *Tractatus de adventu fratrum minorum in Angliam*, ed. A.G. Little (Manchester, 1951); a short moral poem by Henry of Burford (not English by birth) is on p. 31. Henry of Avranches wrote a full-length verse *Vita Francisci*, this volume, pp. 184–5.

9 See this volume, pp. 186, 269–76. For the whole topic, see Penn R. Szittya, *The Antifraternal Tradition in Medieval Literature* (Princeton, 1986), especially ch. 5. Criticism of the friars began early, in Paris in the 1250s, led by William of St. Amour; the nature of the arguments is clear in the *Defensio Fratrum Mendicantium*, attributed to John Pecham or Guy de la Marche (this volume, p. 226). On the possible Franciscan contribution to 'le goût de la pathétique' in devotional literature, see this volume, pp. 207–8.

10 See this volume, p. 68 and n. 4.

11 *De Triumphis Ecclesiae* (this volume, pp. 173–6), 3.227–8, p. 53.

12 See this volume, pp. 166, 187, n. 108, and p. 160 for his teaching of Aristotle.

13 On Grosseteste, see S. Harrison Thomson, *The writings of Robert Grosseteste, bishop of Lincoln, 1235–1253* (Cambridge, 1940), and Southern, cited this volume, p. 68 n. 4. Grosseteste has been credited with two poems on domestic manners (Thompson, pp. 148–50). The first, the *Liber Curialis*, is an extract from Daniel Beccles' *Urbanus Magnus* (see this volume, ch. 2, n. 211). The other is the popular short poem 'Stans puer ad mensam', of which there is a critical edition by Gieben (this volume, ch. 2, n. 209). The evidence for Grosseteste's authorship of 'Stans puer' is in two lines, which occur in most of the several versions of the poem:

> Hec qui me docuit grossum caput est sibi nomen,
> Presul et ille fuit, cui felix det Deus omen

The tense of *fuit* seems to me to rule out Grosseteste's authorship; I put the lines in the category of those which attribute the doctrines of Beccles' *Urbanus Magnus* to 'old King Henry' (this volume, p. 126).

As noted in ch. 2, n. 199, my attention was drawn recently to the attribution of the scientific poem 'Scribo sed ut merear' (this volume, pp. 122–3) to Grosseteste. Bergmann's attribution depends, I understand, on the computus calculations in the poem which correspond to those of Grosseteste, a topic on which I am not competent to judge. If the poem is indeed Grosseteste's, it adds a remarkable, but not impossible, dimension to his literary achievement.

14 R.W. Hunt, 'Verses on the life of Robert Grosseteste', *Medievalia et Humanistica* n.s. 1 (1970), 241–51.

15 See this volume, pp. 176–7, 215–22, 229.

16 David Townsend, 'Robert Grosseteste and Walter of Wimborne', *MAe* 55 (1986), 113–17.

17 J.H. Mozley, 'Susanna and the elders: three medieval poems', *SM* n.s. 3 (1930), 27–52 (Alan's poem on pp. 41–50). His name is pronounced *mews*.

18 On Peter Riga, see this volume, p. 156. Both poems are printed by Mozley, 'Susanna and the elders'. Riga's version is a dramatization, beginning with the judges' accusation, followed by Daniel's reconstruction and proof of what actually happened; Giles'

redaction goes back to the original chronological sequence, and supplies connecting narrative links.

19 Ed. Mozley, 'Susanna and the elders'. On the manuscript, Corpus Christi College, Cambridge, 450, see this volume, p. 307.

20 The *Distinctiones* has not been published. The longest coherent set of extracts is by A. Wilmart, 'Un répertoire d'exégèse composé en Angleterre vers le début du xiiie siècle', in *Mémorial Lagrange* (Paris, 1940), pp. 307–46, with a full account of the genre. There are also extensive extracts in J.B. Pitra, *Spicilegium Solesmense*, 4 vols. (Paris, 1852–8), vols. 2–3 under the *Clavis Melitonis*. For a full study of the verses, see P. Lehmann, 'Mittellateinische Verse in *Distinctiones monasticae et morales* vom Anfang des 13. Jahrhunderts', *Sitzungsberichte der bayerischen Akademie der Wissenschaften*, Philos.-Philol. und historische Klasse (Munich, 1922), Abh. 2 (reprinted in P.G. Lehmann, *Erforschung des Mittelalters* (Stuttgart, 1959–62), 4.317–35). R.W. Hunt, in *Liber Floridus*: *Mittellateinische Studien Paul Lehmann zum 65. Geburtstag*, ed. B. Bischoff and S. Brechter (St. Ottilien, 1950), pp. 355–62, suggests Louth Park as a possible place of composition.

21 Wilmart, 'Un répertoire d'exégèse', p. 333.

22 The Fables are in Hervieux, *Fabulistes latins*, 4, 173–255, 361–416. See A.C. Friend, 'Master Odo of Cheriton', *Speculum* 23 (1948), 641–58.

23 These have been extracted and printed separately by Hervieux, 4, 265–343; there are 195 in all.

24 See this volume, p. 114.

25 See this volume, p. 257.

26 The fullest bio- and bibliographical account remains that of Paetow in his edition of the *Morale Scolarium*, below, n. 37. For John of London and Garland's verses on him, see this volume, p. 159.

27 There is no evidence that he preferred his nurse (France) to his mother (England). In *De Triumphis Ecclesiae* 3.405–6 he writes

Anglia cui mater fuerat, cui Gallia nutrix,
Matri nutricem praefero marte meam

Paetow read *mente* for *marte*, but the MS clearly has *marte*, meaning that Garland simply thought that the French were better fighters.

28 Two useful guides to Garland as a musical theorist are: W.G. Waite, 'Johannes de Garlandia, poet and musician', *Speculum* 35 (1960), 179–95; Bob R. Antley, *The rhythm of medieval music: a study in the relationship of stress and quantity, and a theory of reconstruction with a translation of John of Garland's 'De mensurabili musica'*, Ph.D. thesis (Florida State University, 1977).

29 *CLP*, p. 386.

30 Ed. A. Scheler, 'Trois traités de lexicographie latine du xiie et du xiiie siècle', *Jahrbuch für romanische und englische Literatur* 6 (1865), 43–59, text 142–62, commentary 287–321, 370–9; also ed. *Hunt, 1, 191–203. On Adam and Alexander, see this volume, pp. 72–3, 118.

31 Scheler, pp. 52–3. Now ed. *Hunt, 1, 204–31.

32 Extracts from *Synonyma* and *Equiuoca* in P. Leyser, *Historia poetarum et poematum medii aevi* (Halle, 1721), pp. 312–39; PL 150, 1577–90. See also *Hunt, 1, 136–42.

33 Ed. E. Habel, *Der deutsche Cornutus* (Berlin, 1908). The poem (inc. 'Cespitat in phaleris'), also known as *Disticha*, *Distigium*, was later adapted as the *Novus Cornutus* by

Otto von Lüneburg; ed., with commentary, by *Hunt, 1, 323–48.

34 Scheler, pp. 46–8 (*Clavis compendii*), 50–1 (*Ars lectoria*), 55–7 (*Ars versificatoria*) has extracts. The list of earlier works given in the *Ars lectoria* is printed by Paetow (below, n. 37), pp. 107–8. See *Hunt, 1, 143–50, 157–60.

35 *The Parisiana Poetria of John of Garland*, ed. Traugott Lawler (New Haven, 1974).

36 Edwin Habel, 'Die exempla honestae vitae des Johannes de Garlandia, eine lateinische Poetik des 13. Jahrhunderts', *Romanische Forschungen* 29 (1911), 131–54. Habel's line-count gives 308 lines, but this includes all the headings to the sections.

37 *Morale Scolarium*, ed. L.J. Paetow (Berkeley, 1927).

38 See this volume, pp. 125–7.

39 The rhyme (abba) is cross-shaped; a *cancellum* is a lattice barrier.

40 *Integumenta Ovidii*, ed. F. Ghisalberti (Milan, 1933).

41 See this volume, p. 125.

42 Ed. F. Novati, 'Un poème inconnu de Gautier de Châtillon', in *Mélanges Paul Fabre* (Paris, 1902), pp. 265–78. The ascription in the manuscript (BN lat. 15155) to Walter of Châtillon almost certainly results from the incorrect inclusion of a couplet of Walter's at the beginning. Novati italicizes rhymed lines as unworthy of 'Walter'. The correct ascription is provided by E.F. Wilson, 'The *Georgica Spiritualia* of John of Garland', *Speculum* 8 (1933), 358–77, who has a full study of the poem; she suggests that the poem may have utilized the *De laudibus Beatae Virginis Mariae* (this volume, p. 208, n. 180), but this was written in 1245, probably too late for the *Georgica Spiritualia*, if, as Wilson suggests, the latter was absorbed into the *Epithalamium* (c. 1231–5 ?).

43 *Epithalamium Beatae Virginis*, ed. A. Saiani, Biblioteca di 'Quadrivium', Testi per esercitazioni accademiche (Bologna, 1965–). By 1980 only Books I–VI had been published; the edition is now complete and forthcoming.

44 For a full discussion (to which my account is indebted), see E.F. Wilson, 'Pastoral and epithalamium in Latin literature', *Speculum* 23 (1948), 35–57.

45 It had already been used for allegorical purposes in Martianus Capella's *De nuptiis Mercurii et Philologiae*.

46 In two manuscripts this poem is attributed to Alain de Lille, but the ascription is hesitantly doubted by M.-T. D'Alverny, *Alain de Lille: textes inédits* (Paris, 1965), pp. 48–9.

47 *Epith.* 6. 42; Lawrence of Durham makes the same use of the eclogue.

48 In MS Digby 65 (this volume, p. 237), the poem is preceded by a prose prologue.

49 Similarly, the Virgin places the pen in Walter of Wimborne's hand when he is too overawed to write: this volume, p. 220.

50 This section is heavily indebted to Prudentius' *Psychomachia*.

51 See this volume, p. 208.

52 It is incorporated in the *Commentarius*, ed. Scheler (n. 30 above), pp. 52–3. Another copy follows the text of the *Epithalamium* in MS Digby 65.

53 *The Stella Maris of John of Garland*, ed. E.F. Wilson (Cambridge, Mass., 1946).

54 See this volume, pp. 35, 84, 104.

55 *De Mysteriis Ecclesiae*, ed. F.W. Otto, *Commentarii critici in Codices Bibliothecae Academicae Gissensis* (Giessen, 1842), pp. 131–51. Manuscript versions differ in length.

56 On the combined poems on the sacraments by Hildebert and Petrus Pictor, see this volume, p. 150.

57 *De triumphis ecclesiae*, ed. T. Wright, Roxburghe Club (London, 1856).

58 The date of 1245 is implied at 8. 69–72; in the *Epithalamium* (revised 1229–32) he says

that he has already written about the crusades, perhaps referring to an early draft of the *De triumphis* (Books III–VI). Book VIII begins 'Est liber hic nonus'. At the end of Book VII (7.491–2) he implies that he has almost reached the end of the work:

Divinae menti quae sunt ventura relinquo,
Dum portum properat cymba tenere mea

In the Prologue (191–4) he implies a nine-book arrangement by writing of the perfect number:

Planctus multiplicat primus, causasque secundas
Fert liber, effectum publicat ordo sequens.
Est numeri ratio, triplex ternarius impar
Res incorruptas perpetuasque notat

There are four attempts to summarize the poem (Prol. 85–174, 191–4, 7.495–8, 8.571–90); none of them corresponds to the actual contents of the poem as it stands, except in describing Book I as a lament and listing some of the general themes. A proper edition might clarify some of these problems.

59 The Poitevins, under Hugh de la Marche, whose wife was Isabella, widow of King John and mother of Henry III, revolted against Louis IX of France, thus involving England in war against France.
60 In this popular legend, when Adam was dying, Seth obtained from the angel who was guarding Paradise seeds from the tree of life. The seeds, planted under Adam's tongue, sprouted and produced three trees which intertwined into one. This tree was cut down to form a beam for the temple, but was either too long or too short; it became a bridge, which the Queen of Sheba honoured, and eventually was used for the Cross.
61 Garland's account of the origin of this crusade is idiosyncratic. In 1208 the papal legate, Peter of Castelnau, was assassinated; he was one of a series of papal emissaries sent to combat heresy in the south of France. Innocent III called for a crusade, and the first wave of crusaders arrived in 1209.
62 In the *Dictionarius* (this volume, pp. 163–4) Garland mentions that he had been present at the siege of Toulouse where Simon de Montfort (father of the hero of the Barons' War, this volume, pp. 198–204) was killed.
63 For the lines that imply that this is the end of the poem, see n. 58 above.
64 These are lines that can be read forward or backward, often with satirical effect, as in these lines on Paris:

Parisius proba non pugnat gens, parcere clero
Provida, non curat perfidiam sua lex.
Lex sua perfidiam curat, non provida clero
Parcere, gens pugnat non proba Parisius (2. 715–18)

65 See this volume p. 173 and the quotation from Book III on p. 174.
66 The first full account is by P.G. Schmidt, 'Elias of Thriplow: a thirteenth-century Anglo-Latin poet', *Papers of the Liverpool Latin Seminar* 3 (1981), 363–70. An edition of the *Serium senectutis* is in preparation by Roger Hillas, and I am grateful for having been able to see the edition before publication. Elias ('Tripolitanus') received little attention in the Middle Ages; quotations from the *De vita scholarium atque sua* and *Contra*

nobilitatem inanem were made by the fourteenth-century friar Ringstede and the fifteenth-century bibliographer John Whethamstede, printed by Beryl Smalley, *English friars and antiquity in the early fourteenth century* (New York, 1960), pp. 218–19, 351–3.

67 J.C. Russell, in *BIHR* 8 (1930–31), 109, in one of a series of articles on the DNB. See also his edition of Henry of Avranches, this volume pp. 179–93 and n. 74.

68 See *Sacris eruditi* 10 (1958), 329–52.

69 Francisque X. Michel, *Chroniques Anglo-Normands* II (Rouen, 1836), 99–142; other items here on Waltheof could also be William's.

70 John Whitaker, *The Life of St Neot, The oldest of all the brothers to King Alfred* (London, 1809), pp. 317–38. Whitaker thanks a friend for transcribing it for him from Magdalen College, Oxford, MS 53; in fact, it is an incredibly slipshod transcription and also omits a couplet.

71 ASS 31 July (July 7, 330–40). See Mary P. Richards, 'The medieval hagiography of St Neot', *AB* 99 (1981), 259–78.

72 The poem is unpublished; only the date of the manuscript, Bodleian Lib., MS Laud misc. 515, places it in this chapter. The eleven-line epilogue to this poem was wrongly taken, by Tanner and the DNB (S. Gregory of Caergwent), to be the prologue to the life that follows in the manuscript, Henry of Avranches' verse life of St Hugh of Lincoln (this volume, p. 183). There is nothing to connect this poet with Gregory of Ely, author of the verse life of St Etheldrida (this volume, p. 22): the metres are quite different.

73 See this volume, p. 21.

74 A canon of Henry's writings was first established by J.C. Russell and J.P. Heironimus, *The Shorter Latin Poems of Henry of Avranches relating to England* (Cambridge, Mass., 1935), based on Russell's unpublished thesis. The evidence presented in its favour seems at first sight to be insubstantial and conjectural: for a discussion, see D. Townsend and A.G. Rigg, 'Medieval Latin Poetic Anthologies (V): Matthew Paris' anthology of Henry of Avranches (Cambridge, Univ. Lib. MS Dd. 11.78)', *MSt* 49 (1987), 352–90. Recent scholarship by D. Townsend and P. Binkley, however, has shown that Russell was substantially correct. Attributions by Matthew Paris in the Cambridge manuscript, together with Henry's habit of reusing lines and conceits in several works, enable us to be fairly sure that he wrote all the saints' lives discussed here (except perhaps the long *Vita Thome*), the 'educational' poems, the debates and flytings (except perhaps the first *Clericus et Miles* debate), and most of the occasional poems. We also have external testimony from some medieval catalogues. There is no space here to discuss the whole complex business of attributions. Russell conjectured, probably rightly, that the Cambridge manuscript was copied from a collection compiled by Henry, and so included some material (e.g. part of Alexander of Ville-Dieu's *Doctrinale* and Philip the Chancellor's Heart and Eye debate) that he was interested in; this may explain the 'German' debates. The other large collection of poems has no contemporary notes of ascription (and the librarian Richard James headed it 'Michaelis Cornubiensis Poemata'), but internal examination shows that many of the poems are, as Russell had conjectured, by Henry; see P. Binkley, 'Medieval Latin Poetic Anthologies (VI): the Cotton anthology of Henry of Avranches (B.L. Cotton Vespasian D. v, fols. 151–84)', *MSt* 52 (1990), 221–54.

75 See this volume, pp. 193–8.

76 Bodleian MS Digby 172, 'Ave maris stella vera mellis stilla', this volume, p. 186.

77 D. Townsend, *An Edition of Saints' Lives attributed to Henry of Avranches*, Ph.D. thesis (Toronto, 1985), pp. 51–151.

78 On Reginald of Durham (Coldingham), this volume, pp. 97–8.

79 Ed. Townsend, *Saints Lives*, pp. 152–204. For the source, see D. Townsend, 'An eleventh-century life of Birinus of Wessex', *AB* 107 (1989), 129–59.

80 These lines had an independent circulation; they are quoted (in a sixteenth-century hand) in Cambridge, Univ. Lib., MS ɪl. 1.15, and by Du Cange.

81 Ed. W.F. Bolton, *The Middle English and Latin Poems on St Guthlac*, Ph.D. thesis (Princeton, 1954), but I have used the forthcoming edition by D. Townsend. Guthlac was a popular saint: there are lives in Old English verse and prose, and in Latin by Felix of Croyland and Alexander of Ashby (this volume, p. 132 and note 224). A Peterborough chronicle states that Henry, abbot of Croyland, commissioned two lives of Guthlac, one 'metrico stylo' by Henry of Avranches, the other 'heroico stylo' by Peter of Blois; the latter has been identified with the prose life in Horstmann, *Nova Legenda Angliae* (this volume, ch. 4, note 67), App. ɪɪɪ, pp. 698–719, but it is hard to see how prose could be 'heroico stylo', and abbot Henry's and Peter's dates do not match well.

82 Ed. F. Hervey, *Corolla S. Eadmundi* (London, 1907), pp. 200–23; I have used the forthcoming edition by D. Townsend.

83 Ed. F. Hervey, *The Pinchbek Register*, 2 vols. (London, 1925), ɪɪ, 365–78, which inadvertently omits a folio; I have used the forthcoming edition by D. Townsend.

84 *Metrical Life of St Hugh, Bishop of Lincoln*, ed. J.F. Dimock (Lincoln, 1860); ed. and transl. Charles Garton, Lincoln Cathedral Library Publications (Lincoln, 1986), using the Dimock text. Adam of Eynsham's *Magna Vita* is ed. D.L. Douie and H. Farmer, 2 vols., (London, 1961–2; Vol. ɪ rev. Oxford, 1985); Adam used the earlier life by Gerald of Wales (this volume, p. 95).

85 Compare John of Garland's *De mysteriis ecclesiae*, this volume, p. 173.

86 Ed. Russell-Heironimus, pp. 37–43.

87 Ed. Russell-Heironimus, pp. 44–8.

88 The miracle is described in terms of 'generation and corruption' (see this volume, p. 187 n. 110); for a similar miracle, see on William of Combe, this volume, p. 81.

89 Ed. Townsend, *Saints Lives*, pp. 205–351.

90 It is stylistically unlike his other works; it never echoes the Short Life, even when the same incident is being described, and there are discrepancies, as in Henry II's motive for wanting Becket to be archbishop.

91 The relationship between Becket and Langton is stressed in Henry's poem No. 44 (Russell-Heironimus, p. 54), which says to Langton 'te non a Thoma separet ulla athomus'. Another poem to Langton (No. 9, Russell-Heironimus, pp. 92–3, probably Henry's as it has lines from No. 47, Russell-Heironimus, pp. 85–7) laments that the prior of Canterbury did not like Henry's poem on the Miracles of Becket, possibly referring to the *Revelationes*.

92 Ed. M.I. Allen, 'The metrical *Passio Sanctorum Crispini et Crispiniani* of Henry of Avranches', *AB* 108 (1990), 357–86.

93 'Henrici Abrincensis Legenda S. Francisci versificata', *Analecta Franciscana* 10 (1926–41), 405–521.

94 The version in the Cambridge manuscript is a later revision, written after the death of

Gregory in 1241; there is another (incomplete) version in a Versailles manuscript utilizing the life by Bonaventure.

95 Sat. 10.22; Henry made a similar use of the line in the *Vita Guthlaci*.

96 Like many poets, going back to Geoffrey of Vinsauf, Henry comments on the fact that Innocent's name cannot be accommodated to metre.

97 Ed. D. Townsend, 'The "Versus de corona spinea" of Henry of Avranches', *MJ* 23 (1988), 154–70.

98 Ed. Russell-Heironimus, pp. 48–51.

99 The original Hildegard letter (Epist. 48) is printed in PL 197. 243–53; for a study, see Kathy Kerby-Fulton, 'Hildegard of Bingen and anti-mendicant propaganda', *Traditio* 43 (1987), 386–99.

100 'He, he, vos esse deberetis, ut dictum est, "Mons Sion in quo habitasti in eo". Nam benedicti et signati in coelestibus personis habitaculum esse debuistis, myrrham et thus redolens, in quo etiam Deus habitaret. Sed hoc non estis, sed veloces estis ad lasciviam puerilis aetatis.' (col. 245)

101 The poems on the joys have not been published; 'Anna partu solvitur', AH 40, 114; 'In te concipitur O virgo regia', AH 20, 140 (AH 48, 269–70), possibly by Alexander Neckam (see Hunt, pp. 55–6).

102 See this volume, p. 237.

103 AH 20, 144–7.

104 J.P. Heironimus and J.C. Russell, 'Two types of thirteenth-century grammatical poems', *Colorado College Pubication*, General ser. 158, Language ser. III 3 (Colorado Springs, 1929), 1–27. The original Donatus reads: 'Nomen est pars orationis cum casu corpus aut rem proprie communiterve significans.'

105 Extracts cited by Heironimus-Russell (n. 104). See *Hunt, 1, 120–3.

106 See this volume, pp. 71, 111–12.

107 Ed. Hervieux, *Fabulistes latins*, 3, 468–74. The fables are Nos. 1–5, 15, 19, 37, and 34 in Avianus.

108 The prologue is edited by Russell-Heironimus, pp. 102–4; for the text itself I have used an unpublished transcription by Dr Anna Kirkwood. Henry certainly used the Latin prose translation, but at times has a better understanding of Aristotle's meaning than the laboured prose could have provided. He may have heard lectures on it: John Blund, who lectured on Aristotle in Oxford, is praised in a poem possibly by Henry (No. 127 in Russell-Heironimus' list).

109 The Latin translation reads: Antiquorum igitur hi quidem vocatam generationem simplicem alterationem esse inquiunt; hi vero aliud generationem, aliud alterationem. Quicumque igitur unum aliquid omne esse dicunt, et omnia ex uno generant, his quidem necesse et (= est ?) utique generationem alterationem esse dicere, et quod principaliter fit, alterari.

110 The topos is used also in *Vita Hugonis* and *Revelationes* after Becket's death (on the newly created testicles), and, as a simple contrastive pair, in the Short Life of Becket and *All Saints*.

111 Editions of the two poems in preparation by P. Binkley. The Peterborough catalogue credits Henry with: Versus eiusdem de Decretalibus. Versus de Decretis cum sentenciis eorumdem. A text of the *Decretum* poem is with other poems by Henry in MS Bodley 40, and an extract from it is in the Cambridge manuscript. Ascription to him of the

Decretals poem rests on the Peterborough catalogue and on the fact that it accompanies the *Decretum* poem in MS Lyell 41. Henry's interest in law is shown in a poem to Frederick II (see note 127 below) urging the Emperor to codify civil law just as the Pope was doing for canon law:

> Canonicum ius papa novat; civile novari
> debet pocius, cum sit diffusius (C. 7–8)

112 Mnemonic verses on canon law are not uncommon. See the Appendix to my edition of Walter of Wimborne (below, note 190), p. 311. Peter Binkley informs me of a similar work by Werner von Schussenried, a Vicenza canonist of the beginning of the thirteenth century.

113 Ed. G.W. Leibnitz, in *Scriptores rerum Brunsvicensium illustrationi inservientes* II (Hannover, 1710), 523–32.

114 Ed. H. Walther, *Das Streitgedicht in der lateinischen Literatur des Mittelalters* (Munich, 1920), rev. ed. by P.G. Schmidt (Hildesheim, 1984), pp. 250–3. The separation into two poems is suggested by: Matthew Paris' notice of authorship at the beginning of the second, the change of metre and of judge, and the fact that the second poem makes no reference to the arguments of the first. The most famous verse debate on the merits of clerks and soldiers is the *Phyllis and Flora* (*Carmina Burana* No. 92), of which there is a copy in MS Harley 978 (this volume, p. 238).

115 In *Materials for the History of Thomas Becket*, Vol. 3, RS (London, 1877), p. 5.

116 For epigram and verse-capping competitions, we have the evidence of several stories about Hugh Primas, and Gerald of Wales' account of Maurice of Glamorgan (see ch. 2, n. 105).

117 See below, pp. 193–8.

118 My edition of this poem, from Vespasian D. v, is in progress. John Bordum is known to have been a canon and subdeacon of Angers; see P. Binkley (n. 74 above), n. 66.

119 1–28 Leonini caudati, 29–39 elegi caudati, 40–342 Leonini, 343–452 Leonini unisoni, rhyming entirely on -*ere*.

120 Edition in preparation by P. Binkley.

121 Two short debates with a German connexion were added to the Cambridge manuscript by Matthew Paris. One is a short interchange, first attacking Lambert or Lambekin for his long hair and poetic pretensions, followed by Lambert's reply, attacking the *Britones* but praising the generous 'preclari' and giving thanks to St Alban. The second is presented in the third person as a debate between Conrad and an Englishman. Only their presence in this manuscript suggests any connexion with Henry; the insults are typical of this kind of poetry, but they lack the inventiveness of Henry's other abusive poetry. They are edited by Russell-Heironimus, pp. 28–9.

122 Prologue ed. Russell-Heironimus, pp. 102–4.

123 Only the poem for Blund has been edited; for the others I am grateful to Peter Binkley for his transcriptions.

124 Russell-Heironimus, pp. 129–36.

125 Unless specified, all poems mentioned in this section are in Russell-Heironimus.

126 See this volume, p. 227.

127 Ed. E. Winkelman, 'Drei Gedichte Heinrichs von Avranches an Kaiser Friedrich II', *Forschungen zur deutschen Geschichte* 18 (1878), 482–92. See also above, note 111. The pun on *Henris* was also made by Robert Partes, this volume, p. 77.

128 Ed. P. Binkley, 'Two thirteenth-century Latin *Ferienlieder*', *Scintilla: a Student Journal for Medievalists* (Toronto), 5 (1988), 23–43. The graduation poem is No. 109 in Russell-Heironimus, No. 6 in the Vespasian manuscript; it has not been edited.

129 The Rome-Innocent debate (this volume, p. 188) was written in about 1215; Henry is also credited with a (lost) poem on King John's dispute with the barons.

130 He died after 8 June 1262 and before Easter 1263, according to P. Binkley.

131 See this volume, pp. 53, 96–7, on Serlo of Fountains and William of Glasgow.

132 Russell-Heironimus, pp. 94–5.

133 See Binkley, 'Poetic Anthologies' (n. 74 above), on Vespasian D.V, p. 234, n. 42.

134 'Blaunpayn', white bread, is conjectured by Russell to be a pun on *mich*, a term for a small loaf.

135 For his possible authorship of a poem on the Barons' War, see this volume, pp. 202–3 and n. 157. The poems in Cotton Vespasian D.V, ascribed to Michael by the librarian Richard James, have now been given to Henry of Avranches (see n. 74 above), but it is possible that some of them could have been by Michael or another poet.

136 Ed. A. Hilka, 'Eine mittellateinische Dichterfehde: Versus Michaelis Cornubiensis contra Henricum Abrincensem', in *Mittellateinische Handschriften . . . Festgabe zum 60. Geburtstage von Hermann Degering*, ed. A. Bömer and J. Kirchner (Leipzig, 1926), pp. 123–54. Extracts in Russell-Heironimus, pp. 149–55. The insults are so repetitive that I have given only brief synopses of Parts II and III, which largely repeat (in different words) the abuse of Part I.

137 See P. Binkley, 'The date and setting of Michael of Cornwall's *Versus contra Henricum Abrincensem*', *MAe* 59 (1990), 76–84; this corrects Russell's dating. Dr Binkley has pointed out to me that to some extent Michael modifies his attacks according to the judges: in Part I he is concerned with academic points (grammar, philosophy); in Part II it is legal points that engage him.

138 See this volume, p. 192, n. 127.

139 R.W. Hunt, explaining a joke about Neckam, explains: '"Tu autem" are the first words of a liturgical formula for bringing a lesson to a close' (Hunt (ch. II, n. 180), p. 3, n. 15).

140 Nicholas' surname, and that of a fellow-thief, is printed by Hilka as Suihud, but manuscript readings allow the interpretation Smith or Smud.

141 This may allude to Henry's use of the first line of Ovid's *Metamorphoses* at the beginning of the *Vita Oswaldi*, this volume, p. 180.

142 See below, note 143.

143 *Part I*: 1–120 Leonini, 121–318 collateral, 319–68 Leonini. *Part II*: 369–78 Leonini, 379–434 collateral, 435–6 caudati, 437–40 Leonini, 441–4 trinini salientes, 445–592 collateral, 593–626 runover. *Part III*: 627–34 collateral, 635–42 cruciferi, 643–792 collateral, 793–822 Leonini unisoni, in couplets, 823–922 Leonini unisoni, rhyming in blocks of twenty lines in a vocalic series: *-aris, -eris, -iris, -oris, -uris* (cf. John of Howden, this volume, p. 214), 923–52 Leonini unisoni in couplets, 953–82 dactylici tripertiti, 983–1006 spondaici-dactylici tripertiti, e.g.

> Inclite rex o gallice, flexo crure pudice
> Me tibi vexo filaque texo, rex Lodowice

1007–8 collateral, 1009–1032 trinini salientes, (1033–8, 1041–6 hexametri retrogradi, from a poem attributed to Alain de Lille), 1039–40 collateral, 1047–97 triple rhyme, e.g.

> Si cupias scire, reperire, reperta polire,

1098–107 triple rhyme, unisoni in couplets, on *-ari, -eri, -iri, -ori, -uri*, e.g.

> Dignus culpari, non laudari, reprobari,
> Non acceptari, dampnari, non dominari

1108–206 triple rhyme, 1207–76 runover.

144 See this volume, p. 193.

145 See this volume, p. 29.

146 MS Bodley 233, fol. 107rb; the poem is headed: Versus magistri Michaelis le Poter de Corn(ubia).

147 Ed. Russell-Heironimus, p. 157. The poem is in the Cambridge manuscript of Henry's poems (see n. 74 above), where Matthew Paris has made the marginal note 'Mich.'; this is probably sufficient evidence for the attribution. Matthew refers to the incident of the broken leg in his chronicle for 1243.

148 For a general study, see Richard Vaughan, *Matthew Paris* (Cambridge, 1958). For Matthew's xenophobia, see this volume, p. 158.

149 *Vitae duorum Offarum et viginiti trium abbatum*, ed. William Wats *Matthaei Paris . . . historia major* (London, 1640); fragments of the life of Langton in *Ungedruckte anglo-normannische Geschichtsquellen*, ed. F. Liebermann (Strassburg, 1879), pp. 318–29; C.H. Lawrence, *St Edmund of Abingdon* (Oxford, 1960), with editions of the lives by Matthew, Eustace of Faversham, and others.

150 See this volume, p. 124 and note 204.

151 See this volume, p. 186.

152 Ed. Wright, *Political Songs*, pp. 121–4; the poem is preserved in the *Chronicle of William de Rishanger*, ed. J.O. Halliwell-Phillips, Camden Soc. (London, 1840).

153 *Song of Lewes*, ed. C.L. Kingsford (Oxford, 1890).

154 Cited by Lefferts (see next note).

155 See George W. Prothero, *The Life of Simon de Montfort, earl of Leicester* (London, 1877), pp. 388–91; the hymns are 'Rumpe celos et descende', 'Mater Syon iocundare', and 'Nequit stare sed rotare', followed by a prayer 'O decus milicie'. Texts of both 'Salve Symon' and 'Miles Christi', with a review of literature on Simon, are given by Peter M. Lefferts, 'Two English motets on Simon de Montfort', *Early Music History* 1 (1981), 203–25. There is another text of 'Salve Symon' in Rishanger (n. 152 above), pp. 109–10.

156 F.W. Maitland, 'A song on the death of Simon de Montfort', *EHR* 11 (1896), 314–18; there is no reason to suppose that Walter of Hyde was the author of the poem. The b-rhymes of the poem rhyme throughout on *-a (-ia, -era*, etc.).

157 The poems are printed by Halliwell in his notes to Rishanger's Chronicle (n. 152 above), pp. 112, 114, 118, 123–4, 139–46. I have corrected misprints silently.

158 Russell-Heironimus p. 150, nn. 9–12; the parallels are not very convincing, and the wordplay is characteristic of this kind of poem. The author of the prose chronicle was presumably a monk of Ramsey, and if Michael was a monk, he would surely have mentioned it in the *Altercacio*; of course, it is possible that the prose chronicle and the poems are by different authors. Curiously Russell does not mention the most important evidence, that the poet names himself Michael!

159 His chronicle extends from 1066 to his own day, and is his own work for the period 1256–78; in 1282 he became a canon of Osney Abbey, and the last part of his chronicle corresponds closely to that section of the Osney Annals, for which he was probably also responsible.

160 Wright, *Political Songs*, pp. 128–32; Wright's reading *Wyta* is wrong: the manuscript has *Wyca*. The poem stops abruptly and may be incomplete. Bale (*Catalogus* pp. 355–6; *Index* p. 460) and others credit him with two lost poems, on wine ('Syncerum mihi dede merum') and gluttony ('Prandens in mensa').

161 For a full account, see Jenny Swanson, *John of Wales: a Study of the Works and Ideas of a Thirteenth-century Friar* (Cambridge, 1989).

162 See this volume, pp. 254–5.

163 The first 404 lines were edited by J. Hammer, 'Une version métrique de l'*Historia Regum Britanniae de Geoffroy de Monmouth*', *Latomus* 2 (1938), 131–51. The poem is not a direct versification of Geoffrey but is based on a prose epitome of British history.

164 See this volume, pp. 98–9.

165 The prose narrative closest to the poem is that in BL MS Harley 3860; this is similar to the prefatory material to Walter of Coventry, *Memoriale*, ed. W. Stubbs, RS, 2 vols. (London, 1872–3), I. 3–18. There was almost certainly a third version that lay behind Harley 3860, Walter of Coventry and the poem. The prose narrative that accompanies the poem in three of its four manuscripts is not the source.

166 See this volume, p. 296.

167 See this volume, p. 77 and n. 42.

168 See this volume, p. 198 and n. 149.

169 'Ave gemma confessorum', AH 13, 117–19, No. 43; 'Gaude Sion ornata tympano', AH 25, 246–50, No. 88; 'Iste pastor dignus memoria', unpublished, text kindly supplied by Andrew Hughes.

170 AH 35, 137–52, No. 10. On the form of the psalterium, see this volume, p. 124.

171 See this volume, p. 222.

172 St Simeon Stock (? 1165–1265), general of the Carmelite order, was credited by the antiquaries with two hymns, 'Ave stella matutina' (possibly by Peter the Venerable: see *RB* 51 (1939), 53–69, on p.60), and 'Flos Carmeli vitis florigera' (WIC 6673, Chevalier 6400.

173 For example, see John of Howden, this volume, pp. 208–15.

174 See this volume, pp. 246–8.

175 See this volume, pp. 20, 61.

176 See this volume, pp. 83–4.

177 Hunt (this volume, ch. 2, n. 180), pp. 106–7 and nn. 55 and 57. Neckam recommends the study of Gregory and Anselm.

178 He was also known as Stephen of Salley, where he was abbot, 1223–4. A. Wilmart, 'Les méditations d'Étienne de Salley sur les Joies de la Vierge Marie', *RAM* 10 (1929), 368–415, rpt. in *Auteurs spirituels* pp. 317–60. A. Wilmart, 'Le triple exercice d'Étienne de Sallai', *RAM* 11 (1930), 355–74. Edmond Mikkers, 'Un "Speculum Novitii" inédit d'Étienne de Salley', *COCR* 8 (1946), 17–68; 'Un traité inédit d' Étienne de Salley sur la psalmodie', *Cîteaux* 23 (1972), 245–88.

179 See this volume, pp. 212–13.

180 Edited in *B. Alberti Magni . . . opera omnia*, ed. A. and A. Borgnet, Vol. 36 (Paris, 1898).

181 The name Howden (rather than Hoveden) is confirmed by the metre of his French *Rossignos*; see Louise W. Stone, 'Jean de Howden: poéte anglo-normand du XIIIe siècle', *Romania* 69 (1946–47), 469–519. For discussions of his identity, see A.J. Taylor, in Raby *Poems* (n. 182 below), pp. 270–4; Russell, *Dictionary*. He may be identical with a saintly John, prebendary of Howden in Yorkshire, but as the church was only

established in 1266 it seems surprising that he should derive his name from there. This prebendary has also been identified, by Taylor, with a John of Melton, but contemporary authorities say that he was born in London. The prebendary died in 1275 or 1276. A John of Hoveden was given a prebend at Bridgnorth in Shropshire in 1275; this surely rules out identification with the saintly John, as the latter was buried, in 1275 or 1276, at Howden. Russell mentions two other Johns of Hoveden, alive at the beginning of the fourteenth century.

182 *John Hovedens Nachtigallenlied*, ed. Clemens Blume (Leipzig, 1930). *Poems of John of Hoveden*, ed. F.J.E. Raby, Surtees Soc. 154 (London, 1939), with texts of all poems except the *Philomena*.

183 John of Howden was also an astronomer, author of the *Practica Chilindri*, ed. Edmund Brock, '*Practica Chilindri* or the Working of the Cylinder, by John Hoveden', in *Essays on Chaucer* (London, 1874), pp. 55–81 = *Chaucer Society*, 2nd series, 9, part 2. The link between poetry and technical mathematics is seen also in John Pecham (this volume, pp. 222–6) and of course later in Chaucer. It is evident also in anthologies such the Cerne Abbas collection, Trinity College, Cambridge, o.2.45 (this volume, p. 238), and Digby 166 (this volume, p. 308).

184 Two acrostics on the name MARIA are found in the Cambridge manuscript of Henry of Avranches.

185 Howden himself recast the *Philomena* into French verse as the *Rossignos*, addressing it to the Queen Mother Eleanor (thus, after 1272) and incidentally explaining its name: '. . . because as the nightingale makes out of diverse notes one melody, so does this book make out of diverse matters one harmony. And for this further reason it is called *Nightingale*, that it was made and contrived in a fair orchard in flower, where nightingales were just then singing'.

186 Most cantica vary between twelve and twenty quatrains; Cant. 47, to the Virgin, is a quinquagenum of fifty stanzas. The distribution of rhyme schemes is as follows: abab Cants. 1–10, 21–8, 32–5, 41–5; abcb Cants. 11–15, 31; abba Cants. 16–20, 29–30, 36–40, 46–50.

187 Cant. 42 is based on Dan. 3; Cant. 46 uses Ecclus. 12.

188 The fifteen joys are: Annunciation, Conception, Visitation, Nativity, Salutation, Adoration of the Magi, Presentation in the Temple, Return from Egypt, Jesus with the doctors, miracle at Cana, healing the sick, Resurrection, Ascension, Pentecost, Assumption of the Virgin.

189 See this volume, pp. 246–8, but cf. also pp. 327–8.

190 The little we know about him is summarized in *The Poems of Walter of Wimborne*, ed. A.G. Rigg (Toronto, 1978); see also Townsend (cited in n. 198 below).

191 This metre was popularized for satirical poetry by the ubiquitous *Apocalypsis Goliae* and *De coniuge non ducenda*.

192 Walter could have found Diogenes in Valerius Maximus, 4.3. *ext.* 4 or John of Hauville, *Architrenius* 6. 241–85; in 3–4 he combines the story of Naaman (4 Reg. 5: 27) with Horace, *Sat.* 1.3. 73–4.

193 See John A. Yunck, *The lineage of Lady Meed: the Development of Mediaeval Venality Satire* (Notre Dame, 1963). Some well-known Medieval Latin examples include John of Hauville, *Architrenius*, Books 5–6, Nigel Whiteacre, *Speculum Stultorum* 2585–650, *Carmina Burana*, Nos. 1, 10, 11.

194 A leaf is missing at the end of the poem; this could have contained a conclusion, and

perhaps a signature. The title, supplied by a sixteenth-century hand, is not very appropriate: *de avaritia* would have been better.

195 Compare *De Mundi Vanitate* 103/4–5: lepus erit tunc athleta, / lupus pastor, bos poeta.

196 They were added to Corpus Christi College, Oxford, MS 232 (which contains *Ave Virgo* and *De Mundi Vanitate*) by the same hand that added the *De Mundi Scelere*, and are printed in Appendix 2 of my edition of Walter (n. 190 above).

197 Partial edition by A. Kirkwood, Ph.D. thesis (Toronto, 1989); there are extracts in my edition of the poems, Appendix 3. Quotations were taken from it by the fourteenth-century friars Holcot and Lathbury: see Smalley, *English Friars*, pp. 365–8.

198 For his use of a very recent text, see D. Townsend, 'Robert Grosseteste and Walter of Wimborne', *MAe* 55 (1986), 113–17.

199 See above, n. 180. The compilation has a mainly biblical basis; it lists the Virgin's mental and physical attributes (silence, rest, face, cheeks, legs, etc.) and the images by which she can be described, e.g. cosmic (star, cloud, sea, mountain, snow, dew, moon), domestic (house, window, door, bed, stool, throne), culinary (oven, granary), potatory (tavern, wine), horticultural (plants, trees, fountain), animal (bee, ass, nest), container (medicine-chest, spice-box), vehicular (boat, chariot), martial (shield), and so on.

200 In Bodleian MS Digby 19, the poem has been entirely reorganized into three quinquagena, beginning *Ave, Salve, Gaude*; the poet's signature has been omitted. See my edition, Appendix 1.

201 Compare John of Garland, *Epithalamium*, this volume, p. 170.

202 In these stanzas there is a clear reminiscence of the Archpoet's *Confession*, st. 12, when he asks that wine be placed near his mouth when he dies, with angels to sing 'Sit Deus propitius huic potatori'.

203 This is reminiscent of the scene in the *Alexandreis* of Walter of Châtillon when Hell, aware that a great conqueror is going to conquer it, mistakes Alexander for the Saviour and has him assassinated.

204 The notion of Christ as a thief is in William de Montibus, *Versarius*, No. 1371 'Est Christus latro fur in mundo uel auerno'.

205 *CLP*, p. 391.

206 The *De Palpone* was abbreviated from 200 to 34 stanzas; the *De Mundi Vanitate* from 154 to 66½, and the *Marie Carmina* from 644 to 144. The *Marie Carmina* was also plundered for short hymns by Richard Ledrede (this volume, pp. 247–8) and another editor. For alteration of a different kind, see n. 200 above.

207 His name is pronounced with a soft *ch*; see D.L. Douie, *Archbishop Pecham* (Oxford, 1952); the poems receive little attention in this biography.

208 AH 50, 602–16, No. 398.

209 AH 50, 598–601, No. 397.

210 See this volume, p. 124 and n. 202.

211 AH 31, 111–14, No. 105.

212 AH 50, 598, No. 396.

213 AH 5, 19–22, No. 1.

214 AH 50, 594–6, Nos. 391–4.

215 E. Peeters, 'Vier Prosen des Johannes Pecham, OFM', *Franziskanische Studien* 4 (1917), 355–67.

216 The initials of each stanza form the series A–Z twice; at 22/1 read *Zabuli* for *Saeculi*.

217 See p. 223 above.

218 *Defensio Fratrum Mendicantium*, ed. C.L. Kingsford, in *Fratris Johannis Pecham . . . Tractatus tres de paupertate*, ed. C.L. Kingsford, A.G. Little, F. Tocco, British Society of Franciscan Studies 2 (1910), 148–98. For the attribution to the French Franciscan, Guy de la Marche, see Hans Pflaum, '*Sortes, Plato, Cicero*: Satirisches Gedicht des dreizehnten Jahrhunderts', *Speculum* 6 (1931), 499–533.

219 The first undamaged line of the poem is 'Heu miser quam misere'; it is in Cambridge, Univ. Lib. MS EE.6.6. Pecham's authorship (introduced with the phrase 'ut creditur') is unlikely on metrical grounds: the Goliardic stanzas often have eight syllables in the first half of the line and/or seven in the second half. There is even less reason to follow the catalogue in giving Pecham the poem on old age and repentance that precedes 'Heu miser' in the manuscript: there is no ascription in the manuscript, and the metre, quatrains of single-sound Leonines, is not elsewhere used by Pecham.

220 See above, n. 74 and pp. 199, 202–3.

221 *Gesta Abbatum Monasterii Sancti Albani*, ed. H.T. Riley, 3 vols. RS (London, 1867–69), I, 244–47. For Henry of Avranches' poem to Richard Marsh, see this volume, p. 191; on Hotoft's, see below.

222 See *Annales Monasticae*, ed. H.R. Luard, 5 vols. RS (London, 1864–9), 2, 253, 284–5, 304–27.

223 *Lanercost Chronicle* (see n. 225), p. 32; the poem is quoted anonymously (quodam monacho Dunelmensi) by Matthew Paris.

224 See *Annales Monasticae* (n. 222 above), 4, 414, 495, 503, 506–7, 510–11, 513, 514, 527, 543, 550, 556 (the prophetic verses on pp. 514–5 are in a different metre and probably not by Nicholas).

225 *Chronicon de Lanercost MCCI–MCCCXLVI*, ed. Joseph Stevenson, Bannatyne Club (Edinburgh, 1839), pp. 105–47.

226 On the prose satire on Edward's purge of judges, see this volume, pp. 235–6.

227 Wright, *Political Songs*, pp. 180–1.

228 Wright, *Political Songs*, pp. 160–79; the length varies in different manuscripts, and in one it is adapted to suit Edward III. It was once ascribed to Robert Baston (this volume, pp. 244–5).

229 See this volume, p. 167.

230 The *auctoritas* is from the *Ecloga Theoduli*.

231 Lehmann, *Parodie*, No. 10, pp. 205–11. In the second quotation, Lehmann reads *petencie*.

232 See Russell, *Dictionary*. The poem (inc. 'Synderesis rogitata refer', WIC 18977) is in Bodleian MS Digby 100 among others; it is unpublished. Prol. ed. *Hunt, I, 153–6.

233 See R.W. Hunt, 'Oxford Grammar Masters in the Middle Ages', in *Oxford Studies presented to Daniel Callus*, OHS n.s. 16 (Oxford, 1964), pp. 163–93, quoting a few lines from the *Neutrale*. Hunt was hesitant about the attribution of the *Deponentiale*, but Adam promises a treatise on deponent verbs, and the two poems are adjacent in MS Digby 100. Emden, *BRUO*, conjectured that Nutzard is the same as Adam Shidyard, a Merton scholar. See also (Tony) *Hunt, I, 152–3.

234 There are many anthologies of versified grammar. In addition to Digby 100, already cited, are, for example: St John's College, Oxford, MS 178, fols. 402–11; Gonville and Caius College, Cambridge, MS 136 (76); BL MS Harley 4967; Trinity College, Dublin, MS 270.

235 See my remarks, p. 138, on the importance of anthologies and anonymous texts.

236 Wright, *Mapes*, pp. 54–7.

237 Wright, *Mapes*, pp. 237–42.

238 Wright, *Mapes*, pp. 243–50.

239 A.G. Rigg, '*Metra de monachis carnalibus*: the three versions', *MJ* 15 (1980), 134–42; also Lehmann, *Parodie*, No. 5, pp. 194–5 (the continental version).

240 On Digby 65, see this volume, p. 237. There was also a continental adaptation of the poem to fit nuns.

241 Wright, *Mapes*, pp. 44–5.

242 W. Meyer, '*Quondam fuit factus festus*: ein Gedicht in Spottlatein', *Nachrichten von der königlichen Gesellschaft der Wissenschaften zu Göttingen*, Philologisch-Historische Klasse (Göttingen, 1908), 406–29.

243 See this volume, pp. 143–6.

244 Lehmann, *Parodie*, No. 16, pp. 233–41.

245 Wright, *Mapes*, pp. 69–70.

246 Wright, *Mapes*, pp. 180–2 ('Rumor novus Angliae'). Wright based his text on Titus A. xx (this volume, p. 308) and Vitellius A. x; the longest version is in Bodley 851 (this volume, pp. 307–8) and even this is incomplete, ending in the middle of a stanza. There is a version of thirty stanzas, all in Bodley 851, in Trinity College, Cambridge, o.2.45 (this volume, p. 238). Quotations are based on my own transcription.

247 Wright, *Mapes*, pp. 171–3. The relationship between 'Rumor novus Angliae', 'Prisciani regula', and 'Clerus et presbyteri' (Wright, *Mapes*, pp. 174–9, from Flacius Illyricus) remains to be disentangled.

248 Wright, *Political Songs*, pp. 46–51; critical edition in my thesis, i, 7–10, ii, 203–5; see also Raby, *SLP* 2, 210.

249 Ed. T. Wright, *Early mysteries and other Latin poems of the Twelfth and Thirteenth Centuries* (London, 1838), pp. 93–8; critical edition in my thesis, i, 146–56, ii, 356–70.

250 Ed. Wright, *Early Mysteries* pp. 99–106 with *Descriptio* (n. 249).

251 Ed. Wright, *Early Mysteries* (n. 249), pp. 49–51; see R.H. Hilton, 'A thirteenth-century poem on disputed villein services', *EHR* 56 (1941), 90–7.

252 See this volume, pp. 144, 229, 232; surprisingly, the *Gospel According to the Silver Mark* (Lehmann, *Parodie*, No. 1, pp. 183–8) does not seem to have circulated widely in England.

253 Lehmann, *Parodie*, No. 8, pp. 199–202.

254 See this volume, pp. 146–8, 149–50.

255 *Gawain on Marriage: the Textual Tradition of the De coniuge non ducenda*, ed. A.G. Rigg (Toronto, 1986).

256 See this volume, pp. 139–40.

257 Wright, *Mapes*, pp. 95–106, inc. 'Noctis sub silentio tempore brumali.'

258 Wright, *Mapes*, pp. 93–5, inc. 'Si quis cordis et oculi.'

259 Wright, *Mapes*, pp. 87–92, inc. 'Cum (Dum) tenerent omnia medium tumultum.'

260 Wright, *Mapes*, pp. 251–7. We should note here that the famous debate between Phyllis and Flora on the merits of knights and clerks (*Carmina Burana* No. 92, Wright, *Mapes*, pp. 258–67) is in only one English manuscript.

261 For a general study, see G. Zippel, 'La lettera del Diavolo al clero, dal secolo XII alla Riforma', *Bulletino dell' Istituto storico Italiano per il Medio aevo e Archivo Muratoviano* 70 (1958), 125–79; also Helen C. Feng, *Devil's Letters: their history and significance in church and society 1100–1500*, Ph.D. thesis, Northwestern Univ. (Illinois, 1982).

262 Ed. W. Wattenbach, "Über erfundene Briefe in Handschriften des Mittelalters,

besonders Teufelsbriefe', *Sitzungsberichte der königlich preussischen Akademie der Wissenschaften zu Berlin* (Berlin, 1892), Part I, 91–123 (ed. on pp. 104–16). The letter is in the fourteenth-century English anthologies Harley 913, Bodley 851, and Digby 166 (see this volume, pp. 307–8). For a further example of the genre, see pp. 275–6.

263 Interestingly, the quite genuine expression of dismay by the head of the Friars of the Sack was tacked onto the end of the satirical 'Princeps regionis gehennalis' in MS Digby 166; see *Speculum* 55 (1980), 84–90.

264 See this volume, pp. 153–4.

265 See R.W. Hunt, 'The collections of a monk of Bardney: a dismembered Rawlinson manuscript', *MARS* 5 (1961), 28–42.

266 See this volume, p. 151.

267 The fullest account of this manuscript is by Kingsford, *Song of Lewes* (n. 153 above).

268 See this volume, pp. 157–8 (politics), 157 (xenophobia), 158–9 (mendicant orders), 159–60 (universities).

269 See this volume, pp. 207–8.

4 Edward II to Henry V (1307–1422)

1 Smalley, *English Friars*, pp. 162–3.

2 See this volume, ch. 3, n. 185.

3 *The Works of William Herebert OFM*, ed. Stephen R. Reimer (Toronto, 1987).

4 *Vita Edwardi Secundi*, ed. N. Denholm-Young (London, 1957), p. 29.

5 Ed. Wright, *Political Songs*, pp. 258–61, and in my thesis, i, 160–2, ii, 378–82. Texts of Venantius Fortunatus may be found in many places, e.g. A.S. Walpole, *Early Latin Hymns* (Cambridge, 1922; rpt. Hildesheim, 1966), pp. 167–77, *Oxford Book of Medieval Latin Verse*, ed. F.J.E. Raby (Oxford, 1959), pp. 74–6. For other parodies of these hymns, see WIC Nos. 13611–13618, 20283.

6 The original reads:

> Vexilla regis prodeunt,
> fulget crucis mysterium,
> quo carne carnis conditor
> suspensus est patibulo

7 The original reads:

> Crux fidelis inter omnes, arbor una nobilis . . .
> Flecte ramos, arbor alta, tensa laxa uiscera,
> et rigor lentescat ille quem dedit natiuitas

8 Ed. Wright, *Political Songs*, pp. 268–72.

9 The text is in *Joannis de Fordun Scotichronicon cum supplementis et continuatione Walteri Boweri*, ed. W. Goodall, 2 vols. (Edinburgh, 1759), 2, 250–1. The poem was originally much longer: forty-three lines missing after line ten can be supplied from the fragment of the poem printed by W.D. Macray, 'Robert Baston's poem on the Battle of Bannockburn', *EHR* 19 (1904), 507–8: they concern the English preparations and boasting.

10 See A.G. Rigg, 'Antiquaries and authors: the supposed works of Robert Baston, O.

Carm.', in *Medieval Scribes, Manuscripts and Libraries: Essays Presented to N.R. Ker*, ed. M.B. Parkes and Andrew G. Watson (London, 1978), pp. 317–31; the attributions all go back to Bale, and many are manifestly wrong.

11 Ed. Wright, *Political Songs*, pp. 262–7.

12 Text in *Scotichronicon* (n. 9 above), pp. 254–5.

13 *The Latin Poems of Richard Ledrede, OFM, Bishop of Ossory 1317–1360*, ed. E. Colledge (Toronto, 1974); *The Lyrics of the Red Book of Ossory*, ed. R.L. Greene (Oxford, 1974); *The Latin Hymns of Richard Ledrede*, ed. T. Stemmler (Mannheim, 1975). The Red Book is a collection of legal, historical and diocesan records compiled after 1360. Ledrede probably composed the hymns, or some of them, not long after he left the London Greyfriars, where he had probably seen a copy of Walter of Wimborne (see this volume, p. 248).

14 Eight are in rhythmical asclepiads (see this volume, pp. 247–8), one in the regular Victorine sequence stanza.

15 Greene regarded the proportion of Christmas to Easter carols as relatively low, but his comparison is with vernacular collections; for a Latin songbook, the number of Christmas hymns is strikingly high, and a pointer to future liturgical developments.

16 See A.G. Rigg, 'The Red Book of Ossory', *MAe* 46 (1977), 269–78, a review-article on the three editions. On the *Marie Carmina*, see this volume, pp. 220–2.

17 The half-stanza combines *Marie Carmina* 31/1–2 with the second half of 30/3.

18 The only extant copy of the *Marie Carmina* is in Bodleian MS Laud misc. 368, a fifteenth-century manuscript from Durham. For a detailed comparison of the Ledrede and Paris poems with the original and the short B-text, see my article (n. 16 above). For the tendency for Walter of Wimborne's poems to be abridged, see this volume, p. 222 and n. 206.

19 AH 40, 208–9, No. 233; 46, 266–7, No. 226 (also in AH 52, 202, No. 221).

20 My reading of Rolle has greatly benefited from the study by Nicholas Watson, *Richard Rolle and the Invention of Authority* (Cambridge, 1991); I am grateful to Professor Watson for his advice on Rolle. The standard discussion of Rolle is by H.E. Allen, *Writings Ascribed to Richard Rolle, Hermit of Hampole, and Materials for his Biography* (New York, 1927). Dr Watson provides a much more convincing chronology for Rolle's works.

21 See *English Writings of Richard Rolle, Hermit of Hampole*, ed. H.E. Allen (Oxford, 1931), for a useful selection.

22 Editions of the principal Latin texts are as follows. *Incendium Amoris*, ed. M. Deanesly (Manchester, 1915); *Melos Amoris*, ed. E.J.F. Arnould (Oxford, 1957); *Contra amatores mundi*, ed. P.F. Theiner (Berkeley, 1968); *Richard Rolle de Hampole (1300–1349), vie et oeuvres, suivies du Tractatus super Apocalypsim*, ed. N. Marzac (Paris, 1968); *An edition of the 'Judica me Deus'*, ed. J.P. Daly (Salzburg, 1984); *Richard Rolle's Commentary on the 'Canticle of Canticles', edited from MS Trinity College, Dublin, 153*, ed. Elizabeth M. Murray, Ph.D. thesis (Fordham Univ., New York, 1958); Richard Rolle's *Expositio super novem lectiones mortuorum*, ed. M.R. Moyes, 2 vols. (Salzburg, 1988); A. Wilmart, 'Le cantique d'amour de Richard Rolle', *RAM* 21 (1940), 131–48 (also ed. by G.M. Liegey, 'The *Canticum Amoris* of Richard Rolle', *Traditio* 12 (1956), 369–91).

23 He makes few literary allusions. He once quotes Ovid (*Remedium Amoris* 344 in *Melos Amoris*, ch. 26, p. 78); an anonymous line 'Pontus erit siccus cum pauper habebit amicos' (*Incendium*, ch. 17, p. 197) sounds very much like Walter of Wimborne, but is not in his

extant works. On Rolle's use of Howden, see below, n. 27. He was, of course, well read in literature on meditation.

24 He rebukes Anselm for his recommendation of the monastic life (in *Melos Amoris*, ch. 47, and in his commentary on the Song of Songs). Much of Rolle's writing is self-justificatory: he defends himself against charges of frequently changing his hermitage, of living in the houses of the rich, of gluttony and self-indulgence (warning against the excesses of asceticism), and even of touching women, though he is usually keen to stress the dangers of association with women.

25 This is the chapter that begins 'Though I speak with the tongues of men and of angels, and have not charity, I am become as sounding brass or a tinkling cymbal.'

26 See this volume, pp. 208–15.

27 See Raby, *Minor Poems* (above, ch. 3, n. 182), pp. xxiv–xxvi.

28 *Melos*, pp. 85–97.

29 See, for example, *Incendium*, p. 195.

30 See J.A. Alford, 'Biblical *imitatio* in the writings of Richard Rolle', *English Literary History* 40 (1973), 1–23.

31 This is not the result of naive piety. A biography, written some years after his death, tells us that he studied at Oxford, where he presumably studied theology. His knowledge of the Bible is immense, and he had read widely in other mystical and pastoral writers. Once editorial and typographical errors are removed, his Latin can be seen to be sound, if idiosyncratic; he had full command of rhetorical figures such as *gradatio* and isocolon, and especially rhyme and alliteration. Thus, he had the intellectual freedom to choose what to say and how to say it.

32 In the *Contra amatores mundi* he poses a question that has troubled many readers: why did he bother to write down his experience, when other mystics did not? He suggests that the others may have been reluctant to cheapen their experiences, but he was driven by love to help others gain the same joy. He says that no one, not even the saints, has seen God face to face.

33 *Incendium* ch. 42, p. 277 (cf. *Melos* ch. 55, p. 178). John of Howden's *Philomena*, which Rolle knew (above, n. 27), does not use the symbolism of the nightingale. Neckam (*De Naturis Rerum* I, ch. 51, p. 102) compares the nightingale to the contemplative life, but his bird does not die. In John Pecham's *Philomena* (this volume, pp. 222–3) the nightingale signifies the human soul; it sings until it dies; it sings at the canonical hours rather than at night, and is not singing out of desire for its beloved.

34 Watson (n. 20 above), p. 178, writes that the *Melos* 'both is and is about *canor*. Hence the display of eloquence occurs on two levels: one conceptual, as the reader takes in "information" about *canor*; the other affective, as the reader participates in (is "informed" by) *canor*, through response to the alliterative eloquence the work "unveils".'

35 The passage is on p. 49 of the *Melos*. See G.M. Liegey, 'Richard Rolle's *Carmen prosaicum*, an edition and commentary', *MSt* 19 (1957), 15–36.

36 In some manuscripts the 'Oleum effusum' section was combined with an extract from the *Incendium* and other devotional pieces to form a separate treatise.

37 Stanzas 1–37 are Goliardic quatrains with internal rhyme in couplets; stanza 38 has $4 \times 7p + 5pp$; stanza 39 has four single-sound Leonine hexameters rhyming monosyllabically on -*i*. For the cyclic structure, compare *Pearl*, *Sir Gawain and the Green Knight*, and the *Anturs of Arther at the Tarnewathelan*.

38 I take this to mean: 'The glorious progeny (Christ) of the dripping honey (the Virgin), by right (juice?!) of the Father, is a thousand times sweeter; the sweetness of the hardening (sc. honey, i.e. the foetus) is redolent of cinnamon.' Walter of Wimborne writes often that honey kisses honey and produces honey (*Marie Carmina* st. 13 ff.)

39 AH 52, 345–8, No. 390.

40 See this volume, pp. 205–8.

41 See this volume, p. 75.

42 There are several editions, e.g. *Richard of Bury: Philobiblon*, ed. and transl. E.C. Thomas, revised by M. Maclagan (London, 1888, revised Oxford, 1960); *Riccardo de Bury: Philobiblon*, ed. A. Altamuri (Naples, 1954).

43 The catalogue is printed (without its foreign authors) by Tanner, pp. xvii–xliii. On the contents, see R.A.B. Mynors, 'The Latin classics known to Boston of Bury', in *Fritz Saxl 1890–1948: a Volume of Memorial Essays from his Friends in England*, ed. D.J. Gordon (London, 1957), pp. 199–217; on the authorship, see R.H. Rouse, 'Bostonus Buriensis and the author of the *Catalogus scriptorum ecclesiae*', *Speculum* 41 (1966), 471–99.

44 On his *Prohemia poetarum*, see this volume, p. 297.

45 Bale's first venture in literary history was the *Anglorum Heliades*, written in 1536, a history of English Carmelite writers. An English Carmelite, William of Coventry, also known as Claudus Conversus (fl. *c.* 1360?), wrote a verse history of the order, inc. 'Isidorus annos a principio tibi' (WIC 9593); the first twenty-one lines are extant in MS Bamberg Lit. 153, fol. 160ʳ.

46 For his commentary on John of Bridlington's Prophecy, see this volume, p. 268.

47 One of the books that came to Rede from Trillek was a copy of Walter of Wimborne's *Ave Virgo*. On Rede, Trillek and Sandwich, see F.M. Powicke, *The Medieval Books of Merton College* (Oxford, 1931), especially pp. 31, 87–91. Rede bequeathed his books to Merton College, where forty-three books have been identified as his; four more are in the Bodleian. On private libraries in this period, see Susan H. Cavanaugh, *A Study of Books Privately owned in England 1300–1450*, Ph.D. thesis (Univ. of Pennsylvania, 1980).

48 Beryl Smalley, *English Friars and Antiquity in the Early Fourteenth Century* (New York, 1960).

49 On Ridevall, see the next section; on Holcot's *Moralitates*, see this volume, p. 256. Both Holcot and Lathbury quote from Walter of Wimborne's *Quatuor Elementa*.

50 Thomas Walsingham made extensive use of Seneca's tragedies: see this volume, pp. 297–8.

51 On the *Epistola Valerii*, see this volume, pp. 89–90.

52 *Fulgentius Metaforalis*, ed. H. Liebeschütz (Leipzig, 1926). On Alberic of London, see this volume, p. 125.

53 The *Fulgentius Metaforalis* had an important continental influence. In 1341 the Benedictine (formerly Franciscan) scholar Pierre Bersuire, or Berchorius, completed a moralization of Ovid's *Metamorphoses*, using, among other sources, Petrarch's *Africa*. When this first version was printed in 1509 it was attributed to Thomas Waleys. Bersuire became aware of Ridevall's work and of the French *Ovide moralise*, and in 1359 produced a second edition of his Ovid commentary. For the use made of these mythographers by Thomas Walsingham, see this volume, pp. 297–8.

54 See this volume, pp. 31, 114–15, 163.

55 The major studies are by J.T. Welter, *L'Exemplum dans la littérature religieuse et didactique du moyen âge* (Paris, 1927); C. Bremond, J. LeGoff, J.-C. Schmitt, *L'Exemplum*,

Typologie des sources du moyen âge occidental, fasc. 40 (Turnhout, 1982). The best way to obtain an overview of the genre is to read through Vol. 3 of Ward-Herbert's Catalogue.

56 *Gesta Romanorum* (Oesterley ed., see n. 64), No. 32, Holcot's *Convertimini* (below, n. 63), No. 1; the ultimate source is Seneca, *Quaestiones naturales* 2, 31.

57 *Gesta Romanorum* No. 60, Holcot *Moralitates* (see n. 63), No. 35; the ultimate source is the story of Atalanta, Ovid, *Metam.* 10. 560–680.

58 *Gesta Romanorum* No. 41, from Valerius Maximus, 5, 6 *ext.* 1.

59 *Le Speculum Laicorum*, ed. J.T. Welter (Paris, 1914); see Ward-Herbert 3, 370–405; the ascription to Howden goes back to Bale.

60 *Les Contes moralisés de Nicole Bozon*, ed. L. Toulmin-Smith and P. Meyer (Paris, 1889), pp. 195–227; Ward-Herbert 3, 100–5. The *Liber exemplorum* (Ward-Herbert 3, 414–23) is probably French in origin.

61 See Siegfried Wenzel, *Verses in Sermons: Fasciculus Morum and its Middle English Poems* (Cambridge, Mass., 1978); the *Fasciculus Morum* was probably the direct source for the exempla in BL MS Harley 7322 (Ward-Herbert 3, 166–79).

62 The work is only available in early printed editions; for a list, see T. Kaepelli, *Scriptores Ordinis Praedicatorum Medii Aevi* 2 (Rome, 1975), 392–4; for the date, see L.E. Boyle in *Speculum* 48 (1973), 533–7.

63 The *Moralitates* is available only in early printed editions: see Ward-Herbert 3, 107, and 116–55 for a summary of *Convertimini*. Thomas Waleys' *Moralitates* is not an exempla collection but a series of notes for sermons or lectures; it does, however, include several exempla and was used by other preachers: one of its stories is in the *Gesta Romanorum*.

64 *Gesta Romanorum*, ed. H. Oesterley, 2 vols. (Berlin, 1872); *Die Gesta Romanorum nach der Innsbrucker Handschrift vom Jahre 1342*, ed. W. Dick, Erlanger Beiträge zur englischen Philologie 7 (Erlangen, 1890). The Middle English version is ed. S.J.H. Herrtage, EETS e.s. 33 (1879).

65 The fables are in Hervieux 4, 417–50; for an account of him, see G. Mifsud, *John Sheppey, Bishop of Rochester, as a Preacher and Collector of Sermons*, B. Litt. thesis (Oxford, 1953).

66 Horstman suggested that he was both vicar of Tynemouth and a monk at Tynemouth Priory, and that he then went to St Albans, taking on the mantle of the great line of St Albans historians leading from Matthew Paris to Thomas Walsingham, and that he died in the Black Death 1348–9. V.H. Galbraith, however (in *Essays in History Presented to R.L. Poole*, ed. H.W.C. Davis (Oxford, 1927), pp. 379–98) dismissed the notion that he was ever a monk; our only contemporary authority, Henry of Kirkstede (this volume, p. 254), does not mention that he was a monk and gives his floruit date as 1366. John also wrote a world history, *Historia Aurea*, from creation to 1347; one manuscript of it, Bodley 240, contains another series of saints' lives: some duplicate the *Sanctilogium*, some are expansions (e.g. Edmund), some are additions.

67 *Nova Legenda Anglie*, ed. C. Horstman, 2 vols. (Oxford, 1901). The only known manuscript, BL Cotton Tiberius E.1, was presented to the monks of Redburn by Thomas de la Mare, abbot of St Albans (1349–96), who had been prior of Tynemouth (1341–9). The manuscript is so badly damaged that Horstman was obliged to use the Wynkyn de Worde edition of 1516, thus following its alphabetical organization and its misleading title.

68 A fifteenth-century redactor, once incorrectly identified as Capgrave, reorganized the

lives alphabetically, from Adrian to Wulfstan. Note that Alexander of Ashby (this volume, pp. 131–2) also followed a calendrical order, but began with Andrew on 30 November.

69 John says that he had found many other legends of Kyned in a place in Wales, but the manuscript was worn away by age.

70 See this volume, p. 127.

71 See this volume, pp. 51–61, 96–9.

72 See this volume, pp. 204–5, 296.

73 See this volume, pp. 244–5, 284–5.

74 See this volume below, pp. 262–23. A poet whose work has been almost entirely lost is Robert of Syreston, a monk of Durham, who wrote a poem in honour of the prior John Fossor (d. 1374); five lines have been preserved by Henry Wharton, *Anglia Sacra* (London, 1691), I, 768.

75 See this volume, pp. 294–5, 293–4.

76 Richard Sharpe, 'An *Exortacio ad contemplacionem* from Farne Island', *MAe* 54 (1985), 159–77. The outer limits of the dates are 1195 and the late fifteenth century.

77 *Political Poems* I, 26.

78 Another poem, *Disputatio inter Anglicum et Francum*, inc. 'Anglia faex hominum' (*Political Poems* I, 91–3) is probably of this period. It concerns French manners – hair-style, complexion, elocution, gait, etc. The Frenchman first defends himself against criticisms of his manners, and then the Englishman attacks him for them. Scholars have assumed that something is lacking at the beginning, but it is much simpler to reverse the two speeches: this is a debate in which the Frenchman has the last word (presumably composed by a French author), which has been altered by the English scribe of BL Cotton Titus A. xx to give the appearance of an English win in the contest. It consists of seventy-two non-rhyming elegiac couplets, a metre not in favour for political poetry in England until later in the century.

79 *Political Poems* I, 26–40. The version in BL Cotton Titus A. xx and Bodleian Rawlinson B. 214 contains 394 lines. The relationship between Bodley 851, Titus and Rawlinson (see this volume, pp. 307–8, 312) is complex, especially in the poem on Neville's Cross 'Corda superborum', this volume, pp. 261–2 and n. 81; I am inclined to think that the Bodley version is closer to the original.

80 Edward III used these arguments in a letter to Pope Benedict XII asking for his support; the pope, after a long delay, wisely refrained from commenting on the theological arguments and simply hoped for peace. The legend that Hugh Capet was a butcher is alluded to in John of Bridlington's Prophecy: see my article cited there (n. 90).

81 *Political Poems* I, 41–51. Wright's text, a conflation of the version in Bodley 851 with that in the Titus and Rawlinson manuscripts (n. 79 above), is very difficult to disentangle. The Titus/Rawlinson version has 238 lines; the two versions have many unique lines. Titus/Rawlinson have twenty-six lines before the line 'Corda super-borum', of which the first couplet is found in the middle of the Bodley 851 version of the poem on Crecy:

> Dux Valeys hinnit, Francia grunnit, territa tinnit,
> Francia plorat, falsa colorat, se dehonorat

These twenty-six lines contain the images of Philip as a lion and Edward as an eagle; this conflicts with the imagery in the Crecy poem. What is needed is a parallel edition of both versions; it is very unlikely that Wright's composite poem ever existed.

82 The poet's pun on the name *Percy* 'pierce' ('acies fortes penetravit', 'Percy persequitur') is also seen in John of Bridlington's Prophecy.

83 Ed. in Joseph Stevenson, *Illustrations of Scottish History* (Glasgow, 1834), pp. 63–72.

84 E.g. 5/4–6/1 'Nam patet per exitum qualis fuit fructus. / Fructus parvus affuit . . .' See this volume, p. 228, for concatenation in the poem on the battle of Falkirk in 1298.

85 *Political Poems* I, 40–1.

86 *Political Poems* I, 52–3. In the later Rawlinson manuscript, 1–10 and 11–18 are attached to their respective poems, and the two rhythmical stanzas are incorrectly attached to a copy of the Falkirk poem mentioned in n. 84 above.

87 *Political Poems* I, 53–8. It is one of the poems incorrectly assigned to Robert Baston: see this volume, p. 245 and n. 10.

88 Compare Irish *trogae*, pl. *troga*, glossing 'aerumnae', Middle Welsh *trwc*, *trwch* 'sad, wretched'.

89 Modern research has tended to confirm the story of the seventeenth-century antiquary John Selden that the much-married Joan of Kent (in 1347 she was between two husbands, Thomas Holland and William Montagu, earl of Salisbury, and later became the wife of the Black Prince and thus mother of Richard II) was also the object of Edward III's affections, and that it was in defence of her honour that the Order of the Garter was established. See references in my article on John of Bridlington (next note), pp. 600–1.

90 Ed. *Political Poems* 2, 123–215, with the Ergom commentary; critical edition of the verses by M.J. Curley, *Versus Propheciales: Prophecia Johannis Bridlingtoniensis, an edition*, Ph.D. thesis (Chicago, 1973). See A.G. Rigg, 'John of Bridlington's Prophecy: a new look', *Speculum* 63 (1988), 596–613, for the argument that Ergom is not the author of the Prophecy (also see this volume, p. 268 and n. 95) and that John of Bridlington himself (d. 1379) may have been. Early parts of the Prophecy were incorporated into a chronicle written at Bridlington by 1339.

91 The use of verse prophecies remained popular at all periods. The fourteenth-century *Eulogium Historiarum* (ed. F.S. Haydon, RS, 3 vols. (London, 1858–63), I, 417–20) connects three verse prophecies with the conquest of Ireland and Edward III: 'Ter tria lustra' (6 lines), 'Illius imperium' (4 lines attributed to Alanus Somniator Religiosus), and 'Anglia transmittet leopardum' (13 lines). All three could go back to the Merlin tradition of prophecy (see this volume, p. 47), but the last is closer in its symbolism to John of Bridlington and the literature surrounding Edward III's claim to France; in Rawlinson B. 214 it is associated with Henry VI's similar claim to France.

92 See this volume, p. 261 and n. 80.

93 See this volume, pp. 299–301.

94 See this volume, p. 254; M.R. James, 'The catalogue of the library of the Augustinian friars at York', *Fasciculus J.W. Clark dicatus* (Cambridge, 1909), pp. 2–96. Ergom dedicated his commentary to Humphrey, seventh earl of Hereford, Essex and Northampton (1361–72); he became prior of Bridlington in 1385, but in 1386 went to the papal curia and thence to Naples.

95 See my article cited in n. 90. Briefly my argument is that Ergom was commenting on a defective text of the Prophecy, that several of his interpretations of the number codes are unnecessarily strained (when the answers 1347 and 1348 fit easily), and that most of the poems fit the events up to 1349 much more closely than those up to 1364.

96 Texts in *Formularies which bear on the History of Oxford c. 1204–1420*, ed. H.E. Salter, W.A. Pantin and H.G. Richardson, Oxford Historical Soc. n.s. 4 (Oxford, 1942), I, 108–11.

97 See this volume for his hostility to the friars, pp. 270, 272.

98 H. Furneaux, 'Poems relating to the riot between town and gown on St Scholastica's Day, Feb. 10, 1355', in *Collectanea* III, ed. M. Burrows, Oxford Historical Soc. 32 (Oxford, 1896), pp. 163–87.

99 In the poem the friars are praised for their assistance to the university (107–8). On Tryvytlam, see this volume, pp. 273–4; it should be noted, however, that his asclepiads do not have internal rhyme.

100 *ursina vada* 'bear ford, Bereford'; *vada precis* 'bead (prayer) ford, Bedeford'.

101 From the writers mentioned so far in chs 3–4 we may point to: Walter of Wimborne, John Pecham, Robert Baston, Richard Ledrede, the 'classicizing friars', Robert Holcot, John Ridevall.

102 For an overview, see Penn R. Szittya, *The Antifraternal Tradition in Medieval Literature* (Princeton, 1986). For the *Defensio Fratrum Mendicantium* (before 1274, once ascribed to Pecham), see this volume, p. 226 and n. 218.

103 For Henry of Avranches' versification of the prophecy and Matthew Paris' interpretation of it, see this volume, pp. 186, 198

104 See this volume, p. 237 and n. 263.

105 This may be alluded to by John of Bridlington's line on 1349 'Ecclesie patres solvent hoc tempore fratres' (III.II), which is cleverly ambiguous: will the fathers of the church dissolve the friars, or the other way round?

106 On Fitzralph, see this volume, pp. 268, 272.

107 On verse contests, this volume, pp. 188–91.

108 Ed. P.R. Szittya, '"Sedens super flumina" a fourteenth-century poem against the friars', *MSt* 41 (1979), 30–43; the fiction that the author had been recruited by the friars (see next note) led Bale to attribute the poem to Peter Pateshull. The O-and-I refrain was popular at this time in both Latin and vernacular verse.

109 This fiction, used also against monks, was a popular poetic topos: see my 'William Dunbar: the fenyeit freir', *RES* n.s. 14 (1963), 269–73.

110 Ed. W. Heuser, 'With an O and an I', *Anglia* 27 (1904), 283–319; for a new text and commentary, see my thesis, i, 132–8, ii, 341–6.

111 See note 109 above.

112 Ed. A.G. Rigg, 'Two Latin poems against the friars', *MSt* 30 (1968), 106–18.

113 Ed. H. Furneaux in *Collectanea* III (see above, note 98), pp. 188–209; revised edition with commentary in my thesis, i, 115–31, ii, 333–41.

114 He was possibly the author of the *Cronica sive Antiquitates Glastoniensis Ecclesie*: see the edition by James P. Carley, *The Chronicle of Glastonbury Abbey* (Woodbridge, Suffolk, 1985), pp. xxix–xxx.

115 Ed. Rigg (see n. 112).

116 Unpublished; 'Achab diu studuit' is followed by 'Sedens super flumina' and (added) 'Heu quanta desolatio' (this volume, pp. 281–2). The manuscript, mainly an antifraternal collection, oddly contains 'Belial apostatarum' (n. 119).

117 The rhymes and pattern of lines 1–2 and 3–4 of each stanza (illustrated in the quoted stanza) are repeated in each second stanza. The 'collateral' rhymes of the refrain seem most suitable for chanting.

118 See this volume, pp. 236–7.

119 Ed. Wattenbach (ch. 3, n. 262), pp. 116–21, from Bodleian MS Digby 98 (see n. 116 above).

120 John of Gaunt was a patron of Revesby Abbey; a 'Walter atte Burgh' witnessed a document for him in 1372.

121 *Political Poems* I, 97–122, a composite text based on MSS Rawlinson B. 214 and Digby 166.

122 For Pedro's final fate, see Chaucer, *Monk's Tale*, 3565–80.

123 The symmetry is very strained historically: Henry, Sancho and Thilo were all illegitimate sons of Alfonso, but their legitimate brother Pedro was brother to the Black Prince and John of Gaunt only by treaty.

124 An exposition of the Metamorphoses in Bodleian MS Rawlinson B.214 (which has a text of Walter's poem on Najera just before it) is ascribed by the Bodleian Quarto Catalogue to Walter, but this is untenable; the Exposition is simply a summary of the fables in the Metamorphoses, with no interpretation (Christian or otherwise), and is in prose, whereas Walter makes it clear that his interpretation was in verse.

125 On Alain's probable authorship of the poem ('Vix nodosum valeo'), see M.-T. D'Alverney, *Alain de Lille: textes inédits* (Paris, 1965), pp. 42–4; she prints the extra stanzas by Walter on p. 43.

126 *Political Poems* I, 94–6.

127 See this volume, pp. 299–301.

128 Cambridge, Gonville and Caius College, MS 230 (116), fols. 112^r–116^v. On the metre, see this volume, p. 270 and n. 108; the phrase 'With an O and an I' is not written in the manuscript, but is clearly needed. The date is uncertain: the arguments are appropriate to 1371, when the reformers, led by two Austin friars, convinced parliament of Edward III's right to tax the clergy. Wycliffe was present at the parliament and was already known for his views on possessions, but he had not yet stepped into extreme forms of unorthodoxy. It could be somewhat later than 1371, but the absence of any discussion of Wycliffe's other views means that it could not have been written after 1377. Also, there is no mention of the papal schism.

129 William of Ockham's treatise, 'An rex Angliae pro succursu guerrae possit recipere bona ecclesiarum', was written for Edward III in about 1338–40.

130 *Political Poems* I, 253–63.

131 For literature on the Peasants' Revolt, see this volume, pp. 283–4, 287–8.

132 On this fiction, see this volume, pp. 270–1, 272 and n. 109.

133 John Wells, a monk of Ramsey and prominent anti-Wycliffite, was owner of MS Bodley 851, which contained Walter Map's *De Nugis Curialium*, Latin satire, and the Z-version of Piers Plowman. See this volume, pp. 307–8.

134 *Political Poems* I, 231–49. The metre, 8pp rhyming aabaabbbabba, is that of John of Howden's *Cythara*, this volume, pp. 212–13.

135 Another anti-Wycliffite writer of some literary interest was William of Rymington (DNB s.Rimston); in 1382 he drew up a list of forty-five heretical propositions in Wycliffe's teachings; this is preceded by a verse prologue. He was prior of the Cistercian abbey of Sawley (and thus a successor of Stephen Easton, this volume, pp. 207–8). His *Stimulus peccatoris* is a series of meditations that draws heavily on Anselm (ed. Robert O'Brien in *Cîteaux* 16 (1965), 278–304).

136 *Political Poems* I, 227–30.

137 *auster* 'south, Sud-', *bacca* 'berry, -bury'.

138 *dux stramineus* 'straw leader, Jack Straw'.

139 In Fordun's *Scotichronicon* (above, n. 9), 2, 406–14; in the chronicle the poet is named 'de Barry'. I have used the name given him by Bale.

140 See this volume, pp. 193–8 and n. 144.

141 Four lines (249–52, p. 412) seem to be rhythmical; they rhyme internally on *-atis* but finally on *quili-bet, anili-ter, juvenili-ter, vili.*

142 He was a member of the order by 1376 and died in 1396. In about 1380 he wrote a treatise *Protectorium pauperis* against the anti-mendicant Oxford theologian John Ashwardby; an acephalous copy is preserved in MS Digby 98 (see above, note 116). For his English poem, see EETS 155 (1917), pp. xvi–xvii, 103–4.

143 *Political Poems* I, 282–300; for a synopsis and partial translation, see Glynne Wickham, *Early English Stages 1300–1660*, Vol. I *1300 to 1576* (London/New York, 1963), pp. 63–71.

144 Gower's first version of the *Vox Clamantis* was written some time after 1381. The name 'Troy' for London goes back to Geoffrey of Monmouth.

145 Probably 'Male-bouche', the personification of slanderous gossip, who separates the lover from his rose in the *Romance of the Rose*.

146 Little is known about his life. By 1398 (when he married) he was living in lodgings in the priory of St Mary Overey in Southwark; shortly after 1400 he went blind, and died in 1408. He was certainly not in orders, but his profession (merchant and lawyer have been proposed) is unknown. His name appears in documents from 1378, and he may have been involved in litigation as early as 1365 (the 'Septvauns affair'), but the traditional date given for his birth, 1330, seems unnecessarily early: 1340 or even 1350 are equally possible. He was a friend of Chaucer.

147 The effigy on his tomb wore the collar presented to him by Henry in 1393.

148 *The Complete Works of John Gower*, ed. G.C. Macaulay, Vol. 4 *The Latin Works* (Oxford, 1902), pp. 20–213. As all his Latin works are in this volume I give no further references. For the chronology of his revisions, I follow, for the most part, Maria Wickert, *Studien zu John Gower* (Cologne, 1953): the whole work, including the *Visio*, was first completed some time after 1381, but was revised later, probably after 1399, when parts were rewritten to make it appear to predict Richard's eventual downfall (see next note). The title (Matt. 3: 3) is particularly apt, as John the Baptist was Richard II's favourite saint (see this volume, p. 286). On the metre: Walter of Peterborough used unrhymed elegiacs for his prologue (p. 276).

149 The verse epistle on pp. 1–2 was added, after the final revision, in the presentation copy made for Archbishop Arundel.

150 For example, Nigel Whiteacre *Speculum Stultorum*, Circe's transformation of Ulysses' crew into swine, the Gadarene swine of the Gospel, and the plagues of Egypt.

151 Books II–VII are linked to Book I by reference to the 'heavenly voice' that commanded him to write, but the fact that the title is first given in Book II probably indicates that Book I was a separate work. The absence of any mention of the Schism in the first version of the estates satire led Wickert to date it to before 1378, but a marginal note (at III.375) gives a probably correct allusion to the Norwich Crusade of 1383, and there is an allusion to 'yesterday's deeds' that seems to refer to the Peasants' Revolt.

152 In fact, he also deals with other estates, such as merchants and lawyers. He gives far more attention (two books) to religious orders than to the other estates (8 chapters to knights, 2 to peasants, 4 to merchants, 6 to lawyers), no doubt because there was more

anticlerical, antimonastic, and antifraternal satire on which to draw.

153 See this volume, p. 103, for Burnellus' eclectic rule.

154 See G.R. Owst, *Literature and Pulpit in Medieval England*, 2nd ed. (Oxford, 1961), pp. 93–7; Ward–Herbert 3, 30 (from Jacques de Vitry).

155 This is one of the passages that was drastically revised, probably after 1399, to criticize Richard strongly.

156 For Chaucer's methods, see Jill Mann, *Chaucer and Medieval Estates Satire* (Cambridge, 1973).

157 This is a medieval commonplace; see *Vox Clamantis* v, 53–78.

158 That is, the earls of Gloucester, Warwick, Arundel and Derby (the future Henry IV), supported by the Earl of Northumberland. The Boar is the earl of Oxford.

159 For dramatic effect Gower has removed this event out of chronological sequence to the end of the section.

160 The idea that Richard was in flight is a Lancastrian interpretation.

161 See this volume, pp. 299–301.

162 Other poems in honour of Henry are: 'Rex celi Deus est' (adapted from *Vox Clamantis* VI.xviii, where they were originally addressed to Richard II), 'H. aquile pullus', 'O recolende bene', and 'O Deus immense'. His other late poems include one on the comet of 1402 and the verses for his own tombstone.

163 See Siân Echard and Claire Fanger, *The Latin Verses in the Confessio Amantis: an annotated translation* (Lansing, Michigan, 1991).

164 In *York Historians* 2, 446–63; Raine conjectured that its author might be John of Allhallowgate, who wrote the first part of another verse history of York mentioned in this volume, p. 311 n. 6.

165 See this volume, pp. 52–3.

166 *Political Poems* 2, 114–18. Wright used BL MS Cotton Faustina B.ix, which has seventeen stanzas; I have corrected this from the version added in Bodley 851 (this volume, p. 307), which has twenty-one stanzas and a somewhat better text. The extra stanzas are very hostile to the king and may have been deleted by the Faustina scribe.

167 The stanzas are of eight lines, aaabcccb; the a- and c-lines are rhythmical asclepiads and the b-lines are 8pp. The rhymes are not always exact.

168 S.B. Gaythorpe, 'Richard Esk's metrical account of Furness Abbey', *Transactions of the Cumberland and Westmoreland Antiquarian and Archaeological Soc.* n.s. 53 (1954), 98–109.

169 *dives-durus* = 'rich-hard'; in *est* substitute the tenth letter of the alphabet (*k*) for the nineteenth (*t*).

170 J. Hammer, 'The poetry of Johannes Beverus with extracts from his *Tractatus de Bruto abbreviato*', *Modern Philology* 34 (1936–7), 119–32.

171 It is incorporated into the *Eulogium Historiarum* (above, n. 91), 2, 216–8.

172 See this volume, pp. 204–5.

173 Space given to reigns is as follows: Edward I (1–108), Edward II (109–40), Edward III (141–200), Richard II (201–60). The continuation is in BL MSS Harley 1808 and 2386, both closely related.

174 See this volume, pp. 143–4, 88–93, 93, 128–9, 258, 255–7, and G.T. Shepherd, 'The emancipation of story in the twelfth century', in *Medieval Narrative: a Symposium*, ed. H. Bekker-Nielsen and others (Odense, 1979), pp. 44–57.

175 See this volume, pp. 54, 127–8.

176 M.R. James, 'Twelve medieval ghost-stories', *EHR* 37 (1922), 413–22; James did not print two of the stories. See also H.E.D. Blakiston, 'Two more medieval ghost-stories', *EHR* 38 (1923), 85–7; one of these concerns Lancashire, the other Ely.

177 The fullest account is by V.H. Galbraith, *The St Albans Chronicle 1406–1420* (Oxford, 1937); see also Gransden, ch. 5, pp. 118–56. He wrote (or supplemented) several contemporary histories and the chronicle of the abbey. His *Ypodigma Neustriae*, a history of England from 911 (beginning with Normandy) to 1419, was dedicated to Henry V.

178 His unpublished *Historia Alexandri* was apparently a conflation of the life by Valerius and the 'St Albans compilation' (see this volume, ch. 1, n. 132).

179 An edition is being prepared by Dianne Heriot, Monash University, Australia. The *Prohemia* is unfinished and the extant text, BL MS Harley 2693, seems to have been Walsingham's working copy. There are two accounts of Statius and Claudian; only eight of ten promised Senecan tragedies are discussed; there are gaps, not always filled, for illustrative quotations or new material.

180 *Thomae Walsingham De Archana Deorum*, ed. R.A. van Kluyve (Durham, N.C., 1968).

181 His sources include Alberic of London (see this volume, p. 125; like many medieval writers, Walsingham ascribed this to Alexander Neckam), the Second Vatican Mythographer, Berchorius, Arnulf of Orléans, and other mythographers. Other Anglo-Latin interpreters of Ovid include John of Garland and Walter of Peterborough (see this volume, pp. 168, 277–8). The late fifteenth-century manuscript Rawlinson B. 214 (see this volume, p. 312) also has a fable-by-fable explication.

182 A transcription of the text was made by E.A. Holtze, Ph.D. thesis (Univ. of Nebraska, 1974). The *Dites* was written after the *Arcana*, to which it refers.

183 Here too Walsingham avoids Christian interpretations or moralizations; it is interesting that he nowhere attempts to relate ancient geography to contemporary history.

184 In *Memorials of Henry the Fifth*, ed. C.A. Cole, RS (London, 1858), pp. 63–75, inc. 'Ad Salvatoris laudes'.

185 On Elmham, see Gransden 2, 194–219, C.L. Kingsford, *English Historical Literature in the Fifteenth Century* (Oxford, 1913), pp. 45–50. The prose works include: an unfinished *Speculum Augustinianum*, a history of St Augustine's, complete only to the year 806, but with notes and documents up to 1192 (preceded by a synchronic table); an unpublished *Cronica regum Angliae* in tabular form, in three periods, Hengist-Augustine, Augustine-Conquest, Conquest-present (the extant manuscript breaks off at 1389); he says that he had also written a prose account of the first five years of Henry V's reign, but this is no longer identified with the *Gesta Henrici Quinti*: see J.S. Roskell and F. Taylor, in *BJRL* 53 (1970–71), 428–64; 54 (1971–72), 223–40.

186 *Political Poems* 2, 118–23. There are two short unpublished poems in MS Rawlinson B. 214: forty lines on the years from Brutus to the Norman Conquest and on kings who had died violent deaths; forty-seven Leonine hexameters on the kings of England (one line each) from Ethelbert to Henry V.

187 The six hexameters that follow must have been written later, after 1421, as they spell out acrostics on Henry V and Queen Catherine.

188 Ed. Cole (see n. 184 above), pp. 79–165.

189 For example, *Gesta*: 'Vetus Castrum (i.e. Oldcastle) cum sua vetustate et novitate traditus Sathane'; *Liber metricus*:

Namque Vetus Castrum, cui fit damnosa vetustas,
Profugus inde fugit cum novitate fera,
Traditus hic Sathanae . . . (125-7)

The *Gesta* (see n. 185 above) ends in 1416, and both works have many details not in the other, but there is no doubt that Elmham for the most part followed it closely, recording minor incidents in the same sequence.

190 Cole destroys the chronogram by classicizing the spelling to *Babylon*. Almost every chapter of the *Liber metricus* has at least one, sometimes several, chronograms. On John of Bridlington's use of them, see this volume, p. 267.

191 In the Rawlinson manuscript this is followed by a brief poem 'laudes Anglicane', also possibly by Elmham.

192 He was the dedicatee of Walsingham's *Arcana deorum* (this volume, pp. 297-8).

193 They have been studied, with extracts, by V.H. Galbraith, 'John Seward and his circle', *MARS* 1 (1941), 85-104. My account here is totally indebted to Galbraith's article. The works are: *Hisagoga metrica, Mamilla, Somnium, Metristencheridion*, (lost) *Cathametron* (prosody); *Arpyilogus, Brachilexis Sancte Arpyie, Antelopologie* (allegory and mythology); *Ludicra, Invectiva, Epigrammata* (verse experiments).

194 His correspondents include William Relyk, William Sheffield, Richard Altham, 'J.W.', John Leland, and a Henry. The John Leland (Leylond) to whom he wrote laudatory epigrams was himself author of at least four grammatical treatises and taught at Oxford as a grammarian; he was probably an ancestor of the famous antiquary, and he died in 1428. Another grammarian, Richard Kendale (d. 1431), was credited by Bale with a series of grammatical works, but none seem to be extant.

195 R. Weiss, *Humanism in England during the Fifteenth Century*, 3rd ed. (Oxford, 1967).

196 The predominance of satire in most of the anthologies discussed here and in earlier chapters is the result of a circular process: I was first drawn to the anthologies in search of distribution patterns of satirical, particularly 'Goliardic', poems. There are doubtless many other types of anthology that I have never examined.

197 See this volume, pp. 149-50, 150-3, 236-8.

198 See this volume, pp. 150, 308.

199 Ed. J. Bolte, in *ZfdA* 35, n.s. 23 (1891), 257-61.

200 Wright, *Mapes*, pp. 208-12.

201 Wright, *Mapes*, pp. 147-8; see WIC 3934.

202 See this volume, pp. 143-4, 229, 232, 235, 236-7.

203 H. Walther, 'Versifizierte Paternoster und Credo', *Revue du Moyen Age latin* 20 (1964), 45-64 (texts pp. 54-6). On this manuscript, see this volume, p. 308.

204 *Glastonbury Miscellany*, pp. 117-22. The manuscript itself (see this volume, pp. 311-12) is fifteenth century, but most of the verse is of the fourteenth century or earlier. For references to the St Uritha material, see ibid. p. 100.

205 See this volume, p. 226 and n. 219. It occurs in a grouping of poems in the devotional manuscript Cambridge Univ. Lib. Ee.6.6 (s. xiv, late), which comprise: 'Dum iuuenis creui' (WIC 4883), the poem in question, Pecham's *Philomena*, and 'Cur mundus militat'.

206 Two prominent treatments of the theme in Anglo-Latin are by Lawrence of Durham and Walter of Wimborne (this volume, pp. 58, 216-17), but almost every religious poet expresses it somewhere.

207 Ed. A.G. Rigg, in *MAe* 36 (1967), 249–52. At the time of writing the article (and when writing my thesis) I was unaware of a copy in Sion College, London, MS Arc. L.40.2/ L.12, which confirms that the poem is no later than the fourteenth century: see N.R. Ker, *Medieval Manuscripts in British Libraries*, I: *London* (Oxford, 1969), p. 273. The poem is in the *Glastonbury Miscellany* and was also incorporated into the English treatise 'Disce mori', which contains several Latin poems.

208 *Political Songs*, pp. 224–30; on the manuscript, see this volume, p. 307.

209 Wright, *Mapes*, pp. 229–36; the poem is among those incorrectly ascribed by Bale to Robert Baston. It is preserved solely in Titus A.xx and Rawlinson B.214, the sister-manuscripts described in this volume, pp. 308, 312.

210 *Glastonbury Miscellany*, pp. 123–9 (see also next note). The date is uncertain: Stephen's name is not in any of the lists of monks made in 1338–40, 1377, or 1456. The first half-line often has only five syllables; once the second half-line has seven syllables.

211 *Philomena* (ch. 3, n. 182), stanzas 1091–5; I was not aware of the Howden source when I made my edition; the notes need to be adjusted and the text at 90 should read 'prunas pugnancium et Petrus spreuerat'.

212 Ed. K. Strecker, 'Zwei mittellateinische Gedichten', *Zeitschrift für deutsche Philologie* 51 (1926), 117–19; the manuscript is s. xiv, not s. xiii (see this volume, p. 308).

213 Ed. H. Walther, 'Zur lateinischen Parodie des Mittelalters', *ZfdA* 84 (1952–3), 265–73.

214 Ed. Strecker (above, n. 212).

215 Ed. A.G. Rigg, in *Anglia* 85 (1967), 127–37; in Trinity College, Cambridge, MS O.9.38 (the sole source, see this volume, pp. 311–2) it is adjacent to the dog-Latin 'Quondam fuit factus festus' (this volume, pp. 231–2).

216 Ed. A.G. Rigg, 'Gregory's Garden: a Latin dream-allegory', *MAe* 35 (1966), 29–37. It was written after 1280, the approximate date of Franco of Cologne's *Ars cantus mensurabilis*; the portrait of the eagle may owe something to either Dante or Chaucer.

217 For the Anglo-Latin entries, see this volume, pp. 144, 222–3, 231–2, 304, 305.

218 For a full account, see C.R. Cheney, 'Law and letters in fourteenth-century Durham', *Bulletin of the John Rylands Library* 55 (1972–3), 60–85. For the Anglo-Latin entries, see this volume, pp. 161–2 and ch. 3, n. 206.

219 For a detailed account, see A.G. Rigg, 'Medieval Latin Poetic Anthologies (II)', *MSt* 40 (1978), 387–407. I have revised my opinions on several points of the article; see *William Langland: Piers Plowman: the Z-version*, ed. A.G. Rigg and Charlotte Brewer (Toronto, 1983). Also, the revised date for John of Bridlington's Prophecy (see this volume, p. 265 and n. 90) makes possible an earlier date for Bodley 851.

220 On Wells, see also this volume, p. 281.

221 On Anglo-Latin material in this manuscript, see pp. 88–93, 102–4, 113–14, 193–8, 218–20, 233, 236, 260–2, 294.

222 For a detailed account, see A.G. Rigg, 'Medieval Latin Poetic Anthologies (I)', *MSt* 39 (1977), 281–330.

223 On Anglo-Latin material in this manuscript, see this volume, pp. 102–4, 113–14, 117, 127, 193–8, 220–2, 231, 233, 234–5, 260–2, 264, 278–9. On Rawlinson G. 109, see this volume, p. 150.

224 On the Bekynton anthology, see this volume, pp. 152–3, on Rawlinson B. 214, see n. 222 above, and p. 312.

225 For a detailed account, see A.G. Rigg, 'Medieval Latin Poetic Anthologies (III)', *MSt* 41 (1979), 468–505; this includes an account of Bodley 603 (this volume, p. 150), which

shares the block of Walter of Châtillon with Digby 166.

226 For Anglo-Latin material in this manuscript, see this volume, pp. 80, 226, and n. 218, 234–5, 236, 276–7, 278, 305.

227 See my brief notes on Gower's latinity in Echard and Fanger (n. 163 above).

Epilogue

1 There were moments when this perception seemed less obvious. In 1635 Sir Francis Kynaston translated the first two books of Chaucer's *Troilus* into Latin to make them more comprehensible and to protect them from further linguistic change.

2 W.F. Schirmer, *Der englische Frühhumanismus*, 2nd ed. (Tübingen, 1963); on Weiss, see ch 4, n. 195.

3 See E.F. Jacob, '*Florida verborum venustas*: some early examples of Euphuism in England', *Bulletin of the John Rylands Library* 17 (1933), 264–90.

4 It is interesting that in later copies of Frulovisi's *Vita* his more classical spellings were 'medievalized' into more familiar forms.

5 Ed. Gieben (see ch. 2, n. 209), pp. 71–4.

6 In *York Historians* 2, 469–87, inc. 'Benedicam Dominum mundi plasmatorem'; the first part was written by John of Allhallowgate.

7 For example, I have placed several pieces from the *Glastonbury Miscellany* (this volume, pp. 311–12), such as *Gregory's Garden*, Deverell's *Ingratitudo*, and poems on St Joseph, in the last chapter (pp. 303–6), when they could equally well be mid-fifteenth century compositions.

8 Leicester Bradner, *Musae Anglicanae: a history of Anglo-Latin poetry 1500–1925* (New York/London, 1940), points to the use of rhyme in epitaphs and ceremonial verse.

9 See this volume, p. 65 for the authorship.

10 Ed. in *Snappe's Formulary*, ed. H.E. Salter, Oxford Historical Soc. 80 (1924), pp. 138–44; on the manuscript, see p. 312.

11 See A.G. Rigg, 'Two poems on Sir Richard Gresham 1485–1549', *Guildhall Miscellany* 2.9 (1967), 389–91.

12 For example, there is an incomplete poem on mythography, inc. 'Jubiter et Juno', in Bodleian Lib., MS Digby 64, and BL Cotton Vespasian E. xii, both late fifteenth century; the Vespasian is probably a direct copy of the Digby text. An edition is in preparation by Siân Echard.

13 In *Lives of Edward the Confessor*, ed. H.R. Luard, RS (London, 1858), pp. 359–77, inc. 'Quid faciat virtus'. On earlier lives, see this volume, pp. 12–14.

14 The same point can be made by two commonplace books, both containing scraps of verse, proverbs, weather-lore, local history, moral and theological tags, mnemonics, etc.: Bodley 487, written mainly by John Curteys (1457–1509), who had connexions with Winchester and New College, Oxford, as well as Eton and Cambridge, and BL Harley 3362 (sixteenth century).

15 See this volume, pp. 152–3.

16 A.G. Rigg, *A Glastonbury Miscellany of the Fifteenth Century* (Oxford, 1968); this is an abbreviated version of my D.Phil. thesis (Oxford, 1966). My reason for thinking that it was compiled in Oxford, rather than at home in Glastonbury, is the close textual affiliation with Vespasian E. xii (p. 312) and Bodley 851 (pp. 307–8) in the *De coniuge non ducenda*. In neither my thesis nor my book was I aware of the significance of the booklet

system of compilation, but I now see clearly that several parts of the manuscript were once written separately.

17 For Anglo-Latin material in this manuscript, see this volume, pp. 22–24, 216, 231–2, 234, 243, 272–5, 303–6, and ch. 3 n. 60.

18 For Anglo-Latin material in Bodley 496, see this volume, pp. 65, 102–4, 108–10, 114–15, 311.

19 For a detailed description, see the article cited in ch. 4, n. 222, comparing it with Titus A. xx.

20 For Anglo-Latin material in this manuscript, see this volume, pp. 231, 234, 264–5, 276–8, 298, 299–301.

21 For a full description, see my 'Medieval Latin Poetic Anthologies (III)', *MSt* 41 (1979), especially pp. 498–505.

22 For Anglo-Latin material in this manuscript, see this volume, pp. 42, 75–6, 102–4, 215–16 (this manuscript contains the oldest form of the *De Palpone*), and n. 12 above.

Appendix: Metre

1 This Appendix deals only with metrical forms mentioned in this book. The standard work on Medieval Latin metre is by Dag Norberg, *Introduction à l'étude de la versification latine médiévale* (Stockholm, 1958). For classical metre, see D.S. Raven, *Latin Metre: an Introduction* (London, 1965).

2 The exceptions are John of Garland, whose *Parisiana Poetria* (this volume, pp. 165–6) contains examples of many quantitative lyric metres, especially from Horace, and Thomas Varoye (pp. 284–5), who has a section in the metre of Boethius, *Cons. Phil.* I met. 2.

3 See Serlo of Wilton and Richard Pluto (this volume, pp. 70–2, 111–12). The line quoted here is from Serlo.

4 Examples here are taken from the opening of Joseph of Exeter's *Ylias* (this volume, pp. 99–102); a few lines are used below to illustrate hexameters, 4.I.A.i (a).

5 Medieval poets are often censured for their failure to observe classical vowel quantities. In fact, most of them are sound on length by position; not surprisingly, lacking reference tools, they occasionally made 'mistakes' with natural length, but even here they tried to be careful. Henry of Avranches applied for permission to turn amphibrachs into anapaests (see p. 193).

6 The line is from the Troy poem 'Pergama flere volo'; *Iota* is feminine singular nominative, but must be scanned *lotā*.

7 See pp. 323, 325, particularly on rhythmical lines of twelve and fifteen syllables.

8 See this volume, p. 47.

9 See this volume, p. 235.

10 See this volume, pp. 70–2; this is poem No. 18.

11 On Michael, see this volume, pp. 193–8 and n. 143 for the variety of rhyming patterns, many of which are cited here. The rhyme here (431–2) is collateral.

12 See pp. 24–30 and n. 63 for the abbreviations LMP and WMP.

13 See pp. 244–5.

14 On 'run-over' rhyme, see p. 321.

15 See p. 214.

16 See p. 190 and n. 119.

17 For another odd type, see (d).

18 See pp. 17–20, 54–61.

19 See p. 285 and above n. 2.

20 For another example, see p. 166 (John of Garland).

21 Henry makes use of adonics in his imitations of Old English verse. For other examples of them, see pp. 31, 39. For a full history of this metre in medieval verse, see M. Lapidge, 'The authorship of the adonic verses "Ad Fidolium" attributed to Columbanus', *SM* 3rd ser. 18 (1977), 249–314 (especially pp. 253–71).

22 On hymns, see this volume, pp. 206–7. For the hymn quoted here, by Ambrose, see Walpole (cited in ch. 4, n. 4), pp. 46–49.

23 See p. 302.

24 For another example, see Henry of Huntingdon, this volume, p. 39.

25 See p. 40.

26 See p. 284.

27 See p. 40.

28 On rhyme in Lawrence of Durham's five-foot line and in Glyconics, see pp. 317, 318.

29 Serlo of Wilton, this volume pp. 70–2.

30 From a poem on Simon de Montfort, see p. 202.

31 From the poem on St Hilda, this volume, pp. 22–4.

32 From John of Garland's *Morale scolarium*, this volume, pp. 166–8.

33 See ch. 3, nn. 119, 143.

34 Goodall has *Anglicus* (for *Anglus*) unmetrically; there is another set in lines 219–28. See also pp. 320–1, (f) and (g), for other collateral rhymes.

35 From the *Morale scolarium*, this volume, pp. 166–8.

36 See p. 65.

37 See pp. 265–8.

38 Michael's pattern is also used by Thomas Varoye. Run-over rhyme is also used in a rhythmical poem by Henry of Avranches, this volume, p. 193.

39 See p. 269.

40 See pp. 276–7.

41 See p. 190.

42 See pp. 83–4.

43 An apparent exception is the *Chronicon Metricum* of the church of York (this volume, pp. 293–4), but this has enough monosyllabic rhyme to be reckoned as a rhymed poem.

44 See pp. 260–5.

45 These were written to imitate Old English verse: see pp. 37–8.

46 A problem of definition sometimes arises here. Some well-established lines are sometimes broken by internal rhymes, arranged collaterally. For example, the rhythmical asclepiad, 12pp, rhyming aaaa, is sometimes broken medially into 6pp6pp, rhyming abababab or ababcbcb. Should this be treated as a variant of the twelve-syllable line or as an independent form? I have tried to indicate alternative interpretations by cross-references. In this case, for 6pp, see under 12pp.

47 See pp. 208–12; for another example, see p. 79. It is often found in combination with other rhythmical stanzas, in rhymed offices and in Lawrence of Durham's poem on the Resurrexion (pp. 57–8).

48 For combination with 6pp, see (e) below. For combination with 8pp, see p. 327.

49 See this volume, pp. 215–22. In the *Descriptio Northfolchiae* (p. 234) the stanzas vary in

length, and there are several metrical licences, such as extra syllables, as there are also in Stephen Deverell's poem on Ingratitude (p. 305).

50 See pp. 213–14, where a stanza is quoted, and n. 186 for the rhyme schemes.

51 I owe this observation to Professor John Magee of Columbia University.

52 See p. 124.

53 See p. 228; the last line of this stanza is from the *Ecloga Theoduli*. The poem also has 'concatenation' p. 328.

54 See this volume, p. 224; there is another example on p. 230. The stanza is sometimes laid out, particularly in the *Analecta Hymnica*, as eight lines.

55 See p. 252. It is also seen in a poem on Bannockburn (p. 245).

56 See pp. 85–7 and Dronke's editions. I have also excluded 'Miles Christi' (p. 201) and 'Beati qui esuriunt' (p. 304).

57 See the poem 'Quid sit Deus', this volume p. 138 and n. 236; several stanza schemes are used in Lawrence of Durham's poem on the Resurrexion (pp. 57–8) and in rhymed offices (this volume, p. 206).

58 See this volume, p. 217. The burlesque 'Quondam fuit factus festus' (pp. 231–2) has eight-line stanzas: 2(3(8p) 1(7pp)). Expansion of the number of a-lines, even within the same hymn, is a common feature of the Victorine sequence.

59 On 12pp6pp, see this volume, p. 324 (e).

General index

The index includes (I hope) all persons and places that a reader is likely to want to consult. It excludes minor characters, persons and places of no significance outside their context in the specific work; at the periphery there is some inconsistency (Brutus is in, Corineus is out). In accordance with modern (though not medieval) usage, names of people after 1216 (i.e. in chapters 3–4) are given under their last name; those before 1216 (chapters 1–2), except for cases like Abelard, are under first names. This practice may be irritating, but it is better than having to look up Reginald under Canterbury or Chaucer under Geoffrey. Biblical characters and books may be found under their own name or under Bible.

Topic headings have been selected pragmatically. Some (Christ, humour) are so vast that only major discussions are indexed: such entries should not be regarded as exclusive. Conversely, others (politics/satire, sins/vices, Bible/typology) overlap. If in doubt, read the whole book.

Poems are indexed by first line only when they are commonly referred to in this way, in this book or in catalogues.

The introduction (pp. 1–8) contains mainly my own opinions, and is not indexed. Endnotes (pp. 330–93) are indexed only when they provide information that would not necessarily be expected from the context, that is, when they are more than bibliographical or cross-references.

Index of manuscripts

413